Career
Education for
Handicapped
Children and
Youth

Donn E. Brolin
University of Missouri-Columbia

Charles J. Kokaska
California State University-Long Beach

CHARLES E. MERRILL PUBLISHING COMPANY
A Bell & Howell Company
Columbus Toronto London Sydney

Published by
Charles E. Merrill Publishing Company
A Bell & Howell Company
Columbus, Ohio 43216

This book was set in Kabel and Helvetica.
The Production Editor was Cynthia Norfleet Donaldson.
The cover was prepared by Will Chenoweth.
Cover photo by Tom Hutchinson.

Permissions: p. 9, Figure 1. Reprinted from "A framework for considering some issues in special education," by Maynard Reynolds, *Exceptional Children,* 1962, *28* (7), by permission of The Council for Exceptional Children.

International Standard Book Number: 0-675-08278-1
Library of Congress Catalog Card Number: 78-070623

1 2 3 4 5 6 7 8 9 10 / 84 83 82 81 80 79

Printed in the United States of America

This book is written for all persons concerned with the career development of handicapped individuals—parents, teachers, counselors, administrators, rehabilitation workers, psychologists, business and industrial leaders, and many others. The book is a text for use by university educators in regular and special education, vocational education, guidance and counseling, psychology, rehabilitation, and anyone who prepares their students for working with the handicapped. It should also be most useful for curriculum planners and inservice trainers who design and implement career education in their districts. State department administrators, educational consultants, and numerous community agencies involved in the career development of handicapped individuals should also find this book a valuable resource.

This book presents career education as a whole life process for all handicapped individuals—regardless of categories or labels. We see career education as a sequence of planned learning activities which prepare individuals for varied life roles (i.e., occupational, vocational, family, civic, retirement). We examine all career development needs of the handicapped, not just vocational needs, and provide a mix of daily living (simple budgeting skills), personal-social (communicating effectively), and occupational skills for preschoolers through adults. We define career education as a systematic coordination of all school, family, and community activities to actualize each person's greatest potential. We have tried to present a total approach to career development—its concept, development, and teaching in educational settings. Our book attempts to place career education in the whole curriculum by presenting 22 competencies for different settings (home, school, and community) and four stages of development (awareness, exploration, preparation, placement, and follow-up). In addition, we present strategies and resources for teaching career skills and suggest ways to involve both family and community in career education. This material results from our years of experience as promoters of career education, teachers, counselors, administrators, and researchers.

In part one the text reviews career services and development for a variety of handicapping conditions. In part two we survey career instruction for the handicapped and conceptualize life centered career education in personal-social, daily living, and occupational skills. In part three we present strategies for planning and conducting career education programs. In part four we discuss how community agencies, families, and businesses can assist in these programs. Part five looks to the future of career education.

Our notion of career education as a life-long process arises out of the total career education movement. In 1971 career education was declared a national priority by the U.S. Commissioner of Education, Sidney P. Marland. Since that time it has moved rapidly forward to reform the ills plaguing American education. For its contribution, Congress endorsed career education in the Career Education Implementation Incentives Act (PL 95–207), saying that:

> A major purpose of education is to prepare every individual for a career suitable to that individual's preference . . . career education should be an integral part of the Nation's educational process which serves as preparation for work.

Career education now has its own headquarters—the Office of Career Education in the U.S. Office of Education. All states have career education coordinators, and many are mandating that the concepts be included in ongoing curriculum. The plethora of bills, policy statements, curriculum modifications, organizations and journals, research projects, instructional materials, and national and local workshops reflect the feverish activity in career education in the seventies and into the eighties. We are now on the threshold of making career education an integral part of all education. However, there are many who still resist it and who cry "back to basics," not realizing that career education holds the hope for keeping students in school, interested in learning, and in mastering basic skills.

However, despite these efforts, far too many handicapped citizens continue to have problems joining society as contributing citizens. The ability to conduct their own daily affairs and to make a decent wage are two major problems affecting well over half of our handicapped adults. The need for the schools to do a better job at this is obvious. If handicapped individuals are to achieve their rightful place in this society, much remains to be done. Infusing career education in school can make this achievement more of a reality.

We greatly appreciate the assistance of Gene Conley and Margaret Steck who typed this manuscript. Also, we recognize the contributions of many school district personnel, university and state department leaders, and representatives from the Bureau of Education for the Handicapped (BEH) who have supported and assisted us in our past efforts. And to those who have worked closely with us in our projects over the years, we say thank you.

D. E. B.
C. J. K.

**Dedicated to our wives,
Nancy and Sharen**

Contents

Career
Education for
Handicapped
Children and
Youth

Introduction

Part one presents basic background information about the development and current status of educational services for handicapped individuals; the nature of various handicapping conditions as they relate to career development; and the concept, need, and organization of career education. This information forms the foundation for the career education approach that is presented in subsequent chapters of the book.

Chapter 1 presents some major historical events that have influenced this country's provisions for individuals with handicaps through the years. Various instructional settings are described, as well as a definition of mainstreaming. The chapter discusses the major forces that have molded positive educational change: parent organizations, litigation, legislation, and medical and technological advances. The Individualized Education Program (IEP) and its components and implications for career development are presented. The chapter concludes by identifying several personnel and program changes in education that are projected to increase the number and type of role modifications for educators.

Chapter 2 presents salient information about a number of handicapping conditions. Attention is directed toward the attitudes of various individuals and groups. It stresses that although psychological adjustment to a disability is not an easy matter, handicapped persons can lead satisfying, productive lives if they receive the proper guidance and assistance in reaching career development goals. The remainder of the chapter focuses on the medical, social, psychological, educational, and vocational aspects associated with eight categories of handicapping conditions. It points out that the attitudes of the handicapped individual and society are the two major problems, not the individual's disability itself. The chapter concludes with a commencement address given by a 19-year-old handicapped student from Michigan.

Chapter 3 outlines the case for career education and why it is desperately needed throughout the country for all students. Developments since its inception in 1971 as a national education priority are discussed: four national models, governmental agencies, legislation, new organizations, and other responses. The problem of a universally accepted definition of career education is presented. The authors point out that a person's career is comprised of many roles, one of which is occupation. People also have careers as students, homemakers, and retirees and partake in avocational, family, and civic roles. This chapter, therefore, presents a conceptualization and definition that considers career development needs from a broader perspective than just occupational functioning. Career education concepts, infusion techniques, and a competency based curriculum model are discussed. The proposed curriculum model focuses on 22 career development competencies and 102 subcompetencies, which are classified under three curriculum areas: Daily Living Skills, Personal-Social Skills, and Occupational Guidance and Preparation. School, family and community relationships, and four stages of career development are discussed in relation to their contributions in helping students acquire the competencies. Suggestions for implementing career education conclude the chapter.

The Education of Handicapped Individuals

Over the past two decades there has been a marked change in this country's provisions for handicapped individuals. Public attention through the various forms of media and legislation has focused on numerous aspects of the handicapped individual's life. These aspects include the etiology of the condition; the family's struggle to cope with the situation; infant and child development; methods of instruction; organization of educational programs; peer relationships; vocational training and placement; and success in the adult years.

Education is one element in this total picture, although a singularly important ingredient to the subsequent success of the individual in a complex society. Major changes in the educational structure include increased allocations of monies to support special programs; integration of handicapped students into regular education classrooms; lawsuits to insure that handicapped students participate in daily class activities; and applications of technology in the development of instructional media to assist teachers and students.

Within this continual process of change, several major concerns have emerged, which form the basis for this book. First, career education has sparked new interest in the scope and content of the schools' efforts to prepare individuals for their adult roles and responsibilities. Second, the integration of handicapped students, sometimes referred to as *mainstreaming,* also places certain demands upon personnel within the total school program. For some, these demands are not new. For others, the combination of mainstreaming and career education for the handicapped may require a dual adjustment in curriculum and teaching techniques.

This chapter provides an historical overview of the education and training of handicapped individuals. This overview includes discussions of the various instructional settings; the emergence of the mainstreaming concept; major forces that have influenced society's provisions for handicapped students; and additions to the personnel and programs for handicapped individuals.

HISTORICAL DEVELOPMENT

The history of handicapped individuals is as old as the human race, but their education is a relatively recent achievement. Illustrations of blind Egyptian harpists and singers are found on the walls of tombs that date to approximately 1400 B.C. Individuals with various disabilities have been recorded in other civilizations, as on the pottery of the Incas or Oriental ink drawings. Their hardships are told in the stories of the Greek poets, of whom the most notable, Homer, was blind.

Historical records indicate that the experiences of handicapped individuals were harsh during a period when humans had to strive daily for mere physical survival. The deformed, disabled, and slow-witted were at a constant disadvantage. They were viewed as a burden to the total community and denied any claim to worth and status. The Spartans, who recognized the expedience of the "survival of the fittest," simply required defective infants to be abandoned in the surrounding country or thrown from a cliff. This freed the community of another mouth to feed. Those who weren't destroyed in the Spartan custom had little to look forward to in other Greek city states and the European cultures that followed for the next eighteen hundred years. This situation was due partly to the influence of such prominent philosophers as Plato, who in describing the ideal society, envisioned no place for an individual with handicaps. He recommended in the *Republic* (1941) that:

> . . . the offspring of the inferior, or of the better when they chance to be deformed, will be put away in some mysterious, unknown place, as they should be. (Book V)

Those societies that followed the Greeks only improved the basic "survival doctrine." Occasionally, handicapped individuals were protected or achieved status in royal courts. In the Middle Ages various types of homes and asylums were established by religious orders. This practice stemmed from the Christian belief that humans' divine qualities should be manifested in acts of sacrifice and kindness toward the suffering and afflicted. However, for every individual who may have been assisted, for example, by St. Vincent de Paul and the Sisters of Charity, there were hundreds who were tortured, burned, and punished, viewed as the physical manifestations of the evil powers at work in the world. For every individual who entertained in the courts as a jester or buffoon or with access to the royal family in the role of an escort to the king or tutor of his children, there were thousands who maintained themselves as beggars. It is no wonder that classical art and literature often portray handicapped individuals as thieves, scoundrels, and the refuse of the social system. The vast majority met with little favor or advantage among the councils of the rich, knowledgeable, and powerful.

European Antecedents

The beginnings of education and hope for handicapped individuals can be traced to a cluster of French philosophers, scientists, and physicians who advocated an enlightened view of human beings. The first of these leaders was Jacob Rodriques Pereire, who in 1749 presented his method for teaching deaf mutes to speak and read at the Academy of Science in Paris. His accomplishments received such attention that King Louis XV requested Pereire and his pupil to appear at court (Kanner, 1964). Pereire's work has been identified by some scholars as the beginning of special education as a distinct discipline.

If there are classics in the history of the education of handicapped individuals, then one of the first is the efforts of Jean-Marc-Gaspard Itard with Victor, as documented in *The Wild Boy of Aveyron* (1962). Few texts in special education are without a reference to Itard. His hopes as a humanitarian and rigor as a scientist set an example for the field that has endured the generations. Victor, a boy of 10 or 11 years of age, was captured by hunters in the forest of Aveyron, Southern France, in 1799. He was literally placed on exhibit to the public and curious scientists, who were investigating whether Victor could be a representative sample of Rousseau's "noble savage." The boy was far from noble as he trotted and grunted like the beasts of the forest, ate most anything placed before him after sniffing it, rocked back and forth in his cage, and seemed to be imperceptable of heat and cold.

Pinel, a leading physician of the period and Itard's mentor, put an apparent end to the speculations about the boy's hidden human intelligence within an animal existence by declaring Victor to be an incurable idiot. Itard was of a different opinion, which did not please his mentor, and ventured upon a 5-year experiment to educate the boy. *The Wild Boy of Aveyron* is truly the first documentation of an educator's ideas, successes, and failures with a handicapped child. It stands as the first piece of literature in a long series of novels, biographies, and scholastic works which constitutes a rich treasury of readings about exceptional individuals.

Itard attempted to achieve five goals with Victor. They were to: interest him in a social life through a gradual transition from the life he led in the forest; awaken his nervous sensibilities through intense stimulation and emotion; extend his range of ideas by increasing his social contacts; lead him to the use of speech through imitation but based on necessity; and induce mental operations associated with meeting physical needs through instruction.

Itard did not achieve success in his opinion, and Victor never became a "normal" individual. But, he did achieve significance among future educators and scholars by attempting techniques with what could be described as the most unlikely candidate for success. In reviewing the significance of Itard's work, a physician (Richard Masland), a psychologist (Seymour Sarason), and a social scientist (Thomas Gladwin) termed the efforts and accomplishments *phenomenal.*

> Over the long period of training one could see the development of various ego functions, the capacity to delay responsiveness—in short, one saw the development of a surprisingly complex personality. (Masland, Sarason, & Gladwin, 1958, p. 325)

Itard's efforts characterized a growing interest in the nineteenth century with the *possibility* that the deaf could communicate, that the blind could be mobile, and that the mentally retarded could learn. Other individuals such as Thomas Hopkins Gallaudet, Samuel Gridley Howe, and Edouard Sequin were to continue to expand the means through which handicapped individuals would realize those possibilities.[1]

The American Scene

The expansion of education for handicapped individuals in the United States during the nineteenth century was due to the singular efforts of such men as Gallaudet, Howe, and Sequin. Although the first residential setting, the American Asylum for the Deaf and Dumb, was established in Hartford, Connecticut in 1818, it took almost half of a century before the first day-school classes were initiated in Boston, Massachusetts, as illustrated in Table 1. By 1922 the United States Office of Education had conducted a survey of enrollments in programs for handicapped students in 191 cities with a population of 100,000 or more. These programs enrolled 26,163 students, who were mostly in classes for the mentally retarded.

---

[1] Additional historical reviews appear in Kolstoe (1972a) and Jordan (1976).

The education of handicapped individuals expanded slowly between the two world wars. School districts increased their offerings in all areas of exceptionality but were hindered by the drain on personnel and finances created by the wars and the Great Depression. Nevertheless, two significant events took place during that period, which were to influence the development of future programs and assistance.

Table 1
*Commonly Reported Dates for the Establishment of the First
Day Classes for Handicapped Students*[a]

Deaf	Boston, Massachusetts	1869
Retarded	Providence, Rhode Island	1896
Crippled	Chicago, Illinois	1899
Blind	Chicago, Illinois	1900
Lowered Vitality	Providence, Rhode Island	1908
Partially Seeing	Roxbury, Massachusetts	1913

[a] United States Office of Education. *The unfinished revolution: Education for the handicapped,* 1976 Annual Report, National Advisory Committee on the Handicapped. Washington, D.C.: Government Printing Office, 1976, p. 11, Table 2.

In 1922 Elizabeth Farrell and students enrolled in her course at Columbia University founded what was to become the dominant professional organization in special education, The Council for Exceptional Children (Aiello, 1976). The Council has continually functioned as an advocate for the rights of handicapped individuals and a strong lobby for legislation in conjunction with parent groups.

The 1930 White House Conference on Child Health and Protection provided special education with its first recognition as a notable contributor to the education and well being of children. One of the results of the conference was the creation of a department of special education in the Office of Education, which was filled by Elise Martens. That one-person department has grown into the Bureau of Education for the Handicapped, with a projected budget of billions of dollars.

The end of World War II brought a conclusion to public apathy toward individuals with handicaps. That was due, in part, to the return of handicapped war veterans to a society that remembered them as healthy and able. The contradictions between the traditional stereotypes and reality were such that the nation had to finally deal with the question of whether capable handicapped individuals would be provided with the training and opportunity to achieve those freedoms for which they fought. The organization of the President's Committee on Employment of the Handicapped in 1947 was a beginning in this direction and helped start what was to become the most dramatic period of expansion and activity in the history of the education of handicapped individuals.[2]

It is at this point that we must divert from a general chronological discussion in order to focus attention upon several distinct components that were a vital part in the expansion. Each component has its own story and contributes to the total development of the field. We have divided these components into instructional settings, mainstreaming, parent organizations, litigation, legislation, medical and technological advances, the individualized education program and additions to the personnel and programs.

INSTRUCTIONAL SETTINGS

The varied characteristics and instructional needs of handicapped students, combined with the evolution of programs within school districts, has led to a variety of settings. But one of the dominant concepts that has emerged in the field of special education in the United States is the application of the "least restrictive alternative" to the education of handicapped students. It is based, in part, on the efforts and experiences of European educators and humanists in normalizing the education, work, and social environments in which handicapped individuals must function. The concept requires that a range of instructional alternatives are available to accommodate the specific learning characteristics and requirements of the student. Reynolds (1962) places the various administrative approaches on a continuum of services, extending from the least to the most integrative arrangements relative to the regular classroom (see Figure 1).

Deno (1970) and Dunn (1973) expand upon this "cascade of services" model, thereby moving the field of special education toward advocating environments that best meet the multiple needs and abilities of the individual. The ultimate goal is to place the individual in as normal an educational setting as possible, regardless of the form of disability. The goal is reflected in the specific references to free appropriate public education and individualized education programs contained in The Education for All Handicapped Children Act (PL 94–142), which will be discussed in greater detail later in the chapter. The following is a review of the *major forms* of instructional settings that have evolved over the history of special education.

Hospital and Homebound Instruction

Although these are two distinctly different settings, they share a common characteristic of totally isolating the individual from the regular classroom.

---

[2] Harold Russell, chairperson of the President's Committee on Employment of the Handicapped, won an Academy Award for his authentic role as an injured veteran in the 1946 movie, *The Best Years of Our Lives.*

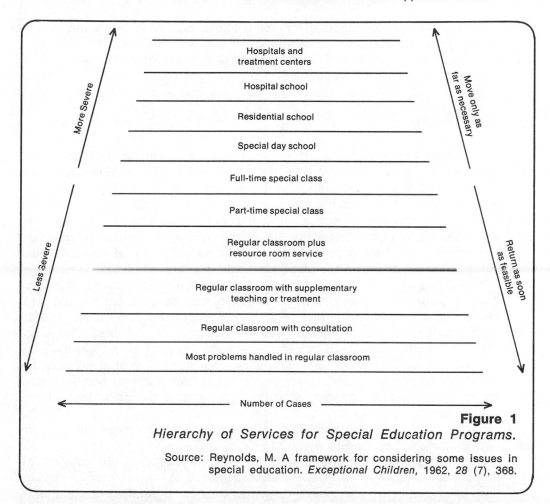

Figure 1
Hierarchy of Services for Special Education Programs.

Source: Reynolds, M. A framework for considering some issues in special education. *Exceptional Children,* 1962, *28* (7), 368.

Even in cases in which hospitals conduct classes for groups of children on a ward, the individual learning requirements of any one child may be such that the itinerant teacher must work with him on a one-to-one basis. Once the student leaves the hospital setting for home, he even loses the small advantage of companionship that a ward setting may offer.

The itinerant teacher must continually seek to conquer the academic retardation that accompanies periods of illness, injury, or postsurgery. This task is made more difficult when the recovery period leaves the student with limited amounts of energy that can be exerted on the lessons. There have been instances when itinerant teachers, who may visit the home for a few hours a week, have had to cancel instruction due to the student's need for companionship and moral support.

Special educators have attempted to incorporate students in daily classroom activities through the use of telephone terminals. The student can monitor the lessons, participate in discussions, and interact with other students and instructors. The increased development of videotapes and video cassettes with adapters for home television opens additional possibilities for individuals, whether young or old, who must spend a part of their "learning experiences" in hospital and homebound settings.

Residential School

It is ironic that within recent years, residential training facilities have come under severe criticism. The irony is that the very beginnings of the education of handicapped individuals are rooted in the training school approach. Some of the leading personalities and programs can be identified with such residential settings as the Vineland Training School in New Jersey or Perkins School in Massachusetts. Many of the residential schools are maintained by private organizations, but the vast number of students educated in these settings have attended public institutions.

The difficulties with the institutional arrangement began to occur principally in those situations in which the facility was responsible for the total life of the individual and there was little prospect that the student would return to the community. Institutions for the mentally retarded and emotionally disturbed began to take on the characteristics of a "warehouse," except that no one drew upon the stored humanity. Training schools for individuals who were blind, deaf, or physically handicapped had less of a stigma because their faculties did return students to the community. However, even these programs came under scrutiny due to the fact that the range of vocational and adult training was too narrow to meet the expanding demands of the society.

As it now stands, it appears that the residential school is not going to be eliminated. In some instances, the characteristics of the residential population have changed. For example, institutions for mentally retarded individuals have attempted to return many of their more able students to the community and are directing more attention to the severely and profoundly retarded. In other cases, such as with outstanding private schools, the total involvement of the staff with the individual offers parents an attractive alternative in their plans for the handicapped youth.

Special School

The concept of an entire school for students with one or more disabilities is an extension of the residential setting, except that the student lives at home. The special school allows the architect to design physical adaptations for individuals with braces or in wheelchairs, to include color tones and lighting to assist those students with visual difficulties, and to add numerous types of structures and rooms to assist individual therapy and instruction. These schools offer the advantages of a concerted emphasis upon both physical design and faculty expertise to meet the instructional needs of the handicapped individual.

For a while, only the largest school systems could build such a physical plant, as they had both the revenue and number of students to merit a separate facility. But not all communities can build and equip such a structure, nor can it service all handicapped students within the school system. The great majority of students remain in other settings within the elementary, secondary, and community college progression, if they are admitted. Also, the special school, like the institution, segregates the handicapped student *and* the specialist from their peers. The idea of the integration of handicapped students has been gnawing at special educators for years and taxes them whenever another special school is proposed.

Special Class

The education of handicapped individuals is usually identified with the "special class," whether you are talking to professionals or students. More handicapped students have been educated in the special class than in any other unique form of programming. Special class assignments allow for an ample amount of opinion among researchers who have tried to identify its successes and shortcomings. The special class is a segregated group of students who meet the definition of a particular form of exceptionality, as established by state law. The maximum enrollment is also designated by law and is under the direction of a teacher, who is sometimes assisted by an aide. The teacher provides the "core" of essential curriculum, whether the class is at the elementary or secondary level. Students have an opportunity, under various plans, to integrate with normal peers in physical education, music, art, home economics, and extracurricular activities. The previous courses are generally regarded as electives, but there are instances when even these subjects are conducted by the special class teacher.

The special class student is closer to the regular classroom in comparison to a corresponding student in the residential setting. However, the element of isolation is still possible. A form of gallows humor in special education is the advice that when a visitor wants to find the special class in a school, he need only ask for the boiler room and look next door. If such locations matched the story, it is no wonder that researchers began to publish what were termed *efficacy studies*. The studies compared the achievements of students in special classes to those of corresponding students who, for several reasons, remained in the regular classes. The studies focused largely upon classes for the mentally retarded and generally reported that the students in special education classes did not achieve the academic levels of their peers in regular classes. The studies were compounded, however, by such factors as selection of students for special classes, methods of instruction, and the criteria for comparison.[3] These studies, combined with the several legal suits and investigations of institutional settings, provided more fuel in the search for other models in the education of handicapped students.

Resource Room

This instructional setting bridges the gap between the student's membership in a special class and integration into the regular class. Students report to the teacher at designated parts of the school day for specific assistance (Hammill & Wiederholt, 1972). Emphasis is placed upon instruction so that the occasion is not used as a study hall and upon the teacher as an enforcer of discipline on behalf of the regular classroom teacher. The room may include various mechanical aids or learning devices that are not available in the regular classroom. For example, blind students can report to the resource room to use a braille writer to record class notes or assignments.

The success of the resource room rests upon the ability of the teacher to provide additional assessment, instruction, and evaluation, which maintain the student's membership and success in the regular setting. An additional function of the resource teacher is to provide consultation to the regular teacher on problems related to instruction and overall program planning. In effect, the role of "consultant" requires that the resource teacher demonstrate competencies in communication with colleagues, as well as evaluation and prescription for student learning.

Regular Classroom

Numerous kinds of specialists are being trained to assist the regular classroom teacher in maintaining the handicapped student in this setting. These specialists include speech therapists, remedial reading teachers, consultants in career development, and resource personnel with responsibilities for particular areas of exceptionality, such as mental retardation or learning disabilities. There is a fundamental logic behind the increased emphasis upon maintaining handicapped students in regular classrooms. There just are not enough specialists to work with every handicapped student on a one-to-one basis or even in the special class. Gallagher (1972) dramatizes this problem in only one area of exceptionality, emotional disturbance, by estimating that it would take 158 years for training programs

---

[3] Bruininks and Rynders (1971) provide a summary of the pros and cons of special class placement for the educable mentally retarded, and Kolstoe (1972a) examines six allegations on the same issue. The two articles capture much of the turmoil that irrupted during the period.

to meet the demand for personnel to provide service to 60% of the children for the year 1975. Gallagher even allows for an increase in the number of specialists who enter the area of behavior disorders, but he does not attempt to calculate similar projections for all categories of exceptionality. The realization that special education could not provide the personnel to meet the needs of handicapped students according to previous models of instruction increased attention upon the regular classroom and lead to the use of the term *mainstreaming*.[4]

MAINSTREAMING

In April 1976 the delegate assembly at the 54th Annual International Convention of the Council for Exceptional Children adopted the following definition of mainstreaming as a statement of policy.

> Mainstreaming is a belief which involves an educational placement procedure and process for exceptional children, based on the conviction that each such child should be educated in the least restrictive environment in which his educational and related needs can be satisfactorily provided. This concept recognizes that exceptional children have a wide range of special education needs, varying greatly in intensity and duration; that there is a recognized continuum of education settings which may, at a given time, be appropriate for an individual child's needs; that to the maximum extent appropriate, exceptional children should be educated with non-exceptional children; and that special classes, separate schooling or other removal of an exceptional child from education with non-exceptional children should occur only when the intensity of the child's special education and related needs is such that they cannot be satisfied in an environment including non-exceptional children, even with the provision of supplementary aids and services.
>
> (The Council for Exceptional Children, 1976)

This action had to be taken by the delegate assembly as the term *mainstreaming* was receiving increased use in both professional and popular publications without a general agreement as to its definition. It was another example of society's penchant for using "catchy" expressions or terms and

---

[4] One way of changing the number of students per category of exceptionality is to modify the definition. This happened in 1973 when the American Association on Mental Deficiency stated that mental retardation began at the second standard deviation below the mean on tests of intelligence. In 1972 a student could be classified as mentally retarded if his performance on a test of intelligence fell between the second and first standard deviation below the mean.

then spending years deciding what they mean. Some parents of handicapped students initially visualized the wholesale elimination of the special schools and facilities that they had worked so hard to establish through efforts with state legislatures and local school boards. Regular classroom teachers envisioned that a wave of students with special needs would break upon their classes and require additional time and skills, which were already sorely pressed. Special educators were torn between meeting the needs of all handicapped individuals, while insuring that the student would receive the best possible instruction.[5]

Hopefully, the definition given here will eliminate much of the confusion and focus attention on three critical points. First, the concept of the *least restrictive environment* should be used to determine the appropriate educational setting. Second, an *appropriate educational setting* is one that meets the unique needs of the exceptional student, which includes integration, as much as possible, with nonexceptional students. Third, a *continuum of settings* (Figure 1) is acceptable in order to meet the varied needs and abilities of the student.

There are some problems in implementing mainstreaming. An evaluation report by Rice (1976) on a series of meetings that included 11 state directors of special education lists four major obstacles as identified by those administrators.

- Regular classroom teacher attitudes toward handicapped students.
- The attitudes and willingness of general administrators toward means of integrating handicapped students.
- The lack of fiscal resources.
- Insufficient number of specialists on the staff.

Of course, these major obstacles overlap. The regular classroom teachers may be reluctant to accept the process of mainstreaming when they are acutely aware that they lack prior experience or assistance from specialists to bolster the daily activities. Administrators may want to integrate handicapped students on a gradual scale if the faculty needs extensive inservice training in order to attend to some serious concerns. These concerns may have to do with:

- The attitudes of regular students toward handicapped individuals;
- modifications in the physical environment to accommodate handicapped students;
- appropriate curriculum materials, evaluation instruments, and teaching techniques;
- the utilization of resource personnel; and

---

[5] The term and the issues it generated have received ample exposure. The reader can refer to the following authors: Reynolds & Davis, 1972; Birch, 1974; Mann, 1974; Nyquist, 1975; Lowenbraun & Affleck, 1976; and Mann, 1976.

- coordination of several programs that interface with the regular curriculum.

One may say that the discussions on the pros and cons of mainstreaming are academic. Mainstreaming—integration—least restrictive environment, whatever the term, will occur because there are major forces at work within the American social and political setting that will move this society toward those goals. It is only a matter of whether we are to achieve first-class citizenship for handicapped individuals as effectively and quickly as possible. The following section examines those major forces in society that are affecting positive changes on behalf of handicapped individuals.

MAJOR FORCES AFFECTING POSITIVE EDUCATIONAL CHANGE

The explosion of services and public attention on behalf of handicapped individuals has not been a matter of chance. There have been and will continue to be distinct forces in American society which foster change and increase the possibilities that handicapped individuals will fulfill their maximum potential. We have divided these forces into three headings for the sake of discussion. In reality, the forces of parent organizations, litigation, and legislation interact with one another and build upon the success that each has fostered within the society.

Parent Organization

It is appropriate to begin a discussion of major forces with a review of the numerous organizations that have been founded by the parents of handicapped individuals. Such organizations date back to the founding of the National Society for Crippled Children in 1921. The major thrust occurred in 1949–50 when the National Association for Retarded Children (now the National Association for Retarded Citizens) and the United Cerebral Palsy Association were organized within a few months of one another. Membership in such organizations is open to parents, students, and professionals and numbers in the hundreds of thousands.

These organizations were a response of the parents to the lack of public action, as illustrated in the absence of school programs, treatment centers, or even skilled personnel who were interested in working with an increasing number of handicapped children. A well-known example of the parents' plight can be found in the story of the beginnings of the New York State Cerebral Palsy Association. A parent advertised daily in several local newspapers that those individuals who were interested in receiving help should call or write to her (Killilea, 1960). There are numerous examples of parents finding each other in order to provide solace and answer basic questions about their children's condition and future. Those same organizations have grown to a point at which they are viable speakers for handicapped individuals and can affect the future through political and social action.

The organizations had initial problems in working with professionals. Parents were forced into combined action because very little was being provided by agencies in which the doctor, teacher, and psychologist were employed. The bitter memories and feelings at first forced parents to rely upon themselves for counsel and direction; but, in time, they learned to use the professional's skill as the organization continued to expand its role and influence. At the current stage of development, numerous parent groups have professionals as consultants and members of their board of directors, although the parents still control the overall intent and direction of policy, as it should be.

Their strongest drive and accomplishments have been to promote legislation from the local level through the statehouses and Congress. Several organizations have active legislation committees that monitor the progress of bills, organize attempts to lobby on behalf of favorable legislation, produce witnesses during committee hearings, and function as a source of information to its members, legislatures, and representatives of the media. These efforts have been rewarded as repeated laws have been passed at all levels of government which support the rights of handicapped individuals.

Parent groups have also served other purposes. For example, they have:

1. Organized educational facilities and services when public schools or agencies were unavailable;
2. promoted public awareness and support for programs and efforts to assist handicapped individuals;
3. supported parents through counseling, guardianship plans, respite care programs, and medical services;
4. promoted research into causes, treatments, education, and other aspects of the individual's life;
5. sponsored training for teachers, teacher aides, community leaders, doctors, and other individuals who may be involved in the care, education, and treatment of handicapped individuals;
6. built permanent structures for sheltered workshops, day schools, and diagnostic centers; and
7. developed programs to prepare the handicapped for such necessary functions as daily care, mobility, recreation, leisure, and raising a family.

Finally, parent groups have established their place as advocates by representing handicapped individuals as plaintiffs in litigation involving public agencies. One of the most prominent suits was that of the *Pennsylvania Association for Retarded Children* v. *Commonwealth of Pennsylvania*, which will be reviewed later in the chapter. The case and decision have been termed *landmark,* and it is appropriate that one of the parent organizations was so intimately involved in a decision that affirmed the constitutional right of every child to an education.

What are the future directions and roles for the parent organizations? Cain (1976) identifies several in his review of the historical position of parent groups. First, there will be more instances of coordinated activity across organizations that had previously been working in isolation. This cooperation was already evident in the areas of vocational training and placement when the Department of Labor awarded a contract to the Epilepsy Foundation of America based upon the department's successful experience with a somewhat similar award to the National Association for Retarded Citizens (*Mental Retardation News,* 1975; *National Spokesman,* 1976). The contracts allow for cooperative training agreements that involve the national organizations, school systems, and business. Both organizations have been exchanging information and ideas with other parent groups so that one would expect continued growth in these awards, as well as cooperation between groups on other common goals.

Second, parent groups will continue to increase their attention to the total life of the individual. The emphasis that has been characterized by the customary "poster child" will change as the organizations and the consumers they serve move toward the problems of adulthood. It is also likely that those organizations that have been founded by adults with disabilities will exert an influence on the parent organizations through mutual action in the areas of transportation, adult education, and employment.

Third, parent groups will change their role to that of initiator and monitor of services as the public sector increases its responsibility as the provider of services. The Department of Labor contracts, for example, illustrate the parent groups' ability to initiate projects when school systems have been unable to meet the needs of handicapped students. It is hoped that with time, these services will be absorbed by the education sector. The role of monitor is already evident in the several cases brought before the bar in which the parent organizations challenged school districts and other public agencies to meet a standard of due process procedures in determining the appropriate education or training program for the handicapped individual. As more laws are passed that clearly establish procedures, parent groups may then focus upon the *quality* of the service, as contrasted to the previous concern with the right to that service.

Litigation

As important as the doctor, teacher, or psychologist may be in the history of special education, the lawyer and judge are not to be denied a valued role. Since 1960 an increasing number of legal suits and judicial decisions have had a direct effect upon the education, training, care, and protection of handicapped individuals. These cases have proliferated to such an extent that the National Center for Law and the Handicapped was established in 1972 to keep track of the litigation and to function in an advisory role to those who wish to initiate similar suits in their own communities. Their bimonthly publication, *Amicus,* contains special reports, reviews of court decisions, and news items on laws effecting the rights of handicapped individuals. Another publication, *Mental Disability Law Reporter,* was introduced to the field by the Mental Disability Legal Resource Center, a component of the American Bar Association Commission on the Mentally Disabled. This bimonthly journal functions as a compendium of legal materials for lawyers, administrators, professionals, and advocates in the area of mental disability.

There is an astounding number and range of cases involving the rights of handicapped individuals. Friedman (1973) provides a review of 44 cases pertaining only to individuals with mental retardation that have either been closed or are pending decision. The reviews are in the following categories:

- sterilization
- right to treatment
- right to education
- right to just compensation for labor
- right to fair classification
- exclusionary zoning
- custody
- commitment

Since Friedman's review, more cases have been filed and decided that have particular bearing upon other areas of disability. Each case, however, contributes to a collective body of litigation, which moves handicapped individuals toward equal protection and participation under the law. In general, this movement has increased the amount of attention and interest among parents, special educators, and other professionals associated with programs in the areas of education, training, or care. Such publications as *A Handbook on the Legal Rights of Handicapped People* (The President's Committee on Employment of the Handicapped, 1976) and *A Primer on Due Process* (Abeson, Bolick, & Hass, 1975) familiarize the reader with specific suits, laws, and procedures that are related to securing equal protection under the law. Although we are interested in each category of legal action, the major focus of our discussion will be with those cases that have established the right to education for all handicapped children. We have limited our discussion to a few significant cases, although some readers may object to the selections. Those readers in search of greater detail and scope to the numerous court decisions should refer to the previous journals, as well as the discussions contained in Cohen and DeYoung (1973), *Harvard Educational Review* (1973), Hobbs (1975), Kirp (1974), Ross, DeYoung, and Cohen (1971), and Weintraub (1975).

A major cornerstone of the right to education litigation is based on the Supreme Court decision in *Brown* v. *Board of Education of Topeka, Kansas* (1954). The decision in favor of the plaintiff ruled that the doctrine of "separate but equal" educational facilities was unconstitutional. State laws could not permit or require the separation of students on racial grounds. Although racial segregation was the predominant concern, the *Brown* case established a principle of equal protection in order for individuals to experience educational opportunity. Education was declared by the court to be the very foundation of citizenship. It is an instrument in preparing the student to perform the basic responsibilities and is essential for later training to enhance success in life. The court stated:

> In these days it is doubtful that any child may reasonably be expected to succeed in life if he is denied the opportunity for an education. Such an opportunity, where the state has undertaken to provide it, is a right which must be made available to all on equal terms.

This same combination of arguments was to be applied at a later date to cases involving handicapped individuals who had been denied equal education because of the unfounded belief that they would not be able to profit from it and contribute to society.

Hobson v. *Hansen* (1968) was one of the first litigations that included special education within the broader issues of segregation and labeling of children. Judge Skelley Wright ruled against the use of a five part track system in grouping students for instruction. The track system was ruled unconstitutional as it deprived students who were black or from lower socioeconomic status an opportunity to experience equal educational service. The school system was unable to demonstrate that the system, in fact, allowed for advancement within and across the tracks or that instruction at the lower levels was meeting the needs of the students. The *Hobson* case established additional precedence for future right-to-education suits in the following ways.

1. It included the idea that school districts had to provide evidence that programs were yielding adequate results. It was not enough for school districts to *intend* to design adequate programs for students.
2. It indicated that the placement of students into appropriate programs had to be substantiated by adequate procedures and supporting evidence. The courts would not accept procedures that violated the constitutional rights of the child or tests that were inappropriate for the intended educational objectives.
3. It forced the field of special education to examine its unwilling partnership in de facto segregation and the practice of placing students into categories of disability.

A third major decision was reached in *Pennsylvania Association for Retarded Children* v. *Commonwealth of Pennsylvania* (1971). The association, on behalf of the parents of 13 retarded children, filed a class action suit in the United States District Court against the state of Pennsylvania for failure to provide publicly supported education for all retarded students. The class action suit was a strategic move by the plaintiff's lawyer, Thomas Gilhool, as the court decision would affect all children with mental retardation in the state. A second strategic move was to base the case on the right of every American child to an education. Through the use of expert witnesses before a panel of three judges, Gilhool was able to elicit testimony that established the ability of the mentally retarded individual to profit from an education and contribute to society. After two days of hearings, a consent agreement was reached between the two parties.

The court ordered the state to provide the necessary education and rejected the argument that there was a lack of funds, personnel, and facilities to meet the educational requirements. The court maintained that if, in fact, the state did not have the resources to educate all the children, then the handicapped children must take a share of the burden with other children but not bear the entire load of the state's financial difficulties. As a postscript to the decision, which further substantiated the plaintiff's contention that there was a general absence of programs, a survey of all eligible children who were mentally retarded and not enrolled in school was conducted by the state of Pennsylvania. The survey indicated that 14,267 children had been denied access to the public schools (Gilhool, 1973).[6]

The *Pennsylvania* case signaled the beginning of a succession of suits in other states for the following reasons.

1. It established the concept that every normal and handicapped child had a right to an educational program appropriate to his ability.
2. It established the precedent that a state has the obligation to provide the personnel and resources to meet the instructional needs of the child.
3. It itemized a due process procedure whereby parents and students would be able to approve or challenge the school system's action on a change of educational status to the extent that the final decision would be settled in the courts, if necessary.
4. It established the necessity of fulfilling an individual's present rights (i.e., those that must be immediately exercised and safeguarded).

The *Pennsylvania* case was a major breakthrough on behalf of the rights of handicapped individuals to receive an appropriate education. A previous case, *Diana* v. *State Board of Education of California* (1970), and a related decision in *Mills* v. *Board of Education of the District of Columbia* (1972) helped this cause. The *Diana* decision led to modifications in state codes related to testing, assessment, and assignment of individuals

---

[6] Lippman and Goldberg (1973) provide an extensive review of the background, development, and impact of the case, including a copy of the final court order.

from minority groups to classes for handicapped students. The *Mills* decision extended the right to public education from the mentally retarded students involved in the *Pennsylvania* case to *all* handicapped individuals. These cases also established a judicial foundation for efforts by organizations working on behalf of various groups of handicapped individuals to first encourage state legislatures to enact further laws. If those laws were not forthcoming, the same groups had the option of turning to the courts. Both of these alternatives required time, effort, and money. Furthermore, as one looked across all the states, he would have observed unequal efforts and results being applied to various groups. What was needed? Simply, a form of legislation that would apply to all states and all forms of disability, with a funding basis to support the necessary education. That form of legislation was in its early stages of development when the *Pennsylvania* case became prominent in the field of special education.

Legislation

The growing urgency of an appropriate education for handicapped individuals can be documented by the increased number of laws that were passed in the states. It has been within the Constitutional design that the states assume the responsibility of establishing school law, districts, procedures, and, in some instances, financial support. In effect, there are 50 state plans and definitions of state and local partnership in the conduct and funding of education for all children, youths, and adults. Thus, states differ in the extent of their support of education for handicapped individuals, as well as medical facilities, research, and employment possibilities.

In 1961 President John F. Kennedy appointed a panel to prepare a "national plan to combat mental retardation." He recognized that the office of the president could be used to develop approaches to a problem that existed in every state when no one state had the means to the solution. The panel's *Report* (The President's Panel on Mental Retardation, 1963) established long-term goals in the following areas:

- research and scientific manpower
- prevention
- clinical and social services
- education, vocational rehabilitation, and training
- residential care
- the law
- public awareness
- planning and coordination of services

The significance of the panel's work and the *Report* was that many of their findings and recommendations were applicable to other areas of disability and, more importantly, were placed into law by Congress. These laws have also reflected the legal decisions by emphasizing equal opportunity for handicapped individuals, whether it be in access to public facilities, education, or employment. Finally, the tens of bills that have passed through Congress have added the necessary financial punch to the recommendations through the allocation of support monies. By the early 1970s the estimated, annual federal expenditures for programs for handicapped individuals by the Department of Health, Education, and Welfare ranged near $1 billion. This amount will increase as state and local educational agencies begin to use the resources contained in additional legislation. The following discussions focus on four of the most significant pieces of legislation enacted during the 1970s.

MAJOR EDUCATIONAL LEGISLATION

The Education for All Handicapped Children Act, PL 94–142 (1975)

The Act has already been hailed as a Bill of Rights by numerous organizations and sponsors who labored for several years in its drafting and passage. It established the federal government's commitment to a full and free appropriate public education for all handicapped children. The term *children* is used in the act, although it includes funds for individuals between the ages of 3 to 21. The legislation is based on the congressional findings that:

- There are more than eight million handicapped children in the United States today;
- the special educational needs of such children are not being fully met;
- more than half of the handicapped children in the United States do not receive appropriate educational services that would enable them to have full equality of opportunity;
- one million of the handicapped children in the United States are excluded entirely from the public school system and will not go through the educational process with their peers;
- there are many handicapped children throughout the United States participating in regular school programs whose handicaps prevent them from having a successful educational experience because their handicaps are undetected;
- because of the lack of adequate services within the public school system, families are often forced to find services outside the public school system, often at great distance from their residence and at their own expense;
- developments in the training of teachers and in diagnostic and instruc-

tional procedures and methods have advanced to the point that, given appropriate funding, State and local educational agencies can and will provide effective special education and related services to meet the needs of handicapped children;

- State and local educational agencies have a responsibility to provide education for all handicapped children, but present financial resources are inadequate to meet the special educational needs of handicapped children; and
- it is in the national interest that the Federal Government assist State and local efforts to provide programs to meet the educational needs of handicapped children in order to assure equal protection of the law.

(Section 601 (b) of the Act)

It is the purpose of this Act to assure that all handicapped children have available to them, within the time periods specified . . . a free appropriate public education which emphasizes special education and related services designed to meet their unique needs, to assure that the rights of handicapped children and their parents or guardians are protected, to assist States and localities to provide for the education of all handicapped children, and to assess and assure the effectiveness of efforts to educate handicapped children.

(Section 601 (c) of the Act)

We do not intend to review every aspect of the Act and its regulations. It is possible that some of the initial regulations will be modified as state and local educational agencies begin to implement the several sections. This is the first time that such a comprehensive form of legislation has been applied to the education of handicapped individuals in the country. Therefore, parents, educators, advocates, and government officials will experience a variety of problems that will need further clarification.

Effective Date

The federal law became effective on October 1, 1977. All handicapped children who require a special education program are eligible for service by the law, but all such individuals between the ages of 3 to 21 must be served by September 1, 1980. However, the age groups of 3 to 5 and 18 to 21 need not be included in the clause if it is inconsistent with a state's law or the order of any court.

Priorities

The first priority under the law is for those children who are "unserved." The next priority is to accommodate those severely handicapped children within each disability area who have been inadequately or inappropriately served.

Funding

The Act supports education for all handicapped children with an entitlement formula by which the federal government provides a gradually escalating percentage of funding for excess cost. The formula is based on the National Average Per Pupil Expenditure (NAPPE) in public elementary and secondary schools times the number of handicapped students between 3 and 21 years of age being served by the local educational agency. The percentage increases by the following years until a permanent 40% authorization is maintained after 1982, as illustrated in Figure 2.

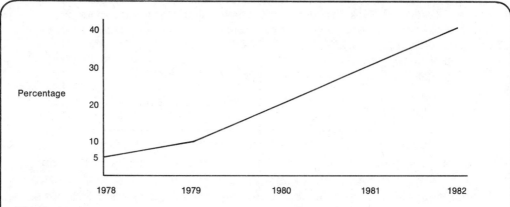

Figure 2
Percentage of National Average per Pupil Expenditure for Handicapped Children through PL 94–142, by Year.

Percentages mean little without dollars. The projected authorization ceilings for the first years of the formula (% of NAPPE x number of handicapped students being served) are illustrated in Figure 3.

These projected allocations represent previously unequaled funds in the history of the education and training of handicapped individuals. Local education agencies (LEA) received monies during fiscal years (FY) 1976 and 1977 through the state education agency (SEA) according to an approved state plan. However, when the distribution formula went into effect in FY 1978, a set percentage, 50%, was "passed through" the state agency to the local agencies. This percentage increased with FY 1979 and will

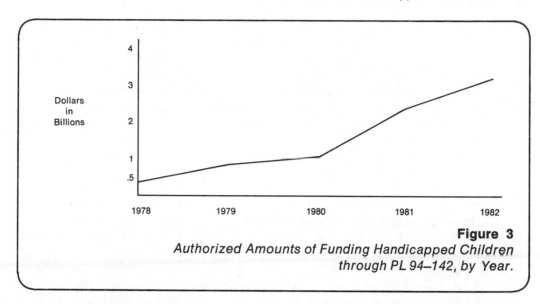

Figure 3
Authorized Amounts of Funding Handicapped Children through PL 94–142, by Year.

remain at 75% for the life of the Act. Incentive monies are also available for those agencies that provide special education and related services to preschool handicapped children.

The funding rests upon the concept of "excess costs" and it, in turn, has met with some sharp criticism from public school administrators. Yates (1977) reviews several of the obstacles in the financing of the law. They range from questions of state's rights and the increased role of the federal government in local education agency policy to the process of pupil accounting and equalization in funding. He raises enough questions to indicate that this segment of the law will require more time and attention than imagined after the first reading.

Application and Assurances

The local education agency will receive monies on the approval of an application to the state education agency, which includes the assurance that: **1.** the funds granted under the law are to cover excess costs above the average annual per pupil expenditure that provides services for handicapped students; **2.** staff development program must be outlined and provided; **3.** schedule of services and the dates by which they will be provided must be outlined in the plan; and **4.** the LEA must include adequate provisions for program evaluation and reporting.

Individualized Education Program

The Act specifically requires LEAs to establish or revise individualized programs at the beginning of each school year and to review their educational provisions periodically but not less than annually. Such programs are to include a written statement of the following components.

1. The student's present levels of educational performance.
2. Annual goals and short-term instructional objectives.
3. Specific special education and related services to be provided.
4. Projected dates for initiation of services and the anticipated duration of each.
5. Appropriate objective criteria, evaluation procedures, and evaluation schedule.

It is in the development of such an individual education program that the team of professionals with the consent of the parents will determine the least restrictive setting. The Act not only requires the individual program but also provides the financial resources so that local educational agencies can develop a continuum of possible environments in which the student will be able to obtain the instructional objectives. The IEP and the services that will facilitate its success are the very heart of the legislation, and we will discuss them further in this chapter.

Due Process Procedures

In the year of the nation's Bicentennial anniversary, a historian made the observation that one of the most important aspects of the celebration was the development of 200 years of law. A key ingredient in this system of law is the concept of *due process.*

> Due process is a course of legal proceedings in accordance with established rules and principles for enforcing and protecting individual rights.

Section 615 of the Act is directed toward the rights of handicapped individuals and their parents and, although not immediately evident, contains safeguards for those who work in systems of public instruction.

An example of the safeguards is contained in Section 615 (e) 3. It specifies that a child shall be placed in a public school program upon initial admission and shall remain there while the procedure of identification, evaluation, and determination of educational program has run its complete course, including impartial hearings and appeals. The procedures prevent instances in which children are held outside the public school program while their fate is being decided. This outside status had the effect of denying them an education.

In reviewing PL 94–142, previous legislation, and court orders, there are several basic elements of due process procedures in programs for handicapped individuals. These are listed in Figure 4. The reader should be aware of the fact that they overlap one another when school systems apply them to the student population.

- The child is represented by a parent surrogate when the: parent or guardian are not known, parents are unavailable, and child is the ward of the state.
- The parents have the opportunity to participate in the evaluation and determination of the child's program.
- The parents receive written and oral notification in their primary language before evaluation, change in educational program, hearings, or review.
- The educational agency has established specified periods of time for the completion of each identified procedure.
- The parents have the opportunity to respond to all notifications and receive written results of identified procedures.
- Impartial hearings will be conducted if the parents disagree with decisions. In conjunction with the hearings, parents can: examine all relevant records; obtain independent educational evaluation; be represented by counsel; cross examine witnesses; produce witnesses; present evidence; receive records of hearings; and, obtain written findings of fact and decision.
- Parents may appeal decisions to an appropriate civil court.
- The burden of proof for recommended action is upon the educational agency.
- The educational agency conducts periodic review of procedures.

Figure 4
Basic Elements in Due Process Procedures.

In reviewing the above elements, educators can begin to anticipate the amount of communication that is required in the whole process of identification, assessment, program planning, instruction, and evaluation. A great deal of accountability is required, especially if parents press the education agency into a hearing or court case. Yet, professionals should not suppose that it is now a given rule that hearings will flourish like the spring grass. Many hearings are a direct result of the lack of communication between parent and educator and can be avoided if the educational agency develops adequate due process procedures for the whole Identification-instruction cycle.

Melcher (1976) speculates on future changes in the laws relative to the rights of handicapped individuals. He projects that laws would be modified to: **1.** enable the handicapped individual to be a direct party in all procedures, **2.** allow a role for third parties to represent handicapped individuals (this could occur in instances when parents or guardians have failed to respond to suggested education programs); **3.** require school districts to facilitate a range of educational programs; and **4.** change the guidelines for compulsory attendance, exclusion, and expulsion.

Many of these changes will be welcomed rather than opposed by professionals. There is little doubt that they are already anticipated by parents and handicapped individuals. Several of these elements are contained in the following laws, which have received less attention in the popular media relative to PL 94–142, but are significant to the success of handicapped individuals in their adult years.

The Education Amendments of 1976, PL 94–482

This Act contains several provisions within a Vocational Education Section that will affect training programs for handicapped individuals. These provisions build upon prior legislation, such as the Vocational Education Act of 1963 and the Vocational Education Amendments of 1968 (PL 90–576). The 1968 amendments required states to spend at least 10% of the basic federal/state grant-in-aid funds for vocational programs to meet the unique training needs of handicapped students. This provision is continued in the 1976 amendments with the stipulation that the 10% set-aside monies can be matched with 50% from state and local funds. This prevents the practice of substituting federal monies for state funds in vocational education programs for handicapped students and should increase the total amount of fiscal support available for future efforts.

The law is also consistent with The Education for All Handicapped Children Act, PL 94–142, in the following provisions.

1. States are directed to use the set-aside funds to assist handicapped individuals to participate in regular vocational education to the maximum extent possible.
2. States are to provide written assurance that the use of funds will be consistent with the state plans that are submitted under PL 94–142. The references to state plans and provisions under PL 94–142 means that the same safeguards contained in that legislation would be extended to handicapped individuals who obtain services through the vocational education section.

The Rehabilitation Act Amendments of 1973, PL 93–112

Section 503

This section is intended to regulate the hiring, training, advancement, and retention of qualified handicapped workers by employers under contract with the federal government for more than $2,500. It requires employers to initiate "affirmative action" for all employment openings, including executive level. Affirmative action can also cover such employment practices as upgrading, transfer, demotion, layoff, and termination. A government contractor holding a contract of $50,000 or more or having at least 50 employees is required to develop and maintain an affirmative action program. This program can be integrated with others but must be reviewed annually. Any changes in the program must be made available to employees and applicants for jobs.

The Act and its regulations outline the several steps that employers must initiate in an affirmative action program, as well as the complaint procedure that can be followed by a handicapped individual in the case of possible discrimination. Documents pertaining to these two aspects of Section 503 can be obtained by writing to the Employment Standards Administration, Department of Labor, Washington, D.C. 20201.

Key aspects of the employer's affirmative action program are that he will:

1. Initiate outreach practices reflecting the affirmative action plan. These practices could include adequate use of employment and placement services, active recruitment through the public media, cooperative ventures with organizations that represent handicapped individuals, and company efforts to expand all employees' understanding of and cooperation in affirmative action;
2. accommodate the job and work environment to the physical and mental limitations of the qualified handicapped worker. Such accommodations may include the elimination of architectural barriers, modifications in the work setting or machine, and changes in the work process;
3. train the worker in routines that are within his general capabilities. This training may encourage qualified handicapped workers to enter the labor force when they previously were denied an opportunity to compete based solely on the presence of a limitation;
4. refrain from discrimination against handicapped workers who are qualified to advance to other levels of employment. This is particularly important in eliminating situations in which handicapped individuals were locked into a certain work role and corresponding economic returns; and
5. refrain from attempting to fulfill affirmative action obligations through the process of subcontracting with sheltered workshops for handicapped individuals. Sheltered workshops are to be considered as another source of manpower for the employer and not as a means of meeting obligations without changing employment policies.

There are also some limitations that should be recognized by the handicapped applicant. First, the handicapped worker must be "qualified" (i.e., capable of performing a particular job with a reasonable accommodation to his limitations). Second, the handicapped applicant must declare himself in order to be covered by affirmative action policies. Even with these limitations, employers and handicapped workers may both experience new opportunities for increasing the skills of the labor force and general productivity.

Section 504

This section has been described as the most comprehensive civil rights protection ever extended to handicapped individuals in America. It affects fundamental modifications in actions and attitudes of individuals in all organizations that receive any funds from the federal government. Such recipients include the several levels of the education community (elementary, secondary, adult, and university systems), hospitals, and social service agencies. The section includes the statement that:

> No otherwise qualified handicapped individual . . . shall, solely by reason of his handicap, be excluded from the participation in, be denied the benefits of, or be subjected to discrimination under any program or activity receiving Federal financial assistance.
>
> *Section 504,*
> *The Rehabilitation Act Amendments of 1973*

Although the Act was passed by Congress in 1973, it took until April 28, 1977, before the final regulations were signed by the then Secretary of the Department of Health, Education, and Welfare (HEW), Joseph A. Califano, Jr. His action was not without some attention as various handicapped individuals and groups representing the interests of handicapped individuals conducted demonstrations in protest over the long delay in implementing the law. Once again, we will not attempt to review all of the regulations but will highlight some of the significant parts.

Program Accessibility. A fundamental principle is that programs must be accessible to handicapped individuals. This includes modifications in class schedules, changes in degree requirements or ways in meeting such requirements, and the use of mechanical devices that enable the individual to participate in the program. Accessibility also includes institutional efforts to integrate the handicapped person as much as possible with normal citizens.

Public Education. Handicapped individuals are to be afforded free public education appropriate to their needs. This part of the section reaffirms similar rights and policies as elaborated in PL 94–142.

Architectural Changes. All new facilities are to be barrier free. By June 3, 1980, remaining facilities are to be modified in order to allow handicapped individuals access to programs and service that are housed in the structures.

Elimination of Discrimination. Program personnel must abolish materials and practices that discriminate against handicapped individuals. These practices may include admission procedures, testing, and interviews related to health, welfare, or social service benefits. The procedures are especially crucial in hiring practices, and employers may not refuse to hire handicapped individuals if reasonable accommodations can be made as previously discussed in Section 503. Employers are also directed to eliminate pre-employment physical examinations related to the extent of a disability as a requirement of employment.

The Department of HEW has taken several steps to assure compliance with the regulations. They have:

1. Developed a technical assistance unit to aid recipients of federal monies in meeting the several regulations;
2. established a deputy for program review in the Office for Civil Rights to insure continuity across the several divisions of HEW relative to compliance with the regulations; and
3. initiated a public awareness campaign that will inform handicapped individuals of their rights, recipients about the regulations, and the general public about changes in the law.

Any person who has a complaint about discrimination on the basis of a physical or mental handicap in a program funded by HEW should file a letter with the Director, Office for Civil Rights, Department of Health, Education, and Welfare, Washington, D.C. 20201.

MEDICAL AND TECHNOLOGICAL ADVANCES

There have been significant changes in the daily lives of handicapped individuals through medical and technological improvements. The use of corrective surgery for physical and sensory damage has assisted individuals to maintain acceptable levels of performance in the classroom, community, and place of employment. The development of medicines to prevent disease, to decrease forms of damage due to illness or injury, and to stabilize one's physical status within the environment have added to the amount of time and effort the individual can devote to learning. Finally, refinements in the use of metals and synthetics for prosthetic devices and other mechanical aides have allowed handicapped individuals greater mobility within the environment and access to forms of work and leisure. Generally, these advances have assisted the process of education by providing handicapped individuals with additional means for gaining necessary information. The following are some notable technological developments that assist handicapped individuals in both the educational and vocational setting.

Optacon

This electronic device converts printed images into tactual representations that can be felt by blind persons (Goldish & Taylor, 1974). The student moves an optical scanner with one hand across a page in a text or telephone directory. The impulses of the printed letters are duplicated as tactile representations, which the student feels by placing his opposite hand on the Optacon device. One of the numerous accessories is a camera module, which allows the user to "read" a cathode ray tube. This benefits those individuals with visual disability who are employed as computer programmers. In 1976 The Bureau of Education for the Handicapped engaged in a proposed 3-year project to teach blind students to read with the Optacon. Between June 1976 and May 1977, over 160 teachers learned to use the device in teaching reading to 200 blind students.

Vocoder

Engelmann and Rosov (1975) report experiments with a device that translates auditory signals into tactual impressions so that individuals with hearing impairment can produce speech. Five metal boxes are attached to the surface of the skin by elastic bandages. Vibrators within the boxes relay auditory factors as pitch and stress to the student so he is able to discriminate between words that are received and produced. Future developments with the Vocoder will further the individual's ability to "hear" by using tactual input.

INVACAR Model 70

The British INVACAR (vehicle) has been used by disabled persons in Britain for 30 years and is presently being imported into the United States. It is designed to furnish greater mobility for individuals with physical limitations. It has an automatic transmission, which can be fitted with 56 variations of controls to suit the particular limitations of the user. It also allows for several possible safety devices, a two-way radio, and space for a folding wheelchair. Additional information is available through the British Embassy Information Department, Washington, D.C. 20008.

Braillemboss

A braille page printer allows the individual access to time-shared computers (Dalrymple, 1975). The mechanism is a basic teletype unit that produces braille instead of printed letters. With appropriate training, blind individuals can work as computer programmers, reservationists, inventory managers, or in any job that includes the functions of entering, manipulating, and retrieving data stored in a computer.

Voice Controlled Wheelchair

Jet Propulsion Laboratory, Pasadena, California, built and tested a wheelchair that responds to one-word commando (*Now York Times*, 1975). The commands are given through a microphone worn by the disabled individual. A miniature computer is programmed with a 32-word memory and accepts such directions as: ready, go, stop, left, right, and forward. The wheelchair is also equipped with a manipulator arm and pincers that can grasp items on command. The funding for the wheelchair was through the Veterans Administration.

The Auto-Com

Wendt, Sprague, and Marquis (1975) describe the initial frustrations and successive experimentations that led to the production of a device which facilitates communication for a student with severe cerebral palsy. The portable Auto-Com includes a magnetic letter board, which is activated when the student places a hand device over a particular symbol. The symbol can be recorded on a typewriter, television screen, or tape printout. The Auto-Com is particularly valuable for students who understand the symbols but may be unable to use expressive language. It was developed by a team of engineering students and professors, the Cerebral Palsy Instrumentation Group, at the University of Wisconsin.

Speech Plus Caloulator

The same organization that produced the Optacon, Telesensory Systems, Inc. (1975), has marketed a hand-held, portable calculator for blind individuals. As its name implies, the device produces the audio representation of the numbers and forms of calculations when their respective keys are depressed. It includes a 24-word vocabulary, memory register, automatic constant feature that enables repeated calculations, and square root.

Emulator

This device enables individuals who are restricted to the use of one finger, as in instances of cerebral palsy or paralysis, to record programs to be used by computers. The individual can work at home or in another setting just so long as he has access to a telephone terminal. A cathode ray tube screen and magnetic tape cassette allow the programmer to display, retrieve, and correct typed information before it is transmitted by telephone line to the computer (President's Committee on Employment of Handicapped, 1975b).

Reading Machine

A prototype model of a potentially revolutionary device has been developed by Kurzweil Computer Products, Inc. The machine performs an "automatic translation of ordinary printed material into full-word English speech" (Office for Handicapped Individuals, 1975). The machine electro-optically scans printed lines, recognizes the characteristics of the material, determines the pronunciation for each word, and produces synthesized speech, which is readily comprehensible after a small amount of exposure. Although the device is in the prototype stage, it is expected that it will first be purchased by libraries or schools, but, after continued development, it will reach a purchase price individuals can afford.

You may infer that many of the previous aids are at the initial development stage, but it is our opinion that the increased attention and financial support that has accompanied the expansion of facilities and program for handicapped individuals will also fuel an equally rapid investment in technological and medical changes. As these paragraphs are being written, other inventors and companies are expanding the use of calculators, video recorders, cassette tapes, audio equipment, electronic scanners, and several forms of print reproduction machines. Numerous magazine and newspaper articles (Kayfetz, 1977; Wollman, 1977) report such space age inventions as:

- Electronic hands for people with below-elbow amputations, which are controlled by the individuals' thought process;
- wheelchairs that can be operated by a breath-flow pattern;
- control systems for the home that respond to oral commands;
- an artificial larynx; and
- an electric typewriter that is triggered by a tongue switch.

Teachers, counselors, and other professionals at all levels of instruction will be able to choose from an expanding array of devices and programs that basically are aimed at increasing the handicapped individual's access to information. Information is a necessary ingredient to success in all phases of life and is definitely required to meet the personal competencies discussed in the chapters on daily living skills, personal-social skills, and occupational guidance and preparation.

INDIVIDUALIZED EDUCATION PROGRAM

One of the far reaching effects upon instruction of Public Law 94–142 is the provision for a written individualized education program (IEP) for each handicapped student who is receiving or will receive special education. The law mandates that each state and local educational agency (LEA) shall insure policies and procedures for developing, implementing, reviewing, maintaining, and evaluating the IEP regardless of what institution or agency provides special education for the student. The IEP should be developed or revised at the beginning of the school year with at least annual review and modification. Although the program will contain references to services and goals to be obtained by the student, parents, and teachers, it should not be interpreted as a binding contract for the school system or agency. State and local educational agencies are responsible for establishing appropriate services so that the individual will achieve specified goals, but the agencies do not violate the federal regulations if the individual falls short of the projected objectives.

The formulation of the individualized education program will be the responsibility of the LEA. Each meeting for the purpose of writing, reviewing, or revising the IEP shall include the following participants:

- One or both of the student's parents.
- The student, where appropriate.
- Other individuals, at the discretion of the parent or agency.

If one adds various state standards to the federal regulations, an IEP could include several of the components in Figure 5 on page 38.

It should be obvious that the IEP is a complex document outlining the present and projected status of the student. A great deal of attention has been focused on it because it has a specific status in the law. Each state must provide the local educational agencies with guidelines; and several national organizations, such as the Foundation for Exceptional Children, which is closely related to the Council for Exceptional Children, have published primers, workshop manuals, and study guides specifically related to the effective design and execution of the IEP (Torres, 1977a). See sample IEP, pp. 36–37.

The IEP should be regarded as an instrument in defining and monitoring objectives and, secondly, an essential prerequisite to gaining financial allocations for the educational services that would facilitate the student's

SAMPLE INDIVIDUALIZED EDUCATION PROGRAM FORM

School District
Responsible _____

Date(s) of meeting: _____

_____

Student _____
(name or number)

_____

Current
placement _____

Eligibility
certified _____
(date)

Period of individualized education program

_____ to _____

Persons present	Relationship to child

Curriculum areas* requiring special education and related services	Present level(s) of performance	Annual goals	Short term objectives	Time required	Objectives attained (dates)		
Area 1							
Area 2							

*If more space is required, use an additional sheet.

A. List any special instructional material or media necessary to implement this individualized education program.

Special education and related services recommended	Personnel responsible (name and title)	Date services begin	Duration
Curriculum area 1			
Curriculum area 2			

Student name or number _____

B. Describe the extent to which the child will participate in regular education programs.

_____

_____

_____

_____

C. Recommended type of placement: _____
   (include physical education)

   _____

D. Provide justification for the type of educational placement.

   _____

   _____

   _____

   _____

E. Actual placement: _____

   _____

F. List the criteria, evaluating procedures, and schedule for determining
   whether the short term objectives are met.

Short-term objectives	Objective criteria	Education procedures	Schedule

Date of parental acceptance/rejection _____

Signature _____

Signature _____

- A statement of the student's present levels of educational performance, including academic achievement, social adaptation, prevocational and vocational skills, psychomotor skills, and self-help skills.
- A statement of annual goals describing the educational performance to be achieved by the end of the school year, according to the IEP. These goals would correspond to the areas of performance as identified in the above component and could include other domains.
- A statement of short-term instructional objectives, which are measurable, intermediate steps between the present level of educational performance and the annual goals.
- A statement of specific educational services needed by the student. This part would include:
  —all specific education and related services that are needed to meet the unique needs of the student, including the type of physical education program in which he will participate.
  —any special instructional media and materials that are needed.
  —the career education program in which the student may participate.
- The date when the above services will begin and the length of time they will be provided.
- A description of the extent to which the student will participate in regular education programs.
- A justification for the type of educational placement that the student will experience.
- A list of the individuals who are responsible for the implementation of the IEP.
- Objective criteria, evaluation procedures, and schedules for determining on at least an annual basis whether the short-term instructional objectives have been achieved.

Figure 5
Components of an Individualized Education Program.

success. However, the IEP should not be entirely "new" to professionals who have had experience with diagnostic and prescriptive procedures, whether they were used in a counseling, vocational, or therapeutic setting. The power of the IEP is that these procedures now have a status in law with an enumeration of guarantees for participation in the planning process by parents and, in some instances, students.

The IEP also provides numerous opportunities for professional personnel to improve educational measures in career development.

- It can be a focal point for parent-teacher cooperation in meeting mutually defined objectives. These objectives will be the primary responsibility of the teacher and other professionals involved in educational services. However, the parents' assistance and areas of cooperation should be identified in order to continue basic themes and activities that were first introduced in the educational setting. The parents' role and efforts will be discussed separately in chapter 9.

- It requires the teacher to specify long-term goals and short-term instructional steps that are required to obtain the goals. The IEP functions as a broad scale marker of the direction in teaching content and skills, as well as a tool in the management of resources. These resources can be interpreted as services (vocational training in cooperation with a community facility), personnel (therapists, instructors from other disciplines), and materials (System FORE individualized instruction, System 80 individualized instruction via teaching machine methods).
- It provides other personnel with an overview of the student's educational program, as well as the career objectives. This total view would be valuable for curriculum coordinators, counselors, therapists, aides, substitute teachers, and cooperating instructions from such disciplines as physical education, home economics, and vocational education. The overview provides a basis for the particular instruction directed at the intermediate objectives that may be the responsibility of the cooperating professionals.
- It contributes to the continuity of educational efforts as the student progresses through the system or moves from one system to another. Each step in the development of the plan and its subsequent evaluation and revision adds an increased amount of information about the student's abilities and difficulties. This composite will hopefully decrease the amount of time and effort that instructors must expend in establishing baseline measures of competence. As a fundamental reference, the plan is extremely helpful for students who must change systems because of personal circumstances or the availability of services to meet their particular needs.
- It identifies the "who, what, when, and how" of educational services and evaluation. "Who" refers to the learner and professionals involved in the instructional process. "What" refers to the forms of instruction, assistance, or review that will be conducted within a given period of time. "When" refers to the period of time covered in the plan or the specific period during which the student will receive designated services. "How" refers to the measures and means by which program planners will determine student achievement. These four questions, which have been greatly simplified in this discussion, are always in the forefront when one considers the multiple needs of the handicapped student.
- It is another means through which the instructor can specify and obtain career development objectives. The sections dealing with statements of educational performance, objectives, and services should contain references to the student's progress in career development.

At this writing, the IEP is in its early stages of application. Professionals are first learning about the various requirements associated with the process of composing the document, projecting goals, and writing intermediate objectives. Its function as a device in managing the flow of services to handicapped individuals will be one of the prime elements for evaluation by the Bureau of Education for the Handicapped. Its role as a tool within educational systems depends upon the success that professionals and parents experience in cooperatively planning programs. This cooperation, with financial assistance, will lead to the availability of services to meet projected goals. But, if the plan is viewed as a perfunctory task that meets another requirement, then there may be little correlation between the goals as identified in the IEP and actual classroom instruction. The goals and objectives can be worded in such a general manner that even casual instruction or the student's maturation will account for his achievement. The IEP is intended to provide another element in a rigorous procedure that includes the progression of assessment, planning, teaching, and evaluation.

OTHER PERSPECTIVES

You may have already identified several trends in the care, education, and training of handicapped individuals interlacing the previous discussions of parent organizations, litigation, legislation, and medical and technological advances. For example, PL 94–142 was enacted to modify procedures, increase the range of opportunities available to handicapped individuals, and integrate many types of professionals into the total education process. We have attempted to identify several changes in education that are projected to increase the number and type of role modifications for educators. They are divided into two major categories, personnel and program, as these constitute the very core of the educational setting.

Personnel

The most obvious observation concerning requirements for personnel is that there are presently not enough teachers, counselors, and administrators with the particular skills to meet the needs of all handicapped students in segregated settings. This factor was discussed previously as a major element in the coining of the term *mainstreaming* and the search for least restrictive environments. But the question is often raised, "If greater numbers of handicapped students are to be served in regular classes, who will assist the teachers in providing the appropriate instruction?"

Such laws as PL 94–142 change the role of teachers and administrators by increasing the range of factors to be considered in conducting programs, as well as the number of students enrolled in the classes. Regular class teachers and, surprisingly enough, some special class teachers will experience changes in their roles, responsibilities, and curriculum. These changes must be accompanied by several types of direct support to the daily instruction of students when needed, as well as other kinds of personnel who can shoulder unique functions in the total process. Hopefully, these personnel will be available in a corresponding ratio to the number of handicapped students that regular teachers are required to integrate into their classrooms. The following is a discussion of some of these personnel.

Administrators of Programs for Handicapped Individuals

One of the most evident changes in the administration of state and local programs is the appointment of individuals who are handicapped to executive positions. Some of these positions are in agencies connected with rehabilitation, vocational training, and social services. There is no magic in these actions, but they are an immediate indication that the interests of the handicapped individual who is served by the agency will have a representative at the top level of administration. Policy always takes a certain amount of time to filter through a bureaucracy. But it would be better for changes to receive sanction at the executive level, as opposed to working their way up from the bottom.

These appointments set an example for administrators in public school systems. Although education is a separate system with its own requirements for advancement, it is not impervious to the demands of parents and advocates of handicapped individuals nor the actions of legislatures. These demands basically require the administrator to be knowledgeable about the needs of handicapped students and efforts to further their integration. It is an old adage that change in each school must begin with the principal. The principal sets the tone for the faculty regardless of the directives from the "front office." The authors of PL 94–142 recognized this fact by requiring that the chief administrator or his representative be involved in the final decisions on the academic placement of a handicapped student.

Resource Specialist

The term is most widely associated with teachers who function in the resource room as discussed earlier in the chapter. The actual physical location of the resource room may vary from school district to school district or with the elementary, secondary, and adult levels. Even the functions of the resource specialist are subject to change, according to the teacher's abilities, prior experience, case load, district philosophy, or designated duties. Some of the responsibilities assigned or identified with the role of resource specialist by school districts are to:

1. Coordinate services provided by the local school for handicapped students;
2. assist regular classroom teachers in the instruction of students;
3. provide direct instruction to students who need additional assistance in addition to regular classroom experiences;
4. assist in the identification and adoption of equipment and materials appropriate to the instruction of the students;
5. initiate parent contacts and coordinate school communications relative to the performance of the student;
6. conduct inservice training of regular classroom teachers relative to the instruction of handicapped students; and
7. function as a team member on interdisciplinary reviews of programs for handicapped students.

There are undoubtedly many more functions that fall into the job description for the resource specialist. They include administration, communication, instruction, and coordination. At the same time, do not forget that each one of these categories contains several components, all of which are to be mastered by the resource specialist.

Habilitation Specialists

Although habilitation personnel may be considered as another form of resource specialist, we prefer to discuss this role separately due to their unique significance in the training and preparation of students for work roles. Second, these specialists often function in facilities and programs removed from the ordinary classroom or school. They may work with other professionals in sheltered workshops, rehabilitation centers, or vocational-technical schools. These assignments require the specialists to be diverse in their prior training and experience in order to communicate and consult with colleagues from different orientations to the needs and abilities of handicapped students.

The labor market is another important concern for habilitation specialists. They must be aware of the fluctuation in the economy at a national and local level, which will have a direct effect upon the employment possibilities for handicapped individuals. Information from the Department of Labor or the President's Committee on Employment of the Handicapped may be of some assistance, but one cannot rely on reports that are after the fact. This means that the habilitation specialist must maintain close contact with those employers who have had a prior experience with handicapped workers and can reflect the immediate status of the local supply and demand in the labor market. In other words, the habilitation specialist, like the resource specialist, is "on the firing line" in so far as the current condition of the handicapped worker is concerned.

The term *programs* refers to the total span of education from the preschool to adult years. Twenty years ago, educators only considered preschool and adult education for distinct categories of handicapped individuals, and even then, the availability of personnel and resources limited the number of such offerings. Today, both the range and variety of programs has been increased across several forms of disabilities. Our discussion is primarily focused on a few prominent components that have received a priority status in legislation and funding. These are early childhood education, programming for the severely handicapped, and career education.

Note that there are other areas of interest that cross these distinct components. We are referring to the teaching methods, materials, and techniques used by professionals at various levels of development. Such approaches as precision teaching, competency based instruction, and behavior modification have been used in all of the programmatic elements. This is because the basic principles involved in each approach are applicable with certain modification across age groups or curriculum areas.

Early Childhood Education

Special educators have long advocated education for preschool handicapped children. It is imperative to the development of children who are deaf, blind, or orthopedically impaired that their education begin as soon as possible. These early efforts are necessary for the deaf child to understand the place of speech in the world of communication, for the blind child to use other senses for mobility and reading, and for the child with orthopedic impairment to learn how to use various prosthetics while gaining an education. All these efforts take time, and the handicapped child must start his education as soon as possible merely to keep pace with the normal child.

The advent of Head Start programs opened new possibilities for those children who did not manifest overt signs of disability but were usually placed in the "mild" range of categories when they entered school. In other words, early childhood programs could identify children with difficulties prior to their entrance into regular education. Second, these same programs held possibilities for those children who previously had been ignored as "uneducable" or who would not profit from the effort, according to some educators. This latter group would include children classified as trainable mentally retarded, cerebral palsied, or multiply handicapped.

By 1968 Congress approved the Handicapped Children's Early Education Program, Part C of PL 91–230, which authorized the funding of 150 preschool projects that were often referred to as the *First Chance Network*. The projects covered the entire range of disabilities and were intended to demonstrate effective intervention strategies and techniques with children, parents, and agencies. Some of the original projects were included in a series of 19 early childhood education institutes conducted by the Council for Exceptional Children in February 1977. These institutes brought together leading educators and faculties for intensive training in such areas as motor, language, and effective development; drug therapy; locating and screening young children; family involvement; teacher training; evaluation, planning, and program development; and strategies for children with various disabilities. The institutes were continued throughout the country to assist local educators, parents, and agency personnel in expanding their programs in early childhood education.

Severely Handicapped

Programs for the severely handicapped rank second only to the "unserved" as mentioned in the priorities for PL 94–142. This status is due to a combination of factors, including the absence of public support, finance, demonstrated programs, personnel, instructional techniques, and materials. Once again, the Congress, through Part C, Section 624, of the Education of the Handicapped Act, PL 91–230, launched the nation on a course that would enable the severely handicapped individual to achieve as much independence as possible. Although the funding and number of projects have been less when compared with early childhood education, one must consider that the population of individuals is also smaller.

The education of the severely handicapped received another form of support through the special publication of the Division on Mental Retardation, The Council for Exceptional Children, entitled: *Educational Programming for the Severely and Profoundly Handicapped* (Sontag, 1977). The publication contains approximately 35 discussions on such topics as community services; the role of parents; programs in rural areas; teaching strategies for infant, preschool, adolescent populations; vocational development; skill areas; and the training of personnel. The combination of a high priority status and the efforts of interested professionals and parents will bring continued emphasis and attention upon the development of programs for severely handicapped.

Career Education

Educators have always been concerned with the ability of handicapped individuals to earn a livelihood. This concern was clouded at times with other issues that interfered with the overall aim of preparing students to integrate into society. The Second World War created a deficit in labor supply, which allowed even handicapped workers to occupy previously unachieved levels of performance. Many of the follow-up studies of former special class students that were conducted in the 1950s and 1960s used those individuals who left school during periods when employers worried less about genetics than production. The results of the follow-up studies were then used to justify expanded special class programs, based on the fact that handicapped workers could contribute to the economy.

School systems began developing forms of work-study programs for handicapped students prior to the Second World War, but the overall expansion of special education was primarily at the elementary school level. It was not until the 1960s that the secondary schools began to receive more attention from parent organizations, legislators, and special educators. They were assisted greatly when the then Commissioner of the Office of Education, Sidney Marland, began to emphasize the importance of career education for all students. The new emphasis in regular education upon career development had great potential for handicapped individuals because it was in line with the efforts of those parents and professionals who had been advocating the right *and* ability of handicapped individuals to maintain employment and contribute to the total society.

CONCLUSION

We have reviewed some of the highlights in the history of the education of handicapped individuals. These highlights include distinct landmarks, significant individuals, and concerted efforts by groups of people. Perhaps the brightest aspect of this chapter is that these actions are not over but truly have just begun. Professionals, advocates, and handicapped individuals feel that they have just opened the gate of possibilities with the passage of the legislation reviewed in this chapter and The White House Conference on Handicapped Individuals. The implementation of the legislation and the recommendations of the delegates to the White House Conference, over half of whom were handicapped individuals, mark further paths to be followed and goals to be achieved.

2

The Nature of Various Handicapping Conditions

There is no one universally accepted definition of handicap or disability. Public and voluntary organizations have their own particular definitions, suited to their purposes and objectives. There are generally many factors that enter into the identification of people as handicapped or disabled or whatever descriptive term is being used to differentiate them from the "able-bodied." Generally, a distinction is made between the terms *disability* and *handicap.* Disability is a medical condition, which may or may not be a handicap. If the person can resume her normal activities, then a handicap does not exist. If the disability prevents the individual from resuming normal activities or it is perceived as such, then it is a handicap. Factors such as body impairment, functional limitations, mental ability, emotional level, communication, environment, self-care, age, education, and social skills are major determinants of the extent to which an individual may be considered handicapped.

The Office for Handicapped Individuals of the Department of Health, Education and Welfare is responsible for examining programs and needs for handicapped persons throughout the federal government. It defines a handicapped individual as follows:

> A handicapped individual is one who has a physical or mental impairment or condition which places him at a disadvantage in a major life activity such as ambulation, communication, self-care, socialization, vocational training, employment, transportation, adapting to housing, etc. The physical or mental impairment of condition must be static, of long duration, or slowly progressive.

This definition is useful because it excludes short duration and minimally limiting conditions, but is still broad enough to accommodate narrower definitions.

Another definition used by rehabilitation personnel throughout the country is stated in the Rehabilitation Act of 1973, which defines "severe handicaps" according to the following:

> A disability which requires multiple services over an extended period of time and results from amputation, blindness, cancer, cerebral palsy, cystic fibrosis, deafness, heart disease, hemiplegia, mental retardation, mental illness, multiple sclerosis, muscular dystrophy, neurological disorders (including stroke and epilepsy), paraplegia, quadriplegia and other spinal cord conditions, renal failure, respiratory or pulmonary dysfunction, and any other disability specified by the Secretary in regulations he shall prescribe.

The above definition is similar to the one presented in the regulations of the Education for All Handicapped Children Act of 1975 (PL 94–142), which describes handicapped children as "mentally retarded, hard of hearing, deaf, speech impaired, visually handicapped, seriously emotionally disturbed, orthopedically impaired, other health impaired, or as having specific learning disabilities, who because of those impairments need special education and related services."

The definitions presented thus far seem to agree that handicapped people are those who deviate from the average in mental, physical, or social characteristics to the extent that they require special education or rehabilitation services in order to develop to their maximum level of potential. They constitute a significant proportion of American society.

The prevalence of handicapping conditions in American society is difficult to accurately ascertain and is dependent upon which definitions and survey methods are used. Results from various studies have been quite diverse and thus, any figures presented can only be considered at best as estimates. Halloran (1978) presents the estimated incidence of handicaps by disability area in Table 2 for school-age populations.

Table 2
*Incidence Level of
Various Types of Handicaps*

handicapping condition	incidence (% of school-age population)
Speech Impaired	3.5
Mentally Retarded	2.3
Learning Disabled	3.0
Emotionally Disturbed	2.0
Orthopedically Impaired	0.5
Deaf	0.075
Hard of Hearing	0.5
Visually Handicapped	0.1
Other Health Impaired	0.06
Total	12.035

Source: Halloran, W. E. Handicapped persons: Who are they? *American Vocational Journal,* 1978, *53*(1), 30–31.

A study by the Urban Institute (1975) of voluntary agencies' figures relative to incidence and prevalence data for populations of concern to them, led that agency to estimate the number of severely handicapped individuals in the United States in 1975 to exceed 10 million persons. They estimate that by 1984 there will be over 38 million severely and moderately disabled individuals in this country.

The best possible estimates appear to substantiate the fact that there are over 10 million handicapped citizens in this country who have severe or multiple handicaps. These are the individuals who need special assistance during their school years to prepare for and secure employment, to earn wages that will permit them to maintain a good, decent level of living for their families, and to gain acceptance as worthwhile, contributing members of our society. Unfortunately, social attitudes toward handicapped individuals often exclude them from participating in normal community, cultural, recreational, and vocational pursuits which are desired by and the right and privilege of supposedly everyone in the American society. Many professional workers in the field consider public attitudes to be perhaps the greatest obstacle that handicapped citizens face in making a satisfactory adjustment in our society. Therefore, before presenting salient information on the various types of handicapping conditions, a discussion on attitudes toward handicapped persons and on the psychological aspects associated with being handicapped (or disabled) will be presented.

ATTITUDES TOWARD HANDICAPPED PERSONS

Much has been written and researched about the attitudes various individuals and groups have about handicapping conditions and individuals. Although the general public has become more aware and tolerant of handicapping conditions today, a pervasive prejudice still exists toward persons with disabilities. Society's role expectations for a handicapped individual are outlined from the sociopsychological viewpoint. Not only is a role enactment provided for the handicapped but another is implied for those dealing with the handicapped. The individual is reinforced for acting "handicapped," while significant others enact the role of dealing with the handicapped. Although there have been advances in the elimination of architectural barriers and transportation problems, there is still a general resistance on the part of the public to make buildings and travel accessible to handicapped citizens. This is only one example of the many barriers they encounter in becoming fully accepted members of today's society. As professional workers we need to become aware of the attitudes of others and ourselves. Thus, we can become more tolerant and understanding of the resistances that occur as we pursue our objectives in designing and providing career education programs for handicapped individuals.

The attitudes people have toward handicapped or disabled persons are generally a function of the interaction between a number of demographic, personality, experiential, and behavioral variables. Learning theory would suggest that these attitudes are learned and that negative attitudes represent an aggressive response to a frustrating situation. Psychoanalytic theory would suggest negative attitudes to be a consequence of personality inadequacies developed in early childhood; and the interaction with the handicapped serves to maintain a homeostasis or psychological equilibrium. Role theory would suggest that negative attitudes are a function of one's life experience and the inability to conceptualize what is appropriate behavior in interacting with the handicapped person. In addition to these theoretical views, there are a number of circumstantial events that contribute to the attitudes of the nonhandicapped toward the handicapped: the handicapped person herself may act inappropriately or invite prejudice; family members or human service personnel may interact in a prejudiced or devaluating manner; or mass media may depict various handicapped individuals as the "heavies" or "bad guys" (English, 1971).

Negative attitudes and discrimination toward the handicapped have existed since ancient times when physique was one of the grounds upon which class and caste distinctions were based (Barker, 1948). Physically handicapped persons were considered inferior, sick, punishable for their sins, and lacking of moral virtue. In many respects, despite a somewhat enlightened society, a large segment of today's population holds similar views. Many people perceive handicapped citizens as different or inferior, despite the increased number of positive statements that they may report in public. By definition, a stigmatized person is one who is not quite human or normal (English, 1971). This can be vividly illustrated if we list several devaluating terms which are frequently heard: *retard, psycho, crip, schizo, spastic, blind as a bat, dummy,* to mention a few. Do such words convey stigmatization? You might also recall the many jokes that are made about disabilities.

Being treated as different or being stigmatized and rejected by society causes many handicapped persons to feel and act like social deviants (Moriarty, 1974). Thus, they need considerable ego strength and personal maturity to withstand the constant pressures inherent in coping with the day-to-day negative reactions they typically face. Wright (1960, 1974) points out that the positive coping aspects of the disabled are often overlooked and the negative aspects of their handicap emphasized. (The less we use labels, the greater the opportunity for handicapped individuals to be considered as acceptable human beings.)

Attitudes toward specific handicaps appear to exist at least with some groups of people. Blind, deaf and mildly physically handicapped persons are perceived more favorably than most other handicaps. Society places much emphasis on intellectual proficiencies, and the retarded individual with her limited skill in this area is labeled and, depending on socioeconomic class, is often stigmatized or institutionalized (Ullmann & Krasner, 1975). Similarly, the public view of the mentally ill reinforces the label and stigma for life. Sarbin and Mancuso (1970), in a review of the literature on attitudes of the public toward mental illness, state that the emotionally disturbed individual is considered a nonperson without rights and privileges. People who are former mental patients, those who are more obviously mentally retarded, and those who are quite physically involved generally evoke negative attitudes and rejection from a large proportion of people.

Employers are particularly sensitive to the appearance of handicapped persons. Many may avoid hiring handicapped individuals because they feel they will add many problems to their situation. For example, some fear persons with epilepsy may have a seizure on the job and the employer will be held liable for any injuries; persons with a history of mental illness may act strangely; persons with orthopedic problems may easily fall and injure themselves; or nonhandicapped workers may be fearful or object to working with persons with handicaps. In addition, many handicapped persons do not project the aesthetic and symbolic factors employers desire (Olshansky, 1973).

The resistance to the handicapped is not confined exclusively to employers and the general public. There is a body of evidence to suggest that members of the helping professions hold many of the typical stereotypes and negative attitudes as well. Greer (1975) studied the attitudes of special education personnel toward different types of deviant persons and found them to perceive various disability groups differently. He found their perceptions of the physically and mentally disabled to be more favorable when compared to their attitudes toward alcoholics. However, they assume a much more "hard-nosed" attitude toward the physically and mentally disabled, while leaning slightly toward the compassionate side in regard to the alcoholic. Smith and Greenberg (1975) studied teacher attitudes and the labeling process and found that teachers of the educable mentally retarded appear to subscribe to different views of adaptive behavior depending on the social class of the child. For those from the upper middle class, a deviancy/nondeviancy model of adaptiveness appeared most appropriate. Outside school behavior likely to threaten the established social structure was considered nonadaptive, while those patterns not posing a threat were considered adaptive. For two lower classes, a competency/incompetency model of adaptiveness appeared most appropriate in that outside school behaviors that represent competency were considered adaptive, while incompetent behavior was judged nonadaptive. "Thus, adaptiveness in the upper middle class profiles appears to be a function of the degree to which the outside school behaviors are consistent with accepted standards of conduct, while in the lower class profiles, adaptiveness is more highly related to the acquisition and demonstration of skill" (p. 323).

Handicapped persons also have had to cope with the attitudes of their family, friends, and relatives. Although, in general, the attitudes of relatives are positive and accepting, many often have a deep-seated or underlying resentment, rejection, or guilt feelings associated with the more positive feelings. This may be particularly true when the handicapped person has presented a form of embarrassment or limitations to the family in their community activities. Some parents develop such negative feelings and low expectations that the child is not reinforced to use her fullest potential.

Obviously, the stigma associated with being handicapped cannot be attributed to any single factor. It is a complex interaction between the able-bodied's personality and their attitude in general. The major concern should really be, "What can be done about it?" There is really no simple answer to this question. The stigma will always exist, but it can be reduced, at least with those people who are receptive to attitudinal changes. English and Oberle (1971) suggest that it is possible to conceptually identify occupational groups that hold markedly different attitudes toward the physically handicapped, using occupational emphasis on "physique" as a criteria for making judgments. Their research suggests that knowledge of the emphasis that various occupations place on physique and other characteristics may help avoid precipitous training and placement attempts in occupations for which handicapped individuals will find insurmountable problems. Members of an occupational group that places a low emphasis on physique (typists) display significantly more positive attitudes toward the physically disabled than one displaying a high emphasis on physique (airline stewardesses).

English (1971) believes that stigma is such a large and complex problem that individuals cannot effectively deal with it as a single entity but rather we should identify specific and relatively small scale action projects. He recommends that human service professionals assume responsibility in dealing with the stigma problem by: **1.** presenting the facts about stigma to the disabled individual; **2.** increasing the amount of meaningful contact between disabled and nondisabled persons; **3.** pressuring the mass media, especially television, to present realistic characterizations of disabled persons; **4.** designing experimental studies, via the mass media, to manipulate attitudes toward disabled persons; **5.** influencing family and significant others to participate in the disabled person's educational and rehabilitation program; **6.** organizing the political efforts of persons who are obviously physically disabled; **7.** disseminating information on stigma to professional and lay groups that will listen; and **8.** continuing further professionalization of the human service areas. For the latter, English recommends developing higher professional standards, sensitizing professional workers relative to stigma, pressuring professional groups to stop exploiting disabilities in poster campaigns, making professional associations more action-oriented and political relative to issues like stigma, lobbying for more legislation on behalf of the disabled, following up on disabled persons who have received special services for transitory moral and economic support, ending irrelevant interprofessional and intraprofessional conflicts, and reconceptualizing and reorganizing institutional structures and policies.

Note that considerable progress has been made in the 1970s relative to English's recommendations. This progress is due to the increased public awareness because of legislation; the political activity of new and renewed coalition groups; efforts of the President's Committee on Employment of the Handicapped and similar organizations; positive media presentations on handicapped persons; higher standards by many professional organizations; the White House Conference on Handicapped Individuals, including the many state meetings leading to the final national conference; and the requirements of individualized written education and rehabilitation programs for each and every handicapped individual served by these agencies.

Despite the above accomplishments, much remains to be done, and the acceptance of handicapped individuals in our society still depends on the ways in which they affect the attitudes of those nonhandicapped persons with whom they associate. Second, the handicapped individual must master the coping mechanisms needed to overcome the many rejections and other negative behaviors she encounters. As Gellman (1974) notes, "the disabled person must be able to withstand the presence of societal bias, in regard to the physically handicapped, which shapes the self-image of the physically disabled and leads him to see himself as unable to achieve. He must be able to avoid seeing himself in the mirror of social prejudice and to escape the self-depreciation which transforms a physically disabled person into a socially handicapped person" (p. 3).

Contrary to the general assumptions about being handicapped, there is evidence that disabled people perceive themselves in much the same way that able-bodied persons do (Weinberg-Asher, 1976). If this is true, and it probably is, career development programs will need to make handicapped persons aware of probable reactions toward their disability, while teaching coping mechanisms. There is also evidence that these perceptions and necessary coping mechanisms will vary according to the particular disability. Harasymiw, Horne, and Lewis (1976) suggest that society apparently needs to clarify the relative position of individuals within it. They suggest "that society is ordered in some way along a basic value continuum such as degree of normalcy, i.e., the ability to conform to majority standards, such as work productivity and conforming value acceptance. Those disabilities that allow for the greatest degree of conformity to the accepted work ethic and are not value-rejective would be most accepted, those that are furthest removed from productive work and are value-rejective and most distant" (p. 101). For example, those who evidence a low rate of productivity, such as certain mentally retarded individuals, would be rejected. In an eight-year longitudinal study of disability group acceptance, Harasymiw et al. found a "remarkable stability of attitudes toward the disabled" among a variety of education and socioeconomic status groups, young and old, professional and laypeople, which was not readily altered.

Attitude change toward the disabled will probably be most successful when efforts are directed toward nondisabled persons in a meaningful way (Siller, 1976). Although information campaigns are often not very effective in achieving attitudinal change, they can be effective if they are designed to communicate a limited amount of information to a specific, carefully defined audience (Yuker, 1976). Donaldson and Martinson (1977), using nondisabled college students as subjects, found both a live and videotaped discussion by a panel of physically disabled individuals to be effective in modifying stereotypic attitudes toward the physically disabled. This technique, along with spending a day in a wheelchair, being blindfolded, or deaf for the same period of time, is used in universities by many professors who are preparing their students for the helping professions. It is an effective method of role reversal and enlightenment. Such techniques could also be used in management seminars in which personnel officers and other businesspersons are provided with these kinds of effective opportunities.

Handicapped people themselves are the most important ingredient to overcoming the negative attitudes and stereotypes that exist in this society. They must learn to cope with reactions without retaliating in a manner that will only result in more rejection and discrimination. Handicapped persons, their families, and professionals must learn to trust and respect each other and then together work toward removing the physical, educational, employment, social, cultural, and many other barriers that exist daily. Much progress has been made, and the enabling legislation has been passed; now we must learn how it can be implemented effectively.

PSYCHOLOGICAL ASPECTS OF HANDICAPPED CONDITIONS

The adjustment that a handicapped person makes to her disability is a personal matter. There is no particular pattern or reaction that certain handicapped individuals have toward their disability because of its unique meaning, their personalities, or environmental situation.

In the case of spinal cord injury, the person's premorbid personality often determines the reaction to the spinal cord disability. The loss of various functions such as reduced sexual ability and lack of control over excretory functioning are particularly serious areas that generate idiosyncratic psychological reactions. The dependency that a spinal cord injury imposes on a person is another stressful experience that will need to be overcome. Cook (1976) studied the research on the psychological characteristics of the spinal cord injured, their problems in adjustment, and psychological reactions to the injury. He found most early studies considered the necessity for such individuals to pass through stages of depression, to grieve over loss, and to work through a period of mourning. No doubt these stages are not unique to the spinal cord injured. The assumption that the cord-injured person must pass through a stage of depression in order to form a satisfactory adjustment to the injury may be erroneous. Of extreme importance to their adjustment is the role of the treatment team and the family to resocialization, and the new role that the individual will need to assume.

Psychologically adjusted handicapped persons accept their limitations, adapt to them, and recognize and use their own strengths. The social isolation a handicapped person may experience, insensitive public attitudes, acceptance of one's limitations, development of new roles and capabilities, avoidance of psychological/physical dependency, feelings of inferiority, and depression can substantially drain valuable psychic and physical energy from handicapped individuals (Bardach, 1976). Therefore, counseling and other psychologically-oriented services are important to help handicapped individuals realize who they are and what their particular assets and potentials are, besides the limitations. Denial, depression, self-pity, projection, repression, and overcompensation reactions are to be expected and need to be dealt with accordingly. However, as indicated previously in this chapter, many handicapped individuals do not suffer from a devastated self-image but rather view themselves in much the same manner as able-bodied persons.

Wright (1960) reviewed research findings on the relationship between disability and negative self-image/poor adjustment and found no consistent correlation. Her explanation of these findings was that disability is only one of many contributions to personal-social difficulties and that disabled persons can gain respect, encouragement, and acceptance from significant persons who provide them positive psychological situations.

With regular classroom teachers becoming more involved in the education of handicapped students, labeling takes on an even more important meaning in the school situation. The effects of labels have been studied by several investigators (Gillung & Rucker, 1977; Foster & Salvia, 1977; Algozzine, Mercer, & Countermine, 1977; and others) in regard to teacher expectations. The major findings of these studies were that labels carry a negative connotation that results in lower teacher expectations and underestimations for the handicapped student. Thus, those who teach the handicapped need to become more aware of the tendency to expect less of those students who carry negative labels when their learning potentials may be much greater than the label would reflect.

We have attempted to explain that although psychological adjustment to a disability is not an easy matter, there are ways in which handicapped persons can lead a satisfying, productive life if they receive the proper guidance and assistance in reaching meaningful goals. There have been some situations in which a handicap has been considered a blessing for certain individuals, because of their tendency to be dependent, taken care of, and pitied by others. For other individuals, a positive self-concept and feelings of self-worth must be restored and coping mechanism learned.

The following sections of this chapter will present concise and, hopefully, salient information on eight categories of handicaps: physical, speech, hearing, visual, learning, mental, emotional, and multiple/severe. Each of these handicapping conditions will be discussed in relation to its medical, social, psychological, educational, and vocational aspects.

PHYSICAL HANDICAPS

The physically handicapped constitute a large and diverse group in this society. Their prevalence is increasing because of our expanding population and medical, biological, and technological advances. Many more of the types of children who in the past died during or shortly after birth are now living and growing up.

Although there are various estimates of the prevalence of physical disabilities, it is difficult to accurately state figures because of the many diverse types and definitions. In 1972 HEW estimated that more than 25 million noninstitutionalized American citizens had some form of limited activity due to chronic disease or impairment, including nearly 2 million children under age 17 who have a chronic condition limiting some degree of activity (Swinyard, 1976).

Persons with physical handicaps include those with congenital anomalies, spinal cord injuries, impairments caused by disease, amputations, cerebral palsy, and other health impairments, such as heart conditions, tuberculosis, rheumatic fever, nephritis, asthma, sickle cell anemia, hemophilia, epilepsy, lead poisoning, leukemia, or diabetes. This section will discuss four impairments that we consider most prevalent and serious in the educational setting: spinal cord injuries, amputations, cerebral palsy, and epilepsy.

Spinal Cord Injuries

The spinal cord is a cylindrical bundle of nerve cells and fibers connecting the brain with the various parts of the body. The cord is located within the canal of the spinal column, which is composed of 33 bones or vertebrae. The vertebral column consists of 7 cervical vertebrae (neck), 12 thoracic vertebrae (upper back), 5 lumbar vertebrae (lower back), 5 sacral vertebrae (pelvis), and 4 coccygeal vertebrae (tailbone). Each vertebrae is separated by cartilage to provide a cushioning effect. The spinal cord is contained within the upper two-thirds of the canal, from the base of the skull to the lower back, and is separated from the bony walls of the canal and its ligaments by a layer of areolar tissue and a set of membranes called *meninges.* (See Figure 6.)

Messages from the brain keep the various bodily functions operating and make body movement possible. Conversely, the body sends messages to the brain to inform it of its position, sensations, temperature, and the like. Between each vertebrae are two nerves that carry impulses from the brain (motor) and two that carry messages to the brain (sensory). Like the vertebral column, the spinal cord is divided into various segments: cervical (8), thoracic (12), lumbar (5), sacral (5), and coccygeal (1). There is one more cervical than the vertebrae column and the coccygeal has one segment as compared with four coccygeal vertebrae (Freed, 1965).

Damage to the spinal cord can occur from tumors of the cord, infections, genetic disorders like spinal bifida, and other neurological conditions. Traumatic injuries, such as automobile accidents, falls, and athletic injuries, which partially or totally sever the cord, will generally result in loss of sensation and paralysis. The part of the body that is affected will depend on the level of the injury to the cord and the severity of the damage. Damage to the neck affects both upper and lower extremities, resulting in loss of feel-

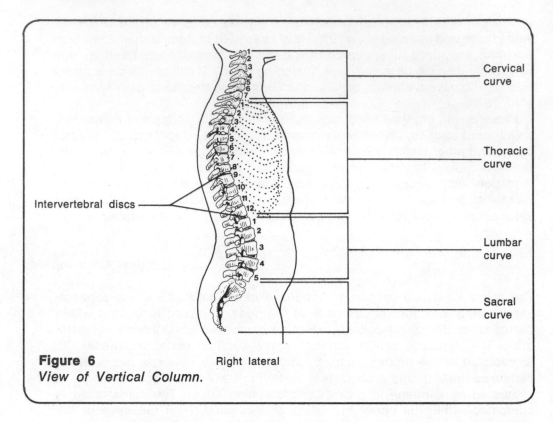

Figure 6
View of Vertical Column.

ing and movement in the body parts below the injury. Injury to the upper back will generally result in some feeling in the upper torso area and arms but still be considered as *quadriplegia,* as does injury in the neck area. Injury to the cord in the lower back generally results in loss of feeling and paralysis in the lower extremities only and is called *paraplegia*. It should be noted that injuries to the vertebrae (backbones) do not necessarily injure the spinal cord itself. Thus, it is possible to have a broken neck or back with no permanent loss of sensation or movement in the body. Unfortunately, there are ever increasing numbers of paraplegic and quadriplegic individuals because of military operations, violent crimes, and automobile accidents in particular (Sword & Roberts, 1974).

A prediction of functional potential can be made from the level of spinal cord involvements, assuming the individual is motivated and free of other complications. Figure 7 depicts what can be expected from individuals with spinal cord injuries at various parts of the cervical (C), thoracic (T), and lumbar (L) areas.

The individual with quadriplegia will always require some attendant care, but many will be able to function outside of the home if transportation is available.

Social adjustment for the spinal cord injured is highly contingent upon learning activities of daily living; that is, eating, dressing, undressing, hy-

C 4   Completely dependent for all needs.

C 5   Dependent for dressing and hygiene activities as well as transfer to and from wheel chair, able to propel wheel chair for short distance on level, able to manage feeding with specially adapted utensils as well as handwriting or electric typewriter.

C 6   Added increment permits activities of C 5 with more ease and with simpler adaptive devices. Wrist motion provides a grasping mechanism to hold large objects.

C 7   Manages transfer, dressing and hygiene activities with minimal assistance. Able to write and use electric typewriter without adaptive apparatus.

T 1   Able to accomplish all manual activities. Requires only minimal, if any, help in transfer, dressing, and hygiene activities. May manage automobile with hand controls.

T 6   Able to achieve complete independence in transfer, hygiene, and dressing activities. Complete independence in use of automobile with hand controls. Ambulation with braces for physiological purposes is a reasonable goal.

T 12   Complete independence in all phases from wheel chair. Ambulatory on level or stairs with bracing of knees and feet.

L 4   May be able to manage without wheel chair. Bracing required for loss of function in ankles and feet.

Figure 7

Functional Potential Expected from Various Sites of Cord Injury.

(Freed, 1965, pp. 272–273)

giene, ambulation, communication, and travel. Limitations in physical strength, dexterity, and locomotion can seriously hinder early social and educational experiences. Inability to handle daily living activities properly, such as drooling, catheters, and others, can lead to certain embarrassing and dehumanizing situations, resulting in rejection from able-bodied persons. Frequent hospitalizations is another problem that detracts from learning and interpersonal experiences. Quadriplegic and paraplegic individuals need to learn socially acceptable bowel and bladder functions. Some paraplegic individuals have the potential to become ambulatory with the help of long leg braces and crutches. Many can learn to drive an automobile fitted with special hand controls. The achievement of this daily living skill is extremely important because it connotes a sense of independence and self-confidence about the driver's future.

Persons who sustain a serious cord injury generally and understandably have a difficult psychological adjustment. It is felt that these individuals go through several reactive stages: denial of the disability, depression, apathy and resentment, hostility, a point when the problem becomes the center of their universe, immature reactions, and finally and hopefully, an acceptance of the disability in which the person decides to build a new life in spite of her handicap. Many individuals must pass through these various stages in order to recover satisfactorily. Others may not pass through this complete progression of stages. Counseling and emotional support from the patient's family and significant others is extremely important during this period. Overprotectiveness and sympathy of an undue nature should be minimized. As indicated earlier in this chapter, there is no specific reaction to a physical disability that can be expected from all or most individuals. It is highly dependent upon the person's characteristics before the accident, the extent of disability incurred, and the person's perception of it, the assistance given from significant others, and a realistic outlook for the future.

Physically handicapped individuals may receive educational services in several settings (i.e., a regular class with supportive services, resource class, self-contained classroom, hospital, home, day-care center, extended care facility, or nursing home). Most intellectually capable and mobile physically handicapped students can be accommodated in regular classes and services and generally have normalization experiences. They may need special meals, bathroom facilities, ramps, transportation arrangements, or recreational provisions.

A large proportion of individuals with spinal cord injuries become unemployed, although many more vocational opportunities are becoming available as transportation, architectural, and employment barriers are improved. People with quadriplegia are becoming more mobile through the use of vans. Simple things like having appropriate parking space may mean the difference between employment and homebound confinement. Those severely handicapped who are young, well educated, and highly motivated stand the best chance of securing competitive employment. Many persons with spinal cord injuries may remain in their own homes doing telephone solicitations, tutoring, and work that requires writing and calculating. Many of these individuals are finding colleges and universities more accessible and providing the services that will permit them to prepare for professional work.

In conclusion, the individual with a serious spinal cord injury presents a difficult challenge to the rehabilitation and educational field. But, with the medical, mechanical, and attitudinal advances that have occurred in recent years, the outlook for those desiring to build a new life and overcome the multitude of problems associated with this disability is much greater than ever before. Much guidance, emotional support, and relevant education will be needed from many sources. But now there is considerable hope for these individuals.

Amputations

Amputations can occur at any age, although the preponderance of their incidence is greater with older individuals. Amputation can be simply defined as surgical removal of a limb or a portion of a limb. There are three major causes of amputation: congenital, traumatic, and disease. There are many children born with congenital deformities requiring the limb to be amputated in adult life and replaced with a prosthesis. The prosthesis is of functional and aesthetic value for social and vocational life. Amputations of the upper extremity are generally the result of industrial or automobile accidents. Most of the amputations occurring in the lower extremities are carried out on people of older age. Frequent causes of lower extremity amputations are vascular insufficiency associated with arteriosclerosis or diabetes, accidents, malignant tumors, acute infection, and thermal injuries (heat and cold).

Amputations are generally referred to in terms of "site of amputation." It is necessary to be familiar with several terms to facilitate communication with rehabilitation workers. Upper-extremity amputations occurring between the wrist and elbow are referred to as below-elbow (BE) amputations. Amputations occurring between the elbow and shoulder are referred to as above-elbow (AE). Lower-extremity amputations between the ankle and knee are referred to as below-knee (BK) amputations; those between the knee and hip are above-knee (AK) amputations. Amputees are further described at unilateral (one arm or leg), bilateral (two arms or two legs), double (one leg and one arm), triple (three extremities), and quadrilateral (four extremities).

The amputee's social adjustment is similar to that of other types of handicapped persons. Acceptance of disability depends much on the individual's insight into her problems and needs. Before and after surgery, most are extremely concerned about the cosmetic effect of the loss of the limb and the restoration of normal appearance. The individual will have to decide whether or not to use a prosthetic device. It is extremely important to provide a supportive atmosphere so self-concept and interpersonal relationships can be adequately restored to an acceptable level.

The individual with amputation experiences a psychological adjustment process somewhat similar to persons with spinal cord injuries. Fink (1967) describes four sequential phases of psychological adjustment: shock, defensive retreat, acknowledgment, and adaptation. Obviously, not all persons with amputations pass through these four stages. Some may, for example, resist any changes in their thinking by using such avoidance mechanisms as fantasy, denial, or rigidity. Counseling is very important to learn more about the disability, for an expression of feelings and fears, and so future plans can be formulated. Some individuals may have to change their life plans, but most will be able to do what they generally had planned to do or were doing prior to the surgery. Adjustment may be said to occur when the individual no longer views herself as an amputee, but as a person with a prosthesis.

Those individuals who are still in school can resume normal classroom activities. Certain physical and recreational activities may have to be changed or curtailed, but substitute involvements that bring similar interactions with peers should satisfy most of their needs for peer interactions and group acceptance.

Over 75% return to their occupations. This may require learning how to skillfully use a prosthesis. Many other individuals will need to establish new vocational objectives. Jobs that involve a substantial amount of upper-extremity activities, especially bilateral function (assembly, drawing, manipulation), should be avoided by those with upper-extremity involvement, while jobs involving substantial ambulation should be avoided if there is lower-extremity involvement (Fishman, 1973).

In conclusion amputation, like other forms of disabilities, is an interpersonal as well as personal process (Chaiklin & Warfield, 1973). Most of these individuals can resume essentially normal lives if they so desire. Professional workers must help them work out effective ways of dealing with their feelings and the stigma associated with their situations.

Cerebral Palsy

Cerebral palsy is one of the most devastating physical disabilities that exists because of the many associated abnormalities that accompany the motor handicap. The condition is essentially a motor disorder that may occur at birth or in the neonatal period or in the early developmental years. The congenital form comprises about 85% of the population and can be attributed to such causes as anoxia, hemorrhage, infection, or birth trauma. Acquired cerebral palsy, accounting for approximately 15% of the population, can be attributed to such causes as meningitis, trauma, or vascular problems. Over 50% of the individuals with cerebral palsy are mentally retarded, 30% have seizures, 50% have visual difficulties, and many others have problems with hearing, speaking, and learning due to visual-motor-perceptual abnormalities (Scherzer, 1974).

There are numerous definitions of cerebral palsy. A general one is that it is a group of medical conditions characterized by nerve and muscle dysfunction. It is not a disease but rather is caused by damage to the part of the brain that controls and coordinates muscular function. Intellectual and sensory impairments often result from the condition. Over 750,000 children and adults in the United States have cerebral palsy; 250,000 are under age 21. The National Institute of Neurological Disease and Stroke, National Institute of Health, estimated in 1972 that 20 out of every 5,000 people manifest one or more of the symptoms of cerebral palsy. One out of every 200 live births results in cerebral palsy (14,000 per year). The annual estimated cost of care and rehabilitation for the total number of children and adults with cerebral palsy is over 1.6 billion dollars.

There are basically five classifications of cerebral palsy: spasticity, athetosis, ataxia, rigidity, and tremor. The person with spasticity is characterized by stiff and difficult movements due to loss of voluntary control of muscles. Approximately 50 to 60% of cerebral palsy victims are of this type. The person with athetosis is characterized by involuntary and uncontrolled movements which are slow, jerky, irregular twisting or writhing in the limbs of the body. Approximately 12 to 18% of cerebral palsy individuals are of this type. The person with ataxia (1 to 10% of the cases) is characterized by inability or awkwardness in maintaining balance or coordination. The person with rigidity displays resistance to almost all movement, and the individual with tremors is characterized by rapid and repetitive movements of the body (McLarty & Chaney, 1974).

It is now recognized that the major motor manifestations of the condition are not present when the precipitating cause occurs but rather emerges upon the maturation of an abnormal nervous system. The spastic condition is not usually recognized before 12 to 18 months of age; the athetoid, 18 to 24 months; and the ataxic form may not be readily discernible before age 3. However, a diagnosis of the major motor types of cerebral palsy can be made much earlier than its obvious presence (Scherzer, 1974).

Until recent years, cerebral palsy was considered to be generally untreatable. However, recent advances have demonstrated that the physical impairments may be corrected in some cases. It has been reported that freezing a small portion of the thalamus has produced restoration of motor functioning in approximately 60% of the 75 individuals on whom Dr. Irving Cooper has operated (McLarty & Chaney, 1974). Although there is no real cure at present, orthopedic surgery, braces, and medications may be effective. Preventive programs are underway to ameliorate birth injuries, blood incompatibilities, prematurity, nutritional deficiencies, and other factors associated with the condition. The United Cerebral Palsy Associations, a national voluntary organization formed in 1949, promotes service, public and professional education, and research and has over 300 affiliates in 45 states. These local affiliates provide direct services to persons with cerebral palsy and their families by offering medical diagnosis, evaluation and treatment, recreation, parent counseling, and general information and education to the community about their needs.

The building of self-esteem is an important component to the social adjustment of persons with cerebral palsy. By virtue of their general appearance and dependency upon others for certain needs, they can become very frustrated with the obstacles that prohibit them from achieving normal goals like everyone else. Verbal communication is often difficult, and other persons must make a concentrated effort to decipher what many individuals with cerebral palsy are trying to convey. Some individuals with cerebral palsy, because of their gait, have been thought to be under the influence of alcohol by the unknowing bystander, and there are instances of inappropriate arrests by the police. Because so many cerebral palsied children have had limited exposure to community life, it is essential that they get around to learn about its characteristics. Being able to learn to handle the necessary daily living skills, including personal care and mobility, is particularly critical for social interactions and development. Attitudinal change is needed within society to enable the cerebral palsied individual to exert her rights and to develop to her fullest potential.

In some instances, the psychological adjustment for persons who are born with cerebral palsy is easier than for those who sustain spinal cord injuries or amputations. The frustrations felt by formerly able-bodied persons who are now unable to perform previous functions is one hurdle that the individual with cerebral palsy need not overcome. This is not to say cerebral palsied persons aren't frustrated. They can succumb to a fostered dependency and overprotectiveness that will never permit them to function in the normal world. Although it is extremely important for parents to love and care for their handicapped child, they must at the same time permit and expect that child to develop as many living skills, social skills, and as much independence as humanly possible. Due to the multiple effects of the condition, there is a greater tendency for cerebral palsied persons to be sheltered and not expected to do much. This is a grave and unjust error by families and significant others and can contribute to the failure of the individual's attempts to meet success. Cerebral palsied persons can be emotionally healthy individuals if they are given the warm support, positive reinforcement, proper learning environment, and guidance they need to set goals for a meaningful life.

The educational program is extremely critical for social and vocational development. It should be remembered that cerebral palsied individuals constitute a diverse group, which includes those with superior intelligence. Many are often denied credit for their level of intelligence as it may not be readily apparent and testable. Preschool education, particularly in self-help and socialization, is highly recommended for these children so they can become ambulatory, toilet trained, and communicative for school programs. Many can benefit and be included in regular classes if the physical setting is accommodating with equipment such as adjustable furniture. Otherwise, they may attend special classes for the orthopedically handicapped, retarded, or other handicaps, which is often the case. In the past many cerebral palsied children were excluded from classes because school districts reported that they could not provide special classes or services. Fortunately, with current legislative mandates, these children will now receive educational opportunities.

Immediately upon entering school, the child should begin to develop the social, physical, problem solving, motivational self-confidence, and other characteristics needed for successful career development. Work habits, attitudes, interests, and goals should be included early in the elementary years, summer prevocational programs, and in workshop and work-study programs during the high school years. Positive and successful work experiences must be provided to override the intense feelings of insecurity and fear that often result from failure in academic, physical, and interpersonal activities. Frequent and periodic vocational evaluations beginning in the early years are necessary so that proper vocational goals and instruction can be provided. While it is difficult to accurately reflect the employment status of this group, it has been estimated that the majority are essentially unemployed as adults. Others are employed in their own households, sheltered workshops, and regular employment. Messner and Haynes (1973) indicate that the individual with cerebral palsy is generally less able to perform semiskilled work than either unskilled or clerical work. Manual dexterity is an extremely important determinant of vocational success, according to these authors.

In conclusion, cerebral palsy is an extremely crippling condition but one for which medical advances are forthcoming. Given the proper conditions and opportunities, cerebral palsied persons, like many other types of handicaps, have demonstrated their capacities for going further than expected in their personal, social, physical, educational, and vocational functioning. While the degree of physical impairment, intellectual impairment, personality adjustment, and education influence their ultimate attainment, most cerebral palsied persons can lead a meaningful and productive life with proper opportunities.

Epilepsy

Epilepsy is a brain disorder characterized by recurrent seizures that impair consciousness. The disorder may consist of involuntary tonic or clonic movements of the skeletal muscle (convulsion), impairment of the state of consciousness, and impairment of autonomic nervous functions. There are two classifications: idiopathic epilepsy, which has no known cause and is probably an inborn hereditary tendency, and acquired or symptomatic epilepsy, which is due to a specific organic disease or damage to the brain (Lorenze, 1965). The latter may be caused by congenital defects, tumors, abscesses, blood clots, head trauma, infections, cerebral vascular accidents, and metabolic disorders. Approximately 75% of all cases of epilepsy are idiopathic, and the total incidence in the United States is estimated at 1% (Grand & Grand, 1974; *National Spokesman,* 1977).

The major types of epilepsy are: grand mal, Jacksonian, petit mal, and psychomotor. Grand mal is the most common (over 50%) and is generally preceded by an aura of less than a minute that signals an approaching seizure. The person loses consciousness, muscles become rigid, and there are rhythmic contractions of the muscles of the extremities (jerking). During these phases there may be tongue biting, bowel or bladder incontinence, and changes in skin color. In most cases, the seizure lasts a few minutes, but it can extend from a few seconds to several hours. A deep sleep may follow the seizure. The incidence of seizures may be several times a day or less than once a year, and they can occur at any age. Jacksonian seizures start in one portion of the body and gradually spread throughout the extremity and sometimes to the whole body. This type of seizure is rarely found in children. Petit mal seizures are characterized by temporary loss or impairment of consciousness generally 5 to 30 seconds. Staring into space with occasional rolling of the eyes or mild jerking movements of the head or upper extremities typify this condition. These seizures are generally daily occurrences, sometimes up to a hundred per day, and occur primarily in children between 4 and 8 years of age. They usually disappear after adolescence but may develop into grand mal or psychomotor epilepsy.

Psychomotor seizures are more common in adults and are the most complex ones. They may include dream states, hallucinations, amnesia, laughing, crying, and changes in perception and thought. They may last several minutes or longer and for many are daily occurrences (Grand & Grand, 1974; Lorenze, 1965).

Most cases of idiopathic epilepsy can be adequately controlled with medications, such as Dilantin and Phenobarbital. Certain surgical procedures have been successful for some cases (Lorenze, 1965). It is estimated that complete seizure control is possible for 50% of the individuals and a reduced frequency or severity in another 30% (Grand & Grand, 1974). About half of the persons with epilepsy have no other limitations. Some cerebral palsied and mentally retarded individuals also have epilepsy. Schlesinger and Frank (1976) list these procedures for an observer to follow if an epileptic individual has a seizure (p. 37):

1. Keep calm. You cannot stop a seizure once it has started. The seizure will run its course. Remember the individual is not in pain.
2. If you can, ease the person to the floor and loosen the collar.
3. Try to prevent him from striking his head or body against any hard, sharp or hot objects, but do not interfere with his movements. Remember, you do not need to physically restrain him.
4. When the person becomes quiet, turn him on his side, face pointed downward so that saliva or vomitus can drain out and is less likely to be inhaled.
5. Do not insert anything between the person's teeth. There may be violent teeth clenching as part of the seizure. Teeth may be broken or gums injured in attempting to introduce objects into the mouth.
6. Do not be frightened if the person having a seizure seems to stop breathing, momentarily. Breathing will be resumed spontaneously. Resuscitation efforts are unnecessary and may be harmful.
7. After the movements stop and the person is relaxed, he should be allowed to sleep or rest if he wishes. He usually returns to his normal activities as soon as he feels capable of doing so.
8. If the jerking of the body does not stop within five minutes or keeps reoccurring, medical assistance should be obtained.
9. If the person is a child, the parents or guardians should be notified that a seizure has occurred.
10. After a seizure, many people can carry on as before. If after resting, the person seems groggy, confused or weak, it might be advisable to accompany him home.

The person with epilepsy can be relatively normal if care is exercised in her daily routine, accommodation to pressures, and interpersonal interactions. Unfortunately, there has always been considerable misinformation, fear, and prejudice about epileptic persons, which perhaps presents the greatest obstacle to their rehabilitation.

As with the handicaps discussed previously, adjustment problems associated with epilepsy are generally associated with a mixture of the individual's personality prior to the onset of the epilepsy, the affect of the epilepsy itself, brain damage, family reactions, and other environmental circumstances that affect the emotional outlook of the individual. Proper guidance and counseling along with supportive services are absolutely necessary to aid in the adjustment for most of these individuals. Psychological reactions such as denial of the disability, dependency, fear, hostility, and depression are to be expected, and the individual must be taught how to live as normal a life as possible with restrictions.

Epileptic children of normal intelligence can be taught in a regular classroom, although it is important for the teachers to be aware of the child's condition relative to the incidence of seizures, medications, physical placement, and stress. Adherence to these necessary items will preclude unnecessary concern about having the child in the classroom.

Vocational opportunities for persons with epilepsy are less than satisfactory. There still is a great deal of prejudice and discrimination among employers, making vocational assimilation difficult for these individuals. Benson (1978) indicates that employment is still a major problem for persons with epilepsy and that employer attitudes and client self-image are the two major problems. However, according to Benson, research reveals people with epilepsy lose no more work due to accidents than their co-workers and that they have higher ratings of job performance than many of their co-workers. The studies of employer prejudice need not be reported here. But the fact that epileptic persons given the chance perform as well or better than other employees is the point of significance. As long as the epileptic person is placed in an appropriate situation relative to hazardous circumstances, she is no greater risk than other employees.

In conclusion, epilepsy is a serious condition, but it can be controlled in most instances through medication; thus, a relatively normal life can be maintained. As with the other handicaps previously discussed, considerable social prejudices still exist to make adjustment difficult. The importance of concentrated attempts at career counseling and preparation during the school years and thereafter is readily apparent.

HEARING IMPAIRMENTS

There is no one definition of hearing impairments that is acceptable to every professional group. Individuals who fall within this classification range from mild (hard of hearing) to profound impairments (deaf). The prevalence of hearing impairments is difficult to state, although the National Association of the Deaf is conducting an extensive study to determine more accurate figures. It has been estimated that 8½ million Americans have a significant hearing loss, including 1 million children who are hard of hearing. The prevalence of deaf people has been estimated anywhere from 250,000 to 500,000. Whatever the actual figures, hearing loss is one of the most common health problems in the United States (Vernon, 1973).

Hearing loss can be classified into three main types: conductive, sensory-neural, and central impairment. Conductive impairment is the loss of hearing resulting from dysfunction in the transmitting of sound through the outer or middle ear. Medical treatment and surgery, if performed early, can be effective with many individuals. The use of a hearing aid generally compensates for the loss of sound that has occurred. Sensory neural impairment is the loss of hearing resulting from dysfunction of the inner ear or auditory nerve. This results in a loss of tonal clarity and loudness, particularly in the higher frequencies. Hearing aids and medical treatment are only minimally successful with most of these individuals. Central impairment results from dysfunction along the pathways of the brain from the brain stem to and including the cerebral cortex. Inability to perceive and interpret sound is the major difficulty. This disorder results from a neurological disorder, and the value of a hearing aid is questionable.

Deaf people lack auditory reception and the acquisition of normal speech in contrast to hard of hearing individuals, who have some functional auditory reception. For deaf persons, communication is usually related to age at the onset of the disability. Those who become deaf after acquiring speech and language are less functionally handicapped. It is important to detect impaired hearing as soon as possible so the most appropriate communication skills can be developed.

Deaf persons can be taught to communicate in three ways: oral, manual, or total communication. Oral communication stresses the use of speech-reading, commonly called *lipreading* and *writing.* There are problems associated with this method because approximately 50% of the sounds of the English language look like other sounds. Manual communication includes sign language, fingerspelling, Seeing Essential English (SEE), and siglish. Sign language is concept-based, with the first letter of the word being signed often formed within a certain spatial positioning. Thus, the same gesture may have a different meaning, depending on the location of the body in which it is being signed. Fingerspelling uses the 26 letters of the alphabet to spell out the word. Seeing Essential English uses signs that correspond to the sound components of English words. Siglish is signed English assembled according to the rules of English syntax. Total communication comes through combining *both* oral and manual methods.

Conditions such as prenatal rubella, meningitis, complications of Rh factor, and prematurity account for one-third to one-half of all deafness that has an early onset. It is also associated with brain damage, learning disabilities, aphasia, mental illness, and additional disorders. The individual may have other disabilities in addition to the hearing loss (Vernon, 1973).

Deafness has always presented a serious social adjustment problem because of the stigma it has unduly received. Deaf people have been depicted as dumb, demons, subhumans, and in many other derogatory ways. One recent study found that 36% of the professional workers in print media and 41% in television in the Washington, D.C. area, and 28% in print and 10% in television in the Los Angeles area still think that deaf people communicate by braille (Russell, 1977). In the same article, Russell reports that a proposal before the Bureau of Motor Carrier Safety in the Federal Highway Administration, Department of Transportation, to permit deaf persons to drive trucks in interstate commerce is opposed by the nation's truckers and their leading customers. The opponents claim that deaf drivers would be difficult to instruct in chemical operations and safety procedures; unable to hear malfunctioning parts or equipment, horns, sirens, or warning bells; and could neither receive nor transmit messages by phone. However, the Wisconsin State Department of Health and Social Services, which made the proposal, counters by saying that noise levels in heavy-duty trucks make hearing insignificant as a safety factor. These are two of many examples of how deaf people are often stereotyped and considered incompetent, thus making social adjustment difficult.

The whole range of personality and achievement is found among deaf people (i.e., good and bad, rich and poor, extroverts and introverts, competent and incompetent). Deaf people may develop an attitude of dependency and passivity due to their sheltered existence in special residential schools, and social isolation. A lowered level of motivation and self-image is understandable; therefore, considerable assistance is often necessary for them to become assertive and to believe in themselves and their potentials.

The education of deaf children presents a challenge to teachers and other school personnel. Unfortunately, it is generally agreed that most deaf children leave the educational system with a far lower level of academic skills than is necessary. Many leave functionally illiterate, and others drop out of public school or transfer to special residential schools for the deaf. Another problem is that although sign language is almost universally preferred by deaf individuals, most residential and day-school programs continue to emphasize speech and lipreading skills. Since more deaf children will be attending public schools in the future, it is important that more schools make provisions for their education. Those few students who can lipread can be accommodated in a regular class that is well lit and where they are close enough to read the teacher's lips. Otherwise, an interpreter, who can relay discussions through manual communication, will be necessary. Remedial programs should be available to develop their communication, writing, and other skills.

Deaf people share many of the same employment problems of other handicapped and minority groups (i.e., limited opportunities, employer misconceptions, lower pay). Those employed are in primarily skilled, semi-skilled, or unskilled jobs; a few work in professional and managerial positions. There are some excellent vocational-technical schools scattered around the country, but they are few in number. More adult education programs need to be established. Better job-seeking skills are also needed by these individuals (Johnson, 1974).

In conclusion, much remains to be done to permit deaf persons to take their place as accepted and contributing members of this society. For the hearing impaired, the task is much easier, although some prejudices exist. But for the deaf, social, educational, and vocational opportunities need much improvement before this group will reach their potential level of adjustment and contribution.

VISUAL IMPAIRMENTS

Visual impairments (malfunctions of the eye or optic nerve preventing a person from seeing normally) constitute a significant and difficult disability among American citizens. Although it is difficult to estimate the exact number of persons with visual impairments, it is generally believed that 450,000 to 500,000 are legally blind, and perhaps up to one million persons are functionally blind. Over 50% of the legally blind persons are 65 years of age or older, whereas between 3 and 10% are under age 21.

A person is considered legally blind if her central visual acuity does not exceed 20/200 in the better eye with correcting lenses or her visual field is less than an angle of 20 degrees (this means if a person can see no more at a distance of 20 feet than a person with normal sight can see at a distance of 200 feet, she is considered blind). Functional blindness is visual acuity greater than 20/200 but not greater than 20/70 in the better eye after correction, meaning a person is unable to read newspapers or watch television. The term *visually impaired* refers to those who can learn to read print. Persons who cannot learn print need instruction in braille (Kirk, 1972). This discussion will not include much about the *partially sighted* individual, although they too can have considerable adjustment problems unless given the proper guidance and assistance they need to be contributing citizens. A person who loses her sight before age 5 is said to be congenitally blind. One who loses eyesight after having seen and mentally recorded a variety of visual images of objects, colors, and natural phenomena such as sunsets and clouds, is said to be adventitiously blind (Roberts, 1973).

There are many causes of blindness. The American Foundation for the Blind (1973) estimates that 14½% of all new cases of blindness are attributable to glaucoma, a disease of the eye marked by increased pressure of the fluid within the eyeball and gradual loss of sight. The onset of glaucoma may go unnoticed, since the condition is usually painless and visual loss comes slowly. Diabetes accounts for 14.3% of new cases of blindness. This is due primarily from retinopathy—diseases of the retina that cause the small blood vessels within to break and hemorrhage. Senile cataracts cause 13.7% of new cases of blindness. Cataracts change the lens from a clear, transparent structure to an opaque one. Fortunately, blindness in newborn children is relatively rare today because of medical advantages. The main causes of blindness at birth are usually rubella (German measles), affecting the mother in the first 3 months of pregnancy; retrolental fibroplasia (RLF), a disease of both retinas; and congenital syphilis. During 1964 and 1965 an epidemic of German measles in this country resulted in thousands of children being born blind or multiply handicapped. RLF is no longer a major problem after research revealed that it was caused by the high concentration of oxygen that was routinely administered to premature babies, not by the infant's prematurity or by prenatal factors. Accidents account for another 1,000 cases of eye injuries that occur each working day of the year in American industries. In addition, there are countless numbers of home, school, and community accidents occurring daily, endangering the sight of children and adults alike. Probably over half of the cases of blindness could be prevented if people were more careful.

A wide range of professional services is required in the rehabilitation process. Basic to the rehabilitation process are four important areas: mobility, communication, techniques of daily living, and optical aids. Mobility training includes physical conditioning, developing adequate spatial orientation, teaching the use of other senses, and learning a method of travel (dog or cane). Communication training involves learning to read and write braille, and to use a typewriter, telephone, talking books, and recording equipment. Techniques of daily living include self-care, housekeeping, home mechanics, and recreation. Optical aids increasing functional vision include braille watches, slide rules, measuring devices, and tools. Sometimes, it is more difficult to rehabilitate a functionally blind, partially sighted, or blinded individual than someone who is born blind because of the former's tendency to cling to the sighted ways of doing things (Johnson, 1965).

Socially, the blind person has difficulty interacting with the general public as so much effective communication takes place visually through facial expressions, glances, and gestures. It is difficult for many to socially interact in unfamiliar surroundings for fear of their embarrassingly tripping or crashing into physical objects and people.

There are many special rehabilitation centers around the country that teach mobility, communication skills, activities of daily living, physical conditioning, and prevocational skills. A myriad of agencies are available to assist the visually impaired citizen in her rehabilitation efforts (MacFarland, 1973). The American Foundation for the Blind records over 300 books a year. Also, the Library of Congress purchases and lends materials to visually impaired individuals free of charge. Through its regional libraries, it distributes printed materials in braille and large type, as well as music scores, record players, records, and tapes to more than 150,000 users each year.

Much has been written about the psychological aspects of this disability. It seems to be the general consensus that being able to accept and adjust to the visual impairment is the greatest obstacle that occurs. Rusalem (1972) reports, "The experience of blindness, for most people, transcends the loss of the physical ability to see. With few exceptions it has serious emotional consequences, generating prolonged distress and intensifying preexisting mental health problems. It tends to reduce status, weaken one's economic position and lessen one's worth to others" (p. 113). According to Rusalem, the blind individual, like others who are handicapped, proceeds through a sequence of adjustment stages in reacting to the newly acquired disability: denial, grief, anger, rejection, and hopefully, eventual acceptance. The individual's adjustment will depend upon her premorbid personality, understanding, and attitude about the disability, family and friends reactions, and hopes and goals for the future. McGowan and Porter (1967) believe that the public attitude toward a blind person is possibly the greatest single determinant of the psychological effects the disability has on an individual. In general, however, the psychological problems of the visually impaired appear to occur no more frequently than those of sighted individuals, and the degree of psychological impact cannot be correlated to the degree of disability (Hardy & Cull, 1974). Scott (1969) believes being blind is a learned social role. The blind "adopt as part of their self-concept the qualities of character, the feelings and the behavior patterns, that others insist they must have" (p. 22). The sighted learn these stereotypes and interact with the blind on that basis.

The majority of children who are blind attend public schools, and a minority attend special residential schools. Several thousand blind persons attend postsecondary educational institutions. The most appropriate educational placement is the one best suited to the individual's needs. The blind child will need special books and educational materials, which can be supplied by the American Printing House for the Blind, the largest publishing house for the blind in the world. In most instances, only minor instructional modifications need be implemented for the blind students. Learning can take place from tactile and sound cues, and notes can be taken by a tape recorder, braille stylus and slate, braillewriter, or by memory, depending on the situation.

The vocational possibilities for blind individuals are much greater than is generally thought. For too long, they have been directed into a few stereotyped occupations. Consequently, education and rehabilitation personnel should try to break the stereotypes that generally plague visually impaired individuals. Many employers fear even meeting a blind person, let alone considering her for employment. Thus, a great deal of education of employers must be done to explain how hiring this individual will benefit the company. Blind persons have been known to be successful in a wide array of occupations, such as sales (including real estate and insurance), cooking (chef), nursing, television repairs, medicine, court reporting, typing, and receptionist, besides piano tuning and singing. These are only a sample of jobs blind persons can do if they are given the opportunity.

In conclusion, blindness need not be feared by either the individual sustaining the disability or the general public, including employers. Blind people can learn to lead a satisfying and productive life. Helen Keller once said, "Not blindness, but the attitude toward the blind is the hardest burden to bear." This indeed becomes their great handicap to succeeding in society. On the next encounter with a blind person, keep these basic principles in mind: "Do not raise your voice when speaking, he is not deaf; don't fumble around to find substitutes for the words *see* or *blind,* they're in his vocabulary too; be considerate enough when entering a room to speak to him and when leaving, tell him so; never grab his arm when walking together, rather, offer your arm so he can follow along" (Wood, 1968).

LEARNING DISABILITIES

The regulations for Public Law 94–142 define a specific learning disability as "a disorder in one or more of the basic psychological processes involved in understanding or in using language, spoken, or written, which may manifest itself in an imperfect ability to think, speak, read, write, spell, or to do mathematical calculations. The term includes such conditions as perceptual handicaps, brain injury, minimal brain dysfunction, dyslexia, and developmental aphasia. The term does not include children who have learning problems which are primarily the result of visual, hearing, of motor handicaps, of mental retardation, or of environmental cultural, or economic disadvantages" (p. 56977). This definition approximates that of the National Advisory Committee on Handicapped Children (1967). The definition is also accepted by the American Academy of Pediatrics.

Hallahan and Kauffman (1976) report that while there is diversity in definitions by various groups and organizations, there seems to be some agreement in regard to the following characteristics of the learning disabled child: **1.** academic retardation, **2.** uneven pattern of development, **3.** there may or may not be central nervous system dysfunctioning, **4.** environmental disadvantage is not a contributing factor, **5.** mental retardation or emotional disturbance is not the cause. Denhoff (1974) believes that regardless of cause or reason, a learning disability is generally the result of excessive demands made upon a child at developmental periods when her associative sensory-spatial-motor language systems are not yet capable of such intersensory performance. Hallahan and Kauffman (1976) suggest that the term *learning disabilities* should "be used to refer to learning problems found in children who have traditionally been classified as mildly handicapped, whether it be emotionally disturbed, mildly retarded, or learning disabled" (p. 28). While their point is well taken, this discussion will center on the definition of learning disability as presented in the federal law.

The generally acceptable prevalence figures of learning disabilities run from about 2 to 3% of the school population (National Advisory Committee on Handicapped Children, 1967; U. S. Office of Education, 1971). Learning disabilities may result from such organic factors as brain damage, genetic variations, and biochemical imbalances. There is also a growing body of literature indicating that environmental factors such as poor nutrition and lack of stimulation contribute to neurological dysfunctioning such as perceptual disorders. A third factor often associated with learning disabilities is emotional disturbance, although this relationship is not clear (Tarver & Hallahan, 1976). In the majority of cases, no specific etiology can be established.

Six major responsibilities of the medical doctor in treating a learning disabled child are: advocacy, early identification, provision for high quality health care, referral and coordination, discrimination of program, and interpretation of medical information into proper perspective for the family (Denhoff, 1974). Specific medications, behavior modification, and child and parent modeling or counseling have demonstrated positive results in many instances. Unfortunately, there are few physicians who feel competent to treat a learning disabled child.

The social development and adjustment of children with learning disabilities depends on the extent interpersonal skills are learned appropriately from family and school personnel. Perceptual, language, cognitive, and motor skills are inextricably intertwined with the development of social skills (Hallahan & Kauffman, 1976). A multitude of characteristics have been attributed to children with learning disabilities: hyperactivity, perceptual motor impairments, emotional lability, general coordination deficits, disorders of attention, impulsivity, disorders of memory and thinking, specific learning disabilities (in reading, writing, spelling, arithmetic), disorders of speech and hearing, equivocal neurological signs, and electroencephalographic irregularities (Bryan, 1974). But, as Bryan indicates, there is little empirical support to these characteristics. According to Hallahan and Kauffman (1976) conduct disorders and school failure are the two most serious difficulties these children face relative to their eventual social adjustment.

The importance of appropriate educational programming becomes apparent for learning disabled children. Accurate assessments of their potential and needs are critical to appropriate educational programming. A systematic diagnostic procedure is necessary to assess the specific learning disability and to organize an appropriate remediation. Kirk and Kirk (1971) recommend the following: **1.** determine whether the child's learning problem is specific, general, or spurious; **2.** analyze the behavior manifestations that are descriptive of the specific problem; **3.** discover the physical, environmental, and psychological correlates of the disability; **4.** evolve a diagnostic inference (hypothesis) on the basis of the behavior manifestations and the correlates; and **5.** organize a systematic remedial program based on the diagnostic inference. Behavioral analysis procedures are demonstrating their effectiveness in remediating basic academic deficiencies, such as omission, substitution, digit reversals, and other problems generally associated with learning disabilities (Stromer, 1977). Thus, establishing an appropriate learning environment for these children generally results in successful educational experiences.

Van Etten and Watson (1977) stress that career awareness must be part of a total curriculum for the learning disabled. They suggest specific materials and activities for career exploration and planning. Attention is just beginning to develop relative to the occupational future for those with learning disabilities. In the case of career education, Bingham (1978) conducted a study comparing two groups of adolescents, those with and those without learning disabilities, at two stages of development. Her results would imply that students with learning disabilities are less mature in their responses to career choices. She recommends that these individuals "be provided with carefully planned experiences and activities that accommodate the developmental differences noted in this dimension of vocational maturity" (p. 342). Presently, little is being done for these individuals. In the future, we should see more activity so that children with this problem are given increased opportunities to reach greater heights in their vocational functioning.

MENTAL RETARDATION

The mentally retarded are a very heterogeneous group, varying widely in intellectual, physical, behavioral, and other characteristics. As with the other handicaps, no one definition of this condition has ever been universally accepted, although the one preferred by these writers is the revised definition of the American Association on Mental Deficiency (AAMD) (Grossman, 1973): "Mental retardation refers to significantly subaverage general intellectual functioning existing concurrently with deficits in adaptive behavior, and manifested during the developmental period" (p. 11). This definition is a correct response to those critics of the first AAMD definition (Heber, 1961), which classified individuals with appropriately measured intelligence scores of less than one standard deviation below the mean as mentally retarded, provided they were also diagnosed as having deficits in adaptive behavior.

The newer AAMD definition uses intellectual performance scores falling two standard deviations below the mean as the cutoff point for the classification of mental retardation, plus the previous requirement of deficient adaptive behavior. Thus, individuals who score, for example, an IQ of 67 or less on the Stanford-Binet or 69 or less on one of the Wechsler intelligence tests would be so classified if they are also deficient in adaptive behavior. Adaptive behavior has always been the fuzzier of the two performance assessments and varies in its requirements according to one's age group. During the preschool years, these behaviors are manifested primarily in maturational attainments; during the school years, in academic achievements; and in the adult years, in terms of vocational and social responsibilities.

The AAMD definition is often ignored by many school systems who prefer to define the condition more in terms of IQ, with a cutoff score anywhere from the high 60s to the low 80s, (which is the old borderline "retardate" of the former AAMD definition). The danger in this position is the more permanent labeling that occurs and the rejection of the realization that for most persons, a lowered test score is a description of present functioning and not an indication of intellectual incompetence. The AAMD definitions recognize the inadequacies of our intellectual measures and the influence of environment and other conditions on one's intellectual performance at various periods throughout life. Therefore, it is our position that mental retardation for many is not a permanent condition, and that what is important is for professionals to determine under what conditions these individuals can most appropriately learn academic, social, daily living, and occupational skills for lifelong functioning. Approximately 3% of the American population can be classified as mentally retarded using the AAMD definition. The prevalence of mental retardation based on a general population of 210 million Americans is illustrated in Figure 8. Over 90% of the individuals labeled *retarded* are only mildly or moderately afflicted. These individuals have the potential for self-care, self-maintenance, and employment, and to be full-contributing citizens if they are given the proper opportunities.

IQ Range	Prevalence
0–20	104,935
20–50	420,000
50–70	6,332,106

Figure 8
Prevalence of Mental Retardation.

Source: Robinson & Robinson, 1976

There are over 200 causes of mental retardation, but most of these account for retardation of the severe and profound types. It is generally accepted that 10 to 25% of retarded persons have a significant central nervous system pathology. Infections, injuries, diseases, chromosomal abnormalities, prematurity, and disorders of metabolism or nutrition are examples of biomedical causes. Phenylketenuria (PKU), hydrocephalus, microcephalus, and Down's Syndrome are examples of resulting conditions. Over 50% of individuals with cerebral palsy can be classified also as mentally retarded. For the majority of persons classified as retarded, no evidence of biological factors or organic conditions is evident. These individuals, who are primarily the mildly retarded, are considered to have cultural-familial retardation, which can be defined as: "An undefined admixture of genetic and environmental variables, including poor nutrition and poor physical health of the mother and child, economic poverty, membership in an ethnic minority and a social class structure at variance with the dominant majority class, and IQ scores and educational attainments at the lower end of the normal end of the normal distribution of intelligence as measured psychometrically" (Milgram, 1972). There are some individuals who may be temporarily retarded because of psychological reasons. Therefore, these individuals must not be treated as permanently retarded; otherwise, their potentials will not be realized.

In 1977 the National Association for Retarded Citizens established the goal of seeking a cure for mental retardation. Roos (1977) states: "The belief that there is no cure for mental retardation has become a self-fulfilling prophecy that has prevented a cure from being found. Now is the time for a new look at the entire problem of mental retardation so that we can capitalize on many of the revolutionary new techniques and examine the evidence that gives us cause for a more optimistic reappraisal." Some examples of future possibilities in combatting and curing mental retardation are: studies in the Soviet Union relative to advances in regenerating damaged portions of the nervous system; new discoveries in teaching people to control their autonomic nervous systems; new understanding of basic cell machinery and ribonucleic acid (RNA) to correct genetic errors; nutritional advances; research in metabolic chemistry and endocrinology, and new surgical techniques, such as the correction of cerebral vascular dysfunctions with the implantation of brain pacer devices and amniocentesis procedures (*Mental Retardation News*, 1977).

The social adjustment of mentally retarded persons has always been a difficult aspect of their career development. Being labeled *mentally retarded* can mean being humiliated, frustrated, and discredited throughout life unless that identity is lost. For many retarded individuals, it is lost when they become successfully employed and productive members of their community. Until recently, retarded people have been essentially denied their constitutional rights. Only in the last several years have significant advances been made in clarifying their legal status in terms of due process and equality under the law. In the past and to a certain degree today, the mentally retarded have been denied the right to: equal access to quality health and social services; conducive residential programs and services; equal education and employment opportunities; marry and have children; equal protection in the criminal justice system; vote (President's Committee on Mental Retardation, 1976). Provision of these rights will assist the majority of retarded persons to be happy and productive members of society.

The psychological adjustment for many retarded individuals becomes difficult when, like anyone else, they are subjected to repeated failure and rejection. When their interpersonal environment becomes overwhelming, the chances of psychological maladjustment increase. Too many people are still confusing mental *illness* with mental *retardation*. Although there have been many attempts to attribute to retarded individuals a distinct group of characteristics, research has revealed no different pattern of personality characteristic of these individuals.

The education of retarded individuals has until recently been occurring mainly in special classes in public/private schools. With the advent of mainstreaming, most mildly retarded students have been given greater opportunity to spend most or all of their school day in regular classes with supportive services and resource rooms made available by special education personnel. Although it has been fairly well established that these students can benefit from this placement, there is still considerable resistance by many regular educators to having them in their classes. Much remains to be done to assure retarded students the normalization and appropriate education that Public Law 94–142 was intended to provide to these and other handicapped individuals.

It has been clearly demonstrated in numerous studies of the performance of retarded persons that they can be productive workers in literally hundreds of occupations if provided with appropriate vocational evaluation, training, guidance, and placement opportunities. Examples of jobs that the retarded have been able to attain that are often beyond typical expectations are: card punch operator, carpenter, clerk, clerk-typist, engineering aide, mail clerk, medical technician, office draftsman, office machine operator, photographic processing aide, telephone operator, upholsterer, and many others (Brolin, 1976). Despite these demonstrations of competency, too many retarded persons are underemployed or unemployed, while experiencing extreme frustration and feelings of self-depreciation. More relevant educational programs and rehabilitation efforts are still needed to assure the adjustment of retarded citizens into society's mainstream.

In conclusion, much has been attained in the last several years to benefit the career development of retarded individuals. As with other handicapped persons, we still have a long way to go, but we are much closer to achieving normalization goals than ever before. (Discussion of the severely retarded individual will be presented later in this chapter in the section on severe multiple handicaps.)

EMOTIONAL DISTURBANCE

An emotional or behavioral disorder is another misunderstood disability prompting much discrimination. The most commonly cited incidence of behavioral disorders is that of Eli Bower (1960), who estimated that 10% of the school-age population needed some type of professional assistance during their school years. However, only about 1% of the school-age children have severe emotional problems requiring intensive intervention programs (Kelly, Bullock, & Dykes, 1977). Gearhart and Weishahn (1976) estimate that there are 1,100,000 emotionally disturbed children in this country, with only 15% receiving needed services. Approximately 2% of the school-age population is emotionally disturbed (U. S. Office of Education, 1971). These children exhibit one or more of the following characteristics: inability to learn, which cannot be explained by intellectual, sensory, or health factors; inability to build or maintain satisfactory interpersonal relationships; inappropriate types of behavior or feelings under normal conditions; pervasive mood of unhappiness or depression; or physical symptoms, pains, or fears associated with personal or school problems (Bower, 1969).

Definitions of emotional disorders, like other handicaps, are difficult to agree upon, particularly since the definition of what is "normal" seems to be out of our reach or comprehension. Generally, emotional disorders may be thought of as mental health problems that cause the individual personal discomfort; interfere with her ability to function at school or in training; interfere with family and other interpersonal relationships; and impair vocational functioning. Some of the various classifications or types of disturbances are: neuroses, psychoses, behavior disorders, and personality disorders. *Neurosis* results in problems in attending to daily activities but are not overly serious. Depression, hysteria, and obsessive-compulsive behaviors are examples. *Psychosis* can be typified by such symptoms as hallucinations, delusions, inappropriate behavior, withdrawal, concern from family and others, neglect of personal hygiene, and dependency. Schizophrenia and manic-depression are examples. *Behavior disorders* are patterns of behavior at conflict with some area of society. Drug dependence and public offenses are examples. *Personality disorders* are long-term patterns of behavior that are in conflict with others. In one study of attitudes toward disabled persons, Tringo (1970) found that the least preferred group was the mentally ill. All types of adverse reactions emanate from the general public, and a full array of negative reactions and perceptions about these people continue to exist today. Being accepted by family, friends, and peers is a major problem. There is a tendency to withdraw from social, recreational, and educational situations because of the rejection that occurs. Low self-esteem, expectations of failure, and inconsistent performance characterize many of the problems faced by these individuals. Thus, it becomes important for professionals working with the emotionally disturbed to establish positive experiences from which they can learn to cope with the demands of community living.

The psychological recovery of the emotionally disturbed individual depends greatly on the family, other significant persons, and societal factors. Blum and Kujoth (1972) discuss the issues of job placement for the emotionally disturbed. A re-education of the public is needed. Many rehabilitated emotionally disturbed persons are still viewed aversely by their communities. Awareness, education, and cooperation with the community has to be part of a career development system for disturbed individuals. The enhancement of self-esteem of the emotionally disturbed person is stressed by Bauman and Grunes (1974) as a result of the social contribution of work and of earning money in society. Medication is an effective treatment for many other individuals, particularly those with more serious disorders. Heredity, chemical imbalances, physical trauma, physiological dysfunctions, and environmental situations are some of the many possible causes of emotional disorders; therefore, treatment varies according to the needs or situation of each person.

A wide range of educational alternatives are required for emotionally disturbed children. Many can function in regular classes if they receive appropriate support services. A study by Gullotta (1974) reveals that regular class teachers appear willing to maintain and help disturbed children as long as they are provided with the necessary support to keep the students in their classes. However, Kelly, Bullock, and Dykes (1977) found that regular classroom teachers need considerably more inservice and preservice training in behavioral disorders to be more competent in their ability to work effectively with them. Many children will need special class services. Morse (1977) indicates that perhaps the most important factor in successful programs for the emotionally disturbed student is the teacher who has some charisma or some particular expertise. He maintains that one of the major problems is too little working together between the school and mental health agencies so that the problems of the family and child are dealt with realistically within their total life dilemma. Another major problem, according to Morse, is the scarcity of vocational education for these students because of the difficulty of maintaining them in the vocational program.

People who have had serious emotional disorders have many employment barriers. Sarbin and Mancuso (1970) generally found that the public was not sympathetic toward persons labeled *mentally ill* (emotionally disturbed). "They look upon such persons with disrespect and are willing to relegate them to a childlike, non-person role. An exemplar of the general public would place a sizable social distance between himself and those persons labeled mentally ill" (p. 167). Questions of whether a former mental patient should reveal her illness to prospective employers are still debatable. The amount of pressure and interpersonal requirements are important considerations in job placement. Many will need continual or periodic follow-up services, including counseling to maintain themselves in the community. Fear of failure and rejection by others will contribute to inadequacies in the work situation.

In conclusion, persons with emotional or serious mental problems carry a stigma similar and in many ways more debilitating than other handicapped persons. Medical and guidance services are extremely important in helping these individuals, who have good potential for functioning successfully in our society. Acceptance by family, friends, and co-workers is critical to their successful career development.

SPEECH AND LANGUAGE DISORDERS

Speech Disorders

Speech disorders are of special concern in the career development of handicapped individual, since they may significantly impair the individual's ability to successfully interact and assume responsible roles in congruence with her ultimate potential for educational and vocational achievement. Hall and Alexander (1974) classify speech disorders as problems of phonation, articulation, fluency, and symbolization, or a combination; they constitute about 5% of the school population. Phonation disorders are distortions of pitch or intensity; articulation disorders are sound production problems; fluency disorders refer to the rate or flow of speech; and symbolization disorders refer to sensory motor areas of speech. Some of the most common speech disorders are discussed below.

Articulation Disorders

This type of disorder constitutes about 60 to 80% of the speech handicaps in the public schools. These disorders can be classified as substitutions, omissions, distortions, and addition of sounds. Speech therapy and classroom instruction can help the child toward more articulate speech (Kirk, 1972).

Vocal Disorders

These disorders are related to vocal quality, pitch, and loudness. Phonation defects (production of sound) may be characterized by the failure of the vocal cords to produce adequate air flow. A voice retraining program is usually beneficial for the correction of these defects.

Cerebral Palsy Symptoms

These consist of a loss of motor control of the voluntary muscle functions of the face, mouth, lips, and tongue, resulting in improper speech articulation. Treatment must be directed toward improving muscle control and coordination.

Cleft Palate Disorders

These are articulation problems resulting from a fissure in the roof of the mouth, which opens into the nasal cavity. This results in a severe speech defect and a cosmetic problem. Rehabilitation for this congenital condition involves plastic surgery, including orthodontic treatment to realign the teeth. Speech therapy is an important aspect of the rehabilitation program and should include the adjustment to the surgical aspects and the prosthesis (an obturator) if there is one.

Stuttering

This is a problem of rhythm and is generally a functional disorder associated with a high degree of tension and anxiety. While the causes of stuttering are difficult to ascertain, there are essentially two major theories: organic and psychological. Thus, treatment may take the form of a psychiatric or psychological approach, with the speech therapist assisting the student in building confidence in her ability to carry on an appropriate speech pattern.

Speech Defects Associated with Hearing Loss

Persons with hearing loss may develop an associated speech disorder and will have to monitor their speech for loudness, pitch, and clarity. Persons born without hearing will need earlier and more intensive speech training than those who learned speech before their hearing loss.

Other problems related to speech disorders include: nodules or lumps on the vocal bands, causing a distortion of sound or deformed vocal bands; dental malformations, such as oversized teeth and improper spacing; laryngectomy, which is the surgical removal of the larynx and the substitution of a mechanical or electric larynx, or esophageal speech; loss of lung capacity due to cancer, emphysema, enlarged heart, or loss of function of the diaphragm.

Diagnosis and treatment of speech disorders requires a team approach and may include: surgery, family counseling, special education, vocational counseling, psychotherapy, speech training and therapy, artificial appliances, and audiology.

The social adjustment of persons with speech disorders depends in part upon the reaction of others toward the disability. Similar to other handicaps, there may be discrimination in social interactions, peer group rejection, and undue sympathy and pity. The individual must regenerate feelings of self-worth and learn how to handle these interactions. Psychological adjustment depends upon handling the depression, negative self-concept, anxiety, and other behaviors that may result from the disability. Individual, group, and family counseling are often included in the therapeutic phase.

The student with a speech disorder must be accepted and encouraged to participate freely in the classroom. The teacher and speech therapist should work closely together in developing verbal communication to the highest level possible. Adult individuals must be directed into occupations requiring a limited amount of verbal interactions. It must be cautioned that there is a tendency to underestimate the speech disordered individual's vocational potential many times, and they are often directed into occupations much beneath their capacities.

Language Disorders

Language disorders constitute a wide variety of verbal deficiencies and are the result of a number of causes, including strokes, head injuries, and neurosurgical interventions. Language disorders occur only as a result of brain impairment. Over a million persons in this country suffer from language disorders and concomitant physical and psychological problems. *Aphasia* disorders constitute the inability to formulate verbal symbols due to organic impairment of the central nervous system. They can be divided into several types: pragmatic, semantic, syntactic, jargon, and global. *Pragmatic* aphasia is a disorder of symbol formulation whereby individuals cannot organize and regulate their expression to a given stimulus, although they can maintain a flow of language and retain the melody and pitch changes of normal speech. *Semantic* aphasia is a disorder of symbol formulation whereby the individual has difficulty in attaching a meaningful verbal sign to a previously acquired concept, and in recalling and using previously acquired verbal forms applicable to the concept, while retaining highly frequent function words and using generally normal speech. *Syntactic* aphasia is a disorder of symbol formulation whereby the individual is unable to use her previously acquired grammatical structure, exhibiting a misuse or omission of function words and grammatical inflections, while being unable to form sentences and phrases. *Jargon* aphasia is a disorder of symbol formulation and expression in which previously acquired sequences of phonemes making up intelligible units of speech are no longer available and are replaced by jargon. *Global* aphasia is a disorder whereby the individual is unable to respond verbally to stimuli except with an automatized word, phrase, or phoneme sequence, and exhibits little or no comprehension and communication (Wepman, 1973).

There are also nonsymbolic language disorders in addition to the symbolic ones. *Agnosia* is the inability to transmit incoming stimuli so as to imitate, copy, or recognize stimuli or match them with identical stimuli. *Apraxia* is the disruption of or inability to transmit a motor pattern along a specific modality, exhibited by difficulty articulating speech and formulating letters in writing.

The most common physical handicap of adult aphasic individuals is hemiplegia (paralysis on one side of the body), or hemiparesis (weakness or partial paralysis on one side of the body). The next most common disability is hemianopia, a limitation in the function of the visual fields. Other after-affects of brain damage include vertigo, tinnitus, optic atrophy, ciplopia, localized headaches, and tremors (Wepman, 1973).

The treatment of language disorders requires a team approach with considerable assistance and support from the family. Therapy must establish day-by-day achievements as daily livings skills are restored. It is important not to establish unrealistic long-term goals that will produce frustration, anxiety, and withdrawal. Some family members make excellent therapists in helping the individual readjust to life.

As with other handicaps, the social adjustment of the person with a language disorder is dependent on many factors, including the development of new interpersonal skills, daily living skills, and family reaction and assistance. Psychological adjustment may be poor or excellent, again depending on the premorbid state before the disability. Realistic goals and family support are significant factors for adjustment. Educational programming is a very important part of the total therapy program, as learning to speak, comprehend, and write become paramount. Vocationally, many language disordered individuals eventually return to their jobs; others need to be retrained and redirected to employment within their capacities. Some are unable to work, at least in the competitive market place.

In conclusion, speech and language disorders range from mild to severe and can result in a relatively dramatic change in life style for the individual and her family. However, with proper treatment and guidance, most individuals can lead a meaningful and productive life.

SEVERE AND MULTIPLE HANDICAPS

In the past few years, attention has become directed toward a long neglected population of handicapped Americans, the severely and profoundly handicapped. A publication of the Division on Mental Retardation of the Council for Exceptional Children, *Educational Programming for the Severely and Profoundly Handicapped* (Sontag, 1977) was a landmark venture into presenting educational models, intervention strategies, and concepts for the education of this population. Formal education for these individuals has just begun. As educational practices become more refined, they should demonstrate the ability of these individuals to be taught and trained as meaningful contributors to the complex society in which we live.

The Rehabilitation Act of 1973 was perhaps the precursor of things to come. It mandates a comprehensive study of methods to prepare individuals with the most severe handicaps who are not normally eligible and to assist individuals with severe handicaps who cannot be expected to be rehabilitated. But under a program of rehabilitation, both can improve their ability to live independently or function normally within their family and community. This Act and the Education for All Handicapped Children Act of 1975 are proof positive that we are moving toward giving these individuals the assistance necessary for them to realize their potentials.

Many individuals with the handicaps discussed previously in this chapter also suffer from concomitant disabilities. Emotional disorders frequently accompany many physical handicaps, sensory handicaps, and mental retardation. Persons with cerebral palsy often have a combination of visual, hearing, intellectual and other handicaps in addition to the physical. Two groups that have been drawing recent attention are retarded individuals who are hearing impaired and those who are deaf and blind. These groups represent a low incidence population but are in dire need of multifaceted services. The actual number of children with severe hearing loss and mental retardation is 15,000 to 20,000 persons under age 21 (Task Force on the Mentally Retarded Deaf, 1973). Most of these individuals are either residing in facilities for the mentally retarded or public and private day and residential schools for the deaf. In both cases, program quality is generally limited, and this group is a minority group within a larger handicapped population.

Individuals who are deaf and blind constitute a real challenge to educators and rehabilitation personnel. These individuals have been receiving services since Perkins School for the Blind in Massachusetts admitted its first such student in 1837.[7] The Industrial Home for the Blind is an outstanding example of a facility that has effectively provided specialized services to adults for over 50 years. In 1967 the Vocational Rehabilitation Amendments authorized the establishment and operation of a National Center for Deaf-Blind Youths and Adults. The Industrial Home for the Blind operates the National Center under an agreement with HEW. In recent years, education and rehabilitation efforts have been directed to all levels of deaf-blind individuals, not just those who are gifted or exhibit advanced intellectual functioning (Spar, 1973). Much work remains to be done to discover effective education and training techniques so these individuals too may find their place in society.

The service needs of the severely handicapped are many and continuous. Weintraub, Abeson, & Braddock (1971) indicate that nearly 900,000 children classified as hearing impaired, mentally retarded, and multiple handicapped are not receiving special service that meet their needs. But the day is dawning when these deficiencies will be corrected, and these individuals will receive their rightful services so they may become accepted members of the human race.

CONCLUSION

This chapter has presented some salient points about persons with various types of handicapping conditions. It is important to emphasize that the concept of handicapped is not homogeneous, i.e., "special educators have begun to question the assumptions about these groupings and the homogeneity of the classes of persons with handicaps" (Martin, 1976, p. 134). Handicapped individuals are really not that different from the non-handicapped in most characteristics. For every handicapping condition discussed in this chapter, the attitudes of the individual and society toward the handicap seem to be the major obstacle, not the individual's disability. Many medical and social advances have been made in the past decade, but much remains to be accomplished.

Perhaps this chapter can best be concluded by presenting the commencement address of Bill Yore, a mentally retarded and physically impaired 19-year-old senior at Lakeshore High School in Michigan. He was one of three

---

[7] Helen Keller was the most famous individual with this handicap and attended Perkins.

students selected as a commencement speaker. His mother and teacher had both tried to discourage him, but he worked for weeks on his speech. He had been in special education programs all of his life, and he had a message he felt impelled to impart. It is a message that all of us need to hear.

> Mr. Reilly, honored guests, ladies and gentlemen and members of the graduating class of 1974. I want to take this opportunity to convey appreciation to you for allowing me to express my feelings this evening.
>
> Tonight represents a dream come true for my parents, friends and relatives. Tonight also represents the attainment of a goal for many interested and concerned teachers, counselors and staff. Tonight also represents the downfall of a diagnosis that was made over 15 years ago. Let me explain.
>
> In 1958, a 4-year-old boy was taken to the University Hospital at Ann Arbor for neurological examinations. After many hours of examinations, tests, x-rays, and waiting, a verdict and sentence was handed down by the University doctors. The parents were informed that their son was mentally handicapped and the best place for him was in an institution. "Your son, at best, may some day be able to sell papers on a street corner," the doctors informed the stunned couple. On the convictions of these parents, through the efforts of devoted teachers and the legislation of interested taxpayers like yourselves, this would-be resident of Coldwater's Home for the Mentally Handicapped was placed in our local school system.
>
> This boy was loved and cared for not only at home, but also at school. Sure, there were hard and rough times. It isn't easy competing with other kids, even when you are normal much less handicapped. But, the love and the patience were there for 19 long years. And, tonight I am proud to stand here and say that I am that boy—almost condemned to an institution. True, I am not an "A" student. But neither am I a dropout. I may never go to college but I won't be on the welfare roles either. I may never be a great man in this world, but I will be a man in whatever way I am able to do it.
>
> For tonight, I say thanks to my parents who prayed and worked so hard. I say thanks to you, my instructors and the staff of Lakeshore High who had the patience and dedication to see me through. I say thanks to this audience for your work, your dollars, and your concern in providing me with an opportunity for my education. And, to you, my classmates, I also say thanks. I will always remember our years together and I hope that you will also.
>
> Remember me as you search for a place in life, for there will be youngsters needing your help as you select a vocation in life. Remember me as you become paying members of our communities because there will be children needing your financial support. And, remember me and others like me in your prayers because in some cases there are not always parents, teachers, and classmates like I have had at Lakeshore High School. Thank you.

He hesitated, lost his place, stuttered, but he went on. No senior in the assembly moved.

3

Career Education

Career education was first proclaimed as a major educational reform in 1971 when the then U. S. Commissioner of Education, Sidney P. Marland, Jr., introduced the concept to a group of secondary school principals at a national education convention in Houston, Texas. Six years later in November 1976 Dr. Marland returned to Houston to keynote the first National Commissioner's Conference on Career Education and expressed amazement at career education's growth. He reported that "there probably never in our educational history has been such enormous movement toward a central concept of reform over such a brief span of time" (Neil, 1977).

Why has career education moved rapidly forward in this short period of time and made accomplishments such as legislation, funding, and a federal office of its own; a flurry of activity at the state and local levels, resulting in definitions, guides, policy statements, and curriculum modifications; endorsements from prestigious national leaders and organizations, including the U. S. Chamber of Commerce; the creation of career-oriented divisions in several professional organizations; feature issues in professional publications on career education; and national workshops and conferences on career education for handicapped and other individuals? Obviously, there is a need for significant changes and improvements in the way educational services are provided to all students, including the handicapped. It is the purpose of this chapter to examine these needs, present a conceptualization of career education that we feel is relevant for handicapped students, and describe a curriculum approach that we believe can appropriately result in the necessary career development services needed to meet these needs.

THE NEED TO CHANGE

The need to improve and change educational practices has been voiced by students, parents, business and industry, handicapped, disadvantaged, and other groups for many years. It is tragic that close to one million students drop out of school every year and that many others remain to the bitter end only because they feel they need the diploma. School has become such a negative psychological experience for so many students that many actually develop poorer self-concepts about themselves, their learning abilities, and their potentials the longer they stay in school. Vogel (1974) indicates that the development of self-esteem is the primary prerequisite to learning, because positive self-feelings need to be present before a person can think about anything else.

American education has been subjected to the following major criticisms:

- Too many persons leaving our educational system are deficient in the basic academic skills required for adaptability in today's rapidly changing society.
- Too many students fail to see meaningful relationships between what they are being asked to learn in school and what they will do when they leave the educational system.
- It best meets the educational needs of that minority of persons who will some day become college graduates.
- It has not kept pace with the rapidity of change in the post industrial occupational society.
- Too many persons leave our educational system at both the secondary and collegiate levels unequipped with the vocational skills, the self-understanding and career decision-making skills, or the work attitudes that are essential for making a successful transition from school to work.
- The growing need for and presence of women in the work force has not been reflected adequately in either the educational or the career options typically pictured for girls enrolled in our educational system.
- The growing needs for continuing and recurrent education of adults are not being met adequately by our current systems of public education.

- Insufficient attention has been given to learning opportunities which exist outside the structure of formal education and are increasingly needed by both youth and adults in our society.
- The general public, including parents and the business-industry community, has not been given an adequate role in formulation of educational policy.
- It does not adequately meet the needs of minority or economically disadvantaged persons in our society. Post high school education has given insufficient emphasis to educational programs at the sub-baccalaureate degree level.

(Hoyt, 1975, pp. 1–2)

These criticisms clearly depict the need for change. In the past, there has been too much emphasis on bringing students to a certain grade level by the end of a school year rather than considering the total constellation of developmental skills needed to make the individual a more effective person. This approach too frequently produces passive-dependent students who become apathetic, irresponsible, or rebellious (Moore & Gysbers, 1972).

The Chamber of Commerce of the United States (1975) states that career education holds the promise for exciting learning, the type that can turn students "on." They list the following problems as reasons why career education offers a promising response for educational reform:

- For too many youth, career exploration begins after leaving school instead of during the early learning years when there is ample time to develop areas of work interest and competence.
- Youth unemployment is consistently four times greater than adult unemployment, and turnover is high.
- Many students are not provided with the skill and knowledge to help them adjust to changes in job opportunities.
- There has steadily developed an increased emphasis on 'school for schooling's sake' . . . education has become, for many students, simply preparation for more education.
- In some schools, much of what happens in the classroom has too little to do with what is happening outside the classroom.
- Seventy-six percent of secondary school students are enrolled in a course of study that has, as its major emphasis, preparation for college—even though only 2 out of 10 jobs between now and 1980 will require a college degree.
- The dropout-failure rate among college students remains among the most stable of all statistics in American education. Forty percent of all who enter college this fall will not make it to their junior year, and 50 percent will never obtain a baccalaureate degree.

(Chamber of Commerce of the United States, 1975, p. 5)

The Chamber reports that 24% of the students attending secondary schools in the United States drop out. They recommend career education for all students to reduce the gap between unrealistic educational programs and career needs and to provide students with insight, information, and motivation concerning specialized training, as well as professional education.

The preceding discussion is intended to reflect some of the national opinion about the need for career education for all students. But what about handicapped students? Martin (1972) predicted from the best possible estimates available that only 21% of the handicapped children leaving school between 1972–1976 would be fully employed or go on to college; 40% would be underemployed; and 26% unemployed. He predicted an additional 10% would require at least a partially 'sheltered' setting and family, and 3% (75,000) to be almost totally dependent. Further need for career education for handicapped citizens was prompted by Viscardi (1976) at the Annual Meeting of the President's Committee on Employment of the Handicapped. He reported that the best available figures indicated that only 4 million of the 11 million employable age handicapped citizens were actually working, and many of these were underemployed. These and other figures reveal that a significantly greater proportion of handicapped individuals are not working when compared to those who are not handicapped.

At the "National Topical Conference on Career Education for Exceptional Children and Youth," Martin (1974, p. 1), speaking in his capacity as deputy director of the Bureau of Education for the Handicapped in the U. S. Office of Education, advocated redefining our basic instructional services to handicapped students so they receive more employment-directed vocational programs. The Bureau gave further impetus to involving handicapped students in career education by establishing that:

> By 1977, every handicapped child who leaves school wil have had career educational training relevant to the job market, meaningful to his career aspiration, and realistic to his fullest potential.
>
> Edwin Martin,
> Bureau of Education for the Handicapped

However, despite this proclamation and a top priority rating given to career education by the U. S. Office of Education, a large proportion of handicapped students are still not receiving the kind of training recommended by Martin. There is no doubt that handicapped individuals need career education and that they need it immediately. Our educational system is failing these students even more drastically than those who are not handicapped.

Career education holds the promise of educational reform because it "relates to all levels of education and infuses occupational relatedness to the curriculum—all curriculums" (Marland, 1976). In addition to its vocational benefits, evidence is also now emerging from evaluations that is demonstrating favorable academic gains by students from career education efforts (Bhaerman, 1977).

DEVELOPMENT AND ORGANIZATION

Career education is not totally new but rather something we abandoned over the years. Career education attempts to get us back on track by making education efforts more meaningful and relevant to the type of preparation individuals will need for living and working successfully in their communities.

Prior to Marland's speech, the Vocational Education Act of 1963 and its Amendments of 1968 were a major stimulus and forerunner of the career education movement, which was launched in 1971. Part D, Section 142(c) of the Vocational Education Amendments of 1968 was particularly significant for promoting the development of prevocational efforts in the elementary and junior high schools, for creating new curricular thrusts in vocational education, and for broadening the relationship of vocational education within the educational sector. Thus, it is not surprising that a major responsibility was assumed by the U. S. Office of Education's Bureau of Adult Vocational and Technical Education (now called Bureau of Occupational and Adult Education) shortly after Marland's proclamation. One significant event in 1971 was the conceptual development of 15 career clusters of the U. S. Office of Education from 20,000 jobs listed in the *Dictionary of Occupational Titles* (Herr, 1976). These were:

- Construction Occupations
  - Manufacturing Occupations
    - Transportation Occupations
      - Agri-Business and Natural Resources Occupations
        - Marine Science Occupations
          - Environmental Occupations
            - Business and Office Occupations
              - Marketing and Distribution Occupations
                - Communications and Media Occupations
                  - Hospitality and Recreation Occupations
                    - Personal Service Occupations
                      - Public Services Occupations
                        - Health Occupations
                          - Consumer and Homemaking Occupations
                            - Fine Arts and Humanities Occupations

Also that year, research and development funds were authorized to design and implement four national career education models: **1.** School-Based, **2.** Home-Based, **3.** Residential-Based, and **4.** Employer-Based. Each of these is described briefly as follows.

The *School-Based Comprehensive Career Education Model* (CCEM) is for all practical purposes no longer in existence. Developed at Ohio State University, the CCEM model promotes a sequential program of career awareness (K–6), career exploration (7–9), and career preparation (10–12). Its objectives are to help students develop: **1.** self-awareness and positive attitudes about self; **2.** occupational awareness and positive attitudes about work, school, and society; **3.** personal characteristics, such as self-respect, initiative, and resourcefulness; **4.** a clearer understanding of the relationship between the work world and education; and **5.** entry-level job preparation skills or further educational opportunities. Basic subjects are structured around the world of work, using the 15 USOE occupational or career clusters mentioned earlier for curriculum reorganization. Over 1,500 goal statements are the basis for learning activities and program implementation. Some of the major criticisms of the CCEM are: **1.** its use of the 15 USOE clusters for curriculum and instructional design, without taking into consideration other occupational systems and theories; **2.** its lack of a theoretical framework (e.g., career development theory); **3.** its focus on preparing people to work at the expense of other important educational objectives; and **4.** its lack of attention to the affective domain (Hansen, 1977). Despite these and other criticisms, the CCEM has had a profound impact on hundreds of schools throughout the country (Drier, Martinez, & Kimmel, 1975).

The *Home-Based Career Education Model* was developed by the Education Development Center in Providence, Rhode Island. Designed for adults who are not in school or working, its objectives are to: **1.** develop educational delivery systems for the home and community; **2.** provide new career education programs for adults; **3.** establish a guidance and career placement system for individuals in occupational and related life-roles; **4.** develop more competent workers; and **5.** enhance the quality of the home as a learning center (Drier, Martinez, & Kimmel, 1975). A mass media communication approach is used to reach and ascertain the career interests of its listeners and viewers. The center offers an extensive bibliography and many audio cassettes, correspondence programs, and other media and aides to inform the model's target group about work and training opportunities (Hansen, 1977).

The *Rural-Residential Model* was developed by the Mountain Plains Education and Economic Development Program. Its major focus is disadvantaged rural families who are chronically unemployed; it provides a wide array of services: career counseling and guidance, training, remedial education, kindergarten, elementary and secondary education, homemaking skills, and many others. The intent of the model is to make the family financially capable of functioning in their community.

The Employer-Based Career Education Model was renamed as the *Experience-Based Career Education* (EBCE) model. Four agencies developed this model: Appalachian Educational Laboratory, Far West Laboratory for Educational Research and Development, Northwest Regional Educational Laboratory, and Research for Better Schools. Its focus is a comprehensive curriculum primarily for those teen-age students who are alienated or unmotivated in school. The EBCE program consists of eight basic ingredients (Henderson, 1976, p. 68):

1. Students' needs, interests, and abilities are carefully and individually examined throughout the year to find out the kinds of learning and experiences that are most appropriate for that student.
2. Community experience sites which agree to participate in the program are thoroughly analyzed to identify the kinds of things students might learn there and under what conditions (for example, level of involvement, employees, hours, people, dress codes, etc.)
3. Information on sites, assessment of student needs, and the concept-oriented curriculum have been systematically cross-referenced so that the ingredients can be mixed and matched to meet the unique needs and desires of each student.
4. Standard high school courses have been re-worked into multiple concepts and objectives which a student can tackle in many different ways.
5. Each student's specific learning activities are carefully described, followed and evaluated.
6. Students use the community to investigate who they are, what the adult community offers, and how to deal with the lifelong series of vocational, avocational, and personal choices which constitute careers.
7. Special career development materials have been custom built so that *planned* occupational experiences in the community are *carefully evaluated* by the student in terms of self-awareness, vocational awareness, with options, decisions, and when appropriate, commitment generated.
8. Finally, the traditional "teacher" has been replaced by a "Learning Coordinator" who has full responsibility for coordination, guiding, counseling, and evaluating all aspects of a student's program.

Hansen (1977) indicates that early formative evaluation of EBCE has been encouraging. Parent, community, and student attitudes and involvement have been positive features. In addition, the Appalachian Educational Laboratory has developed materials for handicapped students. (See chapter 8.)

In 1972 many other USOE units became involved in career education. The Bureau of Education for the Handicapped began awarding contracts for investigations directed at careers appropriate for handicapped students. The Education Amendments of 1972 were passed, creating the National Institute of Education (mentioned earlier) as a major USOE research and development agency. The Amendments also created within USOE's Bureau of Occupational and Adult Education the specific responsibility for several vocational, manpower, and adult programs, including career education (Herr, 1976). Title X of Part B (Occupational Education Programs), which was never funded, addressed and supported virtually all of the theories, philosophies, and implementing measures of career education (Marland, 1976).

In 1973 the National Institute of Education assumed responsibility for the four career education models and all Educational Resources Information Center (ERIC) Clearinghouses. A Center for Career Education was established within the Bureau of Occupational and Adult Education. Dr. Kenneth B. Hoyt was appointed Associate Commissioner for Career Education in April 1974, and in August the Education Amendments of 1974 (PL 93–380) were passed; they authorized: **1.** establishing a U. S. Office of Career Education; **2.** a director to report directly to the Commission of Education; **3.** up to $15 million for career education each fiscal year until June 30, 1978; and **4.** the appointment of a National Advisory Committee for Career Education. This legislation made career education a law of the land and clarified the shape of its leadership (Herr, 1976). Since that time, career education has come of age, prompted by aggressive leadership from Hoyt and other national leaders and a flurry of activities at the state and local levels. Career education position statements, guides, conferences, workshops, and projects have resulted. Some states and local school districts have moved rapidly forward and headlong into career education programs; others have taken a "wait-and-see" attitude. A survey of career education (mandated by Congress in 1974) by the American Institutes for Research found that 60% of the school systems in America are making efforts toward establishing career education, although only 3% of the districts conduct what could be considered comprehensive career education programs.

At the national level, the U. S. Office of Career Education provides significant leadership despite limited funds by issuing stimulating position papers and other monographs; sponsoring workshops and mini-conferences with individuals and organizations of all types; funding special project proposals; and in general, serving as the stimulus for legislative and programmatic developments. The Office of Career Education makes project grants available for the express purpose of demonstrating effective methods and techniques in career education and developing exemplary career education models. It does not fund research and development projects, nor does it provide general operational support for the implementation of career education activities. State educational and local educational agencies, universities, colleges, and other nonprofit agencies are eligible by applying directly to the U. S. Office of Career Education, Washington, D. C. 20202.

The Education Amendments of 1976 (PL 94–482) also became a further boon to career education. Part C of Title III, "Career Education and Career Development" provides federal assistance to states for planning and developing career education and development programs and activities for individuals of all ages, and in the areas of awareness, exploration, planning, and decision making with regard to career opportunities and development.

Ten million dollars was authorized, including up to $2 million for: gathering, cataloging, storing, analyzing, and disseminating information related to careers; analysis of career trends and options; publication of reports and reference works for use in career education programs; and dissemination of the information through seminars and workshops. Money was also used to hire staff people, run the national office in Washington, D. C., for demonstration grants, and to finance a National Commissioners Conference (November 1976) and a number of mini-conferences with various professional and business organizations.

The support for career education was evidenced with the passage of the Career Education Implementation Incentive Act (PL 95–207) in 1977. The law authorized 400 million dollars to be spent over 5 years beginning fiscal year 1979 to infuse career education into school curriculums, and to provide funds for guidance, inservice training, and other guidance activities. State education agencies are required to make sure that career education is part of ongoing local instruction, not just part of vocational education. In developing this legislation, Congress declared: "A major purpose of education is to prepare every individual for a career suitable to that individual's preference . . . career education should be an integral part of the Nation's educational process which serves as prepartion for work." The measure is intended to stimulate more state involvement and commitment to career education at all levels of education.

Several states have passed specific laws prescribing career education, encourage the concept through their budget procedures, or are weighing legislation possibilities. Most states have established a full-time career education staff, and almost everyone has adopted affirmative policy statements on career education (Marland, 1976). Every state has a designated career education contact person who can give interested individuals and organizations requested information on career education activities and funding possibilities. Over 8,000 people from all states attended the National Commissioners Conference in Houston in November 1976, one of the largest ever sponsored by the U. S. Office of Education. Educators, informed citizens, and representatives of government, business, and industry met to exchange ideas about career education approaches toward today's youths and adults.

Career education is growing and has received increased support at the federal and state levels through legislation and funding. There is no reason to doubt that this movement will be curtailed but rather will continue to grow until our citizens are provided with the relevant services they need to become contributing and satisfied members of this society.

CAREER EDUCATION FOR THE HANDICAPPED

Career education for handicapped individuals has also made rapid strides since its introduction on the public education scene in 1971. The activities of the Bureau of Education for the Handicapped in 1972 were mentioned previously (pp. 90–91). In 1973 the Council for Exceptional Children (CEC) jointly sponsored with the American Vocational Association a "National Topical Conference on Career Education for Exceptional Children and Youth" in New Orleans, which attracted several thousand participants, including a large number of government leaders and representatives. This conference was important because it launched career education officially at a national level for handicapped individuals. In January 1975 the Bureau of Education for the Handicapped sponsored an important conference for national and recognized leaders in the field of handicapped education ("Conference on Research Needs Related to Career Education for the Handicapped"). Based on intensive group interaction and problem solving over several days, a list of top-priority needs were identified by the 10 teams of participants and now serve as a focus of BEH efforts.

Legislatively, the Education for all Handicapped Children Act of 1975 (Public Law 94–142) has many implications for securing funds for career education programming. Federal funds are supposed to be used to supplement and expand existing services to handicapped students and to develop a comprehensive series of programming alternatives, including developing close working relationships with parents and other advocacy groups. In addition, the act provides funds for effective inservice training for staff so that different general and special educational instructional and support personnel are adequately and appropriately prepared and trained to carry out the act. This legislation represents a substantial increase in federal commitment to the handicapped, authorizing the following grants over a 5-year period: 1978—$387 million; 1979—$775 million; 1980—$1.5 billion; 1981—$2.32 billion and 1982—$3.16 billion. The act includes protections and assurances in regard to complete due process procedures; individualized, written educational plans; being served in the "least restrictive environment"; nondiscriminatory testing and evaluation; and policies and procedures to protect student confidentiality. All of these are consistent with the career education practices that are recommended in this book.

Title I of the Education Amendments of 1976 contains the amendments to the Vocational Education Act of 1963 and are particularly significant. It requires that funds used for vocational education of the handicapped are expended in a manner consistent with the state plan for the education of the handicapped, as in PL 94–142. It mandates the expenditure of at least 10% of the state allotment for 50% of the costs of vocational education for handicapped persons (meaning the federal share will be 50%). The federal expenditure of funds for vocational education for the handicapped could total $88 million in fiscal year 1978 and $148 million by 1982. States may use funds for program improvement and supportive services to special populations such as handicapped and disadvantaged persons, exemplary and innovative programs, curriculum development, vocational guidance and counseling resource centers, and consumer and homemaking programs. The vocational resource centers are intended to meet the special needs of out-of-school individuals, including handicapped persons. The consumer and homemaking education are intended to be instructional programs, services, and activities at all educational levels for the occupations of homemaking, including but not limited to consumer education, food and nutrition, family living and parenthood education, child development and guidance, housing and home management, and clothing and textiles. These include outreach programs for handicapped persons and are consistent with our advocation of the daily living skills training for these individuals.

In recent years, several other legislative acts directly related to career education, which provide possible sources of funding for career education endeavors, either directly or indirectly to schools, have been passed. The Rehabilitation Act of 1973 requires state vocational rehabilitation agencies to give special emphasis and priority to serving the severely handicapped and authorizes rehabilitation research and demonstration funds to discover, test, demonstrate, and promote utilization of new concepts and devices that will provide rehabilitation services to handicapped individuals. Section 504 of the act was discussed earlier as the civil rights act for the handicapped. The Comprehensive Employment and Training Act of 1973 (PL 93–203) directly funds special educational and training programs for the disadvantaged of which certain handicapped persons may qualify. It is operated under state employment service jurisdiction. Housing funds for the handicapped can be obtained from the Housing and Urban Development Act. Voluntary organizations and foundations are also potential sources of funds for career education programs. Schools and state vocational rehabilitation agencies have had a long history of cooperative programming, and the two agencies must continue these efforts if career education is to be effective for handicapped individuals. An important breakthrough between the federal rehabilitation agency (Rehabilitation Services Administration) and the U.S. Office of Education occurred in October 1977 when the two commissioners of these agencies issued a "memorandum of understanding," recognizing the fact that they have many common responsibilities to handicapped persons. The memorandum proclaimed: "Education agencies are concerned with the overall life adjustment of handicapped young persons within their communities, including their ability to become employed. Vocational rehabilitation agencies are concerned with enabling handicapped individuals—particularly the severely disabled—to prepare for and engage in employment. These concerns are clearly compatible and every effort should be made to coordinate available services." Objectives of the memorandum were: **1.** to assure that handicapped persons eligible for service under the Education for All Handicapped Children Act of 1975 (PL 94–142), the Education Amendments of 1976 (PL 94–482), and the Rehabilitation Act of 1973 (PL 93–112) receive all of the appropriate services for which they are eligible; **2.** to assure that all agencies administering these laws understand that eligibility under one law should not, in and of itself, result in a denial of complementary services under another of the laws; and **3.** to assure that the federal agencies involved are fully committed to aiding state and local agencies engaged in coordinated service delivery for handicapped persons (Council for Exceptional Children, 1977). The Bureau of Education for the Handicapped (BEH) and the Rehabilitation Services Administration (RSA) established a joint work group to develop guidelines on how school districts could coordinate services to handicapped children under the three pieces of legislation. A national study was instituted to identify 10 school districts throughout the country that are effectively responding to these mandates.

Two organizations created in the mid-1970s significantly reflect the importance career education has achieved in the educational sector. The American Vocational Association approved the National Association of Vocational Education Special Needs Personnel (NAVESNP) within its organization. This group is making significant strides in promoting legislation, programs, and inservice/preservice efforts so vocational educators can more adequately serve handicapped and disadvantaged students. The Council for Exceptional Children (CEC) approved its twelfth division in 1976, the Division on Career Development (DCD), to interface with its other divisions and organizations to promote career potentials of handicapped individuals. Both organizations are fast becoming vital forces in the career education movement for handicapped persons. Collaborative efforts, publications, legislation, research, inservice/preservice modifications, and many other efforts have been undertaken as major needs and activities by these new organizations.

The Council for Exceptional Children has given further advancement to the career education movement by appointing a Special Study Committee on Career Education to have dialogue with the U. S. Office of Career Education and to interact at a mini-conference with its director, and by authorizing another National Conference on Career Education for Exceptional Individuals (which was held in February 1979). An intensive Training Institute on Career Education preceded the conference and was repeated several times afterwards. CEC has also published special issues on career education in its journals and monographs. It has also participated in many meetings and conferences on the subject.

There is no doubt that career education is much more than a passing fancy or fad. The movement has not been without criticism and resistance, and the old adage "everyone is for change unless they have to do it" is certainly true in this case. Labor has expressed fear that career education would encourage children to leave school early, child-labor laws and minimum-wage laws would be in danger of revision, liberal education might become the exclusive right of the privileged, and career choices would be imposed on children (Neil, 1977). Others have called it "old wine in new bottles" and just another name for vocational education, which they believe is trying to grab the spotlight. One of the main concerns is that career education means seriously reducing emphasis on traditional academic instruction which, like the other criticisms mentioned earlier, is denied by career education proponents. And we agree:

Career education does not de-emphasize the fundamentals. Rather, it brings meaning to the curriculum by making individuals more aware of themselves, their potentials, and their educational needs.

The Authors

It is our hope that what follows in this chapter will clarify this statement.

TOWARD DEFINING CAREER EDUCATION

Career education was launched without a commonly accepted definition. When Commissioner Marland introduced the term in 1971, his staff had labored over an appropriate term months earlier in response to a White House directive to increase the place of vocational education within the federal role. Marland saw this as an opportunity to promote total reform by embracing vocational education and the occupational aspects of human development for all of education (Herr, 1976). Since that time, career education has become a priority in American education, and numerous attempts have been made to conceptualize and define it at the federal, state, and local levels. No attempt will be made here to present an exhaustive array of definitions that have been advocated and debated throughout the country.

One of the major problems career education has experienced is the widespread tendency of professional workers to conceptualize the words *career* and *occupation* synonymously. Donald E. Super (1976), a recognized pioneer and leader in career development theory, wrote a monograph on career education for the U. S. Office of Education which clearly placed career education into what appears to us a more appropriate perspective. He wrote:

> Career education must take into account the many theaters in which careers take place, the numerous roles which can constitute a career, and the non-occupational roles which acquire prominence in society as that of occupation diminishes. Educators need to think of aptitudes, interests, and values as traits which may be utilized, find outlets, and seek satisfaction in available occupations, avocational activities, in civic activities, and in family activities. We need to ask ourselves which roles seem likely to provide the best outlets for each student and in what combination . . . (and) to ascribing honor and importance to appropriate non-occupational roles as they begin to take on more significance in a leisure-oriented society (p. 42).

In presenting a "Career Development Glossary for Career Education," Super defines *career* as "The sequence of major positions occupied by a person throughout his preoccupational, occupational, and postoccupational life: includes work-related roles such as those of student, employee, and pensioner, together with complementary avocational, familial, and civic roles. Careers exist only as people pursue them; they are person-centered" (p. 20). Thus, a career is multifaceted and consists of occupational, social, leisure, and interpersonal roles—occupations are only a part of one's career.

Goldhammer (1972) identifies several life careers in which individuals engage as members of society. He indicates that there are at least five such careers that should constitute the framework within which *all* curriculum content should be organized. "**1.** a producer of goods or a renderer of services; **2.** a member of a family group; **3.** a participant in the social and political life of the society; **4.** a participant in avocational pursuits; and **5.** a participant in the regulatory functions involved in aesthetic, moral and religious concerns" (p. 129). Bailey (1976) notes that several scholars have identified various classifications of life roles and that the most commonly mentioned are worker, citizen, family member, person and leisure roles. He concludes that the major life roles should be a work role, family member role, learning and self-development role, a social citizenship role—and an educated person.

> One's "career" consists of many roles . . . occupational . . . avocational . . . family . . . civic.
>
> Super and others

Larry Allen, an Arkansas high school student, perhaps best reflected the need for educators to focus attention and efforts on career education in this perspective when he advocated education on learning to live, as well as on earning a living:

> I hope that when the time comes to follow a Career Education plan in public schools we don't limit the concept implied by the term Career Education. In the future, the work careers of Americans will constitute only a portion of our daily lives . . . To lead full useful lives, on the job and off, we must be prepared to develop ourselves into well-rounded individuals.
>
> (Allen, 1973, p. 162)

We are in agreement with the above views in regard to conceptualizing and defining *career* and *career education.* We believe it should comprise a life ethic or life career perspecive rather than exclusively a work ethic. While work is an important part of life and career education, it should not be separated from other life roles and settings in which individuals find themselves. We believe career education should consist of preparation for all aspects of successful community living, including working. The term *career* connotes many *settings* (home, school, occupation, community), many *roles* (student, worker, consumer, citizen, family member), and many *events* (job entry, marriage, and retirement) as conceived by Gysbers and Moore (1973).

Hoyt (1975) defined career education originally as "the totality of experience through which one learns about and prepares to engage in work as part of her or his way of living" (p. 4). In this context, *career* is defined as the totality of work one does in his or her lifetime; *education* is the totality of experiences through which one learns. Thus, career education is conceptualized as considerably less than all of life or one's reason for living. The emphasis is on the four letter word *work* (paid or unpaid), which is defined as "conscious effort, other than that involved in activities whose primary purpose is either coping or relaxation, aimed at producing benefits for oneself and/or for oneself and others" (Hoyt, 1975, p. 3). More recently Hoyt appears to take a broader view of career education than his earlier definition indicates. In "A Primer for Career Education," Hoyt (1977a) redefined career education in a work context, emphasizing that it should be only one of several basic educational goals by teachers and learners. In another publication, Hoyt (1977b) makes it more clear that in career education, the word *work* included *unpaid* work—voluntary work, productive use of leisure time, the unpaid work of the full-time homemaker, and the school work of the student. Thus, Hoyt clarifies his position on work by defining it in a broad sense, something that many conceptualizers of career education have failed to do.

In our opinion, the definition of career education should include the many roles and positions occupied by handicapped individuals during their lifetime. This will distinguish career education from vocational education and place emphasis on the important knowledges, skills, and attitudes students and other individuals need for the various life roles and settings comprising their lives, including that of paid work. For the majority of handicapped individuals, paid employment will be a major part of their career if they receive the necessary occupational guidance and preparation to permit them to earn a decent living. For many other handicapped individuals, paid employment will not necessarily comprise a major part of their career. These individuals, being limited in their vocational functioning, may have a successful career and productive life by learning how to function adequately in avocational, family, and civic pursuits. In this way, career education is for everyone, the focus depending on each individual's unique set of abilities, needs, interests, and ultimate potentials (Brolin & D'Alonzo, 1979).

Over the years, there has been much confusion about the distinction between career and vocational education. Table 3 attempts to delineate some of the major differences between the two concepts based on the writings of Gysbers (1975), Bailey (1976), and Hoyt (1977a).

Thus, career education in this book will be considered as a purposeful sequence of planned educational activities, which assist individuals in their

Table 3
Some Differences between Career Education and Vocational Education

career education	vocational education
Focuses on paid and unpaid work (e.g., volunteer, leisure & recreation, home-making)	Focuses on paid work (although unpaid work is referred to in the Vocational Education Amendments)
Emphasizes general career skills	Emphasizes occupational preparation
Promotes cognitive, affective, & psycho-motor skill development	Promotes psychomotor skills for entry into occupational society
Meets the needs of the learners	Meets the needs of the labor market
Is a system-wide effort, not specific courses or an instructional program	Is defined in terms of courses and is an instructional program
Is taught by all educators	Is generally taught by vocational educators
Focuses on all instructional programs at all levels of education	Focuses on the secondary and post-secondary levels
Involves family, agencies, & business/industry	Involves primarily business/industry

career development (i.e., the process of preparing for various life career roles). It requires the active participation of not only school personnel but the interface and substantial contribution of family, community agencies, business and industry, and other community organizations and their resources. Our definition of the concept is presented below.

Career education is the process of systematically coordinating all school, family, and community components together to facilitate each individual's potential for economic, social, and personal fulfillment.

The Authors

Our conceptualization is consistent with that of The Council for Exceptional Children (1977) whose position statement describes career education as "the totality of experiences through which one learns to live a meaningful, satisfying work life . . . providing the opportunity for children to learn, in the least restrictive environment possible, the academic, daily living, personal-social and occupational knowledges and skills necessary for attaining their highest levels of economic, personal and social fulfillment. The individual can obtain this fulfillment through work (both paid and unpaid) and in a variety of other societal roles and personal life styles . . . student, citizen, volunteer, family member and participant in meaningful leisure-time activities."

INFUSION OF CAREER EDUCATION INTO CURRICULUM

Career education for handicapped individuals should be a major part of their educational program. By now, it should be clear that reference to vocational education is not being made when the term *career education* is used. Vocational education is clearly the training in a wide variety of specific technical and subprofessional skills and, thus, is an important complement to career education. Career education, however, permeates through vocational education, academic education, guidance and other educational learning activities directed toward the individual's total career development.

If career education is to be comprehensively designed and implemented for handicapped individuals in the school settings, several changes need to be forthcoming.

- The total curriculum will need to be sequenced definitively and logically from elementary through post-secondary levels. School personnel from the various levels must combine and coordinate their efforts to provide sequential learning for life competencies.
- There must be a shift from the traditional content-based curriculum to one that is more process-based (i.e., relating curriculum directly to the outside world and focusing on each student's unique ways of learning and becoming motivated). The development of skills rather than knowledge and information must be emphasized.
- Some handicapped students must be permitted to go beyond the traditional period of time until they acquire the necessary competency level for career success. Lifelong learning opportunities must be provided as they need them. Career education is an important part of lifelong learning.
- New methods of realistically providing career-relevant experiences and content within a career education context in both regular and special education classrooms need to be identified and infused.
- Traditional teacher and counselor roles need to be changed, and there must be greater involvement and investment in educational programming from the family, community agencies, and employers.

To implement our career education conceptualization, several key concepts must be incorporated into an educational program. Table 4 presents our work over a 3-year period on a federal project designed to develop an inservice career education training model focusing on handicapped students. The key concepts or propositions necessary for the development of a comprehensive career education curriculum consistent with our definition are identified in Table 4 (Brolin, 1978).

Table 4
Career Education Concepts

- It extends from early childhood through the retirement years.
- It focuses on the full development of all individuals.
- It provides the knowledge, skills and understandings needed by individuals to master their environment.
- It emphasizes daily living, personal-social and occupational skills development at all levels and ages.
- It encompasses the total curriculum of the school and provides a unified approach to education for life.
- It focuses on the total life roles, settings and events and their relationships which are important in the lives of individuals, including work.
- It encourages all members of the school community to have a shared responsibility and a mutual cooperative relationship among the various disciplines.
- It includes learning in the home, private/public agencies and the employment community as well as the school.
- It encourages all teachers to relate their subject matter to its career implications.
- It includes basic education, citizenship, family responsibility and other important education objectives.
- It provides for career awareness, exploration, and skills development at all levels and ages.
- It provides a balance of content and experiential learning, permitting hands on occupational activities.
- It provides a personal framework to help individuals plan their lives including career decision-making.
- It provides the opportunity for the acquisition of a saleable occupational entry-level skill upon leaving high school.
- It requires a life-long education based on principles related to total individual development.
- It actively involves the parents in all phases of education.
- It actively involves the community in all phases of education.
- It encourages open communication between students, teachers, parents and the community.

The concepts in Table 4 clearly reflect that career education is preparation for a satisfying life at all developmental stages. It focuses on career development from the important aspects of attitudes, values, and habits; human relationships; occupational information; and the acquisition of actual job and daily living skills. It is an effort to personalize education and encompasses all disciplines and levels of education along with community involvement.

In terms of learner outcome, the implementation of a career education program as outlined in Table 4 will help students to develop realistic self-concepts and esteem for themselves and others, a realistic and appreciative understanding of the evolving world of work and its opportunities, and a specific focus on one or more clusters of occupations and their educational requirements.

It will help students to know and appreciate the many changing and avocational, domestic, and civic outlets for developed interests and abilities which often supplement, complement, or even supplant paid work in making a satisfying career (Super, 1976).

The CEC Position Paper on Career Education (1978) lists the following objectives of career education for exceptional individuals.

- To help exceptional students develop realistic self-concepts, with esteem for themselves and others, as a basis for career decisions.
- To provide exceptional students with appropriate career guidance, counseling and placement services utilizing counselors, teachers, parents and community resource personnel.
- To provide the physical, psychological and financial accommodations necessary to serve the career education needs of exceptional children.
- To infuse career education concepts throughout all subject matter in the curricula of exceptional children in all educational settings from early childhood through post-secondary.
- To provide the student with the opportunity to leave the school program with an entry level saleable skill.
- To provide career awareness experiences which aim to acquaint the individual with a broad view of the nature of the world of work, including both unpaid and paid work.
- To provide career exploration experiences which help individuals to consider occupations which coincide with their interests and aptitudes.
- To provide exceptional individuals programs with occupational preparation opportunities for a continuum of occupational choices covering the widest possible range of opportunities.
- To help insure successful career adjustment of exceptional students through collaborative efforts of school and community.

A major objective of career education is to make all instructional materials personally relevant by restructuring and focusing them around a career development theme when possible and involving community resources so that every individual acquires the knowledge *and* skills to be successfully employed and/or continue on for further education. Every teacher can incorporate career education concepts into his classroom. It has the potential for bridging the gap between school and the "real world."

A CURRICULUM MODEL FOR CAREER EDUCATION

Conventional American education has generally focused on the question of "What must the individual know?" Students are taught reading, spelling, mathematics, and other skills that facilitate knowledge about history, chemistry, economics, and other topics. The important skills needed for community functioning are largely ignored—what gets taught are the major battles of the Civil War, the parts of human anatomy, and how the President vetoes a bill. While these should be taught, a second fundamental educational need of students is missing that must be met: "What skills are essential to the individual to make him a more effective person?" This is called *process education,* which is "The development of cognitive, affective, perceptual, motor, and social interactive skills" (Bailey, 1976, pp. 40–41).

Based on the preceding discussion, you should not be surprised that we recommend a competency based curriculum design for handicapped students that: 1. emphasizes basic academic skills and the acquisition of daily living, personal-social, and occupational skills; 2. involves a partnership between school personnel, family, and community representatives; and 3. incorporates the elements of career awareness, exploration, preparation, and placement/follow up into its design. Career education should focus on facilitating individual growth and development for all of the roles, settings, and events comprising a person's total life. A curriculum model is appropriate that organizes learner competencies into three primary categories: 1. daily living skills, 2. personal-social skills, and 3. occupational guidance and preparation. Academic instruction is used to develop the skills in these three categories. This is illustrated in Figure 9.

The three-dimensional model in Figure 9 comprises the competencies, experiences, and stages necessary for individuals to achieve their career development potentials. There are 22 competencies that handicapped individuals must acquire to be assured of successful career functioning (see Table 5). These competencies, learned in school, family, and community settings, are acquired through the stages of awareness, exploration, preparation, and placement/follow up/continuing education.

An example may clarify the elements of the model in Figure 9. Competency 1 (Managing Family Finances) could be taught in a math class at the elementary, junior high, and senior high level. Before the competency itself is taught, the elementary teacher should provide the student with a sufficient *awareness* of the importance of this skill, including how people acquire the skill, what kinds of things are involved in learning the skill, and what people can do with this skill (e.g., family responsibilities, job possi-

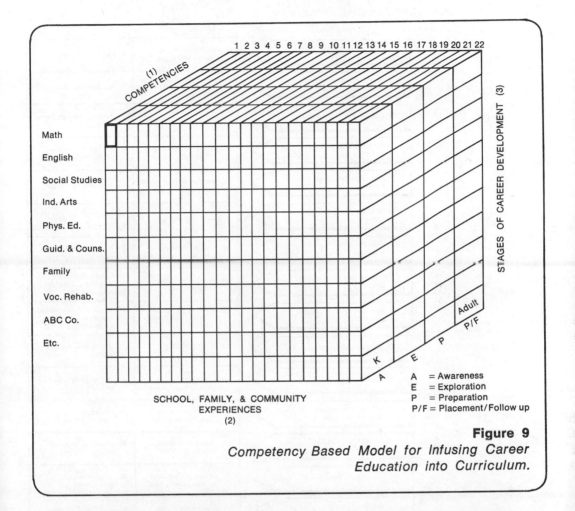

Figure 9

Competency Based Model for Infusing Career Education into Curriculum.

bilities). The student should be more receptive to learning this competency, which begins with being able to "identify money and make correct change." As some basic skills are learned, the student should be provided during late elementary levels with *exploration* experiences in and out of the school situation to observe how other people make "wise expenditures," "obtain and use bank credit facilities," and so on. During late junior high and early senior high, the student should be crystalizing his skills in this competency area (*preparation*) with further complementary community and family experiences. Finally, during the preparation stage, the student is given the opportunity to independently display his skill for this competency. The student may use this competency for primarily family living or may have the interest and skill level for continually becoming employed in this area.

This curriculum model can form the basis for infusing career education experiences or concepts and materials into the total educational program for the handicapped student, whether it be in the school, family, or com-

Table 5
Career Education Curriculum Competencies

Curriculum Area	Competency		
DAILY LIVING SKILLS	1. Managing Family Finances	1. Identify money and make correct change	2. Make wise expenditures
	2. Selecting, Managing, and Maintaining a Home	6. Select adequate housing	7. Maintain a home
	3. Caring for Personal Needs	10. Dress appropriately	11. Exhibit proper grooming and hygiene
	4. Raising Children, Family Living	14. Prepare for adjustment to marriage	15. Prepare for raising children (physical care)
	5. Buying and Preparing Food	18. Demonstrate appropriate eating skills	19. Plan balanced meals
	6. Buying and Caring for Clothing	24. Wash clothing	25. Iron and store clothing
	7. Engaging in Civic Activities	28. Generally understand local laws & government	29. Generally understand Federal Government
	8. Utilizing Recreation and Leisure	34. Participate actively in group activities	35. Know activities and available community resources
	9. Getting Around the Community (Mobility)	40. Demonstrate knowledge of traffic rules & safety practices	41. Demonstrate knowledge & use of various means of transportation
PERSONAL SOCIAL SKILLS	10. Achieving Self-Awareness	43. Attain a sense of body	44. Identify interests and abilities
	11. Acquiring Self-Confidence	48. Express feelings of worth	49. Tell how others see him/her
	12. Achieving Socially Responsible Behavior	53. Know character traits needed for acceptance	54. Know proper behavior in public places
	13. Maintaining Good Interpersonal Skills	58. Know how to listen and respond	59. Know how to make & maintain friendships
	14. Achieving Independence	62. Understand impact of behaviors upon others	63. Understand self-organization
	15. Achieving Problem-Solving Skills	66. Differentiate bipolar concepts	67. Understand the need for goals
	16. Communicating Adequately with Others	71. Recognize emergency situations	72. Read at level needed for future goals
OCCUPATIONAL GUIDANCE & PREPARATION	17. Knowing & Exploring Occupational Possibilities	76. Identify the personal values met through work	77. Identify the societal values met through work
	18. Selecting & Planning Occupational Choices	82. Identify major occupational needs	83. Identify major occupational interests
	19. Exhibiting Appropriate Work Habits & Behaviors	87. Follow directions	88. Work with others
	20. Exhibiting Sufficient Physical-Manual Skills	94. Demonstrate satisfactory balance and coordination	95. Demonstrate satisfactory manual dexterity
	21. Obtaining a Specific Occupational Skill		
	22. Seeking, Securing, & Maintaining Employment	98. Search for a job	99. Apply for a job

3. Obtain and use bank and credit facilities	4. Keep basic financial records	5. Calculate and pay taxes		
8. Use basic appliances and tools	9. Maintain home exterior			
12. Demonstrate knowledge of physical fitness, nutrition & weight control	13. Demonstrate knowledge of common illness prevention and treatment			
16. Prepare for raising children (psychological care)	17. Practice family safety in the home			
20. Purchase food	21. Prepare meals	22. Clean food preparation areas	23. Store food	
26. Perform simple mending	27. Purchase clothing			
30. Understand citizenship rights and responsibilities	31. Understand registration and voting procedures	32. Understand Selective Service procedures	33. Understand civil rights & responsibilities when questioned by the law	
36. Understand recreational values	37. Use recreational facilities in the community	38. Plan and choose activities wisely	39. Plan vacations	
42. Drive a car				
45. Identify emotions	46. Identify needs	47. Understand the physical self		
50. Accept praise	51. Accept criticism	52. Develop confidence in self		
55. Develop respect for the rights and properties of others	56. Recognize authority and follow instructions	57. Recognize personal roles		
60. Establish appropriate heterosexual relationships	61. Know how to establish close relationships			
64. Develop goal-seeking behavior	65. Strive toward self-actualization			
68. Look at alternatives	69. Anticipate consequences	70. Know where to find good advice		
73. Write at the level needed for future goals	74. Speak adequately for understanding	75. Understand the subtleties of communication		
78. Identify the remunerative aspects of work	79. Understand classification jobs into different occupational systems	80. Identify occupational opportunities available locally	81. Identify sources of occupational information	
84. Identify occupational aptitudes	85. Identify requirements of appropriate and available jobs	86. Make realistic occupational choices		
89. Work at a satisfactory rate	90. Accept supervision	91. Recognize the importance of attendance and punctuality	92. Meet demands for quality work	93. Demonstrate occupational safety
96. Demonstrate satisfactory stamina and endurance	97. Demonstrate satisfactory sensory discrimination			
100. Interview for a job	101. Adjust to competitive standards	102. Maintain post-school occupational adjustment		

munity. It requires a master career education plan involving the various disciplines and levels of education to assure that each student acquires all competencies of which he is capable. Procedures for developing this kind of plan will be presented in chapter 7.

Competencies

Twenty-two major competencies contained within the three curriculum areas have been identified in previous research (Brolin & Thomas, 1971, 1972; Brolin, 1973; Brolin, Malever, & Matyas, 1976). This research has been supplemented from several other studies, professional opinion, and 3 years of intensive work on Project PRICE (Programming Retarded in Career Education), a federal project in which the senior author was project director and the junior author a project consultant. These 22 competencies have been subjected to rigorous review throughout the country. Field test results reveal that they generally reflect the major outcomes that should be expected for students if they are to be successfully prepared for community living and working. These competencies and their 102 subcompetencies were developed into a Program Guide (*Life Centered Career Education: A Competency Based Approach*) and published by The Council for Exceptional Children (Brolin, 1978). The competencies, generally referred to as the PRICE competencies, have been reported elsewhere (Brolin, 1974; 1976) and are presented in Table 5. The following discussion will briefly describe the three curriculum areas and the 22 competencies, the relationship of the school with the family and community representatives, and the four stages of career development as they relate to competency attainment.

Daily Living Skills

The competencies that are included under this category are: **1.** managing family finances; **2.** caring for home furnishings and equipment; **3.** caring for personal needs; **4.** raising children and family living; **5.** buying and preparing food; **6.** buying and making clothing; **7.** engaging in civic activities; **8.** utilizing recreation and leisure; and **9.** getting around the community. These are the complementary work-related avocational, family/leisure, and civic roles that were mentioned earlier in this chapter. But their attainment can also lead to many occupational possibilities, too. It is critical for handicapped students to learn these competencies to exist in today's fast-moving society. Too often, educators do not emphasize these areas nearly enough but expect that they will be learned incidentally in the home and elsewhere. For most handicapped students, this doesn't happen. So the school must make a deliberate effort to provide this instruction to the extent it cannot be provided in the home and other community settings.

Personal-Social Skills

The competencies that are included under this category are: **10.** self-aware-ness; **11.** self-confidence; **12.** socially responsive behavior; **13.** interpersonal relationships; **14.** independence; **15.** problem solving; and **16.** communica-tion skills. These competencies relate to helping the student understand who he is, discovering his potentials to solve problems and make decisions, becoming an independent person, and interacting appropriately with others. It is a well-known fact that lack of skills in this area causes the major down-fall of all individuals, including the handicapped, in work and other settings, no matter how competent the individual may be in other skills. Emphasis on this area in the schools is critically lacking, and much remains to be done to meet the requirements of handicapped students.

Occupational Guidance and Preparation

The competencies that are included in this category are: **17.** knowing and exploring occupational possibilities; **18.** making appropriate occupational decisions; **19.** work habits and behaviors; **20.** physical and manual skills; **21.** a specific saleable job skill; and **22.** being able to seek, secure, and maintain satisfactory employment. As mentioned earlier, this area is the one most often associated with the term *career education.* It deserves a major curricular emphasis, but it must be inextricably related to the other two areas because occupational functioning is dependent on the individual's adequate functioning in daily living and personal-social skills. It can be noted that two of the occupational competencies relate to awareness and decision making. (This should be done within a broad context and in no way should force early and specific occupational choices.) Three of the occupa-tional competencies should be tackled almost immediately after the student enters school: Knowing and exploring occupational possibilities, appro-priate work behaviors, and physical manual skills development. The other three should be emphasized primarily at the high school level.

The advocacy of this competency based approach in three curriculum areas does not intend to de-emphasize basic academic instruction. Stu-dents are still taught reading, mathematics, social studies, science, but now there is a specific purpose beyond the traditional one of bringing an in-dividual to a certain grade level at the end of a year or mastering some kind of physical activity. The specific purpose in this instance is the development of 22 important life-sustaining competencies. And every teacher in every subject at every grade level has a stake in each student's career develop-ment. This approach advocates teaching academic skills in relation to the students attaining career education competencies.

The next section discusses the relationship of school personnel, family, and community representatives to the career education effort and the com-petency based curriculum.

School, Family, and Community Relationships

As mentioned earlier in this chapter, a competency based curriculum requires a change in teacher and counselor roles and more involvement from family and community agencies, including the business and industrial sector. Involvement of the student is another aspect of career education that is often overlooked despite its obvious benefits. They, too, must be given the opportunity to significantly influence the direction of curriculum and instruction that will most appropriately benefit them, and to exercise their rights of choice and opinion.

School Personnel

All members of the school community have shared responsibility with meaningful input from family and community. Unfortunately, little is done to assure that there is a systematic application of this responsibility. Many wish to hold on to the traditional mode of imparting knowledge, concentrating on grade level content, and manipulating the classroom environment for that purpose (Moore & Gysbers, 1972). Starting with the top administrators and moving down the chain of command, responsibilities must be clearly outlined and assumed by the various personnel. Regular classroom teachers often display a resistance to having handicapped children in their classes, particularly the slower learners. With the inception and adoption of mainstreaming laws, they feel even more resistant because they feel these children are being pushed on them. They must be shown that these children can be taught without undue strain and that they have very important roles in teaching the child information, knowledge, and *skills* that will result in a successful community career in later years. An effective inservice program and special considerations for teachers assuming such a role must be provided by the administration. Regular class teachers are important in helping the student to develop feelings of self-worth and competence by providing situations where he can learn and be accepted by other class members. Almost every regular class teacher can help the student develop at least one competency. Home economics and industrial arts teachers are particularly significant in the daily living skills and occupational areas, while counselors are integral helpers in the personal-social and occupational guidance areas. Table 6 (Brolin, 1978) presents examples of the types of school personnel who could assist the student *in learning various competencies* at the junior and senior high school levels.

Special education teachers assume a somewhat new role under this competency based career education curriculum that we are advocating. The special educator becomes more of a consultant/advisor to other school personnel, parents, and community agencies and industries by coordinating services and integrating the contributions that school, community, and home can make in meeting each student's career development needs. Specific classroom instruction will still be needed for many students who cannot be appropriately educated in certain regular classes. They will become increasingly important as resource personnel to the regular classroom teachers who will need: inservice assistance, methods and materials consultation, modification and materials development assistance, and the sharing of relevant information on the students' basic academic skills, values, and attitudes. The special educator should also assume a major responsibility for monitoring each student's progress in competency attainment and to direct the energies of the various school staff in assuring their instruction and acquisition.

Family

The handicapped individuals' family is extremely important in their career development and can provide meaningful assistance to school personnel efforts by providing: hands on experiences, positive reinforcement for achievements, a secure psychological environment, community experiences and involvements, participation in family decision making, specific job tasks around the house, an atmosphere which encourages the development of independence, work habits and values, family projects, meaningful leisure and recreational pursuits and many other career development opportunities. The family must work closely with the school personnel to coordinate their efforts sequentially and consistently, assist in the development of community resources, assist as a volunteer or aide in school settings and functions, and serve on advisory and action committees related to career education. Families of handicapped students can help schools in public relations, fundraising, resource development and many other efforts needed to enhance school operations. Chapter 9 is devoted to "Family Contributions," where more information relevant to these ideas is discussed.

Community Involvement

There are a wide array of agencies and organizations that can assist school personnel and families in helping the student acquire the 22 career education competencies. For Daily Living Skills, agencies, organizations, and civic clubs such as YMCA, YWCA, Red Cross, League of Women Voters, Jaycees, Kiwanis, Rotary, Chamber of Commerce, Planned Parenthood, Parks and Recreation, Public Health, 4-H, Boy Scouts, churches, libraries, Girl Scouts, and Campfire Girls are resources that are available and can be used for career education experiences. For Personal-Social Skills, many of the preceding organizations, as well as the following, will be helpful: the state employment service; mental health, counseling, and university organizations. For Occupational Guidance and Preparation, a wide variety of agencies and organizations can be useful: vocational rehabilitation, state employment service, Comprehensive Employment Training Act (CETA) Programs, Community Action Programs, Veterans Administration, rehabilitation workshops,

Table 6
*Possible Competency Instructional Responsibilities**

competency	junior high	senior high
Daily Living Skills		
1. Manage family finances	Business, Math	Home Economics, Math
2. Select, manage, maintain home	Home Ec., Vocational Ed.	Home Economics
3. Care for personal needs	Home Ec., P.E./Health	Home Economics
4. Raise children, family living	Home Economics	Home Economics
5. Food preparation & buying	Home Economics	Home Economics
6. Clothing preparation & buying	Home Economics	Home Economics
7. Engage in civic activities	Social Studies, Music	Social Studies, Music
8. Utilize recreation time	P.E., Art, Music, Counselors	P.E., Art, Music
9. Community mobility	Home Economics	Driver's Education
Personal-Social Skills		
10. Achieve self-awareness	Music, P.E., Counselors	Art, Music, Counselors
11. Acquire self-confidence	Art, Music, P.E., Home Economics, Counselors	P.E., Counselors, Social Studies, Art, Vocational Ed., Music
12. Socially responsible behavior	P.E., Counselors, Music	Social Studies, Music
13. Exhibit interpersonal skills	Counselors	Music, Counselors
14. Achieve independent functioning	Counselors	Counselors
15. Decision making, problem solving	Math, Counselors	Science, Counselors
16. Communicate adequately	Language Arts, Music, Speech, P.E.	Language Arts, Speech, Music, Art
Occupational Guidance & Preparation		
17. Occup. knowledge & exploration	Vocational Education, Home Ec., Counselors	Counselors
18. Appropriate occup. decisions	Business, Vocational Ed., Counselors	Counselors
19. Appropriate work habits & behaviors	Vocational Ed., Math, Home Ec., Art	Home Ec., Vocational Ed., Music

Table 6 *continued*

competency	junior high	senior high
20. Acquire phys. & manual skills	Vocational Education, P.E.	Vocational Ed., P.E., Art
21. Obtain specific occup. skill	Vocational Ed., Home Ec.	Vocational Ed., Home Economics
22. Seek/secure employment	Counselors	Counselors

* Regular educators only. Special education teachers and others should assume these responsibilities as needed.

Governor's Committee on Employment of the Handicapped, and others. Business, Industry, and labor are also a wealth of assistance. banks, grocery stores, department stores, factories, insurance companies, repair shops, gas stations, loan companies, and many others are important to use in daily living and occupational learning activities.

The interaction and interface of these three important contributors to one's career development cannot be overemphasized. It will take considerable time and effort to develop these relationships into an effective, meaningful operating mechanism. But once achieved, the benefits will be greatly realized and the career education of handicapped students fully achieved.

STAGES OF CAREER DEVELOPMENT

Career education is typically depicted as consisting of several different stages or phases. Our model includes four stages of development: career *awareness;* career *exploration;* career *preparation;* and career *placement/ follow up,* and *continuing education.* This is illustrated in Figure 10. It is suggested that these stages begin earlier for many handicapped individuals, especially the more severely involved, since it will take them longer to develop the skills needed for successful functioning.

Career Awareness

During the elementary years in particular, career awareness should be emphasized. In the Daily Living Skills area, students must become aware of the fact that: Money must be managed and used appropriately; a house must be managed and maintained; personal needs must be taken care of properly; raising children and family living requires considerable responsibility; food must be purchased and prepared; clothing must be selected and

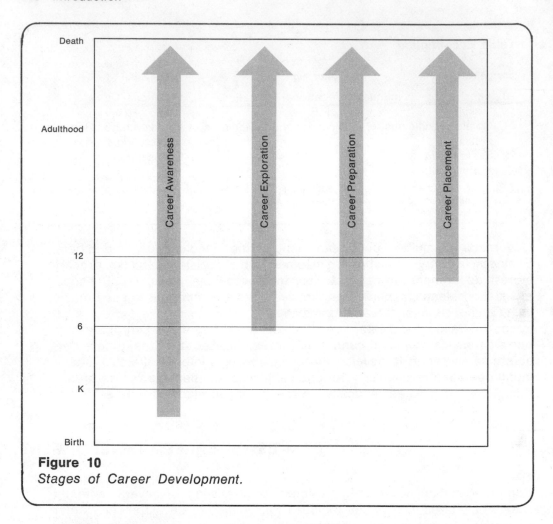

Figure 10
Stages of Career Development.

cared for; there are many civic responsibilities and roles that people must engage in; there are many recreation and leisure activities people can engage in to meet interests and needs; and there are various ways to get around the community, which must be learned.

In the Personal-Social Skills area, the students must begin learning about their feelings and values (self-awareness) and their potentials; develop feelings of self-confidence and self-worth; become aware of the types of socially desirable behavior that is expected in this society; learn what constitutes appropriate interpersonal skills; become aware of the need to become independent in thought and in relationships; become aware of how problems can be approached and solved; and become aware of the need to develop such communication skills as reading, writing, and speaking, so relationships with others are developed.

In the Occupational Guidance and Preparation area, students can begin developing positive attitudes about work; begin seeing themselves as potential workers; become aware of different types of jobs and their requirements; begin developing a work personality by acquiring a unique set of abilities and needs; become aware of the types of work habits and behaviors needed for success in work; and begin developing physical and manual skills.

Attitude, information, and self-understanding are three main elements to career awareness. Attitudes are the foundation on which the career education structure is built. Young children must learn that people make many conscious efforts at producing some benefit for themselves and others, including working. They must learn that people work for many reasons: economic, psychological, and societal. They need to understand that work is good and that it can provide a major source of personal identification and satisfaction. Information helps the student learn the variety of ways people earn a living and how they use their time in avocational, civic, leisure, and other life roles. Self-understanding is important to focus on during this period so the students can begin formulating their relationship to the world and identifying their eventual adult roles, which will enhance effective career development (Kolstoe, 1976).

Career awareness is not that difficult to infuse into the elementary curriculum. To a limited extent, most teachers are already doing it by taking the time to talk about the police officer, fire fighter, mail carrier, doctor, nurse, and homemaker. But the career education concept requires that this be done in a more purposeful manner so that they meaningfully and appropriately help students become aware of career aspects and themselves. Career education must be designed, like any other form of education, sequentially so that whatever happens at each grade level is built upon and leads toward competency attainment.

Career Exploration

Career exploration occurs at the elementary level, but its primary emphasis generally comes during the junior high school years. During this phase, the student begins a more careful self-examination related to his own unique set of abilities and needs, the world of work, avocational interests, leisure and recreational pursuits, and all other roles related to his career development. It is important for school personnel to be able to design curriculum and instructional experiences so self-exploration can appropriately occur. This should include the use of a variety of techniques, experiences, and settings relevant to each individual. The incorporation of community resource is crucial during this stage of career development.

Daily Living Skills instruction should permit exploration of various methods of managing family finances; how to go about selecting and managing the home; methods of caring for the individual's various personal needs; childrearing and family living methods; methods of buying and preparing nutritious food; methods of buying and caring for clothing needs; engaging in various kinds of civic activities; exploring recreation and leisure pursuits of interest; and trying out various modes of community transportation. All of these explorations can be personalized to the individual student and his emerging set of attitudes, values, and needs. These can occur through various courses, field experiences, clubs and organizations, home activities, and other community involvements, such as part-time jobs, hobbies, reading, and conversation.

Personal-Social Skills exploration should help the students to begin to seriously question who they are and to assist them to leave the child status they have assumed during the elementary years. Guidance and counseling functions are important in helping students identify unique abilities, needs, and interests as they relate to their career development. Individual and group counseling activities should be made available for role playing, modeling, values clarification, and other inter- and intrapersonal activities to help students learn more about themselves and others.

Occupational guidance and preparation helps students to carefully examine several occupational clusters and engage in a variety of hands-on experiences, both in and out of school. To learn more about occupational possibilities, students need to observe and analyze them firsthand to really understand their characteristics, try them out in a simulated situation, and talk to employers about the various aspects of jobs and work itself. To select and begin planning *tentative* occupational choices, the student will need the assistance of guidance personnel to receive a thorough assessment of their vocational aptitudes, interests, and needs. At this time, occupational choices can be only generally related to any specific area, as interest and needs will change during the high school years. Students should be encouraged to try various work samples, simulated job tasks, and community jobs, and to develop work habits and behaviors, physical and manual skills, and other skills needed in the work place. Prevocational classes such as industrial arts and home economics will be beneficial during the junior high school years.

Career exploration is the link between career awareness and career preparation. The young student begins to seriously think about his particular set of aptitudes, interests, and needs and how they can be directed toward a meaningful and successful adult role. Carefully planned and sequenced exploration activities and experiences should be available so that by the time the student is ready for high school, a more highly individualized educational plan can be designed; then relevant career preparation can be offered.

Career Preparation

As with the other stages of career development, career preparation is not solely confined to one period of schooling. Like the others, it begins in the early grades and continues throughout life as the person needs it. But, for most individuals, particularly those who do not go on to post-secondary training, the high school years are critical for reaching the necessary level of competency in the three curriculum areas comprising the 22 life career development competencies.

In the Daily Living Skills area, it is important for the student to try to master the nine competencies. Curriculum efforts must be directed to closely monitor and promote the learning of these competencies. Prior to high school, students were made aware of these competencies and had the time to explore and to begin learning them. Home economics, math, business, health, driver's education, social studies, and physical education are particularly relevant courses helpful for attaining the competencies. The students should be taught to be responsible and contributing individuals who are about to embark upon adulthood.

In the Personal-Social area, if previous efforts at the elementary and junior high levels have been satisfactory, the student is now ready to learn those personal-social skills needed for community living and working and to put them into practice. Any specific difficulties students have learning these seven competencies should be identified by the special educator and counselor and procedures designed for their elimination. This may occur in various classroom situations by informing the instructional staff of procedures that should be attempted to improve the deficiency, through direct classroom instruction, or by counseling—individual and group. Regular counseling, role playing, modeling, values clarification, and other techniques are effective with most students. It is important to treat and perceive each student as an independent and nearly adult-functioning individual who is to be listened to and respected. Specific interests and aptitudes should be identified and a life style more clearly delineated.

In the Occupational Guidance and Preparation area, career choices, although still tentative, can be more specifically directed toward vocational instruction. Students should be able to select from a wide variety of vocational courses and community job experiences according the aptitudes, interests, and abilities comprising their work personality. If work habits and behaviors, physical and manual skills, and work values and attitudes have been acquired satisfactorily during the elementary and junior high years, the focus can be on the selection of an appropriate occupational area and specific occupational skill. For some readers, this recommendation of specificity may not be appreciated. This is not an attempt to pigeonhole students. In the process of learning a specific saleable occupational skill, students also acquire a much more positive self-concept, confidence in their ability to learn a specific skill, and other personal-social skills. A final competency, which should not be taken lightly, is being able to know how to seek, secure, and maintain employment. This should be emphasized all 3 years of the high school program and is an important responsibility of guidance and special education workers.

Career preparation for most handicapped students will require a heavy experiential component. The use of community resources is encouraged.

Accurate vocational evaluation is necessary in helping the student to assess the realism of his career choices and training needs. Many handicapped students may need more than the traditional time to be prepared adequately for a successful career and should be given additional time, either in the high school or another setting, which can provide the necessary education.

Career Placement, Follow Up, and Continuing Education

Career placement can occur the last semester of the senior year or later, depending on the student's readiness for this last stage of career development. In most work-study programs, this is usually the time when the student is given the opportunity to be placed on an actual job as if he were being employed as a regular worker. This may be either on a full- or part-time basis and may last longer than one semester, depending on the student's ability level and needs.

Although career placement is most usually associated with job placement, students should also be given the opportunity to assume responsible, nonpaid adult work roles—avocational, leisure and recreation, civic, and other roles—to determine their level of ability and needs in these areas, as well as in paid employment. School personnel should work closely (supportively) with the family. For example, the student should be given specific and significant household responsibilities, which include managing family finances, managing a home, caring for personal needs, family living, food buying and preparation, clothing buying and care/selection, civic involvements, engaging in recreation and leisure-time activities that are self-planned, getting around the community, and developing and maintaining satisfactory social relationships. Although the school and family has probably worked on these competencies together well before this stage, they should now be practiced without the assistance of the family. Thus, it will be important for the family and the school personnel responsible for student monitoring and remedial assistance to work closely together.

The career placement stage pulls it all together. In the case of some students, it will identify where the student still has competency deficiencies and where further instruction is needed. It is the realistic aspect of the career education program and one that may extend intermittently over several years for many of the students. Therefore, it is very important to involve as many community resources relevant and crucial to the student's life career development and success into this final stage if they haven't been involved previously. Most handicapped persons, like other people, will have important lifelong learning and re-learning needs. Provisions must be made to account for these needs. Therefore, follow up and supportive services are an important aspect of career placement.

The four stages of career development interface with the competency based career education-oriented curriculum we advocate. If conducted accordingly, all handicapped students will be given full opportunity to learn the competencies they need to successfully assimilate into this complex society.

IMPLEMENTING CAREER EDUCATION

Career education is gathering steam, but there is much to do before it will become a reality for most students. In times of increased property tax, declining enrollments, and a surplus of teachers, many people are not ready for changes of such magnitude. But, ways must be found to maintain the continued reform of education. Marland (1976) offers the following as personal judgments imperative for career education: **1.** more systematic teacher education—inservice and preservice preparation; **2.** educators must compromise their traditional territorial claims so there can be genuine community involvement in providing students with work-site learning experiences; **3.** counselors should be freed of their paper shuffling chores so they begin engaging deeply in the work of career counseling; **4.** improve our methods of forecasting work force needs so we avoid the dreadful waste and frustrations that come from oversupply and undersupply in occupations; **5.** move from the experimental-demonstration to the operational-installation mode; **6.** resolve the hindrances of obsolete laws and agreements that prevent young people from working, limit the days or hours of school, place unreasonable burdens of liability on cooperating businesses offering work sites for the students, and give excessive emphasis to the credentialing of teachers and counselors, foreclosing the usefulness of talented volunteers; **7.** assess the outcomes of career education and document the evidence that where career education has been systematically installed, academic growth improves dramatically; and **8.** an initiative from educators that will result in career education being implemented comprehensively in their school districts.

Hoyt (1976a) lists 11 strategies for attaining change: **1.** use public opinion polls and research data illustrating current youth problems and societal need as a rational for reform; **2.** emphasize the system-wide need for career education; **3.** utilize an infusion approach to reform; **4.** don't try to "take over" all of education; **5.** emphasize "work," but do so in humanistic terms; **6.** organize career education efforts around the process of career development; **7.** implement career education primarily around the teaching/learning process; **8.** allow teachers the time and the opportunity to be creative; **9.** allow teachers to "sell" themselves on career education; **10.** provide key roles in career education for all professionals in education; and **11.** recognize the importance of collaboration. Collectively, these 11 strategies hold high potential for educational reform and motivating professional educators and the general public to decide for themselves to change their present practices or levels, preschool through adult education (pp. 18–20).

Two key words—*infusion* and *collaboration*—underlie efforts to implement career education. Infusion is the attempt within the formal system of education to make education as preparation for work both a prominent and a permanent goal of all who teach and of all who learn. Collaboration represents involvement among educators, business-labor-professional-government, and the home and family. Hoyt (1976a) introduces a basic idea for career education which he calls the "Marshmallow Principle."

> External pressure exerted on an organization to change its basic structure will, for as long as that pressure is applied, cause the organization's structure to bend and assume a new shape. Once the pressure is removed, the organization will reassume its original shape. Basic change in organizational structure is accomplished only when the key functionaries within that organization make an internal commitment to change.
>
> "Marshmallow Principle,"
> Kenneth Hoyt

Hoyt also believed (like Marland) that any basic changes in American education are contingent on the commitment of classroom teachers to change.

In the case of handicapped students, there are many in the special education area, as well as regular educators, who remain content to make only minor modifications in their educational practices. There are those who believe special education has been offering career education all along, and to those individuals we must reply that this is not true. In the 1960s, out of desperation, work-study or vocational adjustment programs developed in many secondary programs and were a boon to the career development of many handicapped students. The combination of academic and work experience was indeed a positive response to those critics who very accurately called for more than basic academic skills instruction for handicapped students if they were to assume productive work roles as adults. Special educators took the leadership and developed these vital programs; but we strongly believe, based on all available evidence, that this still isn't enough for handicapped individuals. They must also, in concert with academic and occupational skills, learn and acquire adequate personal-social skills and daily living skills as we described earlier to achieve total fulfillment and functioning as a productive human being in today's rapidly demanding and moving society.

To achieve this, present and future school personnel must be trained intensively in career education methodology. There is a long way to go in this area, although Hoyt (1976a) indicates that 24% of all districts have started inservice faculty development. However, Hoyt is bothered by the fact that what is often called career education in a school is frequently only one or two teachers implementing one aspect of career education in their classrooms. He maintains that often what is called career education really is not. The American Institute for Research (AIR) reports that career education is underway in 9,300 of the nation's 16,740 school districts, although these figures may be meaningless if what is being called career education is what Hoyt suggests (Neil, 1977).

If change is to occur, then encouragement and support must begin with administrators at the federal, state, and local levels. These individuals must give those who provide direct services to handicapped individuals the time, materials, training, and recognition for these achievements. Effective in-service training programs are badly needed so professional personnel can learn new skills that were not taught previously in the universities. Institutions of higher learning must respond more rapidly and extensively to the needs of the schools. Too many of these institutions will probably give only passing attention to local needs and continue preparing their personnel in the same manner of the past unless there is enough local and state pressure to do otherwise. Some universities have responded in an extensive manner, most have not.

Much remains to be done if career education is to be implemented properly for handicapped individuals. Hopefully, this book will assist those interested in meeting this important national priority.

CONCLUSION

Career education is a term used for a group of activities, processes, and interventions that occur in different school levels and community settings (Herr, 1977). It is an evolving educational concept, requiring the participation of the entire school community, family, agencies, and the business-industrial sector to be totally effective. Career education is *not* the only education students receive, but it should be a very significant and pervasive part of what is taught. Career education is not intended to replace traditional education but rather to bolster it and make curriculum more directed toward the roles, settings, and events that will comprise their lives. It is meaningful and relevant education.

While still in its infancy, it is already beginning to demonstrate its ability to significantly increase the academic achievement of students, as well as increase career maturity, personal responsibility, self-awareness, and other life-centered goals (Bhaermann, 1977; Herr, 1977). Several studies indicate that parents are the most influential factor in the student's career development (Herr, 1977). Studies of career education for handicapped students are relatively few, and much more work needs to be done in this area to demonstrate unequivocally its impact.

If career education is to become a reality, the following will be required:

- Support from top-level administrators;
- funds and the time to re-direct curricula;
- acceptance of the career education conceptualization and the need to change;
- attitude changes by school personnel relative to the handicapped— inclusion of their parents into policy-making educational decisions;
- change in the roles of various types of school personnel—more teamwork; and
- a greater understanding of the world of work by school personnel— recognition to school personnel who make outstanding contributions in providing career education.

This chapter has attempted to present salient information about career education and to describe its major features, including the authors' conceptualization of a competency based career education approach based on the total life career development needs of handicapped individuals. Career education is the hope and promise for properly conveying educational services to our handicapped citizens and other individuals. It will require changes in our entire system of education, but it does not say what we have been doing is all bad or has to be all thrown out. Rather, it attempts to look at the individual's total career functioning needs. By defining career in a broader perspective, we account for the total needs individuals have for community living and working.

Our conceptualization of career education is that it: encompasses all kinds, types, and levels of education; prepares individuals for all phases of their lives; focuses on interpersonal and intrapersonal skills; extends from preschool through retirement; equips students with saleable skills; provides a balance of content and experiential learning; emphasizes helping people to plan and make decisions wisely; and personalizes education. The four letter word *work* is wholeheartedly supported and emphasized so that students are prepared adequately with vocational skills. But avocational, civic, and family roles are equally important and crucial to occupational and community success. Remember, occupations are a part of one's career, not one's *only* career.

part two

Instruction

Part two presents two major types of information in regard to teaching handicapped students in a career education context: First, objectives and activities that teachers and other school personnel can use in teaching the 22 competencies and 102 subcompetencies presented in chapter 3; second, a discussion of suggested techniques for teaching the various competencies to handicapped learners.

Chapter 4 is devoted to the Daily Living Skills competencies. The competencies in this area are not only important for community living but also relate to vocational possibilities, depending on one's unique pattern of abilities, interests, and needs. The chapter gives many suggestions on teaching the nine daily living competencies and the 42 subcompetencies and how they relate to the IEP. It is recommended that school personnel identify areas of the curriculum that already contain lessons relative to the competencies. A curriculum check sheet is presented, which can be used by the teacher to facilitate a review of texts, programmed materials, or learning aides, and to correspond to the competencies, curriculum areas, and method of instruction under consideration. Examples of lesson plans are also presented.

Chapter 5 discusses the Personal-Social competencies. The seven competencies in this area are those necessary for personal achievement and satisfactory interpersonal relationships, both at work and in family and community living. After suggestions for teaching the 33 personal-social subcompetencies, several strategies for teaching them are discussed: bibliotherapy, classroom discussions and meetings, individualized learning centers, role play and sociodrama, self-concept scales, and values clarification. Particular attention is given to the development of one's self-concept because of its extreme importance to the ultimate success or failure of the handicapped individual.

Chapter 6 focuses on occupational competencies, which are categorized under the heading Occupational Guidance and Preparation. The six competencies comprising this area can be divided into three that relate to occupational guidance and three to occupational preparation. The 27 subcompetencies that relate to five competencies are discussed in relation to suggestions for their provision in and out of the classroom. The sixth, "obtaining a specific occupational skill," is discussed relative to why it is necessary to acquire it before graduation. A section on occupational guidance describes several techniques: counseling, vocational testing, work evaluation, job/task analysis, simulations of business and industry, career seminars, field trips and speakers, and a career information center. Occupational preparation techniques discussed in the chapter are work tasks and projects, vocational education/centers, simulations of business and industry, and on and off campus training.

Daily Living Skills, Personal-Social Skills, and Occupational Guidance and Preparation, combined with basic academic skills instruction, constitute a comprehensive career development curriculum approach to meeting the needs of our handicapped citizens. We are pleased that so many school districts throughout the country are moving toward a competency based career education approach. Several have adopted the 22 competencies that are discussed in detail in the chapters that follow. The CEC has published a guide on teaching these 22 competencies, which the reader can refer to for further information (*Life Centered Career Education: A Competency Based Approach,* Brolin, 1978).

Daily Living Skills are necessary for successful, independent living in modern society. Acquisition of these skills can lead to vocational possibilities for the student, depending on her particular abilities, interests, and needs. It is vital that instruction in these skills be systematically included in daily classroom lessons rather than taught haphazardly or overlooked entirely. The particular learning characteristics of an individual with limitations may require intense and planned development of learning objectives, methods, and evaluation in order to obtain certain levels of performance. But, this effort on the part of teacher and learner results in dividends that can be measured by success in such daily functions as maintaining personal appearance, managing finances, and mobility in the community.

There are nine daily living competencies we have identified as important to the career development of handicapped individuals. They are listed below with their respective competency number shown in parentheses.

This chapter does not contain all possible objectives and activities that teachers can utilize from the time the student enters school at primary

Managing Family Finances (**1**)

Selecting, Managing, and Maintaining a Home (**2**)

Caring for Personal Needs (**3**)

Raising Children—Family Living (**4**)

Buying and Preparing Food (**5**)

Buying and Caring for Clothes (**6**)

Engaging in Civic Activities (**7**)

Utilizing Recreation and Leisure Time (**8**)

Getting Around the Community (**9**)

grades through adult education. Such an elaboration, if possible, would fill this book; and yet, teachers would still have to modify them to fit the needs of individual learners. We have provided a series of goals toward which the daily lesson plans and individual education programs can be directed. Each competency is divided into subcompetencies (42 in all), which contain narrative discussions and suggestions relative to objectives and teaching activities. Teachers should fashion additional objectives and activities to meet the specific abilities and learning difficulties of their students. We have also presented several *Activity Tips* as a teaching example. The *Activity Tip* is only *one* example that can be modified to meet the student's progress through the stages of career awareness, exploration, preparation, and placement. We have not attempted to provide a book of "how to teach handicapped children and youth" with an exhaustive list of activities. However, the discussions of the competencies and appropriate suggestions should enable the teacher and counselor to infuse career concepts and materials into the daily curriculum. The chapter concludes with a discussion of techniques for teaching Daily Living Skills to handicapped learners.

COMPETENCIES

Managing Family Finances (1)

The ability to regulate various financial transactions is a crucial determiner of adult success for the average, as well as handicapped, citizen. It is logical to expect that one result of successful employment will be a specific amount of economic reward. This consideration requires teachers to include numerous activities within the career development curriculum that prepare students for their roles as spender, saver, and manager. The major subcompetencies are as follows:

1.1. Identifying Money and Making Correct Change

The beginning skill for this subcompetency is the successful identification of the several forms of currency. Students with visual disability may accomplish this skill by building a familiarity with the size of metal coins and by folding currency at various corners to indicate denominations. The actual counting and manipulation of coins and bills can begin in the primary grades with arithmetic exercises. Numerous teaching aides and commercial workbooks are available to help teachers initiate activities requiring students to demonstrate their ability to make correct change and use money in various situations. This currency can be provided by parents in conjunction with field trips designed to exercise this ability, or occur when students visit museums and buy their school lunch and snacks. Other objectives related to this subcompetency should include: a. demonstrating ability to make change, and b. identifying the uses of money in society.

1.2. Making Wise Expenditures

The ability to apply prudent choice in the selection of goods and services is valuable in a society that experiences inflation, economic stagnation, and prosperity. This subcompetency focuses upon the student as a consumer who is able to understand tags and labels for evaluating essential merchandise, advantages and disadvantages of discount stores, and strategies for buying during bargain sales. These skills will be essential for those handicapped workers with incomes that place them in lower economic levels. Teachers can acquire commercial materials that include specific exercises in consumer education. But, generally speaking, the instructor should conduct classroom activities requiring students to compare products available at different stores or markets, itemize their family's purchases during a given period of time, or construct a shopping list and record the prices of the items at a given store. These assignments can begin at the primary level, and experience has taught us that they are continually repeated through the adult years. These practices also broaden the student's experiences with decision making relative to products and services. A final consideration for

ACTIVITY TIP: Students can keep a record and calculate their parents' expenditures for a week or their own expenses for a longer period of time. The student should place budget headings on the left hand side of a ruled sheet of paper. The days of the week or months of the year are placed at the top of the page. Dollar amounts are entered for the following budget headings: rent, utilities, food, transportation, clothing, medical, insurance, taxes, entertainment, savings, others. Advanced students can calculate the percentage of expenditures per budget heading.

all consumers is an awareness of common advertising gimmicks and traps. Local consumer protection agencies and groups can provide the classroom with materials and demonstrations that will further supplement this portion of the curriculum. Other objectives should include: a. distinguishing essential items from luxuries, and b. identifying sources of consumer information.

1.3. Obtaining and Using Bank and Credit Facilities

This complex subcompetency includes the use of a checking account, savings account, credit/charge account, and obtaining a loan. Many students will not engage in the latter step until their adult years, but initial familiarity with banks, pass books, checks, deposits, and the like can begin in the elementary grades. Teachers can establish classroom banks and accounts in conjunction with exercises on the use of money. Shopping trips as discussed in subcompetency 1.2 can be financed by checking, savings, or charge accounts maintained through the classroom deposits. All of these exercises rest, however, upon an actual acquaintance with the community's financial establishments. Although teachers have an opportunity to visit banks, savings and loan facilities, and credit unions, it should be obvious that the family has greater access over a longer period of time. Teachers should encourage parents to explain the family's use of these facilities while taking their children with them to make deposits or withdrawals. These efforts can be supplemented through classroom demonstrations by representatives from these establishments. Other objectives should include: a. identifying benefits in saving money, and b. identifying information required in opening a charge account or obtaining a loan.

1.4. Keeping Basic Financial Records

It is possible for successful adults to maintain a minimum number of records. But, they must be able to identify those receipts, bank statements, or contracts that should be preserved in order to plan a budget, meet bills, and file tax returns. The basis to these actions is a personal system of recording and filing. Children are introduced to logical systems when they develop hobbies that include an ordering of events or materials, such as collecting stamps, pictures, or bubble gum cards. Several commercial publishers provide instructional materials explaining procedures in banking, maintaining records, and calculating taxes. The crucial concern for the teacher is whether the student has *practiced* and *uses* a record-keeping system, whether it be with commercial or teacher-made materials. It is only when students incorporate a system into their daily activities that one can be close to success in this subcompetency. Other objectives should include: a. constructing a personal budget for a given length of time, and b. identifying community agencies that assist individuals in developing an adequate record system.

1.5. Calculating and Paying Taxes

The student will not need these skills in authentic situations until she has accumulated financial returns subject to local, state, and federal taxes. However, this should not deter the instructor from conducting classroom activities examining the several kinds of taxes (sales, luxury, gas) that affect the student's earnings and savings. These activities can identify the items that are taxed, the amount, their collection, and use. Secondary school programs should include exercises to build familiarity with income tax forms, procedures for filing returns, and agencies that can provide tax assistance. Other objectives should include demonstrating the ability to complete a tax form.

Selecting, Managing, and Maintaining a Home (2)

A major portion of the average person's salary is directed toward housing. In certain parts of the country, the monthly rent for an apartment or house may exceed the costs for food without considering additional expenses for cleaning fees and utilities. The continual rise in housing costs in excess of the average worker's salary places increased stress upon her ability to maintain independence. The young handicapped person may have to reside with the family for a longer period of time, seek peers who will share in the costs, or enter marriage as a means of "breaking" into independent living. All these situations require the individual to be alert for ways in which she can minimize expenses for maintaining a home. The major subcompetencies are as follows:

2.1. Selecting Adequate Housing

The awareness of a family's needs for living space and facilities begins with classroom activities in the primary grades. Students can draw their homes or apartments, collect pictures of various rooms, and identify the family functions in each part of the dwelling. This general inquiry into one's own home leads to an expanded knowledge of the various types of housing available in the community as children share their projects and accounts. The teacher should continually stress the advantages and disadvantages of each dwelling, which would include discussions of space, costs, utilities, and location. Students in the intermediate grades can gather information through interviews with realty agents or family members and newspaper advertising. Secondary students should continue with specific exercises related to renting a home or apartment, deposits, leases, tenant rights and responsibilities, and community agencies that can assist the individual with more complicated decisions involving the purchase of property. Another objective should be identifying important considerations in renting an apartment or buying a house.

2.2. Maintaining a Home

This subcompetency includes basic skills such as sweeping, dusting, cleaning, and washing household fixtures, furniture, and utensils. The physical skills required in using brooms, mops, vacuum cleaners, and the like can be acquired through practice in the classroom. But a far better learning situation exists in the student's home. Teachers should coordinate their activities and evaluations with those of the parents. This way the handicapped individual receives both the knowledge of household routines and instruments plus repeated practice in maintaining a clean and attractive home. Another objective should be demonstrating a housekeeping routine or system.

> ACTIVITY TIP: Students and parents cooperate in constructing a large diagram of their house or apartment. Symbols representing the various tools required to maintain and clean the dwelling and that the student can use successfully should be entered at the bottom of the diagram. Students can create their own symbols for such functions as sweeping, dusting, and the like. A chart can be added indicating the functions and the days of the week. Parents and teachers can keep track of the student's progress through entries on the chart. Both the diagram and chart can be expanded in scope, depending on the student's abilities.

2.3. Using Basic Appliances and Tools

Home appliances can be divided into those that are used to clean or to repair. The former have already been mentioned in subcompetency 2.2; the latter would include such tools as a hammer, saw, screwdriver, or wrench. The teacher's goal is to develop student competencies with appliances and tools that would be used in the home to maintain cleanliness and insure that doors, windows, locks, and the like are in working order. This means that students would be able to make basic home repairs and improvements, like replacing screens or light bulbs, tightening screws or bolts, and painting doors or walls. These activities lend themselves to cooperative instruction with professionals from home economics and industrial arts, and the special class teacher should make every effort to enlist their assistance. Other objectives should include: a. identifying financial benefits of home repairs and improvements, and b. demonstrating safety procedures in working with tools and appliances.

2.4. Maintaining the Home Exterior

Although the majority of young adults will maintain initial independent living in apartments, they should understand and practice skills that contribute to the preservation of the exterior portion of the dwelling. These skills include mowing, raking, trimming, watering, painting, and removing ice or snow. Students should demonstrate the ability to use various tools (rakes, shovels, lawnmowers) and the safety procedures appropriate to the function of each device. Once again, professionals from home economics and industrial arts should be used in joint planning of instructional activities. Other objectives should include: a. identifying appropriate tools for each procedure, and b. identifying community sources of tools and advice for maintaining exterior conditions.

Caring for Personal Needs (3)

Adequate hygiene, physical condition, and health care are of special importance to those handicapped individuals who are susceptible to injury, illness, or irritation associated with their impairment. These individuals will, no doubt, receive ample cautions and directions from physicians, parents, and relatives, but the teacher should approach the same ground from a different vantage point. The teacher's objectivity will help balance the emotional involvement of those who identify with the handicapped individual and her appearance. The major subcompetencies are as follows:

3.1. Dressing Appropriately

Social standards concerning acceptable attire for both men and women have become less rigorous over the past decade. The increased range of dress places a definite burden on teachers, who must instruct students in the types of clothing appropriate to different weather conditions, social settings, and work situations. Specific activities have been conducted in the elementary grades with children constructing bulletin boards containing displays that illustrate the major forms of dress. The emphasis with such beginning activities should be on the health aspects associated with attire. Adolescents should engage in role-play situations and self-evaluations to become aware of the social ramifications of dressing to meet the occasion. Another objective should include demonstrating competence in selecting appropriate attire.

3.2. Exhibiting Proper Grooming and Hygiene Methods

The child should demonstrate skills in toothbrushing; washing hands and face; using handkerchieves, towels, and napkins; and maintaining a clean appearance. Teachers from intermediate through adult education should continue to build on this foundation and expand the several means of personal hygiene and grooming appropriate to males and females. This is one of the most important subcompetencies since personal appearance is so involved in the acceptance of an individual by peers, adults, *and* employers.

Another objective should include demonstrating the use of appropriate health/grooming aids.

> ACTIVITY TIP: Each student constructs a "Grooming Card," which is carried in a wallet or purse. It is similar to an identification card but contains specific reminders of grooming appropriate to the student's concerns (i.e., hair style, make-up, clean glasses, and the like). Teachers, counselors, and parents periodically check the "Grooming Card" for proper identification!

3.3. Demonstrating Knowledge of Physical Fitness, Nutrition, and Weight

One of the motivating considerations in the development of the Special Olympics for the mentally retarded was the fact that they had received little or no instruction in physical education or recreation in public schools and institutions. The Special Olympics help dramatize that all individuals possess physical competence when that ability is measured against their own standards of achievement. This situation is repeated across other exceptionalities (i.e. blind, deaf, and physically disabled). Proper care and development of the body is vital for the handicapped so that they may be able to meet the physical demands of everyday life. The child should demonstrate knowledge of major body parts and perform exercises or activities that benefit development. Teachers should enlist the cooperation of professionals in physical education, recreation, and home economics as the child progresses from fundamental knowledge through lessons in basic food groups, nutrition, and weight control. Students can maintain their own health charts, recording maturation, eating habits, or games and exercises. Other objectives should include: a. performing activities that maintain appropriate physical fitness, and b. demonstrating eating practices that contribute to proper nutrition.

3.4. Demonstrating Knowledge of Illness Prevention and Treatment Methods

This subcompetency is one of the most complex as it includes instruction about illnesses and their basic symptoms, hazards to health that occur in the home, basic first-aid techniques, and obtaining assistance for various medical problems. The lessons on illnesses will be of significance to those handicapped individuals who must guard against certain dangers in the environment that can complicate the primary disability, for example, respiratory infections for the physically disabled, or an inflamed eyelid for the deaf. Teachers should begin instruction in basic health measures to prevent illnesses or injury in the primary grades. The children's experiences will provide ample subject matter, and the instructor should provide numerous practice sessions requiring the students to contact emergency facilities in the event of illness or injury. The range of subject matter increases as instruction includes first aid, safety considerations, health facilities, and professionals. Local public health facilities or agents can provide demonstrations and audio-visual aides to assist instruction in these competencies.

Raising Children—Family Living (4)

Success in raising a family begins with the individual's experiences in being a family member. Teachers should help students become ardent observers of successful childrearing in their families, relatives, or neighbors. A great deal of the demonstration required in mastering the subcompetencies will be founded on the observational and reporting skills of the student. Teachers can prepare their lessons on successful child-parent interactions based on these student observations. Experience is the best teacher, but observations of others' experiences have also avoided needless trials and errors in situations where room for experimentation is limited. A second important consideration is that teachers in secondary and adult programs provide students with ample opportunity to develop questions about family and children and provide them with enough sources of information so that they may obtain in-depth answers. The major subcompetencies are as follows:

4.1. Responsibilities Involved in Marriage

The focus of the teacher's lessons should be on the personal adjustments that each partner must make during marriage. Students can certainly observe the "give and take" in decision-making processes that occur in their families. They may also have some basis of experience in adjustments with their brothers and sisters, playmates, club members, or peers. Of course, these are all second best, and the situations hedge around the actual experiences accompanying marriage. They do, nevertheless, provide the individual with test situations involving some important elements of marriage, such as cooperative planning and expressing one's opinion. Given this prior familiarity with mutual concern and respect, the teacher may then probe the decisions in marriage that require careful decision making. Shared responsibilities in the home, earning a living, managing the household, visiting with relatives, and family planning are just a few issues for discussion. They certainly provide enough subject material for the hundreds of hours of television that these same students will view through their childhood and adolescent years! Other objectives should include: a. identifying personal adjustments in life style necessary in marriage, b. listing reasons for family planning, and c. identifying sources of assistance in family planning and marriage problems.

4.2. Child-Raising Procedures (Personal Care)

Children have various needs at successive developmental stages. Infant care and feeding, innoculation for diseases, appropriate diet, clothing, exercise, and protection are important considerations throughout the stages of development. These same needs may vary depending upon the particular characteristics of the individual. Students can associate their own life experiences with each topic area to arrive at appropriate practices in working with their future children. This is one way the teacher can attempt to internalize childrearing procedures when in actuality, the main topic of consideration is projected to some time in the future. Other objectives should include: a. demonstrating proper care of a child, and b. demonstrating basic protection measures for a child.

```
ACTIVITY TIP: The teacher or counselor arranges the class
into a "family circle." All students are members of the
same family. Each session is directed toward an incident or
problem that confronts a family (i.e., planning a vaca-
tion, sending a child to summer camp, and the like). Prob-
lem areas should be chosen that have particular importance
to the class. The students can question the professional
for more details but must present possible alternatives to
solving the problem. Various activities can evolve from
the session, such as drawing, writing, and other creative
means reflecting individual and group solutions.
```

4.3. Child-Raising Procedures (Psychological)

In preparing the student to meet the psychological responsibilities of marriage and childrearing, the teacher must develop the student's awareness of some basic emotional needs within self. Discussions of love, support, and acceptance probe the very structure of the student's sense of self and identify the conceptions and attitudes that are a basis for behavior. These encounters may include the student's identification of her needs as a child or at various stages of development, reflections on the behaviors that meet these needs, and the parent's role in providing for this aspect of the child. In understanding their emotional needs as children, students can approach the problem of building a psychological environment that fosters the personal growth of an individual. Other objectives should include: a. identifying potential family problems, and b. identifying community agencies that provide assistance with family problems.

4.4. Family Safety Procedures and Practices

This subcompetency is founded on the active measures one may take, whether child, adolescent, or adult, in protecting the family against potential danger. It includes the identification of emergency situations that can occur in the home (fire, damage by storm) or with members of the family (injury, accident). Each emergency situation includes an appropriate action that should be taken by members of the family. This would include first-aid procedures and contact with rescue, fire, or safety units. Another objective should be identifying the appropriate safety procedures per hazardous situation.

Buying and Preparing Food (5)

This competency relates to the purchase, preparation, and consumption of food. It also involves an area of life that functions as a reward, thus the frequent use of food as a reinforcer for student performance in the classroom. The role of food as both a necessary substance for life and reward for behavior places an additional responsibility on teachers who must develop student abilities in distinguishing between the two. The following subcompetencies are by no means the last word in planning, purchasing, and preparing food, so teachers should expand this area to meet the particular needs and abilities of their students.

5.1. Demonstrating Eating Skills

Society has developed standards of behavior pertaining to eating in the company of other individuals, whether it be in family or public situations. These standards of etiquette are bent only slightly for the handicapped. The individual with blindness must eat peas with the same skill as her sighted companion who can watch them rolling around on the dinner plate. An inability to conform to these standards even with some slight modification to accommodate the disability places the individual in a situation that elicits disapproval and rejection by other members of society. Therefore, the handicapped student should be made aware of these standards and, secondly, demonstrate the ability to use necessary eating utensils and the accessories that are available to assist those with physical limitations. These skills should be taught in the primary grades, reinforced in the home, and practiced in specifically designed field trips in the community. Another objective should be demonstrating abilities in restaurant or other public eating places.

5.2. Planning Proper Meals

It is quite a step from eating properly to planning appropriate foods for breakfast, lunch, and dinner. One should remember that planning need not include the actual preparation of a meal. Even if one is unable or does not choose to prepare foods, it is still advisable that the student know the nutritional value and relationships between food, health, and growth so that she can choose meals that provide the greatest benefits. Many individuals' diets consist largely of "junk foods," which are high in sugar content but low in protein. This is the type of situation that the individual with a handicap must avoid. Second, adequate meals are important for those indivduals who receive supplementary ingredients to their diets, such as calcium for bone development, medications of various sorts, and injections. These supplements interact with other nutrients in such a balanced condition that any careless regard for diet lowers one's performance in mental or physical tasks, as well as endangering health. Teachers should note that this subcompetency is also related to the one on physical fitness, nutrition, and weight (3.3). Other objectives should include: a. developing a list of foods beneficial to health, and b. planning meals within a specified budget.

5.3. Purchasing Food

This subcompetency is related to the one on making wise expenditures (1.2) and provides ample opportunity for teachers to train students on the use of measuring units of food and calculating costs. Unfortunately, students are often emersed in a world of advertisements for foods and "goodies," thus providing the subject matter for daily assignments in purchasing meals at the school cafeteria, calculating the cost of a "bag lunch," or projecting future expenses for after-school snacks. In later years, with the recommended assistance of home economics instructors or representatives from community consumer organizations, students should be exposed to lessons in distinguishing the quality of foods, various types and cuts of meat and fish, and the advantages of sales and specials. Other objectives should include: a. identifying community sources of information about food prices, and b. constructing a shopping list within a budget.

> ACTIVITY TIP: The teacher provides the class with a list
> of basic food items. Students price each item at their local
> store or supermarket. These prices form the basis for a
> series of activities in which students are required to com-
> pare prices of food items, compute costs for a given number
> of items, or select items based on a fixed amount of money.
> The complexity of the activity can be adjusted to the
> ability of the individual student.

5.4. Preparing Meals

The process of preparing an entire meal will include the use of utensils; following directions; identification of various forms of measures; cleaning, cutting, and preparing foods; and the use of devices for cooking and baking. Every school curriculum should train the handicapped individual in the skills of managing the preparation of a meal, either by direct manipulation or instruction. Other objectives should include: a. preparing a meal according to directions, and b. demonstrating kitchen safety measures.

5.5. Cleaning Up

Teachers should impress upon the student that the cleaning process is just as important and should be as orderly as the preparation of foods. After all, the foods move on, but the dirty dishes remain for the next meal. This subcompetency includes the use of various cleaning measures and materials, the disposal and removal of waste products, and the storage of the utensils. This is also an appropriate area of lessons for an emphasis upon the safety factors and measures involved in the entire preparation and clean-up process.

5.6. Storing Food

Proper food storage is useful in the overall management of financial resources and family health. This process requires the student to be aware of methods of storage and the several indications of spoiled food. Teachers can use the numerous instructional aides that are available from consumer organizations or companies that manufacture storage devices. Another objective should be demonstrating techniques for storing food.

Buying and Caring for Clothes (6)

The old expression that "clothes make the man" has undergone some alterations, but it still signifies a cultural standard that serves as a powerful tool in the classroom. Whether it be blue jeans or formal dress, sport shoes or high heels, students from elementary through adult education classes will be interested in fashions, styles, and the latest "in thing" because clothes are related to identity and social acceptance. For handicapped individuals, proper choice or modification of clothing is particularly important to making them more attractive and minimizing any physical deficiencies they may have. The major subcompetencies are as follows:

6.1. Washing Clothing

The principal objective in this subcompetency is to teach students the basic steps in the care of clothing. These measures help contribute to the student's appearance and use of financial resources. Primary grade students can begin with the tasks of washing dust cloths, handkerchieves, and towels to build their knowledge and use of water temperatures and detergents. As students begin to wash their clothes, they will need instruction about the various laundry products and operating washers and dryers. These steps would require cooperative efforts with parents who, in all practicality, are in closer contact with the weekly processing and evaluation of the skills. Another objective should be demonstrating appropriate laundering methods for different clothing.

6.2. Ironing and Storing Clothing

Home economics teachers can assist students with the skills to prepare and iron various types of clothing. Teachers should be prepared to provide instruction about the why, when, how, and where of storing seasonal clothing. Once again, every attempt should be made to coordinate classroom and home instruction.

6.3. Performing Simple Mending

A list of skills for this subcompetency include matching thread color, the mechanics of preliminary planning and basting, simple hand sewing, machine sewing, and appropriate stitches for different types of tears.

> ACTIVITY TIP: Each student should have access to a "repair kit," either at school or home. The classroom or home economics teacher should assign specific repairs to be completed at home, or the student may bring items from home to repair sessions at school. Teachers and parents can monitor materials for the kit, its location, and use according to the abilities and attitude of the student.

6.4. Purchasing Clothing

It is quite possible that the student will have experience or influence over the purchase of clothing and food products far sooner than the other basics of consumer purchases (i.e. shelter, health, transportation, and leisure). The observant teacher will recall the numerous children who accompany their mothers on shopping ventures in the supermarket and clothing stores. These same teachers may face a bitter battle in attempting to counteract the buying prejudices and practices that have already been established in those prior years of impulse buying. If successful, the teacher will have impressed the student with such considerations as appropriate clothing for different occasions; balancing clothing needs with available funds; identification of well-made versus poorly made garments; and other "hints" related to the timing of purchases. Other objectives should include: a. recording one's measurements, b. identifying clothing for a basic wardrobe, and c. planning a wardrobe based on a specific budget.

Engaging in Civic Activities (7)

The participation of the handicapped in civic activities has steadily increased over the past decade. This participation has been encouraged by the success of other groups of individuals who have demonstrated and lobbied for legislation to insure equality in housing, education, and employment. Having achieved significant laws at the local, state, and federal levels, the handicapped must be prepared to continue their roles as advocates in order to translate legislation and regulations into daily social practice. The major subcompetencies are as follows:

7.1. Basic Local Government and Laws

The teacher should develop within each student an understanding of the fundamental reasons for the existence of laws, government, and the various roles and duties of government officials. It may be easy to fall into the trap of emphasizing the consequences of violating a law, but the teacher should devote a great deal of attention to: those officials within the community who can affect change in the law; the means available to citizens to bring about such changes; and those laws that already exist for the benefit of the handicapped. Another objective should be identfying the duties of various civic officials.

7.2. Basic American Government

The teacher may choose to approach the larger federal structure from the same vantage point as in the previous subcompetency. Local and federal structures contain the three major administrative, legislative, and judicial areas, as well as a set of statutes, regulations, and agencies. The student should be made aware of the instances in which federal law takes precedence over local and state laws. Another objective should be identifying appropriate elements of the Constitution and Declaration of Independence.

7.3.   Citizenship Rights and Responsibilities

This is a major element in the entire competency. Subcompetency 7.1 contains a provision for the identification of laws that were enacted to assist the handicapped. The teacher should be familiar with these various pieces of legislation and regulations. But, each right contains a responsibility of citizenship. It is not a one-way street, and students should be made aware of their obligations, which include obeying the laws, voting, paying taxes, and being informed on problems and issues within the society. Another objective should be identifying community services available to the handicapped.

> ACTIVITY TIP: Students can collect an "Advocacy Notebook"
> of pictures, articles, and information pertaining to the
> rights of handicapped individuals. The material should re-
> flect the exanding role of handicapped individuals in
> civic and social functions. It can be gathered from news-
> papers, magazines, or brochures collected on field trips or
> distributed by classroom speakers. Teachers should attempt
> to enlist the cooperation of handicapped individuals who
> have been active in community affairs.

7.4.   Registering and Voting Procedures

The reasons for voting can be emphasized throughout the elementary years. Many secondary students who have the opportunity to register and vote will enroll in training programs. This situation provides teachers with a chance to use practical lesson plans based on student experiences with the process of registering and voting. Another objective should be identifying the dates, issues, and offices to be decided in coming elections.

7.5.   Selective Service Information

Students should be made aware of their obligations as citizens to register for selective service classification at age 18. In some instances, the military may be a possible occupational choice. For example, former students in classes for the mentally retarded have served in the military. Another objective should be identifying information required for registration with the selective service.

7.6.   Rights and Responsibilities of Handling Questioning by Officers of the Law

There are two aspects to this subcompetency: knowledge of the individual's rights when being questioned by officers of the law, and sources of legal assistance in helping the individual answer the questions. It is not an easy combination of skills for the teacher to develop in students regardless of the numerous aides they receive from TV soap operas and movies. Students should role play situations in which they are confronted by officers. Law enforcement officials or members of legal aid associations may also appear in classroom presentations in order to communicate valuable experiences concerning violations and citizen responses during forms of interrogation.

Utilizing Recreation and Leisure (8)

The steady decrease in the number of hours in the average person's work week has given rise to an increase in the amount of time, energy, and attention that those same workers can devote to recreation and leisure. The handicapped individual should be able to share in these experiences. Various professional and parent organizations have placed new emphasis upon physical education, leisure, recreation, and art for the handicapped. Expanded programs, special events, and conferences will contribute to the development of physical abilities, as well as public acceptance of the handicapped individual's participation in society. The activities involved in this competency prepare the individual for yet another area of integration and, therefore, must be considered as distinct and valuable in the overall curriculum. The major subcompetencies are as follows:

8.1. Participating Actively in Group Activities

Adequate participation in group activities depends, in part, upon the individual's physical fitness (refer to subcompetency 3.3) and ability to interact with other members of the group (refer to subcompetency 1.3). It is therefore necessary that the teacher design or adapt games and group activities that contribute to both goals. The student's physical characteristics are a consideration, but we have enough examples from blind skiers to wheelchair basketball players to know that physical constraints are not the only determiner of whether an individual will choose to engage in particular activities. Other objectives should include: a. identifying group activities available in the community, b. demonstrating competence in a selected activity, and c. demonstrating proper care of equipment used in an activity.

8.2. Knowing Activities and Available Resources

Teachers can begin to teach elementary school students about those functions, events, and facilities available in community agencies, schools, or churches. The next step includes cooperative efforts between teachers, parents, and recreation leaders to encourage and include the handicapped in the role of participant, as well as observer. Based on this encouragement, the student can develop an awareness of the range of recreational activities in which she can participate, as well as the resources and facilities that are accessible in the community.

8.3. *Understanding Recreational Values*

This subcompetency is closely linked to the development of self-awareness (refer to subcompetency 1.4). It includes the student's understanding of the role of recreation in the overall development of life. It can function as a balance to the everyday pressures the individual confronts in striving toward a role of independence. But the theoretical understanding can only be internalized if the student has the opportunity to demonstrate an effective use of leisure time through participation in activities, clubs, or hobbies. This once again requires coordinated effort between parent, teacher, and recreational personnel.

> ACTIVITY TIP: Teachers, recreation and physical education personnel, parents, and students should contribute to the construction of a "Leisure Grid," which is reproduced for use by the students. The grid lists the skills required of the student as: 1. participant, 2. observer, and 3. employee per leisure area. Each sport, activity, or hobby provides students with opportunities to record their observations about recreation and employment possibilities. The grid can be supplemented with pictures, newspaper or magazine articles, and student essays.

8.4. *Using Recreational Facilities in the Community*

The primary objective is that the student should demonstrate ability to use recreational facilities and equipment. This may be demonstrated to teachers, parents, or recreational personnel but should be observed on a firsthand basis and not simply reported by the student. A secondary objective is related to the student's competency in mobility and traveling in the community (refer to competency 9).

8.5. *Planning and Choosing Activities Wisely*

Many of the previous subcompetencies related to the utilization of recreation and leisure require actual "field" experiences. Based on these experiences, the student can begin to plan leisure activities. This planning should include factors such as cost, location, travel, physical requirements, use of equipment, and number of participants. The planning and decision making will incorporate the student's experience with prior activities and a testing of her self-awareness (refer to competency 10).

8.6. Planning Vacations

Adults initiate vacations, but children can be included in some of the planning. Children can wrestle with such major questions as, "When should the family take a vacation? Where should we go? Why should we go there? What will we do when we get there? How much will it cost? Do we have enough money for a vacation?" Throughout the questioning process, teachers and parents should present several considerations so that children have an opportunity to understand that the final plan is really composed of several decisions relative to family needs and resources. Another objective should be identifying available sources of information that assist in planning.

Getting around the Community: Mobility (9)

In a society that encourages mobility in its abundant emphasis upon such things as cars, campers, ski trips, and coast-to-coast air flights, it is no wonder that teen-agers and adults place a high value on their ability to move at will. This ability is even more important for those who experience an inconvenience in their attempts to commute between home and places of employment, recreation, or health services. Unique and diligent training is necessary to prepare those with visual, physical, and mental handicaps to exert maximum mobility within the community. This would involve training with guide dogs or a cane, extensive instruction in the use of a car and other forms of transportation, and adaptations to the use of self-driven chairs or carts. The following subcompetencies are based on the assumption that the individual is able to maneuver within the community with or without the assistance of devices such as artificial limbs, mechanical devices, or sonic sensory aides.

9.1. Demonstrating Knowledge of Traffic Rules and
Safety Practices

The basics of traffic rules, signs, symbols, and sounds should be taught in the elementary grades. Their importance is based on safety for all members of the community. Teachers should use posters, field trips, and numerous audio-visual aides in emphasizing the responsibilities of both pedestrians and motorists.

9.2. Demonstrating Knowledge and Use of Various
Means of Transportation

Although the specific kinds of transportation may vary within each community, students should be acquainted with the several means available in the larger region. Teachers should construct lessons on each form, emphasizing their advantages and disadvantages, costs, schedules, availability, and convenience. The lessons should include such aids as tickets or tokens, route maps, and illustrations provided by various carriers. A second important area of instruction would include the student's ability to interpret maps of the community in order to locate directions and addresses. The lessons culminate with actual demonstrations by the students in using appropriate forms of transportation in personal functions such as going to school, work, or recreational activities.

> ACTIVITY TIP: The old treasure hunt game can be used to test the student's mobility skills. Parents, friends, and other teachers can assist on "hunts" that expand from the classroom or home, to the neighborhood, and to the larger community. The hunt should emphasize all aides that can be used by the student in finding the final destination and the role of various community workers in providing assistance.

9.3. Driving a Car

One of the major goals of most high school students is to sit behind the wheel of a car. This goal can be used successfully in developing several other subcompetencies, as well as academic skills. The teacher should work with other instructors to coordinate lessons relative to driver education. This is especially important if driver educators are responsible for instruction in the driver's manual, state examination, and "behind-the-wheel" training. The classroom teacher could be of assistance in teaching the academic aspects of lessons. Other objectives should include: a. identifying appropriate procedures for a driver after being involved in an auto accident, and b. demonstrating ability to make minor repairs on a vehicle.

TEACHING THE DAILY LIVING SKILLS

All of the prior competencies are projected for mastery by the handicapped individual in the adult years. The great challenge of teaching daily living skills is to translate ultimate goals in education into manageable components of instruction for individual students, given the circumstances that teachers encounter during the average day. It is important to consider the teacher's circumstances, as well as the unique learning styles of the several students who comprise the class or therapeutic case load for that day. With increased emphasis upon the integration, normalization, or "mainstreaming" of the handicapped with regular students, teachers, counselors, and coordinators are faced with greater demands upon their abilities to handle the complexities of meeting all students' needs.

The art of teaching has always included a certain amount of management. After all, the instructor must decide on the progression of lessons that will accomplish an objective, materials to be used at specific points in the progression, and alternatives to meeting the intended goals once she and the learner encounter barriers. We have intended to focus our attention in this section on the management of the teacher's efforts in planning programs because of two reasons.

1. The Individualized Education Program plan has emerged as a focal point for conceptualizing the direction that educators and parents should take in providing handicapped students with appropriate instruction and services. The plan, among other things, is a tool in managing diverse sources, and all the participants should be well versed in its strengths and limitations.
2. The numerous demands upon the average educator's time and ability will require her to use every means available to provide students with experiences in the competency areas.

In the remainder of this chapter, we will be suggesting steps for the identification, coordination, specification, and integration of these competencies so that the total school, home, and community become integral sources of these experiences.

The Individualized Education Program (IEP)

The competencies discussed in this chapter, as well as those in the chapters on Personal-Social Skills and Occupational Guidance and Preparation, should be the long-term goals for all handicapped individuals. They comprise a large number of the final goals of educators and, therefore, can provide a broader scope and direction for the yearly and intermediate objective within the IEP. Most likely, the actual competency statements contained in chapters 4 through 6 could appear as goal statements in the plan for students in secondary and adult education programs. Subcompetency 9.3, driving a car, for example, is an appropriate goal in the secondary curriculum area of driver education. This may be specified as an appropriate goal in the planning sessions between the local educational agency (LEA) representative, parents, teacher, and student. Such factors as physical and intellectual ability will play an important part in the development of training devices and programs that will enable the student to obtain the goal. Those same factors, however, may be less important as barriers as compared with previous years because driving a car is considered an adult skill necessary for mobility and chances at employment.

Once subcompetency 9.3 is designated as a final goal, then the several major steps contained in a driver education curriculum can function as the short-term objectives. There is no need for the participants to record every lesson plan on the IEP if a standard curriculum text or manual is used in the course. Progress through the lessons in the text would provide a basis for evaluation.

Driving a car is one of the easiest Daily Living Skills to use as an example since an entire course of study will meet the requirements of the IEP, as well as the subcompetency. Although the formalized training does not begin until the secondary level, students have had exposure to the several stages of career development in the larger competency of getting around the community since the primary grades. For example, the student's *awareness* of traffic rules, safety, and means of transportation in the community should be nurtured in the elementary grades. Field trips, individual experiences with means of transportation to and from school, and family-directed outings can provide *exploration* in mobility and forms of transportation. The actual driver education curriculum is the strongest example of the *preparation* stage, although one should not forget that mobility training also includes the use of other mechanical aides, cane, or a guide dog for certain handicapped individuals. The final stage of *placement and follow up* incorporates the skills and techniques acquired through instruction and applied to the individual's daily living and work situations. The follow-up component can be neglected by school personnel and, yet, it is very important for those handicapped individuals who may be encountering difficulties in adjusting to new environments, routines, or who need periodic evaluation in the use of their skills and means of getting around the community.

This progression of stages is an important consideration since it alerts teachers and parents to the fact that the several parts of a subcompetency may extend from the primary to adult years. For example, the primary level student may not drive a car, but cars, racers, hotrods, and what one may label as the "Cult of Wheels" are important and available in the student's experiences at successive stages of physical, social, and psychological development. A second important consideration is that it reminds teachers and parents to include provisions for nurturing the subcompetencies in their planning and activities. It is most likely that these small provisions *will not* be identified in the IEP. The plan will be geared toward such curriculum skill areas as arithmetic, language arts, and reading. The tendency is for teachers to focus on the established progression of skill components that exist in the dominant curriculum areas. These skills, over time, begin to build and combine with one another so that students can use them to achieve competence. For example, driving a car requires, among other things, gross and fine motor coordination, perceptual abilities, and reading.

It is definitely important that teachers at all levels (primary through adult education) review the competencies discussed in chapters 4 through 6 because of their prior training and present emphasis upon mastery of the academic skills. These skills will continue as dominant parts of the student's program at the elementary levels. The tragedy of the situation is that secondary and adult education instructors *must* concern themselves with competencies for daily living, social-personal relations, and occupational pursuits. These competencies are integral to the handicapped individual's success as an adult. Thus, teachers of adolescent and adult handicapped individuals must often decrease instruction in the academic skills in order to meet demands in the areas of personal-social and vocational skills. This, too, proves to be a difficult assignment if particular competencies require prerequisite ability with reading, communication, or computation.

> The IEP and competencies complement each other.

Both the IEP and competencies discussed in this text can complement one another. First, the competencies require students to combine several academic skills and, therefore, function as long-term objectives to curriculum areas. Why should a student be able to read at a certain level or complete calculations? These abilities enable her to gain a driver's license, manage personal finances, and repair home equipment, all of which are listed as daily living skills. Second, the individualized education program plan is a tool that can be used by various personnel and parents to check whether the student is achieving both the academic skills and competencies. Has the student used the several means of public transportation available in the community? Does she need more instruction in personal hygiene?

The competencies and IEP function as checks against one another. They can be interlaced in such a manner as to add direction to programming, provide objectives for evaluation, and major steps for instruction. The teacher can guarantee that each handicapped student received instruction at appropriate levels in the development of each competency through the following measures.

Identification

The instructor should identify areas of the curriculum that already contain lessons relative to the competencies. In the best of all possible worlds, to borrow from Voltaire's *Candide,* the ideal teacher would have developed specific lessons for each subcompetency to meet the multiple learning characteristics of the student. Such a task would take years to accomplish, and the very idea of writing that many lessons or learning modules discourages teachers from even attempting the activity. This is one reason why publishers are experiencing such demand and success with packaged curriculums or programs for the handicapped.

The daily living skills form the theme material for texts and programmed learning packages in mathematics, reading, language arts, and the like. It is not the intention of the authors of the curriculum texts to work directly with the competencies as we define them, but they, nevertheless, use activities such as shopping, civic participation, and vocations as a motivating element within the stories. These texts and programs should be reviewed so that the teacher can use the several curriculum areas to enhance the competencies and decrease the amount of material that she has to prepare.

Figure 11 contains an example of a curriculum check sheet that can be constructed by the teacher to facilitate a review of texts, programmed materials, or learning aides. Major competency areas are identified by number in the left margin, with specific references to the subcompetencies that are topics within the curriculum materials. The teacher may also elect to emphasize certain competencies during a particular academic year, depending upon the student's stage of physical, social, psychological, or vocational development. Some major curriculum areas have been placed at the top of the form with page references indicating the location of the competencies within the materials. The two remaining columns, *Other Materials* and *Resources,* refer to personnel, activities, or devices that are suggested by the teachers guides that accompany the curriculum texts or are used in conjunction with the lessons.

The teacher should modify the curriculum check sheet to correspond to the competencies, curriculum areas, and method of instruction under consideration. For example, she may elect to use group activities to identify major forms of money (Competency 1) with individual lessons to follow. Note, however, that this is *not* a lesson plan. It is a form to encourage teachers to methodically review curriculum areas and identify competencies that students will encounter during the normal progression of the school year.

Coordination

The instructor should identify competencies that will be taught by other professionals and cooperate with them to meet common objectives. One of the great advantages to teaching the daily living skills is that they appear in so many curriculum areas that one is not alone in the attempt. Other professionals in home economics, driver education, industrial arts, vocational education, physical education, to name a few disciplines, share the classroom teacher's interest in certain competencies. In addition, the family of the handicapped individual can be a source of experiences in the daily living skills.

It would be logical and rewarding to learn as much as possible from the skills and commitments of other professionals and parents. Enlisting these sources requires a certain amount of coordination on the part of the classroom teacher (or counselor, curriculum coordinator, supervisor), but this is a better alternative than attempting to prepare each student for every competency. This form of coordination requires matching the skills of the professional and parent to the needs of the student. This may not be a difficult requirement. Other professionals may have already included certain competencies as a part of their curriculum. Parents may be providing experiences in the home and community that facilitate classroom instruc-

Intermediate _____   Daily _____
Class or Student   Period

DAILY LIVING SKILLS

Curriculum / Competency	Arithmetic	Gross Motor	Language Arts	Reading	Other Materials	Resources
1. Identifying money	p. 15–18					Filmstrip
wise ex- penditure	p. 101–110					
2. Using basic tools		Industrial Arts			Hobby magazines	Parent: Mr. Brown demonstrates use of saws
3. Demonstrating physical fitness		Physical Education			Sports magazines and newspaper	Swimming coach and film of the Olympics
4. Family safety				p. 53–57		Film on control of fires in the home

Figure 11
Curriculum Check Sheet.

tion. The important ingredient is that the coordinator is aware of the efforts and direction provided by these several sources. An additional column could be added to the curriculum check sheet that indicates the efforts of other professionals and parents with the competencies.

On occasion, the coordinator may suggest that lessons or activities be added to the curriculum in, for example, home economics or vocational education. This expansion of competency units is in keeping with the idea that career development is the responsibility of every instructor in all disciplines. It is also in keeping with our experience that the coordinator must seek every opportunity to enlist the interest and efforts of professionals from all disciplines to increase the availability and quality of education for handicapped individuals. It has only been in recent years that an increased number of professionals from skill areas such as home economics, physical education, industrial arts, and vocational education have expanded their programs to accommodate the handicapped student. This increased attention is welcomed by the handicapped individual, her parents, and advocates, but it requires a corresponding refinement of our abilities to coordinate programs and professionals.

Specification

The instructor should include statements concerning the student's career development on the IEP. As mentioned previously, the IEP allows professionals the opportunity to specify present levels of performance in career development, projected objectives, and educational services required to meet those aims. These statements can also include reference to the personnel who are deemed essential to the student's success.

It is recommended that the participants in the formulation of the IEP involve as many professionals as possible in the plan. This involvement provides the student with a greater fund of skills from individuals who are best qualified to teach particular subcompetencies. Instructors from industrial arts, for example, could function as the primary source of information and activities in subcompetency 2.3, using basic appliances and tools, while those from home economics could offer assistance in several major competency areas, such as competency 5, buying and preparing food, and competency 6, buying and caring for clothes. But, it is essential that the professional's participation and role is clearly defined so that the instructor and program coordinator are aware of the expected objectives to be reached through the involvement. Professionals from the area of physical education or recreation may either provide direct instruction to the student or advise the classroom teacher as to the appropriate activities to be conducted during the period in the school day designated for "physical development." In the first situation, the instructor functions as the primary source of direction for the student; while in the second instance, she is a support person to the classroom teacher. This distinction may not appear on the actual student plan, but it must be clearly understood among the participating professionals.

Integration

One of the obstacles to the introduction of career education into the average student's school experience is that it does not have the progressive characteristics of standard curriculums in areas such as reading, writing, and arithmetic. Advocates of career development have attempted to build a sequential chain of career themes and objectives, as discussed in chapter 3, which range from career awareness to career placement and follow up. Several states have published guides for educators describing appropriate objectives for career lessons to be conducted at various stages of the student's experience. The objectives most often conform to a design which allows teachers and counselors to integrate lessons in career development at grade levels and during parts of the school day. It is during these same periods that instructors can initiate activities that are specifically related to the competencies. Thus, if a competency is neither covered in some way in other curriculum areas or by other professionals, the classroom teacher must develop lesson plans that provide the student with experiences in the competency areas.

Lesson plans for any instructional area range from the simplest to the extended design. We have known teachers who merely record the title of an activity on a sheet of paper and consider that a "lesson plan." More than likely, this kind of planning will not place the teacher in high regard with those parents and advocates who demand evaluations of the intermediate objectives as listed in the individual education program plan. The basic plan should include the lesson's objectives, activities, and forms of evaluation. The following is one such plan in the awareness stage in subcompetency 2.1, selecting adequate housing.

Selecting Adequate Housing. (Competency 2, Subcompetency 1)

Objective: The student will identify various types of habilitation available in the community.

Activities: 1. The teacher will present pictures or illustrations of the various forms of habilitation. The names of the dwellings will be provided with the example.

2. The teacher and student (or class) will discuss the characteristics of each example. The participants will decide upon a common definition for each habilitation.

Evaluation: 1. The student will match the name of the dwelling with the appropriate example.

2. The student will describe the characteristics of each dwelling.

This lesson plan only contains the core elements of the competency unit. The reader, no doubt, has already formulated questions in her own mind about the characteristics of the *learner,* as they are variables in the planning and instructional process. For example, what is the learner's age? This factor may influence the depth of discussion concerning the characteristics of the habilitation. Primary age students would need introductory exposure to the kinds of homes in the community, while members of an adult education course could expand this section to reflect their prior experiences and present needs relative to living in the community. What are the abilities and difficulties of the learner? Students with visual disabilities will require tactile representations or models to fully absorb the themes of the lesson. Students with mental limitations may need to see and tour actual dwellings in order to translate classroom discussions and pictures into concrete examples.

The students' abilities and limitations will also affect the form of evaluation that is used by the instructor. Students with learning disabilities in the area of symbolic representation may encounter difficulties in matching the word *duplex* with a picture of the dwelling. The instructor would have to rely upon the student's auditory channel of communication in both teaching and evaluating mastery of the concept.

Note that this basic lesson lacks any designation as to the curriculum area in which it would be taught. A moment's reflection would provide you with a variety of instructors who could incorporate the unit in their curriculum. One example would be the regular classroom teacher, social studies, intermediate level. She may emphasize the characteristics and patterns of home and apartment construction in the larger community or nearby expansion. The industrial arts instructor may approach the same topic from the vantage point of the design and workmanship that is evident in the construc-

Level:	Secondary
Situation:	Handicapped students integrated into regular home economics class.
Period:	Three
Time Span:	Five periods
Objective:	The student will be able to identify basic rights of a consumer (Competency 1, Subcompetency 6)
Activity Title:	"Your Right to Safety"
Goal of Activity:	Students investigate ways in which the consumer's right to a safe food supply is protected.
Activity:	Obtain state and local regulations that protect consumers relative to such products as milk, meats, fruits and vegetables.
	List some of the above regulations on a bulletin board and examples that appear on product containers, labels, or wrappers.
Activity Title:	"What Can You Do?"
Goal of Activity:	Students become familiar with ways in which they can register complaints about consumer products.

Activity: Divide the class into small groups. Students
compile a list of complaints they have had
or heard. (If the groups are unable to identify a sizeable number of complaints, the
teacher may present them with the following
situations:

* You bought a quart of milk that was sour.
* You found a hair in your salad in a
  restaurant.
* You discovered there were fewer paper
  napkins than the number printed on the
  package.
* You found that the "use" date has passed
  for the packaged biscuits on the market
  shelves.)

Students list ways in which they can gain
satisfaction for their complaints. (The
teacher may conduct role-play situations in
which each student presents her complaint
to a store manager or composes a letter to
be mailed to the firm.)

Evaluation: Students list at least five examples of
regulations designed to protect the consumer.
Students list at least three ways in which
they can receive action on a complaint.
Students demonstrate, through written or
verbal means, one form of complaint.

tion and materials of the dwellings. In these instances, one should expect
that the emphasis, activities, and forms of evaluation will vary according to
disciplines of the instructors who use the competencies in their classroom.
That is the way it should be because the competencies were designed to
cover the broad range of a student's educational experience and are not the
unique possession of any one teacher. Some competencies may be more
closely identified with certain disciplines primarily because those instructors
have the skills and facilities that would be of great assistance to the student.
But, the concept of the integration of the competencies requires that numerous instructors attempt to use competency themes as motivating elements
in their curriculums. The above is an example of a lesson plan developed
for the home economics curriculum. It is a modification of subcompetency
7.6, rights and responsibilities for handling questioning by the law, to Include the growing interest in consumer protection.

Notice that the lesson plan has been expanded from the mere "idea on
a piece of paper" to include level of instruction, situation, period of the day.
the amount of time needed to complete the unit, major and minor objectives,
activities for a group that can also apply to individual students, and several
forms of evaluation. These form basic structural elements teachers can

consider and apply to group and individual planning, but they are not the final word.

CONCLUSION

The Daily Living Skills should be the easiest group of competencies to integrate and teach in the normal span of a school year. This is due, in part, to the fact that they are already evident in the curriculums from primary through adult education. However, one must also consider that the instructor has a fund of knowledge and personal experiences in daily living skills that may surpass the offerings of a textbook or filmstrip. Hopefully, this chapter contains an adequate number of suggestions and examples to encourage the use, whether she be teacher, counselor, or parent, to take the evident daily requirements for successful living and shape them into objectives and themes. These endeavors, whether they are based on the instructor's experience or classroom materials, will supply the handicapped individual with the tools to shape the success of her own life.

The Personal-Social Skills curriculum area includes those abilities that are necessary for personal achievement and satisfactory interpersonal relationships. One may say that the Daily Living Skills form the structure to the individual's abilities, while the Personal-Social Skills are the muscle and blood that propel him toward fulfillment. This sense of achievement and fulfillment is the very basis for determining the quality of life. In other words, we cannot judge the handicapped individual's potential for successful, independent living merely on the basis of academic grades or competency scales. We must also add to the balance the ideas he has about his present status, potentials, and the interactions with other people. These thoughts often determine the manner in which other skills will be used and toward what goals.

The seven personal-social competencies we have identified as important to the career development of handicapped individuals are listed as follows with their respective competency number in parentheses.

Achieving Self-Awareness (**10**)

Acquiring Self-Confidence (**11**)

Achieving Socially Responsible Behavior (**12**)

Maintaining Adequate Interpersonal Skills (**13**)

Achieving Independence (**14**)

Achieving Problem-Solving Skills (**15**)

Communicating Adequately with Others (**16**)

The whole question of personal concepts of self, others, and their inter-actions include the elements of risk and trust in classroom activities. Risk is one element in the process of problem solving, while trust is essential to self-respect. Teachers have always estimated risk as defined by such social factors as self-esteem, popularity with peers, and even teacher approval. The student who identifies a personal problem to the teacher or in a group setting is risking himself. Teachers cannot expect students to just gamble with social status based upon traditional methods. The students must be assured through word and deed that their risks do have rewards. The risk-reward interaction, if successful, contributes to the trust that students must build in themselves and other dependable individuals.

These two elements, risk and trust, intertwine the 34 subcompetencies of the Personal-Social Skills curriculum area. Teachers may identify still other factors and objectives that contribute to the student's mastery of himself and his relationships with others. Activity Tips are presented throughout the chapter as teaching examples. The chapter concludes with a discussion of techniques for teaching the Personal-Social Skills.

COMPETENCIES

Achieving Self-Awareness (10)

There is a new sense of freedom in American life, and handicapped in-dividuals are a part of it. They have been the subjects of an increased number of television documentaries, magazine articles, and newspaper reports. Legislation guarantees equal rights in transportation, education, housing, and employment. People talk about the handicapped "coming out of the closets" and entering the "mainstream" of society. But there is an-other shell aside from the structure and restrictions that society imposes upon individuals. It consists of one's body, abilities, limitations, and needs. The achievement of self-awareness has as much to do with escaping the closet and becoming a contributing and productive member of society. The major subcompetencies are as follows:

10.1. Attaining a Sense of Body

One of the first infant behaviors is the exploration of the body and its differentiation from the surrounding environment. This discovery does not end with childhood. Every maturational change requires a modification in the individual's concept of the physical aspects of the body. This continual process includes a changing image of self. Everyone has such an image of the body, as well as certain parts and functions. This body image is visualized as positive when the individual recognizes limitations but still regards the physical shell as an instrument which can be developed and controlled to achieve objectives. This positive body image is a factor that contributes to the individual's sense of ability and worth. Teachers, parents, and therapists can assist the individual in developing a positive body image by providing adequate information relative to the parts of the body, their functions, and the person's unique physical characteristics. It is important that the information is accurate and that it is presented within an atmosphere of support. This support assists the person in confronting the implications of the information and initiating appropriate personal adjustments and objectives. Each stage of development requires different kinds and amounts of information. Children at 7 will not ask the same questions as adolescents or adults at 40 years of age. Their needs vary and, more importantly, the implications of the answers must be matched to the unique physical characteristics of the individual.

10.2. Identifying Interests and Abilities

There is a basic reason for linking interests with abilities. The individual with handicaps discovers his abilities through interests. How can one expect the child to cry, attempt, accomplish, if one does not arouse his interest? Aren't childhood hobbies a means of building confidence through interest? If the handicapped individual is to achieve independence through competent behavior, then he must have numerous experiences with those things he likes to do, can do, and would attempt to do if given adequate support. It is through trial and error, with support, that he can build an awareness of physical and spiritual capabilities. Teachers should plan activities that require students to identify interests, list personal abilities, and plan strategies to implement action toward selected goals (refer to subcompetency 15.2). Another objective should be identifying the interests of others and ranking the interests according to their possibilities for oneself.

10.3. Identifying Emotions

There is a critical beginning to classroom activities dealing with emotions. It occurs when teachers create a nonjudgmental climate in which the student (whether child or adult) feels free to talk about feelings. Students should identify such emotions as happiness, sadness, and anger in the primary grades. They will have had exposure to these emotions long before entering school. Older children should begin to work with the problem of recognizing emotions that are complicated by the fact that they can be expressed in various manners. Students should be involved in role-play situations, or report observations that emphasize various indices of emotions, for example, body language, facial expressions, and tones of voice (refer to subcompetency 16.5). A second major objective should be for teachers to develop the student's ability to distinguish the consequences of the emotion for others, but particularly, for self. For example, an expression of anger by an employer may have different consequences than a similar demonstration by an employee. One may let off steam, while the other may lose a job. Finally, teachers should identify means through which students can release emotions in a constructive manner. An appropriate expression of emotion is unique to the individual. Teachers and parents should anticipate that they must exert a great deal of time and effort in establishing a foundation of trust that will encourage the individual to explore feelings and adequate ways of expressing them. Another objective should be identifying ways in which emotions affect behavior.

> ACTIVITY TIP: The want-ads of the local newspaper are a rich source of ideas related to personal needs. People advertise for various reasons: to gain employment, to sell home furniture, or to join a car pool. Students can cut and paste ads in various categories of their interest or in those identified by the teacher. Advanced students may inquire further from the source of the ad.

10.4 Identifying Needs

This subcompetency includes the physical, psychological, and social domains. There are some minimal needs for physical existence, but it is much harder to describe basic requirements in the social and psychological realms. How do we measure quantities of security, self-worth, esteem, and love? One way to determine the answer to that question is for students to identify their needs, talk about them, draw them, collect examples of them, and examine the ways in which other persons attempt to meet their needs. Varied classroom activities concerning the necessities of life will lead students to a realization about those things that they regard as essential to their lives. Another objective should be identifying several personal values.

10.5. Understanding Physical Self

This subcompetency contains objectives that are specific to the sexual role of the individual. The activities should develop an awareness of the similarities and differences in the anatomy and functioning of the male and female. This subject material has received increased attention among researchers, parents, consumer groups, and publishing firms primarily because of the long absence of discussion of the sexual role for individuals who are mentally retarded or physically disabled. Teachers should be aware of one thing. If they are to encourage classroom or small group discussion and questions, they must be prepared to provide information. Another objective should be identifying sources of information relative to one's future sexual role.

Acquiring Self-Confidence (11)

Handicapped individuals have been confronted for centuries with stories, fairy tales, works of art, and popular expressions depicting them as incapable and despised. In some instances, the handicapped were not even regarded as human beings but as the embodiment of evil spirits. These ideas and stereotypes linger to this day, and it is a rare individual with handicaps who has not had an experience with abuse or pity by peers or elders. Despite these opinions and attitudes, the individual must build a concept of himself as a capable human being in order to reach personal objectives and dreams. The major subcompetencies are as follows:

11.1. Expressing Feelings of Worth

An individual begins to feel worthy when he experiences expressions of value from parents, teachers, and friends. These declarations of worth may be difficult for the nonhandicapped person to formulate. This is because of a habit within the society to establish worth based upon a comparison to someone else, for example, that handicapped individuals cannot run like other children, or they read below the average of the group. These kinds of comparative statements are common in a culture that rewards individuals who demonstrate the drive to excel. The only problem is that "doing better" is often determined in comparison to someone else. Those with handicaps can find themselves at a serious disadvantage if their abilities are always placed in some type of "better than the other person" derby. To lose the race may be interpreted as being less than others and without value. The key to this potential dilemma is found in the parent's and teacher's ability to work with the assets an individual has at his disposal. They must move away from "you versus them" situations to "I can do" experiences. By emphasizing the "I can," the parent and teacher opinions change, with a corresponding influence on the attitudes and values of the handicapped individual. "I can" is a positive statement of value and worth in this society. How many times have we heard stories about individuals who were told they would never walk, run, dance, whatever, only to accomplish that very thing and more? Of course, physical ability is a variable, but so are the attitudes of an individual toward that ability. Teachers and parents should provide opportunities in which students express feelings about the self, accomplishments, successes, and failures. What are the times when students feel good, worthy, or pleased with their accomplishments? What things frustrate them? These expressions provide professionals with an opportunity to gauge subsequent activities designed to increase success experiences. Another objective should be identifying ways in which other people affect one's feelings of worth.

11.2.   *Telling How Others See Him*

Students should be able to report overt expressions, as well as subtle hints, by others concerning their attitudes toward him or his behavior (refer to subcompetency 16.5). Since most of us are concerned with the self, we are more sensitive to communications relative to ourselves, but are more apt to interject our own interpretations. The handicapped individual encounters a particularly puzzling situation when he wonders whether a person is reacting to his personality or to the particular disability. If someone does not invite him to another party, was it because he did not conduct himself properly, or was it due to his artificial limb? He may never get the answer, and repeated instances of these nebulous situations damage the self-confidence. So much of what others think about us is involved in the development of our attitudes toward the self. These attitudes are used as a basis for further judgments. Parents and teachers cannot control the attitudes of others in the world. They have enough to handle with their own. But they can instruct the handicapped student to be observant of the overt and subtle responses that reflect either positive or negative attitudes. Many of the lessons on communication (refer to competency 16) should include

```
ACTIVITY TIP: An effective requires all students to say
positive things about an individual. The class may be seated
in a circle or at their desks, but the student under dis-
cussion should be facing the class. Each student has 15-20
seconds during which time other students say such things
as: "She helped our team win the game." "He came to school
on time every day of the week." "She knew the right answer
to the weekly quiz." This activity helps build class unity,
as well as individual confidence.
```

such reactions that convey attitudes of pity, disgust, condescension, and the like. The lessons should, however, emphasize positive reactions by the handicapped individual, reflecting self-respect. He must guard against reactions that would be interpreted by other members of society as justification for their folly. Another objective should be constructing personal views of others toward him.

11.3. Accepting Praise

To know how to accept praise, the handicapped individual should have legitimate experiences with respect and confirmation of his behavior. Legitimate experiences include those daily activities in home, school, or other environments that *involve* the student as a contributing member. Respect and confirmation of this contribution can derive from family, peers, teachers, or others. These responses are for a singular contribution but should not be the only ones. This means that there should be some statements of encouragement, friendship, and support prior to and following any noteworthy accomplishment. Otherwise, the student is only rewarded for one achievement, and this may be disproportionate to his total effort at home, in school, or on a team. It is easier to know how to accept praise when one has experienced various forms of reward. Other objectives should include: a. listing effects of praise on self and others, and b. demonstrating ability to offer praise to others.

11.4. Accepting Criticism

Criticism can be interpreted in a positive sense when it refers to astute judgments relative to standards. It is more often taken in the negative vein of fault finding. Finding faults does not mean that the person is of any less value, but unfortunately, criticism and faults have always seemed to end up with an individual feeling less than adequate about himself. This is one reason why students in elementary or college classes hate to receive a critical analysis of their assignments. Fearing a potentially harsh review, they produce less than they can. They, in a sense, are already protecting themselves from devaluation. Is it any wonder, then, that when teachers begin to criticize, students become disinterested? Teachers have the arduous task of first convincing students to be open to criticism, and second, differentiating the point at which critical statements are of little value in changing or improving on a mistake. The teacher can accomplish these goals by providing as much respect for the student and his work as critical review. Respect with criticism builds self-confidence. An attitude of respect says to the student: "You are someone." The critical element conveys the message: "You are someone who can improve on this mistake." The improvement reinforces the previous steps in the process. Another objective should be identifying positive and negative effects of criticism on self and others.

11.5. Developing Faith in Self

Students should be aware of their innate dignity. At times, they may have to assert their rights in order to protect that dignity. These actions are founded upon a trust in one's ability to accomplish objectives. This trust begins with the first completed task in infancy and is nurtured through subsequent efforts to accomplish more difficult objectives. More often than imagined, the act of attempting a task strengthens the individual's trust in himself. Developing faith in self is to entertain an objective and seek the means to accomplish it, appropriate to one's ability. For example, the movie *A Matter of Inconvenience* (Stanfield House, 1974) is based on individuals who, without sight or a leg, attempt to ski. The war veterans without a limb use one ski and two poles fashioned with small runners at the ends. The three skis function as supports to balance the transfer of weight at each turn. The females who are blind are followed by experienced skiers who provide instructions on turning, plowing, and breaking. These individuals experience skiing and enjoy themselves. Their accomplishments are judged by them and not in comparison to Olympic competitors. The experience is of value because it accomplishes an objective through a means appropriate to the individual. We are sure that these individuals' self-confidence is extended and that they will attempt other tasks because their trust in their abilities has been reinforced. They are, in a sense, developing faith in themselves. Another objective should be evaluating self in variety of activities.

Achieving Socially Responsible Behavior (12)

Society is held together by laws and understandings relative to the conduct of individuals toward each other. These laws have been gradually increased to extend protection to the handicapped. But, acceptance of the individual depends more upon his ability to demonstrate responsible behavior in various kinds of social situations. The major subcompetencies are as follows:

12.1. Knowing Character Traits Needed for Acceptance

The student should be familiar with those personality factors which generally allow one to participate in a group situation which results in a positive attitude of others toward the individual. What are some of these positive traits? Cooperation, cheerfulness, dependability, would form a solid foundation. There are others, but the individual must discover them for himself. This is where experience with oneself and observation of others are important factors in change. The ability to look at oneself with a critical eye is not reserved for those with advanced degrees. It comes from practice, with encouragement, at home, and in the classroom. Teachers can help students build their observational skills by assigning them projects in which they interview or consider someone of their choice and list outstanding characteristics. Once the characteristics are defined, then teachers can translate them into behaviors students should attempt. Together, students and teachers should work on a plan of practicing and reporting the behaviors. For students who experience problems in performing acceptable behaviors, the teacher may structure a system in which there is a conscious effort to modify the behavior toward prearranged objectives. Another objective should be identifying character traits that inhibit acceptance.

12.2. Knowing Proper Behavior in Public Places

The student should be able to identify the behavior that is appropriate and expected of him in such places as restaurants, transportation facilities, church, recreational settings, and public meetings. Much of this behavior is acquired through imitation of other members of the family or peer group. If it is necessary for the teacher to modify these behaviors, it is crucial that student, teacher, and family agree on common objectives. There are common denominators to acceptable behavior across all public places. Teachers should examine these similiarities in classroom role play encounters, where the student reports on experiences with family or friends, field trips, or critical reviews of televised events. Like a seasoned athlete before the "big game," the student needs practice whether supervised by teachers or parents. Another objective should be identifying reasons for appropriate behavior in public places.

12.3. Developing Respect for the Rights and Properties of Others

This subcompetency includes one of the fundamental concerns upon which the country was founded. It is a continuous subject of interest in television, radio, and newspaper reports and, therefore, offers ample opportunity for teachers and parents to pinpoint the reasons for respecting the rights of others and their possessions. Parents are the initial vital link in this com-

```
ACTIVITY TIP: "Who Owns This?" focuses on situations and
decisions related to ownership of property. School sit-
uations, newspaper articles, and student experiences
provide the teacher with material for discussions and
students' essays. The teacher constructs the situation
and possible questions to consider. For example, a boy
brings a pair of goggles to a swimming pool. He lays them on
a deck chair and goes for a drink. He returns to put them
on, and another swimmer says that the goggles are his. One
pair of goggles and two swimmers. What should the boys do?
```

petency. They are the ones that have to teach children to differentiate between what belongs to them from what belongs to someone else. Teachers will reinforce these basic lessons as instances of ownership will, no doubt, occur in the classroom. Respecting the rights of others becomes more complicated as individuals grow older and begin to exert their own opinions and power in taking command of possessions. This fact will require teachers to initiate lessons and draw upon student experiences, emphasizing the relationship of laws, ownership, and the protection of the community.

12.4. *Recognizing and Following Instructions*

Just about everything a student does in the school setting is preceded by directions. The routine and even monotony of the school situation makes it more difficult for the teacher to impress upon the student that things are different in the employment world. In school, if one doesn't pay attention or forgets an instruction, he may have to do the assignment again, visit the principal, or lose points. The results become commonplace if they are experienced enough times. But, the employment situation offers one consequence despite the previous form of behavior (i.e., "You're fired!"). An equally difficult task is for the teacher to determine whether a student has the ability to accomplish an objective aside from his competence in following directions. Teachers often infer that a student is unable to follow instructions because the total assignment has not been completed. For example, a student is instructed to clean a room in the home economics model house. He is to dust, sweep, and operate a vacuum cleaner. If he did not receive prior instructions in using the vacuum cleaner, he may be unable to fulfill the assignment. One possible teacher response is: "Didn't you hear what I said?" This is one reason why students must be encouraged to ask questions or identify those things they do not know how to do before attempting a task. Employers have often said that an employee who is mentally retarded is easier to work with because he will tell the employer about those things he doesn't understand. Another person may try to fake his way through the job.

12.5. *Knowing His Role*

Several roles are identified across competency areas. Some of these roles would be employee, citizen, parent, relative, and friend. Each role includes responsibilities to specific individuals, as well as groups. The student should be able to describe and demonstrate responsible behavior to individuals identified with the role (employer, parent, child), as well as groups (union, passengers, clubs). This competence would require the student to be actively involved in each role in order to realize its full meaning. For example, a student may be a member of a family by birth, but not in actual practice. Parents have to involve their children in as many family activities and decisions as possible, especially if the handicapped individual is to choose a future role as parent and spouse. Teachers should conduct exercises that place students in situations that provide them with an understanding of the expectations of others for a particular role. For example, community personnel such as police officers, fire fighters, and employers should discuss their expectations of student behaviors and responsibilities in the role of citizen and employee. Another objective should be identifying all possible future roles.

Maintaining Adequate Interpersonal Skills (13)

This competency explores the skills needed to establish and maintain successful forms of interpersonal relationships. It does not propose to include all skills or offer a "cookbook" approach to an area that has received enough attention in books, magazines, and newspapers to fill a lifetime. It is a skill that interacts with the individual's feelings of confidence and independence and is a key to successful career functioning. The major sub-competencies are as follows:

13.1.   Knowing How to Listen and Respond

Communication depends upon the correct interchange of ideas or objects between people. Computers can be programmed to exchange information, but people depend upon the meaning and implications of the message. They accomplish this by attending to the source of the message, as well as other nonverbal clues that may accompany it (refer to competency 16). The teacher should develop several abilities in order for the student to complete this competency. The student should be able to: a. use all available senses in attending, b. develop an adequate means of response, such as speaking, signing, or typing, c. determine the appropriate message (verbal or nonverbal), and d. determine the correct manner of response. Another objective should be identifying effective interpersonal skills.

13.2.   Knowing How to Make and Maintain Friendships

"Dear Abby" columns in newspapers and magazines are filled with the laments of people without friends. "What is a friend? What do students want in a friendship? What can they offer as a friend to someone else? How can they meet people who may become friends? What happens when a friend leaves? Do friends change as one becomes older?" These are just a few of the topic questions for individual and group activities throughout the year. Students can identify what they want in a friendship, various ways of meeting people and sharing interests, and responsibilities involved in being a friend. Teachers should assist students in forming personal solutions to problems, because in the final analysis, the formula for "how to make friends and keep them" is unique to each person. Another objective should be identifying activities that can be shared with friends.

> ACTIVITY TIP: The teacher should draw upon a coming event in a student's life in order to practice interpersonal skills. For example, a class member has been invited to a party given by a relative. All students can relate to this situation and take various roles as participants at the party in order to rehearse appropriate questions and responses. These rehearsals are applicable from elementary school through the adult years and can be applied to a variety of social situations.

13.3. Establishing Appropriate Heterosexual Relationships

This subcompetency focuses on dating. The student should understand the process of dating, various customs relative to the relationship of individuals in the dating situation, and the responsibilites that are included with each role. There are a series of questions that have to be faced by parents and teachers when they counsel young people. "When do I start dating? Should I date this type of person? How do I act on a date? Where do I go on a date?" Those few questions provide enough fuel for years of classroom discussions, heart-to-heart talks, and personal growth. Other objectives should include: a. identifying activities in the community appropriate for dating relationships, and b. identifying ways to demonstrate that one is pleased on a date.

13.4. Knowing How to Establish Close Relationships

The skills for developing close relationships are nurtured in the family. Children learn about personal reactions and respect by observing their parents, interacting with brothers and sisters, or visiting with relatives. Before the primary grades, students may have already developed bonds of various intensities with members of the family, neighbors, playmates, and therapists. The teacher can begin with exercises that identify the different types of relationships that already exist or can be observed in the family and community. Students should formulate answers to such questions as: "What are the characteristics of a close relationship? In what manner do people respond to one another in a close relationship? What is its function?" The obvious indication of these questions is that by probing and observing, the student will develop an awareness of those individual needs that lead to the development of this form of encounter. The final objective would be for the student to maintain a close relationship based on characteristics that are important to him. Another objective should be identifying persons with whom the student could talk about personal matters.

Achieving Independence (14)

There is no magic in the term *independence,* and yet, it looms as an ever present goal in the lives of most handicapped individuals. Writers have debated whether one is ever *truly* independent. Our lives are a mixture of relationships from dependence, through independence, to interdependence. Writers, who already have a measure of freedom, can debate concepts; the handicapped, who only recently have been acknowledged as first-class citizens, would just like to experience the feeling. Independent persons can assume responsibility for their daily affairs in a competent manner. The major subcompetencies are as follows:

14.1. Understanding the Impact of His Behavior on Others

The goal of personal independence includes the student's awareness of those behaviors that promote acceptance or rejection within society. This anticipation is a part of the interactions within a family, social, or employment setting. Teachers and parents want students to understand and foresee the effect their conduct will have on other individuals. Teachers at the primary level can begin with simple exercises in which students identify the way one person's behavior produces another's response. This is not a difficult task since the basic "cat and mouse" cartoons on television and in the comics evolve around a cause and effect. The attraction of these stories is contained in the viewer's anticipation. Children know what is going to happen, and it does. This same principle can be applied to lessons in the classroom. Given a specific behavior, what will be the response? Of course, the subtleties of behavior and communication become more complicated at successive levels of development, but understanding consequences should receive emphasis throughout the educational process (refer to subcompetencies 15.4 and 16.5). Another objective should be identifying several aspects of behavior (i.e., appearance, manner, speech) and their effect on others.

14.2. Understanding Self-Organization

There are numerous proverbs and sayings in our culture conveying the idea that the larger goals are accomplished by taking one step at a time. The process of arranging these steps falls into the category of self-organization. The importance of self-organization is found in the fact that a task, like getting dressed in the morning, has to be repeated daily and is subject to a pattern of behavior that facilitates its accomplishment. Children's puzzles, among other things, convey the idea that there is an organization—a pattern—involved in solving the problem. One may observe that the child after learning the puzzle will perform the exact steps to its completion over and over. It may be because the pattern is the most efficient or the quickest, or it is just the way he likes to do it. Given this fundamental ability to create and replicate patterns of behavior to meet problems, the next step is to provide individuals with an overview of a problem so that they can choose the best course of action. In other words, students look forward to judging current decisions. Completing mazes and the yearly income tax forms are examples of such a whole-part-whole approach. Most of the students will have had experience with organizing behavior. However, such things as commuting, dating, and shopping are subjects for further review, analysis, and organization. Another objective should be demonstrating ability to organize daily activities.

> ACTIVITY TIP: Teachers and parents can cooperate effectively on the familiar "Things to Do" lists that students establish for weekly projects or tasks. The lists provide the student with an opportunity to identify goals and reminders of resources for accomplishing the objectives. They can also be used as sources for classroom discussions related to daily events and accomplishments. Some students may organize such a list for each subject in the curriculum.

14.3.   Developing Goal-Seeking Behavior

One of the most powerful ingredients to the success of the handicapped individual is behavior leading to the accomplishment of a goal. Indeed, the successful individual who obtains a goal despite an inconvenience is often used as a role model for others who have handicaps. In order to replicate those successes, the student should be able to identify goals and execute the appropriate behavior to reach defined objectives. Teachers should discriminate between short and long term, realistic and unrealistic goals. Students should practice the organization of goals, outline behaviors they will need to reach those goals, practice the behaviors, and evaluate the results. Other objectives should include: a. identifying potential barriers to goals, and b. identifying resources that can assist a person to achieve his goal.

14.4.   Striving toward Self-Actualization

We define self-actualization as a point at which an individual is producing as near to his potential as possible, is aware of these accomplishments, and feels a sense of fulfillment in them. The emphasis is upon current talents and abilities and the individual's feeling that he is "doing the best he can." This is a competency that parents, counselors, teachers, and therapists should enjoy working with as it reminds us of the part it plays in our lives. We build self-actualization when we emphasize the positive aspect of children, what they can do as being more important than what they can't, and that each person can feel confident of some success within each day. Self-actualization is not a final end-all goal but a realization that comes through many incidents in which we have achieved and felt satisfaction. So much growth occurs in the first 20 years of life that children and adolescents are too concerned with the physical aspects and whether they are measuring up to standards. The psychological aspects will be realized in later years, but their beginnings are established during those days when children have so little time for them. It is the responsibility of parents and professionals to plant those seeds of discovery. Other objectives should be: a. identifying elements necessary for a satisfactory day, and b. identifying important characteristics for personal growth.

Achieving Problem-Solving Skills (15)

The process of problem solving is intrinsic to education. One may say that all of the basic skills, like reading, writing, and calculating, prepare the student to make appropriate decisions. Problem solving is usually identified with the previous curriculum areas and the sciences. But, several facets of the methodology can be applied to the broad area of Personal-Social Skills in order to help students examine and improve their relationships with other individuals. The major subcompetencies are as follows:

15.1. Differentiating Bipolar Concepts

Bipolar concepts include such examples as good and evil, positive and negative, pro and con. These terms are often bantered about in references to issues and relationships. However, problems and relationships, more often than not, do not fall into such a neat dichotomy. There may be several solutions to a problem or positions on an issue. The favored solutions would be the ones that are of greatest advantage to the individual and his set of values. Students should demonstrate the ability to identify the extreme positions within a problem area, search for as many solutions, and place them on a progression. In using a methodology that includes this ordering of possible solutions, alternatives, or approaches, the student is able to open and expose the several ingredients intrinsic to the problem. Another objective should be examining various positions relative to a group's interpretation of ideas, feelings, and behaviors.

15.2. Understanding the Need for Goals

Parents and teachers should deal with the question, "What are the purposes of goals?" Students should identify ways in which goals affect their lives and relationships with the people around them. Teachers should conduct activities requiring students to set model goals that can be attained within a short span of time so that students can record behaviors and results. Goals can be set in personal behavior, appearance, academic accomplishment, and group participation (refer to subcompetency 10.2). Their attainment is most meaningful when the student is the foremost advocate in their formulation. In other words, goals established outside of the student, by teacher or parent, may be noteworthy or even achieved by the student. However, if this competency is to contribute to the student's move toward independence and responsibility, then he must be in the dominant position of advocate and main participant, while teacher and parent assume the role of facilitator. Another objective should be listing outcomes of attaining goals.

15.3. Looking at Alternatives

At first glance, a problem may appear to have only one or two possible solutions. The student obviously limits the range of advantage if he accepts the visible solutions. The exercises related to the differentiation of bipolar concepts exposed him to the possibility that other solutions or positions are possible in solving problems, but one must search for alternatives. The deep attraction of fictional mysteries, whether they include Sherlock Holmes or Nancy Drew, is that the characters refuse to accept answers that are easily available and seek other possibilities to solve the puzzle. This same principle should be applied to human relationships. Students should demonstrate the ability to seek information and examine alternatives involved in individual and group relationships.

> ACTIVITY TIP: "The Classroom Industry" is one type of project that combines numerous academic areas and personal-social skills, particularly requiring students to engage in problem solving. The students determine the type of service or product they will provide the community. They organize committees for management, production, distribution, and advertising. Every function requires students to solve problems and arrive at decisions. The project can be as complicated as the skills of the students or as much as the faculty allows.

15.4. Anticipating Consequences

The most difficult component to examine in the problem-solving process is the results of a decision. This may contribute to the fact that it is also the most neglected component of the process. How can one examine what is only anticipated? It is at this point that the student's skills of observations and inquiry will be of greatest assistance. For although the individual student may have had little, if any, experience with potential consequences of a course of action, that does not mean that other individuals are lacking in information. Most of the everyday decisions of life are experienced by all of us, and their consequences can be used as guides for those who are first examining similar problems and alternatives (refer to subcompetency 10.3).

15.5 Knowing Where to Find Good Advice

Throughout the discussions of the subcompetencies, teachers and parents have been reminded that students should know the resources in their communities that can provide assistance in personal and family decision making. These resources should meet the following standards: a. they are experts in their given subject area, b. they have had experience in advising members of the community, and c. they can subdivide the decision-making process for their given subject area into sequential parts.

Communicating Adequately with Others (16)

Without adequate communication, the handicapped individual is isolated. No person, handicapped or not, is an island and can reach fulfillment when he is denied the means to convey his thoughts and feelings to others. In the final analysis, one may say that our efforts in education rest upon our ability to develop communication skills in students. With these skills, they can gain protection, companionship, and understanding. The major subcompetencies are as follows:

16.1. Recognizing Emergency Situations

Darley and Latané (1968) developed "The Decision Tree" to account for people's reactions in emergency situations. In order for a person to assist another who is in need, the bystander must: a. recognize that something is happening, b. interpret the occurrence as an emergency, c. assume some personal responsibility in relationship to the situation or person, and d. intervene. A breakdown in any of these steps may result in an absence of needed assistance. This progression provides teachers with a structure for planning training activities. Students must first be able to attend to instances within the environment that are either direct signs of an emergency (fire, earthquake) or could be interpreted as a danger signal (screeching car brakes followed by a loud "thud," an individual collapsing in a restaurant). Assuming that the student does take a personal responsibility for action (which is a test of his values), he should be able to provide the appropriate form of communication with participants ("Can I assist you?" "What do you need?") and emergency personnel ("I wish to report an accident."

"I observed the following things."). These skills can be practiced in conjunction with subcompetencies 3.4 and 4.4. Another objective should be preparing a list of emergency information to be carried by the student.

16.2. *Reading at Level Needed for Future Goals*

The primary objective in this subcompetency is that the individual will be able to read through the use of visual or tactile methods in order to achieve a degree of independence. The reading ability should include symbols within the environments that are important for safety, health, and mobility. A second important consideration is that the symbols and meanings to be mastered facilitate the individual's overall achievement and development of self-confidence. Some students' goals and abilities will include reading Gibbon's *Decline and Fall of the Roman Empire.* For others, reading the shopping specials in the newspaper or braille directions for repairing a car will provide a sense of accomplishment. A teacher should seek every opportunity to use reading material that includes career/vocational themes or skills. This will require the teacher to use discretion as to whether a student should work in a history book or read about car repairs. These decisions will be enhanced if the teacher coordinates his efforts with the opinions of the parents. Another objective should be demonstrating ability to use sources of information (i.e., newspapers, magazines, library).

16.3. *Writing at Level Needed for Future Goals*

This subcompetency emphasizes the production of written or printed symbols in communicating with others. The term *printed symbols* include the use of typewriter, stylus, or other machine and computer assisted production of words and symbols that convey information. Once again, the level of accomplishment should be commensurate with the abilities and ambitions of the individual. From a career/vocational orientation, students should receive training in abilities to complete informal notes, letters, job applications, and a variety of forms they will encounter in applying for credit, completing a lease, or opening a checking account (refer to Competency 1).

> ACTIVITY TIP: A mock "Employment Bureau" should be established in each classroom or school. It could be another learning center in the elementary classroom or part of the career center at the high school and community college level. Students would have the opportunity to practice several skills required in applying for a job. The bureau would maintain job descriptions, employment applications, audio and video cassette recordings or printed transcripts of interviews, and programmed material that provide information related to employment.

16.4. Speaking Adequately for Understanding

In a society that places a value upon verbal skills (singing, acting, political oratory, salesmanship), the individual with speech disabilities or lacking fluency is at a disadvantage, to say the least. Van Riper (1963) identifies the succession of penalties, frustration, anxiety, guilt, and hostility that individuals with speech problems experience in their everyday dealings with other members of society. Even the competent person has occasional "dark days" when he mispronounces the boss' name, flounders among sentences in an interview, or is tongue-tied when meeting a prospective date. Teachers, parents, counselors, and therapists have a formidable task in preparing students to demonstrate: a. proficiency in basic language skills, b. skill in regulating the loudness of voice according to the social setting, c. ability to participate in conversation, and d. a variety of verbal communications related to the expression of emotion, information, and inquiry.

16.5. Understanding the Subtleties of Communication

Teachers should explore the area of "what is meant" in communication as contrasted to the "what is said, signed, or written." In other words, we live in a world of intention. Students have to realize that communications are clouded for reasons of disguise in order to protect. We say things, imply things, but cannot be held accountable. School children soon master the formula that they can only be held accountable for what was said. They realize that communication can occur through many channels and can operate at both the overt and covert levels. The commercial aspect of life is, perhaps, the biggest and most accessible source of lessons for the teacher. The innumerable number of advertisements on radio, television, and printed matter convey messages other than what is stated or pictured. Here are the nonverbal components, the subtleties, of communication. Students should be able to distinguish between the two so that their own communication skills are improved. They should be aware of those instances in which they are producing dual messages (i.e., one level of acknowledged symbols and another one of intended meaning). Another objective should be practicing verbal and nonverbal forms of communication that are congruent with one's feelings.

TEACHING THE PERSONAL-SOCIAL SKILLS

In the beginning of this chapter, we made the statement that professionals must consider the ideas an individual has about his present status, potentials, and interactions with other people in order to add another dimension to classroom instruction. These numerous personal ideas provide teachers and counselors with reflections of the student's self-concept. As so often happens with terms derived from the field of psychology or sociology, the phrase *self-concept* or *self-image* has been absorbed into the mainstream of popular expressions. One may encounter it in newspaper responses to the lovelorn, as well as textbooks for teachers and counselors. This may be due in part to the fact that the basic idea of a personalized picture that one may have of the self, with all the attributes and deficiencies, appeals to the average individual, as well as artists and scientists.

Each subcompetency is one ingredient in the broad spectrum covered by the self-concept. It is appropriate to emphasize the self-concept at this stage of the text, since classroom activities in the personal-social skills include more than a strict adherence to academic performance. Teacher-student efforts in the areas of self-awareness, self-confidence, responsible behavior, interpersonal skills, independence, problem solving, and communication depend upon an accurate understanding of the student's opinions of his abilities and subsequent efforts to meet his level of expectation.

West (1977) reviews 27 teaching strategies for classroom use with the educable mentally retarded. Aside from the use of media and consultant support, 22 of the strategies require direct initiation or supervision by the teacher. The strategies include:

brainstorming	peer tutoring
consensus forming	practice sessions
role play	lecture
discussion	panel
demonstration	simulation
explanation	games
questions and answers	learning packages
recitation	interviews
review of material	projects
hands-on activities	contract teaching
oral reports	learning centers

We will not attempt to review all of the above forms of teaching individuals with special needs. Although West reviewed the strategies in relationship to students in classes for the educable mentally retarded, they are applicable to all students. Many are well known to the reader, while others may be of less importance due to the teacher's style or characteristics of the classroom situation. We are primarily concerned with strategies that encourage students to learn about themselves, their self-concepts, and ways to change with each new piece of information. Some of these strategies appear in the above list. Several have been developed in recent years. These strategies include bibliotherapy, classroom discussions-meetings, individualized learning centers, role play-sociodrama, self-concept scales, and values clarification.

All of these strategies can be used by teachers and counselors to change the behavior of the student and evaluations of the self. All can be used at each one of the four stages of career development (i.e., awareness, exploration, preparation, and placement and follow up). The use of any one strategy will depend upon the teacher or counselor's objectives for a particular individual or group of students. These objectives should reflect an evaluation of the behaviors and abilities of the individual or group. The essential consideration is that the instructor is using an approach through which the competencies are infused into the daily curriculum. The approach also offers a means by which the teacher or counselor can judge whether particular competencies in the personal-social domain have been confronted and, hopefully, mastered by the student. A discussion of the self-concept will be followed by reviews of several strategies.

The Self-Concept

Several prominent psychologists have written about the self-concept and its central position in the development of personality (Rogers, 1951; Sullivan, 1953; & Thorne, 1967). Rogers, a prominent proponent of client-centered counseling, is familiar to teachers and counselors and provided the definition that we will use in this discussion. He spoke of the self-concept as:

> an organized configuration of perceptions of the self which are admissible to awareness. It is composed of such elements as the perceptions of one's characteristics and abilities; the value qualities which are perceived as associated with experiences and objects; and goals and ideals which are perceived as having positive or negative valence.

(Rogers, 1951, pp. 136–37)

The self-concept is generally regarded as the totality of the way one perceives himself, the picture one has of himself. This total image includes our abilities and characteristics, as well as the positive and negative evaluations that are placed on each. The image changes with our experiences; that is, the self-concept is learned, and new learnings change the composite image maintained from one moment of time to the next. Some psychologists and counselors refer to the self-concept as both the image and the process of change so that at any one time, the individual reflects his movements from one experience to another and the affect those learnings have upon the self.

A second important element in this process is that the self-concept is influenced by "significant others," such as parents, teachers, or those who foster change. For example, the 1977 inductees to the Football Hall of Fame in Canton, Ohio delivered acceptance speeches in which they attributed their successes to specific individuals who coached them at the high school, college, or professional levels.[8] In some instances, the athletes doubted whether they would have succeeded as professional football players, let alone achieved such a prominent distinction, without the teaching and encouragement of their mentors.

A third recurring element in definitions and discussions of the self-concept is related to the way we perceive ourself and our environment. The basic component of perception is the physical reception and transmission of sensations to the brain. Individuals with an impediment in one of the senses will experience difficulties in gaining accurate information about the environment. Bateman (1967), with an assist from Carl Bereiter, developed a model of human data processing to illustrate the effects of the absence of vision upon expression. She likened the various human functions to those of a computer so that one's expression (output) is a product of the sensory input, prior knowledge (storage), and procedures for processing (program). The absence of vision limits the amount of input into the system, while individuals with hearing impediments may miss the rules for processing information that are contained in the learning of language. Also, individuals with severe emotional problems (paranoia, hallucinations, and the like) might have difficulty with input processes.

Perception also refers to the psychological interpretations we place upon events or the behaviors of others. For example, one perceives that his host is ignoring him at the party or that people do not want to stand next to him in line for the theater. These interpretations constitute the basis for the ideas we develop about the self. Since perception, whether viewed from the physical or psychological side, is important to behavior, psychologists have postulated that changes in these perceptions will affect behavior. Simply stated, our behavior is based on perception. If a person perceives differently, then he will behave differently.

The final major element in the self-concept is the act of valuing what is perceived. The average American normally refers to this phenomenon as: "The way one feels about himself." People are asked: "And how are you feeling today?" People respond: "O.K." "Great." "Awful." "I have Excedrin Headache No. 82." "Happy." "Can't complain." The self-concept is more than a total assessment, although the above responses may accurately reflect the person's feelings at that moment. It includes numerous component values, which are placed on specific forms of demonstrated ability, aptitude, and disability. Thus, one may be an adequate tennis player, terrible when it comes to completing income tax forms, quick to form an opinion, and a dependable neighbor. These values, or the ways in which one regards himself, are influenced by the appraisals of significant others, and one's subsequent behaviors, in turn, affect the appraisers. With time, the values

---

[8] The individuals were Frank Gifford, Forrest Gregg, Gayle Sayers, Bart Starr, and Bill Willis. Several of these men occupy leadership positions in which they can influence the aspirations and self-concepts of others.

given to the several components can change as the individual encounters new experiences and other appraisals. This is known in the average American lexicon as: "Taking stock," or "Changing priorities." These new or modified values constitute the foundation for what the individual expects to accomplish (aspirations) and tries to achieve (endeavors).

One's personal opinion of ability and subsequent efforts are crucial to career education. You may recall from our discussion of career education in chapter 3 that it includes all those attempts by members of the school, family, community, and business and industry to influence the student's perception of possibilities for functioning in numerous roles in society, as well as those efforts to succeed in those roles. These efforts attempt to expand the student's perception by placing a positive value on all productive roles in the society. The student's behaviors often depend upon the preconceived notions of ability and requirements for success. Thus, advocates of career education are interested in the Personal-Social Skills, as they include the very elements that form a basis for a concept of self.

Special educators have been interested in the implications of self-concept discussions for the personal development of the handicapped since the early beginnings of the theory. Research on the self-concept and individuals with various types of disabilities expanded during the 1960s with the availability of support monies and emphasis upon changes in social policy. The term appears in research in all areas of exceptionality. Several reviewers (Cruickshank & Paul, 1971; Bartel & Guskin, 1973; Lawrence & Winchell, 1973) have identified major complications that have to be resolved before researchers and practitioners can soundly state that their instruments and methods do, in fact, improve the image that the individual has of himself, as well as his corresponding behavior. These can be summarized as challenges in: **1.** defining the several components of the self-concept, **2.** identifying the progressive stages of development of the self-concept, and **3.** improving the validity and standardization of the instruments used to measure the self-concept or its components.

Aside from the above problems, which are directly related to the formulation of self-concept theories and instruments to indicate one's status vis-à-vis the projected developmental stage, researchers also encounter difficulties when they apply their methods to specific categories of disability. If you consider the amount of variation existing among individuals with, for example, behavior disorders or physical disability, then you must be cautious in generalizing research findings. This is also complicated when there are differences of opinion concerning the definition of a disability and its characteristics. For example, the category of "learning disability" is a fledgling in the field of special education. Several attempts have been made at the national level to develop a definition reflecting current understandings of individuals with this impairment. But, given the relative newness of the category (or as some would have it, the label), combined with previously identified limitations in the measurement of the self-concept, one can imagine his reservations while reading a research report on, for example, the effects of mainstreaming upon the self-concept of children with learning disabilities.

Despite these difficulties and limitations, we feel that teachers and counselors should be encouraged to probe the Personal-Social Skill areas that fall within the larger framework of the self-concept. This statement is based largely upon our observations of the status of handicapped individuals within society and their experiences in attempting to shape an image of themselves that includes positive values. Educators must be concerned with the development of the individual's self-concept for the following reasons:

1. In some instances, the individual's disability interferes with his development of an accurate perception of the environment, which includes people's reactions to him. For example, in subcompetency 16.5, understanding the subtleties of communication, we state that educators should train students to be aware of clues relative to others' reactions to them. But, a great many of these clues are in the visual channel, thus placing those individuals with visual disability at a disadvantage in receiving accurate information. There are very few ways in which the visually limited individual can change the behavior patterns of others. Such things as winks, physical gestures, or the raising of an eyebrow have been learned and perfected over a long span of time in order to convey additional information about the meaning or emphasis of another form of communication. Educators must train the individual to rely on other channels of communication to clarify the information and thereby provide a foundation for accurate perceptions.

2. In some instances, the individual's disability limits his interaction with the environment, which may hinder the range of experiences. Experiences provide information about the environment and one's ability to maintain himself within it. One of the benefits of Special Olympics, or programs in physical development and recreation across the spectrum of individuals with special needs, is that they have the opportunity to test themselves. These tests, whether swimming, camping, or racing, allow individuals to gain new insights about their physical and psychological aspects. New possibilities for success are available, and the aura of limitation that constantly surrounds individuals with disability is diminished. These changes will be reflected in modified self-concepts.

3. In some instances, the individual acquires his appraisal of aptitude from the evaluation by significant others in his life. Their opinions of the individual's "special" aspect and its unique effects can supersede the actual limitation. Individuals with disabilities have often been limited more by these reactions and concepts than by the

physical limitation. Those of us in special education can recount numerous stories of students who regarded themselves as less than adequate, based solely upon the opinions of others. For example, have you ever heard the following statements:

> My parents will always treat me like a baby until the day I die.
>
> They've called me names so often that it doesn't bother me. I just don't talk to anyone that's all. They're not missing much, and neither am I.
>
> Most of the time, I wish I was someone else.
>
> After a while, it just isn't worth trying. The teacher will always find something wrong with my work.

4. In some instances, the individual's identity evolves around and depends upon his inadequate status. These inadequacies are first projected by significant others. Parents, relatives, and teachers link the individual's identity to the disability through such references as my "blind child" or "retarded student." At one stage of development, the use of such terms are passively accepted. The terms may even impart some forms of attention and distinguish him from other children. But, at some stage of development, the same individual begins to realize that certain references or labels bear negative connotations and only decrease his value. This realization marks the break in the path. One road leads to increased independence and an identity generated from accomplishments, while the other leads to a status built on labels and stereotypes. We suspect that some of the emphasis of individuals with special needs upon their role or identity as "people first" may be due, in part, to the series of labels from childhood through adult living that always marked the disability prior to any other human characteristics.

5. In some instances, the individual will resort to evasive means in order to avoid devaluation and buttress a self-concept that has been under assault. Our society is characterized as one of accomplishment. We value success whether measured in gold medals at the Olympics, orbiting satellites, or gross national product. If one is unable to accomplish what amounts to the phantom of success, he is in jeopardy. As a society, we are now beginning to realize that the individual has value and his value does not decrease because he is unable to succeed. But, because we are in the early stages of the realization of the relationships between success, value, identity, and self-concept, numerous individuals with disabilities have had to resort to means to mask their shortcomings and evade detection.

Two researchers, Goffman (1963), a sociologist, and Edgerton (1967), an anthropologist, have documented the attempts of ex-mental patients, drug addicts, prostitutes, the mentally retarded, and others with "spoiled identities" to pass in a society that maintains standards for normal behavior and appearance. Goffman devotes a considerable amount of his book to the means by which those who bear a stigma attempt to avoid detection. Edgerton provides extensive histories of individuals who were released from institutions for the mentally retarded, which include behaviors that project competence to the observer. These various "covering" techniques protect the self-concept but, in fact, only form *The Cloak of Competence* (Edgerton, 1967).

It is no wonder that individuals with special needs experience a whole range of contradictory feeling about self when they view their role as depicted in such popular media as magazines, newspaper comics, television, and movies. You can no doubt recall the classic examples of evil in such fairy tales as *Jack and the Beanstalk* (the giant ogre), *Peter Pan* (Captain Hook) or *Rumpelstiltskin.* Comedians have often used the popular stereotypes and expectations that are associated with a certain disability as the focal point of their jokes. For example, Mel Brooks has been associated with several comedy routines and movies. We need not elaborate on them as that would constitute its own chapter, but there is one routine in his movie *Young Frankenstein* that illustrates his use of a stereotype to "play on" the audience. Dr. Frankenstein, Jr. (played by Gene Wilder) returns to his father's home town and is met at the railroad station by Egor, Jr. (played by Marty Feldman). After an exchange of lines relative to the pronunciation of their names, Dr. Frankenstein notices that Egor has a hunchback. He is seized with pity and, touching Egor's back, states that he is a surgeon and can help Egor with his hump. Egor looks puzzled and responds, "What hump?" The public usually laughs at that point, but we wonder whether they realize that they bear the brunt of the joke? Or does the individual who is sitting in the audience with a noticeable physical difference bear the brunt of the joke in the final analysis?

Bibliotherapy

You are probably familiar with examples of disabilities that are central to such classic literature as Victor Hugo's *The Hunchback of Notre Dame* and William Shakespeare's *Richard III.* The characters Quisimodo and Richard III encounter various difficulties, but one would not consider them as sterling examples of an individual's ability to cope with stress in his environment. There are other works of literature that do present the handicapped individual in a favorable light.

Bibliotherapy is one means of assisting individuals with a disability to understand their difficulties by exposing them to works of literature in which characters with limitations confront and, in most instances, succeed in life's challenges. The key element to the process, aside from the physical act of "reading" the book, occurs when the individual identifies with the character or circumstances, transfers insights from the literature, and applies them to his own situation. Bibliotherapy can be used by teachers and counselors to develop an informational background to many of the subcompetencies in the personal-social skills. For example, characters will often reflect upon their need for certain skills, difficulties they encountered in solving problems related to interactions with "normal" people, or the attitudes of others toward disabilities. Students can be asked to relate their experiences to similar events in the book. The external report by the student indicates whether he has gained insight into the circumstances confronting the character and, more importantly, those pieces of wisdom that can be transferred to his own repertoire of behavior.

Bibliotherapy has received expanded interest among teachers, counselors, and therapists who are attempting to broaden the individual's perspective of his situation and potential problem-solving behaviors that increase self-confidence. This interest has been aided by the fact that a greater number of literary works by individuals with a disability and their parents have found their way into print. Biographies of books and poetry appropriate for various ages and disabilities can be found in Brown (1975), King (1975), and Cohen (1977). Professionals should also write to The National Easter Seal Society for Crippled Children and Adults, 2023 W. Ogden Ave., Chicago, Illinois, 60612, for a bibliography of books about handicapped persons that is organized according to areas of disability. This organization has been reviewing such books in its publication *Rehabilitation Literature* so that professionals may research specific works in order to gain more information prior to recommending it to students or their parents. Readers who are interested in expanded discussions of the method should refer to the works of Moody (1971) and Riggs (1971). Other sources include *Bookfinder* by American Guidance Service (Circles Pines, Minn. 55014), which includes a guide to children's literature about needs and problems of youth ages 2–15 and 450 cross-referenced topics, and *Notes from a Different Drummer* (Baskin & Harris, 1977), which contains an annotated guide to juvenile fiction portraying handicapped individuals.

Classroom Discussions—Meetings

One of the most popular means by which teachers and counselors lead students in exchanges on the subcompetencies covered in chapters 4 through 6 is classroom discussions or meetings. Most professionals have participated in discussions during their training experiences and, no doubt, attempt to conduct similar activities with students in small or large groups. However, few have seriously dissected the functions and anatomy of a discussion as thoroughly as Glasser (1969). He devotes three chapters in his book *Schools Without Failure* to "classroom meetings" and their importance for relevant education.

Glasser projects the teacher or counselor as one who leads the class in a nonjudgmental discussion about the important concerns of the students. His suggestions and concepts are applicable particularly to teacher-student activities in the area of personal-social skills. Students are sensitive to the opinions and judgments of teachers and peers in such competency areas as achieving independence, acquiring self-confidence, and communicating with others.

The success of the meetings depends upon the professional's attitude toward their function in the total school curriculum. If they are viewed as an integral part of the daily routine, students and professionals begin to acquire an open and honest attitude toward topics which, under other circumstances, would warrant guarded and evasive behaviors. The professional cannot afford to lead small or large groups into such sensitive topics (and student concerns) as accepting criticism, understanding behaviors, and expressing feelings, without establishing an atmosphere of trust. At the same time, the professional cannot avoid such topics, as these are the very ones that constitute the building blocks in the development of a positive self-concept.

The classroom meetings have particular benefits for those students with handicaps who are being integrated into the regular classroom. Some meetings may provide students the opportunity to explore questions about feelings and attitudes toward individuals who are different. The student with disabilities may not be the best spokesperson for *all* people who share his inconveniences, but he can relate his experiences in the neighborhood and the school. Hopefully, the open and honest atmosphere that encouraged students to exchange views will also help them to accept individuals who differ from the group.

Individualized Learning Centers

Classroom learning or work centers have become increasingly popular as a means of facilitating independent learning. The center is a designated area in which the student works at a specific task at his own rate of speed. Elementary school teachers use this type of programming to direct students into various activities or buttress previous group instructional sessions. It was not until the introduction of Hewett's (1968) engineered classroom that the concept was expanded into what might be considered a model for special education.

Hewett's program was originally designed for students who were classified as educationally handicapped or emotionally disturbed. The program was subsequently modified to meet the needs of individuals with various types of disabilities. The work center concept lends itself particularly to situations in which the teacher must design a minimum amount of knowledge or skill to be mastered by all members of the class, but is faced with the problem of teaching to different rates of learning. In other words, students must have the opportunity to cover the same amount of material at their own speed without imposing their limitations upon other members of the class. The main requirements of the work center are that:

1. Activities can be conducted with a minimum of direct supervision;
2. instructions and materials are available at each center to meet the needs and abilities of the student;
3. students are introduced to the themes in each center as a normal part of their classroom routine;
4. reinforcement of some form is available to encourage continued success and effort; and
5. it is considered an integral part of the curriculum so that the teacher provides assistance and records observations of student behaviors.

The learning center can be within one room or throughout the school. Their themes may include such activities as visual perception, auditory discrimination, listening skills, fine motor skills, communication skills, and arts and crafts (Kokaska & Kokaska, 1971).

Most of the above activities are associated with physical and academic development. However, Noar (1974) describes "The Center for Learning about Me," which helps students practice skills that foster positive attitudes and feelings about the self. The center contains personal grooming materials, as well as a wash basin and mirror. Noar also suggests that teachers use a camera so that students may have their pictures taken at periodic intervals. Students relate to positive images projected on self-pictures and, thus, build better personal images of themselves.

It is possible to establish individualized learning centers that concentrate on themes relative to the subcompetencies of the Personal-Social Skills. For example, a Communications Center may contain a tape recorder on which a student may practice telephoning for an interview or introducing himself to a member of the opposite sex. Each student should maintain his personal tape or cassette, which can be played, erased, and recorded again until he has produced the appropriate level of skill to meet criteria.

A second center may be assigned to personal reflections about self. Students may use the center to record their ideas about daily accomplishments, new goals, or the way others perceive their behavior. These reflections may be written in a log, diary, or notebook, or contained on the personal tape or cassette. In all instances, teachers and counselors must be mindful of the privacy required by students in disclosing ideas about themselves. This type of center will certainly test the amount of trust that has been established between professional and student, as well as student and peers.

Another center may be assigned to listening or viewing video recordings, slide-tape material, or other illustrations appropriate to Personal-Social Skills. Commercial materials are available covering the wide range of behaviors appropriate to dating, controlling one's emotions, problem solving, developing objectives, communicating with friends and employers. At times, teachers and counselors have more material available then they can use in classroom or small group sessions. This type of center would enable students to explore topics of interest at their rate of learning, which may generate more pertinent questions about abilities and areas of improvement. Letting students create their own learning centers can also be a positive experience.

Role Play—Sociodrama

These terms apply to several techniques that include spontaneous responses by participants within a given situation. The early origins of the techniques can be traced to therapists who encouraged their clients to "act out" frustrations, fears, or antagonisms. More recently, educators have found the value of role playing for use in regular classrooms. This is due to the realization that each one of us is expected to assume a wide range of roles during the adult years with very little direct preparation in the classroom. Each role is assigned a set of expected behaviors, for example, employers expect certain behaviors from employees, and pedestrians from motorists. But, what about the reverse expectations of the employees and motorists?

The manner in which children, adolescents, and adults learn the role expectations and appropriate behaviors is often left to chance. Teachers and counselors recognize that most people, and particularly those individuals with handicaps who have had limited opportunity to engage in social interaction, need experiences in which they can "practice at" certain roles. This practice is generally referred to as making believe, but the topics that are confronted in role play are more significant than those associated with the usual "Let's Pretend" themes. One may recall his experiences at the first formal dance of his life or junior prom. Everyone stood around looking for clues as to the appropriate things to do and say. Some prior role play in a classroom may have made the experience less awkward. Several of these themes have been suggested in our discussions of the subcompetencies, so they need not be reemphasized at this point. The remaining discussion will concentrate on basic techniques that can be used in the classroom with all ages of students with disabilities.

Role play provides the student with an opportunity to experiment with his feelings and explore behavior for a given situation while in a protective environment, namely, the classroom. The play allows the student to express feelings that may not be acceptable outside the classroom, to make mistakes, and to be different, by placing him in a role in which he is only acting. After all, most of us know that actors are only filling a part and don't really believe their lines! The key to the encounter between members in the play is the spontaneity of the participants. Although the students assume the role of different characters involved in situations, the teacher and counselor hope that the students will bring their true feelings, attitudes, and responses for the role to the forefront. If the responses are guarded, then the professional has no real basis upon which to judge whether the sessions are successful in demonstrating expected behavior for the role. The ideal situation is one in which the student displays his behavior, receives constructive suggestions, and incorporates the changes. Of course, the final test is whether the practice behaviors were initiated during actual encounters.

Several authors have suggested a series of steps by which professionals should prepare students for role play or sociodrama. We have organized them into the following sequence.

1. Identify the problem. The problem may have already been identified through student input (i.e., "What do I wear at a prom?") or occur in the normal sequence of the curriculum (i.e., "Goals for this school year."). Teachers and counselors should not be without problem topics, given the 102 subcompetencies identified in this book. The important aspect of this initial step is to define the problem so that each student understands its significance for his life.

2. Warm-up. This step is necessary in breaching the identification of the problem and the subsequent involvement in role play. The warm-up prepares the student by getting him interested in the means to solve the problem. "Should he read a book? Will an authority give him the answer? Can the class help him find the answer?" The warm-up brings the class to the realization that the group may be the best source of information in confronting the problem. The question of "What does one say at the junior prom?" may best be answered by the group in a role play.

3. Specify the situation and various roles. Simply stated, everyone should know his part and what is happening. At first, the teacher and counselor may have to carry the bulk of organizing the participants. Students can, with time and practice, adequately project situations and role behaviors, especially concerning those problems that are particular to their age and circumstances.

4. The play. Response and timing are critical to the play. Students must carry the conversations and responses, but teachers and counselors have to judge whether the play is successful, when to bring it to a conclusion, or whether the participants should be encouraged further. There are no "hard and fast" rules regarding these decisions. Students can sense when they are not on the right track, but both students and professionals need practice at the process of role play before it can be a vibrant part of the curriculum.

5. Discussion. The play should generate additional questions: "What happened? Why? What would you do different? Is there another way of reacting in that situation?" These questions and others are intended to amplify alternative behaviors that could apply to all members of the group. The alternative decisions should be discussed and, in turn, could provide the topics for other role plays.

6. Replay. The same situation could be recast and played again. New participants create new possibilities for review and discussion. Eventually, the situation will lose its luster. Teachers and counselors should be sure to end the play before that point so that students maintain a favorable attitude toward the entire process. They are the ones who then can initiate the role play at some future date.

Readers who are interested in further discussion of the use of role playing in the classroom should refer to Chesler and Fox (1966), Shaftel and Shaftel (1967), and Buchan (1972).

Self-Concept Scales

There are several self-concept scales available for use by teachers and counselors at the elementary, secondary, and adult levels. They are primarily intended to measure the beliefs an individual has about himself. We have already discussed the difficulties encountered by researchers in attempting to use the scales with populations of individuals with disabilities. At this stage of the discussion, we are more concerned with the use of self-concept scales or self-report scales as teaching devices rather than measuring instruments.

The scales basically provide students with statements about self. "I am always happy." "I like to go to the movies." "My parents pick on me." The statements can reflect such things as physical ability, mental ability, appearance, favorable qualities, skills, and are usually rated on scales from "always" to "never," "excellent" to "terrible," and the like. Although the statements can include other people, they always reflect the student's feelings about what others do to him or think about him. Thus, teachers and counselors receive the student's interpretation of his present status, the attitudes and behaviors of others toward him, and the values he places on each ingredient. The obvious limitation to the whole process rests in the accuracy of the student's reports. What a student marks on a form may not be what he feels. But, this limitation in "measurement" provides teachers and counselors with the reason for using these kinds of instruments or reports for teaching purposes. The very fact that the student hesitates to complete a form or reports inaccurately indicates an area of investigation.[9]

---

[9] Teachers and counselors should be aware of the fact that a student may refuse to disclose certain feelings on personal grounds. This factor of privacy should be honored.

Self-concept scales can be used as teaching devices in the following ways.

1. Statements on the report form alert the student to possible areas of behavior and attitudes. In effect, the statements act as a stimulus for further discussions, either in small or large groups. These discussions can place greater perspective on one's ranking of status and the perception of various types of ability.
2. Many of the self-concept scales include statements reflecting the subcompetencies of the Personal-Social Skills. Teachers and counselors would be able to gain an approximation of the student's ranking in such areas as self-awareness, socially responsible behavior, and communication. The use of the scales as a form of checklist would provide professionals with another means of marking the progress of the student through the subcompetencies.
3. Responses on the report form can alert teachers and counselors to contradictions between the student's perception of events or attitudes and the perception of others, including professionals. Such contradictions can be matched against further observations and individual counseling sessions. Above all, the contradictions should not be left unattended. Numerous individuals with disabilities have maintained inaccurate views of themselves and the opinions of others toward their limitations merely because their views were not brought to a conscious level of discussion and inquiry that would have exposed the situation.

Values Clarification

Teachers and counselors have always worked in the realm of personal values, which includes their own, as well as those of the student. The way we regard ourselves and the level at which we prize our several attributes are composed of numerous smaller value choices. Values constitute the qualities and principles one thinks are desirable. The valuing process is a means by which the individual balances the necessity of purposeful action with the idealized concept of himself and his direction. Within the past 15 years several authors have published discussions and techniques providing professionals with a means for enhancing student awareness of values, the valuing process, and the importance of both in developing the self-concept. Charles (1976) comments that these strategies help students to clarify their values and to know consciously what they believe subconsciously.

Values clarification is a process that focuses on the student's particular mode of reaching decisions and the special import he places on actions and goals. One of the strengths of this type of approach is that it does not advocate a special set of values which are to supersede those of the student. The approach concentrates on the process so that the student becomes aware of the value, its relationship to other values, and fundamental aspects of change should the student decide to modify his beliefs. The process, according to Raths, Harmin, and Simon (1966), consists of three main behaviors and seven steps.

1. Choosing one's beliefs and behaviors.
   a. choosing freely.
   b. choosing from alternatives.
   c. choosing after thoughtful consideration of the consequences of each alternative.
2. Prizing one's beliefs and behaviors.
   a. prizing and cherishing one's choice.
   b. prizing and affirming one's choice publicly when appropriate.
3. Acting on one's beliefs.
   a. acting with purpose.
   b. acting with a consistent pattern.

An additional strength of values clarification rests on the numerous activities that have been suggested by advocates. The activities, games, or strategies place students in all of the above seven steps. They certainly are applicable to classes for adolescent and adult groups and have been used with elementary grade students. We would recommend that teachers and counselors review the activities carefully if they attempt to engage certain individuals with disabilities, as mental ability and emotional factors are variables in the anticipated results.

We do not have the space to review the numerous activities contained in Raths, Harmin, and Simon (1966), Simon, Hawley, and Britton (1971), and Simon, Howe, and Kirschenbaum (1972). Their labels should be enough to entice the reader:

First Experiences
Alligator River
Proud Whip
Fallout Shelter
I Am Lovable and Capable

The stories and student responses not only emphasize values but they cross such competency areas as communication, self-awareness, and problem solving to name a few. They also serve as a magnet of student interest into the academic areas that are used to report, observe, record, write, and defend one's position. A skilled teacher or counselor will be able to use values clarification as an adjunct to both the instructional and counseling portions of the curriculum.

CONCLUSION

As one reads through the subcompetencies and teaching techniques for the personal-social skills, he becomes aware that they are intertwined with each other. Self-awareness facilitates self-confidence, achievng independence requires problem solving, adequate communication assists in maintaining interpersonal relationships. The subcompetencies also interact with the teaching techniques but at a level that we cannot fully measure and describe.

In order for the teacher and counselor to get the most out of any one technique or combination of learning strategies, he must establish a sense of trust that permeates the classroom. This fundamental sense of trust is essentially important in those situations in which the individual with a disability has been integrated with normal students. We have identified enough instances in the everyday conduct of affairs for the reader to realize that some students are more vulnerable than others, merely because they manifest some behavior or physical sign that distinguishes them from the larger group. Any one injury or insult to the student's sense of integrity only serves to insulate him from those strategies that are intended to expand his awareness. Certainly remarks will be made, feelings will be hurt, and things will be misunderstood as the student progresses through the educational system. But, these events can be tolerated and used to broaden oneself if the teacher and counselor can convey the feeling and understanding that the student is important, valuable, and necessary. Indeed, all the strategies and activities would be nothing without him!

Occupational Guidance and Preparation

Previous chapters have briefly discussed the vocational adjustment problems of handicapped individuals, as well as certain characteristics related to their vocational functioning. It is a well-known fact that handicapped individuals have significant employment problems after leaving school. According to Levitan and Taggart (1977), only two of five handicapped individuals (40%) are employed during a typical year, compared with three-fourths of the able-bodied (75%). They suggest special training be limited to jobs that are good prospects for handicapped individuals and that better jobs are needed so that economic independence can be assured. Thus, we must begin our occupational efforts earlier in the handicapped individuals' school experiences if they are to compete for meaningful employment in today's marketplace.

The six occupational competencies we have identified as important to the career development of handicapped individuals are listed as follows with their respective competency number in parentheses.

Knowing and Exploring Occupational Possibilities (**17**)
Selecting and Planning Occupational Choices (**18**)
Appropriate Work Habits and Behaviors (**19**)
Exhibiting Appropriate Work Habits and Behaviors (**19**)
Physical-Manual Skills (**20**)
Obtaining a Specific Occupational Skill (**21**)
Seeking, Securing, and Maintaining Employment (**22**)

The Occupational Guidance and Preparation curriculum area includes those abilities that are necessary for effective job selection, satisfaction, and functioning. Occupational Guidance and Preparation is what many often define as career education, and while we believe this curriculum area needs much more attention than is presently the case in most schools, it must be amalgamated accordingly with Daily Living and Personal-Social Skills training to assure the individual's total career development. A combination of academic and work-study training is simply not sufficient in today's complex society unless the career education concepts that we propose are infused through the curriculum.

The six competencies comprising this curriculum area can be divided into three that are occupational *guidance* and three that are occupational *preparation* in nature. There are 27 subcompetencies comprising five of the competencies, whereas Obtaining a Specific Occupational Skill does not include an array of subcompetencies, since it is so dependent on the area in which the individual is being trained. Attention will be directed toward this competency later in the chapter.

In the past, handicapped individuals were all too often pigeonholed into an array of stereotyped occupations. Persons with visual handicaps were expected to tune pianos or sell pencils; deaf people to work in noisy factories; mentally retarded people to be busboys or maids at the best; and the orthopedically disabled to work in sedentary occupations, such as on an assembly line or simple office work. Society has greatly underestimated the real potentials of many handicapped individuals, and many unfortunate injustices have resulted because of prejudices, misjudgments, and plain ignorance. Hopefully, these mistakes of the past will be ameliorated as career education becomes a reality across the land for all individuals, including those with handicaps.

This chapter, like the two previous ones, will discuss each of the competencies and subcompetencies comprising our career education model. Narrative suggestions relative to objectives and instructional and guidance activities that might be used are presented. Activity Tips are presented throughout the chapter as teaching examples, as are separate sections on specific occupational guidance and preparation techniques for handicapped individuals. These techniques provide useful suggestions for teaching the student the competencies present below. Once again, the reader is cautioned that these are only suggestions and that the best technique depends on the unique situation and clientele of each helping person.

COMPETENCIES

Knowing and Exploring Occupational Possibilities (17)

Individuals must have a broad perspective of the world of work before they can make satisfying and realistic occupational choices. This competency is closely allied to the career awareness and exploration stages of career education. Students should begin exploring the world of work and specific occupations almost immediately after beginning school. The greater the awareness of jobs and their reinforcing values, the more likely they will develop a motivation and appreciation of the dignity of work and an identi-

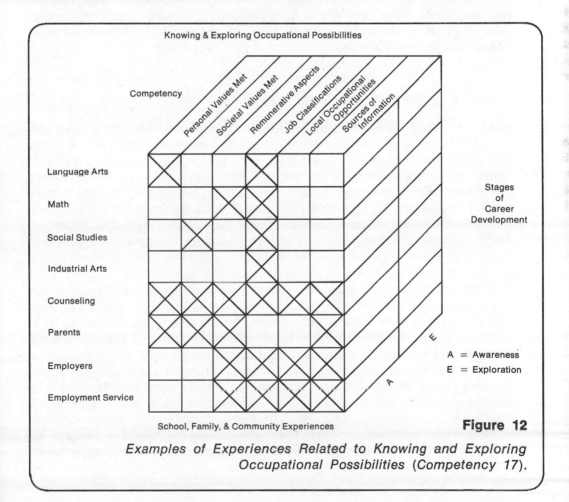

Figure 12

Examples of Experiences Related to Knowing and Exploring Occupational Possibilities (Competency 17).

fication as a part of the occupational world. School personnel, in conjunction with family and community resources, must provide a wide array of awareness and exploration opportunities (i.e., field trips, films, speakers, literature, summer work, role playing, and others) so that occupational possibilities are presented for the student's knowledge and exploration.

A wide variety of individuals should participate in making the student aware of occupational possibilities. The elementary teacher can relate various subject matter to job information. She can also elicit the assistance of the student's parents, employers, and employees who work in various settings throughout the community. Many pamphlets and other media can be used. As students progress in their awareness of occupational possibilities, actual exploration of jobs of interest can be offered in school, family, and community settings. Ideally, most persons who participate in the awareness activities should be involved in assisting students to explore, through hands-on experiences, special interest areas. Figure 12 illustrates what school, family, and community experiences might be provided to assist the student in acquiring the various subcompetencies comprising the competency "knowing and exploring occupational possibilities." The major subcompetencies are as follows:

17.1. *Identifying the Personal Values Met through Work*

Students should learn very early that many personal needs and values can be met by work, which can become a personally meaningful part of one's life. At the same time, they must also learn that some personal needs and values may have to be gratified through leisure and other pursuits. One of the major goals should be to help the student identify and choose a personally meaningful set of work values that foster a desire to be a productive member of society. Values such as a sense of fulfillment, self-sufficiency, worth, positive self-concept, success, self-support, acceptance by others, satisfying social relationships, importance, independence, and monetary gratification are examples of needs that can be met through working. Elementary students can be exposed to the personal needs and values that present workers have met on their jobs through field trips and classroom visits, providing interactions with various types of employed people. Students can begin identifying the kind of personal values they presently possess and how they see themselves meeting their needs through work. It is important in small and large group discussions that students hear about the choices of others and how they arrive at their decisions. Parents are also important in this endeavor. They can discuss the positive aspects of their jobs and what they are missing and wish existed (e.g., more responsibility, variety, physical activity). They should explain how the attempt to meet these missing values and needs is being met. At the secondary level, students who are on job sites and former employed students can be asked to discuss with the class the many features of their jobs. Other objectives that are related to this subcompetency are being able to assist students to recognize the importance of work for: a. economic functioning, and b. building self-esteem.

17.2. Identifying the Societal Values Met through Work

Students should be introduced early to the ways workers affect and help society through their contributions. Students should learn that they can become a contributor to society by producing goods and services that help people to meet their needs. Teaching activities can focus on specific ways individuals from various occupational categories contribute to the betterment of society (e.g., as police officers, fire fighters, food service workers, janitors, farmers, warehouse workers, assembly line workers, clerks, busboys, nurses aides). It is important to cover a wide array of jobs, including those requiring various amounts of skill and training. In this way, students can learn that everyone, no matter what she does, contributes meaningfully to society. Each week, one or more jobs can be highlighted, relative to their societal contributions, through field trips, speakers, and/or class discussions. Representatives of unions and industries, government, the Chamber of Commerce, small businesses, and parents should be extensively involved. Other objectives related to this subcompetency are: a. the ways workers on different jobs are interdependent, and b. the rewards of different occupations.

17.3. Identifying the Remunerative Aspects of Work

Elementary students in general seldom consider the differences among jobs in regard to pay. As students become older and their needs are more clearly defined, this subcompetency takes on an added significance. Inherent in this process is the understanding that remuneration often depends upon such factors as the demand and supply of workers for the job, community needs for the services or goods provided by the worker, and skill from training and/or formal education needed to perform the job. It is important for the student to understand reasons people are paid to work and why there are different pay rates for different jobs. This subcompetency relates to several of those associated with competency 1, managing family finances, in that students can calculate the amount of money they would receive from engaging in an occupation of interest to them and relate it to making wise and necessary expenditures, paying taxes, and the like. Resource persons and parents can assume an important role in the realistic aspects of this subcompetency. Other objectives should include identifying: a. the different kinds of wages (e.g., piece rate, hourly wage, weekly or monthly wage), and b. what personal needs can be met with a salary expected from jobs of interest to them.

```
ACTIVITY TIP: Require each student to secure information
on one job of interest per week for several weeks each
semester. A "Job Information Sheet" should be developed
and then kept by the student. The name of each job inves-
tigated should be recorded on the left side of a ruled sheet
of paper. For each job, the following information is re-
corded: company, salary, training required, hours worked,
and job duties. (Note: This information might be taken
from the Job Analysis Form presented on p. 224 if
it is used.) Parents can help the student investigate the
jobs and complete the sheet. Each week, a class discussion
covers the jobs investigated and possible reasons for
their salary level. A master list of community jobs can be
developed to depict pertinent information relative to
their remunerative aspects.
```

17.4. Understanding How Jobs Are Classified into Different Occupational Systems

Students should be informed during the elementary years about the rudiments of the major categories of jobs, particularly those relevant to their specific interests. At first, jobs can be classified primarily as white or blue collar, skilled or unskilled, and according to type of work, training, or required education. For students in secondary programs, occupational information about job and occupational clusters, which is contained in the *Dictionary of Occupational Titles* (DOT) (1977), *Occupational Outlook Handbook* (1978), and other guides, can add more specificity to classroom activities. A representative from the local employment service should be requested to explain the use of the major job categories and major criteria of other occupational classification systems. Students should be involved in organizing and participating with employers in a careers day program to observe how jobs are classified. Bulletin boards, newspapers, and other media can be used to illustrate different occupational systems. An objective associated with this subcompetency would be to identify education, training, and reimbursement related to various occupational categories.

17.5. Identifying Occupational Opportunities Available Locally

Students should be made aware of the nature of jobs in their community throughout their school career. After identifying community sources of occupational information, students should be requested to secure information from one source for a period of time and write it down, post it on a bulletin board, and present it to the other class members. Newspaper ads, radio announcements, flyers, and community job surveys are examples of such sources. This will enable the student to firmly understand and use all community sources of occupational information while learning those types of jobs and their availability. A close inspection of the nature of the various jobs that are available helps the student learn more about the world of work, job differences, and requirements. Other objectives associated with this subcompetency are for students to: a. identify appropriate sources of occupational information, and b. determine appropriate methods of securing and using such information.

17.6 Identifying Sources of Occupational Information

This subcompetency is closely allied to the previous one. In addition to the community sources listed above, the student should become familiar with such printed information as the *Dictionary of Occupational Titles* (1977), *Occupational Outlook Handbook,* pamphlets from various businesses and industries, and government civil service announcements. These materials provide a wealth of information, which can be brought into the classroom periodically for review and discussion, as well as being available in the school counselor's office. A number of information storage and retrieval systems have been developed. One such system, the *Wisconsin Instant Information System for Students and Counselors,* employs aperture cards, microfilm mounted in an aperture, or keypunch cards. It includes occupational information about a number of nonprofessional jobs and training resources. Another excellent service is provided by commercial publishers, who have developed a host of materials utilizing filmstrips, games, records/cassettes, and guides that require students to identify: a. the kinds of information available from each source, and b. how sources can be used to obtain specific information about a particular job.

Selecting and Planning Occupational Choices (18)

With a broad perspective of the world of work and the development of a positive set of work values, preliminary and tentative occupational choices can begin to evolve for the individual. Although elementary children may promulgate occupational aspirations as part of their career development, it isn't until the secondary years that a serious attempt to identify and begin directing the student toward relevant occupational choices should occur. Many professionals become concerned about encouraging students to make occupational choices too early, believing that they will get pigeonholed or stereotyped by selecting inappropriate work roles. While we sincerely appreciate the concern of those who take this position, we do believe that young adolescents who have learned about and explored occupational possibilities and have developed Personal-Social Skills are ready to think seriously about their future at about the ninth grade level. The key word is *tentative* because one's choices are always changing as a person goes through the process of becoming. It is our conviction that this is an important competency because it brings greater significance to the student's educational program, while reflecting that the individual is someone worthy of societal contribution and adult functioning. Professional guidance and counseling are of paramount importance. The major subcompetencies are as follows:

18.1. *Identifying Major Occupational Needs*

As students acquire the Personal-Social Skills of self-awareness, self-confidence, socially responsible behavior, good interpersonal skills, independence, and problem-solving skills, they should be ready to identify those major occupational needs that are presently part of their work personality. They should be able to determine whether such needs as high pay, independence, achievement, praise, responsibility, authority, ability utilization, advancement, security, social service, variety, and social status are of major importance in their future work. Group discussions on the topic, supplemented with presentations by persons working in various occupations, should be provided so these decisions and others related to an appropriate type of work environment can be ascertained (e.g., outdoor vs. indoor work, blue collar vs. white collar, sedentary vs. standing, urban vs. rural settings). These discussions can serve as a basis for lively and soul searching inquiry. Another objective that can be attempted is to have students identify occupational needs that persons in occupations they are interested in tend to have.

ACTIVITY TIP: Have the class construct a list of occupational needs. Ask various members of the class to define and discuss each need. After all possible needs are identified, construct an "Occupational Needs Inventory" and hand it out to the students. Have them check which needs are "high" and "low." Each need should be explained again before it is rated. The students should then identify their six most important occupational needs. These needs will be referred to as they begin examining their occupational interests and aptitudes later on. (Note: The Minnesota Importance QUESTionnaire would be a good instrument to obtain for this activity. Information about the MIQ can be obtained from the Department of Psychology at the University of Minnesota.)

18.2. Identifying Major Occupational Interests

By ninth or tenth grade, most handicapped students should have a basic idea of occupational areas that would interest them. These decisions are related more to what they think they would like to do, for example, "help people by working in a hospital as an aide or orderly," irregardless of whether the job meets all or most occupational needs and aptitudes. If the jobs identified are not within the capability or need structure of the individual, it will be necessary to identify related but more appropriate ones later on. What is important is that students begin to focus on specific occupational areas and/or jobs based on their knowledge of occupations and self. Interest inventories can be of some value in certain instances, but for the most part, interests evolve from experiences and explorations in the work place. While occupational interests are a personal thing, students can learn how others arrived at such decisions through group interactions. Other objectives that relate to this subcompetency are to assist students to identify: a. occupations that permit the pursuit of personal interests, and b. the occupational needs that can be met from these jobs.

18.3. Identifying Occupational Aptitudes

The utilization of extensive vocational assessment techniques is needed to help students understand their vocational potentials and specific aptitudes. Prior to formalized vocational assessment, students will have had some indication of job areas that they are able to learn and perform successfully. Aptitudes or abilities in the following areas should be ascertained: verbal, numerical, spatial, form perception, clerical, motor coordination, finger dexterity, manual dexterity, and mechanical. *The General Aptitude Test Battery* (GATB) of the U. S. Employment Service is one instrument for identifying the individual strengths and weaknesses of some students. For others, work sample batteries are particularly beneficial and provide a better indication of aptitudes than standardized test batteries, such as the *GATB*. A substantial number of vocational assessment systems are now on the market and will be discussed in greater detail in the Occupational Guidance Techniques section. Another objective associated with this subcompetency should be to assist the student to identify ways of developing needed aptitudes for occupational interests.

18.4. Identifying Requirements of Appropriate and Available Jobs

With a knowledge of sources of occupational information (subcompetency 6) and their major occupational needs, interests, and aptitudes, students should be ready to review the specific requirements and characteristics of appropriate and available jobs. Publications such as the *Dictionary of Occu-*

pational Titles (1977) should be useful for individual and group sessions. These activities can begin seriously during the tenth grade and provide stimulus for independent job searching and decision making. Vocational assessment continues to occupy an important dimension to realistic decision making and planning, as does community resource personnel, who can give an in-depth personal analysis of the job's characteristics. A wide range of commercial games, materials, and packages are available for students. Another objective that should be attempted is to help students identify alternate, related occupations for which they are best qualified.

18.5. *Making Realistic Occupational Choices*

Experiences from the previous subcompetency will help students discover many jobs that really do not meet their occupational needs, interests, or aptitudes. For those that do, a second level of decision needs to be made relative to those of highest preference. The demand for the occupation, required education and training, and other factors become significant at this level. Students should learn the career ladder that the occupation offers and occupations for which they might qualify. These tentative occupational choices should be based on an analysis of the whole person and be systematically arrived at with student, parent, employer, and school personnel input. Professional guidance and counseling is important for this subcompetency. Another objective that should be attempted is for the individual to be able to identify specific work sites where the job(s) of choice is available and to try out the job.

Exhibiting Appropriate Work Habits and Behaviors (19)

This competency is one that transcends the entire educational chain from the early elementary years through adulthood and can be taught by everyone responsible for the individual's career development. Work habits are more than study habits, although there are many similar features. School personnel should make it a point to emphasize to all students the necessity of developing work habits and behaviors that will be needed when they begin responsible jobs. At certain times, it may be advantageous to simulate working environments in the school setting to illustrate the kinds of expectations employers have of competent workers. Field trips and class speakers should also be used for these purposes, and parents can play an important role. The major subcompetencies are as follows:

19.1. *Following Directions*

Employers expect their employees to be able to accurately follow directions. These may be given either verbally or in writing and will range from very simple one-step directions to those that are complex and require several steps to remember and complete. The use of gaming and role-playing techniques is particularly effective in developing these skills. Exercises will need to begin early and be repeated intermittently throughout the grade levels so that the skills are learned and retained, particularly for lower ability students. They should be gradually made more complex as lower order directions are learned. Another objective should be for the student to be able to perform a series of tasks in the home requiring simple to complex written instructions.

19.2. Working with Others

The inability to get along with co-workers and supervisors is one of the most common reasons people fail on their jobs. It is critical that teaching environments provide the opportunity for students to interact in a manner requiring purposeful cooperative efforts in ways similar to the work place. Students must learn work expectations, and the school is a fertile ground

---

ACTIVITY TIP: Set up an assembly line operation with the assistance of industrial workers from the community. The work should be as meaningful as possible, either from the factory or school. Have the workers explain their jobs, particularly as they relate to this competency area. Initiate the work and assess the students on their ability to work along with others, accept supervision, and other subcompetencies that relate to this competency. Some students may be supervisors or assume other roles associated with this type of work. At the end of the day, class discussions should ensue about the group's performance and future efforts. Each student should be rated on work habits and behaviors and provided feedback individually by the teacher to learn strong points and those needing improvement. (Note: Further discussion and ideas related to this type of activity are provided later in the chapter.)

---

for teaching these interactive and cooperative skills. Cooperative work projects and simulated work places can be established to illustrate and promote the development of these skills. Field trips, role playing, and group discussions can be used to demonstrate and discuss the reasons for working with others, individuals' importance in cooperative efforts, and identify positive and negative aspects of working together. Another objective might be to require students to engage in team games or sports where a cooperative spirit is necessary to win the game and to identify critical features of the success of the team.

19.3. Working at a Satisfactory Rate

It is important for the student to learn that people are employed to make money for the employer. This requires that work be done correctly and with sufficient speed. It is important that teachers require students to complete certain work activities within specific time frames in order to form the habit, as well as learn the concept. Time standards can be established for various work tasks in and out of the school and the student's progress charted until criterion is met. Students can participate in establishing reasonable time standards so they understand how and why time or piece rates are determined. Employers and workers are important in conveying the importance of this subcompetency, especially as it relates to earning more money if the job permits. Other objectives associated with this subcompetency should be to help the student identify: a. satisfactory rates required for various jobs of interest, and b. reasons jobs must be performed at certain rates of speed.

19.4. Accepting Supervision

This subcompetency is related to previous ones but is specific to the types of supervision in the work place. This can vary from infrequent and indirect supervision to very frequent direct types. Supervision can be constructive, critical, or unfair. It is important for the student to understand the various forms of supervision and how one should react to these types under different conditions. Role playing provides a viable method for presenting students with various situations and types of supervision so they can learn appropriate ways of responding. After acting out the situation, a group discussion can be used to examine the response and develop other methods of handling the situation. The teacher can also assume various roles of supervising the class members and then gain reaction later to the method. Other objectives that can be attempted for students are for them to: a. observe supervisory policies in several work places and discuss them later with the class, and b. identify various responses that can be used for various types of supervisory practices.

19.5. Recognizing the Importance of Attendance and Punctuality

The classroom situation can be organized to continually emphasize this subcompetency and illustrate the consequences in the work place. A classroom time clock is one method that can be used to promote this concept. The student should learn the importance of attendance and punctuality to the employer (e.g., loss of production time, business income, and meeting deadlines). Students should learn acceptable and unacceptable reasons for lateness and absenteeism, and what to do in both situations. Once again, employers and workers from various businesses and industries can be very effective in presenting their own cases and company policies. Another objective that students should be required to meet is to develop a mock company policies and procedures handbook regarding important work responsibilities of employees.

19.6. Meeting Demand for Quality Work

Students will need to know about quality standards for various types of jobs, particularly those that interest them. They should be expected to meet such standards on their work assignments, understand when and why such standards are not achieved, and work until the standards are met or it is ascertained they are unable to perform at that level. During the elementary years, work projects should be established with quality expectations. Students can be assigned as checkers to ascertain whether work has met the requirements and discussions conducted to point out problems. During the secondary years, job explorations and try-outs should establish expected criteria and the student evaluated under these conditions. Another objective of this subcompetency should be to have the student observe community jobs and their quality standards and present findings in class discussions.

19.7. Demonstrating Occupational Safety

Many employers believe that employing handicapped people will present safety hazards for the company. They are afraid the handicapped individual will have more accidents and that they will be held liable. Thus, considerable emphasis must be given to this subcompetency to minimize the number of potential accidents that could occur and prompt the individual's dismissal. Films, field trips, role playing, and class discussions are particularly important in helping the student to understand potential safety hazards and the necessary precautions needed to avoid unnecessary accidents. Before placement on a community job-site, students should be thoroughly prepared to handle all conceivable accidents that could occur at the work place. It is recommended that this subcompetency be taught at all levels of the school program so that by the time the students leave school, they are well versed in safety practices. Other objectives associated with this subcompetency should require the student to identify: a. major reasons for practicing safety on the job, and b. potential safety hazards that exist in various types of occupations.

Physical-Manual Skills (20)

The types of occupations the majority of handicapped individuals obtain require physical stamina, endurance, coordination, strength, and dexterity. Most jobs available to the lower ability student will require considerable fine or gross motor dexterity, standing, pulling, pushing, lifting, and carrying abilities. The development of adequate physical-manual skills should begin shortly after the handicapped student enters school. Purposeful class activities should be designed to promote the use and development of these skills and, in the process, help students experience a great deal of personal success, pride, and satisfaction. Thus, for many handicapped students, a concerted focus needs to be made in this area. The major subcompetencies are as follows:

20.1. Demonstrating Satisfactory Balance and Coordination

The physical education instructor could assume a major responsibility in evaluating and designing specific individual activities for improving each student's physical capacities. For the more physically involved, consultative services from a registered occupational therapist may be needed so that specific tasks can be designed to measure and develop balance and coordination skills. Students should be required to keep a cumulative record of their performance in the various activities so progress and level can be maintained and understood by each student, family, and instructor. Competitive games and charts may be beneficial to encourage and motivate students by drawing attention to the importance of these skills. Other objectives that should be met are to have students identify: a. the relationship between balance and coordination to the world of work and job performance, and b. requirements of various jobs.

20.2. Demonstrating Satisfactory Manual Dexterity

There are a number of manual dexterity tests on the market that may assist the school counselor, special educator, or whoever is designated for direct-

ACTIVITY TIP: Use the Purdue Pegboard to evaluate and then to motivate the students to develop their manual dexterity skills. Establish a friendly atmosphere of competition with individual and group charts illustrating the students' progress each testing session. Administer the test in a nonthreatening, game-like manner. Give the student three trials to improve herself, using positive challenges and encouragement. Let the student keep the test sheet after recording her right hand, left hand, both hands, and assembly scores. The test should be administered monthly and used to plan physical activities with the student that may enhance physical-manual skills development. (Note: Other tests, including work samples, may be used in a similar manner.)

ing the development of this important skill. The *Purdue Pegboard, Stromberg, O'Connor Tests, Minnesota Rate of Manipulation, Daily Sensorimotor Training Activities* (Stanwix House), *Frostig Move-Grow-Learn* (J. A. Preston), *Pennsylvania Bi-Manual,* and the *Wide Range Employment Sample Test* are examples of standardized and acceptable instruments for evaluating and developing manual dexterity. These instruments should be used early and continue throughout the school program by serving as a basis for determining what work tasks are within the physical capabilities of the student. Other objectives are to assist the student to identify: a. occupations requiring a fair degree of manual dexterity that are of interest, and b. reasons for developing a sufficient degree of dexterity for occupational and community life.

20.3. Demonstrating Satisfactory Stamina and Endurance

This skill is important because most jobs require a given amount of physical and mental stamina and endurance. The physical education instructor can assume a significant role in designing special programs to develop adequate skills in this area. Like the previous subcompetencies, students should be an active participant in their program, charting progress and their attainment of criterion levels of performance. This type of program can be extended to the home where purposeful tasks and responsibilities can be designed that also relate to other subcompetencies. There are several commercial programs available for this subcompetency but are generally unnecessary if the school personnel develop the resources and activities within and outside of the schools to promote these skills. Other objectives that should be incorporated for this subcompetency are to require the student to identify: a. jobs where stamina and endurance are absolutely critical, and b. ways of building these skills to meet individual needs.

20.4. Demonstrating Satisfactory Sensory Discrimination

Many jobs require the ability to distinguish sounds, shapes, sizes, and colors. There are several instruments and programs that have been developed to evaluate and improve skills in this area: *Daily Sensorimotor Training Activities* (Stanwix House), *Frostig Move-Grow-Learn* (J. A. Preston), *Dunnoff School Program* (Teaching Resources), *At Your Fingertips Series* (ACI Films), and others. The *Talent Assessment Program* (discussed later in this chapter) is a work sample/task battery that includes activities in this area and relates performance to vocational potential. Many teachers have also devised their own methods by using everyday objects. The *Bender-Gestalt Visual Motor Test* is recommended for diagnostic purposes to ascertain brain damage and subsequent discrimination deficiencies. Skills in this area should be evaluated and developed early in the school program. Other objectives that we suggest are for students to be able to identify: a. the need for sensory discrimination on jobs, and b. sensory discrimination needed for jobs of interest.

Obtaining a Specific Occupational Skill (21)

There are many professional workers who strongly believe that students should not be prepared to leave the formal educational system with a saleable, entry level occupational skill. Their arguments seem to center around the belief that skill training can be best provided later, that there are too many other types of learning necessary, and that students are too young to be directed toward specific occupational training in the secondary program. While we can admit that these arguments have some degree of validity, it is our contention that at least in the case of most handicapped individuals, the acquisition of a skill is extremely necessary for the following reasons:

1. There are limited training facilities for handicapped persons beyond the secondary level with specialists who can effectively meet the many needs of handicapped individuals.
2. Many post-secondary programs may not appeal to handicapped persons because their facilities are unattractive and dehumanizing, requirements for service are too stringent or unnecessary, the process is too long, or the handicapped person doesn't like being mixed with other more severe problems.
3. Acquiring a specific occupational skill demonstrates to the student, parents, instructors, employers, and significant others that she does have the ability to learn a saleable skill.
4. Training in a specific occupational skill results in the development and improvement in other competency areas (e.g., self-confidence, socially responsible behavior, interpersonal skills, independence, problem solving, communication skills, occupational awareness, work habits and behaviors, and physical-manual skills).
5. Training some handicapped individuals for similar occupational skills of nonhandicapped workers does, in some cases, require more time and diligent effort.
6. It results in a more meaningful curriculum emphasis and makes other instruction more relevant and reality-based.
7. It provides the handicapped student with an extra start on nonhandicapped individuals whom they will be competing against for similar jobs and who have certain advantages over handicapped individuals.
8. It can reveal higher order potentials that can be pursued after the secondary program with training of a more substantial nature.

9. It helps eliminate unfeasible occupational choices early enough so other planning and training more appropriate to the individual can be offered.

Students should generally obtain a specific occupational skill during the high school years. Implicit in the selection of an appropriate training area is a fostering of sufficient self and occupational awareness and interests in addition to the other daily living, personal-social, and occupational skills that are important to the growth of a work personality. Selection should not be random and ill-conceived, but rather a carefully designed process of career development in which student, parents, instructors, and significant others are in general agreement.

Instruction in the Daily Living Skills curriculum area may have revealed special interests and aptitude for occupations that are in the clerical, maintenance, personal care, food service, clothing and textiles, service, recreation and leisure, or transportation fields. Instruction in the Personal-Social curriculum area should reveal the most suitable work environment for the individual (i.e., noisy, calm, pressured, interactive, flexible, restrictive, closely supervised, routine, reinforcing, and impersonal). The Occupational Guidance and Preparation curriculum area should have reflected the student's work values, needs, interests, choices, work habits and behaviors, and physical capacities. Thus, in the process of "becoming," a work personality emerges and forms to the extent that reasonable training choices can be determined.

A number of curriculum guides are on the market that can be used with most handicapped students. They are available in such areas as clothing services, automotive, baking, food preparation, small appliance repairs, small engines, welding, and construction. Thus, vocational education personnel, with assistance from special educators and others, should be able to assume a major role in the instruction of most handicapped students for a specific occupational skill.

Seeking, Securing, and Maintaining Employment (22)

One of the major problems former students with handicaps experience after leaving the formal educational system is their inability to seek, secure, and maintain employment. Efforts at teaching this competency apparently have not been concentrated enough so that students retain this knowledge and ability over time. It is extremely unfortunate, after receiving extensive educational services, that this is many times the major downfall of handicapped individuals in the community. A considerably greater amount of emphasis should be given to this competency in high school programs by beginning its instruction in the tenth grade and continuing each semester thereafter.

There are many commercial materials available for teaching this competency, although school personnel may want to develop their own. The major subcompetencies are as follows:

22.1. Searching for a Job

The ability to develop a logical step-by-step method of searching for a job is a crucial subcompetency. Sources of information about possible jobs is an initial beginning. A concentrated effort can be provided to develop this subcompetency by using bulletin boards depicting these steps and sources of information, field trips to agencies that help people find jobs, role playing, games, and guest speakers on these subjects. Newspaper ads, job descriptions and announcements, other advertisements, and commercial materials on job-seeking skills are available. The Singer Company has produced a *Job Survival Skills Package* and the Minneapolis Rehabilitation Center has developed a job-seeking skills package that also merits consideration. Other objectives related to this subcompetency include: a. identifying steps involved in searching for a job, and b. identifying a specific job through sources and follow through on a job lead.

22.2. Applying for a Job

An important objective in vocational programming should be to prepare the individual to apply for a job. There has been a tendency in the past for professional workers to intervene on the individual's behalf. Mastery of this subcompetency is another indice reflecting the student's ability and independence for vocational functioning. To demonstrate this, the student must become familiar with job application forms and procedures involved in applying for jobs. Beginning in at least the tenth grade, emphasis should be placed on learning words typically used on application forms and interviews. A great deal of time should be spent reviewing and completing application forms, learning a job vocabulary, role playing, and collecting personal data needed for job applications. Another objective that students should be required to meet is to identify those factors they consider important to them in applying for jobs.

22.3. Interviewing for a Job

This important skill is so inextricably related to the other subcompetencies that it requires much more than cursory attention by educators. The use of community resources, particularly employers and workers, is highly recommended in advance of the student's actual attempt(s) at interviewing. The student must understand and learn thoroughly the steps in securing an interview, what to say and do when requesting an interview on the phone or in person, and then what to say and how to handle herself in the actual situation. Role playing, group discussions, films, speakers and demonstrators, games and commercial materials, videotape, and other techniques are all highly recommended to present this subcompetency to students. Other objectives for students should be: a. complete a simulated job interview in an actual business establishment, and b. practice dressing for and transporting self to job interviews.

22.4. Adjusting to Competitive Standards

Students must learn that securing a job does not mean it will be maintained unless performance continues at the standard expected of other workers. This subcompetency can be overlooked, but former students often lose their jobs because of a misunderstanding of what is expected of workers and how they can advance themselves in position and pay. It would be very beneficial to have employers and workers present this kind of information and conduct on-site visits to various job locations to observe such conditions. The student must be aware of the improvement in performance that is expected and how this can be best achieved. Other objectives for students should be for them to be able to identify: a. jobs of interest and their expected standards and improvement, and b. how improvements can be achieved by the individual.

22.5 Maintaining Post-School Occupational Adjustment

This subcompetency is concerned with the potential problems former students may encounter once situated on a job and how they can be dealt with

ACTIVITY TIP: Have students invite former handicapped students back to school to discuss their jobs (or lack of them). The students should be responsible for seeking the former students, inviting them, and developing a set of questions relating to post-school adjustment. Discussions should include the types of problems the former students are encountering, how they handle them, what they feel the students are going to have to do to be successful, and the positive aspects about their present career functioning. Later on, students should have the opportunity to go out into the community with the former students to observe them working (and perhaps living) on their actual jobs. (Note: The former students should also be encouraged to bring in significant people from the community who helped them in their adjustment. It is quite possible, however, that many former students will not be cooperative in such an activity because of their desire to no longer be identified as a handicapped person.)

effectively. Former students are a fertile source of information related to the most significant adjustments they have needed to make. Role play depicting these major problem areas is a recommended technique to use in illustrating effective behaviors. Students should be encouraged to keep a notebook of techniques for future use. This subcompetency should be given considerable emphasis during the latter part of the high school program. Another objective for the student would be to identify sources of assistance for problems that cannot be personally resolved.

OCCUPATIONAL GUIDANCE TECHNIQUES

The three competencies comprising this category are knowing and exploring occupational possibilities (**17**); selecting and planning occupational choices (**18**); and seeking, securing, and maintaining employment (**22**). Each of these competencies and their subcompetencies was discussed in the previous section. You may appreciate the complex nature involved in being able to learn each of these competencies. Knowing about and exploring a wide variety of occupations, for example, is prerequisite to being able to select and plan *appropriate* occupational choices. Thus, students should begin to learn about occupations early and explore many of them through hands-on experiences. Then, tentative occupational choices can be logically determined in the early high school years. The other competency—seeking, securing, and maintaining employment—should be emphasized throughout the high school years rather than be a culminating experience.

School counselors are obvious persons for being responsible for the occupational guidance activities and experiences for handicapped students. Special educators will need to work closely with the counselors and, in many instances, engage in many of these activities with the handicapped student. They will also need to serve in a consultative capacity to the counselor so that appropriate types of experiences are provided. A publication entitled *Guidance, Counseling and Support Services for High School Students with Physical Disabilities* (Foster, Szoke, Kapisovsky, & Kriger, 1977) is recommended.

Attempts to generate lists of specific jobs appropriate for various types of handicapped individuals are generally fruitless. Blind people work in hundreds of different occupations at all levels, including such jobs as phone repair persons, welder, lathe operator, teacher, lawyer, farmer, and others. Homebound individuals have typically been engaged in small crafts and telephone answering or sales work but with the advent of the computer, opportunities as programmers and data entry operators have become available (Kokaska, 1976). A study by Phillips (1975) identifies 515 specific and distinct career opportunities for the deaf in three types of organizations: business and industry, professional and trade associations, and institutions of higher education for the deaf. Occupations such as scientists, teachers, accountants, machine trades, bench work, and clerical and sales are examples of the many possibilities that exist for this group. There is probably no limit to what most handicapped individuals could achieve in employment if there were greater efforts to expand their occupational horizons and provide more relevant and challenging training and employment opportunities.

Occupational guidance should be a continuous and clearly visible part of the educational program. During the elementary years, occupational literature, films and filmstrips, field trips, class speakers, class discussions, career games, home assignments, and class projects and exercises can be provided to make students aware of various occupations and their requirements. During the junior high school years, these activities should continue but the guidance area takes on an even more important dimension. Vocational counseling, vocational assessment, and hands-on work experiences should be initiated for these students. During the high school years, even greater attention should be given to the development of occupational choices, community work experiences, and methods of finding and securing jobs.

Students who have not acquired the three occupational guidance competencies will probably experience considerable difficulties after they leave school. Rehabilitation and other vocationally-oriented programs will likely be necessary to assist handicapped individuals to develop these competencies adequately. This section presents some of the techniques or strategies for helping handicapped students learn more about their vocational potentials and to make rational career decisions.

Counseling

Decision making has been described as the cornerstone of career education. If individuals can be provided with appropriate educational experiences, they should be able to make more effective decisions about their future career and other matters that they will encounter throughout their lifetime. Individuals will be able to learn how to take risks, solve problems, and select from alternatives, if they know enough about themselves, their potentials, and occupational possibilities available in the real world.

It is unfortunate that handicapped students receive such limited purposeful counseling throughout the school years. Effective counseling holds the promise of humanizing the curriculum by permitting a greater understanding of the individual's variety of needs, aspirations, and potentials. The counseling of handicapped persons is essentially no different than for anyone else. We cannot expect it to remain the exclusive purview of the school and rehabilitation counselor, but rather it should be the responsibility of a variety of helping persons. Some basic principles for successfully providing this important service to handicapped persons are the following.

- Trust is the foundation upon which successful efforts take place.
- People can learn to make logical career choices and decisions.

- Helpers must afford the individual respect, understanding, and acceptance.
- Self-concept is one of the most important determinants of career/personal development.
- Individuals are capable of learning new behaviors and extinguishing inappropriate ones.
- Significant others have an important influence on one's behavior and decision making.
- One's psychological needs, beliefs, goals, and values are inextricably related to occupational decision making and satisfaction.
- A personalized, humanistic, systematic and flexible approach is needed to respond to the various characteristics and needs of handicapped individuals.
- A reciprocal relationship between counselor and counselee.
- Recognition of the fact that each student/client is unique and may need a different approach.
- It is a learning process for everyone.

Counseling handicapped individuals requires time and patience in most instances. Rapport between counselor and counselee must be established before other matters can be discussed. Vocational counseling consists of assisting the individual to learn about the world of work; determining appropriate experiences, courses, and persons who can assist in occupational awareness and exploration activities; ascertaining more specific vocational aptitudes, interests, and needs; determining occupational training areas; and instructing in job seeking and securing skills. Handicapped individuals must be heard, as they are in the best position to ascertain their interests and needs and in many respects, their abilities, too. Some important considerations in counseling handicapped individuals for occupational purposes that should be taken into account are:

1. They generally have fewer work experiences than nonhandicapped persons and, therefore, their concept of the world of work may be quite narrow.
2. Many have had a long history of failure and rejection and, therefore, may be unrealistic about their potentials and aspirations.
3. Many of the lower ability individuals may have difficulty understanding more complex verbal interchanges but will try to convey that they are comprehending what is being discussed.
4. Many lower ability individuals can benefit from shorter but more frequent interactions in which specific assignments are given.
5. Audio-visual equipment, blackboards, role playing, and other non-didatic techniques enhance counseling efforts.

The concept of empathy underlies the entire helping relationship and refers to understanding another person from that person's frame of reference. The client-centered approach of Rogers (1961) has many implications for occupational guidance. This approach focuses on the relationship between helper and helpee, which is nondirective and emphasizes the respect, understanding, and acceptance of the helper in providing a climate for experiencing, expressing, and exploring feelings and determining goals and actions. Only from unconditional positive regard (acceptance) by the helper can an individual express feelings, develop more congruence between self-concept and behavior, and begin making rational decisions about career directions. We believe effective occupational guidance and counseling requires more than providing the individual with occupational information, testing, field experiences, and the like. It should be rational, logical, and learning-oriented, involving an open human relationship whereby individuals are listened to while learning how to accept responsibility for themselves. It should be a warm, honest, and personal relationship.

Although many people give input and influence the occupational decision making of the student, a well-trained counselor or special educator is the key to helping the student make rational, realistic occupational choices and training decisions. This does not occur in one or two sessions but must be purposely built into the educational program so it evolves over a period of time and is open to change as new experiences and information are received by the student.

Vocational Testing

A great number of standardized vocational tests are presently available, many of which are useful in helping to determine the vocational aptitudes and interests of handicapped individuals. However, the more severe the handicap, the fewer the number of tests that are applicable. This is particularly true for persons with visual, hearing, and intellectual handicaps. In many instances, it will be necessary to modify tests for certain individuals (e.g., instructions, time frames, scheduling, individual rather than group administration, rapport and reinforcement emphasis, and motivation building). Any time a test is modified, caution must be exercised in its interpretation and validity.

Certain handicapped individuals must be given special consideration in vocational testing endeavors. Many visually handicapped individuals have never experienced shape, color and other visual concepts. Therefore, their set of experiences is quite different from other persons. They often lack the typical set of learning experiences and materials of most individuals. Large print tests should be used with the partially sighted. Special forms of braille tests can be ordered from the American Printing House for the Blind, 1839 Frankfort Avenue, Louisville, Kentucky 40206.

Persons with severe hearing impairments also present testing problems. It will be necessary to determine the individual's communication skills and method(s)—sign language, lip or speech reading, finger spelling. Deaf persons often have been isolated and, consequently, have a limited range of social and educational experiences. Language development may be very poor; thus, tests requiring only a basic reading level and nonverbal test (i.e., no words or items requiring only a basic reading level) are most appropriate. An interpreter may be needed to translate the instructions.

The severely mentally retarded individual presents a testing problem. These individuals have had limited experiences and may have concomitant physical handicaps, such as vision, hearing, speech, coordination, and/or cultural deprivation. Vocabulary level, attention span, frustration tolerance, anxiety, self-concept, and expectancy to fail are some possible problems that must be accounted for before and during testing.

The following discussion highlights some of the more common aptitude/performance and interest/need tests that are used with handicapped individuals.

General Aptitude Test Battery. This group test is comprised of 12 subtests measuring eight aptitudes: general learning ability, verbal, numerical, spatial perception, clerical perception, motor coordination, finger dexterity, and manual dexterity. The battery's sixth grade reading level limits its use with many handicapped individuals. Persons in wheelchairs and those who have upper extremity handicaps are limited on some tests. The GATB is available to certain nonprofit agencies, but formal training is usually required before it is released. The state employment service should be contacted for information.

Nonreading Aptitude Test Battery (NATB). This is a nonreading version of the GATB that can be administered to groups of up to six individuals. There are 14 tests measuring the same eight aptitudes as the GATB. Two deviations from the GATB are: there are no arithmetic problems, and vocabulary items are presented orally. Although the NATB was designed for disadvantaged persons, it has application for certain handicapped individuals. The physically handicapped would be limited as described previously for the GATB. Other limitations are its length of administration and interpretation. Therefore, it is not used much by the employment service. The state employment service should be contacted to ascertain its present status and usage.

Pennsylvania Bi-Manual Test. This performance test requires the individual to assemble 105 nuts and bolts and to place them into holes on a board. It reveals a number of unique motor traits by requiring fine finger dexterity, gross arm movements, and eye-hand coordination. Disassembly is also required for this timed test, which generally takes 10–15 minutes. The test is useful with blind, deaf, mentally retarded individuals and is available from American Guidance Service.

Purdue Pegboard. This performance test measures fine finger dexterity and gross movements of the hands. It requires the individual to place pins in holes with the right, left, and both hands and to assemble pins, collars, and washers on the board in a minute's time. The test takes 10–15 minutes, and there are industrial norms in percentile form. It can be used with the mentally retarded and deaf but is not appropriate with the blind. The test is available from Science Research Associates.

Crawford Small Parts Dexterity Test. This performance test measures fine eye-hand coordination and contains a board with 42 holes and three bins for pins, collars, and screws. The testee uses tweezers to pick up a pin and place it in a hole on the board and a collar over each one. After 36 pins and collars are assembled, 30 screws are placed through a plate with a screwdriver. Percentile norms are available on industrial and other groups. It is a motivating test for many individuals and a worthwhile addition for guidance endeavors. It is available from the Psychological Corporation.

Minnesota Spatial Relations Test. This test consists of four form boards and is designed to measure speed and accuracy in discriminating odd sizes and shapes for mechanical tasks. The testee places blocks in their proper places on each board. The test is timed and generally takes 15–30 minutes. The test would be appropriate for the deaf and mentally retarded but not the blind or those with upper extremity handicaps. It is available from American Guidance Service.

Revised Minnesota Paper Form Board Test. This test consists of 64 two-dimensional diagrams cut into separate pieces. It measures the mechanical ability needed for visualizing and manipulating objects in space. Each diagram has five figures with lines indicating the different shapes out of which they are made. The testee chooses the figure composed of the exact parts shown in the original diagrams. The test can be administered to a group and takes about 20–25 minutes. It is not appropriate for blind individuals, but the deaf and higher functioning retarded persons should be able to take it.

Wide-Range Interest-Opinion Test (WRIOT). The WRIOT is an inventory measuring interests ranging from unskilled through professional occupations. Eighteen cluster areas and seven work attitudes are assessed. The WRIOT has 150 items, each containing three illustrations of men and women of different racial groups engaging in various job activities. The individual selects the job she would most like to do and the one least preferred. The inventory can be administered to groups in 50–60 minutes. No reading other than *least* and *most* and the letters *A, B,* and *C* is required. There are special instructions on use for severely mentally or physically disabled persons. It is not recommended for blind individuals. The inventory is available from Guidance Associates of Delaware.

Minnesota Importance Questionnaire. This instrument focuses on an individual's vocational needs, for example, ability utilization, achievement, activity, advancement, authority, company policies and practices. There are

210 items, and the subject is asked to choose one statement from each pair that is most representative of a characteristic for her ideal job. The last 20 questions ask the subject to indicate whether or not each of the 20 needs assessed by the instrument is important in her ideal job. The MIQ can be administered in 40 minutes and requires about a fifth grade reading level. The instrument is appropriate with most handicapped persons, although blind and lower level retarded individuals are limited in its administration. It is available from Vocational Psychology Research at the University of Minnesota.

Reading-Free Vocational Interest Inventory. This is a pictorial instrument requiring the subject to make one choice from three illustrations. There are several job cluster scales for males and also separate ones for females. The job areas were chosen from those in which mentally retarded individuals have demonstrated proficiency and productivity. There is considerable interest in this instrument, and it is being used widely throughout the country. Norms for public school, residential school, and composite populations are available. It is published by the American Association on Mental Deficiency.

Career Awareness Laboratory (CAL). This is an integrated hardware/software system consisting of six communications matrix network tables for 12 students each; 19 activity games, puzzles, and materials; 19 sound/filmstrips to introduce the basic concepts on which lab activities are based and to provide procedural instruction; three 35mm rear-screen projectors, three audio-visual tables; one group leader's manual; three games and activity books, and 12 participant workbooks. While it was not specifically designed for handicapped students, some evidence is available that would indicate it could be used with some handicapped individuals. The system assists persons to become aware of careers and engages them in decision-making activities. It is available from the Singer Education Division.

Social and Provocational Information Battery (SPIB). This is a series of nine tests and was designed to assess knowledge of skills and competencies considered important for the ultimate community adjustment of mildly retarded students. The nine tests are directly related to five long-range goals of work-study programs at the junior and senior high school level: employability, economic self-sufficiency, family living, personal habits, and communication. There has been considerable research activity by its developers. Irvin, Halpern, and Reynolds (1977) revise the battery for moderately retarded persons and find that both mildly and moderately retarded persons' knowledge of social and prevocational information can be assessed and that it is substantially related to actual performance in these domains. The SPIB is a substantial contribution to the occupational guidance area and worthy of utilization. It is available from CTB/McGraw-Hill

Most standardized vocational tests have their limitations with handicapped individuals. Even the most impeccably developed industrial tests have high reliabilities but very low predictive ability for job success. However, standardized tests of this nature do provide a benchmark and are useful for stimulating work interest and motivation and assessing problem solving, speed, accuracy, frustration tolerance, and one's approach to a work task. Interest tests are just a gauge in the process of helping the individual to identify her interests. Although there is often a tendency to attempt to find one's underlying vocational interests from standardized tests, this would be a mistake unless many other indices are also used. For some students, the *Strong Vocational Interest Blank* (*SVIB*) and the *Kuder Preference Record* may be useful, but in many instances, they require a higher reading and comprehension level than certain handicapped individuals possess. Although interest inventories can be adapted easily for use with blind individuals, there are many items that pertain to only those persons who can see. Thus, there has been little activity to develop an inventory for the blind (Bauman, 1973). One interesting project was conducted at Florida State University, which under a grant from the U.S. Office of Career Education, developed a Self-Directed Career Planning Program to increase the career planning options and opportunities for the visually handicapped. Materials and processes from the University's Curricular Career Information Service (CCIS) have been adapted for use by visually disabled students and adults in various settings (White, 1978). Used judiciously, vocational tests are an important component of occupational guidance services to handicapped individuals.

Work Evaluation

In the past several years, a substantial number of work evaluation systems have been developed to assess vocational potentials of various types of handicapped persons. Their procedures, although difficult to validate, have an advantage over most standardized vocational aptitude and interest tests because of their closer proximity to the world of work. Individuals taking work samples can more readily accept their significance to career planning, and most actuality are related to specific jobs or job families listed in the *Dictionary of Occupational Titles*. In addition, many of the systems do not require the rigid administration and interpretation that standardized tests require, permitting retesting and interpretations as needed. The work sample field is rapidly evolving and warrants serious consideration from school personnel.

The following 10 work evaluation systems have been designed in the 1960s and 1970s and are briefly presented for your information. Requests for more extensive information and costs should be directed to their publishers.

Vocational Information and Evaluation Work Samples (*VIEWS*). The VIEWS was developed by the Jewish Employment and Vocational Service, 1913 Walnut Street, Philadelphia, Pa. 19103. The system became available in 1976 and consists of a battery of hands-on activities to be used in a simulated work environment to assess the work potential of persons with learning disabilities and mental retardation. The unique contribution of the VIEWS is that it does not require a reading ability and incorporates the use of demonstration, practice, and repeated instruction to gain insight into the individual learning style and to relate it to future instructional experiences. The VIEWS reveals changes in learning and performance quality and rates while assessing vocational potential in many occupational areas. Training in the system is required.

JEVS Work Samples. This system was also developed by the Jewish Employment and Vocational Service in Philadelphia. It consists of 28 work samples. They were originally intended for use with culturally disadvantaged youth because the typical tests given by the state employment service were not adequate for this population. They were developed under contract with the U. S. Department of Labor and have been adopted by many of their offices throughout the country. The work samples have also been successful with many physically, emotionally, and mentally handicapped individuals. The samples expose the client to a variety of vocational possibilities and relate the findings to Worker Trait Groups in the *Dictionary of Occupational Titles* (1977). A 2-week training session is required for those who purchase the system.

Talent Assessment Program (TAP). This system consists of 10 work samples. They can be administered in about 2 hours to most handicapped individuals. The system was developed by Wilton Nighswonger, 7015 Colby Avenue, Des Moines, Iowa 50311, to assess the individual's functional characteristics applicable to work in industrial, technical, and service areas. Several individuals can be tested at the same time. Directions are given orally. The system consists of a battery of perceptual and dexterity tests measuring fine and gross finger dexterity, visual and tactile discrimination, and retention of details. It is not intended to be a comprehensive system but does seem to reliably assess many industrial-type aptitudes that are reflective of an individual's vocational potential in these areas. Training is required to use the system and takes 1 1/2 days.

MICRO-TOWER. This is a system of 13 work samples for individuals with mild (educable) retardation through the normal range, adolescents and adults. It was developed at the Institute for Crippled and Disabled (ICD), 340 East 24th Street, New York, N.Y. 10010. A cue-stop cassette tape unit presents the instructions, and a photobook is used to illustrate related occupations and various steps within the work samples. The entire evaluation takes 3–5 days. The work samples are: bottle capping and packing; graphics illustration; making change; message taking; zip coding; payroll computation; electronic connector assembly; record checking; blueprint reading; filing;

want ads comprehension; mail sorting; and lamp assembly. A learning period is permitted before evaluation, which is an appealing feature for individuals with learning problems. There is a feedback of results to the individual, and group discussion techniques are highly encouraged as an integral part of the system. Training is not mandatory.

The Singer Vocational Evaluation System. The Singer Education Division, 80 Commerce Drive, Rochester, New York 14623, an offshoot of the Job Corps Program, began developing in 1966 a hands-on evaluation system of step-by-step programmed work tasks performed sequentially at a series of sampling stations. Reading is not required as the system uses audio-visual techniques to transmit instructions. Some of the work stations are: sample making; bench assembly, drafting, electrical wiring, plumbing and pipe-fitting; carpentry and woodworking; refrigeration, heating and air condi-tioning; soldering and welding; sales processing; needle trades; masonry; sheet metal working; cooking and baking; small engine service; medical service; cosmetology; data calculation and recording; soil testing; photo lab technician; and production machine operating. Each station relates to at least 100 DOT job titles. The system measures both interest and aptitude. More work stations are being developed, although as few as one can be purchased by interested parties. Training is not required but highly sug-gested.

Hester Evaluation System (HES). This system was developed by Edward Hester, Goodwill Industries, 120 South Ashland Boulevard, Chicago, Illinois 60607. It consists of 26 separate tests measuring 28 independent ability factors. The HES measures factor-pure abilities and integrates them with other data to relate the information to the traits corresponding to the Data-People-Things levels of the DOT. A master computer center is available to users to process the results to job possibilities listed in the DOT. The com-puter prints out a list of specific jobs within each Worker Trait Group. The performance tests can be administered in 5 hours by a competent technician. Formal training in the use of the system takes 3 days in Chicago. The system is said to be appropriate for most types of handicaps, including the blind and partially sighted.

The Valpar Component Work Sample Series. The Valpar was developed by Valpar Corporation, 655 N. Alvernon Way, Tucson, Arizona 85716. It con-sists of a series of 16 work samples with more being planned and developed. The work samples are: small tools, size discrimination, numerical sorting, upper extremity range of motion, clerical comprehension and aptitude, in-dependent problem solving, multi-level sorting, simulated assembly, whole body range of motion, tri-level measurement, eye-hand-foot coordination, soldering and inspection, money handling, integrated peer performance, electrical circuitry and print reading, and drafting. The samples are designed to provide an insight into many worker characteristics and are keyed to the Worker Trait Arrangement in the DOT. Two weeks of training is recommended but not required.

Comprehensive Occupational Assessment and Training System (COATS). The COATS is a comprehensive system developed by PREP, Inc., 1575 Parkway Avenue, Trenton, New Jersey 08628. The system has four major components: Living Skills, Work Samples, Job Matching System, and Employability Attitudes. Only the Work Samples component will be discussed here. The work samples assess each individual's interest, performance capability, and general behavior relative to various job situations and have the following titles: drafting, clerical/office, metal construction, sales, food preparation, medical services, travel services, barbering/cosmetology, small engines. All work samples can be administered in one audio-visual station, are individualized, self-paced, and computer-scored. All of the samples are removable, easy to install, and conveniently packaged in compact, lockable formica cubes.

Wide-Range Employment Sample Test (WREST). The WREST was developed in a workshop for the mentally retarded in Wilmington, Delaware and refined by Joseph Jastak. It is distributed by Guidance Associates of Delaware, 1526 Gilpin Avenue, Wilmington, Delaware 19806. It consists of 10 work samples: single and double folding, pasting, labeling, and stuffing; stapling; bottle packaging; rice measuring; screw assembly; tag stringing; swatch pasting; collating; color and shade matching; and pattern making. Its primary purpose is to evaluate dexterity and perceptual abilities. Administration time is about 1 1/2 hours; for groups, 2 hours. Industrial norms, short administration time, and precise instructions are strengths of the battery. The battery is useful for moderately and mildly limited persons. No training is required for its purchase.

McCarron-Dial Work Evaluation System. This system was developed by Lawrence McCarron and Jack Dial and is available from Commercial Marketing Enterprises, 11300 North Central, Dallas, Texas 75231. It comprises 17 separate instruments groups into five factors: verbal-cognitive, sensory, motor abilities, emotional, and integration-coping. The system attempts to assess the individual's ability to function in one of five program areas: day care, work activities, extended sheltered employment, transitional sheltered employment, and community employment. The first three factors can be assessed in 1 day; 2 weeks of systematic observation in a work setting are required for the other two factors. Training of 1–2 weeks is required, depending on the evaluator's experience.

None of these career exploration systems is a comprehensive occupational guidance system. They should be used in conjunction with techniques such as standardized tests and work experiences. However, they are a positive addition to the career development scene, bringing a new and important dimension to career education efforts. In the next few years, substantive reliability and validity information shall become available from most of the publishers of these systems to substantiate their relative merit. In the meantime, we can only suggest that school personnel and other professional workers review the various systems in their entirety and determine the ways they might be used in the career education efforts.

Job/Task Analysis

The use of job analysis and task analysis for occupational guidance may seem somewhat strange but, in our opinion, they constitute an effective method of learning about work, specific jobs, and interest areas. A job analysis is a systematic way of observing jobs to determine what the individual does, how she does it, why she does it, and the skill involved in its performance. Jobs should be analyzed precisely as they presently exist, excluding temporarily assigned tasks. The job should be described in detail, including all tasks and requirements that contribute to successfully performance. Task analysis is the process of breaking a task into smaller steps or skills required to complete the task.

Job analysis can become a powerful career awareness and exploration tool for handicapped students. During each field trip, students should be required to take along a simple job analysis form (such as the example provided on p. 224) to review the work that is observed by the group. In this way, students become aware of the major characteristics and requirements of various jobs. Student job analysis should be reviewed and discussed by the group and teacher before filling in the individual "Job Information Notebook." Students should be encouraged to ask questions of each other relative to their separate analysis. For lower ability students, peer or teacher assistance may be necessary to gather and report the proper information.

As jobs come of interest to individual students, task analysis can be undertaken to determine the minute details. Once again, students become intimately involved in the task and learn a great deal about the nature of work by themselves and from other class members. In group counseling sessions, the analysis can become a central focus of discussion and lively action. As students become more conscious and efficient in analyzing jobs, they should then be able to use and understand occupational literature and other media.

Job and task analysis, as foreboding and complex as it seems, is an important component of an occupational guidance program and should be a part of the elementary as well as the secondary program. It complements other career awareness and exploration techniques and, in our opinion, is a necessary and worthwhile endeavor for all students.

Job Analysis Form

Job Title _____   DOT Title _____
Name of Firm _____   Code Number _____
Date of Analysis _____   Name of Analyst _____

A. Description of Work Performed _____
_____
_____

B. Job Requirements. Circle number of those required and comment if needed.

1. Adding _____
2. Subtracting _____
3. Multiplying _____
4. Dividing _____
5. Make change _____
6. Use measuring devices _____
7. Read _____
8. Write _____
9. Talk _____
10. Follow instructions _____
11. Use telephone _____
12. Lift, carry, push, pull _____
13. Walk, run, climb, balance _____
14. Stoop, kneel, crouch, crawl _____
15. Stand or sit _____
16. Use hand tools _____
17. Operate machines _____
18. Other _____
19. Other _____
20. Other _____

C. Working Conditions. Circle number that describes the job and comment if needed.

1. Extremely hot _____
2. Extremely cold _____
3. Humid _____
4. Wet _____
5. Dry _____
6. Dusty and dirty _____
7. Noisy _____
8. Good lighting _____
9. Good ventilation _____
10. Tension and pressure _____
11. Distracting conditions _____
12. Hazardous _____
13. Work with others _____
14. Other _____

D. Training Required _____
E. Salary _____
F. Hours Worked _____
G. Good features of the Job _____
_____
H. Poor features of the Job _____
_____
_____
_____

Simulations of Business and Industry

Establishing a simulated business in or out of the school setting is a realistic, hands-on experience that can add considerable relevance to both occupational guidance and preparation efforts. Students can assume various roles from the "ground-up" so they can get a broad perspective and appreciation of the types of work responsibilities various jobs require.

One example of a variation of this technique is the "Career City" of the Quincy Public Schools in Illinois. Career City consists of seven mini-buildings, which are located in the Resource Center of an elementary school. A greenhouse, grocery store, bank, bakery, photography shop, barber and beauty shop, and residential house are depicted in 5' x 5' structures, painted and decorated, and transported by special education students from the senior high school program. The major objective of Career City is to supplement the classroom curriculum by providing realistic, hands-on career experiences. The learning activities that ensue provide an array of career awareness experiences for elementary children. They can deposit checks in the bank, grow flowers and vegetables in the greenhouse, and use cameras and viewers in the photography lab. Each career has a packet with all the necessary information and equipment to participate in the many learning activities. Many nonspecial education students also take advantage of this career awareness opportunity. All children seem to relate to each career much better after participating in the career awareness activities of Career City (Bocke & Price, 1976).

One activity that is particularly beneficial for early elementary age children is developing career awareness through an assembly line operation. Students can be provided with information about industry and manufacturing occupations while learning the importance of cooperation in production efforts. An assembly line permits friendly competition and pride in doing quality work that depends on the cooperative efforts of many individuals. Assembly line workers can visit the class, and field trips can be arranged to certain industries.

Another venture for elementary students is to have them set up their own school store. The Plainview Community School in Plainview, Minnesota reports their program in *The Career Education Workshop* (Johnson, 1976). Their first step in organizing the venture was to gain the approval and suggestions from their Career Education Citizen's Advisory Board. The board suggested approaching some local business about their plan for a school store, and it was wholeheartedly supported. The first order was for basic items—pencils, crayons, notebook paper, and erasers. Grades 4 through 6 were placed in charge of the store, and one sixth grade classroom was made responsible for ordering the initial supplies. A board of directors was elected to set up guidelines for operating the store. The board then elected a store manager and personnel director, who developed job assignments and duties: sales people, stock people, and an advertising department. The latter was exciting to the students because of the competition between the rooms to see which could invent the best advertising gimmicks and pro-motions. A second venture by the school was a record shop. The school asked several radio stations to save records that were no longer in use. Students made purchases in cash from the record shop or traded used paperback books. A bookstore and travel bureau were other ventures that the school developed.

Haring (1978) describes a successful teacher-designed career education program at Scottsdale High School (Arizona) that took place in an eco-nomics/free enterprise class while using career education skills and con-cepts. Two hundred seventy-five students formed their own business enter-prises, which became part of a career education program called *PROJECT WORK.* Students produced, advertised, and marketed products and pro-vided services for fellow students or community members. There were 89 companies providing products and services. When the company operation was completed, profits were divided in various ways. Some business enter-prises were corporations and paid their stockholders. Others were partner-ships and others sole proprietorships. Appropriate taxes and licensing fees were paid to the student government. PROJECT WORK was also conducted at a less sophisticated level in the lower grades. Students felt the project was helpful in making them more aware of their interests and abilities and in improving their attitudes and interest toward school and the teachers.

Business simulations can be an extremely effective way to motivate stu-dents to learn academic material, become more knowledgeable about the world of work, and develop occupational interests and skills. They also pro-vide school personnel with an excellent way of integrating handicapped students into business operations and activities with the nonhandicapped. The potentials of this technique are limited only by one's creativity, time, and financial constraints.

Career Seminar

School counselors can be particularly beneficial by conducting "Career Seminars" for handicapped students. Varelas (1976) describes these as having two major purposes: **1.** to help each student become aware of her-self by looking at her individual strengths, interests, values, successes and goals, and **2.** to acquaint students with the many different kinds of careers they may pursue. The experience can be a semi-structured process, meet-ing once per week throughout the semester. Varelas uses a modified human potential seminar group process approach, which focuses on reinforcing the positive strengths and abilities of each student. This technique requires each student to share three strengths, three successful experiences, and her three most important values in life with the group. Students also set short-term goals, which they attempt to achieve each week. A short paper is required covering five specific topics: **1.** a brief description of a career choice, **2.** education required for the career choice, **3.** expected salary of the career choice, **4.** environment and location of the career choice, and **5.** future outlook of the career choice. The key to success is to keep the group experience positive and reinforce individual strengths and abilities. Students begin questioning—"Who am I?" "What is my career choice?" It appears to be a successful method of helping students to grow socially, emotionally, and academically.

One way of fostering thinking about occupations is to have students select an object and identify all the people whose work makes it possible for that object to come into students' hands. The object may be in the category of food, shelter, clothing, toys, or equipment. For example, various occupations that relate to getting an orange into one's hands are: planter, irrigator, picker, sorter, crate maker, manufacturers of trucks or planes, shipping personnel, delivery person, and grocer. Another way of encouraging children to think about occupations is for them to list five or more that they have seen on television and which they feel might be enjoyable. The students then have to provide reasons for choosing them. They may also identify two careers that they do not feel they would like and explain the reasons (*Career Education Workshop,* 1977).

Field Trips and Speakers

We have repeatedly emphasized the importance of students visiting a variety of work places. For all students, but particularly the intellectually impaired, direct experience is important for comprehension and motivation. Field trips should be well planned and an integral part of the curriculum. The field trips should be representative of the various business establishments in the community. It is important to select the relevant business and industries, tour sites, and knowledgeable personnel to speak with the students. The job analysis forms mentioned earlier should be used by the students as they observe people at their work. Prior planning with the company should permit the time for students to observe and record pertinent job analysis information and to speak with some of the people performing the various jobs. The jobs to be viewed should generally be those the group would most likely be able to assume themselves. The importance, characteristics, and opportunities associated with each job should be covered in classroom discussions.

Class speakers are a valuable adjunct to field trips. In some cases, it may be advantageous to have someone from the business speak to the class prior to a tour. She may distribute information, show films, answer questions, identify points of interest, and explain what the students are going to see. In other instances, it may be more beneficial to have the speaker after the trip. Workers should also be invited to such presentations. Former handicapped students are an additional effective way of eliciting student interest and understanding of the industry and its jobs. The students should be prepared for field trips and speakers and be required to study, develop, and present materials related to the industry and jobs they will be observing and discussing. Occupational literature, films, and other media should be reviewed in advance of these experiences.

Career Information Center

A Career Information Center can be an integral part of an occupational guidance delivery system. Students can gather information about occupations and plan their occupational future with a counselor. This learning and planning should relate to what the student is receiving in classroom career-related activities. The center should be a place where students can talk with other students about occupations. It should have sufficient materials so that career-related questions can be readily answered. The establishment of a Career Information Center can be done at a fairly reasonable cost. A host of free materials is available from businesses, industries, and various organizations (e.g., Aluminum Company of America, American Institute of Baking, Association of American Railroads, and Association of General Contractors of America).

Mattson (1976) identifies eight major considerations for establishing a Career Information Center. The location of the center should be in the line of traffic so it is accessible for drop-ins, as well as appointments. It should be near the library but not part of the school's administrative center. *Space* should be large and quiet for reviewing materials, testing, student-counselor planning, parent conferences, and discussions with parents and employers. *Staff* should include a vocational counselor, volunteers, and student aides. There should be an identifiable *budget* for salaries, materials, publicity, equipment, and travel. Some essential *materials* are: *Occupational Outlook Handbook, Dictionary of Occupational Titles,* subscriptions to career-related publications, *Encyclopedia of Careers,* a file of brochures on jobs, several regional newspapers, career-related library books, employment opportunity information, and audio-visual materials on interviewing, job seeking, and the like. *Furniture and equipment* should include copying equipment, bulletin boards, overhead projector, projection screen, microfiche viewer, conference and work tables, furniture for conversational settings, display racks, bookcases, files, and desks and chairs. *Publicity* should consist of a daily bulletin and notices in the staff bulletin and school newspaper, besides bulletin boards, staff meetings, homerooms, and flyers to parents. The center could provide the following *services:* career counseling on an individual basis; career information to classes; career guidance material; administration and interpretation of aptitude achievement and interest tests; financial aid information; military information; information on employment trends, qualifications, and compensation; currculum planning; resource center for faculty, staff, and parents; and liaison between the school and community, business, and other groups.

The Career Information Center can be the hub of activity for career education programming within a school building. For handicapped students, career assessment materials such as those presented earlier in this chapter are a vital component. These work evaluation materials can also be used with many nonhandicapped students.

OCCUPATIONAL PREPARATION TECHNIQUES

Specific and formalized occupational preparation efforts should occur at all levels of the school curriculum. The development of appropriate work habits and behaviors (**19**), sufficient physical-manual skills (**20**), and a specific occupational skill (**21**) constitute the competencies related to this area.

There are a variety of methods for helping the student toward occupational preparation. At the elementary level, we suggest providing several different work projects and home responsibilities. In the junior high school, more complex work projects, on-campus jobs, business simulations, career exploration materials, including the work sample systems mentioned earlier, and home training are complementary techniques. In the senior high school, all of the previously mentioned methods plus vocational education courses, on-the-job training, use of rehabilitation facilities, and a vocational/career development center within the school are additional sources of preparing handicapped students for the world of work. Thus, beginning at the elementary level, occupational activities should be designed in a systematic skill building manner that combines a variety of methods for occupational preparation.

Two publications useful for a detailed review of occupational programs for the handicapped are *Improving Occupational Programs for the Handicapped,* prepared for the Bureau of Education for the Handicapped by the Management Analysis Center (1975) and the Spring 1973 issue of *Teaching Exceptional Children.* Both publications describe a variety of occupationally-oriented programs proven effective with various types of handicapped persons. The first publication is only available from the ERIC Document Reproduction Service, P.O. Box 190, Arlington, Virginia. The second publication can be purchased from the Council for Exceptional Children in Reston, Virginia.

Occupational preparation techniques that should be considered for handicapped individuals are presented next. No attempt has been made to cover all possible methods in this discussion.

Work Tasks and Projects

Teachers can begin the occupational preparation aspect of career development during the elementary years by assigning their students a variety of work tasks. This could include keeping the erasers and blackboards clean, posting and keeping bulletin boards in order, cleaning up and putting away materials, organizing the chairs for various classroom activities, cutting out posters and other classroom materials, and a host of other prevocational tasks. In addition, various work projects can be undertaken during the year, such as collages, Christmas cards and decorations, materials for nursing homes, woodworking and other craft products, horticulture activities, class play responsibilities in getting ready for performances, making Easter eggs, and building model stores and products out of big blocks to sell. Painting products are also a particularly effective prevocational activity as they build physical-manual skills, work habits and behaviors, and personal-social competencies.

Most of the above activities are generally conducted in elementary programs for handicapped and nonhandicapped students. They need to be emphasized even more for handicapped students and in a purposeful manner. When one thinks about all the prevocational activities that can be injected into the curriculum, it is literally amazing. If activities of this nature can be related somewhat to the world of work, students should see their relationship to the kinds of work that exists in the community. In this way, purposeful and systematic sequencing of the various activities can be done and will lend themselves to career education goals and objectives.

The family needs to be closely informed and involved in each series of prevocational activities for their children. They can supplement the school's efforts with work activities in the home. Parents should be encouraged to work with their children on school projects, both at school and home, and to pursue specific interests and aptitudes of the student when the school is no longer able to do so. Cooperative efforts between school personnel and family members will bring closer relationships and appreciation between the two groups and, in the long run, enhance the student's career development.

As the student moves into secondary programs, many work activities should be provided, particularly for students with lesser abilities. There are many other techniques to be used in fostering their career development.

There are several outstanding occupational training programs around the country. The Quincy Public Schools, mentioned earlier, offer a series of "Multi-Experience Centers" for students of various levels. There is a Grooming Center, which provides experiences in the skill development areas of posture and exercise, clothing selection, ironing, and care of nails, shoes, and teeth. The activities prepare the individual for the appearance necessary for finding and maintaining employment. A Furniture Restoration and Upholstery Center permits students to make pincushions, pillows, and footstools, and repair and upholster couches, rocking chairs, and lounges. A Laundry Center assumes the responsibility for laundering towels and uniforms from various departments and classes and are equipped with washing machines, dryers, irons, ironing boards, measuring charts, and cleaning agents. A Health Care Center offers students the opportunity to learn the equipment applicable to a nursing situation (e.g., bed making, bed baths, and temperature taking). A Horticulture Center specializes in the production and use of fruit, vegetables, trees, shrubs, plants, and flowers, in addition to landscaping, gardening, and floral design. Students learn various soil types and cultivation methods and fertilizers. A Food Service Center features the occupations of baker, doughnut maker, candy maker, pizza maker, and cook or chef. Skill development focuses on abilities needed to secure and maintain a job as a waiter, waitress, busboy, cook, cashier, and others. (A Construction Center offers students the opportunity to develop positive work habits, learn safety rules, use various construction tools, construct small products, and learn basic construction skills.) A Production Center is designed for assembly line work and includes such projects as school mailings, preparation of packets, and the assembling of radios, including soldering techniques. Finally, a Maintenance and Repair Center is available to develop practical skills in repairing small appliances, small engines, toys and bicycles (Bocke & Price, 1976).

The Career Development Center in Nassau County, New York, is one of the nation's few modified high schools for handicapped adolescents. The CDC has a strong occupational component and is designed for those students who have failed to benefit from the general curriculum in other district schools. Students take 40 periods of instruction per week, including 18 in occupational education, 12 in core subject academics, and 10 of enrichment electives. Occupational preparation is provided in the areas of small engine and combustion, auto body repair, auto mechanics, electronics, and building maintenance; floral design, greenhouse and landscaping, horticulture maintenance, and equipment repair; health services and office occupations; kitchen, service, short order preparation, and accounting aspects of small food businesses; and multi-occupational units for exploratory activities. A team teaching approach emphasizes building success experiences and subsequent behavior change with a renewed interest in the academic tool subjects of reading, mathematics, and language as they result in occupational functioning. Family involvement is an integral part of the program and has met with tremendous success on a voluntary basis (Colella, 1973).

The Peoria, Illinois Public Schools operate a Mini-Shop to ease the transition of the student from an artificial classroom setting to a practical job training situation. There are three phases: prevocational and academic instructional programming; Mini-Shop instruction, work, and evaluation; and supervised work training experience for sophomores within the high school. In the Mini-Shop, students dualize programs for meeting the unique needs and specifying goals for each student. Behavior charts depicting targets and progress are used to define instruction and establish program directions for each student (Bureau of Education for the Handicapped).

An automotive program for mildly hard of hearing to profoundly deaf high school students is described by McLoughlin (1976). This is a joint venture between the School for Language and Hearing Impaired Children and Automotive High School, both in Brooklyn, New York. Students spend half of each day in the classroom and the other half in the shop where they learn a basic vocabulary of automotive terms; skills in using automotive hand tools; general rules for being successful on the job; repair work on brakes, engines, transmissions, and other automobile parts; and how to disassemble and rebuild automotive parts such as starters, alternators, and carburetors, according to her ability. Classroom work depends on the visual effect of showing the tools and their applications and includes units on brakes, basic automotive systems, front end suspensions, and valve train. There is a basic language, reading, and math program and considerable emphasis on wages, tax information, developing suitable work habits, completing job applications, and job interviewing. Budgeting and planning and driver's education is also available. General Motors, Shell Oil, and Ohio Technical Institute films are shown weekly, in addition to other audio-visual aides. Students graduating from the program find jobs in gas stations, body repair shops, tire shops and other automotive industries.

Another successful program for young deaf adults is described by Dwyer (1973). Twenty graduates from a nearby School for the Deaf began an experimental program at the Blue Hills Regional Vocational Technical School in Canton, Massachusetts. The project staff chose welding instruction for the deaf student's initial vocational experience. A section of five students plus one specialist for the hearing impaired were assigned to the shop program, with 15 hearing students also getting an introduction to welding. After a few months the deaf students were performing so well that they triggered unusual motivation from the hearing students, who volunteered to take sign language courses so they could communicate, learn, and socialize with their deaf friends. Deaf students gained considerable confidence and were admitted to other vocational programs. The success of the ongoing program is apparent, as 85% are successfully employed in careers for which they were trained.

Many schools have begun to operate their own vocational evaluation or assessment laboratories (or vocational centers), using many of the vocational/work evaluation systems discussed in the Occupational Guidance Section, individually developed work samples, standardized vocational interest and aptitude tests, work tasks, and other measures. In most instances, the work sample batteries provide an excellent method of teaching prevocational and vocational skills to the student and are actually of more value in this manner than for evaluation. Work samples and audio-visual units such as the Singer and COATS Systems are useful in motivating students to the world of work and developing occupational interests, physical-manual skills, and work habits. In addition, they provide step-by-step procedures of learning some or most specific occupational skills needed for a variety of jobs. Some school districts have established mobile work evaluation units which, although generally reserved for work evaluation purposes, could be used for occupational training.

Simulations of Business and Industry

The simulated business approach mentioned in the Occupational Guidance Section is also a specific occupational preparation technique. Based on the experiences in a Career City and the job analyses they have conducted, students should develop a relatively accurate idea of the most appropriate job or jobs within a simulated business. Thus, the student can be "hired" within Career City to assume the role of warehouse worker, clerk, bookkeeper, salesperson, assembly line worker, typist, manager, or whatever type of jobs are able to be established within or outside of the school setting. The creation of a career city or simulated business will take considerable creativity, thought, time, cooperation among disciplines, and probably, money. It is a method to attract and benefit students and combine the school and community into an innovative and effective educational technique. Business and industry can be called upon for technical assistance and materials, parents for their expertise and participation, and various types of school personnel can participate and relate their subject matter to the skills needed by the students to succeed on the various jobs within Career City.

On- and Off-Campus Training

The use of the school cafeteria, library, gym, district warehouse, housekeeping, clerical, groundskeeping departments of schools have been a source of occupational preparation for handicapped students in many educational programs. Students are generally placed according to their interest and ability and, in many cases, the work sites function as a prevocational or career exploration experience. But, these placements are valuable in helping to identify student interests and training potentials if enough supervision and objectivity can be provided at the work place. Care must be taken that the student is not used to do some of the unappealing work of others rather than being exposed to all aspects of the job.

Off-campus occupational preparation is a vital part of the school program because of its realistic and competitive aspects. Some students may need the services of a rehabilitation facility (or sheltered workshop) prior to consideration for placement at a real job site. For many of these students, such a placement is advisable because it separates the student from the more academically-oriented atmosphere of the school and requires the student to learn how to get to the agency, meet and interact with other people, respond to the vocational nature and requirements of the facility, and begin to seriously realize that she is getting close to the time of leaving school and finding employment.

Off-campus training should begin as early as possible in the high school program, hopefully by the sophomore year, depending on the individual student and her level and needs. Based on the vocational evaluation and education that has occurred previously, reasonable decisions should be made regarding appropriate work sites and jobs. Vocational planning must be done systematically and not randomly without regard to the needs of the student. The work site must be carefully reviewed by the teacher/counselor and clear understandings made with those individuals for whom the student will interact. Career development at the work site must be assured, therefore, expectations for the student and procedures for reaching these goals must be outlined with the work supervisors.

Many placement personnel believe it is necessary for the students to receive pay for the work they do on off-campus jobs. While this is perhaps desirable, it can also be a hindrance when students think the primary purpose of their working experience is to earn money. They may select certain work experiences primarily because of the money they can receive rather than the intrinsic exploration and preparation values. Other aspects of learning and their benefits can diminish, and in the long run, the students will suffer the consequences if this is seen as the primary and important benefit from this experience. It might be far better to conduct these placements as if the students were taking a vocational education, skill building course. Then, if they do become proficient and productive after a period of time, monetary benefits can be made available. We know this is an issue that provokes much controversy, and we raise it for your consideration and decision in program design.

CONCLUSION

The occupational guidance and preparation of handicapped individuals presents professional workers with an exciting and demanding challenge and a host of techniques depending on the interests, needs, learning styles, and abilities of each individual. It should begin shortly after the student enters the elementary program and gain momentum as the student moves up the educational ladder toward graduation and adulthood. It requires the involvement of all the typical resources that career education demands: school personnel, family and community agencies, and the business and industry sector. It requires innovativeness, time, and money, but most of all, the commitment and cooperation between a host of individuals and resources to assure the career development of the handicapped individual. A further discussion of this curriculum area will be conducted in chapter 8.

Occupational guidance and preparation is a major thrust of the career education concept. When combined appropriately with general academic, daily living, and personal-skills instruction, it will constitute a successful approach to meeting the total life career development needs of our handicapped citizens.

Part III presents information for putting career education into motion. Career education requires carefully planned processes and commitments from a large number of dedicated individuals who really desire to change their educational practices for handicapped learners. It requires a well conceived and substantial inservice training component, the work of several committees, and the development of a comprehensive career education plan for the district and participating schools. Implementation of career education requires a concentration on student and program evaluation procedures to determine its effectiveness and the changes needed. Thus, career education and its appropriate implementation is a complex process but one that can be accomplished by using the guidelines presented in the two chapters that comprise this part.

Chapter 7 illustrates and discusses a suggested process for planning and implementing career education in a school district. A 16-step process is recommended and explained. A Career Education Special Needs Committee, working in concert with a District-Wide Career Education Steering Committee, is suggested for providing the organizational leadership to implementation activities. A detailed organizational structure for career education committees is presented. The chapter gives considerable attention to inservice training procedures, important considerations, and actions needed for successful efforts. The importance of administrative support and input to the development of career education is emphasized in the chapter. A model inservice training program, developed by the senior author, is presented and explained, along with a description and suggested guidelines for developing a Career Education Plan. The importance of receiving and using input from inservice participants in developing the district and school Career Education Plan is emphasized as the key to gaining acceptance for change and implementing career education successfully.

Chapter 8 provides suggestions on how career education can be structured in a K-12+ program by emphasizing academic, daily living, personal-social, and occupational instruction and their interaction. An example of how the competency based approach lends itself to writing Individualized Education Programs (IEPs) is presented. Experience Based Career Education (EBCE) is described, and it is suggested as a feasible model for handicapped students. A successful EBCE project in Iowa is described and depicts the potential of this approach in rural areas. A discussion of various types of student competency measures concludes the chapter. A Competency Rating Scale, developed by the senior author and his associates, is briefly described and illustrated.

The overall goals of education are to prepare the individual to live and work in society. In order to meet these goals, the student must develop necessary daily living, personal-social, and occupational skills as a part of a rewarding and satisfying lifestyle. The student must learn about personal interests, needs, abilities, potentials, and the realities of a modern world. These understandings lead to appropriate decision making about an individual's career. The implementation of the career education/development concept transcends the entire school curriculum. Thus, if career education is to become a reality for handicapped students, educators will need to make changes to implement a meaningful and purposeful career development-oriented curriculum.

Until recently, most school systems have provided students with a content-oriented curriculum approach in which students learn a specific body of knowledge. This approach may not be directly applicable to the student's needs. Our recommendation, as pointed out previously in this book, is to adopt an educational philosophy that is process-oriented. Process education emphasizes the acquisition of specific skills necessary for community living and working and requires educators to decide upon the outcomes they expect from their efforts in precise, measurable terms. This does not negate the importance or need for general education. We believe the educational program must include both general and career education to maximize the student's career development.

Careful planning will be required if significant and positive changes in curriculum are to occur for handicapped individuals. It is not easy to convince people to substantially change their ways of teaching, counseling, or whatever services they have been providing students. They will need to believe in the need to change, be involved in making changes, and be recognized and rewarded for their efforts. The concept of normalizing the educational process for handicapped students is important and will need administrative support. This support should extend from the school superintendent through such administrators as the assistant superintendents, directors and supervisors of programs, and principals.

A career development-oriented curriculum for handicapped students will most likely succeed if education for all students is directed toward similar goals. In some cases, however, this may not be the case, and handicapped students will be receiving a different curriculum focus than nonhandicapped individuals. When this occurs, there will be fewer school personnel involved in the handicapped student's education program than if the entire student body was receiving a career development focus. Thus, we strongly recommend that career education be developed from a broader, more complete concept that encompasses the career development of all students within the school constellation.

This chapter will discuss the salient aspects of career education planning and implementation. It should be recalled that we define *career* in its broader context, as illustrated in Figure 13. A major portion of the material presented in this chapter is based on the senior author's experience in directing Proj-

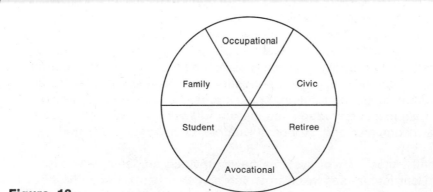

Figure 13
The Various Life Roles Comprising a Career.

ect PRICE (Programming Retarded In Career Education), a 3-year inservice developmental project at the University of Missouri-Columbia from 1974–77. The project resulted in an inservice training program for staff personnel and others and has been published by the Council for Exceptional Children (CEC) as a *Trainers Guide for Life Centered Career Education* (Brolin, McKay, & West, 1978). We appreciate the permission CEC has given to use part of this material in this chapter.

This chapter is divided into three sections: The process of career education planning and implementation; inservice training procedures; and guidelines for the development of a career education plan. We hope that this chapter will help you understand the means through which career education can become a reality in school districts.

THE PROCESS OF CAREER EDUCATION PLANNING AND IMPLEMENTATION

The process of planning and implementing comprehensive career education in a school district involves considerable time, work, and resources by a number of dedicated individuals from the school and community. Close to half of the school districts in this country report they have some form of career education in their schools. But, a closer perusal of these programs often reveals an expanded vocational education or guidance program rather than a totally infused career education operation. The same situation generally exists for handicapped students, although as noted in other chapters, there are some outstanding programs.

Figure 14 illustrates some of the major steps that we believe are necessary for planning and implementing career education in school systems. Each of these steps is discussed next.

Step 1: Enlist Support of School District Leadership Personnel

The initial step in planning for career education requires an organization committee, consisting of staff interested in implementing the concept, to receive the support of top level administrators in the school district. With the current pressures to educate handicapped students in the least restrictive environment, which is generally the regular class, most administrators will be willing to listen to the possibilities career education has for meeting the mandates of appropriate educational programming for these students.

It may be necessary to approach the administration with a proposal that will require, at first, only a small part of the staff and student population until success is demonstrated. Overwhelming proposals for educational change may produce a resistance reaction In some school districts. In

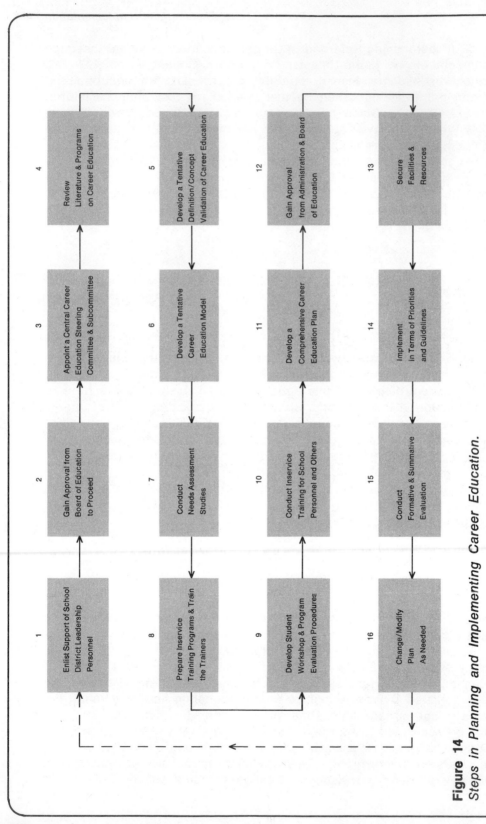

Figure 14
Steps in Planning and Implementing Career Education.

Source: Trainers guide for life centered career education (Brolin et al., 1978).

others, administrators may be willing to attempt a complete overhaul of present practices and support the concept in its entirety.

The career education concept should be promoted as the change agent that can respond to the many criticisms schools are receiving about their lack of relevant curriculum. The focus on career development will link the gap between theory and practice so that curriculum is directed toward living and working in this society. It must be cautioned, however, that career education can be oversold as a panacea for all the ills in education and society.

In addition to administrators, certain other decision-making groups may be needed for their support. Teacher and community groups may be necessary for endorsement before top level administrators approve a career development orientation. Schools often need an outside stimulant to bring about a change.

Step 2: Gain Approval from Board of Education to Proceed

Once the school district leadership personnel have given their backing to the proposal, similar support should be sought from the Board of Education. At this point in time, the only endorsement requested should be to begin organizing for a career development-oriented curriculum in the district or in pilot schools. The board should be presented with the proposed steps in planning and implementing career education as illustrated in Figure 14 so they understand the process. Board members may indicate where they feel they should be involved and make administrative decisions (e.g., career education definition/conceptualization, career education model, inservice training program, and evaluation efforts). The board, as well as the top level administrators, must be assured that they will be kept well informed of progress by the implementors. A timeline for the accomplishment of the various steps would also be helpful. It is recommended that the organization committee gain a commitment to action from the board relative to the kind of activities that will be conducted to ensure program success. This same commitment should be requested of the administrators and other groups identified in Step 1.

Step 3: Appoint a Central Career Education Steering Committee and Subcommittees

A District-Wide Career Education Steering Committee should then be organized to plan, implement, and manage the curriculum development activities for career education. Such a committee may presently exist, but it may not be as comprehensive as we recommend in regard to the needs of handicapped students. It may require an expansion of the committee's activities to include the handicapped and the competency based orientation.

The committee should consist of at least 12 people, including: The person in charge of instruction, Director of Guidance, Director of Vocational Education, Direction of Special Education, Director of Career Education (if any), principals, classroom teachers, one or two students, and community representatives. The community representatives should include parents, as well as those persons from the business/industry sector. There will be a temptation to put numerous people on this committee. This could be disastrous. It would be best to limit the size of the Steering Committee but expand the number of participants on the subcommittees.

The District-Wide Career Education Steering Committee chairperson should be knowledgeable about career education, influential, get people to work together, and have the time and inclination to serve in this responsible position. Members should also be selected with care and informed of the nature of their responsibilities. Typical responsibilities of this type of committee are: deciding upon goals and objectives; identifying tasks and task force groups; setting timelines; coordinating, communicating and evaluating the work of the various subcommittees/task forces; and securing funds and resources.

The Steering Committee may decide to appoint a special subcommittee for the career development-oriented curriculum for handicapped students. We suggest that this is a viable procedure and will refer to such a subcommittee as the Career Education/Special Needs Committee. The chairperson and at least two other members of this committee should also be members of the District-Wide Career Education Steering Committee. This Special Needs Committee will be responsible for developing and promoting the school district career development program and each school building's career education plans for handicapped students. It may assume several of the responsibilities listed previously for the Central Steering Committee. Obviously, the Special Needs Committee should work closely with the Steering Committee in formulating policies and procedures relative to the development of career education activities. The structure of the committees we're talking about, and other subcommittees critical to career education planning, are illustrated in Figure 15.

If the district has a Career Education Steering Committee for all students, it will or should probably have several subcommittees, as described in Figure 15. The Special Needs Subcommittee should in turn have task forces, each relating to the respective subcommittees of the larger Steering Committee. They can provide these subcommittees with various information on handicapped students that relates to their area, as well as relating to the Special Needs Subcommittee. The Building Level Special Needs Committee is involved in implementing career education in each of the schools. These committees should have 4 to 6 members, including special education, vocational education, and guidance personnel, administration, and perhaps one or two students. These committees work with the task forces and the Special Needs Subcommittee in implementing ideas, identifying needs, arranging for staff development training, and communicating with parents and other

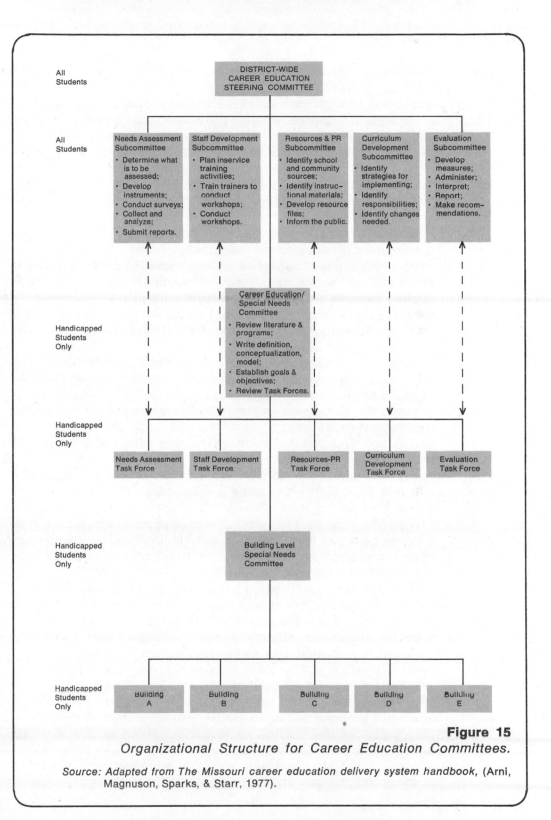

Figure 15

Organizational Structure for Career Education Committees.

Source: Adapted from The Missouri career education delivery system handbook, (Arni, Magnuson, Sparks, & Starr, 1977).

community representatives. Some of these individuals should be on a task force of the Special Needs Subcommittee.

The organization of a network such as the one proposed involves many people and divides the responsibilities so that tasks can be accomplished. Organization and coordination are the keys to the successful delivery of career education to handicapped students. The Special Needs Subcommittee is the important cog in the entire operation. It must determine the needed activities and delegate them to the proper task force or building level committee. Here is a list of activities of the Special Needs Committee.

1. Review literature and programs that appear pertinent for the career development of handicapped individuals;
2. write a philosophy of career education, including conceptualization and definition and a career education model relative to handicapped students and consistent with district policy;
3. compose a preliminary list of career education goals and objectives that can be categorized into three areas: instructional, community involvement, and administrative;
4. present the philosophy, goals, and model to the District-Wide Career Education Steering Committee and the central administration to gain their support and suggestions;
5. approve the Needs Assessment Studies proposed by the Needs Assessment Task Force;
6. review and approve the inservice training program proposed by the Staff Development Task Force;
7. review and approve student assessment, workshop evaluation, and program evaluation procedures proposed by the Evaluation Task Force;
8. review and approve the resources development and public relations proposals of the Resources and Public Relations Task Force;
9. review and approve the curriculum development proposals and activities of the Curriculum Development Task Force;
10. compile, analyze, and prepare written reports from those submitted by the various task forces and submit to the appropriate administrative channels and the Steering Committee;
11. write the Career Education Plan for the District with information provided from various task forces and building committees;
12. present the Career Education Plan to Steering Committee and/or administration and the Board of Education for approval;
13. help secure facilities and resources so that a comprehensive career education program becomes available to handicapped students;
14. help implement the curriculum model in various school buildings according to priorities and guidelines;
15. supervise program evaluation efforts to ascertain curricula effectiveness and changes; and

16. instigate changes and modifications needed to deliver career education to handicapped students.

The above list of responsibilities should reflect the importance of selecting the appropriate people for this committee. As in the case of the Steering Committee, there should be a reasonable number of respected, representative leaders, who have enough expertise and interest in the handicapped individual to fulfill their responsibilities.

Step 4: Review Literature and Programs on Career Education

The Special Needs Subcommittee should move quickly into action so that members learn about career education and their specific responsibilities. These efforts and responsibilities should be publicized so that other faculty and interested community members may anticipate future activities.

Before the committee can formulate their career education definition, conceptualization, and model, members should become familiar with the various philosophies and opinions of leaders in the field and visit school districts that have adopted the career education approach. They need to discuss their readings and observations to determine the most appropriate philosophical basis and model design for their district. As can be determined from the previous chapters of this book, there are a great number of sources of information about current needs and practices. A telephone call to the state coordinator for career education and other state department of education officials may identify other programs in the state that they feel merit a review.

Based on this, the committee should be able to reach a consensus on the career education philosophy and model most appropriate for their particular needs. They can formulate a tentative position statement requiring administrative and teacher/counselor reactions before a final decision is rendered.

Step 5: Develop a Tentative Definition/Conceptualization of Career Education

Definitions and conceptualizations of career education range from a work-centered to a life centered approach. In chapter 3, we discussed this area. We said a career is multifaceted, consisting of occupational, social, leisure, and interpersonal roles; it is not just occupational or vocational education. This feature distinguishes career education from vocational education. Career education prepares individuals for *all* aspects of community life, including work. It is a life centered approach to education, one that infuses all of education.

If the Special Needs Committee chooses this conceptualization of career education, then their definition may be:

Career education is the process of systematically coordinating all school, family, and community components together to facilitate each individual's potential for economic, social, and personal fulfillment.

Step 6: Develop a Tentative Career Education Model

The field has many models of career education. These models will be uncovered as the Special Needs Committee members review materials and visit projects and programs. The school district or state may already have their own model. It is not our intent to review these. Rather, we shall use our model as an example of the infusion of career education into the school curriculum. You will recall that we presented our model in chapter 3 in a three-dimensional illustration (Figure 9, p. 107). The three major components of the model were: **1.** 22 competencies categorized under the curriculum areas of daily living skills, personal-social skills, and occupational guidance and preparation; **2.** school, family, and community experiences; and **3.** four stages of career development—awareness, exploration, preparation, and placement/follow up.

The model we present is designed to provide the student with the competencies necessary for most of the roles, settings, and events comprising his life. It requires basic subject matter to be taught in relation to these competencies. It forms the basis for developing the Career Education Plan, which we will discuss later in this chapter.

It would be advisable for the committee to review the definition, conceptualization, and model of career education with top level administrators, as well as the District-Wide Career Education Steering Committee. All interested parties should have the opportunity for reaction, input, and endorsement. The Board of Education should also review and endorse the proposals of the Special Needs Committee.

Step 7: Conduct Needs Assessment Studies

Needs assessments may be designed to measure a number of different aspects of the educational program. Gysbers (1973) describes three types of needs assessments required for sound program development: **1.** the needs of students; **2.** the status of the current program; and **3.** the professional needs of the staff. These three types can be described by the following questions:

- What do students, educators, parents, and community members see as important education outcomes?
- Is the current program delivering the desired student outcomes?
- What does the professional staff need in order to produce the desired outcomes?

The answer to these questions will guide educational planners toward a person-centered rather than content-centered curriculum (Arni, Magnuson, Sparks, & Starr, 1977).

The District-Wide Career Education Steering Committee and the Special Needs Subcommittee should establish the objectives of assessment studies. However, the Needs Assessment Task Force will probably need to assume most of the duties associated with this activity while informing the Special Needs Committee of its activities and requesting suggestions. The task force will need the endorsement of the Special Needs and Steering Committees, as well as top level administrators, before the needs assessment instruments can be distributed to the respondents. An example of a needs assessment instrument that can be used to measure school personnel's knowledge, attitudes, and commitment toward career education and retarded students is presented in Figure 16. This instrument is one of four developed by the Project PRICE staff for baseline data collection. These data serve as a basis for student and school personnel needs and growth after inservice training and program implementation.

The Needs Assessment Task Force may have to seek additional people to administer the instruments. These individuals should be well trained in the procedure. It is advisable to involve some parents and other community representatives in the study. The ideal assessment is conducted in a face-to-face situation. Some instruments may be administered to a group of individuals under the instruction and supervision of one administrator. In all cases the respondents should receive clear explanations about the reason the needs assessment is being conducted, what will be gained from it, and their responsibility in the process. They should also know how and when they will be informed of the results (Arni et al., 1977).

A procedure must be established for returning the needs assessment instruments to a central location so they can be analyzed and interpreted in a reasonable period of time. No attempt will be made here to explain the various analysis procedures—that can be obtained elsewhere. The results should identify and prioritize educational deficiencies so that a plan of action can eventually be developed to meet these needs and concerns of the various respondents. The data should provide a basis for making accurate and objective appraisals and judgments that can be integrated into inservice training and curriculum modifications.

The decision makers (administrators, Board of Education, Steering Committee, and Special Needs Subcommittee) should receive the specific results of the needs assessment studies. There will probably be certain in-

Figure 16

Needs Assessment Survey.

DIRECTIONS: The following statements are designed to identify beliefs you have concerning career education and/or retarded students. There are no right or wrong answers. Just circle the response which best describes how you feel about each statement. Circle only *ONE* response for each item.

KEY: SA—STRONGLY AGREE WITH STATEMENT
   A—AGREE WITH STATEMENT
   U—UNDECIDED, NO OPINION, NEITHER AGREE NOR DISAGREE WITH STATEMENT
   D—DISAGREE WITH STATEMENT
   SD—STRONGLY DISAGREE WITH STATEMENT

1. A retarded student is classified as such because of lacking ability in the areas of general intelligence and adaptive behavior.   SA A U D SD

2. Selective integration is an effort to move these students into regular classes in an effort to be more accepted by "normal" peers.   SA A U D SD

3. Selective integration will eliminate special services, classes, and programs for these students.   SA A U D SD

4. Career education should systematically coordinate the school, family, and community resources to facilitate each individual's career potential.   SA A U D SD

5. There are few appropriate community resources available to assist teaching career competencies to these students.   SA A U D SD

6. It is unlikely that these students will be thought of as contributing to society.   SA A U D SD

7. Mainstreaming is an effective way to provide career education to these students.   SA A U D SD

8. These students would benefit if a greater emphasis was placed on career education.   SA A U D SD

9. Being labeled "Mentally Retarded" causes these students social and academic problems.   SA A U D SD

10. School personnel should make the decisions regarding proper classroom placement of these students.   SA A U D SD

11. Counselors should be allowed to make career choices for these students.   SA A U D SD

12. Competency training in occupational skills is not important for these students.   SA A U D SD

13. Generally, these students do not look any different than other students.   SA A U D SD

Source: Trainers guide for life centered career education (Brolin et al., 1978).

Figure 16 *continued*

14. Competency training in personal-social skills is important for these students. SA A U D SD

15. The mainstreaming question is more of a civil rights issue than an educational problem. SA A U D SD

16. Relevant teaching is a goal of career education. SA A U D SD

17. These students interfere with the learning of other students in an integrated class. SA A U D SD

18. It is sometimes important for educators to clarify their feelings about these students. SA A U D SD

19. Career education is intended for students not able to succeed in an academic program. SA A U D SD

20. These students create instructional problems for the regular classroom teacher. SA A U D SD

21. It is important that educators understand effective methods of teaching career education skills. SA A U D SD

22. Regular classroom teachers have an obligation to all students in the class. SA A U D SD

23. It is important to develop competency based career instructional units to use with these students. SA A U D SD

24. Career education is just another fad that will soon be forgotten. SA A U D SD

25. Regular classroom teachers are prepared to meet the educational needs of all students. SA A U D SD

26. These students often grow up to be good citizens. SA A U D SD

27. Career education curriculum should be designed around a competency based education plan for these students. SA A U D SD

28. It is important for the family to assist in teaching career competencies. SA A U D SD

29. It is beneficial for educators to understand the major causes of mental retardation. SA A U D SD

30. Competency training in daily living skills is important for these students. SA A U D SD

31. It is important for regular classroom teachers to understand definitions and terminology associated with these students. SA A U D SD

32. These students can learn social behaviors in regular classes. SA A U D SD

33. It is important for regular classroom teachers to develop individualized units of study for these students. SA A U D SD

34. It is beneficial to understand the career potential of these students. SA A U D SD

35. Lecture is a good technique for teaching these students. SA A U D SD

36. It is important to be aware of career problems which these students may encounter. SA A U D SD

37. The need for "mainstreaming" reflects previous educational misjudgment. SA A U D SD

38. There are several ways to integrate these students into regular classes. SA A U D SD

39. Mainstreaming these students will have an adverse effect upon educational achievement of other students. SA A U D SD

40. These students are inclined to be behavior problems. SA A U D SD

Figure 16 *continued*

41. The most important thing you can teach these students is   SA A U D SD
    how to be prepared for life.
42. Currently there is insufficient evidence to justify an opinion   SA A U D SD
    on the mainstreaming issue.
43. It is important for these students to master career com-   SA A U D SD
    petencies prior to departure from school.
44. These students have a right to the services of a regular class-   SA A U D SD
    room teacher.
45. Selective integration will improve the social acceptance of   SA A U D SD
    these students by their "normal" peers.
46. Curriculum development is a waste of time for teachers.   SA A U D SD
47. Educators should develop a teaching plan based upon in-   SA A U D SD
    fusion of career concepts into their subject specialty.
48. These students can benefit from career education experi-   SA A U D SD
    ences provided in a regular classroom.
49. It is beneficial to become aware of the application of career   SA A U D SD
    education curriculum to special populations.
50. Career education and vocational education become identical   SA A U D SD
    programs when dealing with these students.
51. Self-contained special classes for these students discrim-   SA A U D SD
    inate against low socioeconomic students.
52. Career education is relevant to these students.   SA A U D SD
53. Educators would find it useful to be able to identify several   SA A U D SD
    occupations which can be performed by these students.
54. Effective learning experiences for these students can be   SA A U D SD
    successfully developed by regular teachers.
55. It is beneficial to recognize the relationship between career   SA A U D SD
    education and competency based curriculum.
56. It is of value for regular classroom teachers to understand   SA A U D SD
    occasional misbehavior by these students.

formation that can be released to the general public and faculty, so that everyone is informed of the progress and findings.

Needs assessment is the cornerstone for a career development-oriented curriculum. Considerable care and thought must be devoted to the conceptualization of the respondents, questions, the interviewing variable, analysis, and final report.

Step 8: Prepare Inservice Training Program and Train the Trainers

Discussion of inservice activities is limited at this time because the next section of this chapter is devoted to the topic. Inservice training of personnel is critical to the success of any innovative interventions, especially those of the magnitude that are included in career education. As indicated by Mohr, (1971), teachers must be able to participate in the decisions directly affecting their work role if permanent change is to occur. Inservice education provides this opportunity, as well as imparting new knowledges and competencies that will be needed to deal effectively with handicapped students within a career education context. It recognizes the teacher and counselor as important individuals and that posture should influence the inservice atmosphere.

We view inservice training as most effective when the instruction comes from personnel within the school district. As inservice training packages become more available and transportable, school systems will need to depend less on the outside expert who has limited knowledge about the unique circumstances existing in the school environment. But dynamic and effective trainers will be needed if the inservice is to be successful. They must be knowledgeable and adequately motivated conduct the programs. The Staff Development Task Force must identify individuals who will be able to work effectively in this capacity.

Step 9: Develop Workshop, Student, and Program Evaluation Procedures

Conducting successful workshops requires considerable preplanning, effective trainers, and appropriate training materials for the participants. The first step should consist of determining the attitudes and knowledge of the participants before they receive any training. During the workshops, an evaluation sheet can be completed at the end of each session and/or workshop day. If the workshops consist of several days of training, an evaluation of the total inservice program should also be conducted.

Evaluation forms should be as short as possible but effective in gathering worthwhile data. An example of a daily evaluation form used in Project PRICE is presented in Figure 17. A good reference for planning, conducting, and evaluating workshops has been written by Davis and McCallon (1974).

Until recently, little attention was given to evaluating the effectiveness of programs for handicapped individuals. Formative and summative evaluation procedures are needed to assure students of getting a quality educational program that appropriately meets their needs. Formative evaluation, or process evaluation, provides information at intervals so that additions, deletions, or modifications can be made to maximize program success. Summative evaluation, or outcome evaluation, provides information about a program's outcomes so that decisions can be made regarding the continuation, rejection, or modification of the product or program. An in-depth discussion of program evaluation is beyond the scope of this book. Publications by Wellman and Moore (1975) and Wentling and Lawson (1975) provide detailed information on these procedures. A discussion of student evaluation procedures will be presented in the next chapter.

Please rate the general effectiveness of the second workshop by checking one response for each item. Then complete the unfinished sentences expressing your personal reaction toward the workshop.

1. The organization of the workshop was (____excellent; ____good; ____average; ____fair; ____poor).

2. The objectives of the workshop were (____extremely evident; ____evident; ____moderately evident; ____slightly evident; ____vague).

3. The work of the LEA/Trainers was (____excellent; ____good; ____average; ____fair; ____poor).

4. Attendance at this workshop should prove to be (____extremely beneficial; ____beneficial; ____moderately beneficial; ____slightly beneficial; ____not beneficial.

TODAY'S WORKSHOP WAS:	Strongly Agree	Agree	Undecided	Disagree	Strongly Disagree
5. Relevant;	_____	_____	_____	_____	_____
6. Successful;	_____	_____	_____	_____	_____
7. Clear;	_____	_____	_____	_____	_____
8. Practical;	_____	_____	_____	_____	_____
9. Interesting;	_____	_____	_____	_____	_____
10. Excellent	_____	_____	_____	_____	_____

Unfinished Sentences

11. The strongest factor of the workshop was . . .

12. The weakest factor was . . .

13. Overall, I feel that . . .

14. I would like to include . . .

General Narrative Reactions/Comments:

Figure 17
Example of Evaluation Worksheet.

Source: Trainers guide for life centered career education (Brolin et al., 1978).

Step 10: Conduct Inservice Training for School Personnel and Others

The inservice training program developed in Project PRICE will be discussed in the next section.

Step 11: Develop a Comprehensive Career Education Plan

Inservice training should include the drafting of a Career Education Plan for the school facilities involved in the workshops. This must be developed at the grass-roots level if there is to be any real hope of implementing a comprehensive plan within the curriculum. It should be designed to focus on curriculum modifications, instructional strategies and materials, and infusion and collaboration techniques. A separate section in this chapter is devoted to details of developing a comprehensive Career Education Plan.

Step 12: Gain Approval from Administration and the Board of Education

The various comprehensive Career Education Plans developed by the participating school facilities will need to be submitted to top level administrators and the Board of Education for final endorsement. A great deal of written material and verbal input will be generated during the workshops, but after they are completed, it will still be up to the Curriculum Task Force and Committee, in concert with the Special Needs Subcommittee and Building-Level Special Needs Committees, to record their plans in final form. Besides the individual building plans, a District-Wide Career Education Plan may be written by the Special Needs Subcommittee. There may be a considerable amount of work yet to be accomplished after the workshops and task force meetings in order to produce the final Career Education Plan, or plans.

We suggest that the plan be presented to the workshop participants for review, suggestions, and ultimate approval before being forwarded to the administration and Board of Education for approval. Although these groups have been kept informed, they may ask some of the following questions before a final decision is rendered. Can this plan be realistically implemented? What must be done with the budget? Is this what the students, school personnel, parents, and community wants? How does this curriculum for handicapped students interface with that for nonhandicapped students? If these and other questions are properly answered, the administration can seek the support of the Board of Education.

Step 13: Secure Facilities and Resources

The Special Needs Subcommittee should take the following actions upon receiving approval of the plan: Order materials and equipment; establish cooperative relationships with business/industry and community organizations and agencies; inform parents of the final plan and their responsibilities; inform the general community of the new thrust; conduct inservice training efforts for those staff members who will be involved with handicapped students; and secure additional space and/or renovations for those areas identified as having this need.

Step 14: Implement in Terms of Priorities and Guidelines

The appropriate times for starting the pilot or comprehensive program are at the start of the school year, beginning of the second semester, or during a summer session. The program cannot be implemented in its entirety if budgetary, staffing, and resources are unavailable. Thus, priorities must be established. The Building-Level Special Needs Committee will be necessary to insure action, monitor progress, serve as a liaison with the Special Needs Subcommittee, and identify new needs.

Step 15: Conduct Formative and Summative Evaluations

The Building-Level Special Needs Committee should coordinate all evaluation efforts with the help of the Evaluation Task Force of the Special Needs Subcommittee. This includes the implementation of the program and the extent to which students are attaining the competencies and subcompetencies.

Step 16: Change and Modify Plan as Needed

The Curriculum Development Task Force of the Special Needs Subcommittee and the Building-Level Special Needs Committee should meet periodically with faculty and others who are involved in program implementation. Based on their experiences at implementing the goals and objectives of the plan, changes and modifications to the original plan can be made. Those aspects with implications for future inservice and curriculum development activities should be noted for use. It is necessary that the Career Education Plans allow for change, but they should not be disregarded unless the curriculum group decides that there are better alternatives.

This section has presented a comprehensive process of planning and implementing career education within a school curriculum. Two vital ingredients to the success of this endeavor are the inservice training of personnel and the cooperative efforts in the development of a comprehensive Career Education Plan by school personnel, parents, and community representatives.

INSERVICE TRAINING

We believe educational practices will not be altered significantly unless there is a strong and substantial inservice training component built into the design. There have been many fine curriculum guides and other publications written to elicit needed changes in educational practices, but few have provided the necessary inservice education to make any difference in most school districts.

Based on several years experience of conducting inservice activities, we have found the following to be particularly important for successful training endeavors:

1. Obtain firm administrative commitment and support to maximize workshop attendance, cooperation, involvement, and subsequent implementation;
2. notify school personnel well in advance of the educational innovation and the eventual inservice that is going to be offered;
3. select and train a cadre of school district personnel to do as much of the training as possible. They should be dynamic, energetic leaders who have a strong interest and commitment to career education and handicapped students. They must be prepared effectively as they are the key to inservice success. A well-developed *trainer's manual* is essential;
4. select initial participants who are actually willing to work with handicapped students. There is no sense in "forcing" training on those who will not change their attitudes and methods of teaching;
5. provide special incentives for participating in the workshops (e.g., salary credits, college credits, and special recognition);
6. conduct the training outside of the school in a pleasant setting where there are few distractions from everyday business. Eating facilities should be available;
7. limit workshops to 5 or 6 hours per day. Participants become fatigued with a concentrated training program. They should be given the opportunity to move around and relax;
8. vary workshop sessions with a few lectures, warm-up activities, gaming techniques, participant involvement, media, hands-on experiences, and coffee breaks;
9. focus at the beginning on building a teamwork relationship and a cooperative, positive attitude among the participants;
10. provide a variety of instructional materials that are attractive, short, easy-to-read, and well organized. Transparencies, slide/cassette presentations, films and other media can enhance the workshop immeasurably;

11. limit the number of handouts, particularly if they are lengthy and cumbersome. Concise and highly relevant information should generally be disseminated. There should be easy reference to the material during the workshop sessions;

12. avoid making many assignments to the participants between workshops unless they are taking the workshop for college credit, pay or other remunerative aspects, or serving on one of the task forces;

13. emphasize "how to do it" so that participants understand their roles and appropriate conduct;

14. publicize the inservice workshop activities and results in a school bulletin or newsletter or newspaper article, thus providing people with recognition and credit for their efforts; and

15. use Advisory Committees and consultants to give necessary input to designing an inservice training program that can be evaluated for its effectiveness.

Educational change does not occur overnight. In fact, it is a slow process. Innovators must realize that they are not going to dramatically change the system or its major parts in a short period of time. Resistance to new ideas is normal, and people must be convinced that change is needed and a manageable way exists for accomplishing it.

Thus, inservice education that involves the total school staff must be offered so that all individuals are given the opportunity to invest themselves into planning and implementing career education into the school curriculum. The more people are involved in changing educational practices, the more they feel ownership and contribution to a worthwhile educational endeavor. It is important to capture the interest of the faculty and provide them with the knowledge and skills they will need to implement career education successfully.

Some of the major considerations in developing inservice education programs are: Selection of trainers; selection of participants; and organization of the workshop (format, content, and conduct).

Selection of Trainers

It is our contention that inservice training is most effective when it is conducted by personnel from the school districts (i.e., local educational leaders who maximize the input, problem-solving, and decision-making abilities of the participants while using training guidelines and materials). They must be organized and able to divide responsibilities among themselves from session to session so there is a smooth transition throughout each workshop.

The Staff Development Task Force of the Special Needs Subcommittee should be responsible for selecting a cadre of effective trainers, if they do not conduct the workshops themselves. This inservice training team should be composed of educators of complementary talents, for example, a counselor, general and special education teachers, and an administrator. Using a team of local trainers rather than outside consultants provides dedicated leadership within the school district, which increases the chances that the goals of the inservice program will continue after the initial training has ended. The trainers must be personable, enthusiastic, and accepting individuals who can make effective presentations, answer questions, and facilitate satisfactory closure to discussions. Some of the desirable human relations skills trainers should possess include: A sense of humor, enthusiasm, confidence, and ability to listen closely to every group member and provide the necessary feedback responses.

The trainer leader is the general organizer and coordinator of the workshops and orchestrates the various organizational details. The cadre of trainers act as small group facilitators, conduct some sessions, give participants directions, act as reporters of their groups' activities, and contribute to the overall tone of the workshop.

The Staff Development Task Force and trainers (if they are a different group) may devise their own training program, secure and use an existing program, or adapt one that is already developed. (In any case, they will need the time to put together a training program that will lead to the implementation of the goal and objectives, career education model, and the special training needs of various personnel.)

Selection of Participants

The needs assessment surveys and announcements about the inservice program will alert school staff to the projected inservice workshops. Everyone should be given the opportunity to participate. The needs assessment results should be reported to the faculty so the need for the inservice program becomes readily apparent.

The Staff Development Task Force should draw participants from the following categories: educators, family members, community agencies, business, industry, local government, and students. We suggest selecting school personnel from an elementary, junior, and senior high school for each workshop series so that the participants can plan a coordinated and developmental K-12 curriculum sequence to reflect what can and will be done at each level. Several administrators should be involved (i.e., principals, vice-principals, guidance, supervisors, program directors, administrative assistants, and at least one representative of central office). There should be about 10 teachers from each school represented.

Since the career education concept requires family, agency, and business/industry involvement, these individuals should also be involved in the inservice education program. Inservice provides an opportunity for parents to contribute to the schools' endeavors. Parents frequently have negative attitudes about school personnel, believing they are insensitive to the real needs of their children. School personnel, on the other hand, often perceive parents as difficult to deal with and unreasonable. Both sides avoid each other. At workshops of this nature, parents can see how much school personnel care about their children and their education. Parents, conversely, can assist school personnel by indicating their contributions to career development in the home, as well as by influencing community resources.

Representatives from community agencies such as vocational rehabilitation, social services, employment services, sheltered workshops, and public health fields should be invited to the workshops. School personnel generally don't understand the wealth of services these agencies can provide, and agency personnel don't understand the school's goals and direction. These misconceptions can be dispelled when participants meet on a common ground and under a nonthreatening atmosphere.

A concerted effort will enlist the attention of some business/industry leaders. It is important to solicit their participation for career education because of the many contributions they can make to a total program effort as discussed in chapter 10. We also suggest that several student leaders or class officers participate because of their influence in accepting handicapped students in mainstream efforts. These individuals have many ideas for providing acceptance of handicapped students by their nonhandicapped peers.

Organization of the Workshop (Format, Content, and Conduct)

There are many arrangements that will need considerable thought and attention before inservice training begins. Participants should have advance notice and information about the workshops. Administrators must be informed and arrange for substitutes. Trainers must know all their responsibilities. A conducive meeting place with accessible coffee and eating facilities will be needed. Equipment and materials need to be arranged. Publicity should be conveyed through several sources. It may be advisable to arrange for professional growth credits. The success of any inservice program will be enhanced if the wealth of experience of the participants is emphasized through group interactions. These action groups facilitate the exchange of ideas by working through problems and possible solutions (Brolin, McKay, & West, 1977a). Small group discussion is a particularly useful aspect of inservice programs. Through the exchange of information in small groups, trainers can promote the participant's dedication and commitment to the career education purposes of the workshops.

The format and structure should be designed to accomplish the major goals and objectives of the inservice program. Since career education requires the active participation and cooperation of many types of personnel, including those from outside the school setting, a considerable amount of time should be devoted to building strong, positive relationships among these groups. To achieve this goal, we recommend a group process model that maximizes the input, problem-solving, and decision-making abilities of the participants, as illustrated in Figure 18.

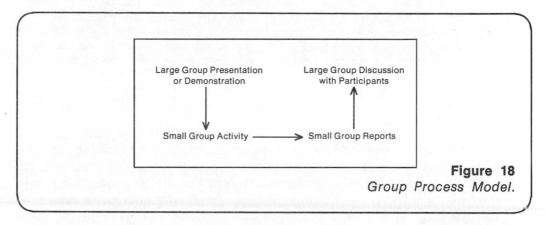

Figure 18
Group Process Model.

The above workshop process assumes that significant action and change in educational services will occur in direct proportion to the active participation of school personnel and other significant persons in the decision-making process. Brolin, McKay, and West (1977b) describe their use of the above model as follows:

> Most PRICE workshop sessions consist of four components: a large group presentation, a small group activity, small group reports and large group discussions. Basic information about the workshop topics (e.g., mental retardation, career education, instructional techniques, resources and materials, etc) are generally presented to the participant's by using information contained in the *Trainer's Manual, Self-Study Guide* and media package. In certain instances, demonstrations are used if they are more effective.
>
> Following the large group presentation or demonstration there is a small group activity to deal more critically with the topic in order to solve problems, gain group consensus, and/or generally learn more about the topic. This group process technique was found to be particularly effective in establishing and maintaining positive communication between the school personnel, parents and community representatives attending the workshops. Using small groups of approximately six individuals and a trainer, carefully selected activities were chosen to meet specific goals and objectives of the session. This scheme promoted a team relationship by working on a common task, working through the task using consensus-forming techniques and deciding upon adequate answers, solutions or alternatives. These tasks were always related to critical problems in developing career education programming for the educable retarded student.
>
> The third part of the session consists of small group reports. A spokesman reports to all participants his group's particular solutions and recommendations on the topic. This activity gives everyone a chance to be heard and for other important ideas to be identified and conveyed to the other groups for their consideration. Often each group strives to establish itself as the greatest problem-solver, which tends to facilitate and strengthen

the small group activity and interject a healthy and amusing sense of competition and cohesiveness into the workshop process.

The fourth component of each session consists of a large group discussion which allows the exchange of ideas and questions from participants on a broader level. This discussion permits a review of the major highlights and consensus of the groups relative to the topic and the opportunity to emphasize the major points that the participants were intended to learn from the session.

(pp. 9–10)

Brainstorming and consensus-forming are recommended techniques for the workshops, especially for small group activities. *Brainstorming* is a procedure that uses a positive, constructive approach in solving problems. No criticism is permitted because the more ideas that are generated, no matter how wild, the better. In a group situation, a recorder should be appointed to write down all the ideas of participants in the several minutes they have to brainstorm solutions to a problem or topic. For example, a humorous practice activity to learn the procedure follows:

A rich uncle just passed away and you have just inherited one million Ping-Pong balls. He didn't want to hand you a great deal of money; he wanted you to have to earn it. You decide not to market the product beyond the limits of your fair city. Thus, to get rid of all these Ping-Pong balls and make a profit, you must uncover numerous ways these balls can be used. Think of as many uses of these Ping-Pong balls as possible in 5 minutes.

We are amazed at the number of creative thoughts that are the products of a brainstorming session on such a topic. Literally hundreds of viable uses have been identified for these Ping-Pong balls in our workshop. In the process, the participants learn the brainstorming technique and start building a warm team relationship while listening to each other's ideas.

The second part of this group process problem-solving approach is *consensus-forming.* Everyone has had a chance to contribute ideas in the brainstorming session, no matter how impractical they may be. But, it is important to identify what the entire group can decide upon as the most appropriate way to market the Ping-Pong balls. In the consensus-forming aspect, each brainstorming idea is considered and those that are clearly unworkable are discarded. Group members may suggest modifications of an idea that will satisfy those who did not approve of the idea in the original form. Eventually, the group will arrive at a consensus on the best solution to the problem. There are some other ways participants can be involved in the workshop process: simulations, role playing, resource persons, demonstrations, panels, buzz sessions, and self-ratings.

The needs assessment studies should be a main determinant of the content of the workshops and the emphasis given to each topic. Some of the major concerns will be how often, how long, and when should the workshops be held? Since career education is so pervasive and will require considerable attitude formation, knowledge building, and curriculum planning from the participants, several inservice sessions stretching over most of a semester should be considered. A 25 1/2 hour inservice program resulted from Project PRICE and was considered the minimum needed to cover these three areas for mildly retarded students. The PRICE Inservice Training Program was conducted in either 4 or 9 days. The 4-day training approach required 6–7 hours per day with the workshops spaced 3–4 weeks apart. The 9-day approach required only 2–3 hours of training at a time and could be conducted after school hours, eliminating the need for substitute teachers. The 20 sessions comprising the PRICE program are outlined in Figure 19.

The type of format selected will depend on several factors (e.g., the school day, incentive factors, available funds for substitutes, and availability of substitutes). The project was the result of 3 years of intensive work and involvement with 12 school districts and several consultants.

1. Orientation. Familiarizes the participants with each other, the purposes of the workshops, the workshop structure, and the nature of the training program. Consists of a welcome, a small group activity for getting acquainted, a large group presentation about the inservice program and evaluation procedures, and questions and answers. The district superintendent should be on hand to welcome participants and lend support.

2. Group Process Techniques. Familiarizes the participants with inservice group process techniques. Consists of a large group presentation on brainstorming, brainstorming activity, large group presentation on consensus-forming, small group consensus-forming activity, group reports on their humorous problem-solving solutions, and questions and answers. The session should be lighthearted and nonthreatening.

3. Mental Retardation. Familiarizes participants with the nature of mental retardation and helps increase empathy for these individuals. Consists of three small group activities, which require each small group to formulate a definition of mental retardation, to identify from a worksheet the major causes of the condition, and to identify personality characteristics unique to these individuals. The various groups then give their consensus on each of the three assignments, listen to a presentation on the topic, and then listen to the group leader give the correct answers to the three assignments. This session begins developing a positive attitude in the participants about working with retarded students.

4. Appropriate Educational Programming. Familiarizes the participants with the concepts and procedures of appropriate programming. Consists of a large group presentation on legislation, court actions, placement, parent assertiveness, labeling, technology, current issues, and the IEP; a small

PRICE Inservice Sessions

session	topic	hours	module
1	Orientation	1½	1
2	Group Process Techniques	1	1
3	Mental Retardation	1½	2
4	Appropriate Educational Programming	1½	2
5	Career Education	1½	2
6	Instructional Strategies	1¾	3
7	PRICE Competency Units	1½	4
8	Resources & Materials	¾	4
9	Personal-Social Skills	1½	5
10	Daily Living & Occupational Skills	1½	5
11	Community Resources	1¼	6
12	Family Assistance	1¼	6
13	Individualized Education Programs	1½	7
14	Student Assessment	¾	7
15	Career Education Programming	1½	7
16	Review of Data	1¼	8
17	Instructional Goals: Responsibilities	1½	8
18	Instructional Goals Resources	1	9
19	Community Assistance-Administrative Goals	1½	9
20	Future Actions & Workshop Evaluation	1	9

Note: If 4 inservice days are selected, there should be five sessions per day.

Figure 19
Project PRICE Inservice Training Format.

Source: *Trainers guide for life centered career education* (Brolin et al., 1978).

group activity on "Desirable Work Characteristics" to depict the different expectations society has for labeled people; small group reports; a videotape of some retarded students and their opinions about their educational experiences; and questions and answers. The videotape is an effective attitude development technique.

5. Career Education. Familiarizes participants with the career education concept and competency based education. Participants formulate a definition in a small group, report their definition and give supporting arguments, listen to a large group presentation on the PRICE definition and the competencies, and questions and answers. State and local definitions are also covered. The session is intended to promote the life centered concept of career education.

6. *Instructional Strategies.* Familiarizes participants with appropriate instructional procedures. Consists of a small group activity and reports from each group, who are requested to select a name and motto; a small group activity of working out a strategy; and a question and answer period, where other strategies for teaching the competencies are identified.

7. *PRICE Competency Units.* Familiarizes participants with instructional guidelines contained in a program guide, now entitled *Life Centered Career Education: A Competency Based Approach.* Consists of listening to a large group presentation explaining the units, developing a unit, small group reports, a large group demonstration on using the *Guide*, and questions and answers. The session encourages the participants to consider what needs to be taught to these students, where, when, and by whom.

8. *Resources and Materials.* Familiarizes participants with appropriate sources of career education materials. Consists of a large group presentation and a materials display organized into daily living, personal-social, and occupational guidance and preparation areas. Local community resources should be displayed and made available for workshop participants.

9. *Personal-Social Skills.* Familiarizes participants with effective techniques. Consists of a humorous small group activity in which members of each small group identify what they consider to be their outstanding qualities, a large group presentation on techniques and involvement in a values clarification activity that can be used in the classroom, a case study to prepare a demonstration of a technique, small group reports, and a question and answer period.

10. *Daily Living and Occupational Skills.* Familiarizes participants with ways daily living and occupational competencies can be acquired. Consists of selecting two of five small group sessions most closely related to their area of specialty and then discussing activities, materials, and resources that are appropriate for teaching the competencies. The session lays the foundation for the future development of the Career Education Plan.

11. *Community Resources.* Familiarizes participants with appropriate community resources. Consists of a community resources panel of agency personnel who react to a list of questions such as what competencies they can help students acquire, eligibility, and costs. A question and answer period concludes the panel's responsibilities. The agency representatives and the inservice trainers should distribute literature. This session permits community representatives to make a significant contribution to the school.

12. *Family Assistance.* Familiarizes participants with ways the family can contribute to the student's career development. Consists of a parent panel explaining competency involvement, problems encountered in teaching their children, assistance they feel they need, and community services they feel they can help the school acquire. Parents attending the workshop should usually make up this panel.

13. *Individualized Education Program.* Familiarizes participants with recent federal/state legislation and IEPs. Consists of a large group presentation on the laws, small group activity to develop an IEP, and questions and answers. At least one trainer must be very knowledgeable about the legislation and IEPs to make this session effective.

14. *Student Assessment.* Familiarizes participants with evaluation procedures for assessing competency or career development. Consists of explaining the PRICE Competency Rating Scale, a small group activity to practice using the scale, small group reports, and questions and answers.

15. *Career Education Programming.* Familiarizes participants with the procedures necessary for creating a functional career education infusion program. Consists of a large group presentation outlining the steps associated with career education planning and other details associated with implementing the concept in a district and school building; a presentation by the Career Education Special Needs Committee relative to their work to date (e.g., formulating a philosophy and definition/conceptualization of career education and goals/objectives); a reaction to the philosophy and goals/objectives by the participants; and a question and answer period to identify other goals and needs. The data collected at this session are tabulated and presented at the next workshop.

16. *Review of Data.* Familiarizes participants with the analysis of data from the previous session. Consists of presenting participants with a list of all agreed-upon goals/objectives, open discussion, presentation of the results of a student competency assessment study, and questions and answers.

17. *Instructional Goals: Responsibilities.* Determines strategies and methods for attaining the agreed-upon goals and objectives and who is to be responsible. Consists of a small group activity to identify strategies/methods and appropriate personnel, parent and community personnel indicating their role, and questions and answers. The trainer reviews each of the 22 competencies to gain group consensus of responsibilities, including subject taught, grade level, and parent and community involvement.

18. *Instructional Goals: Resources.* Determines resources and assistance needed for helping students attain the competencies. Consists of a small

group activity where participants identify what course changes and additions, instructional materials, and assistance from special educators are needed to teach the 22 competencies. A concluding period reviews the major needs.

19. Community Assistance and Administrative Goals. Determines strategies and methods, responsibilities, and other needs. Consists of large group discussion where participants brainstorm possible strategies/methods and who should be responsible. Parents, agency personnel, and business and industry participants convey their commitment, while school personnel meet in other groups to identify staff, facilities and resources, student and program evaluation, staff development, and financial needs that will be required to meet each of the goals/objectives. (The Special Needs Committee will develop these further after the inservice workshops and then present them back to the participants later.)

20. Future Actions and Workshop Evaluation. Familiarizes participants with future actions that will occur and evaluates the inservice program. Consists of small group activity where participants complete a self-contract indicating their willingness to participate in a specific way to include the Career Education Plan in their daily activities. The superintendent should come to this session and indicate support of career education and their efforts.

You can readily see that inservice training requires considerable time and effort to be effective and before it can provide input for building an acceptable Career Education Plan. However, if an extensive inservice training program like PRICE is conducted, the chances of career education becoming a significant aspect of the school's curriculum is much greater.

THE CAREER EDUCATION PLAN

The impact and significance of inservice training will be minimal unless something definitive is accomplished by the participants and put into practice shortly thereafter (Brolin, McKay, & West, 1977a). The Career Education Plan provides the vehicle by which participant input and commitment can be put into motion and career education implemented.

The process of developing a Career Education Plan begins well before inservice workshops are conducted. There are three major time periods associated with the plan's development: **1.** prior to the inservice workshops; **2.** during and between the workshops; and **3.** after the inservice has been completed. There may be an overall district-wide model developed, but each school implementing career education will have to adapt it to meet its own circumstances or develop its own plan based on the agreed-upon guidelines.

The Special Needs Committee of the larger Career Education Steering Committee and its task forces (Needs Assessment, Staff Development, Resources & Public Relations, Curriculum Development, and Evaluation) are responsible for developing and implementing the Career Education Plan. The process is set in motion when the Special Needs Committee and its task forces begin reviewing the literature and programs on career education, developing a tentative philosophy and model for career education, conducting district-wide needs assessment studies, preparing an inservice training program, and deciding upon evaluation procedures for the workshops and the career education program that is developed.

Inservice workshops provide school personnel, parents, students, and community representatives the opportunity to react to the work of the committee and task forces and to help identify needs and activities necessary to infuse career education into the curriculum and the community. This grass-roots input and commitment is important in determining a go/no-go situation in the various schools. Inservice should generate a multitude of ideas about directions that will have to be taken if career education is to be implemented. New faces and leaders the committee will need should surface and help contribute to the development of the Career Education Plan.

After inservice workshops are completed, the committee and task forces must combine the input, investigate other matters that emerge from the workshops, and begin to write the final Career Education Plan or plans. Building committees should write their own plans with assistance from the Special Needs Committee. A suggested outline for writing the plan is presented in Figure 20.

Career education goals and objectives should be consistent with the school district's philosophy and definition/conceptualization of career education. We suggest identifying at least three types of goals: instructional, community involvement, and administrative goals. Participants from the inservice workshops should help determine and agree to them to gain a shared commitment. Examples of each type of goal are as follows:

- *Instructional Goal:* Provide all handicapped students with the opportunity to learn the 22 competencies; integrate handicapped students more appropriately in regular classes; encourage teachers to emphasize career concepts in their subject matter; and provide career awareness, exploration, guidance, and preparation experiences.

- *Community Involvement Goals:* Involve community groups on career education advisory committees and task forces; increase community career education sites; and develop home training materials for parents to teach competencies.

- *Administrative Goals:* Secure adequate staff facilities and resources; inservice staff and community representatives; and conduct frequent assessments of student competency attainment and IEP needs.

CAREER EDUCATION PLAN OUTLINE

Name of School _____ City, State _____

A. School District Philosophy

B. Definition of Conceptualization of Career Education for Handicapped Students

C. Career Education Goals/Objectives
    1. Instructional
    2. Community Involvement
    3. Administrative

D. Instructional Goals/Objectives
    1. Strategies/Methods and Responsibilities
    2. Competency Instruction Responsibilities: School Personnel
    3. Courses Changes/Additions
    4. Instructional Materials Needed
    5. Assistance Needed from Special Educators
    6. Other

E. Community Involvement Goals/Objectives
    1. Strategies/Methods and Responsibilities
    2. Competency Instruction Responsibilities: Community Personnel
        a. Family
        b. Agencies
        c. Business/Industry

F. Administrative Goals/Objectives
    1. Strategies/Methods and Responsibilities
    2. Staffing Requirements
    3. Facilities/Resources
    4. Staff Development
    5. Student Assessment
    6. Program Evaluation
    7. Budget
    8. Other

G. Implementation

Figure 20
Suggested Outline for Career Education Plan.

Source: Trainers guide for life centered career education (Brolin et al., 1978).

The *Trainers Guide for Life Centered Career Education* illustrates how each goal/objective should be broken down into logical steps for implementation, using the guidelines presented in Figure 20. The last component of the Career Education Plan, implementation, reflects the steps or actions needed to incorporate career education in the school. Timelines and responsibilities should be determined so that personnel, facilities, public relations, and other provisions can be provided accordingly. Once the plan is approved by the central administration, materials and equipment will need to be ordered, cooperative efforts secured with various community groups, further inservice programs developed, and public relations efforts conducted.

Once the plan is put into operation for students, formative and summative evaluations will be needed to determine how well the program is being conducted to meet student needs. Feedback of the effectiveness of instructional experiences at school, home, and in the community will determine any needed modifications.

CONCLUSION

Career education planning and implementation is a comprehensive process requiring the involvement of school, parents, and community resources. Solid support from administrative decision makers is an absolute necessity and starting point for career education if it is to be successful. In addition, a competent and committed core of organizers, process of development, needs assessments, inservice training, and Career Education Plan must all interact effectively to result in a change of educational practices and a dedication to career education. If a major impact is to be forthcoming, a large number of individuals, important to the student's career development, must be involved and have a voice in what is developed. Change will occur only if these people believe they have been listened to and have had an impact on what is proposed.

In this chapter we have discussed what we feel are important components to successful career education planning and implementation. The next chapter will focus on aspects related to conducting these programs for the students.

This book maintains that a life centered career education approach is necessary for handicapped individuals if they are to successfully assimilate into today's rapidly changing and demanding society. While the development of occupational skills is critical to competing and surviving in the labor market, the individual must also possess, as equally important, a relatively high degree of personal-social, daily living, and academic skills. Career education offers the opportunity to pull it all together by considering the whole person.

There has always been a concern by special educators for the adjustment of the adult handicapped individual in the community. Kokaska and Kolstoe (1977) Indicate that the vocational aspect of career education has often been emphasized but that the totality of one's life is also a valid area of instruction within the curriculum. In their opinion, career education concepts are particularly important for the handicapped since they often need longer periods of intensive teaching. Thus, "career concepts can be used to maintain a continuity to a curriculum that extends from early childhood through the adult years" (p. 5).

In chapter 3 we discuss the many concepts of career education and our conceptualization of a career education-oriented curriculum. We emphasize the need for students to be able to leave the school system with 22 career development competencies that our research has found as critical to community and occupational success. In order for these competencies to be acquired, we advocate a curriculum approach that is competency based, involves school, family and community representatives, and incorporates the elements of career awareness, exploration, preparation, and placement/follow up into its design.

Each of the 22 life career development competencies can be broken down into subcompetencies, some of which should be taught at the elementary level. Many subcompetencies should be emphasized throughout the student's educational program, particularly those that relate to the various personal-social and occupational skills.

There is no simple recipe as to how career education can be structured in a K-12+ program for handicapped students. In this chapter we will give suggestions, but they can only be used in that manner since every school situation is different. What is important is that school personnel shift from a *content*-based curriculum to one that is more *process*-based. Students should understand how the content is related to their career development, both as a future worker and as a functioning member of society.

CURRICULUM CONSIDERATIONS

The classroom climate is a primary factor in determining the success of career education programs within a school environment. School personnel must realize this fact and set up a systematic way to facilitate an atmosphere that is democratic rather than autocratic, optimizing each person's development in all areas. Magnuson (1974) suggests the following steps in creating a facilitative climate: **1.** Take an honest look at the present climate and determine how it really is; **2.** Ask if each student in the room who will sit in the classroom throughout the year would enjoy being there; **3.** Ask, "What do I do to ensure success for each person?"; and **4.** Ask "How do my students see me?" and "How would I like for my students to see me?" Once these questions have been honestly answered, the teacher will be able to establish a systematic, facilitative environment that should include the beliefs listed on the following page.

Some ideas Magnuson lists for improving the school climate are: *Interact* with your students and be available; *talk* with other teachers about ideas for implementing career education activities; *plan* an all-school project to get everyone involved; work toward making your *faculty lounge* a really enjoyable place to be; and agree on some common ground rules relating to *noise* level.

I BELIEVE:

—It is my responsibility to strive to love, accept and understand each student as a unique human being with unique needs.

—It is my responsibility to plan for creating a psychologically safe learning environment for every student trusted to me.

—It is my responsibility to serve as an adult model who demonstrates compassion and empathy.

—I do have time in my day to encourage success in each student.

—Human interaction between students and students, and students and teachers is an essential part of growing.

—How I teach is as important as what I teach.

—I, by nature of my position as an educator, have power over human lives. It is my responsibility to remain cognizant of this fact and utilize my power in ways that will maximize human growth.

Magnuson, 1974

Career education for handicapped students requires the involvement of all possible school personnel, in addition to family and community representatives. Through the process of conducting inservice workshops and developing a Career Education Plan for the school, this partnership should become established. As we indicated in chapters 3 through 6, career education transcends the entire curriculum and requires competency/subcompetency instruction at all levels. Curriculum emphasis will vary from school to school and student to student, depending on the school's resources, philosophy, preparedness, and the like. Based on our experience, career education instruction in academic, daily living, occupational, and personal-social skills follows the breakdown over the K-12+ curriculum period as depicted in Figure 21. Each of these four curriculum areas is discussed next.

Academic Skills

During the elementary years, handicapped students must learn functional academic skills, such as reading, writing, and arithmetic. There is no question that this must be the primary emphasis during these years as they lay the foundation for the subsequent learning of the daily living and occupational skills needed for community living and working.

At the junior high school level, there should begin a decrease in teaching academic skills per se, although much of this type of instruction can be

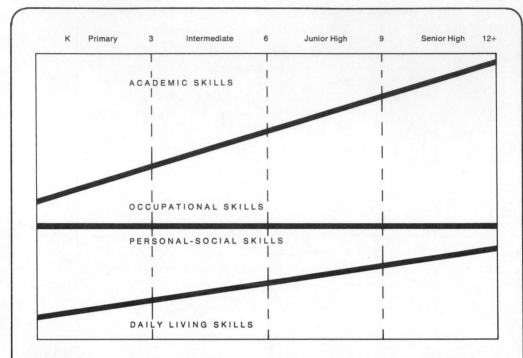

Figure 21
*Suggested Curriculum Area Emphasis for Career Development
at the Various Grade Levels.*

directed to teaching specific daily living and occupational skills. This, of course, will vary with the handicapped student and her potential and need for academic skills instruction. However, at this age, students begin questioning the relative value of what they are learning compared to what they will do later in life.

At the senior high school level, academic instruction should be directed primarily to those subjects not yet mastered well enough and that are critical to community functioning and to those subjects that are of high interest to the student. Otherwise, daily living skills and occupational guidance and preparation should form the greater part of the student's course of study. Teaching academic skills that will result in little further progress is senseless when the other curriculum areas are of such vital importance to the student's career development.

Daily Living Skills

There are several subcompetencies that can be taught during the elementary years in addition to basic academic skills. In the daily living skills area, these include: Identifying money and making correct change; making wise expenditures; dressing appropriately; grooming and hygiene; eating skills; local laws and government; participating in basic leisure and recreational group activities; and traffic laws and safety practices, which are subcompetencies that can be learned, or that can begin to be learned, by handicapped students.

At the junior high level, a much greater emphasis on daily living skills should occur. Learning about bank and credit facilities, home maintenance, adequate housing, use of basic appliances and tools, physical fitness, nutrition and weight control practices, marriage and child care practices, meal planning, preparation and purchasing, clothing purchase and care, citizenship rights, recreational planning, traffic rules, and use of various means of transportation are subcompetencies that can begin to be learned and perhaps acquired by the time they enter the high school program.

At the senior high school level, the student should have learned the subcompetencies that were taught earlier and also those that have not yet been taught or emphasized. Learning how to keep financial records, calculate and pay taxes, maintain a home interior, prevent and treat common illnesses, respond to questioning by the law, plan vacations, and to drive a car are higher order subcompetencies that some students may never learn adequately. Students unable to learn certain competencies/subcompetencies will need to know how they can receive assistance.

Personal-Social Skills

The elementary years are particularly important to handicapped students for developing adequate personal-social skills. The first few years of life are vital to personality development. Handicapped children in particular are vulnerable to the attitudes and behaviors of others toward them, which, in many instances, may be ridicule, hostility, rejection, or physical abuse. Thus, they must learn enough about themselves to feel they are worthwhile persons, as well as how to handle these negative behaviors. This area needs much more attention if handicapped students are going to benefit from educational efforts and attain optimal career development. All seven competencies and their subcompetencies should become part of the instructional program at the elementary level. All school personnel teaching the handicapped student should make it a point to include personal-social development as an integral part of instruction.

If a concerted attempt is made during the elementary years to assist the student in her personal-social skills development, the emphasis may be decreased during the secondary programs. This is not meant to de-emphasize its importance during these years. Rather, we mean to imply that the time spent with students in helping them learn enough about themselves, develop self-confidence, display socially responsible behavior, and other personal-social skills may be reduced. On the other hand, certain students who have not acquired these skills will need a substantial amount of time directed toward this area. Personal-social skills development should continue within the realm of all school personnel, with guidance and counseling persons lending their special expertise in dealing with unusually deficient behaviors.

Occupational Guidance and Preparation

The career education conceptualization highlights the need for elementary programs to provide much more attention to the student's occupational development at this level. Young children are interested in the world of work and actively seek to find out what their parents and significant others do to make a living. We believe many of the subcompetencies in this curriculum area should be emphasized during the elementary years: work attitudes and values; remunerative aspects of working; work habits (following directions, work with others, accept supervision, good attendance and punctuality, quality and quantity performance, safety); and physical-manual skills (balance, coordination, dexterity, stamina).

As the student progresses through the educational system, the occupational emphasis needs to become even greater. At the junior high school level, industrial arts, home economics, and other vocational subjects should be made available to the handicapped student to develop prevocational skills and motivations. Career exploration experiences in the community become important, and the opportunity to try out various jobs in the classroom and community (besides in the home) will increase the student's concept of herself as a future productive member of society. Occupational guidance activities such as those discussed in chapter 6 should be initiated to assist the student in her career development and decision-making.

During the high school years, both occupational guidance and preparation should form at least half of the curriculum for most handicapped students. A Career Information and Assessment Center will help students learn more about jobs, their specific vocational aptitudes and interests, and job-seeking skills and procedures. Such a center should be open at any time for the student, teacher, parent, and community representative, in addition to being an integral part of the student's weekly program. Vocational subjects, work/job samples, on-the-job work experiences in the community, and other activities of this nature should be provided. The entire school faculty should be oriented toward the goal of helping the student prepare for community living and working requirements, and economic, social, and personal fulfillment.

Most of the daily living, personal-social, and occupational skills comprising the competency based curriculum approach can be taught in regular subject matter courses. Daily living skills can be taught in math, social studies, music, art, physical education, English, home economics, home mechanics, driver's education, business, and special education classes.

Personal-social skills can be taught by all teachers, with additional assistance from school counselors and special educators. Occupational guidance can also be received from all teachers, with the school counselor and special educator working cooperatively to assist each student individually. Occupational preparation is particularly dependent on vocational teachers from home economics, industrial arts, agriculture, and auto mechanics, as well as those special programs that the educator has established in the school and community. Well-established work-study programs (vocational adjustment, work experience) developed by special educators can be used for the occupational preparation needs of handicapped students but should not constitute the only source of such training.

We suggest the form presented in Figure 22 be used to identify the benefits of each course the handicapped student takes as it relates to her career development. This form can be used with the Individualized Education Plan that we have mentioned frequently throughout this book and that we will

LESSON PLAN

Student _____ Teacher _____

Subject _____ Grade _____

Curriculum Area	Objectives	Activities/Strategies	Resources/Materials
Academic Skills			
Daily Living Skills			
Personal-Social Skills			
Occupational Guidance & Preparation			

Figure 22
Example of Form That Could Be Used by Teachers to Indicate Their Career Development Instruction.

INDIVIDUALIZED EDUCATION PROGRAM

School District Responsible: Sunset

Student: Joe Dokes

Current placement: Special Education

Eligibility certified: 9/1/XX (date)

Period of individualized education program: 9/15/XX to 12/18/XX

Date(s) of meeting: September 12, 19XX

Persons present	Relationship to child
John Smith	Psychologist
Tom Jones	Counselor
Mary White	Special Ed.
Nancy Black	Home Economics
Gene Blue	Industrial Arts
Mr. & Mrs. Dokes	Parents

Curriculum areas* requiring special education and related services	Present Level(s) of performance	Annual goals	Short term objectives	Time required	Objectives attained (dates)		
Area 1 Daily Living	Partially Competent	Managing Family Finances	1) Keep financial records; 2) Calc. taxes	9/15/XX to 12/18/XX 9/1 to 12/18	12/2 XX	12/15 XX	
Area 2 Occupational	Not Competent	Seek, secure & maintain emp.	1) search for job; 2) apply for job; 3) interview	1)9/15 to 10/8 2)10/10 to 11/1 3)11/11 to 12/15	10/6 XX	10/30 XX	12/14 XX

*If more space is required, use an additional sheet.

A. List any special instructional material or media necessary to implement this individualized education program.

1) Budget book, checks, tax forms, tax guide, samples
2) Job search exercises, job application forms, video-tapes of job interviews

Special education and related services recommended	Personnel responsible (name and title)	Date services begin	Duration
Curriculum area 1 Daily Living	Sam Green, Bus. Ed. Nancy Black, Home Ec. Mary White, Special Ed.	9/15/XX	3 mos.
Curriculum area 2 Occupational	Tom Jones, Counselor Mary White, Special Ed.	9/15/XX	1 mo.

B. Describe the extent to which the child will participate in regular education programs.

Language Arts--10%; Social Sciences--15%; Physical Education--10%

Home Economics--15%; Vocational Agriculture--15% (65%)

C. Recommended type of placement: Regular educational program with no more than
   (include physical education) 35% time out of program.

D. Provide justification for the type of educational placement.

Student needs to acquire a higher level of the following competencies as

indicated on the Competency Rating Scale: #1 Managing Family Finances;

#22 Seeking, Securing, & Maintaining Employment. Regular class placement will

facilitate other competency areas.

E. Actual placement: _____

F. List the criteria, evaluating procedures and schedule for determining whether the short
   term objectives are met.

Short term objectives	Objective criteria	Evaluation procedures	Schedule
1) Keep financial records	Competency Rating Scale	Administer CRS	11/1/XX, 12/1/XX, 12/18/XX
2) Calculate and pay taxes	Same	Same	11/1/XX, 12/1/XX, 12/18/XX
3) Search for job		Same	10/6/XX
4) Apply for job	Same	Same	10/30/XX
5) Interview for job	Same (see CRS Manual)	Same	12/14/XX

Date of parental acceptance/rejection _____ 9/13/XX _____

Signature _____

Signature _____

Figure 23
Example of How Competencies Can Be Presented in the IEP.

discuss again later in this chapter. It has the potential for not only assuring the student of receiving the typical content transmitted in a regular class-room but also of having the teacher relate the subject matter to its impli-cations for career development (daily living, personal-social, and occupa-tional skills).

INDIVIDUALIZED EDUCATION PROGRAMS

The competency based approach advocated in this book lends itself to the development of appropriate Individualized Education Programs (IEPs) for handicapped students. The publications *A Primer on Individualized Educa-tion Programs for Handicapped Children* (Torres, 1977a) and the *Special Education Administrative Policies Manual* (Torres, 1977b) and other publi-cations treat this topic more extensively. It is not the purpose of this chapter to go into such matters in any detail other than to illustrate how the career development competencies can be used in IEP efforts. Figure 23 is an ex-ample of how the competencies can be presented on the IEP.

EXPERIENCE-BASED CAREER EDUCATION

The Experience-Based Career Education (EBCE) model was described briefly in chapter 3 when the four national models were presented (pp. 92–93). EBCE is an alternative program for high school students; it provides them with an opportunity to explore occupations while taking academic subjects for graduation. A major concept of EBCE is that the community can provide a rich array of experiences that, combined with academic courses, will better help students to learn more about who they are, and what they want to become. The model developed by The Appalachian Edu-cational Laboratory (AEL) is discussed here.

Unfortunately, many vocational, cooperative, and work-study programs emphasize training for a specific skill rather than learning about many careers and making many types of decisions. Academic studies are kept in the classroom rather than being allowed to occur in the community. Consequently, the students' choices become limited and their perspective of the world of work becomes too narrow. EBCE attempts to correct this deficiency by going one step further than traditional work programs. It em-phasizes people, jobs, self, and the way communities work within the regu-lar course of study of high school students. Thus, students learn all about these things through direct experience with hundreds of adults in the com-munity (Hyre & Henderson, 1976).

A learning coordinator (LC) works on an individual basis with each student in developing job and academic experiences. A student guide is used in selecting career experience sites. Students select the occupations they wish to explore and are placed with a resource person in that occupation for a period of 2 to 13 weeks, 1 to 3 hours a day. They explore the occupations by observation, hands-on experiences, and by completing their subject requirements. The subject assignments are developed to help the student learn concepts in relation to the occupation being explored.

The key to the EBCE program is the use of several documents that are student-centered and provide a comprehensive, systematic, and individualized academic and career exploration approach to learning. The student guide assists the student in developing, maintaining, and updating her academic and career program. Several cross reference catalogs provide suggested resources that can be used and activities that can be pursued to meet specific subject objectives. A career guide permits the student to conduct a self-directed exploration of career or occupational opportunities. A series of experience site learning guides provide the LC and student with information about job sites and occupations.

Developing an individualized career program for each student requires identifying worker trait groups (WTG) and selecting specific occupations of interest. Four inventories or checklists are used to help the student determine WTGs of interest: **1.** school subjects liked; **2.** an interests checklist; **3.** a temperaments checklist; and **4.** a self-assessment instrument. The results of these instruments are related to a "Worker Trait Group Matrix" from which the student explores occupations from WTGs that appear to be of highest interest.

Developing the academic program consists of selecting mandatory courses for graduation, of interest, or that are related to the occupations being explored. A Basic Skills Inventory identifies any reading and mathematics deficiencies. A "Course Concept Matrix" permits the student to scan all of the concepts and objectives that can be pursued in selected courses. The EBCE instructional system is depicted in Figure 24.

Each student's individualized program is developed according to her subject content interest, occupational interests, aptitudes, academic abilities, basic skills deficiencies, and other criteria. The weekly programs are developed jointly by the student and LC. A weekly assignment is written for each subject and career planning and are completed "on site," at home, or in the library. To receive academic credit in an experiential placement, projects or assignments are developed that relate to the student's occupational placement and the job tasks performed by the resource person. These projects are outlined in a document called an *activity sheet.*

When planning an academic activity, the LC and student must take into account the subject concepts and/or objectives, occupational site, and the tasks performed by the resource person. Three or four concepts are selected for each course and are written to include one objective and one job task to be performed by the resource person. The LC and student decide what activities will assist the student in learning that behavioral objective. The activities are outlined on the activity sheet—defining the problem, gather-

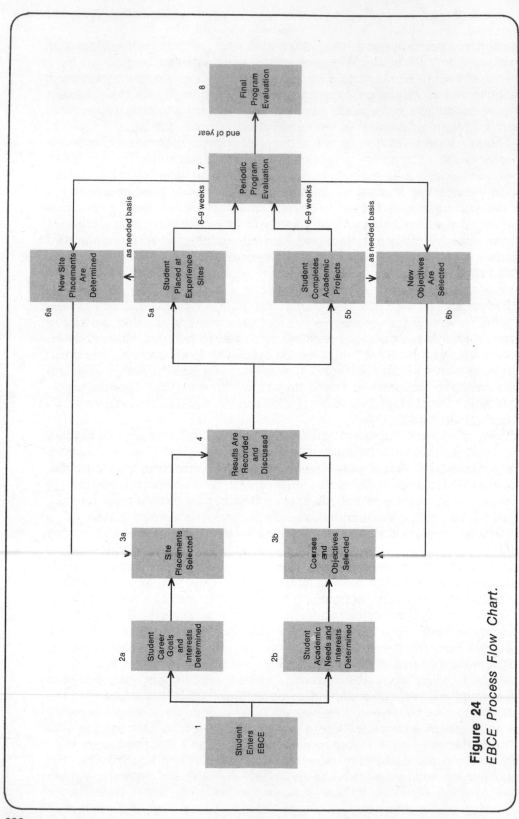

Figure 24
EBCE Process Flow Chart.

ing and analyzing information, generalizing, and communicating. There is also a section on what and how the activity will be evaluated.

The EBCE model is undergoing several trials for use with handicapped students. At Iowa Central Community College, the model is being assessed for its potential in meeting the career education needs of mildly mentally disabled (MD) adolescents in rural secondary schools. Carl Larson (1978), assistant superintendent, provides the following information about this effort.

EBCE-MD began as a by-product of the EBCE-Part D effort. The original EBCE-Part D effort in Iowa was granted to Iowa Central Community College by the Department of Health, Education, and Welfare. The purpose of the grant was to develop career education exploratory experiences for students in rural areas. Early in the development of the EBCE effort it became apparent that a similar career exploratory program was needed for special education students and that efforts should be directed toward the mildly mentally disabled adolescent.

One of the key elements in deciding to develop or modify the AEL model of EBCE was the realization that the business and industry sector of the community was willing to volunteer their resources toward educating the children. Such a resource could not be overlooked as a basis for developing a MD program. Another realization was that the EBCE-AEL model can be adapted to fit a district population group. The EBCE model is highly structured. Certain component parts of it can be modified to meet an identifiable population need area without destroying the model. Iowa Central Community College, 2 years prior to this existing EBCE-MD model, modified the AEL model for the high school dropout population. This was accomplished by substituting the GED and high school equivalency segments for the academic components of the AEL model. A final reason for moving towards an adaptation of the AEL model was the realization that mentally disabled students placed with Work Experience Instructors (WEIs) in a traditional program are essentially locked into a one-career experience during a school year. Using the EBCE-MD model, students can explore a variety of occupations during the critical years of career decision making while they are in the high school stage. Thus, new dimensions can be added to the WEI role and function when the EBCE-MD model is implemented.

When a school with a WEI makes a decision to implement the EBCE-MD program, the first consideration must be to identify student career needs. The Area Education Agencies (AEA) in Iowa are responsible for this task. However, in its career assessing system, the EBCE-AEL model further defines the career goals of MD students. It is important to realize that student needs are paramount in making a decision on how schools implement the program.

The experience site is the key to career exploration. Therefore, the local business/industry community must be oriented to the career needs of mentally disabled students. They also must be oriented to the realization that they have a vested interest in the education of their own children and are a tremendous resource in that educational process. This awareness or orientation to the EBCE-MD program is accomplished by the EBCE staff operating out of the community college.

At the orientation meetings, the business/industry community is asked to volunteer their services by opening their doors to analysis and development of the resources at their fingertips. This development of the business/industry community is accomplished by trained, experienced site analysts from the community college.

Each business is analyzed in-depth and a learning site guide (LSG), especially adapted for mentally disabled students, is developed. The guide provides to the WEI the essentials of the learning structure when the student is placed at the site. It is necessary to develop approximately three to four sites for each student in the EBCE-MD program. Students in the program will explore more than one occupation at a given site. The student spends about 8 to 9 weeks at a given site. Before the student is placed at a new site, she meets with the WEI and redefines her career goals. Records are kept on each student so that the WEI can bring career goals to a sharper focus through proper career site placement. Examples of sites and occupations that the handicapped students experience in these rural areas are presented in Table 7.

The WEIs are trained at Iowa Central Community College by specialists from AEL, with the aid of team members from the EBCE-Part D project. Training is a 5-day process and consists essentially of working through the entire EBCE process (Figure 24). Once training is completed, the WEI is then prepared to go out into the community and develop the necessary number of learning site guides for her students. Technical assistance is provided to each WEI at critical times by the specialists from the AEL, as well as trained personnel from the community college. A newly trained WEI will need technical assistance usually at about the third week after school starts, the end of the first quarter, the beginning of the second semester, and during evaluation at the end of the program.

In a typical program, the mentally disabled student spends (depending on her ability) two to three afternoons at the site. The remaining afternoons are spent with the WEI in designing activity sheets for the work experience program. Activity sheets are designed jointly between the student and the WEI on an individual basis.

Students in the EBCE-MD program may complete academic work in English-communications, math, personal-social skills, and career education. The WEI must work closely with the special education teacher because in the mornings, the mentally disabled student is completing work in home economics, social studies, industrial arts, physical education, math, and English. If the student is pursuing English through the EBCE-MD program, then she would not duplicate that career area with the regular special education teacher.

Basic to the success of any EBCE-MD program is a formation of a local Coordinating or Advisory Committee. This committee should be comprised essentially of members of the business community, parents, and students,

Table 7

Examples of Experience Sites and Occupations for
EBCE-MD Students in Iowa Rural Project

site	occupation
Motel	Maid/Housekeeper
Bakery	Baker
Flower Shop	Plant Care
Supermarket	Carryout/Stocking
Community Hospital	Custodian; Cook/Food Service
Plumbing, Heating, Refrigerations	Repairperson; Plumber
Newspaper	Photography; Advertisement, Display Lay-out
Garage	Lubeperson; Car Clean-Up
Grocery	Produce Person; Carryout; Stocking
Community Schools	Custodian
Job Service	Placement/Filling
Conservation Community	Conservationist
Catalog Store	Sales Person
Dime Store	Clerk; Buyer
Beauty Salon	Hair-dress/Stylist
Carpet Store	Warehouse Worker; Carpet Installer
Lumber Store	Yard Person; Delivery
Service Station	Mechanic
Body Shop	Body/Repair (Fender)
Plumbing & Heating	Plumber
Service and Repair Shop	Mechanic
Cleaners	Presser
Cafe	Short Order Cook/Busing
Heating/Cooling Company	Metal Sheet Repairperson
Manufacturing Co.	Sewing Machine Operator
Flower & Candle Shop	Flower Designer
Water Treatment Plant	Water Treatment Operator
Concrete Company	General Concrete/Light Construction
Body Shop	Auto-body; Fender Repair

Source: Information received from Dr. Carl Larson, Iowa Central Community College
(1978). Reprinted by permission.

with educators serving in a minority. The Advisory Committee can be a sounding board for the project, base for soliciting the other businesses to aid in the program, resource for parents of students in the program needing an orientation to the success of the EBCE-MD, and assist the WEI in matters of decision-making policies and procedures of EBCE-MD.

With modifications, the EBCE model appears to be a viable approach to meeting the career education needs of handicapped individuals.

STUDENT COMPETENCY ASSESSMENT

Evaluation of students is one of the more difficult tasks classroom teachers face. Misuse of tests and recent discoveries regarding the inappropriateness of some tests has led to a general distrust of their results and usefulness. Some states have legislated against the use of traditional tests in public schools. Still today there are literally thousands of tests on the market that purport to measure practically anything.

Table 8

Possible Evaluation Techniques to Be Used by Classroom Teachers for Assessing Educable Retarded Student Behavior in the Domains of Knowledge, Skill, and Attitude

observational techniques

1. rating scale
2. anecdoted records
3. ranking scales
4. case study
5. self-appraisal devices
6. autobiographies
7. professional observation
8. play therapy
9. student conferences
10. follow-up studies
11. scaled data: graphs, charts, percentiles
12. scattergrams
13. expectancy tables
14. projection techniques
15. student projects
16. token economy
17. peer evaluation

18. personal data sheet
19. questionnaires (program-service)
20. student daily record
21. sociometric tests
22. sociometric patterns
23. cumulative records
24. student-kept cumulative records
25. student-parent conferences
26. group guidance (orientation-therapeutic)
27. child study program
28. attitude observation
29. behavior modification
30. modified test procedure (test, re-test)

31. health records
32. utilize community agencies
33. checklists
34. administrative reports
35. informed teacher reports
36. student interviews
37. projective techniques
38. study habit interview
39. sociodrama/psychodrama
40. discussion groups
41. role playing
42. audio-video devices and feedback
43. computer-assisted devices
44. gaming
45. simulated experiences
46. student input/contracts

test techniques

1. scholastic aptitude
2. special aptitude
3. achievement
4. interest inventories

5. personality adjustment
6. reading ability
7. individual interest battery
8. oral tests

9. open ended sentences
10. criterion referenced
11. skill performance tests
12. identification tests

Source: Selected PRICE topical papers for career education (McKay, 1977).

For certain groups of individuals, such as handicapped students, tests may require differential interpretation or revision before they are useful. Performance below the average only means that testing revealed what a person cannot do when compared to people in general. Thus, alternative evaluation activities will be needed to obtain information that will more accurately assess the performance and progress of students and their career development. Table 8 lists possible evaluation techniques for assessing student behaviors in the domains of knowledge, skill, and attitude.

Alternative Techniques

Salamack (1977) lists several alternative evaluation procedures that can be used to de-emphasize quantitative grading techniques and provide a more flexible process for both the student and the teacher These tech niques are generally more useful in assessing the student's career development by tapping areas of knowledge not often sampled by traditional tests. Each are discussed next.

Role Play. The teacher defines objectives to be learned (vocational, educational, social) and establishes criteria for evaluation. Evaluation can be done by the teacher, establishing a checklist form for grasp of concept, use of available information previously presented, enthusiasm, or any other dimension the teacher wishes to measure. Scales of most to least extremes with responses in between could be used. The teacher can create a student form where the viewers of the role-play situation evaluate it in terms of what they learned from it.

Case Conference. The case conference should yield recommendations in regard to specific students and/or to the improvement of the system(s). Objectives can be set in terms of what variable is to change (e.g., reading speed), what treatment shall be used to affect change, who will deliver this treatment, how long a time should the treatment be continued, and criteria for measurement (retest of reading speed). The personnel could then evaluate how effective their recommendations were and the degree of change in the student.

Token Economy. A classroom can be evaluated on its group cooperation toward a given goal (points amassed by a class to earn a special privilege are measurable units). Secondly, the number of tokens that the individual student amasses are measurable. Baseline data can be established and subsequent information can be compared to that initial information showing changes over time.

Behavior Modification. A particular behavior can be pinpointed (example: speaking in class), baseline data can be obtained, a treatment program can be established, and, at the end of the treatment period, data regarding change can be obtained. Rewards can be administered to apply to in-class or out-of-class situations.

Tutoring.   Students can be evaluated on various measures of academic achievement (example: *Thorndike-Lorge Vocabulary Test*) where potential deficiencies exist. After the tutoring treatment, readministration of test materials would show the effectiveness of the tutoring process.

Student Input.   Student and teacher draw up what general information is to be evaluated for all students. Various options of how the information is to be grasped by the student can be presented. The student would make the choice as to what she wants to do for the grade and how much work she is willing to do for it. A contract (agreement) as to these things can be signed by both the teacher and student, and an evaluation can follow from this.

Special Interest Projects.   Students define what their special interests are in a particular area. Their project can be evaluated by the teacher devising a scale on comprehension of major concepts, using other information, ability to generalize from the specific to the general, and the like. The teacher may also devise a scale that would be given to the students, assessing what they have learned from the individual's project. Field trips and tours would make excellent sources of project materials.

Informal Observation.   Teachers can devise rating scales that evaluate the presence and degree of intensity of any number of factors (examples: peer interaction, approach/withdrawal from novel situations). Checklists of descriptive words (e.g., *helpful to classmates*) and scales rating students from one extreme to the other of particular tasks or attributes allow teachers to fit observations into a more evaluative framework. Several observers using the same scales in a variety of situations (or observing the same situation) would give further depth to the observational technique.

Modified Test Procedure.   The teacher can give pretests on presented information that give her an idea of the student's strengths and weaknesses and allow for changing teaching priorities to meet particular needs. Use of the actual test as a pretest item could be done, with the readministration after the completion of the lesson.

Individual Counseling Interview.   Students may be evaluated prior to and after individual counseling experience by any number of psychological tests (example: Q sort, adjective checklist, sentence completion). Teachers and counselors can monitor the student's behavior by rating scales during and after counseling, showing direction and degree of change.

Student-to-Student Teaching. The teacher can pair an advanced student with a slower student to facilitate learning. Prior to beginning this, the teacher can evaluate the level of the "behind" student's performance with either standardized tests and/or teacher-devised instruments. After a specific time, tests can be readministered or alternative forms of evaluation could be used to measure the degree of change.

Parent Conference. The teacher can use observed data about the student gathered prior to the parent conference against the observed rate regarding the student after the conference. Parent conferences involve the parent in the educational process with specific exercises that will enhance the student's mastery of subject matter. Behavior modification systems that incorporate home and skills can be devised, where good behavior at school equates to certain positive consequences at home.

Autobiography. Students can be presented with certain structures to follow in writing (e.g., "What kind of a person am I?" "What do I hope to become?"), or they may just write in whatever perspective they feel most comfortable. These students may present themselves better graphically. For example, the student can draw a coat of arms of her life, filling in various areas of the shield with "the things I do well," or "the proudest moment of my life."

Games. Teachers can take subject matter and transform it into a game that calls upon students' knowledge and abilities. Games can be devised for either individual students, or groups or teams of students. Evaluation could be made on the basis of winning or how close to winning the student(s) come.

A Competency Rating Scale

One of the outcomes from Project PRICE was a rating scale built around the 22 career development competencies presented in this book. This competency rating scale (CRS) was developed to provide a systematic approach to organizing and standardizing the assessment of each student's career development competency level. The 102 subcompetencies are the actual CRS items of the scale. The daily living skills section of this scale is presented in Figure 25 to illustrate its construction. The complete scale and its manual is contained in *Life Centered Career Education: A Competency Based Approach* (Brolin, 1978).

A competency rating scale manual presents several behavioral criteria to use in judging student mastery of each competency/subcompetency. The ratings are performed by those most knowledgeable about student performance in a specific area. The manual contains information relative to types of information needed to rate students, who should do the rating,

Figure 25
Daily Living Skills.

Student Name _____ Date of Birth _____ Sex _____

School _____ City _____ State _____

Directions: The following items are PRICE subcompetencies identified as being important for the career education of educable retarded students. Please rate the student according to his/her mastery of *each* item using the Rating Key below. Indicate the ratings in the column below the date for the rating period. Use the "NR" rating for items which cannot be rated. For subcompetencies rated "0" or "1" at the time of the final rating, place a check (√) in the appropriate space in the yes/no column to indicate his/her ability to perform the subcompetency with assistance from the community. Please refer to the CRS manual for explanation of the Rating Key, description of the behavioral criteria of each subcompetency, and explanation of the yes/no column.

Rating Key: 0 = Not Competent   1 = Partially Competent   2 = Competent   NR = Not Rated
To what extent has the student mastered the following PRICE subcompetencies:

Subcompetencies	Rater(s)								
	Grade Level								
	Date(s)								
								Yes	No
I. Managing Family Finances									
1. Identify money and make correct change	—	—	—	—	—	—	—	—	—
2. Make wise expenditures	—	—	—	—	—	—	—	—	—
3. Obtain and use bank and credit services	—	—	—	—	—	—	—	—	—
4. Keep basic financial records	—	—	—	—	—	—	—	—	—
5. Calculate and pay taxes	—	—	—	—	—	—	—	—	—
II. Selecting, Managing, and Maintaining a Home									
6. Select adequate housing	—	—	—	—	—	—	—	—	—
7. Maintain a home	—	—	—	—	—	—	—	—	—
8. Use basic appliances and tools	—	—	—	—	—	—	—	—	—
9. Maintain home exterior	—	—	—	—	—	—	—	—	—
III. Caring for Personal Needs									
10. Dress appropriately	—	—	—	—	—	—	—	—	—
11. Exhibit proper grooming and hygiene	—	—	—	—	—	—	—	—	—
12. Demonstrate knowledge of physical fitness, nutrition and weight control	—	—	—	—	—	—	—	—	—
13. Demonstrate knowledge of common illness prevention and treatment	—	—	—	—	—	—	—	—	—
IV. Raising Children, Family Living									
14. Prepare for adjustment to marriage	—	—	—	—	—	—	—	—	—
15. Prepare for raising children (physical care)	—	—	—	—	—	—	—	—	—
16. Prepare for raising children (psychological care)	—	—	—	—	—	—	—	—	—
17. Practice family safety in the home	—	—	—	—	—	—	—	—	—
V. Buying and Preparing Food									
18. Demonstrate appropriate eating skills	—	—	—	—	—	—	—	—	—
19. Plan balanced meals	—	—	—	—	—	—	—	—	—

Subcompetencies	Rater(s)								Yes	No
	Grade Level									
	Date(s)									
20. Purchase food	—	—	—	—	—	—	—	—	—	—
21. Prepare meals	—	—	—	—	—	—	—	—	—	—
22. Clean food preparation areas	—	—	—	—	—	—	—	—	—	—
23. Store food	—	—	—	—	—	—	—	—	—	—
VI. Buying and Caring for Clothing										
24. Wash clothing	—	—	—	—	—	—	—	—	—	—
25. Iron and store clothing	—	—	—	—	—	—	—	—	—	—
26. Perform simple mending	—	—	—	—	—	—	—	—	—	—
27. Purchase clothing	—	—	—	—	—	—	—	—	—	—
VII. Engaging in Civic Activities										
28. Generally understand local laws and government	—	—	—	—	—	—	—	—	—	—
29. Generally understand federal government	—	—	—	—	—	—	—	—	—	—
30. Understand citizenship rights and responsibilities	—	—	—	—	—	—	—	—	—	—
31. Understand registration and voting procedures	—	—	—	—	—	—	—	—	—	—
32. Understand selective service procedures	—	—	—	—	—	—	—	—	—	—
33. Understand civil rights and responsibilities when questioned by the law	—	—	—	—	—	—	—	—	—	—
VIII. Utilizing Recreation and Leisure										
34. Participate actively in group activities	—	—	—	—	—	—	—	—	—	—
35. Know activities and available community resources	—	—	—	—	—	—	—	—	—	—
36. Understand recreational values	—	—	—	—	—	—	—	—	—	—
37. Use recreational facilities in the community	—	—	—	—	—	—	—	—	—	—
38. Plan and choose activities wisely	—	—	—	—	—	—	—	—	—	—
39. Plan vacations										
IX. Getting Around the Community (Mobility)										
40. Demonstrate knowledge of traffic rules and safety practices	—	—	—	—	—	—	—	—	—	—
41. Demonstrate knowledge and use of various means of transportation	—	—	—	—	—	—	—	—	—	—
42. Drive a car	—	—	—	—	—	—	—	—	—	—

*Total Possible Score
    (TPS) = N × 2 _____
        *Total Actual Score
           (TAS)   — — — —   — —
      *Average Score
       (AS) = TAS/N   — — — —   — — —

Comments:

Source: Life centered career education: A competency based approach (Brolin, 1978).

when the rating should be done, criteria for rating, a rating key defining numerical rating values, and CRS Record Forms for recording and summarizing ratings, as well as recording demographic data. The rating forms are divided into three career education areas: daily living skills, personal-social skills, and occupational guidance and preparation. The CRS is an experimental instrument at this time, and results should be viewed as adjunctive information rather than primary assessment results. Future development of the CRS may encompass reliability and validity studies and possible transformation to an objective, criterion-referenced instrument.

CONCLUSION

In this chapter we have suggested curriculum and instructional efforts for handicapped students within a career education context. It is important that this instruction begin in the early school years and that it involve a variety of school and community resources. The Experience-Based Career Education (EBCE) Model is discussed and considered to be an approach holding considerable promise for the future. The wide array of work experience sites that can be found in a rural area, as demonstrated by the Iowa project, attests to the potentials that exist by using this model.

There is a great need to incorporate more career education concepts into the writing of Individualized Educational Programs (IEPs). Presently, this is not done enough. We have presented our example of how this can be done. Close monitoring of each student's program and competency attainment is also crucial for career education success. A variety of techniques are available to help educators make these determinations.

Part four will discuss the major resources needed by school personnel to implement a comprehensive career education approach—family; business and industry; and the major agencies, organizations, and instructional sources.

part four

Involvement of
Community Resources

Part four presents the three major sources of needed assistance to the school in developing and conducting effective career education services for handicapped students: the family, agencies/organizations, and business/industry. This information is intended to assist the professional worker in identifying appropriate resources and in using them effectively.

Chapter 9 examines the contributions of the family in the career development of the handicapped with principal attention focused on the parents. Parent power is discussed in light of the several court cases that led to expanded provisions for the education of handicapped students. Several important publications providing helpful suggestions and hints for parents and professional are identified. The influences parents have upon the student regarding career roles and other matters concerned with the realities of the modern world are stressed throughout the chapter, and several suggestions are made for involving family members in the student's educational pro gram and competency development. The Home-Based Career Education Model is mentioned as having several implications for parents and teachers of the handicapped. Suggestions for working with parents are also presented.

Chapter 10 discusses the specific contributions business and industry can make to programs for handicapped individuals, suggestions for involving members of business and industry in their career development, and procedures to follow when educators approach prospective employers. Several business organizations and industries who have committed themselves to career education are identified. Business and industrial personnel can identify trends in the economy, provide job leads, become advocates for the handicapped, provide program consultation, offer work experiences to students, sponsor conferences and workshops, and provide instructional and resource materials for classroom use. Suggestions by which educators can contact and involve members of business and industry are discussed: Community Advisory Committees, Committees for Employment of the Handicapped, civic organizations, school publications such as brochures and news releases, business publications and job fairs, workshops, and institutes. Ways to approach employers and handle resistance are outlined in the chapter. Continuous contact and involvement with employers is an important part of maintaining good relationships and successful student placements.

Chapter 11 identifies some of the major agencies and organizations available at the local, state, and national levels that are important to the career development of handicapped individuals. The number and type of agencies and organizations are actually astounding. Community resources such as service organizations, private social service agencies, vocational-technical schools, community colleges, rehabilitation facilities, and sheltered workshops are particularly important local sources of assistance. This chapter also identifies major informational systems for materials and references on career development. You will find that a large number of resources are available for securing needed information in your work.

9

Family Contributions

The formulation of the Individualized Education Program (IEP) with pro-visions for career development must include the cooperation and approval of the parents. There is a precedent for this cooperation between profes-sional and parent in special education. In the past, children who were diagnosed as blind, deaf, or physically handicapped were often placed in special schools or institutions so that they could begin their education as soon as possible. This concept of early education has expanded to other areas of exceptionality, but its effectiveness depends upon the relationship between the three principal participants: child, parent, and professional. This cooperation must also extend into the area of career development so that students can receive the fullest complement of experiences that provide the basis upon which they will view themselves as producers, consumers, citizens, and parents.

It is interesting to note that each participant (child, parent, and profes-sional) benefits from the continued growth of the other. In other words, there is a reciprocal relationship that exists between the participants, both in the smallest classroom and conference situation, and in the larger context as in group efforts and legislation. Parent groups grew from a lack of services for their children. Those expanding services drew new professionals who increased the number of success stories among children and adults with handicaps. The successes encouraged further expansion of efforts by parents and professionals, thus repeating the cycle but with greater consequences.

This chapter will examine the contributions of the family in the career development of the handicapped. Although the term *family* has wider connotations, principal attention will be focused on the parents. We will explore the efforts of parent groups to meet the vocational needs of the handicapped, the influences of the parents upon the student's concepts, and means by which the teacher and parent can work together to effect success in the competencies.

PARENT POWER

Professionals can find a strong ally for career development in parents. You may recall from the brief review of the history of special education in chapter 1 that parent groups initiated several court cases that led to expanded provisions for an appropriate education for all students. There have been so many battles to fight over the years that it has only been recently that certain parent groups have directed some of their attention and effort to the area of career development. Most of the interest has been in the narrower area of vocational training—work-study programs and job placement. There are some signs, however, which indicate that this scope will become wider as parents probe the full extent of career preparation. If they do pursue the basic areas as discussed in this book (daily living skills, personal-social skills, and occupational guidance and preparation) as it is believed they will, then professionals can expect several changes. Research by Brock (1977) may serve as an example.

He touches on the increasingly important concept in special education, that of the role of parent advocate groups. He implies that if parent groups can lobby for certification standards to be changed so that all teachers receive some training in the education of the handicapped, then those same groups can also impress training programs and state department personnel with the idea that career development should be an important component of that course work. Nichols (1977), a parent and executive director of a development center, provides an extensive and constructive discussion of the concept in the New Hampshire Association for Retarded Citizens *Newsletter.*

> The word 'advocacy' evokes fear in the minds of some, confusion in others and a sense of purpose in still others. Before we allow the word to fall into disrepute or oblivion, perhaps we should explore its meaning and function.

Webster defines 'advocate' as one who 'supports the cause of another.' Threatening? Confusing? On the contrary, the definition is very clear and relatively innocuous. Support can be financial, political or educational. One can advocate anonymously and silently or publicly and vocally. The support can be directed at very general issues (rights for the handicapped) or very specific ones (publicly funded training for handicapped children from birth to 21 years). Parents, educators, legislators, employers, public officials, private organizations and the handicapped themselves can be advocates.

So, it seems, we have cleared up the initial question in two paragraphs— or have we? What about constructive versus destructive advocacy? Is there a way, in our zeal to support a cause, that we can ultimately do more damage than good?

Legislation is often the answer to the problem of guaranteeing rights. But legislation without sufficient appropriation of funds can only serve to cloud the issue. Expensive court battles can follow, wasting energy and public funds and often the service goes unprovided, the rights unprotected.

Constructive advocacy takes time, organization and a clear perception of the problem and the solution. First, we must be sure of what we wish to attain—do we only wish to bring attention to an injustice or do we want some action? Do we want new services or procedures or do we simply want to make better use of those that already exist?

Next, we need to identify the barrier. Is it really a person or is it the policy he must enforce? Who or what is responsible for making the decision? Often we waste our time knocking on the wrong door or arguing with 'non-issues' (such as, 'your retarded child will never learn to read') and overlook the real barrier.

Third, we must strategize how to use existing precedents and other data to show that what we want is possible. We must be able to map out the solution, anticipating all the drawbacks and present it in a clear manner.

Finally, we must be willing to negotiate and compromise in the event of an impasse. Settling for half a loaf now may guarantee the balance in the future. Helping to effect the solution and monitoring that effect may mean temporary sacrifices and long-range commitments.

The handicapped and their parents, because of their unquestionable vested interest, have often been the most successful advocate. Their only purpose is to secure rights for themselves or their children—a purpose that cannot morally be challenged. But, because of the emotions involved, their advocacy is sometimes not constructive. Professionals, however, may remain unemotional about the issues but may jeopardize the constructiveness of their advocacy by directing it toward their own professional survival. We must be careful that partisan politics and personal ambition don't become part of the issue.

Advocacy means supporting a cause and we must advocate in an informative and constructive way that will provide dignity to the word and to those we support.

The above discussion conveys the impression that some parents are highly skilled in effecting changes in systems of government and education. These parents have served on committees to organize write-in campaigns for legislation, conducted direct lobby efforts with legislatures, gained co-operative support from business and industry, convinced celebrities from media and sports to appear at benefits and fund-raising drives, and in general, formed successful organizations to implement and support common goals. It is likely that parents with these experiences and accomplishments will only accept future responses from school personnel to the effect that career development cannot be implemented. It is not likely that these same parents will accept a secondary role in the formulation of the Individualized Education Program (IEP), which is the cornerstone of PL 94–142, The Education for All Handicapped Children Act. The provisions of this law, its safeguards for the rights of the handicapped and their parents, and the drafting of the IEP have already been discussed in chapter 1. However, you should review those discussions, as the law and the process of drafting the IEP will be relevant to career development for the handicapped in the coming years. Parent organizations are providing an ample amount of encouragement for parents to become acquainted with key provisions. Just about every publication that is designed with parents in mind has featured articles on the several components and safeguards and carry such titles as:

PL 94–142: Changes Ahead

New Law for the Handicapped and Some Questions Parents Are Asking About It

Know and Protect Your Child's Rights!

Into the Mainstream: Parent and Child Rights

Parents have also become sophisticated in the combined approach to changing public policy. One of the newly effective means by which parents effect change is through the formation of a coalition of groups. Coalitions grow from the realization that the numerous separate organizations representing specific areas of disability (for example, individuals who are blind, physically handicapped, or mentally retarded) are, in effect, asking for similar changes to be made in programs of human care and education. These changes include institutions, school systems, state departments, local government, and all the regulations and delay that can be associated with the multiple layers of bureaucracy. Coalitions have been formed in some of the larger states (California, New York, Ohio, Illinois) and have brought changes in legislation, monitored fulfillment of mandates, and surveyed the needs of handicapped individuals. The continued success of these coalitions will signal the beginnings of another improvement in the parent movement. Additional information is available by writing: Coalition, Box 1492, Washington, D.C. 20013.

One of the obvious target goals for parent organizations and coalitions would be to effect changes relative to career futures for handicapped individuals. Parents need very little prodding in this area, since the children they sponsor soon grow into adolescents and adults. The preschool and mainstreaming concerns soon give way to discussions about work-study and job placement programs. In chapter 1, there was a discussion of the fact that the Department of Labor awarded contracts to the National Association for Retarded Citizens and the Epilepsy Foundation of America to train and place individuals with these disabilities. These organizations have been exchanging information and ideas with other parent groups so that one would expect future applications from organizations representing other areas of disability or a coalition of advocates. The contracts, efforts, and suggestions about what parents can do to involve themselves will continue to receive dissemination through the newsletters, information centers, and journals of the individual organizations.

One such organization is *The Parents' Campaign for Handicapped Children and Youth,* a national information center which gives guidance and practical hints about special services and educational programs. Through its publication, *Common Sense from Closer Look,* the center keeps parents and professionals abreast of research and support grants relative to the vocational preparation of the handicapped. The center prepares a variety of informational materials, which include the following suggestions for parents of the handicapped.

1. Check with local public schools for existing programs. These programs may include academic training and work-study situations;
2. find out about the services offered through the local office of the state vocational rehabilitation agency. These agencies are responsible for providing aptitude testing, counseling, training, job placement, and other services;
3. investigate programs offered by other organizations such as local chapters of the National Association for Retarded Citizens or Goodwill Industries. Several of these organizations also have contact with school systems, vocational rehabilitation, business, and industry;
4. inquire about work programs sponsored by sheltered workshops. This situation would be appropriate for those individuals who need extra help to cope with their tasks;
5. investigate day activity centers that may be sponsored by local parent organizations or mental health centers;
6. get in touch with organizations composed of parents of handicapped individuals or founded and directed by handicapped individuals. Check with your local chapter of the Easter Seal Society for Crippled Children and Adults for names and addresses of these organizations; and
7. apply for a "fair hearing" under regulations of the vocational rehabilitation agency if local services are inadequate. Be sure to compile a folder of accurate records that will be used to document your case. The folder should include information about:
   a. name, address, telephone number
   b. school history with copies of pertinent records

    c. medical history with pertinent statement from physicians

    d. previous training and a list of occupations appropriate to the demonstrated skills

    e. any telephone calls or visits related to your attempts to gain education and training (the individual should keep a log of the calls and visits).

Other publications include suggestions and hints that parents and professionals can use in developing community interest and support for training programs through workshops. The following topics and questions should be considered in developing a workshop.

1. Basic Questions:
   a. Who is going to be the host?
   b. What are the costs?
   c. Where and when should it be held?
   d. Who is on the workshop team?

2. Organizing the Format and Speakers:
   a. What are the topics?
   b. How much time should be given for presentations, discussions, mini-sessions?
   c. Who will be the chairperson, feature speaker, panel members?

3. Exhibits:
   a. Who should be invited?
   b. Who may be interested?
   c. Where will they exhibit?

4. Advertising:
   a. Will the local radio station provide a public service announcement?
   b. Should the preconference information be mailed or hand-carried to schools and parent groups?

5. Odds and Ends of Conducting a Workshop:
   a. Should there be a registration procedure?
   b. Who will draw signs and placards?
   c. Are there enough workshop packets?

Another parent organization, the California Association for Neurologically Handicapped Children (CANHC), discovered that there was very little effort on the part of agencies and programs to meet the vocational needs of individuals with minimal brain dysfunction or learning disabilities. A report presented by the organization's Vocational Committee (Anderson, 1976a) concluded with these observations.

The battle for realistic vocational preparation for the neurologically handicapped has only begun. In every community, CANHC members and especially parents will have to work with local schools, Rehab Departments, colleges and other agencies to get help for their own adolescents and young adults. CAHNC cannot just *demand* services . . . for professionals and agencies do not yet understand or know what to do. Parents must be prepared to describe the needs, share information about resources and workable programs, encourage teachers and counselors in the efforts to serve our NH young people. Hopefully the materials prepared by the first Vocational Committee will help.

The committee was referring to their efforts in compiling a *Vocational Kit: Steps in Vocational Readiness for Adolescents and Adults with the Hidden Handicap* (Anderson, 1976b). The *Kit* includes 25 articles written by teachers, parents, and other professionals related to activities in the classroom, counseling session, training program, or home. The several articles and suggested activities are organized under the following headings:

1. General Information (including a glossary of terms and bibliography)
2. Tips for Young Adults, Their Employers and Spouses
3. Remediation/Any Age (to facilitate job success)
4. Parents Can Help
5. Employment Information (including resources for training and the use of vocational rehabilitation and job specifications)
6. Survival Academics and Vocational Education.

Additional information is available by writing: California Association for Neurologically Handicapped Children, Box 4088, Los Angeles, California 90051.

The *Kit* represents the attempt of parents to influence classroom instruction and counseling. It grew from a frustration over the fact that students were not being prepared to enter the job market. This example was only true for the state of California, but we are sure that the *Kit* will be purchased throughout the country and used with other populations of individuals with disability. Hopefully, the *Guide, Kit,* and this book will begin to have their effect upon professionals so that the impetus for change need not come from outside the school systems. The following discussions are intended to alert teachers and counselors to the role that parents can assume in career development.

PARENT INFLUENCE

Long before the teacher or counselor ever encounter the pupil, the parents have influenced the student's approach to role models. Children begin to acquire opinions concerning the value of certain occupations when they hear some of the following comments:

> Look at the fire fighter, Johnny. Wouldn't it be fun to be a fire fighter?
>
> We're ready to board the plane to fly to Grandmother's. There's the captain. Doesn't he look grand?
>
> Your sister has to work late tonight at the store. It's really a hard job and I wish she would quit.

The parents' inflections, interest, and estimation of importance clue the student as to the attractiveness of certain roles within one's life. Parents stimulate the "fantasies" of children and adolescents which, at times, includes ideas about jobs, roles, responsibilities, and accomplishments. This happens with the normal student (i.e., the one who does not exhibit overt signs of behavioral or physical deviation). Less is known about whether parents express similar attitudes toward occupations with the exceptional student. One would expect that a certain amount of prior selection does take place as parents screen various roles. The individual with cerebral palsy does not receive the same emphasis upon *being* a fire fighter or police officer as an individual with normal physical characteristics. The individual who is blind does not see the captain or, for that matter, the pilot may not even be pointed out to him. The parent may reflect upon the sister's job, but he may not feel that his son or daughter who is mentally retarded could work in the same store.

Elaboration about any one occupational role is determined by the parents' estimation and projection of the required abilities and behaviors. In some instances, students are not exposed to roles because parents imagine their son or daughter will be unable to handle the responsibilities or meet a certain level of prerequisite attributes. But, parents are often not accurate as to what abilities are needed for a job. The great flaw in this delicate balance is that parents (and educators) often operate upon imagination rather than information. Both need a greater quantity and quality of information about occupations and other career roles, sexism influences, the student's abilities, what other individuals with handicaps have achieved, and the cooperative efforts of home and school in providing the appropriate training.

Second, parents also maintain ideas about whether certain career roles are appropriate for the projected *status* of the family or student. These ideas are not major hurdles in the development of a training program for the majority of students, but they do occur enough times so that educators must consider parent opinions and attitudes in matching students, for example, to jobs. In a survey of work-study coordinators, Kokaska (1968) reports that high school students in classes for the mentally retarded were not placed in certain positions because these jobs did not meet the approval of the parents. Becker (1976) reports a large survey that includes training for 1,438 students in classes for the mentally retarded. The survey questionnaire was returned by 40 work-study coordinators covering 35 school districts in 12 states and the District of Columbia. It was primarily directed at determining the types of jobs to which students were assigned during the 1972–74 school years. The coordinators were also asked to rank 10 problem statements according to their severity. Obtaining the cooperation from parents in carrying out the work-study curriculum was ranked eighth.

The home environment is the primary classroom, and educators must be equally concerned with what *is not* presented to students in that situation as they are concerned with what happens in the classroom. A student with auditory impairment may not work in the electronics field, but parents and educators do not know whether this assumption is true during the student's early developmental years. If parents and educators assume that a certain role is unattainable, they will avoid presenting that model as a feasible choice. The avoidance of discussions, illustrations, and an open exchange of references to the role can limit the students' experimentation and inquiry. Students should receive as much exposure, information, and interaction as possible with the full variety of productive activities that characterize work roles at all stages in the continuum of career development.

In several ways, the parent of an exceptional student is a sharp contrast to the parent of a normal student. One of the early major considerations of the parents evolves around the question of whether the individual will be able to achieve independence as an adult. This is important to all parents, but those with a handicapped child have a very real concern as to whether the disability will hinder independent functioning. If the individual is unable to work, he will be dependent upon the parents or someone else for his physical and, in some instance, psychological support. The economics of this situation receives a considerable amount of attention. The systematic exploration of career roles and functions is one of the first attempts to prepare both parents and the student for later adult status. As such, one can expect to encounter certain forms of resistance. Parents may make such statements as:

It is too early to concern ourselves with jobs.

My child will never be able to manage a home and family.

We're not particularly worried at this time.

These responses do not provide an answer to the long-term considera- tion that all students must be prepared for total life functioning and that one contribution to the process of change can come from the family. The state- ments may indicate a reluctance because the family has not fully resolved or has completely rejected the fact that the student does have a handicap. The parents' response may indicate that they have overestimated the effects of the disability upon the potential accomplishments of their son or daughter. Finally, educators must consider that the parents have to resolve their own feelings of guilt or pain, and their responses may be a protective reaction until such future time when they will be able to deal with the next problem. In all situations, the teacher and counselor must consider the feelings of the parents while continuing to pursue long-term goals that are for the benefit of the student.

> Include parents in shaping educational objectives.

While services and programs for individuals with a handicap have been expanding, basic concepts relative to their encounters with the realities of the modern world have also changed. One of these concepts is the "dignity of risk" (Perske, 1972; Kokaska, 1974), and it has an important bearing upon the interactions between educators and parents concerning goals and programs for handicapped students. The dignity of risk places emphasis upon the fact that individuals develop a sense of value within themselves and in the eyes of their peers by encountering tasks commensurate with their functioning. To deny handicapped individuals the opportunity to learn, venture, or try appropriate tasks is to, in effect, de-value and dehumanize them. This is one reason behind the emphasis within legislation and regulations upon the terminology of "least restrictive environment." Educators and parents are to choose those educational environments that are least restrictive to the development of the handicapped individuals' abilities *and* sense of value.

The often heard expression of the dignity of work also falls within the same conceptualization. Numerous advocacy organizations and handicapped individuals have repeatedly voiced their desires for an opportunity to work as opposed to receiving charity or welfare. The role of work and the positive status of an employed individual are still woven tightly within the fabric of the American society. But, the actual physical process of work, which includes movement, dexterity, and endurance, places certain individuals in situations of risk. The social and interpersonal variables involved in other forms of work even dominate certain occupations and also function as other forms of risk. Teacher and parents sense these elements of risk. The very thought of risk, no matter if it is based on accurate information, is enough to modify the intended goals for handicapped students by teachers and parents.

If teachers, counselors, and parents are to share in the combined effort of preparing students for various career roles fulfilling a level of dignity that is acceptable to the handicapped individual, then they must carefully examine their perceptions of tolerable levels of risk. The process of career development begins in the family, and the question of whether the handicapped individual should attempt a "risk situation" will occur at every stage of maturation. The question cannot be avoided, especially since more and more handicapped individuals are taking their rightful productive places in society. Therefore, it is crucial for educators to encourage family participation in the mutual goals of developing those competencies that will enable the handicapped individual to meet daily challenges and achieve a sense of value.

Thus, educators cannot afford to work apart from the parents. The authors of PL 94–142 and the Individual Education Program (IEP) recognized this by including numerous provisions involving parents in the shaping of educational objectives. But, aside from these guarantees, it would still be to the educators' benefit to actively include parents in decisions and activities that may shape students' future achievements and socioeconomic status.

Throughout the previous discussion, we have concentrated on parents who may be reluctant but yet interested in their child's future. The question may be asked: What can educators do with parents who are uninterested in their child's program? This question is not unique to career development for exceptional individuals. Regular and special educators have had to contend with the question over the years, and the magnitude may increase. One should recall that the post-Korean War high school dropouts (uninterested students) may now be the parents of another generation of children. These children have been nurtured by television and may have even less tolerance for the classroom, especially if their parents see little value in education.

The educators' basic concern in confronting this problem has to be with the quantity and quality of communication between school personnel and parents. Educators can't compel the parents' interest against their will. But, educators can certainly make an eager attempt beyond the traditionally yearly parent-teacher conferences. The parents' lack of interest reflects a complex situation that may involve more than the student's progress with the three Rs. Therefore, the amount of communication between home and school has to increase so that some of the elements of the situation may surface. The quality of communication refers to those face-to-face meetings between educators and parents that allow both parties to deal with problems and concerns.

The requirements of parent approval for the individualized education program actually provide educators with another tool for encouraging parent interest. Parents can be included and committed to responsibilities as designated on the IEP form. But that spark of interest can be extinguished if parents are overpowered in meetings with three, five, or seven educators. In the final analysis, the educators must confront themselves in asking about the "uninterested parents." They must ask themselves such questions as:

Have we repeatedly communicated our concern for the parents' and child's benefit?

Have we utilized other means for encouraging parent interest, such as parent groups and community organizations?

Have we planned our meetings, newsletters, or announcements so that parents receive positive feelings about themselves and child?

These questions and others allow educators to determine whether they have done enough in meeting a problem that may possibly extend beyond their expertise.

Kroth (1978) suggests the following as important factors to consider in designing and planning parent programs:

1. *Heterogeneity.* Parents are not a homogeneous body. The only thing they have in common is a handicapped child. Some will be well read, some will be skilled modifiers, and some will be good listeners. The educators will need to analyze the parent's needs just as the children's needs are taken into consideration, i.e., differential diagnosis should lead to differential programming.

2. *Size.* In general, parent education groups should be kept small. Most programs reported in the literature seem to run from 6 to 10 individuals plus the group leader(s). It is extremely difficult to have meaningful interaction in groups of more than 10. Large groups usually end up being lectures with a one way flow of communication.

3. *Time.* A parent education program should have clear objectives and usually a specified number of sessions. For example, if a teacher can say to parents that they will be involved in a program where they can learn to help their children read and that it will involve four 1 hour sessions, parents seem to respond better than if the goals are vague and the length of commitment is not clear (p. 90).

The following suggestions are directed at involving parents and other members of the family. These suggestions include familiar activities, but you should approach them with a desire to use the parents' influence upon student goals and behaviors.

Initiate an active information program for parents. The information may include suggested readings or reprinted articles related to career development about classroom activities, progress reports on former students who are employed in the community, and reviews of guest speakers in the classroom. These provide parents with a perspective on what may be termed the "career future" of the student. Some school districts have provided parents with suggestions about the kinds of questions that their children may ask concerning the parents' careers, jobs, previous education, duties, and rewards.

Provide parents with a brochure or handbook on classroom activities in career development that can be replicated in the home. The handbook can contain lists of career terms, places to visit in the community related to career development, and household chores that develop the student's daily living skills. The handbook may also contain a checklist of the several competencies discussed in chapters 4–6. The checklist may be accompanied by suggested home and community resources related to the competencies. For example, the resources may include home study guides, manuals, community walking tours of industries or facilities, and guest presentations to organizations.

Present "career/vocational workshops" for parents. These workshops would include information sessions on the several facets of career development, family contributions to career development, possibilities for vocational training, work-study programs, and sources of vocational information that can be acquired by parents. These workshops can also include presentations by former students about their training and current experiences in the labor market, as well as employers of individuals with handicaps.

Conduct parent field trips of training sites, placement facilities, classroom activities related to career and vocational development. Hopefully, these types of visitations will provide parents with firsthand observations of students who are in training and, perhaps, working in selected roles and industries. The observations provide a vital link between what parents have read or been told and what they can experience through contact and conversation with students, trainers, and employers.

All of the above suggestions may provide basic ideas and activities that can be modified to meet the unique educational setting. For example, parent field trips may not be appropriate to an urban situation in which all family members work during the school day. These family members may profit best from a handbook on suggested activities in the home or a newsletter that informs them of weekly television programs related to careers, jobs, or the world of work. Other parents may enthusiastically respond to suggestions for a workshop. These parents will want speakers and will engage in discussions concerning training, prospective employment, and the role of the family. It is important to fit the suggested activity to the characteristics of the parents and the capacities of the professional staff. In some instances, as in the development of newsletters or printed matter, the educators may enlist the services of professional writers and printers.

FAMILY INVOLVEMENT WITH THE COMPETENCIES

Throughout our discussions of the 22 career development competencies and their respective subcompetencies in chapters 4–6, we made numerous suggestions concerning activities that could be conducted in the classroom or home. Parents could be given a copy of this book or an even more extended listing of the activities accompanying each subcompetency. A review of each competency will soon reveal that parents and other family members can significantly contribute to the student's career development in almost all competency areas.

Family members do not have the professional training of the teachers and counselors and, in some instances, may be discouraged when they are confronted with lists of competencies and activities. But, we believe that the competencies can be developed by the family as they occur in the normal conduct of maintaining a home. For example, even before a child can read words, he can read pictures. A special recipe card with words and pictures can help the child develop reading skills. The child can learn to follow pictures and recognize packages such as canned goods, powdered sugar, flour, and salt. One way of teaching the child food concepts is by playing games that ask: "I'm thinking of something on your plate and it's white and square. Can you guess what it is?" Parents can give the child a sense of importance by assigning him tasks such as sponging the table top, scrubbing vegetables, or tearing lettuce into small pieces for a salad. Children can learn safety rules through food experiences, coordination and manipulation skills, and many other competencies related to their career development.

The majority of activities in chapters 4–6 facilitate one or more of the skills involved in the competencies. These skills and competencies should serve as a basis for some of the conversations between teachers, counselors, and parents. They can be included, for example, in the consultations relative to the objectives contained in the IEP.

Career-related topics and competencies can also form the basis of conversations within the family. The Mesa (Arizona) Public Schools (1976) published two brochures for parents entitled, *Talking with Your Child (Teenager) About Your Career.* The brochures included such basic questions as:

Why do you work?

When did you make your career choice?

Who benefits from your career?

What do you see in the future?

The publications also suggest appropriate moments in the day, such as during dinner or on a family outing, when parents can initiate conversations. The discussions will reflect the parents' career history and, hopefully, prompt children and adolescents to deal with their own career futures.

Once family members (father, mother, grandparents, brothers, sisters, and relatives) understand the long-term objectives and some representative examples of daily activities, they can generate other activities that do not appear in booklets or textbooks. These activities would have the unique advantage in that they are particularly appropriate to the individual family, their situation and life style, the student's ability and limitations, and are supported by family members since they are the ones who conceived the ideas.

The following are 10 suggestions that we believe families should consider in helping their handicapped member to achieve the career development competencies contained in this book.

1. Emphasize the *development of coordination, dexterity, balance, and strengths* by providing daily physical exercises or activities (sports, crafts, balance boards, chores around the house). The family should be aware of activities that involve both fine and gross motor functions. These skills can be transferred later to routines that are important for successful employment, daily living, and leisure.
2. Provide a *home workshop* so construction activities can be learned by using hammer, nails, saw, ruler, and drill press. Home workshops also provide the individual with an opportunity to establish a knowledge base relative to the names of tools, tasks, and consequences.
3. Assign *specific jobs/duties* to the individual. The duties should be completed to specifications and within a certain time frame. A second level of expectation is related to the individual's development of a plan of action to complete the job/duties. This plan may include following a routine, maintaining a schedule, and returning tools or utensils to specified locations.
4. *Identify jobs* performed by various workers in the community, *visit job sites,* and *discuss them* in detail at home. Include the family in these discussions and observations. These discussions assist the individual in expressing personal observations and opinions. They also help build work values, interests, and long-term aspirations.
5. Provide a variety of *family projects and activities,* such as camping trips, sports events, travel, and church events to build leisure, recreation, and social skills. These family projects and outings also provide the handicapped individual with an opportunity to communicate ideas and feelings associated with positive experiences. These types of communications are important in helping the individual build positive concepts of the self and his role in society.
6. Insist that the individual *make his own decisions,* investigate alternatives, and understand the consequences. This process of problem solving and decision making is essential to the development of the individual independent status within the family and community.
7. Permit a sense of psychological security by *providing positive reinforcement* for successful work and the opportunity to *participate in family decision making.* Once again, the family should concentrate on building a positive self-concept and confidence in his abilities.
8. *Work closely with school personnel* in achieving educational goals and objectives for the handicapped individual. Several classroom activities are richly supported by the cooperation of the family. For example, teachers often use classroom activities through which students learn about their parents' occupations. The activities may include role play, child-parent interviews, and class field trips to the work locations of the parents. The class functions would also support the family's attempts in building such personal skills as communication and problem solving.

9. Help *develop community experiences* with the school personnel to expand the curriculum opportunities, such as field trips, guest speakers, and work experience.
10. Become involved in *school advisory committees* concerned with curriculum, development of resources, and other career education matters.

Some important limitations to the teacher's activities in the classroom provide support for greater home-school cooperation. For example, many school systems only allow one field trip per year due to financial limitations. However, it is quite possible that under the direction of the classroom teacher, parents can include their son or daughter in family outings to centers of work activity. This form of cooperation provides the educator with a greater array of experiences that can be incorporated in the curriculum.

Of course, the problem of maintaining continuity between the teacher's objectives for a particular field trip in relationship to career development and the actual fulfillment of these objectives can be encountered by the cooperating parents or family members. This goal would require the teacher to provide the family with a basic understanding of career development and the competencies, in addition to the objectives for any particular field visitation. Given these basic understandings, the teacher can tolerate variation according to each family's emphasis upon the observed tasks and skills at a particular field site. It should be remembered that one of the prime objectives in career development is to expose the student to many work settings, and therefore, family involvement and effort increase the possibilities for achieving this goal.

It is also feasible that student responsibilities in the home have been determined during a teacher-parent conference. These duties can be evaluated for the types of skills they develop. Reports between home and school are also important so that parent and teacher appraise and reinforce each other's progress. This would continue to enhance a continuum of effort between the primary training site—the home—and the skilled individual in career development—the teacher. These "homework assignments" should not be taken lightly. They are strong components toward achieving positive self-values. For example, Pollard (1977) suggests that the classroom teacher and students conduct a career education program for the parents. Students can display their projects and demonstrate activities. Parents can participate in the same career activities that students practice in the classroom. Pollard reports that parents of adolescents who were in classes for the trainable mentally retarded were surprised to discover the kinds of work tasks that were conducted in the classroom. These types of discoveries often lead to increased responsibilities in the home, as well as more realistic expectations.

One final comment about teacher-parent cooperation and the role of the family in achieving certain goals. The U.S. Office of Education has supported four models, designed to achieve the overall goals of career education. The Home/Community Base Model is one of the four and has several implications for parents and teachers of the handicapped. First, the model emphasizes the home as a learning center (Simpson, 1973). The importance of values and activities has previously been discussed, but the concept of a *learning center* includes more than just theoretical discussions. The learning center provides a means of communication between the home and an outside source of information. This may be via television, radio, or telephone. It enables parents to obtain appropriate information and assistance relevant to the training objectives that can be accomplished in the home.

Second, the model includes a designated area of the home in which students engage in activities that further their understandings of careers and goals. This may involve such audio-visual combinations as a slide projector and cassette tape recorder or a designated program on a television channel. It certainly can be used to provide information relative to many of the sub-competencies

Third, the model implies that the whole family is a career learning team. Parents and siblings are involved in furthering career pursuits and, thus, provide model roles and experiences that impact upon the handicapped individual. Once the family understands the basic dynamics of the situation, combined with the projected competencies for the individual, they can figuratively stretch their experiences and understandings to include the individual.

Finally, the home program seems most appropriate for individuals with certain types of handicaps because of their need for tutoring assistance beyond the scope of the ordinary school. The home-based model would develop another learning environment which, although outside of the physical boundaries of the school, would be coordinated with the teacher's efforts toward mutually determined objectives.

WORKING WITH PARENTS

Working with parents of handicapped individuals is a crucial part of career development. The encounters between professionals and parents should include singular meetings or a determined series of sessions extending over a long period of time. For the professional, the purpose of these meetings is to:

- Exchange information related to student characteristics, achievement, program development, or instances in the home or classroom that may affect the individual's continued academic and social progress; and
- develop plans to solve problems that include cooperative efforts by school personnel and family.

Many articles were published in the 1960s and 1970s related to the role of the counselor with the family of the handicapped individual. Compendiums of several of these articles have appeared in publications by Noland (1971); Gowan, Demos, and Kokaska (1972); Browning (1974); Buscaglia (1975); and Stewart (1978). One can find some common themes reiterated in these publications:

- Help parents focus on the qualities of their exceptional children and youth that are more like other children and youth than different from them. The exceptional aspects are important but secondary. That type of orientation is not an easy accomplishment, as parents have a great deal of psychological investment in their offspring. Damage, injury, and differences have to be reconciled with the parents' *image* of their sibling. By focusing on the individual qualities of the person, parents can be aided in adjusting their goals and expectations. The numerous examples of success by individuals with handicaps in the society, the expansion of parent organizations, and technological advances have also helped parents in the process of adjustment. Nevertheless, every family must tread its own course in moving from such initial negative reactions of mourning, denial, guilt, rejection, shame, and frustration to productive actions on behalf of the exceptional individual. The professional in the counseling role is a vital ingredient to this transition;

- help parents work through their *feelings* about the many obstacles that stand between projected goals and daily accomplishments. Parents of exceptional individuals can be overcome by the numerous medical reports and school evaluations identifying damage, limitations, or failures. This type of information can contribute to feelings of failure and resentment, which only serves as yet another obstacle toward concerted efforts by the family and school personnel. The professional's attention to the parents' feelings provide a basis of communication, understanding, and acceptance. The emphatic relationship between professional and parents has helped solve problems by allowing the latter to free themselves of concerns that interfered with the adequate solutions;

- offer perspective on the total expanse of the exceptional individual's life so that parents can identify the relationships between stages of development. Of course, daily problems have to be solved and each step in the developmental sequence has its own unique characteristics. The professional's contribution is to identify parental measures that can be taken to modify behavior or achieve success and the potential benefits for future goals; and

- function as a resource to assist parents and handicapped individuals achieve goals. Each year brings additional resources into the community on behalf of handicapped individuals and their parents. These resources include financial assistance, varied forms of instruction, medical and legal assistance, and vocational training. The average parent cannot be expected to know of all the resources. However, it has been the experience of numerous professionals that parents can pursue appropriate avenues of support and assistance when they have been alerted to the community resources. At times, parent organizations have been instrumental in spreading such information through contacts with professionals in school systems and community agencies.

In addition to these broad themes for professionals, numerous publications contain specific suggestions for counselors working with parents of individuals who are entering a stage of development or manifest particular forms of disability. One of these by Patterson (1956), a parent of a mentally retarded individual, was specifically intended to alert professionals about their own preparation for the parent conference. These pointers were expanded into 10 commandments for counselors by Jordan (1976). The two lists appear in Table 9.

The pointers and commandments help focus attention upon the attitude and procedures that enhance the relationship between counselor and parents. Parents need the opportunity to express their feelings about their son's or daughter's handicap, gain confidence in the counselor, and attempt constructive planning. The counselor's concern, behavior, and techniques can

---

Table 9
Pointers and Commandments for Counseling with Parents

pointers for professionals	the ten commandments
1. Tell us the nature of our problem as soon as possible.	1. Be honest in your appraisal of the situation and explain it without unnecessary delay.
2. Always see both parents.	2. Deal with both parents, since they are a natural unit.
3. Watch your language.	3. Be precise, but do not be unnecessarily technical in your explanation.
4. Help us to see this is OUR problem.	4. Point out who must be responsible ultimately.
5. Help us to understand our problem.	5. Help the parents grasp the issues.
6. Know your resources.	6. Keep in mind the referral agencies that can be of assistance.
7. Never put us on the defensive.	7. Avoid precipitating ego-defensive reactions in the parents.
8. Remember that parents of retarded children are just people.	8. Do not expect too much too soon from the parents.
9. Remember that we are parents and that you are professionals.	9. Allow parents their quota of concern and uncertainty.
10. Remember the importance of your attitude toward us.	10. Try to crystallize positive attitudes at the outset by using good counseling techniques.
(Patterson, 1956)	(Jordan, 1976)

contribute to the parents' overall success during the meetings. As parents become more accepting of their situation and the counselor's efforts, they can concentrate increased amounts of attention on the student's needs and accomplishments associated with the competencies identified in chapters 4–6 as critical for career success. The mastery of competencies in the areas of daily living, personal-social, and occupational skills should constitute the long-range objectives for student instruction in the classroom and home. The parents' worries and questions chiefly center around the competencies:

Will my son be able to drive a car?

What shall we do when our daughter reaches the dating age?

Should he have his own allowance?

Who will hire my son?

Will our child be cut-off from the rest of the students in the class because of the differences in appearance?

There is an endless list of questions raised by parents in counseling and program planning sessions. At first you may say that these same questions are raised or are secretly considered by *all* parents. The differences rest largely in the handicapped individual's physical or emotional ability to meet identical challenges. For example, all parents may wonder about their child's ability to hold a job in the adult years. But, the parents of a child who is blind or mentally retarded will justifiably pursue answers to questions of employment at an early age in the developmental sequence. Some parents of handicapped individuals spend years of effort in preparing their children to accomplish certain competencies that normal students master in a semester.

The use of the competencies as described in this text within the IEP afford a sound basis on which professionals and parents can meet to exchange opinions and plans. Parents may not be able to initiate measures within the home that prepare the student in all of the 22 competencies, but they should be able to understand the total direction of the school program and identify competency areas that lend themselves to immediate efforts within the home. The student's attainment of the 22 competencies can be a reference point for teacher-parent conferences related to the individual education program. Both participants can start the IEP conferences with a common ground of understanding about the short-term and long-term objectives for the student. Both participants can share a common framework of understanding that defines the intended goals of school and home activities. Daily problems in adjustment or academic assignments take on a new measure of meaning when parents and professional are able to identify the relationship of these smaller parts to the overall direction of the curriculum.

The counselor or teacher should consider the following suggestions in conducting, planning, and evaluating activities related to the competencies and the IEP:

*Provide an evaluation of the student's current status relative to the compe-
tencies to be achieved during the school year.* Professionals must also be
careful to identify the several variables that may be limiting an adequate
appraisal of student competencies in the school, training, or home situation.
Many of these limitations may be raised by parents who attempt to initiate
activities and observe accomplishments. For example, a student may have
the responsibility of "cleaning his room," but the parent may be unable to
observe the student's progression due to other responsibilities in the home.
These are the kinds of problems that teachers and parents must rectify,
although they cannot be classified as major stumbling blocks to progress.

Determine forms of reward for the parents. The simple attainment of a
level of behavior by their child may be an ample reward for a parent. The
first spelling test, colored picture, date, and driver's license often provide
just as much positive feelings in the hearts of parents as in the students
who achieved the goals. The counselor, nevertheless, should allow for instances in which parents receive direct recognition for their part in the
process aside from the student achievements. The meetings at which teacher
and parent review yearly progress on the IEP can be used for appropriate
opportunities to provide parent rewards.

*Involve as many family members as possible in the planning and progress
of activities designed to train students in the competencies.* Many of the
experiences with competencies in the daily living skills and personal-social
skills can be supervised by peers and relatives. This procedure allows for a
greater number of "teachers" in the total training process of the student.
There has been increasing emphasis upon the "team concept" in special
and regular education, across different professions, and between the school
and home. Activities and observations related to the competencies provide
an ample number of instances in which the team can be expanded within
the family.

*Emphasize the importance of career development as a process that extends
from childhood through adult years.* Parents of young children will have
difficulty visualizing the fact that all major competencies are worded in
terms of adult experiences. These parents must see that every attainment
at an early age decreases the amount of training and instruction that must
occur at later stages of development. The concept of career development is
that adult skills and competencies have their early origins in the elementary
grades and, therefore, teachers and parents need not wait until high school
to begin with important competency areas.

Encourage parent questions and suggestions. This procedure promotes
parent involvement in the student's mastery of the competencies. It also
functions as another indicator of the parents' involvement and activities in
the home related to the competencies and IEP. If parents are attempting to
conduct and supervise activities to achieve objectives on the IEP, then they

will encounter problems. Professionals should be aware of these problems and prompt parents to relate the difficulties in the planning conferences.

Present as much information as the parents can handle.   Professionals can promote questions with other items of information, such as new resources in the community or changes in school procedures. But, parents can be overwhelmed with the amount of information that is related to a particular disability, types of training programs, or activities to be conducted in the home. It would be better that parents are eager to hear, find information, and generate their own questions and suggestions as contrasted to a situation in which they are overwhelmed and defeated.

Develop a schedule of activities that parents can follow, which coincides with the classroom lessons.   This is another advantage to the IEP conference. Parents and professionals can plan coordinated activities to achieve common objectives related to the competencies.

Figure 26 is one example of a schedule of family activities for the same Daily Living Skills that were presented in Figure 11. The schedule is specific to the individual student and family situation, whereas the Curriculum Check

Jane
_____
Student

Oct.-Nov.
_____
Week or Month

DAILY LIVING SKILLS

Competency	School Assignments	Family Activities	Family Comments
1. Identifying money	Arithmetic assignments will be sent home	Take Jane on weekly shopping at supermarket	
2. Using basic tools	Find examples of tools	Practice naming appliances; father and brother include Jane in repairing car	
3. Demonstrating physical fitness	Reading assignment on home safety	Practice safety measures for the home related to fires	

Figure 26
Family Activities.

Sheet in chapter 4 provides the teacher with an overall view of the competencies that intersect various curriculum areas.

The parents' schedule provides them with an estimation of those classroom lessons that will be carried into the home through daily assignments or exercises. It also acts as a check upon the parents' involvement and student progress in "out-of-school" functions, such as, for example, Jane's swimming lessons at the YMCA. It is not a perfect device but does provide another link in the communication between teacher and parents. It also establishes ways by which the family can contribute to the development of the competencies through activities suggested by the parents during the IEP conference. This element interjects a certain amount of accountability into the relationship of parents to the IEP.

CONCLUSION

This chapter has emphasized the important role of the family in the career development of handicapped individuals. Parent groups have increased their attention and efforts in the broad career areas of daily living skills, while also focusing upon vocational training and placement. You, the reader, whether parent or professional, should be able to turn to several of the national and state parent organizations for information and publications. These organizations, in turn, will find willing companions in the quest for career development in those school systems and agencies that are initiating career education programs and expanding their efforts in vocational training.

The position of the individual education program in career development should be viewed as a centerpiece in the communication between teacher and parent. The IEP functions as a means through which the competencies can be translated into obtainable objectives and daily activities. Hopefully, teacher and parents will be able to devise activities that can be conducted in the classroom and home environments, which reinforce each others' attempt to obtain mutual objectives. This process of communication between teacher and parent is meant to be ongoing and rewarding, which may explain why those who wrote the law and regulations that gave birth to the IEP specified that the participants were to establish short-term and long-term objectives, as well as dates and time frames. In one sense, these requirements may be viewed as insurance that the school system and teacher will complete their part of the contract. We would rather view them as a way to bring teacher, parents, and students together to discuss, plan, and even dream about what *can* be accomplished.

10
Business and Industry

The necessary cooperation between business, industry, and education has always been an integral consideration of leaders in career development. This collaboration and the several benefits that can be derived from it have been explored in numerous discussions within the professional literature of these fields. Sidney Marland, in his address at the Commissioner's National Conference on Career Education (1976), was quite specific as to the benefits that the business sector could assume as a major collaborator. He stated that business should be involved in:

- Developing better manpower for its own needs;
- creating an improved environment for the work force by reducing unemployment; and
- improving the purchasing power of the public.

Educators and their students can reap rewards by including the expertise and experience of individuals from business/industry who are involved in the successful production of goods and services. The question is not whether each sector could profit from one another's involvement in providing career education for America's public but rather what are the most appropriate means of working together toward mutual objectives?

There are several national efforts being conducted from this sector that have direct bearing on the career education of handicapped, as well as other students. Some of the more important organizations and industries are the following:

- The *Chamber of Commerce of the United States* adopted career education as a major priority in 1971 and published a monograph entitled *Career Education: What It Is and Why We Need It* (1975). The Chamber has taken a leadership role in promoting and supporting federal career education legislation, and without its support, there probably wouldn't be such legislation now. A significant activity of the Chamber has been its involvement with local affiliates in helping them to implement career education in their communities. Thus, at the local level, the Chamber may be a very important resource for schools to involve as they design career education efforts for their students. Information can be obtained by writing Chamber of Commerce of the U.S.A., Education and Manpower Development Committee, 1615 H Street, N. W., Washington, D.C., 20062, or from your local unit.

- The *National Alliance of Businessmen* (NAB) is another excellent source for career education assistance. They have had the disadvantaged individual as a major focus for the purpose of preventing unemployment problems by sponsoring work-study programs for youth; a Youth Motivation Task Force Program involving successful businesspersons from disadvantaged backgrounds; and Career Guidance Institutes for high school counselors, which offer career education infusion materials developed by classroom teachers. Information can be obtained by writing NAB, 1730 K Street, N.W., Washington, D.C. 20006.

- The *American Telephone & Telegraph Company* (AT&T) has been a leading industry in supporting and participating in career education. One endeavor of the company has been the production of films, which are free on loan to schools by contacting the local telephone company. They also developed a career awareness book at the elementary level on working in a telephone company.

- The *General Motors Corporation* (GMC) has established a policy to help students become better citizens by increased self-awareness, improved decision-making capabilities, and occupational skills through a national career education effort. GMC has committed itself to providing classroom speakers and materials on specific careers, offering plant visits, cooperating with school personnel, and serving on industry-education advisory councils. Information can be obtained by writing GMC, Education Relations, General Motors Building, 3044 West Grand Blvd., Detroit, Michigan 48202.

Many other large national companies have or are developing programs related to the career education effort. General Electric Company, New York Life Insurance Company, and the Bell System are some examples. The Bell System has developed a multimedia program entitled "A Career is Calling," which consists of a 27-minute film concentrating on the specifics of several jobs in the system. A teacher's book, consisting of eight spirit master activity sheets, delves into the self-evaluation and self-knowledge students must acquire before they can be happy and effective on a job in the Bell System or anywhere. Thus, the business and industrial sector is an excellent resource for career education.

This chapter contains three major sections related to these mutual objectives. The sections will identfy:

- Specific contributions that business and industry can make to programs for handicapped individuals;
- suggestions for involving members of business and industry in the career development of handicapped individuals; and
- procedures to follow when educators approach prospective employers of handicapped individuals.

CONTRIBUTIONS TO PROGRAMS FOR HANDICAPPED INDIVIDUALS

The resources and personnel within the sectors of business and industry are so extensive that educators must be clear in their own minds about the objectives and means of collaboration. It is better to have identified objectives and possible joint efforts before approaching members of business/industry. At the same time, one should be open to suggestions that are presented by these same members. In other words, educators should approach business/industry with an opening statement such as:

> I have an idea on ways that we can work together in the career development for handicapped individuals. Do you have additional suggestions?

This is contrasted with the question: "What should we do?" which may only serve to alert businesspersons to the fact that the educator has not done her "homework."

This section includes discussions of several ways in which business/industry can assist educational programs. The following list provides suggestions for building a collaborative effort between major sectors in career development. Each suggestion is discussed further below.

Ways Business/Industry Can Assist Educational Programs:
- Identifying Trends in the Economy
- Furthering Contacts with the Business and Industry Sector
- Becoming Advocates for Handicapped Workers
- Serving as a Classroom Resource
- Providing Program Consultation
- Providing Work Experiences
- Participating in Conferences and Workshops
- Providing Instructional and Resource Materials

Trends in the Economy

Educators are always interested in trends, whether they be related to student fashions or the birth rate, which determine enrollments for years to come. In so far as the vocational futures of handicapped workers are concerned, educators must be attentive to the overall condition of supply and demand in the labor market, as well as specific shortages within particular categories of employment that offer opportunities for handicapped workers. Reports on employment by categories, age groups, and industries are available through several government agencies, although the Department of Labor has the principal responsibility of providing the public with a continual assessment of the labor situation. You should be aware of such government publications as the *Monthly Labor Review* and *Occupational Outlook Quarterly* and place your name on the mailing list for special reports and reprints from the regional offices of the Department of Labor, Bureau of Labor Statistics.

Community members of business and industry are an important source of information as they can translate major trends in the economy and labor force into the affects such movements may have upon job development and training for individuals with special needs. Businesspersons are often able to identify surges in demands for workers with particular skills, changes in job classifications, modifications of skill requirements due to the introduction of new machines or work routines, and the growth or contraction of the local economy. All of these factors affect the training, placement, and projected employment of handicapped workers.

Teachers, counselors, placement personnel, and other educators associated with the several aspects of career development may not be expected to know every machine and routine ranging from the electronics to the fast food industry. However, their familiarity with labor force data, general requirements for jobs within industries, and current conditions within the marketplace will enhance conversations with local leaders in business and industry. This familiarity also provides a basic foundation for understanding the observations and recommendations from business people relative to changes in procedures and practices within the educational community.

Contacts with the Business and Industry Sector

Self-reliance ranks as a major thread in the collective American personality. Most Americans believe that a person's own efforts account for her success or failure, whether she falls into the white or blue collar categories. It is no wonder that such terms as *clout, influence,* and *pull,* to name a few, are used in a derogatory fashion to identify individuals who have advanced in the organization or achieved an objective based on means apart from their work skills.[10] Educators would be fooling themselves if they did not imagine that meeting people in business and industry for the purpose of securing contacts was a necessary function associated with developing jobs for handicapped workers. American workers may regard their success on a job as due to their own efforts and ability, but individuals with special needs have stated that they would first like to have a chance at a job!

Individuals from one walk of life or professional endeavor (education and rehabilitation) need an entree to another sector (business and industry) simply because the normal training and pursuit of professional goals does not bring members of one sector into frequent contact with those from the other one. Bankers are more acquainted with other bankers than they are with teachers because most of the working day and, very often, their social life includes other bankers. Thus, it is a question of how an individual from the world of education is going to meet individuals in business and industry who will be amenable to efforts at training or employing handicapped workers. One answer is to use all possible leads and contacts within business and industry.

Educators can use the resources of vocational rehabilitation, sheltered workshops, youth training programs, and just about any organization that has contacts with the business and industry sector. Such contacts are important as they:

1. Economize on the educator's time and energy, which are needed to complete other responsibilities; and
2. provide an element of support for the employer interview.

One can approach an employer independently and achieve favorable benefits for the program. However, the chances for success are enhanced

---

[10] These same terms, as well as the expression "It's who you know that counts," are not confined to the world of work.

if the placement personnel is recommended or endorsed by another businessperson.

In their extensive review of rehabilitation and job placement of handicapped individuals, Zadny and James (1976) distinguish between formal and informal sources of job leads. Contacts between members of business and industry (employers) fall in the category of informal sources and are also characterized by Zadny and James as "underused." These underused channels may provide better results simply because the commonly used sources must support greater numbers of job seekers. The two categories of sources appear in Table 10.

Table 10 is appropriate to our emphasis upon contacts within the business and industry sector, whether professionals are considering the placement of clients, students, or just plain job seekers. It emphasizes the fact that the underused sources of information are those that may be categorized as *personal contacts* between professionals, workers, and businesspersons with prospective employers. As program personnel develop greater contacts with community organizations, advisory groups, and members of the business and industry sector, they essentially operate in the underused channels of information and avoid excessive competition from other applicants for jobs.

Table 10
Used and Underused Sources of Job Leads

commonly cited sources	underused sources
Newspaper want ads	Past employer
State Employment Service	Past clients
Private employment agencies	Counselor's acquaintances
Help wanted signs	Employers cited by employers
Yellow pages	who have hired clients
Trade publications	Counselor co-workers
Unions	Service persons
Civil Service bulletins	Client family and friends
Business pages of newspaper	Workers at business hiring
Employers who have hired clients	clients

Source: Jerry J. Zadny and Leslie F. James, *Another view on placement: State of the art 1976.* Portland, Oregon: School of Social Work, Portland State University, 1976, Table 4, p. 29. Reprinted by permission.

Advocates for the Handicapped Worker

Representatives from business and industry have functioned as spokepersons for the handicapped individual's success at employment. The following statements are taken from literature advocating this success

When the handicapped individual's abilities are matched with the requirements of the job, he is no longer handicapped . . .

Dr. Ralph T. Collins,
Eastman Kodak Company

This is not a charity situation . . . it is a moneymaking part of our operation . . .

Laundry Owner

There's no reason why a disabled person can't function, and there's no reason why it isn't good business . . .

Charles Vail, Jr.
Industrial Corporation

A second form of endorsement is gained through the presentation of the "Employer of the Year" awards by such organizations as the President's Committee on Employment of the Handicapped, Governor's Committee on Employment of the Handicapped, and National Association for Retarded Citizens. The broad objective of increasing training and employment opportunities are furthered through newspaper and magazine stories, interviews, and media coverage generated by these awards.

Some educators have followed the example of the above national and state organizations in building their school programs. In an attempt to gain public awareness of their "Project Success," a work training and placement program, the Roland (California) Unified School District used a public relations firm to prepare a sample speech that members of the Advisory Committee (which included local businesspersons) could deliver to fraternal and business organizations in support of the project (Wright, 1973).

Classroom Resource

Chapters 4 through 6 contain suggestions for using representatives from business and industry as classroom resources. These learning activities will most often include the traditional vehicles of field trips or visitations by skilled personnel to the classroom to demonstrate techniques, materials, and tools. Several school systems have provided their teachers with a Community Career Education Directory. The directory contains information on local businesses and industry, including address, telephone number, major industry or work activities, suggested hours for field trips, availability of guest speakers for the classroom, and the name of the person to contact. Educators from elementary through secondary school can use such a directory in furthering student awareness of the many careers and specific job functions in community industries.

Members of business and industry can also provide valuable opinions about materials, training manuals, or instructional guides used by teachers in the classroom. For example, placement personnel may review application forms or provide suggestions on training students for interviews. Plant supervisors can provide suggestions on training procedures used in school or workshop environments to prepare students for entry into the world of work. Vocational educators are usually in step with changes and modifications in selected industries, but personnel from various companies can continue to advise them on changes in materials, machines, or routines that should be reflected in the training program.

There is one rule that educators should keep in mind whenever representatives of business and industry are sought as classroom speakers, consultants, or hosts to tours of students, faculty, or parents. It is: *Prepare* your resource persons. They must know what is expected of them. This preparation may include an interview with program personnel, printed or visual information about their role, and an estimation of the person's importance to the goals of career development for exceptional individuals. This kind of information helps members of business and industry to use their time and resources with greater efficiency. It may also influence their decision concerning continued involvement with the school system.

Program Consultation

The total expanse of a career development program, including vocational training and placement, requires several skills on the part of educators. These skills are certainly brought to the forefront in such program components as student evaluation, program evaluation, management of resources, and cost analysis. In addition, specific problems may occur relative to minimum wage laws and the work-study assignments, cooperative agreements between the school system and other agencies, and post-placement evaluation of former students and their employers.

It is to the educator's advantage to receive opinions from members of the business and industry sector on mutual problems and solutions. This consultation may be especially valuable due to recent changes in affirmative action policies and guarantees in the hiring of the handicapped worker. Although state and federal agencies can provide the basic requirements and interpretations of the law and regulations, businesspersons can furnish examples of the application of affirmative action with specific, local situations. These examples constitute a stronger basis of understanding for educators when they attempt to place students in similar firms.

Representatives from business and industry can also advise program directors about the competencies required by teachers or other personnel to adequately prepare students for the job market. Jobs, skills, and work roles are in constant change, and those that prepare students to enter such a fluid market must also command certain competencies.

Work Experience

If there is one ingredient that stands out as the prominent link between business/industry and education system across the country, it is their cooperation in work experience or work-study programs for students. Business/industry has been active in collaborative efforts to develop endeavors such as field experience, student internships, summer employment, and on-the-job training. It is in these programs that students get the hands-on experiences that test their interests in particular jobs; provide a source of evaluation for supervisory personnel; train abilities with tools and tasks; and furnish the student with a relevant reward for the amount of energy that is invested in the experience. It may be a cliché to say "experience is the best teacher," but it is evident that every significant program for handicapped individuals involves the work experience situation.

There are two significant points that program personnel should consider in establishing a series of work experiences for their students. First, a sequence of experiences should be available so that individuals from elementary school through adult education can be involved in appropriate positions meeting their level of maturity, interest, and ability, One should not think of work experience as *tho* final stage of a training program. Ideally, it should be an integrated element that is available at various points in a continuum. Such a series of experiences provide the individual and program personnel with several forms of evaluation relative to intended occupational roles. It also allows the student to experiment with work roles that may be of benefit at later stages of development, as in the instance of a change of occupations.

> Work experience is *not* the final
> stage of a training program . . .

Second, work experience is a training device. If program personnel use a work-study placement to "break" open an employment spot, then they have lost it as a training experience for other students. We are well aware of the temptation to place students in employment when the same firms indicate that there are openings. But, the real value of work experience is that a number of students can be cycled through a series of work tasks that have been identified and evaluated by supervisors and educators. This knowledge becomes a standard by which other students can be measured and trained. Eliminating a training site or series of experiences only forces educators to repeat the laborious effort of locating another cooperative businessperson, establishing communication with supervisors, and investing additional time that could have been used in finding employment.

One variation on work experience is the involvement of faculty members in similar on-the-job routines. For example, Kern High School District, Bakersfield, California, financed the placement of its vocational instructors in work-study positions In community businesses. Since these instructions were to train students before they were placed in the community, it was logical for the district to make sure that the teachers knew about the work routines and tasks that would be required of the students. The inservice training of the faculty allowed them to work on jobs that they would later teach to their students.

IBM Company conducts a summer work-experience program for deaf college students who are preparing for programming careers. It is felt that employers will be more receptive to hiring these individuals if they have proven themselves in a real work environment. They are paid a standard hourly rate. Managers and staff participating in the program are oriented on such topics as residual hearing and hearing aids, speech difficulties, and language difficulties. The program is deemed successful by IBM, which employs a considerable number after graduation (Jamison, 1977a).

Conferences and Workshops

This is one of the most common means of bringing people together to discuss themes, problems, issues, or actions related to career development for handicapped individuals. These events can be used to explore such concerns as:

- Business/industry and education partnership in career development for handicapped individuals;
- preparing handicapped youth to meet the changing job market;
- education's role in retraining the employee who is disabled while on the job; and
- the requirements imposed by legislation.

Various organizations within the business world, as well as individual companies, have sponsored conferences and workshops in the broad area of career education for American youth and workers. However, the 1977 White House Conference on Handicapped Individuals, although sponsored by the federal government, included recommendations pertinent to extended cooperation by business/industry with education in career development of handicapped workers. Some of the delegates' recommendations also provided additional themes for joint conferences and workshops. The President's Committee on Employment of the Handicapped (1977a) reports the following recommendations:

- There should be a national public awareness program to give recognition to employers who hire disabled people;
- there should be training for supervisors, emphasizing the utilization of handicapped workers;
- there should be more transitional employment concepts (such as psycho-social centers for the mentally restored and occupational training centers for the mentally retarded); and
- there should be some way to assure that vocational schools, sheltered workshops, and other places of training are teaching the skills that really meet the needs of local employers.

Instructional and Resource Materials

Business/industry and education have cooperated for several years in the preparation of students for work roles. Although the cooperation has been greater in programs for normal and gifted/talented students, there are indications that the collaboration will expand to handicapped individuals due to the active encouragement of the President's Committee on Employment of the Handicapped, school personnel, and organizations such as the National Association for Retarded Citizens.

Hensley (1977) reviews the professional literature and cites numerous instances in which leading companies and business organizations have taken an active role in furthering career development in the work force, as well as students in community school systems. These activities include:

- Policy statements supporting career education;
- work experience;
- tours and field trips;
- continuing education;
- projects that support career education activities that include business/industry and education;
- conferences and workshops;
- resources for classroom speakers; and
- published instructional and resource materials to be used in the classroom.

The latter activity includes such organizations as the American Society for Training and Development, National Association of Manufacturers, and the Business Industry Community Education Partnership, as well as such companies as International Telephone and Telegraph, General Electric, Mountain Bell, and Wells Fargo Bank of California. Readers interested in the original sources for many of the above activities should refer to the bibliography accompanying Hensley's review.

We need not elaborate on the kinds of materials related to career education that are provided by organizations and companies. Any description would soon be outdated as materials are changed or are exhausted. The important thing to remember is that these materials will exist as long as business/industry is involved in the career development of the American worker.

INVOLVING BUSINESS AND INDUSTRY

The previous section identified the various advantages that members of business and industry could provide an educational program of career development. This section offers suggestions relative to the means through which educators can contact and involve members of business and industry in career development efforts benefiting the entire community. The following list provides suggestions; each is discussed next.

Ways Educators Can Involve Business/Industry:

- Invite to serve on a Community Advisory Committee
- Requesting input from Committee for Employment of the Handicapped
- Presentations to Civic Organizations
- Issue publications about program (e.g., brochures, reports, news release items)
- Advertising in business publications
- Conducting job fairs, workshops, and institutes

Community Advisory Committee

The role of the Community Advisory Committee in the total career development program can be a significant factor in its success. If school personnel anticipate acceptance of the individual with special needs in the community and support for school programs, then the Advisory Committee must be more than a perfunctory group whose members' names enhance the stationery of the program director. Campbell et al. (1971) and Phelps (1976) state that the committee can provide valuable service by:

1. Reviewing program components, such as instructional materials, facilities, equipment, and cooperative training agreements;
2. identifying community contributions, resources, and effective measures of public relations; and
3. developing evaluation designs to be included in the total program.

There is no hard and fast rule as to how many members should be on the committee or for what length of time they should serve. The most likely consideration would be to include representatives of the major industries in the community that may employ graduates of the program. However, school personnel should not fall into the assumption nor convey the impression that the members of the committee are obligated to find jobs for students or hire a certain number of graduates. The members principal role is to assist the program and function as advocates for handicapped workers in the community. The following list of suggested members of the committee represents a cross section of the major groups of individuals who are interested in student success or can directly influence the training procedures.

1. Personnel or employment managers who would be able to advise educators about application forms, interview procedures, and employment trends;
2. supervisors who are in direct contact with handicapped workers

and can identify potential difficulties for handicapped workers in work settings;

3. directors or managers of a firm that employs a number of handicapped workers who would speak to businesspersons about the company's successful experiences in employment or accommodation;

4. members of parent organizations who are strongly interested in the career development of the handicapped and could bring support for school programs through coalitions of parents and handicapped workers;

5. members of community agencies involved in the training and placement of handicapped workers who could provide information on the challenges faced by the adult individual with special needs;

6. member of an insurance firm acquainted with the practices and rates for industries that employ handicapped workers;

7. individuals with handicaps who have succeeded in the work world and can provide unique insights into the program's training and placement components.

One final word about the committee. Educators should not expect that since each member has a particular expertise in the area for which she was chosen that she will automatically know about the numerous issues and problems revolving around career development for special needs individuals. The members should be placed on a sequential series of information sessions, informing them about the school program, community efforts, and the national scene. At times, members of the committee may conduct these sessions. But the overall direction must be planned initially by the school personnel, until such time that the committee members exercise their interests and request information in specific areas.

There are some unique examples of the extent to which community committees can become involved in the job success of handicapped individuals. Zuger (1971) reports the development and activities of a Committee for the Specialized Placement of the Handicapped, Institute of Rehabilitation Medicine, New York City. The committee consists of approximately 25 members, representing large and small companies, legal firms, banks, manufacturers, insurance companies, retail stores, and a daily newspaper. These community members meet regularly to interview handicapped individuals who are ready to enter the labor market. But their strongest contributions rest on personal commitments to suggest leads or employment possibilities for the individual. This does not mean that the committee members are obligated to employ the candidates. That procedure may, over a span of time, discourage members from active participation or exhaust employment openings. Zuger attributes the success of the committee to the:

1. Availability of its members for the regular meetings, discussions, and suggested actions to achieve the individual's employment objectives;

2. commitment of its members to provide employment leads; and
3. vigorous follow up of committee members by institute personnel in order to maintain communication relative to the progress of the committee, as well as individual workers.

Committee for Employment of the Handicapped

There are three levels of the committee: president's, governor's, and mayor's. These committees serve as a powerful ally because members of business and industry serve on subcommittees such as employment, education, communications, and medical considerations. The committee also provides educators with contacts to members of government agencies, labor, veterans organizations, fraternal, and religious groups—in other words, all groups that may be interested in the several issues that surround efforts to promote employment for handicapped workers.

The activities and influence of the local committee may vary, but there is a continual flow of ideas and support materials from the president's and governor's committees that should assist the educator's efforts in furthering contact with business and industry.

Civic Organizations

This term is used broadly to include all organizations interested in furthering the general well being of members of the community. The organizations serve as fertile ground for contacts with members of the business community, simply because both the educator and businessperson share a common desire to improve conditions for members of the community. This mutual respect and regard provide educators with an opportunity to present the benefits of the training and placement program and pursue possible leads for further involvement with business and industry. Several program directors have told us that some of their strongest supporters or best leads to employment possibilities have occurred when a businessperson approached the educator after a presentation to a civic group.

We suggest that educators regard presentations to civic organizations as a major public relations project. This attitude requires the speaker to use any form of audio-visual technique or publication that would involve the audience. We also suggest that:

1. The presentation should emphasize major points, as the audience may be "lost" if bombarded with figures and details;
2. the speaker involve the audience by stimulating their desire to ask questions about career development, training, placement, or job success;

3. materials be available should members of the audience wish to read at their leisure or contact other sources of information; and
4. former or current students of the program be included in the presentation in order to dispel possible misconceptions about the abilities of individuals with special needs.

Program Publications

It is the educator's continual objective to keep the goals and achievements of the students in the forefront of community attention. This can be accomplished through personal presentations, as discussed in the previous section, face-to-face meetings with civic leaders, and interviews with businesspersons and parents. Publications, however, provide a ready reference when the educator is unavailable and present the program to the larger public, which also includes members of business and industry. There are several kinds of publications that should be a part of the educator's attempt to advertise career development and involve members of business and industry. These publications would include:

1. An attractive brochure that provides an overall view of the program, its intents, and *advantages* for the reader. The brochure can be a part of employer contacts and interviews, which will be discussed later in the chapter. They are for general distribution and may include pictures of students at work to convey the impression that one of the goals and accomplishments of career development is successful employment.
2. Several types of reports that provide "hard data" about the program. This information is necessary to justify expenditures and is valuable to administrators, teachers, members of the Community Advisory Committee, and members of the community who are interested in the ways in which their tax dollars are spent. The most frequent topics for these reports include:
   a. Successful placements by work titles;
   b. identification of business firms that have hired handicapped workers; and
   c. total number of earnings of former students for a particular period of time, which may also include the amount of tax dollars these students returned to the community.
3. News release items that can be used by the local media in direct reprints, broadcasts, or that can provide the basis for a feature story. The news release can advertise the availability of qualified workers, such as a "work wanted" advertisement. The advertisement may include the unique accomplishments of the student, such as the completion of a training program for mechanics or computer operators.

Business Publications

This form of involving business and industry is an extension of the previous attempts to publicize career development in the school system. Several industries and companies have their own publications. Anyone who has ever sat in a doctor's or dentist's office may have spent a long period of time paging through what are termed the *trade journals*. Articles about handicapped workers have appeared in many of these publications. Educators at the local and state level should be aware of such journals, as they serve as another means of advertising efforts in career development and indirectly building a familiarity on the part of potential employers.

Job Fairs, Workshops, and Institutes

Several organizations (parent groups, associations formed by individuals with special needs, government agencies) have attempted to educate employers and other personnel in business and industry about the positive qualities of handicapped workers. These organizations have combined their talents, contacts, and efforts to meet the following objectives:

1. Inform employers about ways they can meet recent changes in the law related to affirmative action for handicapped workers;
2. display the achievements of other employers who have hired handicapped workers;
3. provide a meeting place in which employers can interview prospective employees with handicaps;
4. provide a forum to discuss common problems experienced by both employers and employees;
5. discuss the local or regional employment situation relative to job openings and projected changes in the demand and supply of labor; and
6. increase employers' knowledge about the abilities and skills of an untapped segment of the labor force.

These efforts may be organized in the traditional conference format, presented over local or educational television, or through the increasingly popular "job fair." The job fair is a central location at which representatives from business and industry interview applicants. It benefits individuals with handicaps by providing several interview possibilities within one location. Business and industry also record gains as firms are able to fill openings in their work force with qualified individuals.

Another attempt at increasing job possibilities was conducted by the Epilepsy Association of Central Maryland through a grant from the Department of Special Projects of the Maryland State Department of Education (*National Spokesman*, 1977). The association recruited employment specialists from private industry to conduct a series of 25 educational seminars designed to take the mystery out of neurological disorders and decrease the resistance to hiring individuals who have them. The seminars are arranged to meet the needs of those who make policy decisions on employment, evaluate individuals, function as line supervisors, and interview prospective employees. One should expect that the several organizations that represent the interest of individuals with special needs will continue to use various forms of training vehicles in order to increase the employer's understanding and employment possibilities for handicapped workers.

The major focus of this section is the means by which educators can contact and involve representatives of business/industry in career development activities. The following are some important considerations permeating the numerous attempts.

- *Involve members of business/industry as soon as possible in the career development of handicapped individuals.* There are several reasons for this recommendation. First, their active cooperation and commitment may be stronger if they know they were approached in the formative stages of a program or project rather than as symbolic representatives. Second, they may be able to suggest important changes or ideas of support while the program or project is in the developmental stages. This is especially crucial if the project actually includes provisions for cooperation with business/industry. This may sound ridiculous, but there have been instances in which educators have spent considerable time planning a project, preparing staff and students, identifying training experiences and appropriate industries, and then approaching business/industry with the expectation that employers, supervisors, managers, and businesspersons would just fit right into their plan. We do not recommend this course of action.

- *Maintain a continuity in communications with members of business/industry.* Business executives are accustomed to a certain degree of punctuality, and supervisors want precision. Both are especially discouraged when they are approached by several representatives of the same program or project. Just imagine what your response might be if three of four salespersons for the same product called you on the telephone during your office hours. The continuity of communication is also important once individuals are involved in the program, as emphasized in our discussion of the Community Advisory Committee.

- *Publicize the link between business/industry and education as much as possible.* Of course, any efforts at publicity should be approved by the principal agents involved in the program or project. Once approved, educators should use as many sources as possible within the community, area, state, region, and nation. We specifically call your attention to successive stages of information, as each contains a corresponding vehicle for communication with the public. For example, the community may have a small, neighborhood or local newspaper and radio station; an area may be covered by a large city newspaper, television station, and several AM-FM radio channels; a state would include official publications by members of the legislature or speeches entered into the official proceedings; the region may be covered through professional publications that pertain to the particular industry; and the nation includes the release of information through the agencies of the federal government, related to education and employment of the handicapped, and to career education. Such publication of an existing collaboration between business/industry and education can assist future expansions in programs, as well as the employment of handicapped individuals, as will be discussed in the following section.

- *Utilize as many resources as possible that can encourage the involvement of business and industry.* The previous discussions of publications, presentations, and committees include references to the many agents within a community who can operate as advocates for training programs. These advocates, whether they be civic groups, parents organizations, or influential citizens, will need the information and encouragement of educators. Furthermore, educators must be aware of the potentials for the total involvement of the community and coordinate the activities with the goals of career development for handicapped individuals.

APPROACHING THE EMPLOYER

The majority of employers for handicapped individuals are in the business and industry sector of the community, so it is only appropriate to discuss measures to increase their favorable attitudes toward handicapped workers in this chapter. One of the most important factors in the change of employer attitudes has been the success of handicapped employees on a wide assortment of occupational tasks. The professional and popular literature report modifications and accommodations in work settings so that individuals in wheelchairs or with prosthetic aides may work in offices and on assembly lines. Other expansions in job opportunities and success can be attributed to the fact that one employer decided to provide a handicapped employee with a chance to prove her ability. Thus, the reader can encounter reports of electric welders who are blind, computer programmers who are severely handicapped or deaf, offset press operators who are mentally retarded, and physicians with cystic fibrosis.

Employers have always been an important part of the total picture of adult success of the handicapped individual, but it has only been within recent years that professionals in all disciplines associated with training

> Ways to Approach Employers:
> - Study employers' apparent receptivity toward handicapped individuals
> - Decide on most appropriate method of contact
> - Prepare "sales" presentation
> - Be able to counteract employer resistance
> - Maintain employer contact after placement

and placement have developed more sophisticated approaches toward influencing employer decisions. Much of this sophistication is really an adaptation of techniques used by members of the business community to market their products with the general public. We do not like to use the word *product* to denote a handicapped individual, nor are all the selling methods completely favorable to our tastes. You will, no doubt, be able to choose those methods that best represent your philosophy and personal style and, thus, open areas of employment for the handicapped worker. The above list provides suggestions for approaching employers concerning job possibilities for handicapped individuals. Each suggestion is discussed further in this section.

Qualification of Prospective Employers

Placement personnel should be well informed of the potential employer's type of business, number of employees, and current projections of the firm's earnings or success. This information can enter into the conversations between employers and placement personnel and indicate to the former that the placement person is attempting to stay abreast of developments in the community and economy. However, the information is most important in providing the advocate with a determination of whether she should even attempt a placement. For example, the firm may already be well staffed in particular skill areas that match those of the prospective employee, or the firm may be experiencing a favorable upswing in business and about to expand its labor force. This kind of information decreases fruitless attempts at placement.

There are other clues that may indicate an employer's acceptance of handicapped employees. These may be:

1. The employers' participation in organizations or fund-raising attempts associated with areas of exceptionality;
2. the existence of ramps at work sites to facilitate employee movements;
3. designated parking areas for handicapped drivers; and
4. other architectural changes that indicate the firm's attempt to meet the needs of handicapped individuals, whether they are employees or prospective customers.

The process of matching students to jobs, as well as influencing employers' opinions about hiring handicapped workers, requires a great deal of time and enthusiasm. One would not want to waste an entire morning on attempting to develop a job when some prior review of the above considerations may provide better alternatives. A second subtle element in the elimination of wasted effort is to maintain a positive attitude toward job development. Such activities as visiting with employers, attending civic functions, and keeping abreast of the local economy can tax the placement person if they do not lead to increased opportunities for handicapped workers. The placement person must be aware of her success-failure ratio in order to prevent any decrease in enthusiasm and effort that may be attributed to a lack of review of essential factors. These factors include knowledge about the employer, applicant, and interview techniques.

Contacting the Employer

There are several ways of contacting employers, but their success is measured by whether the placement person has gained an appointment to explain the merits of her program or trainees. Sigler and Kokaska (1971) identify four major means of contacting employers with appropriate examples: 1. mail, 2. telephone solicitation, 3. personal calls, and 4. referrals.

The *mail approach* can be further divided into several forms of pre-approach letters, which introduce the program or sender with a statement of intent to establish further contact with the employer. The letter can include a response form, which the employer mails to the sender. The disadvantage of the mail approach is that the employer has prior knowledge of the intent of the sender and can take various measures to avoid any face-to-face contact. However, the letter can be combined with a referral from another employer, information about the program, and the honest intent of the placement person to avoid wasting the employer's time. This type of letter should be followed by a telephone or personal inquiry.

Telephone solicitation can be combined with the pre-approach letter and referrals and precede personal calls. The essential part of this technique is that the delivery be assertive and positive, with as much information conveyed in as short a time as possible. The following is an example:

> Ms. Businessperson, my name is Mr. Placement person with Success School District. We have a program that trains individuals to work in your kind of company. I would like to see you for 30 minutes, at your convenience, to explain how our program and students can benefit you. Do you have an opening on your calendar?

Personnel should develop their deliveries to meet the requirements of the firm and practice "jumping" the various hurdles, such as telephone operators and appointment secretaries, that block contacts with employers.

Personal calls can be effective, since it is difficult for an employer to say she won't see the placement person when both are in the office. Personal calls can also be dangerous if the employer considers it a definite intrusion on her schedule. Personnel must extradite themselves from such situations with assurances that they were in the neighborhood with other scheduled interviews and simply had the time and opportunity to call on this additional employer. This personal call should be followed by an attempt to establish a definite time for an appointment.

Referrals rank as one of the most successful methods, since they can be preceded by a favorable work report or letter from the employer's associate or friend. The use of a referral, in a sense, obligates the employer to give the placement person an initial chance. However, it also obligates the placement person to present as strong and polished delivery as possible, since the employer can always inform her friend about the interview. The advocate who fails to make the appointed time, is ill prepared, and blunders through the delivery may experience a compounding of refusals for appointments, as well as loss of her initial source of referral.

Techniques for the Appointment

Business appointments are similar to classroom presentations in that the placement person must be well prepared to accomplish her objectives through selected means. Several authors suggest techniques that can be used in the interview (Payne, 1977; Payne & Chaffin, 1968; Payne, Mercer, & Epstein, 1974; Sigler & Kokaska, 1971). Payne (1977) suggests techniques that could be used with employers that fall into three categories.

> Conformist . . . materialistic . . . sociocentric employers

The categories are derived from Graves' (1970) levels of existence, and the appropriate means of counseling and managing individuals who exhibit behaviors for a particular classification. The three categories include:

1. The saintly conformist who is conservative, a pillar of the community, and manages the business in an autocratic fashion;
2. the materialist who is production-oriented and conducts herself like the "sharp" businessperson should dress and behave; and
3. the sociocentric who is people-oriented and judges success in terms of how well the employees get along with one another, but may be limited because she does not like to make unilateral decisions on hiring handicapped workers.

Knowledge about behavioral or managerial characteristics fall within our previous discussion of qualifying the prospective employer. Modifying the presentation according to the viewer has always been the mark of a "top" salesperson and is in no way unique to the field of job placement of the handicapped. But first of all, one must develop a presentation that includes facts, figures, diagrams, and whatever means that will convince the employer that the handicapped worker is backed by a system of training and support. The following suggestions should be considered in preparing the sales presentation.

Build rapport with the employer. Although the primary goal is to place students in an employment situation, every employer can benefit the program and the employment of handicapped workers several ways. The employer may eventually become a member of the Community Advisory Committee, provide skilled advise for classroom activities, or allow her business to be a training site. Compatible relationships with employers help facilitate actions that have benefits for the training program.

Keep the presentation short and simple. Concentrate on developing a delivery that includes the basic elements of the program or individual. Such aids as charts, pictures, and visuals may be included, but one should not attempt to overload the employer with needless statistics and examples. There is a first line of essential information that allows the employer to understand the *who, what, where,* and *why* of the program. A second line of information supports answers to basic questions the employer may raise about the program or applicant.

Speak in terms the employer can understand. Professionals must be certain to avoid medical or psychological terms that can only confuse the employer or that lead her to questions that divert from the objective of the presentation.

Emphasize the benefits for the employer. These benefits may be reflected in a specific training program that prepares the applicant for work tasks in the employer's firm, increases successful attendance records, or expands production capacity. These benefits should be supported by information contained on the charts or other audio-visual aides.

Build employer responses in the affirmative. In other words, get the employer to respond to questions you may ask with a "Yes" answer. Positive responses build a receptive attitude on the part of the employer and also give necessary feedback to the placement person. We would hope that the employer would find it very difficult to say "No" when you finally request her participation after a long line of "Yes" responses.

Stay with the objectives of your delivery. If you are asked a question, respond with a statement that may be near the answer she wants but is closer to your purpose. For example, "Mr. Educator, how can you train those people?" Response: "Ms. Businessperson, you would be surprised at how rewarding it is. Our students have proven themselves to be dependable on such jobs as . . . ."

Emphasize success with the training and placement of handicapped workers. The employer has to be assured that sho will hire a worker who is the product of a training approach or group of professionals that prizes success. Past and current achievements by other students provide a valuable source of information to answer employer questions about the program gains.

If you were referred to the employer, emphasize that the referral was based on the student's ability. This is in keeping with the goals of attempting to place individuals who demonstrate the various work abilities that are prized by the employer. Of course, if the employer is going to hire her first employee from the training program, that employee should be one of the best workers so that the employer's experiences can lead to other referrals.

Emphasize your availability for further discussion or assistance. You should leave the employer with the opinion that your primary responsibility is to the handicapped worker, but you are also concerned with maintaining favorable relations with the employer. It is possible that the placement person can benefit the employer in other matters related to the hiring of handicapped workers, such as affirmative action policies.

Be truthful and objective about the worker's disability, but avoid initiating lengthy discussions if the limitation is not relevant to the performance of the work tasks. The regulations on affirmative action have helped decrease the tendency on the part of employees or applicants to hide certain forms of disability and placement personnel to be defensive in their presentations to employers. Nevertheless, several questions should be considered in qualifying the employer.

- Has the employer hired other individuals with similar disabilities?
- What type of work tasks will be expected of the applicant and can their successful completion be affected, in some way, by the disability?

- Will the employer regard personality factors to be important to the work task?
- Will the applicant's failure to reveal the disability disqualify her if it is discovered at a later date?

The final answer as to whether the employer should *always* know about the employee's special status is certainly a personal issue that must be decided between the placement person and the applicant before either enters the interview situation or completes an application for employment.

Employer Resistance

Securing employment or training opportunities for individuals with special needs requires that placement personnel identify the employer's:

- Particular needs and requirements for employees; and
- doubts and misconceptions about handicapped employees.

The first element will vary according to the particular industry or occupational task. For example, the owner of a fast food service may stress speed of delivery, appearance, and a pleasing manner in dealing with customers, while the production manager of an electronics firm will be concerned with accuracy and the ability to withstand fatigue. These unique requirements will surface during the interview between the placement person and prospective employer. They are also linked to the employer's questions and doubts about the handicapped worker's ability to meet the established criteria.

The many kinds of objections have been discussed in the professional literature (Sears, 1975), speeches (Jamison, 1977b), and publications by the President's Committee on Employment of the Handicapped and the Department of Labor. The objections may include specific references to the applicant's lack of ability, or more global reflections of stereotypes about certain forms of disability. The placement person should be able to anticipate possible negative responses or attitudes based on her experience and the professional literature. Most objections can be traced to the employer's misunderstanding of terms and a lack of exposure to the abilities of individuals with special needs. In such instances, the placement person should meet objections or puzzled expressions with honest and firm answers, while emphasizing the applicant's ability to accomplish work tasks.

Some of these doubts and misconceptions will be examined in the following paragraphs. These statements, in various forms, have been reported by professionals and researchers in the fields of special education, vocational placement, and rehabilitation. These are not the prevailing attitudes of employers but rather their occasional requests for better information and insight.

I need somebody with initiative.

In a survey of 200 community employers in Baltimore, Maryland, Stewart (1977) concludes that employers in certain industries are more interested in positive work attitudes and motivation to work among employees than their technical skills. Employers often picture the handicapped worker as incapable of learning new things, taking responsibility, or coping with forms of pressure. In some instances, these demands may be outside of the person's present capabilities, but it would be best for the school personnel to determine the kinds of initiative that may be required for each job. One employer's concept of initiative may be another's idea of recklessness!

Could somebody like that really handle this job?

The employer's knowledge of a worker's disability can create doubts about the latter's skill in certain situations, as well as the total competence of the worker. The placement person can gain an advantage in these situations if she is familiar with the job specifications, confident of the applicant's abilities, and capable of matching the two to the satisfaction of the employer. Prior work experiences or a trial period on the job may help convince the employer that the handicapped worker is able to meet job requirements.

Our supervisors aren't counselors or therapists.

Employers may recognize that the individual has the physical skill for the task and yet wonder about the social-personal variables that are involved in the work setting. The employer's concerns may be justified, as in the placement of individuals with a history of personal problems. In these instances, the placement person will have to identify the amount of support that the employer can expect from outside sources to insure the success of the individual and decrease the concerns of the employer and fellow workers. This objection may also be countered if the applicant does not need any special supervision or help but simply has the skills for the job.

My insurance company won't let me hire handicapped people *or* my workmen's compensation rates will skyrocket.

There are several forms to these rejoinders, which usually involve the affect of the handicapped employee upon the safety records of a particular business or industry. In fact, neither workmen's compensation nor group insurance rates are affected by the employment of handicapped workers. The rates are based on employer's accident records and the types of activities in which they are engaged (Department of Labor, no date).

The President's Committee on Employment of the Handicapped has provided business and industry with a number of examples in which employment of handicapped workers has not adversely affected safety records or insurance rates. Bennett (1972) provides one of the first salvos on the "insurance rate worries." He reviews seven common obstacles to hiring handicapped workers but emphasizes a report by the North American Mutual Insurance Alliance. This alliance of 100 insurance companies maintains that impaired individuals have fewer injuries on the job and, when placed on suitable jobs, do not affect insurance rates. In fact, the insurance companies encouraged hiring the handicapped worker.

Another widely quoted survey of the work performance of handicapped individuals was conducted by E. I. du Pont de Nemours and Company, America's sixteenth largest employer (Sears, 1975). The 8-month study gathered data on 1,452 employees with disabilities such as blindness, heart disease, impaired vision, paralysis, epilepsy, impaired hearing, total deafness, and orthopedic problems. The major findings are:

1. There are no increases in compensation costs or lost-time injuries, important factors in insurance rates;
2. most handicapped workers require no special adjustments to the work place;
3. 96% of the handicapped workers rate average or better in safety, both on and off the job. More than one-half are above average. Sears states that the study found the disabled worker to be more safety conscious than the average employee;
4. the handicapped worker wants to be treated as a regular employee and does not want to be singled out for special privileges;
5. 91% of the handicapped workers rate average or better on job performance; and
6. 79% of the handicapped workers rate average or better on attendance.

The Sears article contains such dynamic data that Zadny and James (1976) recommend it should be required reading for every rehabilitation counselor and many of their clients.

> I want to know that the employee I hire will stay with me.

An employer can never be certain that any employee, able or disabled, will complete a certain period of employment. People find other forms of employment and experience numerous changes in their living conditions that can affect their duration of employment with any one firm. Placement personnel can refer to the applicant's previous record of attendance in school or training programs. Another form of support again is based on the du Pont study, which indicates that the handicapped workers rate average or better on turnover in 93% of the cases.

> I'll have to change my entire operation.

The imagined change is often far greater than the real one. For example, Krents (no date) reports on the results of a survey that found that it took 1 cent per square foot to make a building accessible to handicapped in- dividuals, while it cost 13 cents a square foot to clean the floors. The survey was conducted by Mainstream, Inc., a Washington, D.C. based, nonprofit firm, that assists companies in hiring and accommodating handicapped workers. The employer may resist change, but she may be in violation of the regulations for Section 503 of the Rehabilitation Act of 1973, which establish affirmative action in the employment of handicapped individ- uals. Placement personnel can assist employers by providing them with the latest publications on affirmative action and the several attempts to use handicapped workers by altering job sites and including modifica- tions to facilities. These publications are available from the President's, Governor's, and Mayor's Committee on Employment of the Handicapped.

There are other objections that prospective employers can raise when confronted with the possibilities of hiring handicapped individuals. But, those forms of resistance that are based on rumors or stereotypes are being met with solid evidence to the effect that the individual, when properly trained for a work role, can be an asset to the company instead of a lia- bility to society.

Maintaining Employer Contact

Assuming that the educator has established contact with employers, de- veloped the Community Advisory Committee, and recorded successful placements of students, the next major step should be maintaining a pur- poseful relationship with employers. These contacts can lead to benefits to the program, such as employer endorsements or suggestions for modifica- tions and improvements. Follow-up contacts further integrate the expe- riences of the employer with handicapped workers into the overall training program and, therefore, assist placement goals for future students.

Program directors can assure themselves of contact with employers through a consistent method of inquiry via the telephone, mail, or personal visits. The inquiry need not be extensive but should provide the employer with an opportunity to elaborate on particular problems or concerns. It is best to start an inquiry with a standard array of questions or topics that prompt the employer and allow for discussion. The following topics constitute basic areas of inquiry and discussion.

Responsibilities.   What kinds of duties are assigned to the employee? This information is valuable for future advertising with potential employers and the general public. It also alerts program personnel to jobs, duties, and abilities that former students have been able to exhibit after leaving a sequence of training experiences. Personnel have often altered their perspectives about the abilities of students and potentials in the work world due to information received from follow-up studies.

Success.   What is the level of achievement of the employee? Is the employee more successful at some tasks than others? Employers are aware of production rates and success factors, as these elements determine the costs involved in the final product. Program personnel must continually strive to develop performance rates in their students that are compatible with employed individuals in a given business or industry.

Needs.   Are there specific areas of improvement needed by the employee? These areas may include the vocational, personal, or social skills of the worker. However, the interviewer must know two things about these needs once they are identified. First, is the employee's status in jeopardy? Employers may recommend improvement but will not dismiss an employee because she does not fraternize with other workers. Second, is the training program able to provide assistance in achieving new goals? This assistance may include additional training, if the employee wants to renew a relationship with her former teachers and counselors, or a referral to another community agency.

Communication.   Is the employee successfully communicating with supervisors and co-workers? Communication is necessary for understanding tasks and, therefore, constitutes a vital element in successful employment. Note that the emphasis in this area of inquiry is on *successful* communication and not on the form of communication.

Acceptance.   Is the employer pleased with the work performance of the employee? This constitutes the proverbial "bottom line" to the entire follow-up process. Employers should not be forced into predicting whether they will continue to employ certain individuals, as there are several forces acting upon an industry or business that are a part of those decisions. A secure job one day may be changed a few months later, regardless of the employer's satisfaction with the employee. If the interviewer is able to obtain information on the five basic areas of inquiry, as well as further insights offered by the employer (which may include projections on the economy, industry, or business), then program personnel will be able to determine employer satisfaction with graduates from the training sequence.

A second benefit from a continuous involvement with employers relates directly to the length of employment of the former student. The greater the interest of personnel in the training program with the experiences of the worker and employer, the more likely are the possibilities that the individual will remain on the job. There are several situations in which the worker may need some initial assistance by program personnel and tolerance by the employer. These situations may occur when the worker is:

- Experiencing the first form of employment;
- changing occupations or employers;
- increasing the amount of responsibility;
- changing the kinds and sequence of tasks due to the introduction of new machinery or routines; and
- beset by other concerns outside of the job, which nevertheless, influence performance.

Counselors, educators, and rehabilitation personnel can have a significant influence in the above situation as they function as valuable references and sources of support. They may suggest alternate forms of behavior on the part of worker and employer or involve other professionals in the several kinds of adjustments needed to maintain the worker in an employee status.

In addition, handicapped individuals can experience difficulties justifying post-placement attention by program personnel. These difficulties can include:

- Teasing and other disrespectful remarks by fellow employees;
- lack of social sophistication;
- environmental or structural impediments;
- adjustments to work schedules, routines, and overall surroundings;
- levels of anxiety promoted by personal desires to succeed on the job;
- transportation difficulties;
- adjustments in the individual's nonwork life to facilitate personal health and energy while on the job; and
- initial difficulties in communication with supervisors or fellow employees.

There are undoubtedly more difficulties and situations that program personnel can identify and counteract in their attempts to maintain former students in successful employment. Certain general problems occur across all groups of workers, and others are specific to industries or characteristics of the individual. Our main point is that these factors can only be identified if program personnel maintain a vigorous and consistent follow-up effort with employers. The benefits of such a policy accrue for the program, employer, and exceptional individual.

CONCLUSION

The actual involvement of business and industry in career education for handicapped individuals is in the very first stage of development. Yes, business and industry has been hiring handicapped workers for many years and will undoubtedly increase that practice due to Sections 503 and 504 of The Rehabilitation Act of 1973. But, employment is only one aspect of career development, although a singularly important component. Yes, business and industry has been actively involved in career education, but the vast majority of instances have been with students in regular education. Once again, handicapped individuals are near the end of the line in this aspect of career development. The suggestions contained in this chapter will hopefully provide educators with both the skills and enthusiasm for bringing business/industry, and education into numerous collaborative efforts in career development for handicapped individuals.

One of the major contributions of the career education concept is the requirement that a great number of community agencies and organizations be identified and included in the career development efforts of the school. In addition to drawing upon considerable expertise not readily available in the school setting, there are several particularly significant reasons for substantial and active involvement of community agencies and organizations. First, these agencies and organizations have funds, equipment, contacts, and a constituency far beyond the resources of the school. Second, the agencies and organizations are able through appropriate encouragement by educators to assist in the improvement of the school's curriculum and courses. Third, the agencies and organizations are sometimes able to lend financial support for pressing needs the school encounters in implementing career education. Fourth, the negative attitudes and misconceptions of the general public relative to the school's operation and handicapped individuals will be counteracted as these agencies and organizations become partners in career development efforts.

Numerous civic, professional, and private nonprofit organizations and governmental agencies are found in most middle-sized and large communities. Besides the many local avenues for career development, there are several state and national resources that local personnel should use for additional information, literature, contacts, funding possibilities, and, in some cases, direct services.

This chapter identifies and describes some of the major agencies and organizations at the national, state, and local levels that can be included in career development efforts with handicapped individuals. Information about most of the agencies and organizations is presented in Table 11. The chapter also briefly discusses some of the major informational systems that are useful for materials and references on career development.

GOVERNMENTAL AGENCIES

A number of governmental agencies are important in promoting and supporting programmatic efforts in the career development of handicapped individuals. Personnel at the local level should be aware of the relevant information, professional literature, funding, and technical assistance that is available from each of these agencies. Table 11 outlines federal agencies important to the career development of handicapped individuals.

The *Bureau of Education for the Handicapped* (BEH) is responsible for administering and operating the federal program for educating the nation's

Table 11
*Federal Agencies Important to Career Development
of Handicapped Individuals*

agency	department/branch
Bureau of Education for the Handicapped (BEH)	HEW/Office of Education
Bureau of Occupational and Adult Education (BOAE)	HEW/Office of Education
National Institute of Education (NIE)	HEW/Office of Education
Office of Career Education (OCE)	HEW/Office of Education
Office of Developmental Disabilities (DD)	HEW/Office of Human Development Services
Office for Handicapped Individuals (OHI)	HEW/Office of Human Development Services
Rehabilitation Services Administration (RSA)	HEW/Office of Human Development Services
Veteran's Administration (VA)	Veteran's Administration (VA)

handicapped children. It is responsible for identifying national priorities and implementing the Education for All Handicapped Children Act (PL 94–142). The *Bureau of Occupational and Adult Education* (BOAE) administers the 10% of vocational education monies mandated for the handicapped that must be matched in amount by the states. The *Office of Career Education* (OCE) provides technical assistance for conceptualizing, planning, and operating career education programs. It also has some funds for demonstration and planning projects at state and local educational agencies, colleges and universities, and other organizations. The *Rehabilitation Services Administration* (RSA) administers the state-federal program of vocational rehabilitation, including a network of regional offices and state agencies that receive matching federal funds based on an established formula. RSA also has funds for research and demonstration projects directed at providing more effective rehabilitation services to handicapped individuals, including school populations needing better career development services.

The *Developmental Disabilities Office* (DD) is responsible for assisting states in planning and implementing programs for the developmentally disabled (autism, mental retardation, dyslexia, cerebral palsy, and epilepsy). Project grant funds are available for public agencies and nonprofit organizations to demonstrate new and improved techniques. The *Office for Handicapped Individuals* (OHI) serves as a point of coordination within the Office of Human Development Services and publishes a valuable document entitled *Programs for the Handicapped,* which reports events, techniques, programs, legislation, publications, and other important matters for the handicapped. The *National Institute of Education* (NIE) conducts and funds research and development activities in career education. It has produced curriculum modules, the Experience-Based Career Education models, materials to eliminate sex bias in career counseling, and materials assessment documents.

The above agencies are all located within the Department of Health, Education, and Welfare in Washington, D.C. Specific information can be obtained by writing the individual agency. One other important federal agency is the *Veterans Administration,* which offers a broad range of programs, including medical care, rehabilitation, education and training, income support, and other benefits for eligible disabled veterans and their dependents. VA regional offices and centers are situated throughout the country.

A historic "memorandum of understanding" between RSA and the U.S. Office of Education was released in October 1977, with the intent of pursuing methods by which the two delivery systems could achieve greater cooperation and complementary services. The commissioners of these agencies transmitted memorandums to their state directors, requesting them to seek immediately a coordinated service delivery for handicapped persons. Since both agencies require written programs for each handicapped individual, the groundwork has been laid for coordinating the delivery of services among these systems. The directive read:

In order that education and vocational rehabilitation agencies may integrate the goals of the IEP and the IWRP, the plans should reflect short-term and long-range objectives for career development, vocational skill training, personal adjustment, and job placement. To effect this integration, education agencies must provide guidance to those preparing IEPs and establish local contact with VR agencies. And VR agencies must similarly assure that appropriate IWRPs for persons who should complete their plans for special and vocational education, are developed in conjunction with education agencies.

Council for Exceptional Children, 1977

Thus, it appears that the wheels are beginning to turn in favor of consolidated and cooperative efforts within and between agencies, so that the many pressing needs of handicapped citizens will be better met. But, the wheels of change move slowly and often reluctantly. Hopefully, this will not be another meaningless and momentary declaration by those responsible for its implementation.

At the state level, several agencies are available to assist in the career development needs of handicapped individuals. Most of the agencies are extensions of the federal agencies discussed previously and are more accessible to the practitioner. Their titles and identity in the department structure will vary from state to state. Some of the more important agencies are the following:

- *Special Education.* Administers the state program for the education of exceptional children; offers technical assistance to school districts and programs; conducts seminars and workshops; disseminates information; engages in student identification and needs studies; promotes the development of professional services; and promotes, writes, and enforces legislation.

- *Vocational Education/Handicapped and Disadvantaged Program.* Administers the federal/state legislation that relates to vocational education for the handicapped and disadvantaged (called *special needs*); promotes the development and funds programs in secondary/post-secondary educational settings; works closely with universities in developing personnel training programs, conducting special projects, developing and disseminating materials, and other activities of career development.

- *Vocational Rehabilitation.* Administers RSAs federal/state program of assisting physically and mentally disabled persons become gainfully employed. To be eligible, a person must have: **1.** a physical or mental disability that interferes with getting or holding a job, and **2.** a reasonable chance of being able to work in suitable employment after services. Services include: **1.** medical evaluation, including mental/emotional status; **2.** evaluation of vocational potential, training, and placement needs; **3.** medical, surgical, psychiatric, and hospital care if needed to maintain or secure employment; **4.** artificial limbs, braces, wheelchairs, and hearing aids if necessary for work; **5.** vocational training, including tuition and fees, books, and supplies at universities, colleges, commercial and trade schools, rehabilitation facilities, or on-the-job; **6.** maintenance for daily living costs and transportation for medical treatment or vocational training; **7.** job placement equipment, such as job-related tools and licenses; **8.** individual guidance and counseling; **9.** coordination of services; **10.** help in finding employment; and **11.** on-the-job follow-up. While there is no age limitation, most vocational rehabilitation clients are between 16 and 65.

- *Bureau for the Blind.* Administers the vocational rehabilitation program for blind and visually handicapped persons of all ages by offering services similar to VR in addition to those special services needed by blind individuals (mobility training; communication skills, such as braille, talking books, tape recorders, telephone; activities of daily living, such as grooming and hygiene, social etiquette; physical conditioning; and prevocational skills.

The above are state agencies that persons working with handicapped individuals should know about and interface with to develop and conduct meaningful career development services. In addition, the following agencies may be helpful: **1.** *state employment/job service,* which provides direct employment and counseling services, appraisal of employment capabilities, preparation for interviews; job development and modification, a Manpower Development and Training Program; Youth Opportunity Centers, and the Bureau of Work Programs for vocational training of unemployed youths 16 to 21; **2.** *Work Incentive Program* (WIN), which is generally administered jointly by departments of social services and the employment/job service to provide job skills, training, vocational education, and job placement for adults and youths in households receiving Aid to Dependent Children (ADC) benefits; and **3.** the *Governor's Committee on Employment of the Handicapped* (GCE), which conveys to the governor and general public the pressing needs and desires of the handicapped.

At the local level, many of the above agencies and organizations have offices in moderate- to large-size cities. Agencies such as vocational rehabilitation, public health, employment service, mental health centers, social services/welfare, and diagnostic services provide an array of daily living, personal-social, and occupational assistance. In addition, local government officials and political parties can be influential in promoting more adequate career development services for handicapped citizens.

ORGANIZATIONS

There are a great number of private, nonprofit, volunteer organizations and others dedicated to the advancement of services to handicapped individuals. Many of these organizations were started by parent groups and other concerned citizens who felt special attention was needed in a specific area of need.

Some special national committees and centers that promote the career development of handicapped individuals are: **1.** *The President's Committee on the Employment of the Handicapped,* which has over 600 volunteer organizations and individuals representing business, handicapped persons, industry, labor, media, medical, education, rehabilitation, religion, veterans, and youth, and other groups promoting education, rehabilitation, and employment opportunities for handicapped individuals; **2.** *The President's Committee on Mental Retardation* (PCMR), which advises and assists the president on all matters pertaining to mental retardation and disseminates public information; and **3.** *The National Committee, Arts for the Handicapped* (NCAH), an educational affiliate of the John F. Kennedy Center for the Performing Arts, which operates as the national coordinating agency for the development and implementation of arts programs for handicapped children and youth, including those that pertain to their career development.

Table 12 identifies some of the major professional organizations that we believe are particularly important to the career development of handicapped individuals. We have indicated the type(s) of handicap served by each organization, journals and newsletters, and special features.

Several of the national organizations listed in Table 12 have state chapters that implement their philosophies and policies. Particularly significant are the state associations of the Council for Exceptional Children, American Association on Mental Deficiency, National Easter Seal Society, United Cerebral Palsy Associations, National Association for Retarded Citizens, and the National Rehabilitation Association. Each of these organizations has a large constituency of professional workers and parents who focus on the improvement of services, professional standards, legislation, workshops and conferences, informational bulletins and newsletters, and many other matters significant to the career development of handicapped citizens. Some of these organizations have their own executive director and, perhaps, a small staff that works with communities, including their local affiliates, in meeting the objectives established for their agency.

Some cities will have local affiliates of the state and national organization. The Association for Retarded Citizens and United Cerebral Palsy are such examples. These organizations generally receive considerable guidance and support from the state and national organizations to carry out their policies and objectives. Both the ARC and UCP have sponsored day-care facilities, sheltered workshops, and other direct service programs at the local level. If you do not know whether any of the organizations listed have state or local chapters in your area, write the national office for information. They may also provide other resources that can be of assistance to you.

Table 12
*Professional Organizations Important to Career
Development of Handicapped Individuals*

organization and address	handicaps	publications	features
Alexander Graham Bell Association for the Deaf 3417 Volta Place, N.W. Washington, D.C. 20007	Hearing	*Volta Review, World Traveler*	Promotes environments and programs by providing information services to parents, educators, libraries, hospitals, clinics and others.
American Association of Workers for the Blind 1511 K St. Washington, D.C. 20003	Visual	*Blindness, News and Views, Contemporary Papers*	Renders assistance in promoting, developing, and improving services to blind persons, and publishes proceedings of international meetings.
American Association on Mental Deficiency 5201 Connecticut Ave., N.W. Washington, D.C. 20015	Mental Retardation	*Mental Retardation, American Journa' of Mental Deficiency*	Promotes legislation, seminars and conferences, services and standards for facilities, and professional standards.
American Coalition of Citizens with Disabilities 1346 Connecticut Ave., N.W. Washington, D.C. 20036	All	*The Coalition,* newsletter	Promotes advocacy, referral services and information, and publication distribution. An umbrella organization of and for handicapped.
American Foundation for the Blind 15 West 16th St. New York, N.Y. 10011	Visual	*New Outlook for the Blind, Washington Report,* newsletters	Serves as a clearinghouse for information on blindness, and promotes research activities, talking books, aids and appliances, public education, a lending library, legislation and action programs.

Table 12 (Continued)

organization and address	handicaps	publications	features
American Printing House for the Blind 1839 Frankfort Ave. Louisville, Ky. 40106	Visual		Provides literature and appliances to blind people on a nonprofit basis, publishes and distributes embossed books and other educational materials.
American Psychiatric Association 1700 18th St., N.W. Washington, D.C. 20009	Emotional	*American Journal of Psychiatry*	Promotes medical education and career development, services, research and development, professional education, public information.
Association of Rehabilitation Facilities 5530 Wisconsin Ave. Washington, D.C. 20015	All	*FOCUS on Facilities*	Conducts educational seminars and conferences, assists members in developing and improving their services.
Boy Scouts of America North Brunswick, N.J. 08902 (Handicapped Division)	All	Several on various handicapped	Promotes involvement in same activities as non-handicapped, including cubbing, scouting, exploring, camping, civic activities recreation, job preparation.
Council for Exceptional Children 1920 Association Dr. Reston, Va. 22091	All	*Exceptional Children, Teaching Exceptional Children,* newsletters	Distributes materials, provides technical assistance, conducts training institutes and conferences, promotes legislation, provides 12 divisions of special interest groups.

Table 12 (Continued)

organization and address	handicaps	publications	features
Council of Organizations Serving the Deaf P.O. Box 894 Columbia, Md. 21044	Hearing	Newsletters, directories, Annual Forum proceedings	Serves as a clearinghouse for members, legal counseling, adult education, parent counseling, vocational training services, research, annual forum.
Disabled American Veterans 3725 Alexandria Pike Cold Spring, Ky. 41076	Physical	*Disabled American Veteran's Magazine*	Promotes welfare of service connected disabled veterans and their dependents through several special programs.
Division on Career Development 1920 Association Dr. Reston, Va., 22091	All	*Career Development for Exceptional Individuals,* newsletter	Works with other CEC divisions and various organizations to promote research, legislation, professional training, techniques and training materials.
Epilepsy Foundation of America 1928 L St., N.W. Washington, D.C. 20036	Physical	*National Spokesman*	Offers 19 categories of programs in medical, social, and informational service areas.
Federation of the Handicapped 211 West 14th St. New York, N.Y. 10011	Physical	*Spotlight*	Promotes vocational rehabilitation through homebound, training, group work and recreation, and a learning capacities service.
Foundation for Exceptional Children 1920 Association Dr. Reston, Va. 22091	All	*Focus*	Promotes action-oriented and research projects, students assistance, and various types of materials

Table 12 (Continued)

organization and address	handicaps	publications	features
Foundation for Exceptional Children, continued			development endeavors.
Girl Scouts of the U.S.A. 830 Third Ave. New York, N.Y. 10022	All	*Girl Scout Leader Magazine* (several publications on handicapped)	Typical girl scout services with needed adaptations.
Goodwill Industries of America 9200 Wisconsin Ave. Washington, D.C. 20014	All	newsletter	Provides vocational rehabilitation services for employment and personal growth.
Joseph P. Kennedy, Jr., Foundation 1701 K St., N.W. Washington, D.C. 20006	Mental Retardation		Promotes and funds biological and behavioral research, promotes programs of physical fitness and recreation, such as Special Olympics, public awareness.
Junior National Association of the Deaf 814 Thayer Ave. Silver Springs, Md. 20910	Hearing	*Junior Deaf American, Silent Voice*	Promotes young deaf people to use their potential, conducts conferences, camps, and workshops.
Muscular Dystrophy Association of America 810 Seventh Ave. New York, N.Y. 10019	Physical	*Muscular Dystrophy News*	Promotes research for curing and treating, patient services, recreation, and clinics.
National Association for Mental Health 1800 North Kent St. Arlington, Va. 22209	Emotional		Sponsors research, social action, education, and service to improve the care and treatment of mentally ill.

Table 12 (Continued)

organization and address	handicaps	publications	features
National Association for Retarded Citizens 2709 Ave. E. East Arlington, Tex. 76011	Mental Retardation	*Mental Retardation News, Action Together, Information Together, Information Exchange*	Focuses on public education, family counseling, and clearinghouse activities.
National Association of the Deaf 814 Thayer Ave. Silver Springs, Md. 20910	Hearing	*Deaf American*	Serves as clearinghouse for information, provides experts, conducts studies and workshops to help improve services and resolve problems.
National Association of the Physically Handicapped 6473 Grandville Ave. Detroit, Mich. 48228	Physical	newsletter	Promotes legislation, employment, barrier-free design, publicity, housing, education and research, recreation and sports, transportation.
National Association of Vocational Education Special Needs Personnel c/o American Vocational Association 1510 H St., N.W. Washington, D.C. 20005	All	*Journal for Vocational Special Needs Education,* newsletter	Promotes legislation, technical information, staff development, and special workshops to help vocational educators be more effective with handicapped and disadvantaged.
National Braille Association 85 Goodwin Ave. Midland Park, N.J. 07432	Visual		Produces materials in braille, including special vocational materials for blind workers.

Table 12 (Continued)

organization and address	handicaps	publications	features
National Easter Seal Society for Crippled Children and Adults 2023 West Ogden Ave. Chicago, Ill. 60612	Physical	*Rehabilitation Literature, Easter Seal Communicator*	Conducts extensive program of service, education, and research at national, state, and local levels, including public awareness workshops and conferences.
National Federation of the Blind Suite 212 1346 Connecticut Ave., N.W. Washington, D.C. 20036	Visual	*Braille Monitor*	Promotes research into legislation for blind, advocacy, public education, assistance to public officials, scholarships to blind students.
National Industries for the Blind 1455 Broad St. Bloomfield, N.J. 07003	Visual		Coordinates production activities of 83 workshops, researches and recommends new products, procures subcontract work and promotes evaluation and training programs for blind persons.
National Industries for the Severely Handicapped 4350 East West Highway Washington, D.C. 20014	All		Provides technical assistance to workshops in producing commodities or services for sale to federal government, researches and develops commodities that can be produced in sheltered workshops.
National Paraplegia Foundation 333 N. Michigan Ave. Chicago, Ill. 60601	Physical	*Squeaky Wheel*	Distributes information, sponsors medical and scien-

Table 12 (Continued)

organization and address	handicaps	publications	features
National Paraplegia Foundation, continued			tific conferences and educational seminars and publications.
National Rehabilitation Association 1522 K Street N.W. Washington, D.C. 20005	All	*Journal of Rehabilitation,* newsletters	Promotes legislation, provides a forum through publications and conferences, research, and stimulates professional training endeavors.
National Society for the Prevention of Blindness 79 Madison Ave. New York, N.Y. 10016	Visual	*The Sight-Saving Review, The News, Wise Owl News*	Promotes community services, publications, public information, lay and professional education, research, census information, and educational program descriptions.
National Therapeutic Recreation Society 1601 N. Kent St. Arlington, Va. 22209	Physical	*Park and Recreation Magazine*	Promotes recreation and leisure services for handicapped.
National Wheelchair Athletic Association 40–24 62nd St. Woodside, N.Y. 11377	Physical		Formulates and maintains rules governing wheelchair athletics, rule changes, keeps records, and selects and sanctions meets.
Paralyzed Veteran's of America 7315 Wisconsin Ave. Washington, D.C. 20014	Physical	*The Paraplegia News*	Promotes elimination of architectural barriers, special housing, litigation, sports and

Table 12 (Continued)

organization and address	handicaps	publications	features
Paralyzed Veteran's of America, continued			recreation programs, and transportation.
Professional Rehabilitation Workers with the Adult Deaf 814 Thayer Ave. Silver Springs, Md. 20910	Hearing	*Journal of Rehabilitation of the Deaf, Deafness Annual,* newsletter	Promotes services, research, professional training, legislation, and public information.
United Cerebral Palsy Associations 66 East 34th St. New York, N.Y. 10016	Physical	*The Crusade, Word from Washington*	Provides professional service program assistance in regard to research and professional training, infant care centers, vocational programs, governmental activities, and public information/education.
Vocational Evaluation and Work Adjustment Association 1522 K St., N.W. Washington, D.C.	All	*VEWAA Bulletin,* newsletter	Promotes standards for vocational evaluators and work adjustors, disseminates and publishes information, promotes training efforts of field personnel.

Resources at the local level will vary according to the size, location, and particular circumstances of each individual city. The Comprehensive Employment and Training Act (CETA) has helped local communities develop career education programs for disadvantaged and certain handicapped youth in junior and senior high schools. This program requires CETA sponsors to maintain close relationships with both the school and the local business/labor/industry community. Figure 27 illustrates possible resources and services that can be used at the local level for career development.

As indicated in chapter 10, *industry, labor,* and *business* resources can provide students with community work experiences and observations; help

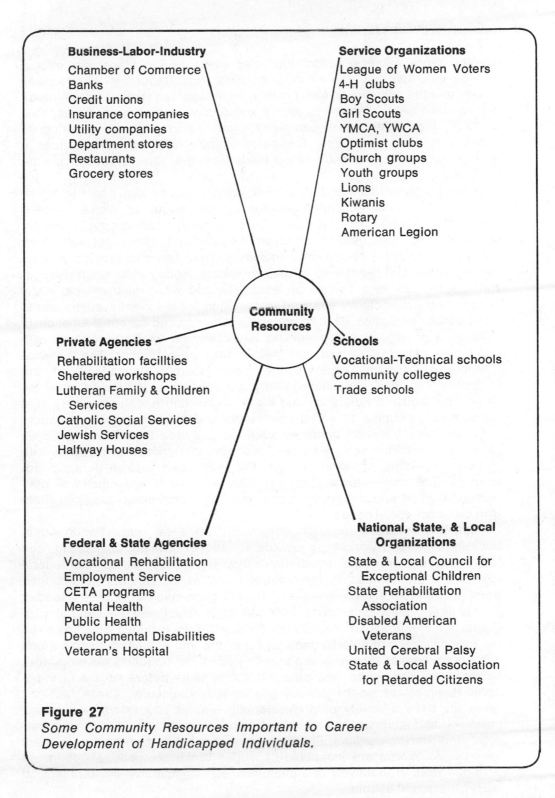

Business-Labor-Industry

Chamber of Commerce
Banks
Credit unions
Insurance companies
Utility companies
Department stores
Restaurants
Grocery stores

Service Organizations

League of Women Voters
4-H clubs
Boy Scouts
Girl Scouts
YMCA, YWCA
Optimist clubs
Church groups
Youth groups
Lions
Kiwanis
Rotary
American Legion

Community Resources

Private Agencies

Rehabilitation facillties
Sheltered workshops
Lutheran Family & Children
   Services
Catholic Social Services
Jewish Services
Halfway Houses

Schools

Vocational-Technical schools
Community colleges
Trade schools

Federal & State Agencies

Vocational Rehabilitation
Employment Service
CETA programs
Mental Health
Public Health
Developmental Disabilities
Veteran's Hospital

National, State, & Local Organizations

State & Local Council for
   Exceptional Children
State Rehabilitation
   Association
Disabled American
   Veterans
United Cerebral Palsy
State & Local Association
   for Retarded Citizens

Figure 27
*Some Community Resources Important to Career
Development of Handicapped Individuals.*

develop more career-oriented curricula; assist in job placement efforts, provide volunteers for the school; and elicit support for career education throughout the community. Many community resources such as banks, credit unions, insurance companies, utility companies, department stores, restaurants, and grocery stores can give students information and experiences in the daily living skills area. These sources are also a powerful influence for obtaining additional and needed funds from the government and private sectors.

Service organizations and other *civic groups* can be significant in developing viable career education programs. The League of Women Voters, 4-H, YMCA, YWCA, Optimist Club, church groups, youth groups, Lions International, Kiwanis, Rotary, American Legion, and others generally look for projects that will benefit the community. They can also provide schools and agencies with the talents of their members. *Rotary International Magazine* (1976) features a special on education and work relationships. Many of their units are actively engaged in assisting local school systems implement career education. The American Legion adopted career education in 1976 as a priority, and its members have become vitally concerned with the future of today's youth and their career development. The National Council of Churches explored the topic "Career Education and the Churches" in 1975 and subsequently established a National Center on Christian Studies in Education and Work. In the future, churches may hold considerable promise as a vital community resource for career education.

Private social service agencies such as Lutheran Family and Children Services, Catholic Family Services, and Jewish Services are available in some communities to assist families and individuals resolve personal adjustment problems, interpersonal conflicts, and social and emotional difficulties. Trained social workers, using individual and group methods, help with personal-social needs.

Vocational-technical schools, community colleges, rehabilitation facilities, and *sheltered workshops* provide vocational training, counseling, and job placement services. Vocational schools, in response to the federal legislation, are increasing their capacity to assist various handicapped persons in developing competitive skills, although much work is still needed in this area. Many community colleges have developed meaningful programs for handicapped individuals. Rehabilitation facilities and sheltered workshops are particularly important for the more limited handicapped person who needs intensive and slower paced instruction to develop work habits, vocational skills, and personal-social skills before receiving vocational-technical or on-the-job training in the community. These facilities generally have a variety of professionally trained counselors, evaluators, teachers, and supervisors who provide work opportunities as both a treatment and training medium. Sheltered workshops may provide employment for individuals who are incapable of working in a competitive setting but who can work productively in a sheltered, semicompetitive environment, at least for a period of time.

Halfway residential houses are available in some communities for individuals who need a certain degree of supervision while receiving vocational training and other career development services elsewhere. Some provide daily living and personal-social instruction, particularly if they are affiliated with a rehabilitation or sheltered workshop. A small staff may be available for individual and group counseling.

In general, the list of community resources for career development is extensive. The list in Figure 27 is not all inclusive but represents the many resources that are available to help handicapped persons.

INSTRUCTIONAL RESOURCES

An identification and discussion of instructional resources can never be complete. Information and materials are being created at such a rapid pace it produces frustration for both researchers and practitioners. A few years ago the dominate question was: "Is there anything available?" This question has been refined to: "What should I use from the number of items that are available?" We will not be able to supply the answer to the second question because the use of materials, devices, and assessment tools is related to intended goals and the characteristics of the individual learner. However, we do hope to provide a broad base of understanding about sources of information. This is an important consideration because many products and publications developed for nonhandicapped individuals can also be used in teaching handicapped learners.

Instructional resources can be divided into four categories: Information systems; books; career education projects that have resulted in publications; and films, audiotapes, learning devices, and other instructional materials available from commercial publishers. Journals on and publishers of commercial career education materials are listed in Appendixes A and B. Recommended reading materials appear in Appendix C. We have not attempted to review or list any films, audiotapes, learning devices, and the like as we feel you can readily secure this information elsewhere.

In this period of the information explosion, your first step of inquiry should be with a system that can bring you to the current status of information relative to a given topic. The usual term given this condition is *the state of the art.* This is the primary goal of an information system (i.e., to enable the user to determine the state of the art at a given moment). An information system usually provides the following functions:

- Collects materials such as reports, papers, documents, guides, bibliographies, books, instructional devices, and dissertations;
- abstracts and indexes references and descriptions of the collected items and/or references;

- provides access to abstracts through printed copies or visual display; and
- distributes information such as bibliographies, position statements, and copies of items in hard cover or microfilm.

Table 13

Information Systems for Materials on
Career Development for Handicapped Individuals

organization	location
Educational Resources Information Centers (ERIC)	
• ERIC Clearinghouse on Adult, Career, and Vocational Education	Ohio State University
• ERIC Clearinghouse on Handicapped & Gifted Children	Council for Exceptional Children
National Center for Career Education (NCCE)	Missoula, Montana
National Center for Law and the Handicapped (NCLH)	South Bend, Indiana
National Information Center for Special Education Materials (NICSEM)	University of Southern California
National Network for Curriculum Coordination in Vocational-Technical Education	
• Northeast Curriculum Coordination Center	Trenton, N.J.
• Southeast Curriculum Coordination Center	Starkville, Miss.
• East Central Curriculum Coordination Center	Springfield, Ill.
• Midwest Curriculum Coordination Center	Stillwater, Okla.
• Northwestern Curriculum Coordination Center	Olympia, Wash.
• Western Curriculum Coordination Center	Honolulu, Hawaii
National Resource Center for Materials on Work Evaluation and Work Adjustment (Materials Development Center)	University of Wisconsin-Stout
NIU Information Program in Career Education	Northern Ill. Univ.
Parents' Campaign for Handicapped Children and Youth	Washington, D.C.
Regional Resource Centers/Specialized Offices (RRC/SO)	Various locations
The Center for Vocational Education	Ohio State University
The Council for Exceptional Children Information Center (CEC)	Reston, Va.
Wisconsin Vocational Studies Center	University of Wisconsin-Madison

The initial steps for the potential user are to identify the system that collects appropriate information or materials, contact the system in order to gain access to the collection, and present the request according to the system's specific instructions.

Information systems that we believe can best provide materials and references related to aspects of career development are listed in Table 13 and are described in the remainder of this chapter. Each of these systems defines its own mission and procedures, but one must not forget that they exist for the purpose of providing information. Sometimes just a simple letter of inquiry will be answered with a packet of material.

You are encouraged to secure the following publications that contain information on resources for career development: *Barriers & Bridges,* California State Department of Procurement, Publications Section, P.O. Box 1015, North Highlands, California 95660 (Phillips, 1976); *Directory of Organizations Interested in the Handicapped,* Committee for the Handicapped/People to People Program, La Salle Building, Connecticut Avenue & L Street, Washington, D.C. 20036; *Ready Reference Guide: Resources for Disabled People,* Rehabilitation Services Administration, HEW, Washington, D.C. 20201; and the *Occupational Outlook Quarterly,* Summer 1977.

INFORMATIONAL SYSTEMS

Educational Resources Information Centers (ERIC)

ERIC is a national computerized network of centers that acquire significant educational literature, select the highest quality and most relevant materials, process (i.e., catalog, index, and abstract) the items for input to a data base, and disseminate information upon request. Their services include functions such as abstracts, computer searches, document reproduction, indexes, and production of microfiche (a small printed negative that must be read with a viewer). The educational literature may include things such as articles, bibliographies, books, conference proceedings, curriculum materials, guides, and reports.

The educational information is disseminated through two publications: *Resources in Education (RIE),* and *Current Index to Journals in Education (CIJE). RIE* is a monthly journal which includes abstracts of documents, research, and programs, with an index to the abstracts. *CIJE* is a monthly publication which includes annotations and indexing of articles from over 750 professional education journals.

You should also be aware of another publication: *Thesaurus of ERIC Descriptors,* which contains the ERIC subject headings used to index and retrieve documents and articles.

Two ERIC Clearinghouses sponsored by the National Institute of Education (NIE) will be of particular interest if you are searching for information on career development for handicapped individuals.

ERIC Clearinghouse on Adult, Career, and Vocational Education. The focus of this clearinghouse is career education, formal and informal at all levels, encompassing attitudes, self-knowledge, decision-making skills, general and occupational knowledge, and specific vocational and occupational skills; adult and continuing education, formal and informal, relating to occupational, family, leisure, citizen, organizational, and retirement roles; vocational and technical education, including new subprofessional fields, industrial arts, and vocational rehabilitation for the handicapped. The center has several bibliographies and information analysis papers on career development. Address: The Center for Vocational Education, The Ohio State University, 1960 Kenny Road, Columbus, Ohio 43210.

ERIC Clearinghouse on Handicapped and Gifted Children. The focus of this clearinghouse is aurally handicapped, visually handicapped, mentally handicapped, physically handicapped, emotionally disturbed, speech handicapped, learning disabilities, and the gifted; behavioral, psychomotor, and communication disorders, administration of special education services; preparation and continuing education of professional and paraprofessional personnel; preschool learning and development of the exceptional; and general studies on creativity. Address: The Council for Exceptional Children, 1920 Association Drive, Reston, Virginia 22091.

The National Center for Career Education (NCCE)

NCCE is a private, nonprofit corporation that assists local institutions, state agencies, and other interested organizations in interpreting career education needs, developing career education curricula, and designing plans for implementation. Located at the University of Montana, NCCE gathers information about and materials from these projects, provides a practical system for practitioners to assess these materials, based on local needs, and assists in implementing efforts through training and technical assistance. Information can be obtained by writing NCCE, P.O. Box 7815, Missoula, Montana 59807.

The National Center for Law and the Handicapped (NCLH)

The center was established in 1972 under joint funding by the Bureau of Education for the Handicapped and the Division of Developmental Disabilities, Office of Human Development. It was established to insure equal protection for all handicapped citizens and provides:

- Legal assistance through direct intervention in selected cases or indirectly through consultation with attorneys, organizations, or individuals involved in the litigation;
- legal and social science research activities; and
- programs and processes of public education and professional awareness.

The center's publication, *Amicus,* advances the purposes of NCLH by informing readers about the effects of legislation, decisions in litigation, research on legal provisions, and the activities of the staff in workshops and conferences. Address: 1235 N. Eddy St., South Bend, Indiana 46617.

National Information Center for Special Education Materials (NICSEM)

The center features a computer-based on-line interactive retrieval system that stores information pertaining to instructional materials and assessment devices which can be used by teachers, parents, and other educators. The on-line interactive element enables the individual to search the data banks through the use of appropriate terms and questions. Access to the system is through terminals, which are located in every region of the country. State departments of special education and regional resource center personnel are able to identify the access terminal nearest the teacher or parent who inquires for more information.

The official list of terms used in the search of approximately 25,000 abstracts of materials stored in NICSEM is available in the publication *Instructional Materials Thesaurus for Special Education.* These terms include references to print and nonprint materials. Examples of the latter would be: kits, films, video cassettes, audio cassettes, filmstrips, games, toys, and transparencies.

NICSEM contains information on: child use instructional materials, teacher training materials, measurement and evaluation, and assessment and instructional materials that can be used by parents. This is in keeping with the requirements for designing and implementing individualized education programs for every handicapped student as specified in the regulations for PL 94–142.

NICSEM has also produced several bibliographies of learning resources relative to age levels, skills, and areas of exceptionality. Although these bibliographies may be available through state or local information and materials centers, they will also be entered into the ERIC system. Address: University of Southern California, University Park, Los Angeles, California 90007.

National Network for Curriculum Coordination in Vocational-Technical Education

This network comprises six regional centers (listed in Table 13) with the responsibility of identifying information and materials relative to vocational-technical education. A curriculum search can be initiated by an individual teacher or researcher and usually proceeds through the local education agency to a state liaison representative who contributes to the regional and national network in the following ways:

- *Communication.* The state liaison representative (SLR) provides information to the national network on new materials, developmental activities, and needs for the state. At the same time, the SLR distributes materials and information to the local education agencies within the state. Thus, the SLR stands as a key link between the needs and changes within a state and the capabilities of a national network to assist and profit from local efforts.
- *Administration.* The SLR assists the national network and local education agencies in identifying priorities for material and curriculum development. The decisions on priorities are based on data collected within the state relative to needs. This requires various strategies of assessment and evaluation, which is another crucial responsibility of the SLR.

Once again, educators are encouraged to contact the state liaison representatives for the network as most of the exchange of information will be between the state and local levels.

National Resource Center for Materials on Work Evaluation and Work Adjustment (Materials Development Center)

The center is the national resource for the collection, development, and dissemination of literature, materials, and procedures on work evaluation and adjustment. It mainly provides services to those personnel who work with handicapped individuals in rehabilitation facilities and sheltered workshops. Among its many publications are updated annotated bibliographies, special monographs, and media packages on work evaluation and adjustment. Information can be obtained by writing: Materials Development Center, Institute for Vocational Rehabilitation, University of Wisconsin-Stout, Menomonie, Wisconsin 54751.

NIU Information Program in Career Education

The first ERIC Clearinghouse in Career Education was established at Northern Illinois University and then moved to the Ohio State University.

Many of the directories, information analysis reports, and informal bibliographies originally developed by the first ERIC staff have been continued and made available to interested readers. A list of these publications is available upon writing to: 201 Gabel Hall, Northern Illinois University, DeKalb, Illinois 60115.

Parents' Campaign for Handicapped Children and Youth

The publication *Common Sense from Closer Look* is the major voice of the Parents' Campaign, which is funded through a grant from the Bureau of Education for the Handicapped. Its purpose is to provide information service to parents of handicapped individuals and other interested professionals and citizens. Other information packets include such publications as:

* *Practical Advice to Parents*
* *Know Your Rights*
* *Disabled Adults: How to Get Help*
* *Preparing for the World of Work*
* *Workshop Planning Guide: How to Set up a Conference in Your Community on Jobs and Job Training for Handicapped Youth*

Information can be obtained by writing: Box 1492, Washington, D.C. 20013.

Regional Resource Centers/Specialized Offices (RRC/SO)

The beginnings of these 16 centers and two specialized offices can be traced to the HEW's funding in 1964 of a network of regional and local special education materials centers. These centers were to identify and even develop materials that could be used in the education of handicapped individuals. The number, role, and function of these centers has changed since the early beginnings. For example, in 1974, the combined Learning Resource Center network consisted of 13 Regional Resource Centers and a Coordinating Office, 13 Area Learning Resource Centers, and five national units. With the passage of PL 94–142, the RRC/SO was modified and charged with the responsibility of assisting states in the development of the individualized education program.

Center personnel can provide technical assistance, demonstration, consultation, and other forms of information distribution related to identification, diagnosis, and prescription of educational programs. These functions will rely heavily upon the methods and materials that have been identified by the system of centers and are available for students of a given age and ability. These services in support of the state efforts also work to the advantage of local education agencies in their efforts to provide effective services to handicapped students. The RRC/SO are listed in Appendix D.

The Center for Vocational Education

The center's mission is to increase the ability of diverse agencies, institutions, and organizations to solve educational problems relating to individual career planning and preparation. Some of its major divisions include: research and development programs, special projects, personnel development, evaluation, and information and field services. The latter division houses the ERIC Clearinghouse on Career Education and publishes *Abstracts of Instructional and Research Materials in Vocational and Technical Education (AIM/ARM)*. This publication reports relevant articles and materials in abstract and index form from a wide range of topics in vocational and technical education.

The center offers an extensive collection of publications, including such specific topic areas as career education, career guidance, and disadvantaged and handicapped. Information can be obtained by writing: The Ohio State University, 1960 Kenny Road, Columbus, Ohio 43210.

The Council for Exceptional Children Information Center (CEC)

As the major professional organization in the education of exceptional individuals, CEC publishes materials in both print and nonprint formats that facilitate continued improvement in services. A list of the products include:

- *Exceptional Child Education Resources (ECER)*. This resource contains documents and articles listed in the basic ERIC publications *Resources in Education* and *Current Index to Journals in Education*. In addition, ECER contains information about commercially published books, films, tapes, and dissertations;
- topical bibliographies based on the references in ECER;
- professional books and tape cassettes on instructional methods and materials, administrative procedures and programs, training of personnel, legislation and legal procedures, and projected changes in education and training of handicapped and gifted individuals;
- the several journals and newsletters related to the 12 divisions within CEC. The two prominent journals are *Exceptional Children* and *Teaching Exceptional Children;* and
- custom computer search of the ERIC data bank upon individual requests.

The Council has expanded its offerings to professionals and the general public through a Center for Information, Technical Assistance, and Training on the Exceptional Person. The center offers the following services:

- *Information.* These services range from publications to customized searches and products (refer to *The Council for Exceptional Children Information Center*).
- *Technical Assistance.* These services include short- and long-term consultation on specific problems and projects.
- *Training.* These services may include institutes, workshops, self-instructional packages, and presentations by qualified speakers.

Information can be obtained by writing The Council for Exceptional Children, 1920 Association Drive, Reston, Virginia 22091.

Wisconsin Vocational Studies Center

The center utilizes the special resources of the University of Wisconsin to solve problems in the delivery of vocational, technical, and career education, to citizens of all ages in communities of the state and nation. In recent years, the center has conducted training workshops and published reference and instructional materials related to the modification of regular vocational programs to meet the needs and abilities of handicapped individuals. Two outstanding products of the center have been a 16mm color film, *Just the Beginning,* and a series of booklets, *It's About Time (Insert category of disability) Came Out in the Open.* Both products focus on the abilities of handicapped individuals and the kinds of academic and support services that are needed for successful integration with regular students. Information can be obtained by writing: University of Wisconsin-Madison, 321 Education Bldg., Box 49, Madison, Wisconsin 53706.

CONCLUSION

Community interest and involvement in career education is not new. As Hoyt (1976b) indicates, "it seems more legitimate to ask whether the education system will work with the broader community in career education than to ask whether the community is willing to work with the formal education system" (p. 25). Those who have professed that there are neither the resources nor the community support are mistaken. The resources are there if the time and attention is given to developing the necessary contacts, relationships, and methodologies for using them appropriately.

In communities with limited resources, state and national organizations may become more significant. Hopefully, the preceding discussion has made it clear that these organizations are available to assist if they are contacted for relevant purposes. The amount of free technical assistance, materials, and referrals to other helpful sources by these associations and organizations is often overwhelming. The number of different organizations serving as advocates for one or more handicapped types is substantial, and they are extremely receptive to assisting community personnel.

Career education requires school personnel to collaborate with those outside of their internal structure. It requires certain individuals to assume a coordinating role if all the necessary resources are to be appropriately orchestrated. While we are the first to admit that this is no easy task, it is indeed a necessary one if we are to offer the comprehensive and relevant curriculum that handicapped learners so richly deserve.

We are encouraged by the vast number of articles, projects, books, reports, guides, instructional materials that are presently available. We are concerned, however, how they are little known and used by those who work with handicapped persons daily. Those of you who become familiar with the resources presented in this chapter and the Appendixes will hopefully identify and secure useful information and tools for your work.

part five
Conclusion

Part five consists of one concluding chapter that briefly summarizes our conceptualization of career education and what constitutes a comprehensive approach, some of the major issues presently existing and needing to be resolved so that career education can move forward, and directions we believe the field will take as we move into the 1980s. We identify some research that is in progress and that is illustrative of the rapid movement into solving some of the complex problems facing us and delimiting career education's progress.

In chapter 12 we call for more leadership and support from the major federal agencies whose goal is to meet the needs of our handicapped citizens. While these agencies have made substantial contributions in furthering career development opportunities for handicapped persons, they have not done nearly enough, although they have such an authority. We are hopeful these agencies will be even more responsive in the near future, and there are indications that they will. Much remains to be done if the career education needs of persons with handicaps in this society are to be served appropriately. If people are willing to change and work together, we will meet these needs.

This book has attempted to present a total approach to conceptualizing, developing, and conducting career education for persons with handicaps. The central focus has been 22 career development competencies, which we firmly believe must be learned by these individuals to be successful in community living and working experiences. The available evidence on the adjustment of handicapped persons clearly reveals that the majority are presently either unemployed or considerably underemployed, settling for jobs below their levels of potential.

A central theme of this book has been our broad conceptualization of the term *career*. We define one's career as the constellation of the various, major roles that individuals are expected to assume in their lifetime, including an occupation. Thus, career education consists of helping individuals learn the skills needed for productive activity in home, occupational, community, and avocational settings. While this concept may be difficult for some people to understand and accept, it distinguishes career education from vocational education. An adequate way to distinguish the two terms is by describing "career education as preparing people for living" and "vocational education as preparing people for an occupation."

This broad concept of career education, endorsed by many professional leaders, is not intended to discourage educators and others so that they believe it is impossible to provide or that it is something that has been done all along. It is not impossible and we have not been doing it.

Throughout the book we have attempted to identify and explain what we believe constitute the components of a comprehensive and appropriate career education approach for handicapped and other persons. This includes the following:

1. Competency based instruction, focusing on the daily living, personal-social, and occupational skills needed for successful community living and working;
2. involvement of all possible school personnel in providing services in the least restrictive environment and designing subject matter to include career implications;
3. considerable parent/family involvement for curriculum and instruction building, competency teaching, and community resource development;
4. extensive use of community agencies and professional and civic organizations having personnel and resources for career education;
5. use of a wide array of business and industrial resources both in and out of the school setting;
6. systematically planned and sequenced career awareness, exploration, preparation, and placement/follow-up opportunities, which are available throughout the individual's lifetime;
7. cooperative curriculum and instructional planning by a variety of educators, students, parents, agency personnel, and members of business and industry;
8. extensive inservice training of school, community, and family members for attitude, knowledge, and skills development so that cooperative efforts can be implemented and maintained;
9. use of more instructional resources and materials that are now available for career education; and
10. frequent and appropriate student evaluation to determine competency achievement and to plan instructional procedures.

The 22 competencies advocated in this book include daily living and personal-social, as well as occupational skills for career development. Close inspection of these competencies will reveal their relation to and development of occupational interests and skills. This should have been apparent in our discussion of the competencies in chapters 4–6.

SOME MAJOR ISSUES

There are several issues that need to be resolved if career education is to be effectively implemented and conducted in various schools, agencies, and institutions throughout this country. Brolin and D'Alonzo (1979) identify six important issues:

1. *Should career education be primarily job centered or life centered?* Presently, there seems to be three views about career education: It is vocational education; it is an expansion of vocational education; or it is a complete educational approach focusing on the various roles, settings, and events in which productive work activity occurs for individuals. In our opinion, the latter view is most appropriate. For many handicapped individuals, their career may consist exclusively of avocational, family, and civic work activities if they have limited vocational abilities and opportunities. They are still able to lead a satisfying, meaningful, and productive life by functioning in this manner.

2. *Should career education be a separate program or permeate throughout the educational process?* Many professional workers believe that career education is something taught in a course one or two hours each day. The other position advocates career education concepts and materials to be infused throughout curriculum and that all school personnel modify their courses to incorporate them in instruction. It is probably much easier to develop a separate course rather than adopt the infusion approach. In our opinion, however, career education for handicapped students is almost everyone's responsibility, and it must be infused in school, home, and community settings. Although it is not the only education the students receive, it should be a very significant and pervasive part of what is taught.

3. *Who has the responsibility for handicapped students?* Although many special educators may find it difficult to abrogate their responsibilities to these students, the career education approach and the Individualized Education Program requirements clearly specify shared responsibility. The IEP requires other school personnel and the student's parents to collaborate and monitor the program. With other school personnel becoming so involved, special educators may now be able to concentrate on other important areas (e.g., parents, community, severely handicapped, career assessment). In our opinion, special educators should not readily abandon their responsibilities to these students. Someone knowledgeable about handicapping conditions and the individual's needs must be substantially available to monitor progress and see that these needs are met.

4. *Does career education aid or hinder mainstreaming efforts?* Although there is no definitive research in this area, it would seem that career education enhances the assimilation and achievement of handicapped students since they generally learn best when instruction is related to the real world and hands-on experiences. In our opinion, career education is the vehicle by which successful mainstreaming can take place.

5. *What should be done with present courses, materials, and teaching approaches?* Career education requires school personnel to take a hard look at what they are doing and why so that courses can be modified, materials added or eliminated, and new teaching methods used. It does not call for a wholesale abandonment of present practices. Rather, it adds greater relevance to the curriculum and requires a more democratic environment. In our opinion, school districts must develop more systematic and comprehensive career education plans so that courses, materials, and instruction are presented in an effective scope and sequence.

6. *How can personnel be trained?* Will universities and colleges and other training sources be able and willing to adequately prepare special educators, general educators, counselors, administrators, and others who need career education and handicapped instruction? What constitutes an effective delivery system, and how and who will do the training? These are major concerns of those in the field. When these concerns are coupled with declining school enrollments, teacher layoffs, budget crunches, and the like, we encounter major obstacles in implementing effective career education. In our opinion, the key to career education's success is staff development training. Local school districts must provide their own inservice trainers to teach their faculty. State and local administrators must convince universities to prepare their graduates for this responsibility.

The most critical issue is whether or not career education results in a significantly better outcome for handicapped students than what they presently receive. A common sense positive expectation is the best we can give to this concern at the present time. Unfortunately, to the best of our knowledge, research in this area is scarce. If evidence becomes available, then administrators, educators, parents, politicians, and many others will have to respond and begin working together to meet these students' career development needs.

FUTURE DIRECTIONS

Major societal changes do not occur overnight. Support from administrative decision makers, time to redirect curricula, attitude changes, cooperative efforts, and a recognition of the direction of change are but a few of the many needs existing in most communities. We have just begun to make significant strides in providing handicapped individuals with a free and appropriate education. But, when we compare the state of the art to that of a few years ago, the progress is quite remarkable. However, if career education is to become a reality for handicapped learners allowing them to reach their optimal level of career development, dramatic changes in our service delivery system will be required.

The following are offered as directions we believe will occur in the field and are of an absolute necessity if career education is to move forward in the 1980s.

1. Applied Research. Career education must establish its efficacy but presently there is a paucity of available empirical research. Critical research needs were the topic of a national conference sponsored by the Bureau of Education for the Handicapped at the Educational Testing Service in Princeton, New Jersey, from January 17–19, 1975. Eighty-six special and vocational educators, rehabilitation workers, and researchers identified the following as top priority research topics:

- Attitudes that impede the handicapped person's opportunities for career development and employment (families, employers, labor unions, peers, educators, community, and the handicapped persons themselves);
- critical incidents or factors that lead to maintenance, improvement, or loss of jobs;
- decision making, problem solving, and development of coping skills;
- development of better articulation among all agents involved in services for the handicapped;
- how handicapping conditions limit career potentials;
- how teachers can be motivated to implement career education;
- how parents can be trained to work effectively with their child;
- post-placement counseling effectiveness;
- personnel development needs;
- retention techniques for job-seeking, readiness, maintenance, and mobility skills;
- effectiveness of such teaching technologies as television and audio-visual aids;
- teacher competencies needed to integrate leisure-education;
- effective counseling techniques;
- who should deliver counseling services; and
- how leisure time complements the career development process.

The conference participants viewed career education as a developmental process, beginning from the early identification of the handicap, through programs of preparation and intervention into retirement. They considered living and leisure skills as important adjuncts to preparation for work. A state of the art paper by Brolin and Kolstone (in press) reveals only minimal research activity occurring in these areas.

2. Cooperative Efforts. We should see more cooperative efforts between various agencies, organizations, business and industry, and the parents of handicapped learners. Certainly, directives from the U.S. Office of Education and the Rehabilitation Services Administration relative to cooperative planning between education and rehabilitation agencies should provide a stimulus. Also, another USOE statement issued in 1978 promulgating "an appropriate comprehensive vocational education for all handicapped persons" should be a boon for securing more and better services from vocational educators. If the various agencies begin working together in greater harmony and respect for each others' contributions, services to handicapped persons will meet their career development needs. Territorial rights, professional jealousies and rivalries, theoretical differences, and many other long-standing problems must be eliminated.

3. Expanded Agency Services. Community colleges, vocational-technical schools, rehabilitation agencies, and workshops are becoming more available for handicapped individuals. A continuum of services should become a greater reality for these individuals as agencies start working more closely with secondary programs in providing transitional services and lifelong learning opportunities for those leaving and who have left the school setting. There appears to be a much greater recognition of the importance of independent living skills training and other lifelong learning needs in basic academic, personal-social, and occupational skill areas.

4. Community Learning Experiences. There should be greater recognition of the contribution of the learning laboratory that is available in the local community. The Experience-Based Career Education (EBCE) Model is an excellent example of the use of the community for relating career development needs to the classroom. As educators become familiar with business and industry and other resources, community personnel are more likely to become involved with the school.

5. Accountability. At the present time, service providers experience various degrees of accountability for their services and its failures. The handicapped person is often blamed for any unsuccessful efforts when the fault may be with the service provider. Also, employers will be more closely monitored to determine their response to Sections 503 and 504 of the Rehabilitation Act of 1973 and the regulations passed in 1977. The Office for Civil Rights (OCR) should become a vital force for this purpose. In the near future we should see handicapped people and their advocates demanding the rights and privileges that have too long been denied. Thus, career education efforts will need to provide an accountability component to demonstrate its effectiveness with handicapped learners.

6. Individualized Education Programs. At the present time, IEPs are not being written with comprehensive career development goals and objectives in mind. This should change, however, as there is considerable concern from career education proponents, indicating that much attention will be directed to this important area in the future.

7. Parent Involvement. Educators will actively include parents in decision-making and curriculum procedures, providing information programs (readings, reports, newsletters), and will train them to work intensively with the children at home and in concert with school objectives. Educators will need to develop appropriate materials for parents to use with their children.

8. Personnel Preparation. Effective inservice and preservice models will be developed for training school, family, and community personnel for career education. Every educator should be required to complete a specified inservice and/or preservice program in career education for handicapped individuals. School districts will have to assume a greater responsibility for training their personnel.

9. Severely Handicapped. There should be a considerable increase in career education services as educational technology becomes more precise and effective with these individuals. The American Association for the Education of the Severely and Profoundly Handicapped, formed in the mid-1970s, has increased attention to this area. The technology is being developed, and a substantial number of researchers and practitioners are giving their full attention to career development practices.

10. Professional Constituency. A large constituency of advocates and promoters of the career education movement for handicapped individuals is being built (e.g., The Division on Career Development of the Council for Exceptional Children (CEC), and the National Association of Vocational Education Special Needs Personnel (NAVESNP) of the American Vocational Association). These groups represent special and vocational educators who are particularly devoted to supporting legislative priorities and funding for meeting the career development needs of handicapped persons. By working together and with other professional organizations and groups, these two advocates can maintain a focus on career education as a national priority.

11. Career Guidance and Assessment. School and rehabilitation counselors must become involved in career counseling and assessment services. The career assessment systems mentioned earlier need to be validated to prove their usefulness. If that can be done, they should provide an excellent vehicle for identifying career interests and aptitudes so appropriate instructional procedures can be designed. Schools are beginning to employ career educators and vocational evaluators for the handicapped.

12. Placement and Follow Up. Employment opportunities should increase because of legislation, business and industry involvement, public awareness, and the efforts of various advocacy groups. The key to opening up employment opportunities, however, is the school's ability to implement and conduct effective career education services for these individuals.

Numerous career education materials have been marketed and will continue to be developed. More refinement and field testing is needed to establish those materials that are particularly effective. New scientific inventions are making it possible for handicapped individuals to be mobile and communicate effectively with their environment. Reading machines and low vision aids for the blind and visually impaired, electronic aids to help the physically handicapped manipulate and function within their environment, teletypewriters, hearing aid adapters for the deaf and hearing impaired, and other dramatic breakthroughs are helping handicapped individuals become independent, productive members of society.

Leadership from the U.S. Office of Education, particularly the Bureau of Education for the Handicapped (BEH), Bureau of Occupational and Adult Education (BOAE), and the Office of Career Education is needed to stimulate model programs, to expand training opportunities, to disseminate successful techniques, and to encourage universities and school districts to make career education their top priority. There are indications that this will be done in the future. Research is presently being supported by these agencies, holding several possibilities for the field, such as:

- Development of a "Career Accessibility Model" to increase job options for the mildly mentally retarded in the Marketing and Distribution Cluster and to enable students to enter at any point and receive appropriate career information, instruction, and/or placement;

- examination of the validity of the cognitive content of career education, development of a comprehensive inventory of cognitive career education skills with curricular implications, and development of a formative assessment instrument in career education;

- development of a comprehensive career education model, assessment tools, and validation and dissemination procedures to meet the needs of orthopedically handicapped children, pre-K–12;

- adaptation of materials and processes from a university Curricular Career Information Service to demonstrate that successful methods of career education and career guidance for sighted students can be made available and successfully used by visually disabled students; and

• demonstration of independent living training for people with multiple development disabilities to break down barriers of acceptance in order to become a contributing, growing, and capable person.

There are many other federal and state funded research projects that hold promise for the future career education of handicapped persons (Brolin & Kolstoe, in press). Some particularly relevant projects are:

• "Teaching Interpersonal and Self-Management Skills to Mildly Handicapped Adolescents as Part of a Career Education Curriculum."
• "The Development, Field Testing, and Dissemination of a Leisure Education Curriculum for Severely Handicapped Children and Youth."
• "Development of Research Utilization Modules to Improve Education Services through Camping for the Physically Disabled."
• "Evaluation of Retarded Student Achievement in Career Education Programs."
• "What's the Difference in Career Education?"
• "Mainstream Handicapped Students into the Executive High School Internship Program."

Further evidence of the generation of career education activities around the country was demonstrated by the large number of proposals submitted for presentations at the National Topical Conference on Career Education for Exceptional Individuals held in St. Louis, Missouri, in February 1979. Over two hundred and twenty-five proposals were submitted by local, state, and national agencies and organizations for consideration. The majority of proposals centered on the following topics: personal preparation, curriculum, secondary programming, career education models, and instructional techniques. Unfortunately, very few research proposals were submitted. But, this demonstration of activity in the area of career education certainly is heartening and reflective of the rapidly increasing momentum that career education is gathering throughout the country.

CONCLUSION

The vast majority of handicapped individuals in this country can become productive, contributing members of society. For some of these individuals, paid employment may not be their major role. But, whatever the individuals' career potentials, they should be maximized to the fullest. Employment need not be the sole criterion for successful outcomes of educational efforts with handicapped students if they can be productive and satisfied in such roles as family member and worker, citizen, and active participant in leisure and recreational pursuits.

Career education is the hope and promise for the handicapped citizens who reside in our society. It is a total educational concept that brings meaning to curriculum efforts by making individuals aware of themselves, their potentials, and their educational needs. It does not replace present educational practices but rather helps make all instructional material personally relevant by restructuring it around a career development theme.

There is much to do! We are on the threshold of substantial improvements in our educational delivery system. Each of us has an important role to play in the career education movement. Let us meet this critical challenge.

SELECTED PROFESSIONAL JOURNALS EMPHASIZING OR CONTAINING INFORMATION ON CAREER EDUCATION/DEVELOPMENT

Journals with an Emphasis on Career Development

Career Development for Exceptional
Individuals
Division on Career Development
The Council for Exceptional
Children
1920 Association Drive
Reston, Va. 22091
Two times yearly

Career Education Journal
Division of Educational Planning
Development and Evaluation
Department of Defense
Office of Dependents Schools
2461 Eisenhower Ave.
Alexandria, Va. 22331
Twice a year

Career Education News
Bobit Publishing Co.
65 E. Palatine Rd.
Suite 101
Wheeling, Ill. 60090
Twice monthly, September
through June, monthly during
July and August

Career Education Quarterly
National Association for Career
Education
Room 1502
School of Education
Boston University
765 Commonwealth Ave.
Boston, Mass. 02215
Quarterly

Career Education Workshop
Parker Publishing Co.
Rt. 59A at Brookhill Drive
West Nyack, N.Y. 10994
Monthly, September through
June

Illinois Career Education Journal
Illinois Office of Education
Department of Adult, Vocational
and Technical Education
Springfield, Ill. 62777
Quarterly

Journal of Career Education
College of Education
University of Missouri-Columbia
Columbia, Mo. 65201
Quarterly

News from NACE
The National Association for
Career Education
Office of Career Education
Glassboro State College
Glassboro, N.J. 08028

Newsletter
Division on Career Development
The Council for Exceptional
Children
1920 Association Drive
Reston, Va. 22091

Newsnotes
The National Association of Vo-
cational Education Special
Needs Personnel
American Vocational Association
1510 "H" Street, N.W.
Washington, D.C. 20005

Journals with Information Related to Career Development

Accent on Living
P.O. Box 726
Bloomington, Ill. 61701
Quarterly

Achievement
Disabled Action Group
8585 Sunset Dr.
Suite 65
Miami, Fla. 33143
Monthly

American Rehabilitation
United States Rehabilitation
Services Administration
Ordered through Superintendent
of Documents
Washington, D.C. 20402
Bimonthly

American Vocational Journal
American Vocational Association
1510 "H" St., N.W.
Washington, D.C. 20005
Monthly, September through
May

CANHC-GRAM
Association for Neurologically
Handicapped Children
Box 4088
Los Angeles, Ca. 90051
Monthly

Common Sense from Closer Look
The Parents' Campaign for
Handicapped Children and
Youth
Box 1492
Washington, D.C. 20013
Two times yearly

Disabled USA
The President's Committee on Em-
ployment of the Handicapped
Washington, D.C. 20210
Monthly

*Education and Training of the
Mentally Retarded*
Division on Mental Retardation
The Council for Exceptional
Children
1920 Association Drive
Reston, Va. 22091

Four times yearly in February,
April, October, and December

Exceptional Children
The Council for Exceptional
Children
1920 Association Drive
Reston, Va. 22091
Eight times a year, September
through May, excluding
December

Exceptional Parent (The)
Psy-Ed Corp.
20 Providence St.
Boston, Mass. 02116
Bimonthly

Journal of Rehabilitation
1522 K Street, N.W.
Washington, D.C. 20005
Bimonthly

Journal of Rehabilitation of the Deaf
Professional Rehabilitation Work-
ers with the Adult Deaf
814 Thayer Ave.
Silver Springs, Md. 20910
Quarterly

Journal of Special Education
Grune & Stratton
111 5th Ave.
New York, N.Y. 10003
Quarterly

Mental Retardation
American Association on Mental
Deficiency
5201 Connecticut Ave., N.W.
Washington, D.C. 20015
Bimonthly

New Outlook for the Blind (The)
15 West 16th St.
New York, N.Y. 10011
Monthly, September through
June

Paraplegia News
Veterans of America
935 Coastline Dr.
Seal Beach, Ca. 90740
Monthly

Personnel and Guidance Journal
American Personnel and Guidance
Association
1607 New Hampshire Ave., N.W.
Washington, D.C. 20009
Monthly, September through
June

Pointer (The)
4000 Albemarle St.
Suite 510
Washington, D.C. 20016
Three times yearly

Programs for the Handicapped
Office for Handicapped Individuals
Rm. 338D Hubert H. Humphrey
Building
200 Independence Ave., S.W.
Washington, D.C. 20201
Six times yearly

Rehabilitation Gazette
4502 Maryland Ave.
St. Louis, Mo. 63108
Annual

Rehabilitation Literature
National Easter Seal Society for
Crippled Children and Adults
2023 W. Ogden Ave.
Chicago, Ill. 60612
Monthly

Rehabilitation/World
Rehabilitation International USA
20 W. 40th St.
New York, N.Y. 10018
Quarterly

School Counselor
American Personnel and Guidance
Association
1607 New Hampshire Ave., N.W.
Washington, D.C. 20009
Five times a year

Teaching Exceptional Children
The Council for Exceptional
Children
1920 Association Drive
Reston. Va. 22091
Quarterly

Vocational Evaluation and Work
Adjustment Association Bulletin
1522 K Street, N.W.
Washington, D.C. 20005
Quarterly

Vocational Guidance Quarterly
National Vocational Guidance
Association

1607 New Hampshire Ave., N.W.
Washington, D.C. 20009
Quarterly

Volta Review
Alexander Graham Bell
Association for the Deaf
3417 Volta Place, N.W.
Washington, D.C. 20007
Seven times a year

PUBLISHERS OF COMMERCIAL MATERIALS ON CAREER EDUCATION/DEVELOPMENT (SELECTED LIST)

List of Publishers

AAHPER Publications-Sales
1201 16th St., N.W.
Washington, D.C. 20036

ACI Films
35 West 45th St.
New York, N.Y. 10036

American Guidance Service
Publisher's Building
Circle Pines, Minn. 55014

The Arden Press
8331 Alvarado Dr.
Huntington Beach, Ca. 92646

Argus Communications
7440 Natchez Ave.
Niles, Ill. 60648

Benefic Press
10300 West Roosevelt Rd.
Westchester, Ill. 60153

Burgess Publishing
426 S. 6th St.
Minneapolis, Minn. 55415

California Literacy
248 E. Main St.
Alhambra, Ca. 91801

Changing Times Education Service
1729 "A" St., N.W.
Washington, D.C. 20006

Channing L. Bete Co.
45 Federal St.
Greenfield, Mass. 01301

Charles E. Merrill Publishing
1300 Alum Creek Dr.
Columbus, O. 43216

Classroom World Publishing
c/o B and R Education
404 Admiral Blvd.
Kansas City, Mo. 64106

Developmental Learning Materials
7440 Natchez Ave.
Niles, Ill. 60648

Dick Blick Company
P. O. Box 1267
Galesburg, Ill. 61401

Edmark Associates
13249 Northup Way
Bellevue, Wash. 98005

Educational Achievement Corp.
P.O. Box 7310
Waco, Tex. 76710

Educational Activities
P.O. Box 392
Freeport, N.Y. 11520

Educational Projections Corp.
3070 Lake Terrace
Glenview, Ill. 60025

EPS Inc.
2304 East Johnson
Jonesboro, Ark. 72401

Fearon Publishers
6 Davis Dr.
Belmont, Ca. 94022

Finney Publishing
3350 Gorham Ave.
Minneapolis, Minn. 55426

Follett Publishing
1010 West Washington Blvd.
Chicago, Ill. 60607

Frank E. Richards Publishing
324 First St.
Liverpool, N.Y. 13088

Golden Press
850 Third Ave.
New York, N.Y. 10022

Guidance Associates
757 3rd Ave.
New York, N.Y. 10017

Guidance Associates of Delaware
1526 Gilpin Ave.
Wilmington, Del. 19806

Guidance Econ. Instruct. Materials Ctr.
Texas Tech University
P.O. Box 4067
Lubbock, Tex. 79409

H and H Enterprises
Box 3342
Lawrence, Kan. 66044

Hallmark Films & Recordings
The Educational Division
1511 E. North Ave.
Baltimore, Md. 21213

Home Econ. Instruct. Materials Ctr.
Texas Tech University
P.O. Box 4067
Lubbock, Tex. 79409

Houghton Mifflin
1900 S. Batavia Ave.
Geneva, Ill. 60134

Instructional Materials Laboratory
#8 Industrial Education Bldg.
University of Missouri-Columbia
Columbia, Mo. 65201

Instructo Corporation
Paoli, Pa. 19301

The Instructor Publications
P.O. Box 6099
Duluth, Minn. 55806

Interpretive Education Division of
    Illinois Envelope
400 Bryant St.
Kalamazoo, Mich. 49001

Intext
257 Park Ave. South
New York, N.Y. 10010

John Day
257 Park Ave.
New York, N.Y. 10010

Kimbo Educational
P.O. Box 246
Deal, N.J. 07723

King Features
236 E. 45th St.
New York, N.Y. 10017

Lawson
9488 Sara St.
Elk Grove, Ca. 95624

Learning Concepts
2501 N. Lamar
Austin, Tex. 78705

Mafex Associates
111 Barron Ave.
Johnstown, Pa. 15906

Math Shop
5 Bridge St.
Watertown, Mass. 02172

McGraw-Hill
Gregg-Community College Division
1221 Ave. of the Americas
New York, N.Y. 10020

McGraw-Hill
Webster Division
1221 Ave. of the Americas
New York, N.Y. 10020

McKnight and McKnight
Box 854
Bloomington, Ill. 61701

National Association for Retarded
   Citizens
Publications
P.O. Box 6109
Arlington, Tex. 76011

New Readers Press
Laubach Literacy
Box 121
Syracuse, N.Y. 13210

Pennant Educational Materials
4680 Alvarado Canyon Rd.
San Diego, Ca. 92120

PENNscript Production Center
5301 Jonestown Rd.
Harrisburg, Pa. 17112

J. C. Penney
Educational and Consumer Relations
   Department
1301 Ave. of the Americas
New York, N.Y. 10019

J. A. Preston Corp.
71 Fifth Ave.
New York, N.Y. 10003

Research Press Company of
   Champaign
P.O. Box 9075
Washington, D.C. 20003

Research Press
P.O. Box 3177, Department L
Champaign, Ill. 61820

Scholastic Book Services
904 Sylvan Ave.
Englewood Cliffs, N.J. 07632

Science Research Associates
259 East Erie St.
Chicago, Ill. 60611

Scott Foresman
2000 East Lake Ave.
Glenview, Ill. 60025

SEIMC
Cooperative Educational Services
Agency #5
Elmwood, Wis. 54740

Singer Education Division
3750 Monroe Ave.
Rochester, N.Y. 14603

Singer-Society for Visual Education
1345 Diversey Parkway
Chicago, Ill. 60614

The Soap & Detergent Association
475 Park Ave., South at 32nd St.
New York, N.Y. 10022

Stanwix House
3020 Chartiers Ave.
Pittsburgh, Pa. 15204

Steck-Vaughn
Box 2028
Vaughn Building
Austin, Tex. 78767

Superintendent of Documents
U.S. Government Printing Office
Washington, D.C. 20402

Teacher/Education Center
230 E. 9th St.
Cincinnati, Ohio 45202

Teaching Resources Corp.
100 Boylston St.
Boston, Mass. 02116

TQ Publishers
3912 Ramsey
Corpus Christi, Tex. 78415

Trend Enterprises
P.O. Box 3073
St. Paul, Minn. 55165

U.S. Depts. of Agriculture and Health,
    Education & Welfare
Washington, D.C. 20201

U.S. Dept. of Labor
Bureau of Labor Statistics
Washington, D.C. 20212

Warren's Educational Supplies
980 W. San Bernardino Rd.
Corina, Ca. 91722

Western Publishing
School and Library Department
850 Third Ave.
New York, N.Y. 10022

Wilson Educational Recordings
H. Wilson Corporation
555 West Taft Dr.
South Holland, Ill. 60473

Wisconsin Department of Public
    Instruction
Supervisor, WISC Project
126 Langdon St.
Madison, Wisc. 53702

Xerox Corp.
600 Madison Ave.
New York, N.Y. 10022

appendix C

SELECTED READINGS: BOOKS

Albright, L., & Clark, G. M. (Eds.). *Preparing vocational and special education personnel to work with special needs students: A teacher education resource guide.* Urbana, Ill.: Bureau of Educational Research, University of Illinois, 1977.

Altfest, M. (Ed.). *Vocational education for students with special needs.* Fort Collins, Colo.: Department of Vocational Education, Colorado State University, 1975.

Blum, L. P., & Kujoth, R. K. (Eds.). *Job placement of the emotionally disturbed.* Metuchen, N.J.: Scarecrow Press, 1972.

Brolin, D. E. *Vocational preparation of retarded citizens.* Columbus: Charles E. Merrill, 1976.

Browning, P. L. (Ed.). *Mental retardation: Rehabilitation and counseling.* Springfield, Ill.: Charles C Thomas, 1974.

Campbell, L. W., Todd, M., & O'Rourke, E. V. *Work-study handbook for educable mentally retarded minors enrolled in high school programs in California public schools.* Sacramento, Ca.: State Department of Education, 1971.

Carroll, A., Gurski, G., McIntyre, K., Male, M., & Stern, M. *The secondary resource specialist in California: Promising practices.* North Hollywood, Ca.: FOREWORKS, 7112 Teasdale, 1976.

Christensen, N. A., DuBois, P. A., & Austin, M. *Selected bibliography for vocational training and placement of the severely handicapped.* Palo Alto, Ca.: American Institutes for Research, 1975.

Compton, D. M., & Vinton, D. A. *Employment of handicapped people in leisure occupations.* Washington, D.C.: Committee on Recreation and Leisure, President's Committee on Employment of the Handicapped (n.d.).

Eau Claire Joint School District No. 5. *Career development-special education.* Eau Claire, Wis.: Eau Claire Joint School District No. 5, 1973.

Hull, M. E. (Ed.). *Programming for the handicapped: Accomplishments, commitments and forecasts.* College Station, Tex.: College of Education, Texas A & M University, 1977.

Kolstoe, O. P., & Frey, R. M. *A high school work-study program for mentally subnormal students.* Carbondale, Ill.: Southern Illinois University Press, 1965.

Lake, T. P. (Ed.). *Career education: Exemplary programs for the handicapped.* Reston, Va.: The Council for Exceptional Children, 1974.

Lambert, R. H., Tindall, L. W., Davis, K. E., & Ross-Thomson, B. *A bibliography of materials for handicapped & special education* (2nd ed.). Madison, Wis.: Center for Studies in Vocational and Technical Education, University of Wisconsin, 1975.

Lippmann, G. K., & Porter, G. C. *How to establish competency model programs for the delivery of vocational services to the severely multihandicapped.* Austin, Tex.: Lippmann/Porter, 109 E. 10th St., 1976.

Moore, J. J., & Engleman, V. S. (Eds.). *Administrator's manual. Programming for handicapped students at the secondary level: Responding to public laws.* Salt Lake City, Utah: The Southwest Regional Resource Center, University of Utah, 1977.

Phelps, L. A., & Lutz, R. J. *Career exploration and preparation for the special needs learner.* Boston: Allyn & Bacon, 1977.

Phillips, L. *Barriers and bridges: An overview of vocational services available for handicapped Californians.* Sacramento, Ca.: California Advisory Council on Vocational Education, 1976.

The President's Committee on Employment of the Handicapped. *Pathways to employment.* Washington, D.C.: The President's Committee on Employment of the Handicapped, 1977.

Towne, D. C., & Wallace, S. *Vocational instructional materials for students with special needs.* Portland, Or.: Northwest Regional Educational Laboratory, 1972.

U.S. Office of Education, Bureau of Education for the Handicapped. *Selected career education programs for the handicapped.* Washington, D.C.: Government Printing Office, 1973.

U.S. Office of Education, Bureau of Education for the Handicapped. *Improving occupational programs for the handicapped.* Washington, D.C.: Government Printing Office, 1975.

U.S. Office of Education, Bureau of Education for the Handicapped.

Proceedings of the conference on research needs related to career education for the handicapped. Washington, D.C.: Government Printing Office, 1975.

U.S. Office of Education, Office of Career Education. *Monographs in career education.* Washington, D.C.: Government Printing Office.
> *A primer for career education* (n.d.);
> *An introduction to career education: A policy paper of the U.S. Office of Education,* (1975);
> *Career education and vocational education: Similarities & contrasts* (n.d.);
> *Career education and the business-labor-industry community* (1976);
> *Career education and basic academic achievement* (1977);
> *Career education and the meanings of work* (1976);
> *Community resources for career education* (1976);
> *K-12 classroom teachers and career education: the beautiful people* (1976);
> *Perspectives on the problem of evaluation in career education* (n.d.);
> *Refining the career education concept* (1976); and
> *The school counselor and career education* (1976).

Urban, S. J., & Tsuji, T. (Eds.). *The special needs student in vocational education: Selected readings.* New York: MSS Information Corporation, 1974.

West Virginia State Department of Education. *Expanding options for handicapped persons receiving vocational education: Run into the future run.* The proceedings from West Virginia's Training Institute. Institute, W. Va.: West Virginia College of Graduate Studies, 1977.

appendix D

REGIONAL RESOURCE CENTERS

	states served:
Northwest Regional Resource Center Clinical Service Building, Third Floor 1590 Willamette St. University of Oregon Eugene, Or. 97401	Alaska, Hawaii, Samoa, Guam, Trust Territory, Washington, Idaho, Oregon, Montana, Wyoming,
California Regional Resource Center 600 South Commonwealth Ave. Suite 1304 University of Southern California Los Angeles, Ca. 90005	California
Southwest Regional Resource Center 2363 Foothill Dr., Suite G University of Utah Salt Lake City, Utah 84109	Nevada, Utah, Colorado, Arizona, New Mexico, B.I.A., Schools

	states served:
Midwest Regional Resource Center Drake University 1332–26th St. Des Moines, Iowa 50311	North Dakota, Oklahoma, South Dakota, Iowa, Nebraska, Kansas, Missouri, Arkansas
Texas Regional Resource Center Texas Education Agency 201 East 11th St. Austin, Tex. 78701	Texas
Mid-East Regional Resource Center George Washington University 1901 Pennsylvania Ave., N.W. Suite 505 Washington, D.C. 20006	Maryland, Delaware, West Virginia, North Carolina
Mid-South Resource Center University of Kentucky Research Foundation Porter Building, Room 131 Lexington, Ky. 40506	Kentucky, Tennessee, Virginia
District of Columbia Regional Resource Center Howard University 2935 Upton St., N.W. Washington, D.C. 20008	District of Columbia
Southwest Regional Resource Center Auburn University at Montgomery Montgomery, Ala. 36117	Louisiana, Mississippi, Alabama, Georgia, South Carolina, Florida, Puerto Rico, Virgin Islands
Pennsylvania Regional Resource Center Pennsylvania State Department of Education 443 South Gulph Rd. King of Prussia, Pa. 19406	Pennsylvania
Great Lakes Regional Resource Center Michigan State Department of Education P.O. Box 30008 Lansing, Mich. 48902	Minnesota, Wisconsin, Michigan, Indiana
Illinois Regional Resource Center Northern Illinois University DeKalb, Ill. 60115	Illinois
Ohio Regional Resource Center Ohio State Department of Education 933 High St. Worthington, O. 43085	Ohio
Northeast Regional Resource Center New Jersey State Department of Education 168 Bank St. Hightstown, N.J. 08520	Maine, Vermont, New Hampshire, Massachusetts, Rhode Island, Connecticut, New Jersey

states served:

New York State Regional Resource Center   New York
New York State Education Department
55 Elk St.
Albany, N.Y. 12234

New York City Regional Resource Center   New York City only
City University of New York
33 West-42nd St.
New York, N.Y. 10036

Specialized Offices

Specialized Office for Materials Distribution
Audio-Visual Center
Indiana University
Bloomington, Ind. 47401

Media Development Project for the Hearing Impaired
318 Barkley Memorial Center
University of Nebraska-Lincoln
Lincoln, Neb. 68583

References

Abeson, A., Bolick, N., & Haoo, J. *A primer on due process.* Reston, Va.: The Council for Exceptional Children, 1975.

Aiello, B. Especially for special educators: A sense of our own history. *Exceptional Children,* 1976, *42*(5), 244–252.

Albright, L., & Clark, G. M. *Preparing vocational and special education personnel to work with special needs students: A teacher education resource guide.* Urbana: Bureau of Educational Research, University of Illinois, 1977.

Algozzine, B., Mercer, C. D., & Countermine, T. The effects of labels and behavior on teacher expectations. *Exceptional Children,* 1977, *44*(2), 131–132.

Allen, L. A 1972 high school graduate looks at career education. In L. McClure and C. Buan (Eds.), *Essays on career education.* Portland, Or.: Northwest Regional Laboratory, 1973.

A matter of inconvenience. Santa Monica, Ca.: The Stanfield House, 1974. (Film)

American Foundation for the Blind. *Facts about blindness.* New York: 1973.

Altfest, M. (Ed.). *Vocational education for students with special needs.* Ft. Collins: Department of Vocational Education, Colorado State University, 1975.

Anderson, L. E. CANHC Vocational Committee Report, 1972–76. *CANHC Gram,* 1976, *10*(6), 5. (a)

Anderson, L. E. (Ed.). *Vocational kit: Steps in vocational readiness for adolescents and adults with the hidden handicap.* Los Angeles: California Association for Neurologically Handicapped Children, 1976. (b)

Arni, T. J., Magnuson, C. S., Sparks, W. C., & Starr, M. *Missouri career education delivery system.* Jefferson City: Missouri Department of Elementary and Secondary Education, 1977.

Bailey, L. J. *Career & vocational education in the 1980's: Toward a process approach.* Carbondale: Southern Illinois University, 1976.

Bardach, J. L. Psychological adjustment of handicapped individuals and their families. *State White House conference workbook.* Washington, D.C.: The White House Conference on Handicapped Individuals, U.S. Department of Health, Education and Welfare, Office of Human Development, 1976.

Barker, R. The social psychology of physical disability. *Journal of Social Issues,* 1948, *4*(4), 28–38.

Bartel, N. R., & Guskin, S. L. A handicap as a social phenomenon. In W. M. Cruick-shank (Ed.), *Psychology of exceptional children and youth* (3rd ed.). Englewood Cliffs, N.J.: Prentice-Hall, 1971.

Baskin, B. H., & Harris, K. H. *Notes from a different drummer: A guide to juvenile fiction portraying the handicapped.* New York: R. R. Bowker, 1977.

Bateman, B. D. Visually handicapped children. In N. G. Haring and R. L. Schiefelbusch (Eds.), *Methods in special education.* New York: McGraw-Hill, 1967.

Bauman, G., & Grunes, R. *Psychiatric rehabilitation in the ghetto.* Lexington, Mass.: Lexington Books, 1974.

Bauman, M. K. Interest inventory for the visually handicapped. *Education of the Visually Handicapped,* 1973, *5,* 78–83.

Becker, R. L. Job training placement for retarded youth: A survey. *Mental Retardation,* 1976, *14*(3), 7–11.

Bennett, K. W. Lamebrain hiring thwarts handicapped. *Iron Age,* 1972, *210*(3), 36–37.

Benson, H. A. Epilepsy and employment: Placement problems and techniques. *American Rehabilitation,* 1978, *3*(4), 3–8, 32.

Bhaerman, R. *Career education and basic academic achievement—A descriptive analysis of the research.* Washington, D.C.: Office of Career Education, U.S. Government Printing Office, 1977.

Bingham, G. Career attitudes among boys with and without specific learning disabilities. *Exceptional Children,* 1978, *44*(5), 341–342.

Birch, J. W. *Mainstreaming: Educable mentally retarded children in regular classes.* Reston, Va.: The Council for Exceptional Children, 1974.

Blum, L. P., & Kujoth, R. K. (Eds.). *Job placement of the emotionally disturbed.* Metuchen, N.J.: Scarecrow Press, 1972.

Bocke, J., & Price, D. Experiential approach for the exceptional adolescent. *Thresholds in Secondary Education,* 1976, *2*(3), 12–13.

Bower, E. M. *Early identification of emotionally handicapped children in school.* Springfield, Ill.: Charles C Thomas, 1960.

Bower, E. M. *Early identification of emotionally handicapped children in school* (2nd ed.) Springfield, Ill.: Charles C Thomas, 1969.

Brock, R. J. *Preparing vocational and special education personnel to work with special needs students: State of the art, 1977.* Menomonie, Wis.: University of Wisconsin-Stout, 1977.

Brolin, D. E. Career education needs of secondary educable students. *Exceptional Children,* 1973, *39,* 619–624.

Brolin, D. E. *Preparing the retarded in career education* (Project PRICE, Working Paper 1). University of Missouri-Columbia, September 1974. (Ed 096 777)

Brolin, D. E. *Vocational preparation of retarded citizens.* Columbus: Charles E. Merrill, 1976.

Brolin, D. E. *Life centered career education: A competency based approach.* Reston, Va.: The Council for Exceptional Children, 1978.

Brolin, D. E., & D'Alonzo, B. J. Critical issues in career education for handicapped students. *Exceptional Children,* 1979.

Brolin, D. E., & Kolstoe, O. P. *Research in career education for the handicapped: The state of the art.* Columbus: ERIC Clearinghouse on Career Education, Center for Vocational Education, The Ohio State University, in press.

Brolin, D. E., Malever, M., & Matyas, G. *PRICE needs assessment study* (Project PRICE, Working Paper 7). University of Missouri-Columbia, June 1976.

Brolin, D. E., McKay, D. J., & West, L. L. Personnel preparation for career education of handicapped students, *Journal of Career Education,* 1977, *3*(3), 52–74. (a)

Brolin, D. E., McKay, D. L., & West, L. L. Inservice training of educators for special needs children. The PRICE Model. *Career Education Quarterly,* 1977, *2*(1), 6–17 (h)

Brolin, D. E., McKay, D. J., & West, L. W. *Trainers guide for life centered career education.* Reston, Va.: The Council for Exceptional Children, 1978.

Brolin, D. E., & Thomas, B. (Eds.). *Preparing teachers of secondary level educable mentally retarded: Proposal for a new model.* Final Report, University of Wisconsin-Stout, Menomonie, 1972.

Brown, E. F. *Bibliotherapy: Its widening applications.* Metuchen, N.J.: Scarecrow Press, 1975.

Brown v. Board of Education. 347 U.S. 483 (1954).

Browning, P. L. (Ed.). *Mental retardation: Rehabilitation and counseling.* Springfield, Ill.: Charles C Thomas, 1974.

Bruininks, R. H., & Rynders, J. E. Alternatives to special class placement for educable mentally retarded children. *Focus on Exceptional Children,* 1971, *3*(4), 1–12.

Bryan, T. H. Learning disabilities: A new stereotype. *Journal of Learning Disabilities,* 1974, 7, 323–324.

Buchan, L. G. *Roleplaying and the educable mentally retarded.* Belmont, Ca.: Fearon, 1972.

Buscaglia, L. *The disabled and their parents: A counseling challenge.* Thorofare, N.J.: Charles B. Slack, 1975.

Cain, L. F. Parent groups: Their role in a better life for the handicapped. *Exceptional Children,* 1976, *42*(8), 432–437.

Campbell, J. Reorganization at HEW. *Disabled USA,* 1977, *1*(4), 6.

Campbell, L. W., Todd, M., & O'Rourke, E. *Work-study handbook for educable mentally retarded minors enrolled in high school programs in California public schools.* Sacramento: California State Department of Education, 1971.

Career education workshop. Career Clips. February 1977, 14–15.

Carroll, A., Gurski, G., McIntyre, K., Male, M., & Stem, M. *The secondary resource specialist in California: Promising practices.* North Hollywood, Ca.: FOREWORKS, 1976.

Chaiklin, H., & Warfield, M. Stigma management and amputee rehabilitation. *Rehabilitation Literature,* 1973, *34*(6), 162–166; 172.

Chamber of Commerce of the United States. *Career education. What it is and why we need it from leaders of industry, education, labor and the professions.* Washington, D.C.: 1975.

Charles, C. M. *Individualizing instruction.* St. Louis: C. V. Mosby, 1976.

Chester, M., & Fox, R. *Roleplaying methods in the classroom.* Chicago: Science Research Associates, 1966.

Christensen, N. A., DuBois, P. A., & Austin, M. *Selected bibliography for vocational training and placement of the severely handicapped.* Palo Alto, Ca.: American Institutes for Research, 1975.

Cohen, J. S., & DeYoung, H. The role of litigation in the improvement of programming for the handicapped. In L. Mann and D. A. Sabatino (Eds.), *The first review of special education* (Vol. 2). Philadelphia: Journal of Special Education Press, 1973.

Cohen, S. *Special people.* Englewood Cliffs, N.J.: Prentice-Hall, 1977.

Colella, H. V. Career development center: A modified high school for the handicapped. *Teaching Exceptional Children,* 1973, *5*(3), 110–118.

Committee for the Handicapped. *Directory of organizations interested in the handicapped.* Washington, D.C.: U.S. Government Printing Office, (n.d.)

Compton, D. M., & Vinton, D. A. *Employment of handicapped people in leisure occupations.* Washington, D.C.: Committee on Recreation and Leisure, President's Committee on Employment of the Handicapped (n.d.).

Cook, D. W. Psychological aspects for spinal cord injury. *Rehabilitation Counseling Bulletin,* 1976, *19*(4), 535–543.

Council for Exceptional Children. U.S. Commissioners pursue systems linkage. *Insight,* December 19, 1977, *12,* 1.

Council for Exceptional Children. *Position paper on career education.* Reston, Va.: CEC, 1978.

Cruickshank, W. M., & Paul, J. L. The psychological characteristics of brain-injured children. In W. M. Cruickshank (Ed.), *Psychology of exceptional children and youth* (3rd ed.). Englewood Cliffs, N.J.: Prentice-Hall, 1971.

Dalrymple, G. F. The braille computer terminal: Its application in employment. *New Outlook for the Blind,* 1975, *69*(1), 1–10.

Darley, J. M., & Latané, B. When will people help in a crisis? *Psychology Today,* 1968, *2*(7), 54–57; 70–71.

Davis, L. N., & McCallon, E. *Planning, conducting and evaluating workshops.* Austin, Tex.: Learning Concepts, 1974.

Denhoff, E. The responsibility of the physician, parent, and child in learning disabilities. *Rehabilitation Literature,* 1974, *35*(8), 226–230.

Deno, E. Special education as developmental capital. *Exceptional Children,* 1970, *37*(3), 229–237.

Department of Labor. *Occupational outlook handbook 1978–79 edition.* Washington, D.C.: U.S. Government Printing Office, 1978.

Diana v. State Board of Education of California. C-70 37 RFP, District Court of Northern California, 1970.

Dictionary of occupational titles (4th ed.). Washington, D.C.: U.S. Department of Labor, 1977.

Dole, R. Handicapped Americans: Speech of Hon. Robert Dole of Kansas in the Senate of the United States, Monday, April 14, 1969. *Congressional Record.* 91st Congress, First Session, 7p.

Donaldson, J., & Martinson, M. C. Modifying attitudes toward physically disabled persons. *Exceptional Children,* 1977, *43*(6), 337–341.

Drier, H., Martinez, N., & Kimmel, K. *An orientation to career education.* Columbus: The Center for Vocational Education, Ohio State University, 1975.

Dunn, L. M. (Ed.). *Exceptional children in the schools: Special education in transition* (2nd ed.). New York: Holt, Rinehart & Winston, 1973.

Dwyer, W. A. Career development for deaf adults: Blue Hills breaks the communications barrier. *American Vocational Journal,* 1073, *18,* 37–39.

Eau Claire Joint School District No. 5. *Career development—Special education.* Eau Claire, Wis.: 1973.

Edgerton, R. B. *The cloak of competence.* Berkeley: University of California Press, 1967.

Employer education seminars designed to build job opportunities in Maryland. *National Spokesman,* 1977, *10*(3), 3.

Engelmann, S., & Rosov, R. Tactual hearing experiment with deaf and hearing subjects. *Exceptional Children,* 1975, *41*(4), 243–253.

English, R. W. Combatting stigma toward physically disabled persons. *Rehabilitation Research and Practice Review,* 1971, *2*(4), 19–27.

English, R. W., & Oberle, J. B. The development of new methodology for examining attitudes toward disabled persons. *Rehabilitation Counseling Bulletin,* 1971, *15*(2), 88–96.

Fink, S. L. Crisis and motivation: A theoretical model. *Archives of Physical Medicine and Rehabilitation,* 1967, *48*(11), 592–597.

Fishman, S. The amputee. In J. F. Garrett and E. S. Levine (Eds.), *Rehabilitation practices with the physically disabled.* New York: Columbia University Press, 1973.

Foster, G. G., & Salvia, J. Teacher response to label of learning disabled as a function of demand characteristics. *Exceptional Children,* 1977, *43*(8), 533–534.

Foster, J. C., Szoke, C. O., Kapisovsky, P. M., & Kriger, L. S. *Guidance, counseling and support services for high school students with physical disabilities.* Cambridge, Mass.: Technical Education Research Centers, 1977.

Freed, M. M. The central nervous system: Disorders of the spinal cord. In J. Meyers (Ed.), *An orientation to chronic disease and disability.* London: Macmillan & Co., 1965.

Friedman, P. *Mental retardation and the law: A report on status of current court cases.* Washington, D.C.: Government Printing Office, 1973.

Gallagher, J. J. The search for the educational system that doesn't exist. In *Imprint: A series of special interest papers.* Arlington, Va.: The Council for Exceptional Children, 1972.

Gearhart, G. R., & Weishahn, M. W. *The handicapped child in the regular classroom.* St. Louis: C. V. Mosby, 1976.

Gellman, W. Projections in the field of physical disability. *Rehabilitation Literature,* 1974, *35*(1), 2–9.

Gibson, R. L. *Career development in the elementary school.* Columbus: Charles E. Merrill, 1972.

Gilhool, T. K. Education: An inalienable right. *Exceptional Children,* 1973, *39*(8), 597–609.

Gillung, T. B., & Rucker, C. N. Labels and teachers expectations. *Exceptional Children,* 1977, *43*(7), 464–465.

Glasser, W. *Schools without failure.* New York: Harper & Row, 1969.

Goffman, E. *Stigma: Notes on the management of spoiled identity.* Englewood Cliffs, N.J.: Prentice-Hall, 1963.

Goldhammer, K. A careers curriculum. In K. Goldhammer and R. Taylor (Eds.), *Career education: Perspective and promise.* Columbus: Charles E. Merrill, 1972.

Goldish, L. H., & Taylor, H. E. The optacon: A valuable device for blind persons. *New Outlook for the Blind,* 1974, *68*(2), 49–56.

Gowan, J., Demos, G. D., & Kokaska, C. J. (Eds.). *The guidance of exceptional children* (2nd ed.). New York: David McKay, 1972.

Grand, S. A., & Grand, A. K. Epilepsy. In R. E. Hardy and J. G. Cull, *Severe disabilities: Social and rehabilitation approaches.* Springfield, Ill.: Charles C Thomas, 1974, 14–38.

Graves, C. Levels of existence: An open system theory of values. *Journal of Humanistic Psychology,* 1970, *10*(2), 131–155.

Greer, B. G. Attitudes of special education personnel toward different types of deviant persons. *Rehabilitation Literature,* 1975, *36*(6), 182–184.

Grossman, H. (Ed.). *Manual on terminology and classification in mental retardation* (Rev. ed.). American Association on Mental Deficiency Baltimore: Garamond/Pridemark Press, 1973.

Gullotta, T. P. Teacher attitudes toward the moderately disturbed child. *Exceptional Children,* 1974, *41*(1), 49–50.

Gysbers, N. C., *The three faces of needs assessment: Periodicals, programs and staff.* Paper presented at a joint ERIC-CAPS American Research & Guidance Association Conference, Ann Arbor, 1973.

Gysbers, N. C. Career education. In D. Brolin (Ed.), *Proceedings of Project PRICE trainer's workshop* (Working Paper 5). University of Missouri-Columbia, July 1975. (ED 109-838)

Gysbers, N. C., & Moore, E. J. Career conscious individual model. *Life career development: A model.* University of Missouri-Columbia, 1973.

Hall, P., & Alexander, G. Handicapping speech disorders. In R. E. Hardy and J. G. Cull (Eds.), *Severe disabilities: Social and rehabilitation approaches.* Springfield, Ill.: Charles C Thomas, 1974.

Hallahan, D. P., & Kauffman, J. M. *Introduction to learning disabilities.* Englewood Cliffs, N.J.: Prentice-Hall, 1976.

Halloran, W. E. Handicapped persons: Who are they? *American Vocational Journal,* 1978, *53*(1), 30–31.

Halloran, W. E., Hull, M. E., Charles, F. H., Lampe, A., & Morgan, C. A. *The Vermont guide for teaching adolescents with special needs.* (Final report, Project No. 5-0125, Contract No. OEG-0-71-4147 603). Burlington: Dept. of Vocational Education and Technology, University of Vermont, 1975.

Hammill, D., & Wiederholt, J. *The resource room: Rationale and implementation.* Philadelphia: Buttonwood Farms, 1972.

Hansen, L. S. *An examination of the definitions and concepts of career education.* Washington, D.C.: National Advisory Council on Career Education, U.S. Government Printing Office, 1977.

Harasymiw, S. J., Horne, M. D., & Lewis, S. C. A longitudinal study of disability group acceptance. *Rehabilitation Literature,* 1976, *37*(4), 98–102.

Hardy, R. E., & Cull, J. G. Vocational rehabilitation of the blind and severely visually impaired. In R. E. Hardy and J. G. Cull (Eds.), *Severe disabilities: Social and rehabilitation approaches.* Springfield, Ill.: Charles C Thomas, 1974, 75–117.

Haring, D. *Learn and earn with Project WORK.* Paper presented at the meeting of the Career Education Workshop, January 1–3, 1978.

Harvard Educational Review. The rights of children: Parts 1 & 2, 1973, *43*(4).

Harvard Educational Review. The rights of children: Parts 1 & 2, 1974, *44*(1).

Heber, R. *A manual on terminology and classification in mental retardation. American Journal of Mental Deficiency Monograph,* 1961.

Henderson, H. L. American youth in transition. *Kappa Delta Pi Record,* 1976, *12*(3), 67–69.

Hensley, G. Enhancing business and industry participation in career education. In *Two studies on the role of business and industry and labor participation in career education.* Washington, D.C.: National Advisory Council for Career Education, U.S. Government Printing Office, 1977.

Herr, E. L. *The emerging history of career education: A summary view.* Washington, D.C.: National Advisory Council on Career Education, U.S. Government Printing Office, 1976.

Herr, E. L. *Research in career education: The state of the art.* Columbus: ERIC Clearinghouse on Career Education, Center for Vocational Education, Ohio State University, 1977.

Hewett, F. M. *The emotionally disturbed child in the classroom.* Boston: Allyn & Bacon, 1968.

Hobbs, N. (Ed.). *Issues in the classification of children: A sourcebook on categories, labels, and their consequences* (Vols. 1 & 2). San Francisco: Jossey-Bass, 1974.

Hobbs, N. (Ed.). *Issues in the classification of children.* San Francisco: Jossey-Bass, 1975.

Hobson v. Hansen. 393 U.S. 801 (1968).

Hoyt, K. B. *An introduction to career education: A policy paper of the U.S. Office of Education.* Washington, D.C.: Office of Education, 1975.

Hoyt, K. B. Refining the career education concept. *Monographs on career education.* U.S. Department of Health, Education, and Welfare, U.S. Office of Education, 1976. (a)

Hoyt, K. B. Community resources for career education. *Monographs on career education.* Washington, D.C.: U.S. Office of Education, 1976 (b)

Hoyt, K. B. A primer on career education. *Monographs on career education.* Washington, D.C.: U.S. Office of Education, 1977. (a)

Hoyt, K. B. Community resources for career education. *Occupational Outlook Quarterly,* 1977, *21*(2), 10–21. (b)

Hoyt, K. B. Why Johnny and Joann can't work. *Occupational Outlook Quarterly,* 1977, *21*(2), 1–3. (c)

Hoyt, K. B., Pinson, N. M., Laramore, D., & Mangum, G. L. *Career education and the elementary school teacher.* Salt Lake City, Utah: Olympus, 1973.

Hull, M. E. (Ed.). *Programming for the handicapped: Accomplishments, commitments, and forecasts.* College Station: College of Education, Texas A & M University, 1977.

Hyre, C. S., & Henderson, N. L. *An alternative curriculum.* Paper presented at the Annual Meeting of the American Educational Research Association, San Francisco, Ca., April 22, 1976.

Illinois Office of Education. *A teacher's handbook on career development for students with special needs: Grades K–12* (2nd ed.). Springfield, Ill.: Office of Education, 1977.

Irvin, L. K., Halpern, A. S., & Reynolds, W. M. Assessing social and prevocational awareness in mildly and moderately retarded individuals. *American Journal of Mental Deficiency,* 1977, *82*(3), 266–272.

Itard, J. M. G. *The wild boy of Aveyron.* (G. Humphrey and M. Humphrey, Eds. and trans.). New York: Appleton-Century-Crofts (Prentice-Hall), 1932, 1962. (Originally published in Paris by Gouyon, 1801.)

Jamison, S. L. IBM work experience program for deaf people. *American Rehabilitation,* 1977, *2*(5), 3–5. (a)

Jamison, S. L. Professional careers for deaf people in business and industry. Paper presented to the California Governor's Committee for Employment of the Handicapped, San Francisco, Ca., April 22, 1977. (b)

Johnson, D. S. Visual disorders. In J. S. Meyers (Ed.), *An orientation to chronic disease and disability.* London: Macmillan & Co., 1965.

Johnson, J. School stores: A vital part of your career education program. Paper presented at the meeting of the Career Education Workshop, March 4–5, 1976.

Johnson, R. K. The deaf. In R. E. Hardy and J. G. Cull (Eds.), *Severe disabilities: Social and rehabilitation approaches.* Springfield, Ill.: Charles C Thomas, 1974, 149–173.

Jordan, T. E. *The mentally retarded* (4th ed.). Columbus: Charles E. Merrill, 1976.

Kanner, L. *A history of the care and study of the mentally retarded.* Springfield, Ill.: Charles C Thomas, 1964.

Kayfetz, V. Swedes test ingenious electronic hand. *Los Angeles Times,* November 4, 1977, pp. 6, 11.

Kelly, T. J., Bullock, L. M., & Dykes, M. K. Behavioral disorders: Teachers' perceptions. *Exceptional Children,* 1977, *43*(5), 316–318.

Killilea, M. *Karen.* New York: Dell, 1960.

King, F. Treatment of the mentally retarded character in modern American fiction. *Bulletin of Bibliography,* 1975, *32*(3), 106–113; 131.

Kirk, S. A. *Educating exceptional children* (2nd ed.). New York: Houghton-Mifflin, 1972.

Kirk, S. A., & Kirk, W. D. *Psycholinguistic learning disabilities: Diagnosis and remediation.* Urbana: University of Illinois Press, 1971.

Kirp, D. L. Student classification, public policy, and the courts. *Harvard Educational Review,* 1974, *44*(1), 7–52.

Kokaska, C. J. *The vocational preparation of the educable mentally retarded.* Ypsilanti: Eastern Michigan University Press, 1968.

Kokaska, C. J. Normalization; Implications for teachers of the retarded. *Mental Retardation,* 1974, *12*(4), 49–51.

Kokaska, C. J. Recent expansions in careers for the handicapped. *Thresholds in Secondary Education,* 1976, *2*(3), 14–15; 23–24.

Kokaska, C. J., & Kolstoe, O. P. Special education's role in career education. *Journal of Career Education,* 1977, *3*(3), 4–18.

Kokaska, S., & Kokaska, C. J. Individualized work centers: An approach for the elementary retarded child. *Education and Training of the Mentally Retarded,* 1971, *6*(1), 25–27.

Kolstoe, O. P. *Mental retardation: An educational viewpoint.* New York: Holt, Rinehart & Winston, 1972. (a)

Kolstoe, O. P. Programs for the mildly retarded: A reply to the critics. *Exceptional Children,* 1972, *39*(1), 51–56. (b)

Kolstoe, O. P. Developing career awareness: The foundation of a career education program. In G. B. Blackburn (Ed.), *Colloquium series on career education for handicapped adolescents.* West Lafayette, Ind.: Purdue University, 1976.

Kolstoe, O. P., & Frey, R. M. *A high school work-study program for mentally subnormal students.* Carbondale: Southern Illinois University Press, 1965.

Krents, H. Selected comments. In *How to communicate to and about people who happen to be handicapped.* Washington, D.C.: The President's Committee on Employment of the Handicapped, n.d.

Kroth, R. Parents—Powerful and necessary allies. *Teaching Exceptional Children,* 1978, *10*(3), 88–90.

Lake, T. (Ed.). *Career education: Exemplary programs for the handicapped.* Reston, Va.: The Council for Exceptional Children, 1974.

Lambert, R. H., Tindall, L. W., Davis, K. E., & Ross-Thomson, B. *A bibliography of materials for handicapped and special education* (2nd ed.). Madison: Center for Studies in Vocational and Technical Education, University of Wisconsin, 1975.

Larson, C. Personal communication regarding the EBCE-MD Model. Ft. Dodge, Iowa: Central Community College, March 1978.

Lawrence, E. A., & Winschel, J. F. Self-concept and the retarded: Research and issues. *Exceptional Children,* 1973, *39*(4), 310–319.

Levitan, S. A., & Taggart, R. Employment problems of disabled persons. *Monthly Labor Review, 100*(3), 1977, 3–13.

Lippman, L., & Goldberg, I. *Right to education: Anatomy of the Pennsylvania case and its implications for exceptional children.* New York: Teachers College Press, Columbia University, 1973.

Lippman, G. K., & Porter, G. C. *How to establish competency model programs for the delivery of vocational services to the severely multihandicapped.* Austin, Tex.: Lippman/Porter, 1976.

Lorenze, E. J. The central nervous system: Disorders of the brain. In J. S. Myers (Ed.), *An orientation to chronic disease and disability.* London: Macmillan & Co., 1965.

Lowenbraun, S., & Affleck, J. Q. *Teaching mildly handicapped children in regular classes.* Columbus: Charles E. Merrill, 1976.

MacFarland, D. C. The blind and visually impaired. In J. F. Garrett and E. S. Levine (Eds.), *Rehabilitation practices with the physically disabled.* New York: Columbia University Press, 1973.

Magnuson, C. Creating a facilitative classroom climate. In *Career education methods and processes.* Columbia: University of Missouri-Columbia, 1974.

Mann, P. H. (Ed.). *Mainstream special education: Issues and perspectives in urban centers.* Reston, Va.: The Council for Exceptional Children, 1974.

Mann, P. H. (Ed.). *Shared responsibility for handicapped students: Advocacy and programming.* Coral Gables, Fla.: University of Miami Training and Technical Assistance Center, 1976.

Marland, S. P., Jr. Career education update. Speech presented at the Commissioner's National Conference on Career Education, Houston, Tex., November 8, 1976.

Martin, E. W. Individualism and behaviorism as future trends in educating handicapped children. *Exceptional Children,* 1972, *38,* 517–525.

Martin, E. W. Foreword. In T. P. Lake (Ed.), *Career education: Exemplary programs for the handicapped.* Reston, Va.: Council for Exceptional Children, 1974.

Martin, E. W. A national commitment of the rights of the individual. *Exceptional Children,* 1976, *43*(3), 132–135.

Masland, R. L., Sarason, S. B., & Gladwin, T. *Mental subnormality: Biological, psychological, and cultural factors.* New York: Basic Books, 1958.

Mattson, H. A. Career information centers for students. *Career Education Workshop,* December, 1976, 11–13.

McGowan, J., & Porter, T. *An introduction to the vocational rehabilitation process.* Washington, D.C., U.S. Department of Health, Education and Welfare, 1967.

McKay, D. J. (Ed.). *Selected PRICE topical papers for career education.* (Project PRICE, Working Paper 8.) University of Missouri-Columbia, February 1977. (ED 143 175)

McLarty, C. L., & Chaney, J. A. The cerebral palsied. In R. E. Hardy and J. G. Cull (Eds.), *Severe disabilities: Social and rehabilitation practices.* Springfield, Ill.: Charles C Thomas, 1974.

McLoughlin, A. Automotive trades for handicapped students. *Career Education Workshop,* November 1976, 5–6.

Melcher, J. Law, litigation, and handicapped children. *Exceptional Children,* 1976, 43(3), 126–130.

Mental Retardation News, National Association for Retarded Citizens, January, 1975, 1.

Mental Retardation News. National Association for Retarded Citizens, March-April, 1977.

Mesa (Arizona) Public Schools. *Talking with your child (teenager) about your career.* Mesa, Arizona: Center for Career Development, Mesa Public Schools, 1976.

Messner, S. A., & Haynes, U. Cerebral palsy. In J. F. Garrett and E. S. Levine (Eds.), *Rehabilitation practices with the physically disabled.* New York: Columbia University Press, 1973.

Milgram, N. A. M. R. and mental illness—A proposal for conceptual unity. *Mental Retardation,* 1972, 10(6), 29–31.

Mills v. Board of Education of District of Columbia. 348F. Supp. 866 (D.D.C., 1972).

Mohr, P. *Current research and development efforts in in-service training and curriculum planning.* Washington, D.C.: U.S. Department of Health, Education and Welfare, Office of Education, 1971. (ERIC Document Reproduction Service No. 083 148)

Moody, M. T. *Bibliotherapy: Methods and materials.* Chicago: American Library Association, 1971.

Moore, E. J., & Gysbers, N. C. Career development: A new focus. *Educational Leadership,* 1972, 30, 1–8.

Moore, J. J., & Engleman, V. S. (Eds.). *Administrator's manual. Programming for handicapped students at the secondary level: Responding to public laws.* Salt Lake City: The Southwest Regional Resource Center, University of Utah, 1977.

Moriarity, J. Role of stigma in the experience of deviance. *Journal of Personality and Social Psychology,* 1974, 6, 849–855.

Morse, W. C. Serving the needs of individuals with behavioral disorders. *Exceptional Children,* 1977, 44(3), 158–164.

National Advisory Committee on Handicapped Children. Conference sponsored by Bureau of Education for the Handicapped, U.S. Office of Education, Washington, D.C., September 28, 1967.

National Spokesman, Epilepsy Foundation of America, August 1976, 1.

National Spokesman, Epilepsy Foundation of America, July 1977, 1–11.

Neil, S. B. Clearing the air in career education. *American Education,* 1977, *13*(2), 6–9; 13.

New York Times, May 4, 1975, pp. 1; 31.

Nichols, D. L. What is advocacy all about? *New Hampshire Association for Retarded Citizens Newsletter,* February 1977.

Noar, G. *Individualized instruction for the mentally retarded.* Glen Ridge, N.J.: Exceptional Press, 1974.

Noland, R. L. (Ed.). *Counseling parents of the ill and the handicapped.* Springfield, Ill.: Charles C Thomas, 1971.

Nyquist, E. B. *Mainstreaming: Idea and actuality.* Albany, N.Y.: State Education Department, 1975.

Office for Handicapped Individuals. *Programs for the handicapped,* 1975, *75*(5), 9.

Official actions of the delegate assembly at the 54th Annual International Convention of the Council for Exceptional Children, *Exceptional Children,* 1976, *43*(1), 41–45.

Olshansky, S. The disabled in the labor market. *Journal of Applied Rehabilitation Counseling,* 1973, *4*(3), 164–170.

Patterson, L. L. Some pointers for professionals. *Children, 3*(1), 1956, 13–17.

Payne, J. S. Job placement: How to approach employers. In R. Carpenter (Ed.), *Colloquium series on career education for handicapped adolescents, 1977.* West Lafayette, Ind.: Special Education Section, Department of Education, Purdue University, 1977.

Payne, J. S., & Chaffin, J. D. Developing employer relations in a work-study program for the educable mentally retarded. *Education and Training of the Mentally Retarded,* 1968, *3*(3), 127–133.

Payne, J. S., Mercer, C. D., & Epstein, M. H. *Education and rehabilitation techniques.* New York: Behavioral Publications, 1974.

Pennsylvania Association for Retarded Children v. Commonwealth of Pennsylvania. 334, F. Supp. 1257 (E.D.Ua., 1971)

Perske, R. The dignity of risk and the mentally retarded. *Mental Retardation,* 1972, *10*(1), 24–27.

Phelps, L. A. *Instructional development for special needs learners: An inservice resource guide.* Urbana: Department of Vocational and Technical Education, University of Illinois, 1976.

Phelps, L. A., & Lutz, R. J. *Career exploration and preparation for the special needs learner.* Boston: Allyn & Bacon, 1977.

Phillips, G. B. Specific jobs for deaf workers identified by employers. *Journal of Rehabilitation of the Deaf,* 1975, *9,* 10–23.

Phillips, L. *Barriers and bridges: An overview of vocational services available for handicapped Californians.* Sacramento: California Advisory Council on Vocational Education, 1976.

Plato. *The republic.* (*B. Jowett, trans.*). New York: Random House, 1941.

Pollard, N. E. Career education in the classroom. In R. Carpenter (Ed.), *Colloquium series on career education for handicapped adolescents, 1977.* West Lafayette, Ind.: Special Education Section, Department of Education, Purdue University, 1977.

The President's Committee on Employment of the Handicapped. *Hiring the handicapped: Facts and myths.* Washington, D.C.: U.S. Government Printing Office, 1975. (a)

The President's Committee on Employment of the Handicapped. Of men and machines. *Performance,* 1975, *15*(8), 9–11. (b)

The President's Committee on Employment of the Handicapped. *A handbook on the legal rights of handicapped people.* Washington, D.C.: U.S. Government Printing Office, 1976.

The President's Committee on Employment of the Handicapped. *Newsletter,* September 1977. (a)

The President's Committee on Employment of the Handicapped. *Bibliography of secondary materials for teaching handicapped students.* Washington, D.C.: U.S. Government Printing Office, 1977. (b)

The President's Committee on Employment of the Handicapped. *Pathways to employment.* Washington, D.C.: U.S. Government Printing Office, 1977. (c)

The President's Committee on Mental Retardation. *Mental retardation: Century of decision.* Report to the President. Washington, D.C.: U.S. Government Printing Office, March 1976.

The President's Panel on Mental Retardation. *Report to the President: A proposed program for national action to combat mental retardation.* Washington, D.C.: U.S. Government Printing Office, 1963.

Raths, L. E., Harmin, M., & Simon, S. B. *Values and teaching.* Columbus: Charles E. Merrill, 1966.

Reynolds, M. C. A framework for considering some issues in special education. *Exceptional Children,* 1962, *28*(7), 367–370.

Reynolds, M. C., & Davis, M. D. *Exceptional children in regular classrooms.* Minneapolis: Department of Audio-Visual Extension, University of Minnesota, 1972.

Rice, J. An interstate consortium of directors of special education confront the problems of mainstreaming. In P. H. Mann (Ed.), *Shared responsibility for handicapped students: Advocacy and programming.* Coral Gables, Fla.: University of Miami Training and Technical Assistance Center, 1976.

Riggs, C. *Bibliotherapy.* Newark, Del.: International Reading Association, 1971.

Roberts, A. *Psychosocial rehabilitation of the blind.* Springfield, Ill.: Charles C Thomas, 1973.

Robinson, N. M., & Robinson, H. B. *The mentally retarded child: A psychological approach* (2nd ed.). New York: McGraw-Hill, 1976.

Rogers, C. R. *Client-centered therapy: Its current practice, implications, and theory.* Boston: Houghton-Mifflin, 1951.

Rogers, C. R. *On becoming a person.* Boston: Houghton-Mifflin, 1961.

Roos, P. NARC to seek cure for mental retardation. *Mental Retardation News,* 1977, *26*(2), 1.

Ross, S. L., Jr., DeYoung, H. G., & Cohen, J. S. Confrontation: Special education placement and the law. *Exceptional Children,* 1971, *38*(1), 5–12.

Rusalem, H. *Coping with the unseen environment.* New York: Teachers College Press, 1972.

Russell, H. The chairman's column. *Performance,* 1977, 27(8), 18–20.

Salamack, M. Alternative techniques of classroom assessment. Possibilities for evaluating EMR students in the classroom. In D. J. McKay (Ed.), *Selected PRICE Topical Papers for Career Education,* (Project PRICE, Working Paper 8). Columbia: University of Missouri-Columbia, February 1977. (ED 143 175).

Sarbin, T. R., & Mancuso, T. C. Failure of a moral enterprise: Attitudes of the public toward mental illness. *Journal of Consulting and Clinical Psychology,* 1970, *35*(2), 159–173.

Scherzer, A. L. Early diagnosis, management, and treatment of cerebral palsy. *Rehabilitation Literature,* 1974, *35*(7), 194–199.

Schlesinger, L. E., & Frank, D. S. *On the way to work: A guide for the rehabilitation counselor.* Washington, D.C.: The Artists and Writers Syndicate, 1976.

Scott, R. A. *The making of blind men.* New York: Russell Sage, 1969.

Sears, J. H. The able disabled. *Journal of Rehabilitation,* 1975, *41*(2), 19–22.

Shaftel, F. R., & Shaftel, G. *Role-playing for social values.* Englewood Cliffs, N.J.: Prentice-Hall, 1967.

Sigler, G. R., & Kokaska, C. J. A job placement procedure for the mentally retarded. *Education and Training of the Mentally Retarded,* 1971, *6*(4), 161–166.

Siller, J. Attitude toward disability. In H. Rusalem and D. Malikin (Eds.), *Contemporary vocational rehabilitation.* New York: New York University Press, 1976.

Simon, S. B., Hawley, R. C., & Britton, D. D. *Composition for personal growth.* Amherst, Mass.: Education Research Associates, 1971.

Simon, S. B., Howe, L. W., & Kirschenbaum, H. *Values clarification.* New York: Hart, 1972.

Simpson, E. J. The home as a career education center. *Exceptional Children,* 1973, *39*(8), 626–630.

Smith, I. L., & Greenberg, S. Teacher attitudes and the labeling process. *Exceptional Children,* 1975, *41*(5), 319–324.

Sontag, E. (Ed.). *Educational programming for the severely and profoundly handicapped.* Reston, Va.: The Council for Exceptional Children, 1977.

Spar, H. J. The deaf-blind. In J. F. Garrett and E. S. Levine (Eds.), *Rehabilitation practices with the physically handicapped.* New York: Columbia University Press, 1973.

Stewart, D. M. Survey of community employer attitudes toward hiring the handicapped. *Mental Retardation,* 1977, *15*(1), 30–31.

Stewart, J. C. *Counseling parents of exceptional children.* Columbus: Charles E. Merrill, 1978.

Stromer, R. Remediating academic deficiencies in learning disabled children. *Exceptional Children,* 1977, *43*(7), 432–440.

Sullivan, H. S. In H. S. Perry and M. L. Gawel (Eds.), *The interpersonal theory of psychiatry.* New York: W. W. Norton, 1953.

Super, D. E. Career education and the meanings of work. *Monographs on Career Education.* U.S. Department of Health, Education and Welfare, U.S. Office of Education, June 1976.

Swinyard, C. A. Treatment of the physically handicapped. In *State White House Conference workbook (Health Centers).* Washington, D.C.. The White House Conference on Handicapped Individuals, U.S. Department of Health, Education and Welfare, Office of Human Development, 1976.

Sword, S., & Roberts, M. M. Spinal cord injured patient. In R. E. Hardy and J. G. Cull (Eds.), *Severe disabilities: Social and rehabilitation approaches.* Springfield, Ill.: Charles C Thomas, 1974.

Tarver, S., & Hallahan, D. P. Children with learning disabilities: An overview. In J. M. Kauffman and D. P. Hallahan (Eds.), *Teaching children with learning disabilities: Personal perspectives.* Columbus: Charles E. Merrill, 1976.

Task Force on the Mentally Retarded/Deaf. *Airlie House Conference report.* Washington, D.C.: Office of Mental Retardation Coordination, November 1973.

Telesensory systems. *Newsletter,* October 1975, *9,* 1–2.

Thorne, F. C. *Intergrative psychology.* Brandon, Vt.: Clinical Psychology Publishing, 1967.

Torres, S. (Ed.). *A primer on individualized education programs for handicapped children.* Reston, Va.: The Foundation for Exceptional Children, 1977. (a)

Torres, S. *Special education administrative policies manual.* Reston, Va.: The Council for Exceptional Children, 1977. (b)

Towne, D. C., & Wallace, S. *Vocational instructional materials for students with special needs.* Portland, Or.: Northwest Regional Educational Laboratory, 1972.

Tringo, J. L. The hierarchy of preference toward disability groups. *The Journal of Special Education,* 1970, *4*(3), 295–306.

Ullmann, L. P., & Krasner, L. *A psychological approach to abnormal behavior* (2nd ed.). Englewood Cliffs, N.J.: Prentice-Hall, 1975.

United States Bureau of Education for the Handicapped. *Selected career education programs for the handicapped.* Washington, D.C.: U.S. Government Printing Office, 1973.

United States Bureau of Education for the Handicapped. *Improving occupational programs for the handicapped.* Washington, D.C.: U.S. Government Printing Office, 1975.

United States Department of Health, Education and Welfare. *Selected career education programs for the handicapped.* Washington, D.C.: Bureau of Education for the Handicapped, 1972.

United States Department of Health, Education and Welfare. *Ready reference guide.* Washington, D.C.: Office of Human Development, Rehabilitation Services Administration, 1977.

United States Department of Labor, Employment and Training Administration. *Placing handicapped applicants: An employment service handbook.* Washington, D.C.: U.S. Department of Labor, n.d. (Mimeograph).

United States Office of Education. *Estimated number of handicapped children in the United States, 1971–72.* Washington, D.C.: Bureau of Education for the Handicapped, 1971. (a)

United States Office of Education. *Estimates on the number of children served/unserved in 1971–1972, fiscal year projected acturities.* Washington, D.C.: Bureau of Education for the Handicapped, 1971. (b)

United States Office of Education. *The unfinished revolution: Education for the handicapped.* In *1976 Annual Report.* Washington, D.C.: National Advisory Committee on the Handicapped, U.S. Government Printing Office, 1976.

Urban Institute. *Report of the comprehensive needs study of individuals with the most severe handicaps.* Manuscript for publication submitted to the Department of Health, Education and Welfare, June 9, 1975.

Urban, S. J., & Tsuji, T. (Eds.). *The special needs student in vocational education: Selected readings.* New York: MSS Information Corporation, 1974.

Van Etten, C., & Watson, B. Career education materials for the learning disabled. *Journal of Learning Disabilities,* 1977, *10*(5), 10–16.

Van Riper, C. *Speech correction: Principles and methods* (4th ed.). Englewood Cliffs, N.J.: Prentice-Hall, 1963.

Varelas, J. T. The career seminar: Ideas and techniques. *The Career Education Workshop,* April 1976, 1–4.

Vernon, M. Early profound deafness. In J. F. Garrett and E. S. Levine (Eds.), *Rehabilitation practices with the physically disabled.* New York: Columbia University Press, 1973.

Viscardi, H. Paper presented at the annual meeting of the President's Committee on Employment of the Handicapped, Washington, D.C., April 30, 1976.

Vogel, J. Learning and self-esteem: You can't have one without the other. *Learning,* 1974, *2*(7), 68–69.

Weinberg-Asher, N. The effect of physical disability on self-perception. *Rehabilitation Counseling Bulletin,* 1976, *20*(1), 15–20.

Weintraub, F. J. Recent influences of law regarding the identification and educational placement of children. In E. L. Meyen, G. A. Vergason, and R. J. Whelan (Eds.), *Alternatives for teaching exceptional children.* Denver: Love, 1975.

Weintraub, F. J., Abeson, A. R., & Braddock, D. L. *State law and education of handicapped children: Issues and recommendations.* Arlington, Va.: The Council for Exceptional Children, 1971.

Wellman, F. E., & Moore, E. J. *Pupil personnel services: A handbook for program developmental and evaluation.* Columbia: University of Missouri, 1975.

Wendt, E., Sprague, M. J., & Marquis, J. Communication without speech. *Teaching Exceptional Children,* 1975, *8*(1), 38–42.

Wentling, T. L., & Lawson, T. E. *Evaluating occupational education and training programs.* Boston: Allyn & Bacon, 1975.

Wepman, J. W. Rehabilitation and the language disorders. In J. F. Garrett and E. S. Levine (Eds.), *Rehabilitation practices with the physically disabled.* New York: Columbia University Press, 1973.

West, L. Suggested teaching strategies for classroom use. In D. J. McKay (Ed.), *Selected PRICE topical papers for career education* (Project PRICE, Working Paper 8). University of Missouri—Columbia, 1977. (ED 143 175)

West Virginia State Department of Education. *Expanding options for handicapped persons receiving vocational education: Run into the future run.* Proceedings of the West Virginia Training Institute, West Virginia College of Graduate Studies, 1977.

White, P. A self-directed career planning program for the visually disabled. Tallahassee, Fla.: The Florida State University, 1978, personal correspondence.

Wollman, P. Electronic advances aid handicapped. *Los Angeles Times,* November 6, 1977, pp. 5; 6–8.

Wood, M. *Blindness—Ability not disability.* Public Affairs Committee, 1968.

Wright, B. A. An analysis of attitudes—dynamics and effects. *The New Outlook for the Blind,* 1974, *68*(3), 108–118.

Wright, B. A. *Physical disability—A psychological approach.* New York: Harper & Row, 1960.

Wright, W. H. *Project success* (EHA Title VI-B, No. 19-73452-1423-2-01. Final Report). Rowland Heights, Ca.: Rowland Unified School District, 1973.

Wrobel, C. Personal correspondence, 1977.

Yates, J. R. Financing of public law 94–142. *Education and Training of the Mentally Retarded,* 1977, *12*(4), 396–401.

Yuker, H. E. Attitudes of the general public toward handicapped individuals. In *State White House Conference workbook.* Washington, D.C.: The White House Conference on Handicapped Individuals, U.S. Department of Health, Education and Welfare, Office of Human Development, 1976.

Zadny, J. J., & James, L. F. Another view on placement: State of the art 1976. *Studies in Placement Monograph No. 1.* Portland: School of Social Work, Portland State University, 1976.

Zuger, R. R. To place the unplaceable. *Journal of Rehabilitation,* 1971, *37*(6), 22–23.

✤·THE·✤
PEEBLES
PRINCIPLES

⚹ THE ⚹
PEEBLES
PRINCIPLES

*Tales and Tactics from an Entrepreneur's
Life of Winning Deals, Succeeding
in Business, and Creating
a Fortune from Scratch*

R. Donahue Peebles
with J. P. Faber

John Wiley & Sons, Inc.

Published by John Wiley & Sons, Inc., Hoboken, New Jersey.
Published simultaneously in Canada.

Wiley Bicentennial Logo: Richard J. Pacifico

For general information on our other products and services or for technical support,
please contact our Customer Care Department within the United States at (800) 762-2974,
outside the United States at (317) 572-3993 or fax (317) 572-4002.

Wiley also publishes its books in a variety of electronic formats. Some content that appears
in print may not be available in electronic books. For more information about Wiley
products, visit our web site at www.wiley.com.

Library of Congress Cataloging-in-Publication Data:

Peebles, R. Donahue, 1960–
    The Peebles principles : tales and tactics from an entrepreneur's life of
winning deals, succeeding in business, and creating a fortune from scratch
/ R. Donahue Peebles, with J.P. Faber.
        p.   cm.—(Wiley trading series)
    "Published simultaneously in Canada."
    ISBN 978-0-470-09930-8 (cloth)
    1. Peebles, R. Donahue, 1960– 2. Businesspeople—United
States—Biography.   3. Real estate developers—United States—Biography.
I. Faber, J. P. (James Paris), 1954–   II. Title.
HC102.5.P384A3 2007
658.4'21—dc22

                                                                    2006103102

Printed in the United States of America.

10   9   8   7   6   5   4   3   2

❖ Contents ❖

❋ *Prologue* ❋

I was not born with a silver spoon in my mouth. I came from what most people would describe as a middle-class home, an only child in a one-parent household. But by the time I was twenty-seven I was a multimillionaire, and by the time I was forty-five I was worth more than a quarter of a billion dollars.

This book is the story of how I created that wealth, beginning with nothing. It is also a book about how to get rich, following the principles I learned over more than two decades of building my personal fortune. It is the breakdown of the deals that created that fortune and how I won those deals. It is a handbook of tales and tactics for a twenty-first-century entrepreneur.

Perhaps not everybody wants to get rich, but I would say that this particular desire is somewhere close to the core of the American dream. I know that I wanted to be rich when I was young. I wanted to achieve a financial stability that would free me from the worries over money that I experienced growing up. I wanted to leave that field of gravity forever.

My dream came true with my first big deal, when I was twenty-seven, which turned me into a multimillionaire. I have since consummated deals that dwarf my first win, but I have never had that same feeling.

1

I remember that day vividly, when I signed a letter of intent with the city of Washington, D.C., to develop an office building on Martin Luther King Avenue. The bricks and mortar were still to come, but that document meant I would own half of a multimillion-dollar project and would be receiving a mid-six-figure income annually for decades to come.

When I returned to my apartment, at about eight o'clock, a group of my friends were there. To celebrate, my girlfriend had gotten a cake from the Watergate Bakery, a white chocolate mousse cake, and a few bottles of champagne. It was a moment worthy of celebration, a breakthrough moment, the biggest event of my business career to date. It meant that my financial future was set from that moment on. I could quit right there if I wanted to; making half a million a year was more than I'd ever envisioned as a kid, when I was a teenager living with my mother and helping her make ends meet.

That night, lying in bed, I thought about it all. I thought back to how I was so impressed in high school when I learned that Walt Frazier was making $300,000 a year playing basketball. I'd wished that one day I could do that, and here I was, on my way to making more than that. It was just such a sense of relief. I was done. I didn't have to do another thing except make sure the construction company actually built the building. What a great moment.

It was more than just the money too. In that moment I was vindicated: The road that I had taken—to quit college after one year, to forgo the pursuit of a medical career in favor of real estate—had proven to be the correct one. The risks had paid off. As I lay in bed I even calculated how many years I would have been in medical school, followed by an internship and residency. At that point I would have been in my first year of internship, struggling financially. Now, with one deal, I was going to make more money each year than top doctors.

It was a bigger moment for me, perhaps, than someone from another background. I did not come from poverty or ignorance, but neither did I come from affluence, the kind that allows children to enjoy a sense of indifference about money. My mother and I had been on our own since she and my father divorced when I was five years old. Although my father was gainfully employed as a government clerk and auto mechanic, he never supported us. My mother did that, through a variety of jobs in the industry that I would end up choosing: real estate. She worked variously as a secretary, a broker, and a midlevel executive at Fannie Mae. We lived mostly in and around Washington, D.C., with a couple of years in Detroit, and our fortunes went up and down as her career changed. We did very well in Detroit, for example, when she had her own real estate brokerage. Later, when we moved back to Washington, she was a secretary again, and again we had to worry about money.

My point is that from the age of thirteen on I was aware of our financial limitations, about being able to afford the necessities of rent, groceries, and school clothes, and from that age on I wanted to make sure I could avoid those same worries when I became an adult. Fortunately, my mother was a very bright woman. Both she and the other members of my extended family—especially my grandfather, a hotel doorman who sent four of his five daughters to college—believed there were no limitations to what I could achieve in life. They gave me a great sense of self-confidence and ambition, and did the sorts of things, like my mother teaching me to play chess when I was in grammar school, that pay off so handsomely in later years.

This book is not an autobiography, however, except to the extent that such information helps readers understand that I entered the economic jungle with no resources beyond my native smarts, a decent education, and a good family background. This book is rather about the methodology of creating success and wealth and an explication of those methods.

I know I have had my fair share of good fortune, and I am thankful for it. But I believe the principles that guided me are principles that can help anyone to achieve success. I don't believe you need to be born with any special advantages, or any special instincts, other than a basic amount of intelligence and a drive to succeed.

I have written this book to share my principles with those who also aspire to make something of their lives in this land of opportunity called America. I do a lot of public speaking, and what I try above all to convey is the idea that the number-one challenge of the entrepreneur is *belief*. If you believe in yourself, and believe that anything is possible, then the road to success is wide open.

What follows in this book are the deals that took me from a wage earner to a world shaker, from a single man in a tiny apartment to a happily married man with a loving family and a substantial fortune. I learned something from each one of the deals I describe, as I hope you will. While the profession I chose was real estate, I believe that the same principles apply to any entrepreneurial endeavor.

Many people will say you have to be lucky to get rich, and I agree. But understand that luck, as a dear friend and mentor once told me, is "where opportunity and preparation merge." This is the kind of luck required to be a successful entrepreneur. My hope is that this book will give you the principles you need to prepare for the opportunities that will undoubtedly cross your path.

Good luck to you all. May the next big deal be yours.

✷ 1 ✷

From Ground Zero:
The First Deal

The basics for success in any business are threefold: Learn the industry, get into the mix of it, and go forward full of confidence. But that only takes you as far as the first deal. What you need after that is something very important, and it's not money. You won't have any money, anyway. Not if you started like I did, with nothing.

My first big deal made me a multimillionaire.

Before that, my net worth was similar to that of most people: what I could generate in wages by providing services. But I never took my eyes off the prize, and it only took me a little more than half of my twenties to achieve my goal of becoming a multimillionaire before the age of 30.

I started in my chosen profession of real estate by becoming a residential appraiser and then a residential sales agent. I was nineteen when I started. The fact that it was real estate is not important. What is important is that, regardless of the business you're in, you have to learn it. And the best way to learn it is to get into the mix. I learned the business from ground zero, in the trenches.

There are lots of ways to get into the real estate business. One way to learn is like Barron Channer, a young man who now works for me, who got his MBA from Wharton. He started as an intern with us, a bright young college kid, and got his foot in the door that way. That's one way to learn the business, through formal education.

I didn't have the educational background, and I also wanted to start at an early age and to get into the business on the ground floor. I didn't get to work in a nice environment like the one we're providing for Barron. Instead I went to work doing home appraisals for my mother, who was a real estate professional, and then for another appraisal firm. For the most part we did housing appraisals for HUD-insured loans and VA-insured loans. The VA—the U.S. Department of Veterans Affairs—was more middle class; HUD—the U.S. Department of Housing and Urban Development—was lower income. We would go into these areas that were rough, really rough.

That was in Washington, D.C., and it's where I learned the business. Today I have projects in lots of other places around the country, including Miami, San Francisco, Detroit, and Las Vegas, but it was in Washington—where I still own buildings—that I honed my skills. It was in Washington, too, where I learned the art of politics.

I was actually born in Washington, D.C., in 1960, the year that President John F. Kennedy took office. My mom moved us to Detroit for five years when I was eight, but when I was thirteen we went back to Washington. I lived there from that point on, except when I went to Rutgers University in New Jersey for a little less than a year in 1978.

In Washington I got my first taste of politics and learned how the political process works, up close and in person. Thanks to my mother's early understanding of the importance of developing political access and her skills of persuasion, I became a Congressional Page when I was sixteen. I spent my eleventh and twelfth grades on Capitol Hill, attending the U.S.

Capitol Page School on the top floor of the imposing Library of Congress building across the street from the U.S. Capitol. It was quite an experience.

My mom got me my job as a page through Congressman John Conyers Jr., a Democratic member of Congress whose Fourteenth Michigan District included about half of downtown Detroit, where we had lived. I had met him when I was a little kid. In fact, Conyers did not have sufficient seniority at the time to appoint me, so he called in a favor from a more senior member of Congress, Representative Gus Hawkins. Hawkins was the first African American to represent the State of California in Congress. He was a major civil rights leader and the co-author of the Humphrey-Hawkins Full Employment Act. I worked as his page for six months.

After that I wasn't about to leave Capitol Hill. The sense of power and excitement was just too much for me to return to ordinary teenage life. Fortunately, while I worked as a page, I developed a friendship with another California member of Congress, Representative Ron Dellums. He was a very cool congressman, a tall, well-dressed, and charismatic social activist. Ron is now the mayor of Oakland, California, and I am proud to say that I helped him raise funds used to run his successful campaign in 2006. I extended my stay on the Hill by another three months as his intern. I closed out my senior year as a paid staff aide in Conyers's office.

The time I spent in the halls of Congress was an education in the power of relationships and how they make politics work. I got to come across people like Tip O'Neill, then Speaker of the House, and Jim Wright, the House Majority Leader, and the flamboyant Charlie Rangel of New York. I also saw Marion Barry in those halls a few times, especially when I worked for Ron Dellums, who was Barry's good friend. Though I didn't know it then, this acquaintance would help me later on.

First, however, I had to learn my trade. After my abortive first year as a premed student at Rutgers, where I promptly ran out of both interest and money, I came home to learn the property appraisal business from my mother. In those days you didn't need a license; it was much less regulated than today. All you needed was experience, working as an apprentice to another appraiser—though you could take classes at American University or the University of Maryland, or with the American Institute of Real Estate Appraisers or the National Association of Independent Fee Appraisers, which sponsored courses at local universities. I took the courses, but I mostly learned through my mother and a guy named Charlie Merkle.

The appraisal business is a great one if you want steady income. Anyone who refinances or applies for a new mortgage has to have an appraisal done. My mother and Charlie appraised housing for Fannie Mae, the massive government sponsored mortgage corporation, and HUD and similar organizations as well as for local and national banks. If you were on an approved list of appraisers, you would get assignments on a rotating basis, for a set fee. At the time I think it was $90 for HUD appraisals and $150 for Fannie Mae assignments. I acted as a sort of subcontractor; I did the work, and they would review and sign off on the appraisals. I did jobs for my mother for $30 each and then later for Charlie at $60 each, so you can see why I was eager to work for Charlie. I found him through an ad in the paper, and it turned out I had seen him when I was going to the HUD offices, dropping off appraisals for my mother.

After a couple of years of doing this, I was ready to start my own appraisal company. I had served my time as an apprentice, learning the business and taking courses along the way. I had also become a real estate sales agent. But now I wanted to make more money and achieve the financial freedom that comes with it. The problem was that in order to launch as an independent appraiser, you needed to be approved by HUD. To get that approval, you needed connections and clout. Since this was Washington, those kinds of connections had to be political. I was going to have to get involved in politics and to make myself known in the community. And this is just what I began to do.

The year was now 1982. Mayor Barry was running for reelection, and I saw this as my opportunity. I would get involved by helping him get reelected.

Barry was in for a tough race, or so it seemed. He had been mayor for four years and was running for a second term against Patricia Harris, ironically enough a former secretary of HUD under President Jimmy Carter.

There was a big contrast between the two of them. Harris was perceived as a polished, articulate, and well-educated person, whereas Barry was seen as a rough guy from the streets. A lot of business leaders thought Harris would win the race, and people were climbing over each other to support her. But I thought Barry would win, because I felt the residents of Washington were more concerned with who was going to make their streets safe, get their trash picked up, and make sure they had decent schools and the like. Barry came across as better suited to deal with the drudgery of municipal politics, plus his efforts to rebuild downtown and the inner city were winning him lots of points among the voters. It's hard to see it now, but back then he had the image of a mayor who could make the city work.

I started getting involved in Barry's campaign by organizing events for him. My big day came when I held a "Meet the Mayor" event in the party room of my apartment building. The gathering was for residents of the area around Connecticut Avenue and Van Ness Street in Ward 3, a predominantly white district that was among the most affluent in the city. We served refreshments, drinks and so forth, and a few hundred people showed up for the opportunity to meet and talk with the mayor—including the heads of some local community and condo organizations, which thrilled me. Barry and his wife came, and I gave a speech introducing him. It cost all of about $1,000, and I got a couple of other people to cosponsor it with me.

As I mentioned, I had met Barry before as a teenage page, but this was when I began to develop a real relationship with him. The meet-and-greet event was a success, and I wanted to follow up on it. I knew from my Capitol Hill days that repetition and familiarity were extremely important in building political relationships but that fundraising was the best way to be taken seriously. Of course, fundraising was a tough task for me at the time, because I didn't know a lot of people who had money. Then I came up with a great idea.

Washington isn't like most other places in the United States, where you are prohibited from spending more on your campaign than you collect. In Washington you are allowed to deficit spend on your campaign, and Barry was doing just that. He would have bills to pay. I also knew that many of the city's major businesspeople were supporting Patricia Harris. But since I believed that Barry would win, I felt these same people would later flock to redeem themselves with the mayor.

Convinced of this, I scheduled a fundraising event for Barry a couple of days after the Democratic primary. This was the contest with Harris, and since the city was about 90 percent Democratic, winning it was the equivalent of winning the race. So I targeted everyone who had given $250 or more to the Harris campaign and invited them to a postprimary, $500-a-head breakfast at the Capitol Hilton just north of the White House. We did our mailing and then Barry won overwhelmingly; in fact, he beat Harris nearly four to one!

A couple of days later the fundraiser took place, and just as I thought, all the people who had supported Harris showed up in droves. It was standing room only; we had to bring in extra chairs and tables. I think we raised about $100,000 for Barry that morning.

This put me on the mayor's radar in a big way. When he spoke to the packed room, he thanked me for organizing the event, and right then I began to develop a relationship with his campaign staff—the very people who would run the D.C. government after the election. These were the people who could help me get on the HUD approved list so I could start my own firm, and I let them know about my ambitions in real estate.

Sure enough, a few weeks after the election, I got a call from a member of Barry's staff. She said there was an opening on the city's Real Estate Commission; would I be interested? Of course I would be, I told her, and she said that I'd get a call from a person named Betty King, who ran the board's office. She called and I sent her my résumé.

A few days later Betty King called back to say there was a problem: I was not qualified to serve on the Real Estate

Commission, since the post required a broker's license, and I only had a sales license. Instead, she thought I'd be more qualified to serve on the property tax appeal board, that in fact it would be perfect for me. There was only one small hitch: When she checked, they had just filled the only vacancies available, and the names had already been sent up to the mayor's office for his approval and signature. I asked when there would be another opening; she said in about two years.

I hung up and thought, I don't have two years to wait. So I called the deputy mayor for economic development, a guy named Ivanhoe Donaldson. I had gotten to know him as the mayor's former campaign chief, and now he was one of Barry's top advisors, a very powerful man in local government and politics—in fact, second to only the mayor. I had also met Ivanhoe when I as a teenager, at a political event hosted by my mother. I told him about the tax appeal board, that it was something I'd like to do and was qualified for, and that I'd like his help in getting appointed. He said he'd look into it and follow up, and that's just what he did. I got a call a couple of days later, again from Betty King, saying that she had some very good news: She was so impressed with me that she'd convinced the mayor to put me on the tax appeal board. My name was going to be sent to the city council for confirmation in the next day or two.

That's how I got on the property tax appeal board. It was a very prestigious position for me. It literally meant that I was qualified to review all the assessed properties in Washington, D.C., and it began to put me into the mix, interacting with major real estate players in the city.

More important, it helped me start my firm. I could now update my résumé to show HUD that I was on the property tax appeal board. Since I was qualified to review all of the properties in the city of Washington, D.C., for tax purposes, why wouldn't I be qualified to appraise some of the low-income housing there, too? I still had to call one of my friends from page school who was now a special assistant to Representative Dellums, whom I'd worked for as an intern. With my new appointment in hand, I got him to write a letter in the congressman's name and then follow it up with calls to the area director for HUD. The director agreed to meet with me, and after a few interviews and conversations, she finally put me on the list.

Now that I was on the HUD list as an approved appraiser, I was guaranteed a minimum level of work. Any lender making a HUD-insured loan has to use an appraiser from that list, and as I mentioned, HUD makes the assignments on a rotating basis. It also gave me an official status that allowed private banks and financial institutions to use me as an appraiser. I felt like a made man. I was on my way.

This all occurred in 1983. Barry had won the election and was sworn into office in January. During the spring of that year that I was appointed to the board, and shortly afterward I got on the HUD appraiser list. I was twenty-two, turning twenty-three. I quit working for Charlie Merkle and I started working for myself, initially out of my home. It was a thrill; I was beginning to generate a dependable source of income.

I did more than just produce a steady income, however. I was aggressive and ambitious, I worked hard at my new business, and I put every penny back into it. Initially, HUD tried me out with a few assignments and then increased my volume. I got more and more jobs because I was quick and reliable. As my business grew, I hired a couple of people, including my cousin, who was in college. I got so good at appraisals that within a couple of years I was being paid to review the compliance of HUD-approved lenders and underwriters. HUD even contracted me to review the work of other appraisers who were my peers.

As good as the appraisal business was going, however, it was my work on the tax appeal board that fascinated me.

The way it worked was as follows: Each year the city of Washington, D.C., through its Office of Assessors, reappraises all of its property at 100 percent of fair market value. This annual event includes all 165,000 commercial properties in the city. It is a massive process.

For the most part, the city underestimates the value of properties. But in some cases, it overestimates—or so the owners feel—and these assessments can be appealed. Remember, we are talking about properties worth tens of millions of dollars, even hundreds of millions of dollars, being assessed by underpaid city employees. And whereas residents pay as little as 1 percent of fair market value in annual property taxes, commercial properties pay as much as 5 percent. So you can imagine the magnitude of money involved.

In terms of timing, the city assessments are finished by March 1, with an appeals deadline of April 15. The board on which I served must then hear all of the appeals and make its decisions by June 1; at that time the tax base has to go into the city's revenue projections. So from April to June is an extremely busy three months, after which the board doesn't meet until the following year. And to give you an idea of how powerful the board was, we were giving back about $50 million annually in property tax refunds, of which about 90 percent went to commercial property owners.

Despite the enormous power and importance of the tax appeal board, however, it was not run with any degree of efficiency. To quote the old German politician Bismarck, if you like either sausages or laws, you don't want to know how they are made. I could say the same about the tax appeal board when I arrived. The chaos shocked me. It was operated, at best, like a bad phone company. Petitioners were told to come down to be heard between 9 A.M. and noon or between 1 and 5 P.M., and often even those hours were not kept. The place was filled with people who had to wait for hours to be heard. You had to take off at least half a day of work, if not the whole day. It was like a zoo, with all sorts of characters milling around.

At the close of my first season on the board, an opportunity arose to change this: The chairman's term was up. The previous mayor had appointed him, and now he would have to be reappointed by Barry. I was young and new at the game, but you didn't have to be a seasoned veteran to understand that things needed improvement.

My first reaction was to go to a board member who had come on at the same time as I did, an older guy who had worked appraising properties for the post office and had then retired to go into business for himself.

"Look," I said to him. "We need to make a change in the chairmanship, and we should get the mayor to do it. If you're interested, I think you're the man for the job."

"No, no, no," he said. "I'm not interested. Why don't you go for it?"

I hadn't considered it, but he said he would support me if I wanted the position. I said yes, as long as he would back me. He agreed, so I took my shot.

I went back to Ivanhoe Donaldson, the deputy mayor

for economic development, and scheduled a meeting. I told him I wanted to be chairman of the board. I said I was qualified and that I'd be a good choice because, as a supporter of the mayor, I'd have his best interests at heart and wouldn't make him look bad. The current chairman, I pointed out, ran the board in a terribly disorganized fashion; it was time to change things.

Donaldson said he was inclined to support me but that I would have to make the decision easier for the mayor. It was a classic lesson in politics: I'd have to get some of the business leaders whom the mayor respected to call him on my behalf, and then he, Donaldson, could go to the mayor and push for the appointment. I'd met some of these people during the fundraiser I gave, and some of them had come before the board. I called on them and asked for meetings; I even met with some of their law firms. I convinced them I was a good person for the job; they called the mayor for me and wrote letters. Then Ivanhoe scheduled a meeting for me with the mayor, in his office at City Hall.

I'll never forget that day. I went into Barry's office, the first time I'd ever been there, and it blew me away. It was huge, far bigger than any congressman's office, overlooking the Washington Monument and the White House, with a ceiling that was probably 20 feet high. I was awestruck but still determined to make my case. I think the mayor got a little bit of a kick out of this young guy who was in there trying to convince him to do this. I remember him asking me how old I was, and I said I was twenty-four.

"People are going to think I'm crazy," he said.

"But I won't let you down," I told him. "You will never be embarrassed by what goes on there. I will do a great job for you, and you will get a lot more out of me than you would with anyone else. Even if it's not me, you should pick someone else. Just don't reappoint this guy, because it's not in your best interests."

It was the truth, and Barry knew it.

I told him again I would work hard for him and do a good job, that I had some good support in the community, and that I wouldn't let him down. Then I shook his hand and left.

After the meeting, I learned that Barry had been elected president of the National Conference of Black Mayors and that they were going to be holding their midwinter conference in Washington. I talked to one of his aides and said, "You know, Barry should hold a reception welcoming all these mayors to Washington." Fine idea, the aide said, but who was going to pay for it?

That's when a light went on in my head. I said I'd raise the private dollars to do it. I couldn't afford to pay for it all myself, but I committed to the event on the spot. I went back to my office and started to call everybody I could think of to raise money. And I got it done. The mayor held his event and I sponsored it, along with some other people, welcoming the National Conference of Black Mayors to the D.C. Convention Center. That got me in front of Barry yet again, and at that point he began to seriously consider me. About a month later, I got a call again from Betty King, congratulating me on the mayor's decision to make me chairman of the property tax appeal board.

That was in December. The previous chairman, Samuel C. Reynolds, exited the board gracefully, and later I hosted a going-away party for him. I had learned that it's best never to burn bridges and be generous in victory. Many members of the board, especially the more senior ones, liked Reynolds, and I wanted to show them the proper respect as well. This was important, as I would need their support in my efforts to make significant changes at the board.

After the farewell party, I began to focus on how I would improve things. First I made a few personnel changes. Several seats had expired, and Barry allowed me the flexibility of naming some of the new board members. One of the persons I put there was the brother of my friend who worked for Congressman Dellums and who had helped me get my HUD approval. His brother was a real estate zoning lawyer who had worked for the city attorney's office, so he was well qualified. This is one of the important rules of politics: Don't forget those who help you, especially by returning the favor.

I then created four vice-chairman positions on the board and made each a committee head. This created a better organization, with more individuals carrying responsibility. I appointed two of the senior board members as vice chairmen and two of the guys who had joined the board when I did.

Next I reorganized the way the board was run. Once we started our three-month session, it was a marathon, from 9 A.M. in the morning until 6 or 7 at night. As I had pointed out to the mayor, appointments were loosely made, with people waiting hours to be heard. I changed this so that everybody got an appointment for a specific time.

In order to hear all the cases, the fifteen members of the board traditionally broke out into five, three-member panels. Before I was chairman, the panels were set up without rhyme or reason, some with senior people and others with only junior board members.

I made sure that every panel had some qualified people. More important, I insisted that each panel give clear explanations for the decisions its members made. Before I was chairman, some panels made decisions that had no apparent basis. I remember one of the first newspaper calls I got was about an old department store that had been assessed at $45 million. The board knocked that assessment down to $8 million, and a few months later it sold for $48 million. I looked at the decision and couldn't come up with a basis for it. All I could tell the *Washington Post* reporter was that it had been done before my time. I made sure we organized ourselves more professionally after that.

I was chairman for the four remaining years of my tenure on the board, at which time I asked not to be reappointed. By then Barry and I were good friends, and I was building my first office building. It didn't make sense for me to stay there anymore; I had reformed and professionalized the board, and I had an idea about starting a private tax appeals business of my own.

But my tenure was supremely important to my career. It made me one of the most powerful local government officials in the real estate industry. It also provided me access to the city's wealthiest and most successful business leaders; this helped me become a major political fundraiser for Barry and other local politicians. Even without the political advantages, I was now in the midst of things, and came to understand the business of development through the property tax appeals that I heard and got to examine. As chairman, I heard only the major appeals. Consequently I developed an understanding of how large commercial property transactions worked. And I knew that's what I wanted to do. So, once again, I started searching for an opportunity.

I had been looking at two different development deals. One was in Georgetown, right down the street from my office. (I had opened an office as my appraisal business grew.) It was an old incinerator site right on a hill overlooking the Potomac River. Twenty years later it would be redeveloped as a Ritz-Carlton Hotel and residential condo project, but then it was still owned by the city, and had been abandoned for many years. The other deal involved a public library branch and a police substation, sitting together on a very valuable piece of commercial property right in the west end of downtown. This site remains undeveloped today. I had approached the city about both properties when I came across the opportunity that would lead to my first building, an office tower at 2100 Martin Luther King Jr. Avenue.

When I opened the offices for my appraisal business, I leased more space than I needed, so I sublet the excess. One of the tenants was a real estate broker who introduced me to some potential investors for the two commercial property deals I was looking at—three guys who had offices in Chevy Chase, Maryland. Meanwhile my other subtenant, a mortgage broker who had served on the appeals board, came to me with *the* big opportunity. He had a client with a vacant piece of land in Anacostia, an economically neglected area targeted for redevelopment by Barry. It was primarily African American and had once been a thriving commercial corridor, but had deteriorated after the 1968 riots.

The city had already targeted the area for redevelopment and had leased office space in a building that was undergoing renovation. The empty site owned by tenant's client was across the street from that building; apparently the city had targeted it for redevelopment as well. A local developer was negotiating to buy the site from my tenant's client, and they were haggling over the price. The landowner wanted $900,000, but the developer only wanted to pay $750,000. The developer said there was no other use for the property because the neighborhood was so run down, and he was right. He told the landowner that he was the only person who would ever buy it from him; to prove the point, he showed the landowner a letter signed by Barry, as mayor of Washington, committing the city to leasing office space in a building on that site if the developer could put one there.

My tenant showed me the letter and suggested I make an offer to the landowner. I thought about it and asked myself: If Marion Barry wants to lease space in Anacostia, why wouldn't he lease it from me? So I called my three investors—Stephen Maged, Stephen Greenleigh, and Gus Papaloizos—and asked them if they would like to partner with me in an office building preleased by the D.C. government. We would develop it and own it, but lease it before we started. They said they'd be very interested. So I set up a meeting with the landowner at Maged and Greenleigh's office.

When the landowner got there, I reminded him of my position—I was beginning to gain some prominence at the time—and said that if the mayor was willing to sign a deal with this other developer, he'd certainly be willing to sign one with me. I told him that I could clearly finance the deal through my partners. I also agreed to pay him the $900,000 he wanted for the property. In exchange, he'd have to give me time to make my deal with the city.

It worked. The seller was convinced we could do it, and signed a contract. It was to become my classic structure: their price, my terms. He agreed to give us a normal due diligence period, to check out the deal and arrange financing, and then time beyond that if we agreed to pay whatever it cost him to carry the property until we got the deal done.

I then wrote the city a letter, the mayor a letter, and the city council person in that ward a letter, advising them all that I now had the property under contract and that I knew the city wanted to lease office space in that location. The city had offered to pay $22.50 per square foot to the original developer, so I offered them a deal at $18.75 per square foot. And I said I would build a bigger building, so it would have a greater economic impact on the community.

My partners and I actually had a big argument about offering the lease for less. They wanted to go in at the same price, but I said we couldn't do it. Because of my relationship with Barry, we would have been crucified. We had to make the offer so defensible that Barry could never back out; if he did so, he'd look like a fool. The way around it for us was to put up a building of 100,000 square feet instead of 22,000 square feet. We'd make more money even if we kept the numbers per square foot down for the city. I had to fight my partners on that one, but I prevailed and in the end it saved the deal. Because when we announced that we controlled the property and wanted the city lease, all hell broke loose.

For starters, the city council person for the ward was upset because she was a friend of the other developer. I remember Barry calling me up—he and the city administrator were in his office and had me on speaker phone—and telling me: "Don, I was just with [the ward council member] and she stormed out of my office yelling and screaming about this deal in Anacostia."

"Well, Mr. Mayor," I said, "I was simply out there buying a property and trying to do a deal. But if it's creating a problem for you, and if you want me to, I'll walk from it. I was only trying to do what you said."

"What do you mean?"

"Well, you wanted to economically empower the neighborhood, you wanted to support African American–owned businesses, and I'm an African American–owned business. I'm also a supporter of yours and your friend. Most important, I'm charging the city a lot less money. But if you want me to walk from the deal I'll walk from it, if it's that important to you."

"Will you lose any money?"

"Yes, I will," I said.

"Then no, I don't think you need to walk from the deal."

At that point the negotiations began. During the process, somebody—most likely the disgruntled developer—leaked the story to the *Washington Post* that I was getting an inside deal. An investigative reporter from the *Post* called me up. He'd already talked to some of Barry's friends and political supporters. When I got the call, I calmly called one of the mayor's aides whom I had worked with on the board and asked how I should handle it. I'd never done something like this before.

"My recommendation would be to go and talk to him," she told me, "but tape record it so there are no mistakes about the facts."

And so I did, scheduling a meeting and going over for an interview that seemed to last for hours. I was as forthcoming as I could be and kept reiterating that it was a less expensive deal for the city, that the city had already made a commitment to go into the neighborhood before I was in

20

the picture, and that the mayor was not doing me any favors. The story appeared on the front page of the *Washington Post* the next day, right on 1A.

The story didn't hurt at all, as it turned out. Actually it helped. Barry wasn't worried about it. He had already talked to me the evening before, to tell me it was a one-day story. And it put some pressure on him to move things along. We'd already signed a letter of commitment, but after the story came out we quickly finished documenting the final version of the lease.

As far as getting the deal done with my investors, that was another story. While it was my idea to do the office building, and I had seen the opportunity, I was missing one key ingredient to getting it done: the money. Actually I lacked two missing ingredients: I had no money and no track record. I needed a partner who had both. So I came to agreement with my three investors where I would deliver the deal and they would supply the money and credit, and we'd split the ownership 50/50.

The problem was that when it came time to close on the deal, they wanted to limit my share to the minimum requirement for a minority partner, which was 25 percent. We had also committed to contribute 10 percent of the profits generated by the project to a local nonprofit community development corporation (CDC) as well as donating the existing historic storefront to them after we developed the project. My new partners wanted the 10 percent to come from my side of the ledger as well.

The ensuing negotiations revealed an important lesson for me, and for anyone who wants to succeed in business. I was in a position of relative weakness, economically speaking. I *needed* the deal. But when it comes to negotiating, you have to act like you're in a position of strength even when you're not. If you work for Credit Suisse or for Lehman Brothers, and you control a lot of money, it's easy to negotiate a deal. If it doesn't work out, there are no consequences. When you are on the other side, and you need the other person's money, it takes finesse.

If that's the case, you must have a couple of things. First, you've got to have a very good deal and you've got to have some greedy people on the other end who want to maximize their dollars. You've also got to be willing to walk away. And I mean walk away with nothing and have to start all over again and find somebody else.

There is one other thing you should do, especially for a first deal: You should protect yourself by hiring someone who has done it before and who knows the business. I hired a lawyer who had done big real estate transactions so many times that he knew what was reasonable and what we could get. He even had a client base so that if these investors didn't do the deal, he would take me to someone else and they'd do it and give me 50 percent without flinching.

I might not have carried it off without this attorney. Back then I was not very confrontational; I figured some money was better than none, and I was desperate to get the deal done. But my attorney, Louis Pohoryles, convinced me to believe in the value of my deal and my contribution to it.

This advice was particularly important because I had made one colossal mistake. When it came to putting the property under contract, my investors put it in their names and agreed they would assign it to a joint venture, once we made our deal. I would never make that mistake again, and controlling the property—usually by way of an option to buy—would become the basis for my future deals. But for now, I remember the sting when they pointed out how they controlled the property.

Fortunately, my attorney fired right back that *we* controlled the tenant. And that proved to be a more important lever.

"You know what?" he told them. "There isn't a shortage of land in southeast Washington right now. We'll find some land elsewhere, and we'll take the tenant and go somewhere else."

The money guys had to think about it. They could keep the property and not do the deal with me and make no money; the property in Anacostia, without my tenant, wasn't worth the money they were paying for it. They knew that and they knew that Barry wasn't going to screw me. There was no way he was going to do a deal with three rich white guys from Maryland who were kicking the small minority guy out, especially one who was his close friend. So the negotiations really came down to a matter of playing hardball and staring them down.

We held a meeting in the boardroom in Lou's offices, which took up an entire floor of a downtown high-rise. The boardroom was a large, glass-walled space that opened onto the lobby, with a long conference table that accommodated thirty or forty people. I was nervous because I had never negotiated anything close to a transaction of this size, and I was humbled by the sense of power the law firm exuded.

Maged and Greenleigh attended, taking seats on one side of the table, while I sat with my attorney on the other side. They were an impressive pair: Greenleigh, a former justice department lawyer who had attended Yale Law School, graying at the temples, and Maged, a wheeler-dealer entrepreneur with a beard, dressed in Armani.

Lou began the meeting, saying he just wanted to talk about the deal. "The deal we propose is a 50/50 deal together. Don's bringing the tenant, he found the property, he found the project, and you guys will go and get the financing. You will build it collectively and everybody will make a lot of money."

"We offered Don 25 percent and we're giving the community development corporation another 10 percent," Greenleigh said. "And that's it; we're not giving another penny more."

"Well, if that's the case, I guess this meeting is over. Don will take his deal to someone else," Lou told them.

Talk about hardball. A few sentences later Maged and Greenleigh walked out. I went home disappointed but Lou told me not to worry, just to continue moving the deal forward with the city as if nothing were wrong.

I had to wait Maged and Greenleigh out for over two weeks. Finally Maged called and suggested we get together for a drink. We met down the street from my apartment, at the Westin Hotel. Maged made an offer of 40 percent for me and 10 percent for the CDC, which was called the Southeast Neighborhood Development Corporation. I said that if we went 50/50, I'd deal with the CDC myself. He agreed. It would be 50/50 across the board, including all fees, and I would be co-managing partner with Maged. I got along well with him from that point on, and we worked together as a team. That was another great lesson for me: Don't take negotiations personally, and don't get emotionally worked up. If the final deal is a good one, and both parties come out winning, the rough and tumble of holding your own doesn't leave any scars. In fact, it may earn you a measure of respect.

The agreement I reached with the CDC was that their 10 percent interest would come off the top once we reached a certain level of income and that it would come from my share of that excess income. As it turned out, the Southeast Neighborhood CDC failed as an organization, and their interest went to the Anacostia Economic Development Corporation. I ended up buying that interest out for $250,000 a few years after the launch.

We signed the deal, and construction of the building at 2100 Martin Luther King Jr. Avenue was started in 1987. I was twenty-seven. It would take eighteen months to complete the office tower, but it immediately began producing income in the form of a developer's fee that my partners and I split 50/50. More important, the deal, on paper at least, made me an instant multimillionaire.

As it turned out, it was a great deal for everyone. The investors put down only $250,000 in cash and borrowed the rest, and we created a building that today is worth $40 million and has produced an annual mid-six-figure income for me—and a similar income for my partners—each of the past eighteen years. I retain my 50 percent interest to this day. After I did the deal, I went and bought myself a reward for all the hard work: a $1 million house in Washington's Embassy Row neighborhood, the future site of many political fundraisers.

EPILOGUE TO CHAPTER 1

My early years taught me numerous lessons, among them that you must believe in yourself, that you must put yourself into the mix, and that you have to play politics in whatever business or industry you become involved in. Those years also taught me that it really does matter whom you know and whom you help—and who helps you—along the way. These things do bear fruit and do come back to you.

Another thing I learned was that, if it's your goal to be an entrepreneur, you need to put yourself in position to be an entrepreneur. That means being free to pursue opportunities as they arise. Being an independent sales agent, for example, is an entrepreneurial career. You don't really have a boss, you're not a nine-to-five worker, and consequently you can manage your own schedule. As an appraiser I was my own boss. Even before I started my company I was actually not an employee of Charlie Merkle but an independent subcontractor. It gave me the flexibility to work on the tax appeal board. I had control of that most valuable commodity: my time.

These are long-term, strategic considerations. On the short-term, tactical level, I learned some very important things as well.

The first was that, in any deal you go into, you've got to protect yourself. If you want to swim with the sharks, you have to bring a shark cage along or run the risk of being eaten alive. This can be something as simple as a confidentiality or noncompete agreement or a copyright or trademark. In my case the shark tank was a savvy, take-no-prisoners lawyer. He was necessary because of my blunder in failing to secure my share of the property in the beginning and because of my own uncertainty in the face of tough negotiations.

He taught me another important lesson: In any negotiations, you have to be able to stick to your guns.

A lot of entrepreneurs, working on their first deal, accept terms that are less than what they want—or deserve. This is only natural. In the hunt for the first major deal, there is tremendous internal pressure to get something done, to break that barrier and go on to the next level. There is also a need to make some kind—any kind—of financial headway.

At these moments, you must have the courage to not back down. You must present the appearance of strength at your weakest moment. Ultimately it comes down to the courage to walk. There is a saying in poker that sometimes you have to be willing to sleep in the streets. This means you have to be willing to lose all your money. A hand is sometimes so good you have to call it and no good if you don't.

This leads to the most important thing I learned in my first big deal. To continue with the poker analogy, if you want to have a strong hand, one worth betting on, you've got to hold some of the top cards. In other words, you have to control some key element of the deal. It may be an option, it may be a lease, it may be a patent, it may be a copyright, it may be a personal connection; when you come to the table to negotiate with investors—and you will have to, to raise capital—you must be essential to the deal you are making. In the case of the 2100 MLK property, it was my relationship with the tenant, and hence the future cash flow, that made the whole thing work. That control was more important than the money.

PEEBLES GROUND RULES

- Always believe in yourself.

- Master your business.

- Put yourself into the mix.

- Protect yourself from the sharks.

- Be your own boss in your profession.

- Be prepared to lose everything.

- Appear strongest in your weakest moments.

Peebles Principle #1: Control the Deal

When going into any major deal, you need absolute control over some key element. If you want to win as an entrepreneur, never negotiate a deal unless you are essential to it.

✷2✷

The Washington Marriott:
No Money Down

My second big deal took a lot of creativity and a fair share of nerve. But it taught me that, if you are willing to take on the early risk, you can make your money going into a deal, not just at the other end.

By the end of the 1980s I had closed down my property appraisal business. Doing low-cost residential appraisals, which meant that I had to go into the field personally, wasn't consistent with my new image as a developer. I wanted to elevate my career.

Since I was now enjoying a steady stream of income from the 2100 Martin Luther King building, and since my term with the tax appeal board was over, I decided to invest in a new, more upscale business. It would make use of my old understanding of property values, my new understanding of the appeals process, and of all the contacts I had made along the way. I decided to start a tax appeal business.

The proposition was simple enough: I would argue cases for property owners who wanted to appeal tax assessments. I would take their cases on a contingency basis. If I lost, the client would pay nothing. If I won, they would pay me between 25 and 33 percent of what they saved. What was equally attractive to me was the rhythm of the business: From January to March you'd market yourself to clients, mostly by taking them to lunch; in March the tax assessments were sent to these potential clients; in April you filed their appeals; in May you argued them; in June the decisions were issued and you billed your clients. From then until the end of the year you were free to pursue other projects, or take a nice long vacation, or both.

In my first season I argued cases for twelve clients, and I won eleven of them. My clients were thrilled. I earned $400,000.

What happened next would teach me a superb lesson in the use of media. One of my competitors called up the *Washington Post* and pointed out how successful the former chairman of the tax appeal board—a friend of the mayor's—had been in winning cases for clients. The *Post* thought this would make a great story because it raised the question of conflicts of interest and the whole concept of "revolving doors" between the public and private sectors.

I had already learned from my first story in the *Post* that it's always better to embrace the press than run from it. In my case I had nothing to fear; I was proud of my successes, and I had already cleared the conflict question with the city attorney. He would actually go on record saying that it wasn't a conflict. What I instead saw was an opportunity to get publicity for my business that I couldn't buy, or if I did pay for would cost me a fortune.

When the story came out, it backfired for the competitors who had "leaked" it. They were an old-line law firm, and they expected that my clients would flee from the controversy. Boy, were they wrong! What the article said was that I was doing nothing illegal and that my success rate was twice that of my competitors. What my competitors failed to realize was that real estate developers are entrepreneurs. As long as it wasn't illegal and didn't look bad, they would go with whoever saved them the most money. Demand for my services soared.

At about this time I met my wife, Katrina, and I really credit her with the ultimate success of my tax appeal business. I had looked at it as a stepchild to my career as a developer and hadn't made a big effort to grow it. In 1990, after my first tax appeal season, we got engaged, and we broke the old rule of separating business and pleasure. Katrina immediately recognized the potential of the company and, utilizing her journalism and marketing background, helped expand it into the largest property tax appeals business in the city. Among her ideas was the creation of *The Peebles Property Tax Letter*, a quarterly report like *The Kiplinger Letter*. It positioned me as an expert. Over the next five years our business would grow from a dozen clients to more than four hundred a year, generating about $4 million a year in revenues.

Before that happened, however, the next big opportunity revealed itself.

In the late summer of 1992, I got some information from a friend of mine who was a commercial real estate broker. She was a good friend whom I'd known then for maybe six or seven years. I'd met her socially in the arts circle—she was active in the Washington Project for the Arts—and as a broker she had talked to me about a couple of deals in the past. That summer she called me and said there was an opportunity downtown, where she knew I'd been in the market looking for a property.

"I've got something good for you," she said one afternoon. "It's a building downtown that the Resolution Trust Corporation [RTC] has taken back, and they're going to sell it off."

There were a few complications, including the fact that the University of the District of Columbia (UDC) had broken a lease on the property, but she knew I was no stranger to the ways of the D.C. government.

What was interesting was the deadline for the bid. It was August at that point, and the bids—sealed bids—were due in the middle of September. Now, in Washington, everybody's gone in August, nobody was focusing on deals, and very few people were in the process of buying real estate that summer. I was done with my tax business for the year, so I thought I'd take a shot at it.

The property was on the corner of 9th and F streets, an old historic building dating from about 1890. It was one of the first savings banks in the city—the ten-story Riggs Bank building—and was on the National Register of Historic Places. At 900 F Street, it was in the east end of downtown (kitty-corner to the National Portrait Gallery), which was the original downtown before development moved west. Over the years the west side of downtown had become a more desirable location, and the east end had decayed. But when redevelopment got hot in the 1980s, it came back east, with a lot of new retail. That's where the available land was. And it had reached to within a few blocks of this property. I liked the idea and decided to pursue it.

The first thing I needed was a partner. The original loan amount on the building before the RTC had foreclosed on it was around $16 million. I wasn't going to bid anything close to that, but even so, I still didn't have the cash to buy the property at that time.

At this point the tax appeal business wasn't throwing off the cash I needed, and besides my share of 2100 Martin Luther King, the only buildings I owned were my houses on Board Branch Road and Q Street (my then current and former residences). That was all. I hadn't bought anything else at that point and had never owned anything in downtown D.C. But I knew I had to be downtown to be a major player. And for that I needed to find an investor.

So I started putting out feelers for partners. I contacted various developers and some of my business clients—one in particular who said he thought I walked on water when it came to tax appeals. Ultimately they all thought it was too big of a risk, that the area was still too uncertain in terms of future development. Finally, I talked to my co-managing partner in 2100, Stephen Maged, to see if he was interested. I was very glad at that point that we had remained friendly partners, because it turned out that his partner Gus Papaloizos—the third wheel of the three Maryland investors in 2100—had an uncle who wanted to invest in real estate. Steve thought he might be able to put something together.

Meanwhile I was getting married to Katrina, with the date set for September 12. For our honeymoon we went to Montana, where I had purchased a vacation home for us; Katrina's parents had a vacation home there as well, in a town called Big Fork, in the northwestern part of the state. We went there for two weeks, and it was during that time that Steve, and Papaloizos's uncle, came in. We needed a $250,000 deposit, and they posted it. For my part I had to get the bid documents notarized in Big Fork and off to the RTC, but there wasn't a notary to be found. I ended up having to go to a place called Kalispell, and I submitted the bid even though it was my honeymoon.

About two months went by and we heard nothing. We had bid very low—$5 million for a 150,000-square-foot building—hoping we'd be the lone bidder. There were no requirements either for a minimum bid or a minimum number of bidders. It turns out there was one other party, but they had bid even less! So, the good news was that we had placed the winning bid. The bad news was that the RTC did not want to sell the building that cheaply; at one point it had been worth $20 million.

Now, during this time, Bill Clinton was running for president. In a stroke of good fortune, Katrina and I had hosted a fundraiser for him at our home on Broad Branch that past spring. In fact, we came back to Washington in late September from our honeymoon because we were co-hosting another fundraiser for him at the historic Corcoran Gallery of Art. Later, after he won, Katrina and I were hosts at the presidential inaugural; we hosted a VIP party and one of the balls, and we were corporate sponsors. We were actually with the Clinton campaign in Little Rock on election night. So we had a lot of access to Clinton and his team, something that would help with the deal.

We would need that access because, months after submitting the winning bid, the RTC still refused to sell. I was indignant. I had won the bid fair and square, and had invested time and money doing so. They said it was too low, and noted that only two bidders had come forth. Again, that was hindsight; there had been no minimum requirement for number of bidders or size of the bid.

Several more months went by, and by then the RTC had filed a lawsuit against the UDC for breaking its lease for the building. This was not good for me, since I was buying the building with the lease in place; I had planned to go to the

D.C. government and enforce the lease or get them to settle. The clock was now beginning to tick.

So I talked to Matt Gorman in the treasury department. I had met Matt during the Clinton campaign. He was a campaign person who had gone to work for the administration and now reported to Roger Altman, who was then deputy secretary of the Treasury. I asked Matt to look into this and he did, and suggested I write a letter laying it all out. Katrina and I worked late into the night to write the letter, as he suggested, and in it I argued my case persuasively, and to the right person: Altman had jurisdiction over the RTC. Ultimately he agreed that I was entitled to the bid that I had won.

In the end, it took until March of 1994 to sell me the building that I had won in September of 1992. But that time lag turned out to confer its own set of advantages.

The first thing that happened was that my partners, Maged and the uncle, were getting impatient. They weren't happy with the progress of the deal, and they wanted to take control of it from me. We were at a standoff, however, because while trying to negotiate a partnership agreement between us, the bid was in my name. They basically said that if I insisted on control, they would take a pass and I would have to immediately pay them back their deposit. They didn't think I could come up with the money. But it had been a great year for my tax appeal business, thanks to the national real estate meltdown that was in full swing by 1993. Everybody wanted to lower their tax assessments, and they were appealing right and left. I wrote Maged and the uncle a check for $250,000 and took over the deal myself, 100 percent (it had previously been 50/50).

Later that year I won the ruling from Deputy Secretary Altman. They agreed to my original bid of $5 million but wanted to negotiate my provision that the RTC finance $4.5 million of it through a seller take-back note for five years. We ultimately compromised at 85 percent seller financing for a mortgage of $4.25 million, and we signed a contract in late 1993, with an eye to closing in early '94. That gave them time to clean up various legalities associated with the sale. It also gave me the time to pursue the UDC.

The UDC had originally leased the building for their school of business, but they had since acquired a building that abutted their uptown campus, so they moved the business school there. When I bid for the building, I included the rights to the lease from the date of the bid; so, once I had a contract in place, those rights now belonged to me— or soon would, upon closing.

I went and met with the chairperson of the UDC Board of Trustees, Michelle Hagens. She was a fellow developer I knew who had the best interests of the city at heart. I met with her and another member of the board, and explained that I now owned the rights to the lease. My offer was that if they gave me cash at the closing, I would settle for 50 cents on the dollar. But if they made me sue, I would never settle, and I would end up getting the disputed funds plus my attorney fees, the late fees, and the interest as well.

The UDC owed $2.7 million on the lease. They agreed to settle with me for $1.25 million at closing.

When it came time to close on the deal, I would still need $750,000 in cash for the equity portion. For that money I went to my bank, BB&T, then called Franklin National Bank. I had a relationship with the president of the bank, who was a real entrepreneurial banker, and a relationship with the bank's executive vice president. I had met them earlier in the political environment and had gone to them a few years earlier when I was looking for a new relationship with a bank. They had begun to give me small lines of credit, but $750,000 was the largest loan I ever borrowed from them. I secured it with my partnership interest in the 2100 building, but that partnership was not particularly liquid. So it was basically an unsecured loan. Still, they agreed, going forward on the good faith that: (1) I knew what I was doing; (2) the downtown was going to come back; (3) I had bought the property well; and (4) I had a tax appeals business that gave me a lot of cash flow so I could pay the loan down, even if the project was not successful.

The closing took place on March 31, 1994. The purchase price for the building was $5 million. I put down the $750,000 from BB&T bank and borrowed $4.25 million from the RTC in the form of a note. Then the UDC brought a check for $1.25 million to the closing, which I put into an account as an interest-reserve against the RTC loan. We agreed that I would use it for predevelopment and marketing costs for the building and as a reserve against interest and real estate taxes. It meant I could carry the property for about three years while I searched for a development deal.

So, if you look at the cash I had to put down at closing, combined with the UDC money, I actually made a profit of $500,000 the day I closed. I got my $250,000 deposit back at closing as well, so, in effect, I closed my first deal in downtown Washington, D.C., with no money. I sent bottles of Dom Perignon champagne to the brokers and lawyers involved, and did an announcement in the business magazine *Regardie's*, which was then the hottest publication in town.

The celebration was short-lived, however. Next came the saga of how to actually make the property work.

Because the building was in downtown D.C., I tried to

lease it to the federal government. I tried the Social Security Administration, the Justice Department, and then several other government agencies. I also tried to find private sector tenants. But the office market was soft at the time, and we were saddled by an additional burden: The building didn't have any parking. As an historic building, it had been constructed before there was any underground parking. That made it tough to compete for tenants.

Nothing worked for a year and a half, and by that time I was spending a lot of time in Miami working on my Royal Palm Hotel deal, which I will describe later. For the sake of this transaction, the Royal Palm project put me in contact with a lot of people in the hospitality industry and made me realize that the solution for the D.C. building was to make it into a hotel; the parking requirements are minimal by comparison. As it turned out, one of my tax appeal clients was a company called Hospitality Partners, which managed hotels on a franchise basis for major brands. I approached them, and they came back with a proposal for a Hampton Inn. It didn't intrigue me; I wanted an elegant, luxury hotel. So I waited.

Now, during the time I pursued the bid for 900 F Street, the city was busy with its own agenda. Marion Barry had left office in January 1991, and Sharon Pratt Dixon was sworn in as the new mayor. During her four-year term, the city had embarked on a major effort to lure the Washington Bullets from Maryland back to the city. Part of the deal included building them a new basketball arena, on a site that was literally two blocks from my property. The city ultimately succeeded, though it was not until 1995, when Barry was back in office (he won again in 1994), that the newly christened (far more politically correct) Washington Wizards moved to their new home.

The deal had been publicized well in advance, of course, and that created activity in the east end of downtown, where the real estate market was starting to come back. More and more people were buying in that area, because that's where the opportunities were. When the law firm Arnold & Porter announced they were going to move their firm's headquarters two blocks from our site, I knew the time had come. That was in 1996, after I had won the Royal Palm project, and the hotel market nationwide was making a comeback.

I called back Hospitality Partners, and they took another look at the property. Their analysis of the area showed that the environment would now support a Marriott or Courtyard by Marriott. We decided that a Courtyard would be better because it would still command a top rate as a business hotel, but would cost less because we wouldn't have to build all the meeting and public space of a full-service Marriott.

By this time I had spent a lot of money winning the Royal Palm bid, and I was still carrying the 900 F Street building. I had also bought a lot of other real estate near the site. So money was going out but not as much was coming in, and I needed to do something soon.

The solution was Jim Donohoe of Donohoe Construction. His firm had built the 2100 Martin Luther King building for me, and he was an investor in Hospitality Partners. I offered him a part of the building for a price he couldn't refuse—$1.5 million in cash plus assumption of 45 percent of the outstanding debt for a 45 percent interest.

That may not seem like a good price for a building that I had paid $5 million for several years earlier. But it did a couple of important things. First, it gave me a cash infusion. Second, it tied both Hospitality Partners and Donohoe Construction to the project, since they ended up taking the 45 percent share together as a limited liability company (LLC) partnership. So, it would encourage the best hotel management deal from Hospitality Partners and would keep construction on time and within budget, since Donohoe would build it. (In fact, Donohoe agreed to guarantee the debt for construction and to cover any cost overruns.) Finally, the agreement called for me to get additional amounts of money after we closed on the construction loan; I would get reimbursed all of my costs, including the expense of carrying the property from the time I acquired it, which amounted to more than $1 million. And because I would be the developer, I would receive an additional fee of $500,000 for that function.

We would later sell off half the project for $8 million in mezzanine equity, and by early 1997 we had a deal and could do the project. We got our plans approved by the city's Historic Preservation Board (including retaining the bank vault and turning it into a meeting room), and by 1999 the work was finished and the hotel ready for occupancy. In addition to more than $2.5 million I made along the way, I would end up with 28.5 percent ownership without any liability, creating another excellent stream of income to use for future investments.

For the grand opening we held a ribbon-cutting ceremony with Bill Marriott and Anthony Williams, then the new mayor of Washington, along with several city council members. It was quite gratifying. We were part of the new wave of development in downtown Washington, and we had restored a beautiful historic structure. The night before the opening I checked into the hotel with Katrina and our son, Donahue III, when it was empty, with nobody there other than staff gearing up for opening day. It was a terrific moment for me.

EPILOGUE TO CHAPTER 2

The hotel at 900 F Street, which is today officially known as the Courtyard Washington Convention Center, has been a tremendous success. It outperforms most of the Marriotts in its class throughout the country, including in Washington, D.C., and it's been a good cash cow for us. It produces hundreds of thousands of dollars in net income every year, and I have no liability and no management responsibilities.

The project also taught me a few things that I had begun to figure out with the 2100 Martin Luther King building. First, if you can gain control of a deal, you can use other people's money; for the Marriott, I put the bid in my name, while my partners put the deposit down. Second, it confirmed that you have to recognize your limitations and bring in someone who's done it before. I'm not a hotel expert, so I brought in one as a partner.

The birth of the Courtyard by Marriott also showed the value of creativity in a deal. I thought it was very creative to tie the builders and managers of the hotel to the project as investors, which gave them a vested financial interest—and not just on the up side. I wanted them to have significant dollars at stake, so I negotiated a provision that no matter what the cost overruns were, Donohoe had to put up my share. And as for any operating deficits, if the hotel ran at a loss, Hospitality Partners would have to put up my share. Bringing in Hospitality Partners and Donohoe as partners also maximized my time. I was too busy with the Royal Palm in Miami to have to manage the Marriott project; I had to bring in not only somebody who could do it, but someone who would be honest and motivated. The only way to do that was to have them put their money in and their name on the line as a guarantee.

Having said that, however, the overriding Peebles Principle that came from this deal is: Taking the early risk produces the greatest rewards. Sometimes the only way you can create wealth is to take the early risk, when most people—and most companies—don't have the appetite for it. Being a pioneer in any new business environment means going in early, when it's risky, but that means you can get in for very little. Later, when it's safe and there is momentum, then it costs considerably more to get in—whether it's buying stock or leasing a retail outlet. The price that I had bid—$5 million for a property that had been on the market for triple that—meant I had already made my profit at the moment of purchase.

I would also add two notes to this deal.

The first one is an ironic note: My grandfather was a doorman at the Wardman Park Hotel on Woodley Road in Washington for forty-one years, now the Marriott Wardman Park. I like to I think about that and what it says about opportunity in America, how a doorman's grandson could become the owner of a Marriott in Washington.

The second is a financial addendum—call it following good money after good. After I bought the old 900 F Street bank building, I bought other sites around it. I assembled three buildings next door to the property, another four within the square block, and one more across the street. When I tried to purchase the nearby Woody's Department Store site, the *Washington Times* did a story about me, with a little box entitled "Mr. Peebles' Neighborhood." Ultimately, years later, I sold these buildings, for huge profits.

PEEBLES GROUND RULES

- Creating cash flow leads to bigger deals.

- Use the media rather than running from it.

- Whenever possible, use other people's money.

- Be creative, especially in negotiating contract concessions.

- Be prepared to litigate to enforce your rights.

- Always tie your partners to the success—and failure—of a deal.

- Be prepared to be patient and endure.

Peebles Principle #2: Make Your Money Going In

The best risk to take in any deal is the early risk, when you can get in for the least. Do this and you make your money at the front end—which is where you want to make it—and not at the back end.

❧ 3 ❧

North Capitol and
G Streets: *Carpe Diem*

A lot of people say that luck is what makes the difference between those who are successful and those who are not. I think luck plays a big part, but luck means nothing if you aren't ready to act on a good opportunity when it presents itself.

Now let's go to the beginning of 1994, I think it was February. Jeff Cohen, a friend of mine, took me to lunch to meet a guy named Chris Roth. Cohen was a local entrepreneur, a developer who also had founded and sold a couple of banks in Washington. In fact, his bank, City National Bank, gave me the mortgage on my first home on Embassy Row. He was a very big supporter and personal friend of Marion Barry, and that's how I originally met him, during the 1982 Barry campaign. He thought it would be good to meet Roth, since Roth was with Trammel Crow, one of the nation's biggest real estate firms. Cohen was playing matchmaker.

As it turns out, there was a deal that Trammel Crow had been monitoring. Roth brought up the idea over lunch, and we discussed it in the following weeks. The city of Washington, D.C.'s, Redevelopment Land Agency—also known as the RLA—had awarded a project to a group that included a guy named Fred Ezra and a company called Richmar. Ezra was also a supporter and personal friend of Barry's. This group was to redevelop a site at North Capitol and G Streets. But though they had won the bid, they had been unable to finance their project for quite some time. It was hard to get anything financed in the office building market then; because of the nationwide real estate collapse and the subsequent banking crisis, few banks were making commercial real estate loans. We were beginning to come out of it, but the country was still in a recession.

Roth knew about the deal because Trammel Crow had built, on a fee basis, an office tower right next door: the headquarters for the American Psychological Association (APA), a large, national nonprofit advocacy organization. Trammel Crow wanted to develop the adjacent city site as well, the one that Ezra and Richmar controlled. Trammel Crow wanted to buy out their interest. Thanks to the APA, they had what the bid winners didn't: the financial backing to build it. Trammel had convinced the APA that it would be a good time to develop a building next door so that they'd be assured of future space to grow. What Trammel Crow wanted were the fees to develop, lease, and manage the new building. And they couldn't do this with Ezra and Richmar in place. Ezra was a leasing agent and wanted those fees, while Richmar was a developer and wanted those fees also. The solution was to buy them out. There was room in the deal for that, since the winning bidders' option to buy the property was for well under its market value.

There was only one snag, besides the fact that Trammel Crow and the APA needed a minority partner to win the RLA contract: They had to have city approval for the winning bid to be transferred to them rather than having the project go out for bid again. Their solution was to approach me. Why?

By that time I had a very good relationship with the new mayor, Sharon Pratt Kelly, and several of her top administrators, and I was politically influential with a number of the city council members. In many ways I was, at that time, at the height of my influence as a premier local political player. So once Trammel Crow decided they wanted to buy out the interests of the winning bidders, the key became getting the city to approve the transfer. And for that they needed me, or someone like me. Otherwise the city was simply going to pull the plug on Ezra and Richmar and start over.

The essence of this deal was speed and my ability to act swiftly. The bidders' deadline was fast approaching, and if they forfeited, the city would take back the site. That also put pressure on Ezra and Richmar to take a deal or risk getting nothing, and it also put pressure on the APA, lest they should lose this opportunity.

I negotiated a deal where ultimately I would get 25 percent ownership in the project (without any capital investment), the APA would get 74 percent, and Trammel Crow would get 1 percent plus the development and leasing fees. I would get a smaller development fee, about a quarter of a million dollars paid in a lump sum, and then another quarter of a million dollars over a year or so. The APA would prelease a third of the building to secure financing and then Tramell Crow would sublease it to other tenants; Trammell Crow would also lease the excess space to other office tenants.

Since my job was to get the transfer approved, I approached the director of economic development, who then went to Mayor Kelly. Although the mayor had not yet asked me, it was understood that the mayor wanted me to chair her campaign finance committee. I was unable to do that, because one of my friends who was a council member was running against her.

Kelly was nonetheless happy with the project; she was up for reelection in the environment of a down economy, and people were looking to her for action. She needed to have some results, and what made our proposition attractive was that we could start construction right away. The fact that we could get a major development project going at a time when no one was building was a feather in her cap. This would be the first new major commercial office building built in Washington since the 1980s, and it was in a high-profile spot—about six blocks north of the U.S. Capitol, next door to the historic Union Station transportation hub.

I had several meetings with the director of the department of housing as well as the RLA and got their support. It then went before the redevelopment agency board, and we got it approved.

The building we ultimately agreed to put up was 280,000 square feet and would cost $55 million. Trammel Crow and the APA went after the financing, which they raised on Wall Street with certificates of participation—bonds—that were guaranteed by the APA and underwritten by the investment banking firm, Dillon and Reed.

As it turned out, Kelly lost and, to most people's surprise, Marion Barry made his now-famous comeback (he had served six months in jail) and gotten reelected. So the building was completed under Barry's term, in the fall of 1997. But it was still a win for everybody involved, including the original bidders, me, the APA, and Trammel Crow, all because we acquired the land so inexpensively.

We bought the land from the city for $3 million, when in fact it was worth about $10 million. We paid another $2 million to Ezra and Richmar; they got paid one sum when we closed and another when we started construction. I had an option that I could exercise in 1998 to force the APA to buy out my interest, which I exercised, and they paid me out a little under $3 million. The APA was happy because they got a $10 million site for, in the end, $8 million. And Trammel Crow was able to earn all the fees associated with the financing, developing, and leasing of the property. We even paid Jeff Cohen a fee for making the introduction to Roth; he made maybe two hundred grand or so.

There is another footnote to this deal that gave me particular satisfaction. I had helped start a janitorial services company with a young man whom I had initially met when he was cleaning my offices; he then worked for me for a number of years. As part of the deal, I made sure that his company got the contract to do the janitorial services work in the new highrise.

I also made sure my tax appeal company got the right to do the tax appeal work for the building.

EPILOGUE TO CHAPTER 3

I kept the description of this deal deliberately short, partly because many of the details of what I had to accomplish don't illustrate any new principles—though they did confirm much of what I had already learned. The need for patience and endurance, for example: This deal began in early 1994 and did not really pay off until I cashed out in 1998, though I did earn some development fees along the way.

Also, I needed to do some hard negotiating, in particular with Trammel Crow and the APA. They wanted to reduce my portion of the deal to 15 percent, even though the city had requirements for minority partnerships with standards of 25 percent or better. They wanted me to go in and argue 15 percent with the city and I wouldn't do it. Ultimately they gave in on that point. I also got Trammel Crow to provide guarantees for the completion of the project, which dramatically reduced my exposure.

The reason I could get these concessions was, of course, that even though this deal was brought to me, I had control of it through my ability to get the bid assigned to our group. I had the most valuable commodity in the transaction: political connections. Perhaps someone else could have gotten it done in a longer time frame, but with the clock running, I was the go-to guy.

I learned a few things watching Trammel Crow, too, and came to understand how the company operated—and my relative advantage as an entrepreneur. When companies get as big as TC, they can't be entrepreneurial; they've got to do business just to earn fees to keep their overhead covered and their people busy. When you are a smaller company, you can be more selective. I wasn't interested in earning fees; I was interested in owning. And because I understood TC's motivation—to earn income needed to keep their operations running—Trammel Crow worked out fine for me. Their interests were parallel to mine, and if you can align your interests with those of your contracted partners, then you have the basis of a successful deal. TC developed the building, the building was completed, they earned their fees and kept jobs for their people. I cashed out.

Also, as with other deals, I didn't put a dollar in. That is a constant lesson for an entrepreneur: try to put the least amount of your own money into any deal. While I always look at my upside and what the profit potential is, I also pay attention to what my financial exposure is going to be. I try to limit it, so it's not a surprise for me later.

What this deal does illustrate, as a new principle, is the importance of being in the right position at the right time. Ideas and deals are the same in this sense: As opportunities, they exist for only so long. You have to be able to seize them. In this deal, I moved on the idea instantly, immediately.

A lot of people who aren't successful make the excuse that successful entrepreneurs have better luck, as if success in business is similar to winning the lottery. I think the odds are much better in business, but that the so-called stroke of good fortune comes only to those who are ready for it. In a very real sense, luck is a matter of putting yourself in the right place at the right time. Then seize opportunities that come your way before they fade away. That is the art of the entrepreneur.

PEEBLES GROUND RULES

- The best contracts are between parties who have parallel goals.

- If you understand the motivations of the party across the negotiating table, you can cut better, stronger deals.

- Always try to limit your financial exposure, especially in terms of guarantees and responsibilities.

- Pay as much attention to the upside as the downside; scared money never wins.

Peebles Principle #3: Being Lucky Means Being Ready

Opportunities come to everyone, but the winner is the one prepared to take advantage of them when they arrive. Put yourself in the right place at the right time, and you can seize these opportunities.

✤ 4 ✤

The Barry Stigma:
Time for a Change

Not all deals succeed. Sometimes, despite your best efforts, the situation changes and you lose. In times like these, you have to assess the circumstances honestly. Sometimes you have to remake the model.

The American Psychological Association building was completed in 1997, long after the term of Mayor Sharon Pratt Kelly. But the deal was closed in 1994, during her tenure, and it remains part of her era. The next era, for me and for the city, began later that year with the return of Marion Barry.

In September of 1994, Barry ran in the Democratic primary for mayor of Washington, D.C. He did this despite the nationwide broadcast of videotapes that showed him smoking crack cocaine. He also did this without my support; I publicly supported his opposition, City Councilman John Ray.

I still contributed $30,000 to Barry's political action committee, by the way. I figured I owed it to him. He had come to me for a donation, and I told him I didn't think he should run for mayor. Nonetheless, if that's what he wanted to do, here was some money. I would still support Ray, however, because I had committed to do so and was going to follow through with that.

Primary election night rolled around. It was September 13, and Katrina and I were watching the returns at home on television. We had a little gentleman's—or gentleperson's— bet going. She predicted that Barry was going to win, while I thought that Ray was going to win. We had been invited by both candidates to join them for the returns but decided to stay on the sidelines.

At around 9:30 P.M. I got a call at the house. It was Barry.

"What did I tell you? I've won!" he yelled on the phone. And sure enough, Barry had captured 47 percent of the vote, while Ray had gotten 30-something percent.

"I'm going to the convention center to give an acceptance speech," he continued. "Why don't you, you and Katrina, come down and meet me there."

So we went down there, and he invited us up on the platform with him. There Katrina and I were, up on the stage with Barry and his wife, with all the hoopla of the victory celebration. It was a perfect display of practical politics. You may prefer one candidate over another, but you have to work with the winner.

Barry himself was nothing if not a big-picture pragmatist. He had won the primary, but now he needed help, because now he was faced with Republican opposition in the form of Carol Schwartz. Ordinarily a Democrat would be a shoo-in, but with Barry's new notoriety, Schwartz had a viable chance. Meanwhile, I had emerged as the premier local political fundraiser. I had raised money for most of the major city council members as well as for the governor of Maryland, Paris Glendenning, and for Bill Clinton, who had been to my house. I had become a major player, and Barry needed me.

The first thing he asked me to do was host a unity breakfast, to bring the Democrats together to fend off Carol Schwartz. I hosted the breakfast at the Renaissance Hotel (which belonged to one of my tax appeal clients) for about seven hundred people. I did a few other things, too, but to make a long story short, Barry was reelected as mayor.

Once back in office, Barry made it a top priority to continue the effort to bring the Washington Wizards basketball team to downtown D.C. The city had already tried to do this under Mayor Kelly, and the team's owner, Abe Pollin, along with the *Washington Post*, had endorsed the idea. Although the city had enjoined its redevelopment agency to award a city-owned site for the arena, however, it had remained undeveloped. Barry saw it as an opportunity to show what he could get done and consequently put a lot of energy into the project.

One problem was that the arena would require the demolition of two city office buildings. Together, these housed about seven or eight hundred employees. The city had to relocate these people, and they had to do it quickly in order to start construction. So the city held a competition on where to relocate the employees.

I had been in the market working with a subsidiary of Starwood Hotels, Starwood Capital, then in its early stages. We had collectively worked on a deal to buy two office buildings, 1121 Vermont Avenue and 801 North Capitol Street, where I thought we could put the district government employees. We bought them very cheaply—the country was still in a real estate recession, and D.C. was no exception—so we could be very competitive in pricing our proposal to the city. Like many other municipalities whose revenues were based on real estate taxes, the city was having financial trouble, so economics were important. It had hired an outside consultant, a brokerage firm, to evaluate ours and other proposals. The firm they hired was actually The Ezra Companies, headed by the same Fred Ezra from whom we purchased the North Capitol and G Streets project.

Before we submitted our proposal, a developer named John Akridge had already put in a bid. He had acquired options on some properties farther up the street from us on North Capitol. He had submitted those buildings, and public opinion was that he was the guy who was going to win, a proverbial shoo-in. We came in with a better price and undercut him. So the city started negotiating with us both simultaneously and evaluating us both. As it turned out, our deal was $58 million less expensive for the city over the term of the lease.

It made sense for the city to select us, and that is what the consultants recommended. They negotiated a deal with us and submitted it for approval to the city council right before their summer recess in June. Akridge found out about it and went ballistic. He started hiring lobbyists to lobby against us, and he called the *Washington Post*—no fan of Barry's by that point—and used the media to portray this as a Barry insider deal.

At that time, the chairman of the city council, Dave Clark, aside from being a man of integrity, was also a good friend of mine. He felt the city should go forward with our project, so he kept the council in session while the city attorney reviewed the documents and the mayor's office worked out some final details.

During this same period of time Congress was creating

an oversight committee to review the City of Washington's finances. This spooked the city's bureaucracy and its officials, and since the profile of our deal was becoming higher and higher, they dragged their feet on it. Bureaucrats aren't courageous by nature, and these didn't want their names in the paper, so everybody just sort of slowed down. Clark finally had to let the council go into summer recess prior to a vote being taken.

Nonetheless, that summer Barry signed the lease himself. The laws at the time gave the council a certain period of time to approve or disapprove a lease, and if they didn't disapprove it, it was deemed approved. The council wasn't going to be back in session until that September, so Barry approved it himself in order to move the project forward. He asked me to go ahead and build out the space so that I'd meet the timetable for the arena.

Over the summer, however, the pressure against the deal heated up. The PR efforts by Akridge intensified, the *Washington Post* ran a couple of editorials, and I even went on Fox Morning News live to defend the deal. The new financial control board came in and reviewed our lease. They now had the right to review contracts, and though ours was already in place—and technically no longer in their domain—Barry submitted it to them for review anyway. And they criticized it, like an auditor would, nitpicking a couple of areas they thought were problematic or would expose the city financially. They noted how the city was exposed to cost overruns, which of course it was if, for example, more tenant improvements were requested. They didn't talk about the overall deal, and they didn't compare our deal to any other. The *Washington Post* ran a story about it on the front page, reporting that the control board had criticized us.

By the end of the summer, the mayor had lost his nerve and had decided to withdraw my lease. He had buckled under the pressure, and he didn't even bother to warn me ahead of time. I found out about it on the television news.

I was incensed. I could understand why Barry didn't want any appearance of impropriety now that he was back in office. But he could have submitted the contract to the city council, where I had the votes needed to approve it, and thereby deflected the limelight of responsibility. More than one official publicly urged Barry to submit it to the council so they could make the decision.

But Barry didn't want to be seen as favoring me, now the target of attacks. In retrospect, I suppose I should have been prepared for his decision: When all other things are equal, you can rely on a politician to protect his or her interests. At the time, however, it felt like an unforgivable act because it violated my sense of what political loyalties are all about. Unless it goes against the interests of the people you represent, you don't sacrifice friends. I didn't consider my bid to be a violation of the public trust. But Barry after making his comeback was overly sensitive to the glare of publicity. So he pulled the lease, and it cost me. It also ruined my relationship with Starwood, because I had told them to go ahead with the project and build it out to the city's specifications. I could have sued the city but didn't. We took our hit financially and moved on.

Ultimately, the city held a new competition for the leases. I submitted again, and we were the low bidder again, but they gave it to somebody else. At first I blocked it at the city council level, where I had considerable influence, until Barry called me and asked me to release some of my votes there because the arena had to go forward. He promised me another tenant, but that never happened.

What did happen that fall was an epiphany for me. It was a watershed event in my career. I had spent the previous four years, after Barry left the mayor's office in disgrace, trying to shed my image as his protégé. I had broadened my horizons and become connected and active with other politicians, with Governor Paris Glendenning of Maryland, with Mayor David Dinkins of New York, with Mayor Willie Herrington of Memphis, and with Mayor Bill Campbell of Atlanta. I had walked up Georgia Avenue with Bill Clinton when he was president-elect, touring economically neglected areas in the city. I thought I had freed myself of the Barry stigma, but now I was pulled back in, at least in the public eye. And because of that I couldn't win a deal in Washington, D.C., even when I was $58 million less expensive than the competition.

I came to the unpleasant conclusion that, at least during the next four years under the Barry administration, I wasn't going to be able to do business in D.C., not without an exceptional amount of scrutiny. The political connections that had helped me thus far had become a liability, creating too high a profile for me. It was even beginning to affect my tax appeal business. I realized that it was a time for a change.

I told Katrina that we needed a long vacation.

"Let's go to Miami," I said. "Everybody is talking about South Beach. It sounds like it'll be fun."

And so began the next phase of my career. I would go to Miami Beach and try the Peebles Principles in a city where I knew absolutely no one. It was a perfect petri dish, a blank slate, and it would prove to be the stage for what was perhaps my most perfect deal, and certainly my most challenging: the Royal Palm Hotel.

EPILOGUE TO CHAPTER 4

My early successes in Washington were predicated on my ability to control deals, and this, in turn, was based on my ability to control some essential aspect of the deal. The simplest perspective is to think of each deal in the classic terms of supply and demand. You've got to control one or the other.

In the example of the 2100 Martin Luther King deal, I controlled the demand—in this case the tenant, which was the city government of Washington. In the example of the Marriott Hotel, I controlled the supply—in this case a prime historic building that I had acquired well below market value. With the North Capitol and G Streets building, I had sway over both sides of the supply-demand paradigm, with an option on the site and influence with the city administration for its lease commitment.

The fact that my industry was real estate and that the supply-and-demand formula was realized as buildings and tenants is merely circumstantial. The principles remain the same for any industry. If I were in the commodities business, my control over supply might be an option on some raw material. In the entertainment industry, I might control content via a contract for a manuscript or the copyright of a song. If I were in the online business, I might control supply, in the form of a desirable audience attracted to my popular Web site. The principle—that you need to control some key element in any deal—remains the same.

Now, with the arena lease deal, I had reached a place where my control of the dynamics was weakened, perhaps fatally. I was no longer able to control the demand for this particular project. And there were other entrepreneurs offering other sites, so I couldn't lock up the supply side either. In such a circumstance, I had to rethink the premise of my model. It was no longer working, at least not in the City of Washington, D.C. I would have to change it or change the venue where I was applying it. I decided on the latter course of action, and would soon be vindicated.

PEEBLES GROUND RULES

- In business and in politics, be pragmatic. Be prepared to work with the winner.

- In business and in politics, self-preservation trumps friendship. Be aware of the other person's self-interest.

- To control a deal, you need only command one side of the equation, either the demand or the supply. But you must own at least one.

Peebles Principle #4: If the Key Doesn't Work, Change the Lock

Not every deal succeeds. If you have failed with one approach, look at the elements. Don't be afraid to do a reality check on any situation, and be flexible enough to change.

✳ 5 ✳

The Royal Palm:
Never Say Die

South Beach in the mid-1990s was a Wild West for developers. There were opportunities everywhere and a mad rush to grab them. Only by stretching my skills to the limit could I win big in this environment. In the end what it took was perseverance and intense attention to detail.

After the debacle with Barry in Washington, I needed to get out of the city for a breather, so Katrina and I went for a long break to Miami Beach. We had previously stayed at Ian Schrager's Royalton Hotel in New York, so when I heard he owned the Delano on the ocean in Miami Beach I booked a suite for Katrina and myself. After a week of sub-par service and them wrecking my Ferrari (which I had shipped from Potomac), we switched to the Astor Hotel.

This was in October of 1995. We ended up spending two weeks in Miami Beach, and we enjoyed it so much Katrina and I decided to look for a vacation home there. The Delano concierge referred us to a real estate broker, and he took us around to look at different properties. We ended up settling on an apartment in a building called the La Tour at 41st and Collins. It was a new building, just completed, and we rented a three-bedroom plus den apartment overlooking the ocean. We spent our first time in the apartment in November, around Thanksgiving, with our year-and-a-half-old son, Donahue III, and my in-laws.

I noticed that things were beginning to happen in Miami Beach. There was a lot more construction than in Washington, which was dead by comparison, so I thought I should look for some business opportunities in the area.

Now, I still had a very successful property tax appeal business in Washington, which was generating millions of dollars annually. My bank was lending me money against that cash flow, allowing me to acquire numerous buildings in Washington during the real estate recession. There was a limit to this, of course. I was buying at great value because they were vacant properties, but that meant they didn't produce any cash to service the debt. I had purchased between $30 million and $40 million worth of properties, but there wasn't enough activity going on to develop them. I needed to go somewhere there was action and movement, and Miami Beach seemed a likely place.

We began flying to Miami frequently, and I looked at several properties; I even made an offer for one at 39th Street and Collins Avenue but was turned down. Nothing really happened before the end of 1995, when we went down for a week to celebrate New Year's.

New Year's Day fell on a Monday that year, and I remember sitting in the living room of our apartment the day before, on New Year's Eve, reading the Sunday *Miami Herald*. They had something called "The Neighbors Section," and the cover story was titled "South Beach: Real Estate on Fire." The cover of the section showed a broker standing in front of the Shorecrest Hotel with a big "For Sale" sign. Inside there was a companion article about the Shorecrest, sort of a case study. It said how the owner had paid

$900,000 for it a few years before and how it was now on the market for $3.9 million. Wow. They also noted that it was right next door to the Royal Palm Hotel, a property that had been set aside for African American ownership. Wow again. I had never heard of a minority program where they specified the race; in Washington it would have been any minority. African American only? I wondered, how many African American developers were there? Not many. And how many were reading the *Miami Herald* right then? Very few, I imagined.

I would later find out how this unique situation developed. Several years earlier Nelson Mandela had been snubbed by the City of Miami, refused an official visit because he was perceived to be a communist—an inflammatory issue among Cuban voters in South Florida. The upshot was a black tourism boycott of Greater Miami, which turned out to be so painful that the City of Miami Beach established a $10 million fund to create a hotel development opportunity for a black developer. It was their olive branch, their peace offering.

At that point I was still in the dark as to the cause, but I saw what could be a good opportunity. The Royal Palm had already been purchased by the city for the black hotel-development project, and the Shorecrest was right next door. I knew from my experience in D.C. that if you want to build anything, you've got to assemble property. People are spoiled in South Florida, where there are vacant lots that are buildable all on their own. To build a sizable structure in downtown Washington, you've got to buy three, four, or five different properties, and deal with difficult property owners in the process. So, I set up an appointment to see the Shorecrest the following Tuesday and got a copy of the request for a proposal (RFP) on the Royal Palm hotel project.

When I went on that Tuesday to inspect the Shorecrest I noticed that both the Royal Palm and Shorecrest sites were skinny, so slender that in order to make an efficient property you would have to buy them both. Clearly, I needed to buy the Shorecrest. The area was still run down, but the future was unmistakable for anyone with a little vision: The Il Villagio luxury condominium was being built just to the south, and just to the north the 800-room Loews convention hotel—another city-backed project to bring life to the beach—would soon begin construction.

Still, vision was necessary because the Shorecrest was really run down. It was like a welfare hotel; there were actually chickens running through the lobby. There were prostitutes living in the hotel, and when I went to the roof deck they were there, sunbathing in the nude. It was a mess, but it was on the ocean, and I decided to buy it. I got back into my car and called Katrina. I was on the speaker phone, looking in the rearview mirror, and I saw a small spot on my forehead. I told Katrina that I must have gotten bitten. But when I touched the spot it jumped.

"My god," I said to Katrina. "I've literally been in a fleabag hotel."

That day I called one of the law firms we work with in Washington and got them to recommend a local lawyer; they connected me with Stuart Hoffman. I met him that Saturday in his offices at Holland & Knight. While Katrina chased Donahue around their 30th-floor offices and terrace, Stuart and I got to know each other a bit, and hit it off, so I hired him to represent me on the Shorecrest purchase. A few days later—within a week of seeing the property—I'd made an offer to buy it.

Having had experience in winning competitions in

Washington, I knew I needed a top team to put together the Royal Palm RFP. So I started assembling people. I called Jim Donohoe of Donohoe Construction, who had built the 2100 MLK building (and would later build out the Marriott Hotel with me) and asked him to join as the construction firm. I also asked Hospitality Partners, the hotel management company he held an interest in (and that would later set up the Marriott management) to come and help win the Royal Palm project.

My team building continued. Stuart Hoffman's firm represented Arquitectonica, Miami's award-winning modern architecture firm, and they introduced me to the CEO, Bernardo Fort-Brescia. We met over lunch at the Sheraton on Brickell Avenue, in the heart of Miami's financial district. I was from Washington, so contemporary architecture was almost foreign to me, but I liked Bernardo. I also liked the idea that he had his offices on Miami Beach and that he was a local architect with international recognition. So I hired him. Then he referred me to a good publicist for the public relations side of things.

With these elements of the team together, I began to negotiate to buy the Shorecrest property, which also involved a leasehold interest. Basically, there was a property owner, a family out of New Jersey, and a leaseholder, the party that owned the hotel itself. The leasehold owner was a guy named Cyrus Mehre. He and his brother had invested in other properties along the beach, and he lived in a Mediterranean villa on Pine Tree Drive. I went to his home to negotiate, and we had several sessions where he would try to get me up in price and get me to put down a bigger deposit.

In the end, it was the arrogance of the city and the Hyatt Hotel team—my main competition in the bidding—that made it possible for me to do a deal with Mehre. And this is where the intrigue begins.

The city, everyone knew, had set aside $10 million to support the award of a hotel to an African American group or individual. Everyone knew that the city had purchased the Royal Palm Hotel for that purpose, as part of a package deal that would also include the Shorecrest.

What everybody did not know was that the city had spent $5.5 million buying the Royal Palm. That meant they only had $4.5 million left to buy the Shorecrest. And that wasn't enough. Why? Because Cyrus Mehre and the landowner—the Cardona family in New Jersey—felt their property should command the same price as the Royal Palm, which was adjacent to the Shorecrest on a piece of property that was the same size. Mehre told the city as much, but the city wouldn't listen. They simply threatened to condemn the property. The Hyatt team, which was the hands-down favorite to win the bid before I arrived, also lowballed Mehre. They told him they were going to win the project and that their offer was the best deal he was going to get. So Mehre was pissed off. And that gave me the window of opportunity I needed: I convinced him that if he sided with me and gave me the option to buy his property, I would win. More important, I agreed to pay Mayer the price he wanted—$4 million—and to pay the Cardona family trust the price they wanted: $1.1 million.

It wasn't a bad deal at $5.1 million. I gave Cyrus Mehre $250,000 as a deposit and the Cardona family a $100,000 deposit, with the provision that I wouldn't have to close until ninety days after my selection for the project. These were great terms; the best part of the contract was that if I failed to win the project, I would get my money back. Mehre agreed to this because he believed I would win, plus he would make more money, and—probably most satisfying— it gave him a chance to get back at the city for screwing with him. He would get to eat his cake and throw it at them, as well as punish the Hyatt team for their arrogance.

For me, this was the critical lever I was looking for in the deal. When I was ready to submit my response to the RFP, I would have control of the Shorecrest. The project, at least as envisioned by the city, could not go forward without me.

As it turned out, that did not mean the bid was a shoo-in for me. This was Miami Beach, the Wild, Wild West of Florida real estate, where no one was watching—except for a guy named Arthur Courshon. He was the head of the selection committee for the project, and he did not want me to win.

Courshon was chairman of Jefferson National Bank (which has since been sold) and they had been the owners and mortgage holders of the Royal Palm Hotel, the very same one the city had purchased as part of the deal. Courshon had also been head of the selection committee which awarded that other city-backed endeavor, the Loews hotel project, to the Tisch family. Hyatt, our main competitors on the Royal Palm, had been a bidder for that project, and a lot of people thought they offered a better financial deal for the city. But Courshon gave it to Tisch, allegedly for political considerations, and then promised Hyatt they would get the Royal Palm deal as a consolation prize. While the Miami Beach City Commission had the final vote, it had a history of never turning down the selection committee's recommendation.

Even without Courshon's endorsement, the Hyatt team

was a formidable opponent. Their minority partner was Eugene Jackson, chairman of the Unity Broadcasting Network. He was putting up the money for his group. They also had South Beach Deco–district pioneer Craig Robins, who hailed from a longtime Miami Beach real estate family and had considerable political pull in the city.

I was going to have to work very hard to get my message through.

My time frame was tight. The deadline for the RFP was originally March 1 but fortunately was postponed until April 1. I was flying down to Miami Beach every week for at least a couple of days, meeting with everyone I could. I met the top editors at the *Miami Herald* as well as the publisher. I began to meet each of the Miami Beach city commissioners. After hiring Holland & Knight, I hired another law firm for land use, and asked them to introduce me to some specific banks. I saw that Ocean Bank and Capital Bank were making loans on the beach—their signs were in front of several buildings—and they seemed very entrepreneurial; Ocean Bank had financed the building where I had my apartment. So I asked to be introduced to these two banks, and both ended up signing commitment letters to finance the project.

I started going to different business organization lunches as well and meeting other politicians. I had lunch with the chairman of the Miami-Dade County Commission and sat with the Miami Beach city manager. I met the head of the Kiwanis Club and the head of the Miami Design Preservation League. I was making the rounds, letting people know who I was, telling them that I had a contract to buy the Shorecrest, that I was bidding on the Royal Palm, and that I wanted them to know what I was doing. I was consensus building and becoming localized in Greater Miami.

To hedge my bets, I even met with the Hyatt team. I did control the Shorecrest, after all, so if they actually won, they would have to deal with me sooner or later.

I went first and talked with Craig Robins. He had been involved with an earlier team—the HCF group—that had actually won the bid for the project during a previous round of bidding. At that time the bid had been only for the $10 million prize. Once the prize was won, the Royal Palm and the Shorecrest were targeted for the project. The city ultimately threw out the HCF award—alleging the team lacked the financial resources to complete the project—but went ahead and bought the Royal Palm anyway. I met one of the HCF team's investors, African American banker John Hall, and he introduced me to Robins.

I remember going to meet with Craig in his South Beach offices. He struck me as a little bit offbeat: He was very artsy looking, with tight and colorful clothes, the opposite of what you'd think of as a developer. He also came across as very arrogant; this was the city where he grew up and where his dad was a successful businessman. He told me flat out that as a newcomer, I didn't stand a chance of beating him, period. He also said he was offering the HCF team a chance to participate and that I should think of joining his group. I went back to Hall and convinced his partners to join me instead, so that we could make it an all African American–owned team.

I thought of working out a deal with Craig, but this proved impossible. I remember one evening I was at the Forge restaurant on Miami Beach, a very exclusive place that caters to celebrities and powerful businessman. Craig was there with Nick Pritzker from the Hyatt Corporation. Pritzker's family had started and built the Hyatt chain. I remember thinking that even though I was a millionaire, I was competing against a billionaire. It was the kind of David and Goliath contest that most people walk away from. But though I was impressed, I wasn't awed. I was too confident for that. I just walked over and told them both that we should work together.

"If both of us go after this deal," I told them, "one of us is going to lose. I believe we have a better shot of winning this together. I control the Shorecrest, so it makes no sense for us to try to knock each other off. I'm not in the hotel management business, but Hyatt is, and you want that brand here, so let's do it together."

I think Nick Pritzker wanted to do it, but Craig talked him out of it. I believe this was mainly out of competitiveness; he was letting his emotions cloud his judgment. I could see that Craig was going to be a problem, especially because he had political relationships on the beach. However, after speaking with them both that night, I was confident that neither of them had what it took to beat me, not even teamed together.

My land use lawyer told me I needed to hire some lobbyists; I wasn't accustomed to this in D.C., mostly because I didn't need them there. I agreed, as long as they did the hiring, not me. She introduced me to a lobbyist named Michael Milberg, and the law firm hired him.

By serendipity, Milberg used to be the general manager of the Royal Palm, and he knew the family that owned it and where all the bodies were buried. He was city commissioner Neisen Kasdin's campaign manager, and Kasdin was a city commissioner with mayoral aspirations. Milberg also had a good relationship with David Pearlson, another commissioner. As soon as he joined our team as a consultant he gave me some good tactical advice.

He told me that Craig Robins had a brother, Scott Robins, with whom he did not get along. So I met Scott. He was the complete opposite of his brother: more businesslike, more professional, not at all arrogant, very level-headed. He was also a broader thinker and not so self-absorbed. Scott also had something to prove—that he was a smart guy in business. Scott and I got along well, and he joined our team. I felt more comfortable then, because he canceled out Craig on the political side. After that it was just me versus Eugene Jackson.

I wasn't going to leave that contest—our credibility as African American entrepreneurs—up for grabs either. I needed to bolster our team's credentials.

I first teamed up with two local business people out of D.C., one of whom owned an aerospace information services firm and the other a partner in one of the largest black-owned accounting firms in the country. While these were good partners, we still needed some pizzazz. Through Bill Clinton I had met Clarence Avant, who was then the chairman of Motown Records. I couldn't think of any other African American company that transcended ethnic lines the way Motown did. I asked Clarence to join the project. He agreed to come in, and that gave me entertainment star power. We needed that Motown sizzle, and we got it; we were even planning to put a Motown Café restaurant in the hotel.

Katrina had professional photographers come to our offices and take each of our pictures, which we submitted along with our financial statements. We were an impressive group of high-net-worth individuals and successful entrepreneurs; collectively we had a net worth of more than $120 million. It was quite a team. (To my pleasant surprise, seven years later my own net worth would exceed this total.)

Finally—and I say finally, even though it was only a matter of three months—the day arrived for the RFP submission. I had asked Katrina, who is very organized and detail-oriented, to help put the bid together. She hired a design firm to do all the graphics for our submission, and the final document was like a work of art, eighteen inches wide with a strip of metal and screws to bind it.

The weekend before the deadline we had a party at our apartment for the entire team, and I had a copy of the complete RFP there so that everybody could see it. We catered the event with champagne and hors d'oeuvres, and displayed the RFP on a coffee table out on the deck. The following Monday, April 1, I personally went to the City Hall and right before 5 P.M. handed the RFP in. The city clerk then opened it up ceremonially.

There were eight of us bidding altogether, each group consisting of a team that comprised a hotel brand, a minority partner, and other partners such as bankers or builders. There was a bid from the Ritz-Carlton, one from the Regal, one from DoubleTree, and another from Wyndham. There was Clarion Hotels, and a Marriott group as well. Then there was the Hyatt group with Eugene Jackson and my group, with Crowne Plaza.

I felt good about my chances. I felt I could certainly hold my own against the other minority partners, since I was the only one who had developed a sizable building on my own. Second, I controlled the Shorecrest, and out of the seven bids, five included a plan to develop both the Royal Palm and the Shorecrest. Despite the RFP's stated requirement that the Shorecrest had to be privately acquired, four of my competitors were bidding for both and asking the city to condemn the property I controlled. Finally, when I submitted my RFP response, I had a letter of commitment from Ocean Bank to finance the project, a letter of commitment from Capital Bank, and a term sheet outlining financing conditions from Nations Bank. Nobody else, including the Hyatt team, had a single loan commitment. I felt I was in a great position: I had the experience, the financing, a 100 percent African American team, and control of the property next door.

Predictably, the Hyatt team wasn't going to let things rest while the bidders prepared for the next stage in the process, a series of formal presentations at the Miami Beach Convention Center. During this phase they unleashed a PR campaign against me; they let it be known to the commissioners that I was a friend of Marion Barry, which made me friends, by association, with Minister Louis Farrakhan. It was an effective ploy, because right at that time Farrakhan was orchestrating the Million Man March to Washington. It was headline news, and the message was that if I was selected, you could expect a groundbreaking attended by Marion Barry, Jesse Jackson, and Louis Farrakhan. I was painted as anti-Semitic. Some of the Jewish businesspeople and politicians I met looked at me like I had murdered somebody. When Milberg found out they were being told I was anti-Semitic, he did his best to counterspin the rumor.

Not that Hyatt didn't get theirs during this period of the process, by the way. The Wyndham group hired a PR guy Randy Hilliard, who was known locally as the prince of darkness, and he started spreading the word that the selection was rigged for Hyatt. He also did some research on their team and hit paydirt: it turned out that Eugene Jackson had defaulted on a housing project loan in Miami-Dade County for $450,000 and had an outstanding judgment against him. The *Miami Daily Business Review* did a front-page story about it, showing the housing project all boarded up, with these poor black people in front of it. It looked like a scene from a third world country, in some African or Caribbean nation, with barefoot kids and graffiti everywhere. This was Jackson's one piece of property in South Florida, and it had more then 250 housing code violations. It looked pretty bad. Additionally, it was reported that Jackson had an IRS lien against him for $3.9 million.

This was right during the period when the eight applicants were given a chance to make their cases. Everybody got to set up in a different room at the convention center, and the selection committee went from room to room. Courshon had his chair brought from his office; it was a big, baby blue high-backed chair, and it was brought to the convention center by truck and wheeled from room to room. Oftentimes the chair would match his baby blue suede shoes.

When it came time for the Hyatt presentation, Courshon was not to be deterred, not by the article on Jackson or anything else. The city had hired a consultant from Tishman Hotels out of New York, and he sat at the table with the staff people. Part of their job was to ask questions, and so he asked Jackson about the newspaper article.

"Mr. Jackson," he said, "we have all read about this default judgment against you. This is of great concern to us. Can you please explain it?"

"Well, I was trying to help the poor, my people," Jackson said. "I was trying to do a good thing for the community and things just didn't work out. We're working at it, and we're doing the best we can to help our community."

It was just a bullshit answer, and everyone knew it.

Then Courshon interrupted the questioning and asked: "But, Mr. Jackson, that hasn't affected your ability to get financing for this project, has it?"

Now, Jackson had submitted no financing commitments, no financing proposals, nothing. So this question was a setup, a soft, slow pitch. It was so blatant that even Jackson didn't catch on at first.

"Pardon me," he said. "I don't understand the question."

Courshon pitched it again, even more slowly. "You can still get financing, even with this, can't you?" he asked.

"Oh, yes, yes, of course," Jackson replied. Courshon was right in there, doing his best.

After the presentations were complete, a process that took several days, the selection committee publicly deliberated the merits of the proposals. Courshon was there, trying to sway everybody toward the Hyatt deal. I noticed that the one African American on the selection committee, Carole Anne Taylor, was absent. She had been in our corner, with the all–African American team, but was removed from the selection committee because of an alleged conflict of interest, though the actual problem was never clearly defined. I was stunned, knowing that Courshon had remained on the committee despite the incredible conflict that it was his bank that had held the loan on the Royal Palm.

Jonathan Mariner, the CFO for the Florida Marlins baseball team at the time, replaced Taylor. He would later say that Courshon had tricked him. The other members of the committee were Maurice Weiner, an investor who owned the Grove Isle hotel, Vincent Scully, an architect who was a professor at Yale, and Ed Marquez, the county's chief financial officer.

So they voted, and did it with a ranking system. It basically came down to our team, the Hyatt people, and the Wyndham team. Everybody rated Wyndham number 3, so the only variations were on the number 1 and number 2 choices. Weiner ranked me number 1 and Hyatt number 2, as did Marquez; then Scully, Mariner, and Courshon all rank Hyatt number 1 and us number 2. I lost by one point.

I couldn't believe it. I couldn't believe that Mariner, the only African American on the committee, has voted against the only all–African American team to submit. And I couldn't believe that Professor Scully has voted against us, which he said he did strictly on the grounds of architectural merit, even though our firm, Arquitectonica, produced a vastly superior design that was sensitive to the historic structures on the site and in the adjacent Art Deco Historic District.

I was stunned. I had put so much effort into this only to lose. My lawyers tried to console me, saying the Hyatt team and the city had to deal with me anyway, that we'd make it all up in the condemnation, and not to worry. Then Wyndham's Hilliard came over—he was nick-named the Prince of PR Darkness and we had hit it off reasonably well—and he said, you know, Hyatt doesn't have this. They still have to go before the city commission.

"I'll deal with Hyatt and Eugene Jackson," he said. "Let's just focus on the enemy. I can knock them off."

He actually convinced me there was still a chance, so the Wyndham team and our group agreed not to attack each other—even though Milberg said the city commission never overturns a decision by its selection committee. There's always a first time, however, and once I recovered from the selection committee loss, I told myself that I wasn't going to let Courshon win this way. There was a week or two before the city commission would make its official decision and the three finalists would get to go before the city commissioners themselves. It was time to start counting votes.

The first thing we did was to turn up the flame on the PR side, beginning with Vincent Scully. He said he selected the Hyatt for architecture. Now, originally he said how great Arquitectonica's solution was, to have two different buildings, as opposed to the one big building that would block the corridors to the ocean. I didn't understand his change of heart, but I sat Milberg and my land use attorney down and asked them who the high authority was in this regard. They said it was the Miami Design Preservation League.

"Let's get them to weigh in," I said.

"They've never done that before in a competition like this. They don't want to pick sides," Milberg said.

"Well, now is the time to pick sides," I said. "Let's go to them and ask them to conduct a charrette [a public design workshop where the community can offer input], evaluate all three of us, and pick which one they like the best."

The architect Bernardo felt good about his chances, so he and I got the Miami Design Preservation League to conduct the review. The result: They voted eleven to one to recommend us, and agreed to write a letter and to make a recommendation to the commission.

I thought that I dealt with the design issue and canceled Scully out. Next came Mariner, whom I still believed should have voted in our favor. I got a few of my partners and allies to go and meet with him, including Carole Anne Taylor and John Hall; they asked why he voted the way he did. He claimed that Courshon misled him about how the vote worked. To prove his point, he wrote a letter to the city commission saying as much. As a committee member, he urged them to substitute their own judgment for that of the citizens' selection committee. That seemed to cancel out his vote.

Meanwhile, Hilliard continued to go after the Hyatt team, digging and digging until he discovered a $3.9 million federal tax lien against Jackson. Now, Jackson had been saying he didn't need partners because he was putting up all the money himself, some $20 million in cash. Naturally, when the *Daily Business Review* ran with the tax lien story, it questioned his credibility.

Also along the way, I got another piece of advice: Call *Miami Herald* publisher David Lawrence and meet with him. I did, and met with him at his *Herald* offices, where I went though my case: I had control of the Shorecrest, I had financing commitments (whereas the Hyatt had none), I had successful experience as a developer (while Jackson had a blemished record at best), and my 100 percent African American team (the only one) best matched the intent of the deal. As I learned from my deals in Washington, the media can be a great help to you if your work is on the up and up.

Lawrence, it turns out, was a member of the Partners for Progress, a group that participated in settling the tourism boycott. So for the *Herald* to just sit by and watch this project, so important to the community, be awarded as a political consolation prize to the Hyatt team . . . well, I knew that Lawrence could not stomach it. The paper would have to weigh in on this one.

Sure enough, the day before the final presentation to the city commission, the *Herald* ran an editorial. The *Daily Business Review* also ran an editorial, making no bones about how the Hyatt bid should be thrown out. The *Herald* was not as aggressive in their editorial, but they did point out that Jackson's problems raised serious questions and that there was another team that deserved serious consideration, a 100 percent African American team—our group—and that the city commissioners should carefully evaluate the proposals based on merit.

The next morning the three finalists went before the city commission. It was the same thing as before: We each had a room in the convention center, and we got to have them a couple of hours early to prepare. We decorated ours, putting video screens up and bringing in our sound people so we could play Motown music in the background. We wanted to create the Motown vibe.

The commissioners started coming in, and they seemed to like it. Then Mayor Seymour Gelber came in and he didn't like it, at all. I remember thinking how, as a man in his late seventies, he was a little out of touch. He sat down and I could tell he was mad at me.

"Turn the music off," he barked. "Turn it off!"

So we turned it off, and then I got up and made my presentation. I thought it was a great one, even with the mayor furious. After we had gotten selected as number 2, I had spent another $200,000 on the effort, not only on a final lobbying and PR campaign, but on constructing a scale model of the buildings in record time. The model was sitting there, sparkling in the spotlights, while we played a video of the project. The video was terrific, with a Motown soundtrack and a computer illustration of what the two buildings would look like together with other yet-to-be-built buildings along either side. It ended with the song "Ain't No Mountain High Enough." Just spectacular.

When we finished, the mayor ignored normal protocol—

which was to allow the commissioners to ask their questions first—and launched right into me.

"I have a question for you, Mr. Peebles," said Mayor Gelber.

"Sure, Mr. Mayor," I said.

"Are you going to . . . will you . . . give us the Shorecrest Property?"

"Pardon me, Mr. Mayor?"

"If you are not selected, will you give us the Shorecrest Property?"

"Well," I said, "hopefully I will be selected. But if not, I intend to build on the Shorecrest property regardless. My bid to the city was only for what you own, the Royal Palm. I gave you information on the Shorecrest property in our RFP, but for informational purposes only. We submitted for the Royal Palm . . ."

"If you are not selected, will you give us the Shorecrest property?" the mayor repeated, raising his voice.

"Mr. Mayor, I am only submitting for the Royal Palm, which is what you own. In the Shorecrest I'm going to do a hotel condo, whether you guys select us or not."

"So," he said, "you're not going to give us this property? You would hold up the African American hotel deal for that?"

"I look at it differently. Hopefully you'll select me, and you'll have both properties done by one developer. If not, you'll have two African American–owned hotels, the one I do at the Shorecrest and whoever you pick for the Royal Palm."

"You're holding the sword of Damocles over our head!" he yelled.

"Mr. Mayor, you've got this all wrong. You should look at this from a different perspective. You've got a qualified

African American–owned team, financially qualified, that wants to build your hotel so badly they went out and did something you guys couldn't do. They bought the adjoining the property and have invested hundreds of thousands of dollars doing it. That should be an example of my desire to really build this hotel for you."

"No, you're holding the sword of Damocles to our head. You better give us the Shorecrest or else!"

"Mr. Mayor," I said. "This is America, and I have the right to own property. I own this property and we plan to develop it."

"You're going to ruin this hotel for our city!" he screamed, and stormed out.

The mayor had lost his cool completely. People in the audience, including those from the *Miami Herald* and various community organizations, were shocked. I made it a point to remain calm and polite, and the louder the mayor spoke, the softer and more gentle I had become. I learned long before that you should never get emotional when conducting negotiations.

Commissioner Kasdin, who was then vice mayor, took the podium.

"Mr. Peebles, on behalf of our city, I apologize to you for the conduct of our mayor. It was completely inappropriate, and I apologize to you for the way you have been treated. If you like, I am going to preside over the rest of these proceedings."

So Kasdin presided, and the other commissioners asked questions, and they commended me on my work. Then they listened to the other two other presentations and called it a day. The vote was scheduled for a public hearing a couple of weeks later.

It was now time to assess the situation and handicap the votes. There were seven in all, including the mayor, and they stacked up like this:

Commissioner Nancy Liebman was clearly with Hyatt, as was Mayor Gelber. That was two against us.

Commissioner Sy Eisenberg was rock solid behind us, and so was Commissioner Kasdin. That was two for us.

Commissioner David Pearlson seemed likely to vote our way—Milberg had helped run his campaign—but he hadn't declared. He was in play.

Commissioner Marty Shapiro? The Wyndham's publicist had run his campaign, so we figured he'd vote for them.

And Commissioner Susan Gottlieb? At first we weren't sure. Milberg had a good relationship with her, but so did some of the Hyatt folks. So we worked and worked on her, and talked to her out of the anti-Semitic rumor about me. Plus we had the Miami Design Preservation League endorsement, which she respected. We also had one of her key advisors supporting our bid. In the end we believed she was with us.

So that was the tally: three votes for, two votes against, one uncertain, and one for Wyndham. The way I figured it, the one for Wyndham—Marty Shapiro—would vote for them in a first round, they'd be knocked out, and then he'd go for us in a second round. I'd win by four to three, minimum.

Courshon, meanwhile, wasn't finished. At the last minute he hired Kroll Security Services to do background checks on all of us, to see what kind of dirt he could find. He figured that since I was close to Marion Barry, there had to be something.

He was wrong. The report came back with nothing except

more judgments on Jackson. So they held back the report until the morning of the vote—though Milberg got me a copy of it from the city the day before the vote.

When I got the report and saw that it could only benefit us, I figured we had everything sewed up.

Later that day, the day before the final vote, I received a couple of frantic calls. My office was calling me, Katrina was calling me, and my lawyer's office was calling me, all to let me know that Eugene Jackson was trying to reach me. He must know he's beaten, I thought. I dialed the number they had left me.

"Oh yes, Mr. Peebles, Mr. Jackson wants to speak to you right away."

Jackson was in his car, on his cell, when they connected the call.

"I wanted to tell you that you've been a worthy opponent, you've done a good job here," he told me. "And after I win tomorrow, hopefully we can sit down and work out a deal for the Shorecrest. And you're welcome to be on my team. There's room for everybody if you want to come on and join my team and bet with us."

"Hey, thanks, Gene, for the call," I said, thinking to myself, What an arrogant son of a bitch. "And by the way," I said, "if I should get lucky, if by some strange coincidence or happenstance I should win, you're welcome to be on my team as well."

"Yeah, yeah, yeah, okay, we'll hook up tomorrow, after the vote. Let's hook up and see if we can't work out a deal on the Shorecrest.

"Okay."

I remember telling Katrina that this guy didn't know what was actually happening; he was completely out of touch. And I realized at that moment a hugely important principle: The reason Jackson would lose, with everything going for him, was that he had entirely delegated the project. He had let his "Miami people" handle everything, including wooing the city commissioners. When we presented to the Miami Design Preservation League, for example, he didn't show up, and I remember pointing that out to them.

"There is only one developer here, giving you the respect to come here personally," I told them. "And that's me."

And I did that time and time again, when I would meet with community groups. I'd tell them that development is a business with problems that come up. Who's going to be here to solve them? I'm here right now, I would say. Has anybody else come to you to ask for your support, other than through a subordinate? Did Nick Pritzker come here? Did Eugene Jackson? I was there, while they delegated.

This is a hugely important business lesson. There are certain things so important that you cannot delegate them. In a competitive environment, when you're trying to get something from somebody, you've got to ask personally. That's why you see the President of the United States going all over the country, to small towns, asking people for their vote. And that's why I beat Jackson. He had lost even before the vote, and he didn't know it.

I, on the other hand, knew I was going to win. I went to bed knowing that I was going to win. Katrina could hardly sleep, but not I. The next day she told me she was amazed, and jealous, watching me sleep so peacefully.

The meeting was set for 10 A.M., Wednesday, June 5, 1996, and my team was there early. Everybody was on edge. Some people were sitting down, the rest milling on the terrace outside the commission chamber. I came in relaxed, taking it easy. Courshon was sitting down, so I went over to him. We talked.

"You made your mistake by buying the Shorecrest in advance," he said. "You shouldn't have done that, people thought you were arrogant. That was your mistake."

"I don't know about that," I said. "I think the only reason I'm in the game right now, in spite of you not wanting me to be in it, is because I got the Shorecrest. And whoever they pick today has got to deal with me."

"Well, we'll see. We're going to have some interesting negotiations to do if you're not selected. And if you are selected, we're going to have some interesting negotiations."

Then Jackson walked in, wearing a purple suit. I will never forget it. I told Katrina, who was sitting next to me: "Now I know we're going to win. I am not going to be beaten by a guy in a purple suit. I don't care if this is South Beach or not."

Jackson came over and shook my hand. He was a tall guy in his early fifties, maybe six foot five, kind of gruff. "Good job," he said. "And remember, we've got to talk after this."

"I'm sure we will," I said. "Good luck."

Then we went into the commission's chamber. It was packed. The media was there, the community leaders were there, all the assembled teams.

Then the proceedings began.

First the commissioners got a brief report from the city manager, who then deferred to Courshon to make the presentation on behalf of the selection committee.

Courshon spent about an hour discussing the various merits of the projects and why the selection committee chose the Hyatt. He was smart about it. He tried to neutralize the fact that I was the only one with financial commitments.

"I believe Don Peebles can get it financed, and I believe Otis Warren [Wyndham] can get it financed, and I know that Gene Jackson and the Hyatt can get it financed," he tells the commission. "I believe you have to give Don Peebles the benefit of the doubt, that he can put the financing together. So I believe they all can finance it."

"So that's not the issue," he says. "What it really boils down to is architecture, nothing else. All of them can get it financed. But it's architecture. And you have Vincent Scully, one of the premier architectural professors in the country, on the committee, and he says Hyatt's is the best design. So I am deferring to him."

Now, Courshon was a lawyer and a banker, and he is very smooth. He argues well. Then the commissioners get some public comments.

The Kiwanis Club comes up, and they talk about certainty, and how my team appears more certain to get the hotel done. Then some minority businesspeople come up and speak on my behalf, about how we've finally got a talented African American team with the financial wherewithal and everything else in place to get it done.

Finally the Miami Design Preservation League comes up. They tell the commission that they've never done something like this before but are compelled to by the quality of the Arquitectonica design and the poor solution of the Hyatt team. They conclude by saying that the Hyatt design is completely inappropriate for the Art Deco neighborhood, while the Arquitectonica solution is completely appropriate.

After that, each of the three teams gets a moment to speak and then it comes time for the vote. I'm sitting with my attorneys, partners, and Katrina, while Gene Jackson, Courshon, and the Hyatt lawyers are all sitting together.

Each commissioner speaks, and makes his or her position clear.

Kasdin goes first. He says how it's important that this project go forward and that in his opinion, the solution must be someone with financing and someone who controls the Shorecrest so the city wouldn't have to condemn it and get into a lawsuit. And that means Peebles. You could see Courshon and Jackson start wiggling a little bit, even though Kasdin isn't that big of a surprise.

Then Liebman gets up and criticizes the Miami Design Preservation League for getting involved in the city's business and says Hyatt had the best solution. No surprise there, or when Gelber gets up and says Hyatt had the best solution.

Next Pearlson announces that it's the toughest choice he's had to make in his career and that he doesn't know how he is going to vote.

The Hyatt team is feeling a little more positive now. They are thinking they have at least two votes, and Gottlieb will make three. They're counting on her. So they are shaken when she gets up next and says she is sick of the city taking so long to get the project under way.

"I want this thing to move forward," she says, "and there is only one team that can move it forward, and that's Peebles."

Then Marty Shapiro starts talking. He says how it's a tough decision, so tough that the city went out and hired investigators to investigate these people. "I saw this investigative report that we just got this morning. We know Gene Jackson already had judgments for tax liens, millions of dollars in judgments. We find out now in this report he has another million-dollar judgment. With all due respect, Mr. Jackson has liens and judgments up the wazoo."

He then says that the Peebles team seems to have a good proposal "but, apparently he is a lifelong protégé of Mayor Marion Barry of Washington, and that sends chills up my spine." So he picks Wyndham.

Finally, Sy Eisenberg steps up to the podium.

"I'm just going to vote," he says. "I've already made my decision, and I'll vote and you'll know how I vote after I vote." Period.

Courshon and Jackson are now visibly nervous. But Courshon has one last curve ball to throw. He explains how they are going to vote. Instead of each commissioner simply picking a winner, with a majority needed to win, Courshon now instructs them to rank each applicant 1, 2, or 3. The numbers will then be added up, and the lowest total will win. He explains this will help the city rank the teams, so that if they can't make a deal with team number 1, they can do a deal with team 2, and so forth. What it really means is that commissioners can now lower my ranking from second to third and sink me with a higher total.

The commissioners are each handed a piece of paper, and they start to write down their rankings. It is a fascinating scrimmage to watch, and all eyes are on them. Eisenberg leans over and sees Mayor Gelber rank me number 3 and Hyatt number 1, in an obvious attempt to manipulate the numbers. But since Eisenberg sees this, he changes his ranking for Hyatt from number 2 to number 3. Liebman does the same as Gelber: Hyatt 1, me 3. On my side, Gottlieb follows Eisenberg's lead and ranks me 1, Hyatt, 3. Pearlson ranks Hyatt 1 but puts me second, and Kasdin does the same, except with me 1 and Hyatt 2. Basically, those two guys are trying to be fair and make everybody happy because they both want to run for mayor. Finally, Shapiro ranks Wyndam 1, me, 2, and Hyatt, 3.

The clerk tallies it up and gives the total to the mayor. The mayor examines it and makes a harummph sound, looking disgusted. He authorizes the clerk to read it out loud:

"Peebles Crowne Plaza, thirteen; Hyatt Jackson, four-teen; and Warren Wyndam, fifteen."

I had won, by one point.

The chamber breaks out in applause and I stand up and start shaking hands. I'm swarmed with people congratulating me. Kasdin comes off the dais and congratulates me. Gottlieb congratulates me and leans over to say "Don't let me down. I know you're going to get this done." Eisenberg comes over and shakes my hand, and Pearlson comes over and shakes my hand too.

Then I notice the Jackson table. Their attorney has his head hanging down, and Courshon is slouched in his chair like he is dying. Jackson is walking out, dejected. I go over to him and hold out my hand and say: "What a tough battle."

He refuses to shake my hand. "You and I have mutual friends in the black business community," he says. "I'm going to go around and tell everybody what you did to me. What you did to me isn't right."

"Gene," I say, "we were competing here and I won fair and square."

"What you did wasn't right!" he snarls, and then storms out.

I did a bunch of interviews, and after about forty-five minutes my team and I walked over to the Van Dyke Hotel on Lincoln Road. We went up to the club on the second floor and had celebratory drinks and lunch.

That was how I won the Royal Palm deal.

I would have another set of struggles getting the hotel built, especially from the city; after the vote, Mayor Gelber threw one last hatchet in my back. Saying what an outstanding job Courshon had done for the city in heading up the selection committee, he announced that Courshon would be the chief negotiator representing the city in the deal with Peebles. Wow.

I would also later continue to grow my business and political influence on Miami Beach as I moved into other projects, notably the Bath Club. Learning from my fundraising days in Washington, I would help organize and finance Commissioner Kasdin's campaign for mayor, a post he would win in less than two years. In that race he would defeat Commissioner Pearlson, who would leave town and move to the Northeast.

But these are for another story.

This day was mine.

EPILOGUE TO CHAPTER 5

What I loved about the deal for the Royal Palm was how compact it was; the starter pistol went off on January 1, with an RFP due in ninety days, followed by two months of presentations and a decision shortly thereafter. It was a horse race—and I was on virgin turf. I had no network in South Florida. The Peebles Principles would be tested on this one.

Nonetheless, I obviously came very close to losing the competition and the deal. I actually did lose on the first round, when the selection committee voted its recommendation, and it required a serious gut check to keep pushing in those final few weeks.

This was an important lesson of the Royal Palm, the idea that you can never give up until it's really over, until that fat lady actually belts it out. It's classic Americana, really, the underdog baseball team pulling it off with a ninth-inning streak. You can never give up until the absolute end, and you can't leave any stone unturned. You still might find the solution under that last rock.

By the same token, you can't kowtow to those with more apparent power and wealth. You can respect them, but don't be in awe. When you are an entrepreneur, you will come up against lots of people who are better established. You can't let that intimidate you. You are going to have more fire and desire than them, and you can be a lot more nimble.

What this deal best highlights, however, is how the last few steps of any transaction are frequently the most important. The fact that you have finished 95 percent of a task doesn't mean anything if you don't wrap up that last 5 percent. You have to execute right to the end. You can never leave it to chance.

It all comes down to what you might call the finishing touches of any deal, also known as the details. There is no such thing as overkill in this type of environment. It doesn't matter that you've written a great contract or a great novel, if the words aren't spelled and punctuated correctly. Cars don't sparkle until they have been detailed. All the training an Olympic athlete goes through doesn't matter if he or she breaks even the smallest rule.

PEEBLES GROUND RULES

- Don't quit even if it seems like the end; endurance is key.

- Don't be intimidated by better established rivals.

- Make your serious requests in person.

- Never stop looking for a way to win.

- Don't get sloppy at the end: The last five yards are more important than the first.

- Remember that you are the final gatekeeper on the quality and image of your deal.

Peebles Principle #5: Be a Bulldog on Details

Never underestimate the importance of dealing with key details yourself, especially final details, and especially when it comes to influencing people whose help or support you need.

❧ 6 ❧

San Francisco:
A Bridge Too Far

Doing deals is also about partnering, and you had better choose a partner you can rely on. I came across a great opportunity in San Francisco in the late 1990s, but it came with a partner I should never have trusted. I learned another lesson from that too: Go with your instincts.

When I won the Royal Palm, I got a lot of media exposure, locally and nationally, and as I had discovered earlier, that often leads to important contacts. I found the inverse to be true as well: The media was a great source of ideas and contacts for me.

Early in 1997, one of those leads came my way through a guy who was working with me on the Royal Palm. He'd read an article about an African American who had won the site to build a major hotel just south of Market Street in San Francisco. The area was becoming a real estate hot spot—it's roaring today—and the future hotel would be right across the street from the Moscone Convention Center and directly next to the Museum of Modern Art.

The name of the guy who had won the bid was Otho Green. He was a successful government contractor but a novice developer who'd never done anything of this magnitude before. Given this inexperience, my colleague who'd read the article suggested I give the guy a call and introduce myself, and see if there was an opportunity for us to do a deal. So I called Otho and congratulated him. I told him I was now emerging in the hotel business with the Royal Palm and that if there was anything I could do to help him to let me know. We agreed to get in touch if he ever came to Miami or if I was ever in San Francisco.

As it turned out, I was in San Francisco a few months later, looking at a request for qualifications to build a new hotel at the San Francisco International Airport. I was there to attend the bidders' conference for the project and made a short vacation of it with Katrina at the Huntington Hotel on Nob Hill. I called Otho Green while I was there, to set up a time for us to meet in person, just to get acquainted.

He called me back early one morning at the hotel. He was in Phoenix, Arizona, meeting with hotel executives from Doubletree Hotels, to see if they wanted to partner with him on his deal. This was on a Tuesday morning, and by the end of that week he said he had to put up a $400,000 deposit with the San Francisco Redevelopment Agency for the site he'd won. That deposit, by the way, gave him the right to buy the site for about $7.5 million. It was easily worth more than twice that.

"Well, if you only need $400,000, then let's talk," I told him. "Why don't we get together later and see if we can do a deal. Don't make a deal with Doubletree until you've given me a shot to see if we can work together."

"Do you have $400,000 to put up?" he asked.

"Of course," I said.

"Then I'll meet you later today."

He flew back from Phoenix and came by the hotel late in the afternoon. He was in his late fifties, maybe early sixties, with an ego way out of proportion to his abilities and position. I remember that he was very concerned about his image, and that he wanted the project ownership entity, no matter what, to be called The Green Group.

We talked conceptually about his deal, and we came to an understanding: I would put up all the money, I would secure the financing, and we would joint venture it. He would own the commercial space and the parking garage and be paid a lump sum of cash up front in the amount of $7.5 million. I would pay the city its $7.5 million price as well, and I would do the rest of the deal with the hotel operator. This would be a major high-rise building, a $150 million–plus project.

Because I had been working with Marriott on the airport hotel bid, I gave them a call to see if this new convention hotel project would be of interest to them. I called their West Coast development guy whom I was working with on the airport deal, to see if he was still in town. He was.

"I want you to see this site, it's really something," I told him. "This could be just where you'd like to put a JW Marriott."

"I'm on my way," he said.

He looked at the site and loved it, and said he thought he could get a deal done. I called my attorney and had him draft a document for Otho Green and me to formalize our understanding. We didn't have enough time to do a full partnership agreement, so it was basically a memorandum of understanding. It outlined the deal we had discussed and also stated that if we were unable to reach a meeting of the minds and work out a deal in good faith, then either party could terminate. I would then get my money back.

The papers were drawn up by my Miami attorney, Stuart

Hoffman, and reviewed by a prominent local attorney, Bill Coblentz. I met with him before I cut the deal and he'd done some research on Otho Green. He informed me that he had heard things about Otho's reputation along the lines that he was in over his head, that many of the city officials didn't really like him, and that I should be very careful. In fact, he recommended that I not do the deal with him.

I didn't care. The land that he could buy for $7.5 million was probably worth around $20 million at the time, and the right to build a high-rise in San Francisco, directly across from the Moscone Center and literally next door to the Museum of Modern Art was too good to pass up. I knew it was a great opportunity, and we had a chance to make a fortune. In spite of the rumors regarding Otho's experience, I decided to go ahead.

The clock was ticking, so the next day I had the money wired to Coblentz's trust account and he issued a certified check to me for the redevelopment agency. Otho Green had stopped by the hotel to sign off on our memorandum, and afterward we drove together to Coblentz's office. He waited in the car while I went upstairs to get the cashier's check. I gave him the reimbursement he needed, and the agency the $340,000 deposit they required. We actually drove to the agency to drop off the check, and I used the opportunity to introduce myself to some of their executives. Otho then dropped me back at the hotel and I thought, Hey, this is the beginning of a good relationship.

Needless to say I was shocked to hear, early the next week, that Otho was trying to back out of our deal. Even though we had signed our agreement, and even though I had put up a nonrefundable deposit with the city and personally bailed him out, he was still negotiating with Wyndham.

I called a friend of mine, a hospitality industry investor I'd met in Miami who had done business with Wyndham. I asked him who was running the company, and he put me in touch with the chairman and CEO, Jim Carreker. I called him.

"I understand your company is trying to do a deal with Otho Green on the Third and Mission Street site in San Francisco," I told him. "I just want to let you know that I have a partnership with him, under contract, so you should probably be communicating with me as well."

"I really don't know what you are talking about, Don," he told me. "But I'm happy to look into it."

We ended our conversation friendly enough, but nothing came of it. Wyndham went on pitching Otho Green to get out of my deal. And Green didn't stop there; he was also trying to do a deal with Pacific Union, a local San Francisco firm, and there were probably others.

In the meantime I was pushing things forward with the city. The redevelopment agency needed to approve the assignment of the project to our new joint venture entity, and so we scheduled a hearing for a few weeks later. I'd taken Katrina home to Miami and then flew back to San Francisco to learn whatever I could, and meet with whomever could help.

One of the people I met with was an early partner of Otho Green's. He was a guy named Steven Williams, a former State of California official who had a long relationship with San Francisco Mayor Willie Brown when he was Speaker of the California Assembly. We had lunch at The Big Four Restaurant at the Huntington Hotel, where I was again staying.

The introduction to Williams had come from the project's architect, Jeffrey Heller. Heller had offered his architectural services to the project on spec, so as to enable Green to submit his winning bid, and he felt Green was going to blow the deal with the city. That would mean a dead loss of the time and money that Heller's firm had put into developing the design and architectural plans. He saw me as the person who could make the project happen. Therefore, he suggested I meet with Williams. Over lunch, Williams told me the history of how he had started with Otho Green and how he had used his political connections to help win the Mission Street deal, and how Ortho had turned around and shopped the deal to other potential partners.

Needless to say, I was now not surprised when Otho called and tried to back out of the deal. "I want to renegotiate or give you your money back," he told me over the phone.

"I don't want my money back," I replied. "We made a deal and you need to live up to it."

But he refused. He wouldn't go forward on the deal we had. He wanted a better one. I said no.

Now, during this time, I had been lobbying the redevelopment agency to approve the assignment of the project to me. Here was a city with an African American mayor, Willie Brown, and yet no African American had done a development of any significance in downtown San Francisco—or anywhere else in the city, for that matter. And none had done a high rise. This was going to be historic.

Now, however, with Otho's refusal to honor our agreement, I had no choice but to go back to the redevelopment agency and ask them to take the item off of their agenda.

Disgusted, I called one of my attorneys, Tim Francis; Tim was well connected in African American political circles. He had brought me into a hotel deal in New Orleans and had also been working on my team at the San Francisco International Airport. I told him what was going on. In a case of it's a small world, after all, Tim knew Willie Brown through Marc Morial, who was then mayor of New Orleans. Tim and Morial were close friends, Morial and Mayor Brown were friends, so it was a game of connect the dots: Morial called Brown for Tim and arranged for me to meet the mayor and discuss the Mission Street hotel situation.

We met in the mayor's conference room. The mayor was there, of course, as was the executive director of the San Francisco Redevelopment Agency. Steven Williams was at the meeting, as were Heller and Tim Francis and another member of the mayor's staff.

Now, Otho Green's attorney was married to the mayor's chief of staff, so Green thought he had an in with the mayor. But he didn't. I explained to Mayor Brown what had happened. And I remember how he leaned over and told his redevelopment director that this was just the kind of thing he didn't want going on.

"Why is this Otho Green speculating with city land?" the mayor asked. "If Peebles is willing to pay him $15 million for the land, we should be getting that extra $7.5 million, not him."

The mayor went on to say that he'd like nothing better than to see the redevelopment agency terminate Otho Green's rights and award the project to me directly. And what the mayor asked, the agency did. Right after that discussion, they put a hearing on their agenda to terminate The Green Group from its rights to the site and the project. After the meeting, Francis was so excited and confident I would get the deal he asked to put his own money into it.

He actually invested $100,000 in the project. This was probably all of his savings; it was a lot of money to him, but he was convinced Brown was with us and wanted his piece of the rock.

Naturally, after the redevelopment agency scheduled this hearing, Green wanted to talk to see if we could work things out. This was in October of 1997, and I was right in the middle of fighting for a letter of intent from the City of Miami Beach for the Royal Palm Hotel project. I was busy as hell just as Green tried to renegotiate a new deal at the last possible moment. I said I wouldn't sign anything other than a definitive agreement, which made it even more complicated. Nevertheless, our lawyers and their lawyers worked together until the morning before the redevelopment agency hearing. At 5 A.M. we finally finished. But it was too late. The hearing went forward anyway.

Early that afternoon, Katrina, Donahue, and I flew back to our home in Maryland, where we had moved after my falling out with Barry. That evening I got a call from Williams advising me that the redevelopment agency had voted to terminate Otho Green's development rights. They also authorized the issuing of a new RFP. I would ultimately bid on that, but in the interim I had to sue Green for the deposit, just as he had to sue the redevelopment agency for the same. They finally agreed to settle with him, but not until I signed off on it, which I did. Green was so broke that I ended up letting him keep his $60,000, gave him roughly another $20,000, and spent $20,000 on lawyers. So I ended up recovering approximately $300,000 of the original $400,000.

I subsequently bid on the project, about a year or so later, with Carlson Hospitality, the owner of Radisson

Hotels, as my hotel partner. I also joined forces with two local minority businessmen, a housing developer and a lobbyist, both of whom had close relationships with Mayor Brown. And while Radisson was not a luxury hotel brand, the Carlson Companies was one of America's largest privately owned companies, so I had high hopes the board would follow through with their intention from the year before and give me the deal. Unfortunately, it would not prove so simple.

First, as I said, Radisson was not perceived as a high end brand, and we ended up in a stalemate: The first round of votes split three to three (with one abstention) between our group and—you guessed it—the Wyndham group, which still wanted the project. In order to break the deadlock, the redevelopment agency hired a consulting firm to evaluate the proposals.

Now, the agency had originally ranked three teams as the top three finalists: my team, the Wyndham team, and one backed by Peninsula Hotels. The was an additional bid for the project that did not make the cut, one that was put forward by a guy named Dick Friedman, a developer out of Boston. His company had developed the Charles Hotel in downtown Boston, and they had hired Brown's top campaign advisor to join their team. Friedman complained about not making the final cut and made a subtle threat to sue the city if they did not include him in the final round. He supposedly went directly to Brown on this, through his campaign connection. Regardless, the final list was suddenly increased to four and Friedman's group was on it.

So the consulting firm conducted interviews and did its research on all four finalists. They ended up concluding that our group offered the best financial deal for the city as well as the strongest financial team, mainly due to Carlson's commitment to guarantee the financing needed to build the project. They gave Brown a preview of their report, and he allegedly directed them to go back and give him more flexibility. The final report was issued the Friday before the vote was scheduled and indicated that while we were stronger in these two areas, it didn't matter. It concluded that the city would ultimately be able to negotiate better deals with the other groups and that because of the strong location and market, the other bidders would not have too much difficulty attracting capital. After reviewing the report, I knew something was going on behind the scenes. I thought it was just Brown pacifying his former campaign advisor on Friedman's team, who incidentally would be working on his upcoming reelection campaign. Just before the agency meeting, however, I discovered that a far stronger political force was at work.

It turns out that Friedman was an old friend of Bill Clinton and that Clinton routinely borrowed Friedman's house in Martha's Vineyard as a summer escape pad. It also turns out that Willie Brown was running for reelection as the mayor of San Francisco and was concerned about the race. He felt he needed Clinton's help in the campaign. From there you don't need a road map: Friedman contacted Clinton, and Clinton tracked down Willie Brown, who happened to be in London at the time. When it came down to finally deciding who got the project—in fact, right in the middle of the meeting—the executive director of the redevelopment agency put a cell phone up to the microphone. It was the mayor, who promptly instructed the redevelopment agency to select Freidman. They did, and Friedman got it.

That is how I lost the San Francisco convention hotel deal.

Ironically, I had been an early supporter of Clinton back when he was running for the Democratic Party nomination. But it never occurred to me that the President of the United States would intervene in a local real estate bid.

In thinking about it afterward, I could hardly fault Brown. The city would still get its money for the land and still get its hotel. In such instances, where the choices are fairly close, it's hard to avoid making a political decision. It was the President of the United States asking for favor!

Such is the danger when you don't close out a deal at hand.

EPILOGUE TO CHAPTER 6

I learned a number of things from the failure of this deal, not the least of which was that you need to be very careful about whom you choose to partner with in business. Worst of all, since I was warned about my partner's reputation before I entered into the relationship, I was blinded by my ambition to do a big deal in San Francisco.

In the case of Otho Green, I rushed to do the deal because I liked it so much. I saw an opportunity to make a whole lot of money, so I took a greater risk in terms of documentation. I should have realized that I was in the position of strength; this guy definitely needed the money, and I should have made him and his lawyer work harder on making the deal binding. If you do business with somebody who has a bad reputation, you've got to make sure to dot your i's and cross your t's. There is no point in signing a contract if it's not completely binding.

Another lesson I learned was to never overestimate your position of strength when it comes to political relationships. As long as it does not violate the public trust, and in situations where most other things are equal, most politicians will ultimately act in their own political self-interest. Therefore, in tough situations, you can count on their support only as long as both of your interests are parallel. I learned this with both Brown and Barry.

The tragedy in all of this is that Otho Green would have made millions of dollars. He would have been set for the rest of his life. I was prepared to put $7.5 million into acquiring the property (Freidman ended up paying the city $15 million for it, by the way) and to give Green another $7.5 million up front as well as a share of the profits. His double-dealing cost him the opportunity of his lifetime.

At the time I thought he was just being greedy, but since then I'm not so certain. In retrospect, I think it was a little bit of the proverbial crabs-in-a-barrel mentality. I was a younger African American and he was an older African American; he wanted to be in control and I was going to steal his thunder. So I don't think he really wanted to see me succeed. What he really wanted was to do business with a big, national company that imbued him with credibility and recognized the ownership entity as The Green Group. This was important for his ego and his sense of self-worth—even if it meant him getting far less money up front and owning just a sliver of the deal.

PEEBLES GROUND RULES

- Do your people due diligence; know your partners.

- Avoid doing business with people who have bad reputations.

- If you cut deals with questionable parties, always make sure the legal documentation is thorough.

- There is no point in signing a contract if it's not completely binding.

- Remember that politicians, in the absence of other decisive factors, will act in their own self-interest. Make yours parallel.

Peebles Principle #6: Listen to Your First Instinct

If your gut tells you that a deal is too risky or that your partners seem untrustworthy, pay attention, step back, and reflect. If you go ahead anyway, do so with extra protection, especially in terms of documentation.

❧ 7 ❧

The Bath Club:
Give Them
What They Want

In any negotiation, it is supremely important that you understand what the other parties want. That was clearly the case in my barrier-busting Bath Club deal, which I won because I understood that it was about much more than the money.

By 1999 I had completely relocated to Miami. It was now my home and I had established offices downtown in the signature Bank of America building. This is a tall, semicircular tower that is lit up at night with spectacular colors that change every week or so. Our suite was on the forty-sixth floor and had commanding views of all Miami as well as Biscayne Bay and the Atlantic Ocean beyond.

Besides being beautiful and conspicuous, the building had an infamous history, even by Miami standards. It was originally built as headquarters for high-flying CenTrust Bank, which went bust in the early 1990s along with its flamboyant president, David Paul, who subsequently spent eleven years in federal prison for banking and securities fraud. His office was an icon for the bank's excesses, with a $13.2 million Peter Paul Rubens hanging in it (paid for by the bank) and gold-plated fixtures in the lavatory (also paid for by the bank). I had part of his old suite, the floor beneath the penthouse; that top slice was taken by B of A for their private banking center. I would actually become one of their best private banking customers.

One afternoon, late in the day, I got a call from Michael Browarnik and Stacy Robins. Michael was a real estate investment banker who secured financing for commercial projects (he had previously arranged permanent financing for my Royal Palm project).

Stacy was a real estate agent whom Katrina and I had met right around the time we got married. We had been staying at the Marlin Hotel on Collins Avenue, back when it was one of the few luxury hotels in Miami Beach; the Robins family had built it with legendary Island Records producer Chris Blackwell, the guy who discovered Bob Marley. Stacy gave us a tour of South Beach before it became the "in" place to be, and I got to know her later when I did business with her brother Scott.

The two called and said they had a deal for me, a perfect deal. The famous Miami Bath Club was on the market and going to be sold. CB Richard Ellis was marketing it, and their target was $10 million.

For those unfamiliar with the history of Miami Beach, the Bath Club was a notoriously exclusive social bathing club on 5.5 acres of oceanfront land about ten blocks north of the Fontainebleau Hotel. The club was founded in the 1920s by Carl Fisher, the developer who started Miami Beach, and Herbert Hoover, before he became president. It was an enclave for society icons and captains of industry from the Northeast and Midwest, their roost when they'd come down for the winter social season. At first not even locals were permitted, but more poignantly, the bylaws stated that "colored people" were not allowed on the property, not even as servants. They could only come as far as the loading dock, to drop off their employers' luggage. There were no Jewish members allowed either. The legacy was still so strong that when it was discovered, in the early 1980s, that Mayor of Miami Maurice Ferre was a member he was lambasted in the local press for belonging to such a racist club.

By the time the deal was presented to me, those policies had been abandoned, partly due to the changing times and partly due to the club's need to attract more members. Ironically, I had been part of that change.

I had been a member of the Bath Club in 1996 when Katrina and I had an apartment across the street on Collins Avenue. Laurinda Spear, the wife and partner of Arquitectonica CEO Bernardo Fort-Brescia, suggested we join and introduced us; her parents were active on the board. The chairman of the club, Doug Bishoff, gave us a tour. I remember being underwhelmed on the walk-through, but the access to the beach was easy so we joined.

Shortly afterward I got a phone call from *Miami Herald* columnist Joan Fleischman, who asked: "How does it feel to be the first African American member of the Bath Club?"

Now, I didn't even know what a restricted club was. We didn't have that sort of thing back in Washington, so she explained the club's history. The next day the paper ran her column about how I was the first ever African American member of the Bath Club and how the club wanted to show it was now more open, accepting a broader membership, etc. They wanted to use me to make the point.

So I was familiar with this great piece of property, and when the deal was presented to me, I knew it was a great opportunity. I knew what a heck of a symbol it would be

Posing for a school picture in 1966, age six.
(Carmody Hills Elementary school photo)

Detroit, summer 1967, me, my
aunt Hilda McIntosh, cousin
Keith, cousin Karl, and my uncle
Dr. Carol McIntosh.
*(From Don Peebles' personal
collection)*

Surrounded by three beautiful women—
my aunt Edith Tucci, my mother Yvonne
Poole, and my Aunt Carolyn—after my
graduation ceremony from Alice Deal
Junior High School, June 1975.
(From Don Peebles' personal collection)

President Jimmy Carter presenting me my high school graduation certificate of achievement at the White House Rose Garden, June 1978.
(White House photographer)

With D.C. Mayor Marion Barry at City Hall in 1984 at the swearing-in ceremony after my appointment as chairman of the Board of Equalization and Review.
(D.C. mayors' official photographer)

With Mayor Barry and developer Douglas Goldsten at a fund-raising event that we co-hosted for the mayor's reelection effort.
(From Don Peebles' personal collection)

My first development project at 2100 Martin Luther King, Jr. Avenue.
(Photo taken by Eric McKan of EVM Maintenance Services)

With Katrina, President Bill Clinton, D.C. Mayor Sharon Pratt Kelly, and her husband James Kelly in 1992 at our estate in Washington, D.C.
(Photo taken by Louis Myrie)

James Kelly, D.C. Mayor Sharon Pratt Kelly, New York Mayor David Dinkins, Katrina, and I at a fund-raising event for Mayor Dinkins held at our Washington, D.C., estate in 1993.
(Photo taken by Louis Myrie)

The office building at 10 G Street, N.E. built in partnership with the American Psychological Association and Trammel Crow Company.
(Photo taken by Eric McKan of EVM Maintenance Services)

The Marriott Courtyard Hotel in
Washington, D.C.
*(Photo taken by Eric McKan of EVM
Maintenance Services)*

Giving the commence-
ment address on May 20,
2000, when I received my
honorary Doctorate in
Business Administration
and Hospitality
Management from
Johnson and Wales
University.
(Photo taken by Johnson and Wales)

Groundbreaking ceremony for
the Royal Palm Hotel, August 1998.
*(Photo courtesy of a Peebles Atlantic
Development Corporation employee)*

The Royal Palm Hotel, front view.
(Arquitectonica International)

The ribbon-cutting ceremony at the grand opening of the Royal Palm Hotel in May 2002, with Peter Calin, attorney H.T. Smith, Miami Beach Mayor David Dermer, Donahue, III, Katrina, attorney Marilyn Holifield, Intercontinental Hotels president Steven Porter, Union Planters Bank president Aldolfo Henriquez, and Ocean Bank vice president Joy Venero.
(Dana Bowden Photography)

The 2003 YMCA boys' basketball team that I coached.
(From Don Peebles' personal collection)

May 2004, after receiving the Black Enterprise Company of the Year
award in Dallas, Texas, with Black Enterprise chairman/publisher
Earl Graves and son Earl Graves Jr.
(Black Enterprise)

Donahue, III at eight years old introduces me at the Bath Club
groundbreaking ceremony while media and guests look on.
(Andrew Goldstein Photography)

Summer 2006, disembarking from our jet on the way to our summer home in Santa Fe, New Mexico.
(Photo taken with my personal camera)

The Lincoln, an office building I built in partnership with Scott Robins.
(Mark Morais)

The Bath Club project looking from the Atlantic Ocean.
(Mark Morais)

The rear exterior of our Coral Gables home, Casa Arboles.

for me, an African American, to buy it. It would mean a great deal of publicity, and that could only increase my visibility and clout in the local real estate business. I knew the Bath Club would have an impact for me. And I knew it would make me a fortune.

I was no longer a member, and that was, in essence, the problem that had prompted the sale: declining membership. Not only had membership stagnated, the club had gone into debt to renovate the facilities to make them more attractive. Nothing seemed to work, however, and shrinking membership plus debt resulted in cash flow problems. They needed to sell.

The asking price of $10 million, however, surprised me. It was quite low for such a big piece of oceanfront land right in the middle of Miami Beach. Even then it should have been worth at least two or three times as much. The reason for the low price? A little bit of homework revealed something that had backfired for the club.

On Miami Beach, you are taxed at the highest and best use of your property. The Bath Club consisted of a one-story clubhouse, sort of an old mansion, with a small wing of two-story cabana efficiencies. It was originally zoned RM3, which permitted a huge high-rise building with no height restrictions. Unfortunately for the club, that potent zoning came with matching taxes. So in the early 1990s the club voluntarily downgraded its zoning to RM1, which gave them a handsome tax cut but restricted any future development to four stories in height. They figured they could always rezone if they wanted to sell or rebuild.

They figured wrong. A decade later came the Save Miami Beach campaign, put on the ballot by a young lawyer named David Dermer, which required that voters approve any new zoning for high-rises. It meant an end to pell-mell high-rise construction on the beach, and overnight it dropped the value of the Bath Club's property from $40 million to $10 million.

Nonetheless, as you might expect with CB Richard Ellis marketing it worldwide, the club got a lot of offers. They had perhaps a hundred inquiries and rumor had it they even received an offer of $40 million subject to rezoning. They got some other big offers too, but these were also contingent on rezoning.

With all the competition, I knew this would require some thought. I remember coming home to Katrina the night after that phone call from Stacy, sitting outside and asking her what she thought.

"What do you think it would take for us to win? What's the issue?" I asked. "It's not so much the money. I mean, there are 160 members, and when you divide it up it wouldn't come to much." (The club was $5.5 million in debt, so each member would get about $28,000 of the $4.5 million left over from a $10 million purchase.)

"I think it's more of an embarrassment to them," she said. "Maybe if there was a way to save face that would do it. Maybe if there was a way to save the club. That could be the solution."

Katrina had hit it. If we could set up something where the club could continue to exist and pay their debts and dues, it should prove very attractive to the members.

As it turned out, this was indeed the solution and the way in which we outfoxed the scores of other bidders for the project. All they could imagine was that the biggest offer would win. They could only picture the sellers' motives in terms of their wallets. They couldn't see that the Bath Club members were not trying to make a score but were selling only as a last-ditch alternative to declaring bankruptcy, which would have really been an embarrassment. I was sure they would much prefer carrying on with their beloved beachside club, and once I figured that out—with Katrina's help—I had the inside line on the deal.

It was an immensely important lesson that I would never forget. In any deal, it is vital to understand what the other parties want. Sometimes this comes down to doing some basic research about the people and/or companies you are dealing with; other times it may take a little creative thinking before the light goes on. Either way, you have to figure out what's motivating the people on the other side of the table. Once you do, then you have to figure out how to get it to them.

As fortune would have it, by that time I had done several historic properties, so I already understood the value of restoration and had a track record to prove it. So I offered to preserve the clubhouse, and let the members keep it, at the same time giving them full access to the improved facilities. (At that time I planned to build a hotel, and they would be able to use the new pools, gym, spa—all the services, including discounted food and beverage services.) I would build around the Bath Club, restore it, add amenities, and keep the members-only beach club itself intact.

I also knew that, second to keeping their clubhouse, their traditions and their dignity, the Bath Club needed cash right away. It was a pressing issue for them. So in addition to my plan for restoration, I offered to put up a big deposit that could not be refunded unless we found environmental contamination. They accepted and from that point on they began to negotiate with me exclusively.

I negotiated with their previous chairman, Doug Bishoff, the man who had given me my first tour of the club (and who happened to be a lawyer), and their current president, Jamie Helman, a real estate developer from Boston. Ultimately Helman took the lead in the negotiations. Having offered them what they wanted, the big agenda item for me was the timing. I didn't want to close on the sale before getting the site rezoned.

Like the other bidders who had offered $30 million and $40 million, the success of the deal depended on rezoning the property. As I was making my offer, I did some research on the city's zoning laws and hired a local zoning attorney. The opportunity looked good; the attorney felt that the Bath Club's RM1 designation was a case of spot zoning at its worst because every other property on that stretch of Collins Avenue was RM3. State law prohibits spot zoning because it can be considered prejudicial against one owner. The attorney also had some calculations about what could be grandfathered in from the old zoning.

Perhaps most important, we found we could go for an RM2 zoning without triggering a public vote. It wasn't RM3, and it would still require the approval of the city commission—and that during a time when the electorate was in a downsizing mood—but the RM2 status would let us build twenty stories high. That was enough to turn the project into an amazingly profitable venture.

As you know, I was no stranger to the city commission by this time. Anti-growth mood or no, I still had some strong relationships among the commissioners, and I figured I could get the votes I needed. Still, before I committed to the Bath Club contract, I wanted to work out my chances with the commission, playing the strategy like a game of chess.

There were seven Miami Beach City commissioners, and the vote threshold for rezoning was five-sevenths. So I needed five yes votes.

First, I had my friends on the commission who had voted in favor of the Royal Palm bid. There was Susan Gottlieb, who was pro-development and who was related to my zoning attorney by marriage. She was solid. Marty Shapiro had also voted for me before, I had established a good rapport with him, and I felt I could count on his vote. I had become good friends with Neissen Kasdin too. He was now the mayor, and I had significantly helped him with his election. I asked him where he stood, and he said he was supportive.

That made three out of the five I needed.

Next I went after Nancy Liebman, who had been an opponent of mine for the Royal Palm bid. First of all, she was the historian activist of the commission, so I thought the proposal to restore the Bath Club might appeal to her. Also, we had developed a strong relationship the year before when she had been running for reelection. I had originally backed an opponent of hers, but when she personally asked me to back off, I did.

That act on my part was now going to pay off. As it turned out, she and I had quite a bit in common when it came to politics. I had always practiced the Lyndon Johnson way of politics: Reward your friends and punish your enemies. Even your friends get a hierarchy of treatment. Nancy followed the same rules, which is what I hoped to get from politicians I supported.

When the Bath Club deal came up, I went to see her and ask for her commitment. As expected, she applauded my effort at historic preservation; before she was elected to the commission, Nancy had been at the forefront of the creation of the Art Deco Historic District in South Beach. Also, as a Jewish person, she despised the club's history of exclusion and loved the fact that a black person was buying it. Because of that restrictive history Nancy had refused to ever step foot in the club, but I convinced her to tour the property with me. I told her that given the club's racist history, it was even more important to preserve it as a reminder of just how far Miami Beach had come. So she committed to support the project, and it was a solid commitment. Even if all the other commissioners changed their vote, Nancy would keep her word, no matter what.

So now I had four of the five votes I needed.

Next I contacted Commissioner José Smith, a real estate attorney with a no-nonsense personality and a high level of ethical integrity. I had met José a couple of years earlier when he was beginning to run for the office of commissioner and I had been one of his early supporters. While this fact would not guarantee his support, it would give me access to him. I knew José would look at the issue objectively, so I was confident I could get his vote. I met with him and he committed to support it based on how I represented it to him. If I was not accurate, all bets were off.

So that was five. Of the other two commissioners, I figured antidevelopment commissioner David Dermer—the man behind the Save Miami Beach campaign that had tanked the value of the Bath Club's property in the first place—was a likely no. Still, I wanted him to be a quiet no. So I visited with him and explained the project as forthrightly as I could. Though he would not promise to support it, he appreciated my candor and my respect, and thus began a long friendship.

Finally there was Simon Cruz. He was also newly elected,

and I was developing a relationship with him as well. He and I had several things in common: He had lived in Washington, D.C.; we had both attended Rutgers University; and we were both in real estate. He also indicated he was inclined to support me. So I had at least five votes, and probably six.

With the political landscape under control, I pushed to complete the deal with the Bath Club. I had Mayor Kasdin talk to Bishoff and Helman, to let them know that I would most likely be able to win the city commission vote. Helman also lived a few doors away from Commissioner Cruz, and Cruz confirmed that opinion. Bishoff and Helman now had confidence in my ability to get the deal approved, so we got down to details.

In essence, I applied the same tactics that I applied in the Royal Palm deal when I got the option to acquire the Shorecrest hotel: their price, my terms. Their price was $10 million, but they didn't need all that money right away. All they needed right away was the cash to pay their bills.

The deal we agreed to was this: I would refinance their loan, pay all their back taxes, and pay all the brokerage fees up front. The Bath Club would then give me eighteen months to close on the deal—I needed this to get the zoning changed—during which time I would pay the ongoing interest on the loan I had refinanced as well as their ongoing taxes. At the end of the eighteen months, if I didn't close, they would then have another eighteen months to sell the property to a new buyer and pay off the loan. I agreed to cover the club's expenses during all this time. For three years, the club would basically be off the hook for about $500,000 in annual interest and tax payments.

It was something of a gamble for me, even with the city commission apparently ready to vote in my favor. If I couldn't get the zoning changed in time, and I backed out, I could lose the interest and tax payments I had put up—though I could get some or all of that back if they ended up selling for substantially more than the original $10 million price. (We had a sharing agreement for the surplus.) However, I could still buy the property for $10 million at the eighteenth-month break point. I figured that even if it were used for a single-family home site, it would probably be worth more than $10 million by then; Leona Helmsley, after all, had just purchased a one-acre home site on nearby Star Island for $12 million. Bottom line, while I was taking a risk on the front end of the project, I was significantly mitigating my financial exposure. In the worst case, I would lose about $2 million—a lot of money but not the end of the world, and much better than having to commit $10 million for the purchase *plus* for the cash for interest, taxes, and other carrying expenses. This way I could see how the real estate market would perform over time; because I set the price a year and a half before closing, I could purchase with hindsight—truly a rarity!

Once we came to an agreement, the Bath Club member-ship had to approve it, and they did so, 159 out of 160 votes in favor. I signed it and we agreed to make a joint an-nouncement of the pending sale. It ran on the front page of the *Miami Herald*, with commentary from the head of Florida's Anti-Defamation League. He was quoted on how barriers had been broken and how the founding Bath Club members must be turning over in their graves.

I had known it would be a big statement for me as an African American to buy the Bath Club, but perhaps not as big as it turned out. It became a national news item. National Pub-lic Radio picked it up, for example, and I got calls from as far away as California from friends who heard the program.

Next we went forward with the architectural plans. I initially used Arquitectonica, which was smart, since Laurinda's parents were on the Bath Club board, and the membership knew her and husband/partner, Bernardo. Then I started meeting with community leaders, historic boards and so forth, to win their support. We also prepared a report for the city's Historic Preservation Board as to why we wanted the club to be designated a historic site. It was actually the first time in the city's history that any property owner had voluntarily requested historic designation, and we knew that would give Liebman a comfort factor not only to support and vote for us but to champion the project. It also won us the loyalty of the city's historic preservation officers as well as the city's director of planning. Even the conservative Miami Design Preservation League supported the project, since we were going to preserve and not demolish.

Next was the rezoning process itself, the application to change the zoning from RM1 to RM2, which would double the density of the project. We also had to make a text change in the city's zoning restrictions; the zoning charter limited RM2 sites to ninety feet, and we wanted to go up two hundred feet, since that was the predominant height for the area where we were located.

To assuage neighboring residents, I made it a point to meet with every group associated with property in the area, from condo boards to neighborhood associations. Among other things, I promised to create an open access path to the beach through the property, something that had previously existed in the neighborhood but that had been sealed off when the old Pritikin building just south of the Bath Club site was sold. As a result of these meetings, we had no community opposition except from the owner of the site directly across the street, since it would impair the ocean view for some of the units in his proposed building. The commission would later chastise him and his attorney for their opposition when their turn came. As they say: When living in a glass house, don't throw stones.

We were now well into the summer of 1999, and I basically had until the end of the year to win the vote from the Miami Beach City Commission. Having previously politicked the commissioners, I thought I had things pretty well under control. But nothing is finished until the fat lady sings, as they say, and she was suddenly out of breath.

Despite the Hollywood portrayal of politics as a cutthroat game of back-room deals and nasty betrayals, I think most good politicians play it according to the Lyndon Johnson rules I've already discussed: You don't go back on your promises, and you always watch out for your friends. I was about to find out that not all politicians play by the rules.

A few weeks before the commission was to hold its vote on the Bath Club zoning issue, I had a conversation with Mayor Kasdin—several actually—during which he tried to convince me to wait until after the November mayoral election to hold the vote. He was running for reelection and was worried that by supporting me on the Bath Club vote, he would be perceived as pro-development. This was not exactly political gold in the current anti-growth environment.

I explained that because of deadlines with the Bath Club, I didn't have time to wait. The City of Miami Beach requires two statutory votes for charter amendment changes, with at least thirty days in between, and requirements for public notices and mailers to the citizens. Mathematically I wouldn't have enough time to close the deal, and that would force me to ask for an extension. With property values rapidly rising, the Bath Club could simply say no, sell the property for a better price, and I'd be out of the picture. It was an enormous, multimillion-dollar risk for me.

Kasdin's problem was that he was running for reelection against his fellow commissioner Marty Shapiro, and although Kasdin thought the project would be a good thing to help revive the midbeach area, he didn't want Shapiro to use the issue to label him as the pro-development mayor he was. I assured him that Shapiro would also vote in favor of the Bath Club. In fact, as I explained to the mayor—who typically votes last—he almost certainly would follow a commission unanimous in its approval of the Bath Club. Even Commissioner Dermer, who had gotten elected with a slow-growth, nongrowth platform, was now in favor. (He had told me that he liked how I was buying a club that had discriminated against Jews and blacks). Reluctantly Kasdin agreed to keep it on the agenda for October and support it.

Kasdin then asked me to help raise money for his campaign, which I had done before. I told him I couldn't do it this time because of the conflict with Shapiro, who had been an ally.

The evening of the vote arrived, and I attended the commission meeting. Kasdin kept putting off our item. During the break, Nancy Liebman came up to me and told me that Kasdin was whispering in the ears of the commissioners, trying to get a deferment of the Bath Club vote. He was saying that it was for my sake, because I didn't have the votes I needed. I asked her and several of the other commissioners to block the deferral.

With the commission back in session, our agenda item came up. Kasdin took the podium and declared there wasn't time for it and that it wasn't the right time anyway, because it was so controversial. The audience members, many of whom were there for this item, were practically booing. Nonetheless, in deference to the mayor, Commissioner Cruz stepped up and made a recommendation for deferral, and Commissioner Smith backed him up. Commissioner Gottlieb had a fit, said she had to leave, then literally got up and left.

Now there were just six commissioners. Kasdin called for the vote on deferral but Dermer, Liebman, and Shapiro voted against it, so it didn't pass. The item had to be considered, and various presentations about the project were then made, along with favorable recommendations from the city planner and the head of the city's Historic Preservation Board. We made our presentation, and other people came up and testified, including historic preservation groups and condo associations, and all were in favor of us. Only one person testified against us, a lawyer representing the proposed condo project across the street.

Kasdin couldn't stall it any longer and had to call the vote. Each commissioner, one after the other, voted in favor. So I had my five votes in favor. It was done.

Then the mayor took the microphone. Kasdin made a speech about how there was no better developer than me, but about how important it was, at this particular time, that he vote no.

I was shocked. He had decided, in the end, to use his vote to show up Shapiro and Dermer, the two anti-development commissioners. The record would show that while they were voting for a rezoning that would allow denser development, Kasdin was voting against it.

I could have let it go. I had won my vote, after all, and I would be able to go forward with the Bath Club deal. But I had been publicly betrayed by a political friend and ally. In politics and business both, you have to send the message that your word is a commitment and can be respected, and that you won't tolerate others breaking their words. If I had let Kasdin do what he did publicly, then I wouldn't be able to successfully work with other city commissioners in the future. Additionally, I did not want Shapiro and Dermer to think I had worked with Kasdin to set them up for the vote so I could win and Kasdin could vote no to make them look bad.

The Bath Club vote was the last item on the agenda, and it was almost midnight. I thanked all the people who supported me and then the commissioners started leaving. I thanked each one of them, except Kasdin. The next day I called Marty Shapiro and told him I'd support his mayoral campaign. He had kept his promise, and I wanted to come through for him.

This created a bit of an uproar among the commissioners, especially those who were Kasdin supporters. Nancy Liebman in particular asked me to talk with the mayor and bury the hatchet. I agreed; the message had been sent. Kasdin and I met, and I agreed to limit my support of Shapiro to a campaign contribution of $10,000 or less.

That should have been the end of it. But at the second commission vote to designate the Bath Club historic, Kasdin lambasted the project and announced that I was supporting Shapiro for his vote. I told the commissioners that Kasdin had also asked for a contribution and had voted against me when I refused. This led the commission to pass a motion requesting that the state attorney's office investigate Kasdin for misconduct in office.

Kasdin still needed to prove he was right. The week before the election, he sent a direct-mail piece to the voters in the hope of making an issue out of my campaign contribution

129

to Shapiro, trying to convince them that a big developer was influencing this nongrowth candidate. "Peebles Buys Mr. Not for Sale's Vote" was the headline of the mail piece. Wow.

I couldn't just let this pass. Sometimes you have to fight fire with fire, so I mounted an overnight mailing to the same voters, pointing out how the mayor was politicizing my Bath Club project, why the project was good, and how his behavior was improper. I also put out a television commercial to let voters know that the city commission had unanimously referred allegations of Kasdin's official misconduct as mayor to the state attorney. "The investigation is pending," the commercial announced.

Ultimately, Kasdin beat Marty in the runoff and was sworn in for a second two-year term. But I was satisfied. I had let the community know that I valued loyalty and that if you went back on your word, there would be serious ramifications. Even Craig Robins, who had been my opponent in the Royal Palm bid, asked me to leave Kasdin alone. "You've made your point," he told me.

In fact, when the rezoning issue came up again for a second round of votes, Kasdin voted for it and it passed unanimously.

When I closed on the Bath Club deal early the following year, it won the Ernst & Young/*South Florida Business Journal* land deal of the year for 2000.

It would also turn out to be extremely profitable, as I predicted. Even before the first spade of earth was turned, the rezoning increased the value of the land to more than $32 million, so right off I made $20 million. After I developed it as a condominium with four beachfront mansions, I would make even more. How much? The total cost of the project was $165 million, which included the $20 million land markup and $6 million to $7 million in fees I would earn as the developer. I had to split the remaining $75 million or so in profits with several partners I took in along the way, but in the end I cleared a total of somewhere around $60 million. You've got to do a lot of deals in downtown Miami to get those kind of numbers.

EPILOGUE TO CHAPTER 7

The Bath Club deal illustrates a number of the Peebles Principles, including the first and foremost principle: You need to control the deal. I was able to get an option on the purchase, and though it was an expensive one—I would have gone through more than $2 million if I had walked away—it gave me eighteen months to get the property rezoned. I controlled it during that period.

The deal illustrates the second Peebles Principle as well: By taking the early risk you make your money going in, not on the other side. The Bath Club was a great opportunity because it had a lot of hairs to it, which means it had a lot of problems. If I couldn't get the zoning changed, we would have to build it to look like the Pentagon—as flat as the profits would be. My willingness to take on that early risk was the entrepreneurial act that created the value.

Nonetheless, I did mitigate my financial exposure by delaying the closing until I knew the outcome of the rezoning. Therefore, I wouldn't be forced to buy the property if the rezoning effort failed. This may seem like something obvious—that you should limit your potential losses—but forgetting this ground rule can prove dangerous.

131

Another ground rule showcased here is the importance of maintaining a war chest of political currency. It was essential to our success. Few people choose to develop the resource of politics—and by *politics*, I don't mean just relationships with actual politicians. I mean relationships with the people in any industry who can influence your deal, for good or bad: the gatekeepers, the decision makers, the bottlenecks, the key executives. Consider such relationships like fire insurance for your home: You maintain it hoping never to use it, but if you ever have a fire you are extremely pleased you acquired it.

Having made these observations, however, I'd still have to say there are two new principles here of even greater importance.

The first is that you must never run from an attack. You have to respond immediately. I learned this first with the media, when the *Washington Post* would investigate a deal. By facing the attack I could control the damage—or even turn it to my advantage. The same is true in business and politics. Not only do you reduce damage, but your willingness to fight back becomes a deterrent. Like the atom bomb, after you use it once, you don't have to use it again.

The second principle is even more fundamental to winning deals and the negotiations that lead to them. This is the principle that you must go out of your way to understand what is in the other party's head and what is motivating them to do the deal. In addition to leading you to a win-win conclusion, which is the best scenario in any deal, understanding the other party's motives is the best leverage you can have. It works every time.

PEEBLES GROUND RULES

- Business is not just about numbers. Creativity can be very important.

- In addition to thinking about how much money you can make from a given transaction, carefully consider your financial exposure. Be aware that this may exceed the immediate cash you've put on the line.

- Maintain political relationships even when you don't need them. They may prove to be good insurance in critical situations.

Peebles Principle #7: Respond Quickly to Attacks

Call it the bully principle: If someone is attacking you, take them on immediately, even if the fight is a costly one. That will save you from all kinds of trouble later on.

Peebles Principle #8: Get Inside the Others' Heads

Understanding what the other parties want takes creative thinking, but ultimately it's your key to successful negotiations. Find out what they want, and then give it to them!

✻8✻

Perseverance:
The Saga of Royal Palm

High hopes with my opening bid for the Royal Palm in 1995 were nearly ground to a halt by a marathon of challenges that taught me the enormous importance of patience in dealing with adversity—and the invaluable art of turning setbacks into opportunities.

When the Royal Palm hotel project was awarded to me by the City of Miami Beach, my mood was euphoric. I had come into a new city and beaten enormous odds, and at that point everything looked terrific. There was just one thorn left in my side, deftly inserted by Mayor Seymour Gelber, right in the midst of that celebratory moment. In the same breath that he announced the award, he also appointed Arthur Courshon, the antagonistic head of the selection committee, as the city's chief negotiator for the deal.

To this day I am not sure if it was naiveté or maliciousness that prompted the mayor to appoint Courshon, nor does it matter. The result was the same. I was saddled with a negotiator who had favored another candidate for the project and who still wanted me to fail.

Courshon, as I have said, was a smart man, and he was still furious that I had bested him in the selection process. Consequently he began a long campaign to wrestle the spoils of victory from me. His principle tactic was delay, to drag the process out. He would put off meetings for months at a time, and when he finally did agree to meet, he required that my staff and I fly to his vacation home in Boone, North Carolina. He even had consultants fly in from New York to conduct the city's business there.

Courshon came up with hurdle after hurdle and then made periodic reports to the city commission, saying that things weren't where they should be but that he was working on it. Then the lawyer representing the second-place bidder, the one Courshon had favored, would try to get the commission to pluck us off and choose them instead. (Ironically, after he sold his bank, Courshon would have his offices in the lawyers' suite in the same building where I happened to have my corporate offices.)

It was a good strategy on Courshon's part. He wanted to make the process so cumbersome that I would eventually quit. In the end he managed to drag things out for more than two years; although we won the award in June of 1996, we didn't get a nonbinding letter of intent from the city until March of 1997. Then it took until October of 1997 to get the definitive documents done, and we didn't get physical possession of the property until August of 1998! Even this was possible only because I had threatened to litigate, which brought Mayor Gelber back into the picture. He was leaving office that November and wanted to get the project done under his watch, as part of his legacy. So he put pressure on Courshon, his personal friend, to get it done.

The delays did hurt me, of course, and created more than a few headaches. It took so long to get the project signed off that my individual partners grew uncomfortable and became unwilling to spend more money. Things also became strained with my hotel partner, Intercontinental, under whose Crowne Plaza brand the property was slated to operate.

The initial investment breakdown went as follows: When we won the bid, Intercontinental agreed to lend us $5.8 million; I put in $1.2 million; and my individual partners agreed to ante up another $5.2 million as we needed it. But as time dragged on, those partners became less enthusiastic about meeting their commitment. Their economics had probably changed. One of the things about a deal is that, unlike wine, it doesn't get better with time. Once you have an agreement, it needs to be closed out in a timely fashion. That principle applies to real estate as well as to other industries. When you look at it, I beat out the initial bidder on the 2100 Martin Luther King project because he didn't close the deal out. If he had closed the deal with the landowner, I'd never have had a chance.

So Courshon's strategy to drag out the deal was having the desired effect. Things started unraveling. Because my bank loan commitments expired multiple times, I had to keep going back to extend them; the banks grew increasingly frustrated and began to question my credibility. My deal to close on the Shorecrest was likewise postponed, and I had to keep going back to those sellers and ask for more time. Cyrus Mehre, the seller of the leasehold (and the hotel itself) wasn't happy about it. He gave me more time, but it was costing me $50,000 here, $100,000 there. The landowner, the Cardona Trust, tried to put us in default and increased their price; this led to litigation.

It was also affecting my other deals, too, because it consumed so much of my time. Courshon forced me to pay such great attention to the Royal Palm that I could hardly do anything else. My life's work at that point really became the hotel, and it was very stressful. Then, as I feared, my partners finally balked at putting in their $5.2 million.

That could have spelled disaster. But I knew there was at least one other party that stood to gain tremendously if the hotel was built, and that was Intercontinental. Due to the rapidly escalating land and hotel prices in South Beach, if the Royal Palm were not constructed, they would find it very difficult to ever again put the Crowne Plaza brand on the ocean there. So I went to Intercontinental and asked them to go from being a lender to being a partner in the deal and replace the equity shortfall.

Intercontinental agreed to put up the additional $5.2 million, but at a big price: 49 percent ownership of the project, in addition to their right to manage the hotel. Because I was determined to secure this deal, I accepted their proposal. The ultimate structure was a $5 million loan at 15 percent interest, compounded annually, and an equity investment of $6 million at 18 percent interest, also compounded annually. On the plus side, I would have the right to buy them out at a later date, with a return on their investment. On the minus side, their management contract was now locked in for twenty years, even if I paid them back. Still, it wasn't a bad deal, everything considered. In effect, they became a mezzanine lender, with obligations to fund further capital if needed.

Finally the time came to look behind the curtain. Right up until August 1998, when I took possession of the building, Courshon and the city had prohibited me from performing any invasive testing of the building's structure. The city had certified the building's structural soundness, and it had signed off on any environmental concerns. In effect, the city gave the building a clean bill of health, in writing. The problem was that its conclusions were dead wrong. When the general contractors finished the interior demolitions, they uncovered the ugly fact that the structural concrete was damaged beyond repair. The steel inside had corroded and swollen, and the pressure from inside was popping the concrete. Beach sand had been used to make the concrete, as was the custom at the time, and the salt had corroded all the rebars from within. We delayed things while we got a better understanding of the structural issues, and during that hiatus we discovered there was contaminated soil on the site. Despite city assurances to the contrary, underground fuel tanks on the site had leaked.

At this point almost any other developer would have walked from the deal, and most people would have understood. It had the opposite effect on me. I decided then and there that I was going to build the hotel and get it up and running, no matter what. My professional image and my personal reputation were both on the line, plus this was an important project for the city and for the minority community as a whole. I knew once I completed the project, it would put me on the national map. If I gave up, however, nobody would read the fine print and the press wouldn't give me fair coverage, no matter how inequitable the deal was. Who'd believe that someone like Courshon would have been given the leeway to drag things out like he did? Who would want to do such a thing anyway? I would simply have been known as the guy who took a $10 million property from the city in a minority set-aside deal and couldn't get the job done. I was determined to succeed.

As it turned out, the two years of delays that Courshon

engineered would prove more costly than I imagined. Forget about the hidden structural and environmental problems; when I finally began building, I was caught in the midst of a major nationwide escalation in construction costs. I would also miss a time period when the hotel business in Miami blossomed; instead I launched the Royal Palm in the face of the 9/11 impact on travel.

The numbers told the story. When we originally bid on the project, we estimated the cost at $59 million. When we finished the project, it cost close to $85 million.

That whopping jump in the price tag came from a variety of sources, including the cost of carrying the project for so long and some hefty construction-cost overruns. But it did not include the fact that the $11 million put up by Intercontinental had, by 2004, grown to more than $23 million—the compounding of the interest on their $5 million loan and $6 million equity investment.

That was the bad news. What I was to discover, however, was the good news, an essential lesson that would propel all my future thinking on what it takes to be a successful entrepreneur: the power to turn setbacks into opportunities.

Let me start with the setbacks that took place with the general contractor, Clark Construction.

We had selected Clark from three contractors we had prequalified; two were from Florida, while Clark was based in the Washington, D.C., area. I selected Clark because they proposed the lowest fee and overhead. They also had a long history of performance in my hometown and had built some significant Miami projects, including the Miami Beach Convention Center and the building that housed our Miami offices.

I would later find out that their Florida operations were not up to par with their operations in D.C. I would also learn, yet again, that you get what you pay for. I have always made it a point to pay for the best in professional services. In the case of Clark, I was painfully reminded that when a company significantly underbids the market, they look for ways to make it up. You are far better off paying up front so you can plan for those expenses in your budget.

When the hotel was finally finished, in early 2002, it was several years behind schedule. Our position was that Clark was accountable for a large number of those delays; Clark's position was that all the delays were caused by design errors, structural defects, and the contaminated soil. They wanted $25 million to cover cost overruns; we thought they deserved closer to $4 million.

To be fair, there were serious issues with the design, in addition to the structural and contamination issues. But there were also lot of problems with Clark. For example, the subcontractor responsible for installing the windows didn't get proper approval ahead of time, so the window installation was delayed. Nonetheless, other subcontractors were allowed to go ahead installing drywall and air conditioning systems—with no windows in the building! A lot of damage resulted from rain, creating additional work to repair and replace what had already been done. They had other problems, too, with late deliveries of materials and poor-quality work, all the result of bad organization and weak management. So we refused to pay for more than our fair share of the setbacks.

Now, while the Clark situation seemed like a bad scenario that could have cost us tens of millions of dollars, good things came from it as well.

The first was that because some of Clark's claims were legitimate—including the errors and omissions by the engineer—the architectural firm's insurance company paid us $5 million, the limit of their policy. This was shortly after the hotel's completion, right when the hotel market was collapsing in the wake of 9/11. I used that cash to carry the hotel until the situation stabilized. Otherwise I'd have had financial problems with the hotel from the day it opened.

The second thing was that, with all the cost overruns and construction delays, the executives at Intercontinental started losing their nerve. As a 49 percent equity partner, they'd be required to cover almost half of any cost overruns, which meant nearly $12 million if Clark won all its claims. They didn't want that kind of exposure. So we worked out a solution: I bought back their 49 percent interest, for which they took a note, and I agreed to put up the rest of any cash necessary to finish the project. It cost me a couple of million dollars—I put up another $1.2 million and deferred my development fee of $1 million—but I again owned most of the hotel. (I still had a few minority partners.)

Also, as part of the new arrangement, Intercontinental gave me the right to terminate the twenty-year management contract they had extracted when I needed their equity. If that contract had remained in place, I could never have sold the hotel to anyone who wanted to bring in their own brand or convert the building to condos. So I bought out Intercontinental's equity and management control using their money—advantages that had come my way thanks to the apparent setback of Clark's claims.

The third opportunity arose from the structural defects and soil contamination. These seemed like nightmares at first, but the City of Miami Beach had significant liability exposure to me because they had misrepresented the condition of the building and had indemnified me from any losses due to adverse soil conditions. I submitted a claim to them for approximately $20 million, and after nearly two years of negotiations we reached an agreement.

The city wanted a solution that did not require them to write a check, so we settled on two things. First, the city agreed to waive and defer portions of the ground rent. Second, and more important, the city removed any restrictions on turning the Shorecrest Hotel suites into condominiums. Courshon had insisted on this restriction; it was one of the roadblocks designed to make it more difficult for me to finance the development of the hotel. With the settlement it was gone! Had that limitation remained, the hotel's value would have been considerably less and the company that eventually bought the hotel—for condo conversions— would not have been interested.

In the meantime, Clark had entered into mediation with us over their claims, and we almost settled with them for about $7.5 million. It was not a bad settlement, but at the time I didn't have the cash to give them. The banks wouldn't give me the money then either; this was right after 9/11, and everyone was concerned about the hotel industry. If I had to pay the $7.5 million, I would have had to sell the hotel. So we went to court instead and exchanged federal lawsuits.

Again, at the time, this seemed like a lost opportunity. Eventually, Clark won a $16 million judgment, a lot more than the $7.5 offer. But by that time the hotel market had recovered and I'd been able to carry the property and ride it out. With the hotel performing and producing cash flow, plus the tremendous improvement in South Beach's hotel market, the Royal Palm had gone up in value to past $125 million; back in 2002, at the time of Clark's offer, it was probably worth between $75 million and $80 million. Had I sold it, I would have made no money, and even if I could have gotten a loan to pay off Clark, it would have cost me 20 percent. So, if you do the calculations, by the time all was said and done, the Clark litigation was cheaper even than a mezzanine loan.

Something else took place at the tail end of the long, drawn-out Clark litigation, something that changed everything for the better: the arrival of Robert Falor and his offer in late 2004 to buy the hotel.

It was not an offer I had solicited; I had been busy pursuing other solutions. I'd been talking to Hyatt about coming in and buying the Royal Palm with me and doing a hotel-condo conversion. And I had called Jonathan Tisch, whose family owned the next-door 800-room Loews hotel, pointing out how he could end up with 1,200 rooms and own the market. But both groups passed on the $110 million entry fee to become my partner—at least $10 million too high, they said—even though Hyatt wanted to be in South Beach in the worst way, and even though Tisch would never get another chance like this again, not right next door. I thought it was a big mistake for both.

In the end I negotiated a deal with a private equity group called BlackRock to finance a condo conversion that I would do myself. That's when the offer came in from the Falor Companies.

Robert Falor had come to Miami at the height of its condo fever. He was the self-described king of hotel-condo conversions, and he was doing deals all over town, taking hotel properties and turning them into private condos or condo hotels. He was using other people's money, and he was creating millions in new wealth, a formula that worked so long as the market kept soaring.

By this point BlackRock had agreed to lend me $114 million to do the condo conversion, and I was looking at a potential $40 million to $60 million profit. So when Falor came to the table, I wasn't willing to consider anything less than $125 million. Fortunately, he came in with a first offer of $126 million, which we negotiated up to $127.5 million, plus their agreement to pay the brokerage commission.

The sale could not take place, however, until I had clear title for the property, and that was being held up by the Clark Construction judgment.

Before Falor arrived on the scene, we were trying to wrap up that litigation, knowing that a settlement would be required prior to any deal on the hotel. We pressed the federal judge in the case to bring it to trial. He had a very busy calendar, so for the sake of expediency he suggested trial by magistrate. We agreed. It turned out to be a big mistake, however—or so it seemed, once again, at the time.

As I was to learn, a magistrate is like an apprentice judge. They normally do bail hearings and so forth. Ours was probably the most complicated case this magistrate had ever heard—and he got it wrong. After a brief, two-week trial, he took a simplistic approach and decided there couldn't be more than one party responsible for the delays. Since the architect admitted some responsibility, and since contaminated soil and structural defects also slowed the project, and since these weren't the contractor's responsibilities, he agreed in the spring of 2004 to the contractor's claims. Our legal staff concluded he was wrong, but he nonetheless gave a judgment to Clark for $16 million: $11 million for their delay claims, plus another $5 million for legal costs and interest.

Naturally, we appealed this judgment. But in order to withhold execution of the judgment during the appeal, we had to post a $20 million bond—the $16 million plus another $4 million in contingency fees. Fortunately, Falor was making his offer just as the judgment was made final. So, rather than come up with the cash ourselves, we went back before the magistrate and asked if we could post the bond when the sale closed. To his credit, the magistrate gave us until February 5, 2005, to post the bond, the day when we were scheduled to close with Falor. That was a big relief—though I had already inured myself against the judgment. First, I'd gotten the $5 million from the architect for their errors and omissions. Second, I had held back $5 million of Clark's money, cash that I had already budgeted to pay them. So in essence the judgment wasn't as bad as it really seemed—the net financial hit to us was really the $6 million in interest and attorney's fees. And we were appealing it.

Falor, in the meantime, was running into a little trouble. He came to me on about the first of February and said his group needed another week or ten days to close, that their lender needed more time to document the loan. I remember thinking how this should come as no surprise, since nothing connected to the Royal Palm was easy. My next reaction was to worry: This could mean big trouble for the judge's ruling on posting the bond for Clark. Then I took a deep breath and began to look for what opportunities this new setback would present.

First, if Falor missed the closing deadline, I could keep a $2 million deposit his group had given me. I could then do the hotel conversion myself, using the financial commitment

I'd previously gotten from BlackRock. (Interestingly enough, my investment banker had actually introduced Falor to BlackRock, and they were now providing him the mezzanine financing to buy and convert the hotel.)

Instead I gave the Falor Companies another twelve-day extension, but for a price. First, they had to release their initial $2 million deposit from escrow and agree in writing that the money would remain mine even if they couldn't close, for any reason. Second, they had to post another $1 million deposit, which would be released to me on closing and which would also be mine if they didn't close by February 16. Finally, they had to pay me $250,000 to cover my costs for the twelve-day extension—my legal fees and so on—kind of like a penalty that wouldn't count toward the purchase price. They gave me all that and I gave them an extension to February 16.

Then my lawyers went back to the magistrate and begged for another extension until February 17 to post the Clark bond. Amazingly, he gave it to us, but said this would be the last time, period.

Two weeks later I was scheduled to have a lunch meeting with Falor and his financial partner, Guy Mitchell; Falor had said it would be a "get acquainted" luncheon for his partner to meet me. It was on a Wednesday, a week before the closing, and we were supposed to meet at Bice Restaurant in the Grand Bay Hotel in Coconut Grove. As it turned out, I had to cancel just as I arrived, in order to deal with an emergency at the Miami Beach City Commission—they had just voted to renege on a tax structure deal we had cut with the city manager—but I rode from the Grand Bay with both of them. We talked in the car.

What Mitchell and Falor revealed was another snafu:

Their equity investors were now giving them problems and were changing the deal. They wanted me to think about putting in some equity and giving them a short-term note, like thirty to sixty days. I told them I'd think about it. I then went into City Hall and convinced the commissioners to reconsider their previous vote and unanimously vote again in my favor on the tax issue; it was another case where a personal presence is called for when you need someone's vote. (It was such a turnaround that the *SunPost* newspaper ran a column in its next edition entitled "Power to the Peebles"—but I digress.)

Over the next couple of days Falor and Mitchell came up with a figure: They wanted me to put in $11.5 million. That was the amount that one of their equity investors, a company called Ashford Hospitality, had originally committed to provide. Ashford got cold feet, Falor explained, because they weren't convinced the hotel-condo conversion would work. They wanted me to make up the shortfall.

My first response was that, since Falor and Mitchell were only putting up $6 million themselves, there was no way I'd do a deal with them where I had more money in than they did. I told them I wouldn't even entertain the idea unless they contributed more. I wanted them to put in at least another $3.5 million, and then I'd consider putting in $8.5 million—though I'd have to think about the terms.

I next contacted Intercontinental, whose local executives just wanted to get their cash out and move on. Given the BlackRock term sheet, I was indifferent as to whether we would complete the deal with Falor, as I would just as soon do the condo conversion myself.

"We have a problem," I told them, and I explained the shortfall. "These guys aren't going to be able to close," I continued. "We can either let them default, keep the deposit, and go and refinance the deal ourselves, or we can make the loan to them. I'm really not interested in making a loan to them personally because it's going to use up a lot of the cash I'd be getting from the deal. But you guys should consider doing it."

The Intercontinental executives said they would consider it, but only if their brand stayed on the hotel—the concession they had given up in our last round of negotiations. Well, that was never going to happen, since Falor's whole business plan was to do an ultra high-end boutique hotel.

"There's no way they're going to let you in," I said. "But I'll ask."

As expected, Falor said no. And as expected, Intercontinental said no, that they wouldn't put up, or leave in, any more money. This meant our options were either that I put it up or we didn't close, or that Falor would go and get a new equity partner—which would mean a gap of about thirty days, during which time the Clark bond would have to get posted.

I'd already told Intercontinental that I wouldn't post the bond myself, that we'd have to post it together, and that it would come to about $20 million. This was the last thing their regional executives wanted, to go back to their London headquarters and ask for approval to post half of a $20 million bond. They were looking to pull money out of the deal, not put more in.

I continued talking with Falor and Mitchell, and I met with them at Mitchell's home in Coral Gables that week and again at his home that weekend. Mitchell had just bought an $11 million house in Tahiti Beach, a super-luxury enclave in Coral Gables, and he always wanted to have meetings there, probably to demonstrate his financial wherewithal. He was a pretty laid-back guy, almost a little bohemian, but he still wanted to make that big impression.

"Look," I told them. "I'm not interested in making a loan. If you want a loan go to a bank. I'm not a mezzanine lender. Nonetheless, I'm willing to consider it." I reminded them that I had already introduced them to BlackRock, which was providing them with $22 million in mezzanine financing. But I knew that Falor and Mitchell were up against a wall and that I could extract significant concessions if I made an offer that solved their problems. These concessions could make me significantly more money in the long run by tying me to the future upside of the condo conversion project. If structured properly, I could have the best of both worlds: cash now from the sale and future profits from the conversion.

What I offered them was a note, but for $8.5 million rather than the $11.5 million they first suggested. In exchange I wanted half the deal and no liabilities. They came back with an offer of 40 percent of the deal; not half, but enough.

That weekend before the closing we hammered out the numbers: I would leave $8.5 million in the deal, in the form of a note that would bear 10 percent interest. They had sixty days to pay it back. If they failed to meet the deadline, I would keep 40 percent of the project, nondilutable, and with no liability for cost overruns (that would come out of their 60 percent.) I would also get approval rights over every major decision. The real kicker was that even if they did pay me back within the sixty days, I would still retain 12.5 percent ownership in the project in perpetuity, no matter what, again nondilutable. This included 12.5 percent of the profit from the condo-hotel unit sales as well as from hotel operations.

We structured this agreement at Mitchell's house that Saturday, and I basically told them that this was it, take it or leave it. I could have pushed for more, and probably gotten it. But it was important not to squeeze Falor too much, because we were going to be partners and he would be managing our partnership. I didn't want to be too abusive of his current position of weakness; doing so would probably provoke him to return the favor when his position grew stronger. I stood to make a significant amount of money from his efforts, and it was important for us to have a good relationship going forward. In any business transaction, one of the fundamental elements is that there must be two winners: you and the other party. If not, the losing party will never forget it and will always look for a payback opportunity.

Next I went back to one of the senior executives at Intercontinental and reminded them that the deal would not close without one of us leaving money in and that I'd think about under what circumstances I'd do it. I basically said I was willing to put the money up with Falor, but that I would then have to restructure the Intercontinental deal.

I talked to the hotel executive that Sunday afternoon and then laid out the structure of a deal via e-mail to him that night.

Here's what I offered Intercontinental: $15 million flat.

Under the existing arrangement, you may recall, I owed Intercontinental $23 million, most of which came from their original $5 million loan, the subsequent $6 million in equity, and the 15 percent and 18 percent in respective interest returns compounded over the years.

But that was only if the deal closed, which it couldn't unless I loaned Falor the money he needed. And if I was going to do that, Intercontinental would have to accept my offer of $15 million. This was turning into a game of high-stakes poker, with each delay from Falor turning into another opportunity for me.

I laid this out for Intercontinental in an e-mail that Sunday night before the Wednesday closing, and I got an e-mail back at the end of the following day. It said they would run the offer up the flagpole but that it was going to be problematic. I fired back an e-mail reminding them that the closing was happening in two days and that they'd better make a decision fast so I'd have time to document the transaction. I also reminded them that if we didn't close, we'd have to post the bond for Clark (proceeds from the sale would otherwise cover it). So instead of getting $15 million now, they would get nothing, plus have to guarantee half of that $20 million bond.

I told them that if they were ready to help post the bond, however, we could blow Falor off and do the condo conversion ourselves and make a lot more money. They just had to make a decision.

They came back to me that same evening at around eight o'clock and said they had to get $16 million, that their president insisted on it. Now, I had already wrestled with whether I should offer them $15 million or $15.5 million, so it wasn't far off. And I didn't want to insult them—though I didn't want them to feel they had any leverage over me either. I also had one more bargaining chip: I had set up a provision where, if the deal didn't close, I had the right to refinance the project and give them $14 million and send them on their way. They had agreed to this because it also called for them to get a percentage of profits if I sold the property within a year. So they knew that if Falor's deal walked away, then Intercontinental would only get $14 million at the present time.

In the end we reached a compromise. I accepted the $16 million figure the next morning, but required them to pay all the expenses for transferring the ownership and management of the hotel to Falor. I thereby saved $7 million. More important, I ended the deal with Intercontinental on good terms, with both of us coming out feeling like winners.

Now that this arrangement was in place, I went back to Falor and worked out a new partnership agreement. We had one last meeting before the closing and went through all the partnership issues. Falor was very reasonable, and I was too, because I'd been in his position before. It only took us about an hour to tie up the loose ends and make the deal.

And what a deal it was. Because I'd put up the $8.5 million with Falor, we'd gotten $7 million knocked off the transaction with Intercontinental—which meant that the $8.5 million I'd put up was really a net investment of $1.5 million. So when this was paid off in sixty days, it meant an immediate profit of that $7 million, plus the value of my permanent 12.5 percent of the deal, which was worth between $12 million and $15 million. However, if they didn't pay off the loan, then my $1.5 million investment would have purchased 40 percent of the hotel, worth between $40 and $50 million!

So here was a last-minute situation that could have been an insurmountable obstacle and could have killed the deal: Falor's inability to close out their private equity money, resulting in a shortfall of $11.5 million. Instead it became a huge opportunity disguised as an obstacle. In about a week, from my aborted lunch with Falor and Mitchell to the closing, we had added at least $19 million in profits (the $7 million back from Intercontinental plus $12 million worth of Falor's condo-hotel), and as much as $57 million in profits (the $7 million plus $50 million worth of the condo-hotel).

To be honest, when I thought about it, I was a little bit saddened by the prospect of selling the Royal Palm. I'd lived with the hotel for more than nine years (from mid-1995 to early 2005), I had overcome every one of the obstacles put in front of me, and I knew the condo-hotel concept would work. But I was going to make a lot of money and didn't have a lot of time to ponder. We had to underwrite Falor's deal quickly, which we could do because we knew the hotel better than they did, and we knew the market exceptionally well. So we underwrote the deal, documented it, and went to the closing.

EPILOGUE TO CHAPTER 8

This deal was fraught with litigation, and that issue deserves commentary. Litigation is a valuable tool in business, and if used properly, it can help level the playing field. For example, when I threatened to sue the city, the mayor finally stepped in and put an end to Courshon's shenanigans.

Basically, because of the time and money consumed, and because the outcome is uncertain, most governments and businesspeople do not like litigation. This is especially true if they are wrong and are trying to use their superior resources (i.e., those of governments and large companies); juries are generally composed of average people who don't like to see big government and big business abuse the little guy.

Litigation can also buy you time, as was the case with Clark Construction. It also comes with significant risk, however, as the same case shows. To this day my lawyers and I feel the magistrate made the wrong decision and gave Clark at least $12 million more than they deserved. But we could do nothing about it: If played out all the way through trial, litigation takes the decision making out of the hands of the business parties involved and puts it in the judge or jury's hands. Therefore, the litigation card must be played carefully and sparingly.

However, while these observations are important, this final stage of the Royal Palm saga illustrates two new Peebles Principles that are far more significant to the deal-making process.

The first is the incredible importance of endurance. This was an exceptionally long struggle, but just as in the Marriott Hotel deal—when my impatient investment partners allowed themselves to be bought out for their original $250,000—my partners in this deal allowed themselves to be bought out for a fraction of what they could have made had they stayed the course. This is a fundamental rule for the entrepreneur: Do not lose your nerve, remain true to your convictions, and do not fall victim to deal fatigue.

The second rule may be even more essential: Setbacks can become opportunities. The cost overruns that the Royal Palm suffered—the shocking discovery of structural problems and environmental contamination—actually created an environment to get a better deal from Intercontinental. And when Falor was having trouble closing on the purchase, it gave me the opportunity to cut a better deal with him.

One final note about the Royal Palm saga: When I finally opened the hotel in May of 2002, my old nemesis Arthur Courshon showed up. He was in his eighties then and had not aged well. I think he showed up purely out of curiosity. He came over and talked with my family, and me, at the table where we were sitting. He actually congratulated me on my success. It was as if he took a perverse pride in having set up so many obstacles, which I had managed to overcome. I was kind to him. I had nothing to lose.

PEEBLES GROUND RULES

- Don't celebrate a victory too soon; no deal is done until it's really done.

- When it comes to closing deals, delay is the enemy of the entrepreneur—unless you use it to stretch out your financial obligations.

- When you are negotiating with several parties at once, never share the details between the groups. That knowledge is power.

- Litigation is a great tool for leveling the playing field, especially with oversize adversaries. But beware: It also takes the decision-making power out of your hands.

Peebles Principle #9: Be the Last Man Standing

Most deals take far longer than expected. Often the difference between failure and success is simply the fortitude to endure and to see things through to the end.

Peebles Principle #10: Turn Vinegar into Wine

Don't despair when problems arise—they frequently create great opportunities. Be alert to these silver linings, especially as they relate to other parties and fellow travelers in a deal.

❦ 9 ❦

The Lincoln Road Project: *The Power of Allies*

Giving the reins to other people can be the mark of a seasoned entrepreneur—as long as they are the right partners. Sometimes you have no other choice, if your political persona grows too large. That was the case in my deal to develop an office tower off Miami Beach's famed Lincoln Road pedestrian mall.

By the summer of 1998 I had begun construction of the Royal Palm Hotel, and as such I was part of the new building boom and general renaissance of Miami Beach. I had foreseen this when I arrived in the city several years earlier, and it was very gratifying to see it come to pass. I was far from alone in this prediction, of course, or in the efforts to make it happen, and the cumulative result was a revival of the city as a residential and retail hot spot. All the efforts, public and private, were beginning to pay off.

A particularly bright spot in this transformation was the rebirth of Lincoln Road Mall, one of urban America's truly great outdoor shopping and dining promenades. It runs almost the entire width of Miami Beach, a people-only pedestrian corridor with interesting architecture, boutique retailers, and tropical landscaping. After its heyday in the 1950s, it went into a four-decade decline. Now it was coming back with a vengeance.

With so much bustle going on, it was clear that more parking would be needed. The existing merchants of Lincoln Road were already feeling the pinch because of parking problems for their customers, and more retail was on the way.

Consequently, the city of Miami Beach was planning to issue a serious of requests for proposals (RFPs) for parking lots adjacent to Lincoln Road Mall. Some of the city's private developers, in fact, had been encouraging the city to deal with the issue; among them were myself, along with lobbyist Michael Milberg, and the father-son development team of Joe and Michael Comras. The idea was for the city to offer several parking lots to the private sector, which would turn them into parking garages with commercial space.

Everybody who was interested in the deal had more or less picked the parking lots they wanted to develop. The Comras group had their eye on several properties, including one on Washington Avenue, and I had looked at some that I wanted, including one on Michigan Avenue.

I had a few problems, however. The first was that I was knee deep in the Royal Palm at that time. As I said earlier, it was becoming an all-consuming project for me. I also realized that it was going to be harder for me politically to win the parking lot RFPs. The Royal Palm had been a political Donnybrook; it was a very visible project that had brought a lot of attention to me. I thought it would be harder for the city to award another project to me right at that time— though I knew I could at least get it on the table.

Still, I was sure that such a project could succeed. What the city had called for were proposals on how to maximize the utility of their parking lots. The idea was to enhance these public parking facilities, which were just outdoor lots, providing not just more spaces but better utilization of the land. My idea—and that of the Comras group also—was to construct an office building on the site, in combination with a parking garage. From my own experience, I knew there was demand for quality office space on Miami Beach; when I went looking for a place to locate my company there, I couldn't find any class A office space available. I ended up in downtown Miami. So I knew there was a growing market for office space as Miami Beach matured, plus I knew how to build it.

I still needed a partner to act as the public persona for the bid, and I started thinking about who would be a good ally. Then I heard from Milberg that Scott Robins was thinking about bidding on one of the lots. It made sense to work with Scott; he'd been part of my team on the Royal Palm bid, and we'd developed a bit of a friendship. Milberg set up a meeting—he had introduced me to Scott initially for the Royal Palm—and it went well. Scott was somebody I could trust. He was an honorable, ethical person, a good businessman, and a generally nice guy. Plus, his ego was balanced, so we could coexist pretty well. Added benefits included his intimate knowledge of the construction market in South Beach and the fact that he was politically well connected. Between his political connections and mine, it would be harder for the commissioners not to support us.

I had another reason to work with Scott. Even though he was part of the winning team, he ended up making no money off the Royal Palm. He was going to do some historical renovation of the property, but in the end it wasn't possible for him to work with the general contractor, Clark Construction. This new deal gave us an opportunity to work together and this time he could make some money doing it.

We agreed to join forces and bid on a couple of the city parking lots: one at 17th Street and Michigan Avenue and another one at 17th Street and Lennox Avenue, both parallel to Lincoln Road Mall. We also looked at acquiring other properties that were adjacent to the city lots. Once Scott and I reached an agreement, we brought in Arquitectonica to design the project as an office building with parking and ground-level retail. We also brought in Stuart Hoffman as our lawyer, since he had represented me on the entire Royal Palm project, and he knew his way around the political landscape.

With this team in place, I felt completely liberated. I had a smart partner with capable people around him, and I knew my interests were protected. I became more of an advisor and let Scott be the lead; we negotiated an arrangement where we were equal partners but with him designated as the managing member and the construction manager for the project. He really ran the deal, which freed me up to continue my work on the Royal Palm. It also kept me in the background. Milberg, in the meantime, got 2 percent of the deal for bringing us together and helping with the politics. That would end up putting a nice piece of change in his pocket.

We put together the RFP response as a team, with some help from my staff, but from then on Scott took the lead, making all the presentations and going through the selection committee process. Things seemed to be going well until the day the commission was scheduled to vote on the awards. Scott called me from the commission chamber to say they had just awarded Comras his site but had decided not to go forward with any of our properties. The commission didn't have to award all of them at that time, so they just deferred. Scott was crestfallen. He was on his cell phone, so I asked him to go into the chamber and pass the phone to David Dermer, one of the city commissioners who had voted for the delay.

I told David that I was involved in the project and asked him to call for a recess. I wanted to talk to him during the break; I was sure he didn't have all the facts. Scott actually got the mayor, Neissen Kasdin, to call a recess, and then I spoke to commissioners Dermer and Simon Cruz, letting them know how beneficial the project would be for the city and its residents and for the merchants on Lincoln Road. Not only were we going to jump the number of parking spaces from about a hundred to more than seven hundred, we were going to add jobs and contribute to the tax base. Scott made similar appeals to the commissioners that he knew.

At the end of the break Dermer went back and made a motion to reconsider the award, explaining that he had received more details about it. Since he had voted against it on the first round, he was allowed to make such a motion. The commission reconsidered it and voted to go forward with one of our sites, the one at 17th Street and Michigan.

After that I had Stuart negotiate the deal with the city. He had negotiated the ground lease for the Royal Palm and went back to the same cast of characters, the same outside council, city attorney, assistant city manager, and so forth. Scott negotiated with them as well, and Stuart kept me in the loop by copying me on e-mails that I needed to see. Once that was wrapped up we went out and looked for financial partners. I brought it to Credit Suisse, which had financed the Bath Club, and we almost sold the project prior to construction, as a build-to-suit deal for Starwood Urban. In the end Scott made a deal with LNR, the commercial branch of Miami-based home-building giant Lennar.

Scott went to LNR when he found out they were going to finance the parking garage/office building that the Comras group intended to build on 16th Street and Washington Avenue. They were interested in our deal as well but didn't want the conflict of interest, with the two buildings competing against each other. They suggested we partner up with Comras, which is what we ended up doing: We each owned half of the other's interests, with each partner remaining in charge of developing their respective projects. LNR put in all the cash, so they took the lion's share of the total, 80 percent for them and 20 percent for our group. But we weren't putting any money in—we actually were able to pull our initial cash out as well as earn development fees— so that was fine with us. Plus, if we exceeded certain return hurdles, the split got significantly higher on our side.

Comras completed their building first, in 2003, and it became the headquarters for LNR. We were a little bit behind them—they had started first—but we were done in the same year, and we started leasing as soon as we were finished. It was a terrific-looking building, with a corner of curved glass walls, and since I had helped design the appropriate footprint for the floor space, I knew the layout was right. We put retail on the street (today it houses the trendy, upscale Lucky Strike bowling lanes and a branch of Colonial Bank) and we increased the city's stock of parking slots by more than 600 spaces. We had done what we set out to accomplish, increasing the tax base, creating jobs, putting more retail on the street, and adding an attractive building to the skyline.

Then LNR decided they wanted to buy our group out of the building on 17th and Washington, where they had placed their corporate headquarters. They wanted to own it outright. Together we negotiated a deal in which they would buy us out of that building, and we would buy them out of the other one on Michigan.

By sheer serendipity this arrangement proved highly lucrative for our group, with a nice twist of irony. Because LNR had leased out so much space in the Washington Avenue building, it was worth more than the Michigan building. Plus, they bought us out first, so we could use our $3 million in profit to reduce the price of the Michigan Building. In the end we paid about $32 million to buy them out, with financing from Credit Suisse.

In the meantime the office market on Miami Beach just kept getting hotter, and we were able to lease out the building. The market looked so good, in fact, that Scott came to me and suggested we sell while the tide was high. We went to Cushman & Wakefield and CB Richard Ellis, the top two brokers in the local market for commercial properties, and asked them for proposals. I happened to know the guy who ran the commercial investment property division at Cushman—he was a commissioner at the temple where I coached my son's basketball team—and he called me and told me he really wanted to represent us, and thought he could get us a top price.

Both companies submitted proposals, but I liked the Cushman team better for this type of deal—they were more disciplined, institutional-type guys—and I liked my friend's aggressive take on going after a top price. We had a target in mind of selling in the mid- $60 millions, which would give us about a $30 million profit. I thought if that was the expected price, we should set up some incentives for doing better. I'd had significant experience, and success, in doing this in D.C., and it was another area where I could be helpful to Scott as a partner. We negotiated a below-market rate commission for any price up to $64 million, and then we let the commission escalate up to 4 percent as the prices got higher.

It worked like a charm. Within a month we had several bids over $70 million, including an initial bid of $76 million from a German pension fund. After the pension fund went through due diligence there was a partial re-negotiation, and we ended up settling at $74.5 million. The city had to approve the sale, which it did with some hand holding from Scott and Stuart, and we closed on the deal in June of 2006. It was the highest price per square foot for any office building ever sold in Miami Beach or Miami-Dade County, and it earned us a profit of $40 million. That meant $20 million for Comras and $20 million for Scott and me, or about $10 million each; we gave Milberg his share of $400,000, a nice reward for facilitating the introductions and helping at City Hall.

In general, I don't believe in the idea of easy money, and even this deal took about five years from start to finish. But, relatively speaking, this was very easy money, because I never had to face any management hassles or operational details. They were handled by my partners. What I invested, besides an initial $250,000 (which was returned to us at the initial closing of the LNR joint venture), was my experience, my political connections, and my creative solutions. The best thing I did was pick a partner who was certain about what he knew and willing to get advice about what he didn't know. He was comfortable having smart people around him in fact, he wanted smart people around him—and he had a high level of integrity. He was also quite motivated to establish himself as a major business player in the market. So it all worked out very well.

EPILOGUE TO CHAPTER 9

Naturally enough, a fair number of the Peebles Principles were evidenced in this transaction—you really can't win without employing some of them—though they were a bit more subtle than in earlier deals. As far as ground rules go, I would add a variant to the dictum about keeping your greed in check, and that would be to keep your ego in check. I was comfortable getting very little recognition, and I didn't care about LNR taking my name off the buildings, which they did due to my controversial political profile. All right, I admit I was a little insulted, but in the end I made the most money. About 80 percent of that $40 million should have been LNR's. Instead we got it.

Also evident here is a very astute management of the political process. Understanding how to use political power in a sophisticated fashion is less about winning deals per se than it is about creating the level playing field that gives you the opportunity to win those deals. My investment in the politics of Miami Beach allowed me to get a fair hearing on our RFP. I had built some credibility in the political arena, and Commissioner Dermer in particular knew I wasn't going to tell him something that wasn't true or waste his time with something that wasn't in the city's interest.

What the Lincoln deal most aptly illustrates and what I learned most from of it, however, was a full understanding of the pluses of picking the right partner. In my experience with Otho Green in San Francisco, I had learned the consequences of picking the wrong partner. This was the reverse. With Scott managing the process, I learned that I didn't always have to be the person running the deal. Essentially, I did no work other than strategizing and making some phone calls. It freed me up to go ahead with the Royal Palm, without worrying about the Lincoln Road building. And that's how a good partnership should work.

PEEBLES GROUND RULES

- Remember that, even more than capital, time is your most valuable commodity.

- Finding good people, as both partners and employees, lets you save time.

- Politics is not about guaranteeing a win; it's about securing an even playing field so that you *can* win.

Peebles Principle #11: Use the Power of Good Partnerships

Entrepreneurs are the gunslingers of capitalism and generally like to go it alone. But if you can find a good partner, one with energy, intelligence, and integrity, he or she can profoundly amplify your power.

✤ 10 ✤

San Francisco Redux:
Diamond in the Rough

Seeing the potential of something—an idea, a place, a product—is the essence of being an entrepreneur. We see value where others do not. And simply because someone else couldn't make an opportunity work doesn't mean it was a bad idea. Just south of San Francisco I discovered this truth in a small town where I ended up making an astonishing profit.

In the summer of 2003 we were all going on vacation—my wife, Katrina, and our two children Donahue III and our infant daughter Chloe (we now had a little girl) flying north toward Bridgehampton, New York, where we had rented a house for the summer. We were in a Legacy jet, a long and roomy aircraft with three compartments: a dining area, a lounge area, and a forward cabin. There was plenty of room, so I brought along Daniel Grimm and Baron Channer of my staff. I figured we could do some business on board; on our way to Bridgehampton we were planning to stop in Detroit to look at a property we were considering acquiring, and I wanted my family to see the city where I spent many of my formative childhood years.

I was sitting with Daniel and Baron in the front cabin, going over paperwork. Sifting through a stack of mail, I came across a flyer for a hotel property in the San Francisco

Bay area, in a little town called Pacifica. The town is less than twenty minutes south of San Francisco and within fifteen minutes of the San Francisco International Airport, and the property for sale was the Lighthouse Point Hotel. It was branded by Best Western and sat right on the ocean.

I remember looking at the aerial photos and thinking that the place was beautiful.

"Man, this is a great piece of property," I said out loud. "And they're only asking for eleven million."

From the plane I placed a call to the San Francisco office of Colliers, the brokerage company, and asked to see the property. A short conversation later I told Daniel to fly out to San Francisco and check it out.

The following week Daniel went out there; it was a trip that would earn him a lot of money. We have an incentive program in our firm that gives a slice of the action to anyone who uncovers a new deal—and by that I mean a really new deal, not one that a broker offers, or that somebody calls in, or that I assign. It's when you find a property that is basically not on the market. If we purchase it, the finder gets a fee of 1 percent of the purchase price and 1 percent ownership. In Daniel's case, due to his seniority, it was a 2 percent ownership and finder's fee.

After arriving in San Francisco, Daniel rented a car and drove to Pacifica. Besides looking at the hotel, which did not particularly impress him (foggy, poor architecture, not much to the town in terms of amenities), he also met with the president of the local chamber of commerce to gather information about the community. Daniel explained why he was there, and the guy basically said that if we wanted a really nice piece of property, he'd show us where to look. He then told Daniel about a huge vacant site, an old rock quarry on the ocean, right next door to the hotel. Daniel checked it out, then returned to make his report.

"The hotel is not going to work for us, but wait till you see this piece of property," he said, showing me aerials of the quarry. "It's eighty-seven acres on the ocean, and I think we can get it for $20 million or so."

The price was a steal. A parcel that size on the ocean in Florida would cost hundreds of millions of dollars.

"So, what's the catch?" I asked.

It turns out that the property had been under contract by the Trammel Crow Company, the large national institutional developer, for just over $20 million. They had wanted to build a mixed-use project that included a residential community there, but in order to build housing, they had to win a public referendum. This is no-growth-California country, after all. So they put the property under contract and put the proposition on the ballot for a November 2002 election. Unfortunately for them they lost, badly, and dropped the deal. They had determined that residential development was key to the project's success, and when they lost the vote they terminated their purchase option. When Daniel discovered the property, it had yet to be put back on the market.

Now, another developer might have been discouraged by that news. But I knew Trammel Crow and wasn't surprised that they couldn't get it done. I had partnered with Trammel Crow in Washington, D.C., on the American Psychological Association Building, and I knew how they operated. They were not exactly a risk-taking company. They operated more like a large institutional bureaucracy than a tight-knit entrepreneurial corporation. And what they couldn't see were other opportunities in the deal.

What Daniel had discovered, and what Trammel Crow presumably knew, was that while it would take a vote to put housing on it, the property was already zoned for commercial development. A total of 2.1 million square feet of space, to be exact, which opened up all sorts of possibilities—especially in the hospitality sector.

I suppose I should not have been surprised by their unwillingness to proceed without the residential element. At the time the housing market was on fire, breaking sales and appreciation records quarter after quarter. At the same time, the aftermath of 9/11 and the bursting of the technology bubble had wrecked havoc on the Bay area's hotel market. In order to move forward with a hotel plan, a person would have to look well beyond the current conditions and take a leap of faith that Americans would get back on airplanes and fly again and that the technology sector—which defined the Bay area economy—would recover.

"Well, let's go and take a look at it," I said. "Who cares if it goes residential or not? It's a great hotel site. Half Moon Bay is just thirty miles or so to the south, they're in an inferior location, and the Ritz-Carlton is doing very well there. So, let's take a closer look." I also wanted to see the $11 million Light House Point Hotel. How bad could that be?

Katrina and I flew out and looked at the hotel first. It was, as I said, a Best Western, and consequently it could have been stepped up. But I wasn't sure if it was worth the effort. It was a very cold location on the ocean, not at all a beach environment. It was scenic, and you could surf there, but it was no place for umbrellas or sun tan oil—or anything else for the guests to do, for that matter. And because it was on a small site, an acre or less, there was no space to create any outdoor activities for guests.

Then I saw the quarry site. What a piece of property! It was a great, rugged piece of land right on the ocean, a limestone quarry for more than two hundred years. In fact, in 1907 they used limestone from there to help rebuild the city of San Francisco after its famous earthquake and fires of 1906. Before that its stone had been used for the buildings on the Presidio in San Francisco, where Katrina had grown up.

The man who owned it was named William Bottoms. He was elderly, about ninety years old, and had purchased it twenty years earlier. It was still a quarry when he bought it, and he'd been trying to figure out a way to develop it or sell it for a significant profit ever since. Trammel Crow, it turns out, was actually the second real estate group to fail in the attempt to win over Pacifica voters.

I loved the site, and told Daniel to go for it. He contacted Bottoms and they began negotiating. I wanted to have a long due diligence period, so we could get the approval for housing, and we were talking a price of between $18 million and $20 million. After his last experience with Trammel Crow, however, Bottoms was unwilling to give us a due diligence period long enough to go through the public voting process. At first that was a sticking point, but Daniel confirmed again the astounding information that this beautiful, shoreline property was zoned for 2.1 million square feet of commercial use, with no vote required. At $20 million, that comes down to less than $10 a developable square foot. In Miami it would cost at least $200 a developable square foot—or about $400 million—for a comparably zoned and located piece of property.

"You know what?" I said. "Let's go ahead and buy it. Even without the residential usage, the site is a steal at $20 million."

We began moving documents back and forth, pushing things forward, when suddenly their side went quiet. We simply didn't hear from them. I thought, Hell, someone else is buying it, we didn't bid high enough. But I was wrong. In the middle of the negotiations, we later learned, William Bottoms had died.

We still wanted the property, of course, so we called Bottoms's lawyer. We asked if the estate was still selling the property. The answer was a resounding yes.

Two things were in our favor. First, we found out that William Bottoms was a pretty tight person when it came to money. Apparently he didn't spend much on the luxuries of life or his family. Consequently, his surviving wife and son wanted to liquidate, with a quick close and no contingencies. They wanted to get some cash, and soon. We also found out there was a reclamation requirement with the state that meant the family had to post a financial assurance for reclaiming the quarry. About $1.4 million was needed, and though it would be returned when the property was graded for development, the family still had to come up with the cash now.

Knowing these things, we made an immediate offer. We also agreed to take over the responsibility of putting up the reclamation bond. I knew I could post a letter of credit that would be canceled once we began to grade the property for construction, so that became part of the negotiation.

As for the offer itself, I remember Daniel saying that we should offer them something in the teens. I suggested we offer them something even lower and take our shot. They wanted cash right then, and we could always raise it back up if they said no. So we offered them $7 million.

They came back at just around $8 million. I would have

taken it, too, but I thought we shouldn't let them feel we were too anxious. Though a letter of intent was going back and forth, we still had to document the contract, and if we took something too quickly, they might feel they could go out and get a better price for it. So we countered with $7.4 million and ended up settling on $7.5 million.

It was an incredible price. Even without the surrounding land, 2.1 million square feet of commercial space at $7.5 million comes to $3 a developable square foot. At the time, the 261-room Ritz-Carlton Hotel and Resort at Half Moon Bay (located more than twice the distance from San Francisco) sold for over $500,000 per hotel room. Generally a quarter of the sales price is attributable to land value; that would indicate a land value of $125,000 per hotel room. Based on a 400-room facility on our site, the hotel component of the land would be worth at least $50 million alone. Even without the hospitality mathematics it was a very cheap price, unheard of. So we contracted for a sixty-day due diligence and then a close ninety days after that. I ended up extending the due diligence period by thirty days, during which time I gave them a small amount,I think it was $25,000—while I lined up my financing.

The financing turned out to be a revelatory experience as well, illustrating again not only how setbacks can produce benefits, but also the true philosophical difference between corporate and entrepreneurial thinking.

I first approached the Credit Suisse Private Equity Group, my partner on the Bath Club, and offered them the deal. I met with the managing director of the real estate division, and we structured a partnership. I would contribute the land, which we agreed to value at $17 million to $20 million. We would then move forward on a 50/50 basis, sharing the cost and the profits. I liked this deal because I'd get an immediate cash payment of at least $10 million for land value, right to my pocket. Then, going forward, I could rely on a sizable institution to help me finance and execute what amounted to a major development deal, one that would involve a political campaign and a complex array of housing and commercial space. It was a big deal, and I was looking for a partner of substance to defray the risks and re-sponsibilities.

Then one of the executives at Credit Suisse who had to approve the deal got cold feet. He was worried that we didn't have the residential zoning locked up, that it was too much of a risk. The group had their team come back to us to renegotiate.

By that time I had already lined up a simple land loan from Bank of America, as a backup, so I told the people at Credit Suisse to forget it. If I was not going to be able to take cash out of the deal at closing, I would be better off doing the deal myself and owning 100 percent. I went ahead with the closing and ended up getting a $16 million loan from a private equity group called Ambit. It was a four-year loan at 12 percent interest, and it included not only the purchase price but also the carrying costs and the money I'd need to conduct my political campaign with the voters. Am-bit was so confident about the collateral value of the prop-erty that they closed the loan without an appraisal, before any rezoning and with no equity interest. They figured, quite accurately, that the land just as it was would be worth considerably more than their loan.

When Bank of America was processing our loan re-quest, they had ordered an appraisal of the site. They hired CB Richard Ellis, an international real estate consulting and brokerage firm, to do it. I instructed my staff and the bank not to reveal our purchase price to them. I didn't want it to affect their judgment. "You guys all have to commit to being quiet on this," I told them. "Everybody's got to commit." The appraiser kept calling, of course, and asking Daniel for the price. I was adamant about not revealing anything.

When the appraisal came in, it was eye-popping. Without any rezoning or improvements, CB Richard Ellis apprised the property at $85 million—the property I had just purchased for $7.5 million. Which meant that, on paper, we had already made a profit of $77.5 million. I could only shake my head at Credit Suisse's cold feet. Even with a value of $20 million for my contribution of the land, they would have instantly made more than $30 million. But that is the way executives at large corporations think. Their mind-set is to not lose any money; they simply have no appetite for significant risk because if they are wrong, they could lose their job. My mind-set is to make money, and though I try to mitigate my chances of losing, that risk is always there. It's like being a boxer. You can't win a fight without going in there and getting hit. You should expect to get hit and stand ready for it.

The other immediate result of the appraisal was the reward to Daniel. By virtue of our company policy, he had just earned himself a $1.7 million bonus: 2 percent of the purchase price (2 percent of $7.5 million, or $150,000) plus a 2 percent ownership interest (2 percent of $77.5 million—the appraisal minus the purchase price—or $1.55 million).

Now came the fun part: the campaign to rezone the land and put it to its best possible use.

Trammel Crow, as I said, had a deal to buy the land for just over $20 million subject to getting voter approval for residential units. They lost that vote 66 percent to 34 percent. I felt I could do a lot better job campaigning than Trammel Crow, but I still wanted to find out why they lost. It was time to do more homework.

I had Daniel get me everything he could about what happened with Trammel Crow: the planning board report, the city council transcripts, newspaper articles, anything. And I sat down for a couple of days, reading transcripts, newspaper articles, and so forth, and reading the development agreement Trammel Crow had entered into with the city. And then I understood why Trammel Crow had lost.

They lost first because they were an institutional company, operating like a franchise, and the local people in charge were not experienced enough for a process like this. Second, Pacifica is a peculiar town: they like to say no just to say no. The publisher of the local paper, the *Pacifica Tribune*, once told me: "Pacifica never misses any opportunity to miss an opportunity." The concept Trammel Crow had proposed would have greatly benefited the city, but the no-growth side was blind to it. Third, Trammel Crow didn't invest nearly the amount of money necessary to win the election; I think they spent about $200,000, which is nothing for the millions at stake. Fourth, anticipating victory, they tried to cover their downside by stipulating a way out of building a hotel on the site as well as other commercial structures. If they chose not to build the hotel, they would have been faced with a relatively insignificant financial penalty.

This last part was key, and to understand why it hurt them, you have to understand Pacifica.

Pacifica was, and is, a small bedroom community (population: 40,000) that should have been a thriving suburb of

San Francisco. Instead, their virulent antigrowth philosophy had almost bankrupted the city. They had the lowest funding per student of any school district in the county, placing them at the bottom eleventh percentile of the entire state. They couldn't afford to maintain their own fire department and had to co-op it with a neighboring city. Their police department was 20 percent understaffed. Their roads had potholes everywhere and the city was dirty, with trash all over the place. This was a revenue-strapped city, and creating a new tax base with a big hotel on the Bottoms property was an attractive solution to the more progressive and moderate residents. By excluding these exciting opportunities in their proposal, Trammel Crow lost the support of many in this key group of voters.

Trammel Crow didn't understand this. They just wanted to do the housing, so they stipulated that if no hotel went up, they would face a penalty of $500,000 per year for three years. That was it.

Another problem was that neither Mr. Trammel Crow, nor any of his family members, had ever set foot in Pacifica; I had been spending one week a month on average as we moved through the development process, and understood the potential—as well as what the city wanted.

Compare my project to theirs. My plan began with a hotel, and that project alone would produce about $6 million a year in bed taxes. And that was just for starters.

To really flesh things out I hired Duany Plater-Zyberk, the world-renowned architecture firm of the "New Urbanism" movement—the trend toward small, environmentally green, walkable communities that mix retail, work, play, and residential. They are famous for their design of Seaside, the perfectly planned, quaint beachfront community in

Florida's Panhandle that was used as the setting for Jim Carrey's movie *Truman*. They are also active in rebuilding some of the neighborhoods in New Orleans.

In May 2006 I had them come in and do a weeklong charrette, or architectural workshop, that was open to the public; in fact, I mailed invitations to every resident in Pacifica. The result of the charrette was a blueprint for a charming, self-contained town, a sort of smaller Carmel-by-the-Sea, with the following dimensions: 131 single-family homes, 42 town houses, 140 apartments, 42 live-work spaces, several hundred thousand square feet of commercial space, a 350-room five-star hotel, and over 45 percent of the land left as open, undeveloped space. The town center would have restaurants, retail, office space, and a movie theater. Plus, the buildings would be the most environmentally sensitive possible; we'd even use special solar panels that would work in super-foggy Pacifica. Duany and his group had actually helped develop these new green building standards. Once our site—an old, bottomed-out quarry and not virgin land—was reclaimed and made green again, it would bring an intense level of environmentally correct development to Northern California for the first time! The build out would be expensive, but it was also groundbreaking stuff. If the plan could be realized, everybody would win.

Prior to the charrette, I agreed to go forward with whatever project resulted from the process. I had initially envisioned a resort hotel overlooking the ocean, retail on the flat area of the site that fronted Highway 1, and 200 single-family luxury homes scattered around the hills with dramatic views. Consequently, the play unveiled on the final day of the charrette was a bit of a surprise to me. Among other things, all of the apartments and live-work units would be money losers, and giving away nearly half of the site for open space would limit future expansion opportunities. However, I had agreed to go with the result of the charrette and I kept my word; I embraced the plan.

Even with the less lucrative elements included, the project would create enormous value for me. It also would create an additional $17 million in annual taxes and 3,750 new jobs—this, in a city where the annual budget/tax base was $24 million and where there were a total of just 3,500 existing private sector jobs. In one fell swoop, my project would double employment in the city and increase its annual budget by 70+ percent. It would revive and rejuvenate the community, and set the town on a firm financial foundation for years to come.

This is heady stuff, and would seem like a no-brainer for the city's 21,000 registered voters. But this is California, and Northern California at that, and as I said, Pacifica had a reputation for an antigrowth attitude that was extreme even by Bay area standards. It was going to take a concerted effort, and I was certainly not going to take things for granted. In my loan from Ambit, I had $2 million earmarked for the campaign, and after the June 2005 close on the property, I began a lengthy effort to educate and win over the voters.

I started by interviewing people to run my campaign—people who had run Willie Brown's mayoral campaign in San Francisco, people who had run California Assembly campaigns, even one of Governor Schwarzenegger's coordinators for that area. I ended up settling on a company that wrote to me after seeing an article on the purchase in the San Francisco newspaper—another example, by the way, of what the media can do for you.

Davies Communications specializes in running campaigns for developers who have ballot initiatives—one of those firms found "only in California," where everything is done by referendum. The company CEO, John Davies, was formerly a member of the California State Assembly and remains a top Republican strategist. His team put together a campaign plan and staffed it with top people.

Having learned that if you need a person's vote you should show enough respect to ask for it in person, I began meeting every city leader I could find—in politics, business, civic associations—along with every resident I could meet, spending ten days out of each month at first. By summer, the polls showed us making real progress.

As the election approached, I began spending half of each month in Pacifica. I treated it like I was running for mayor: I went door to door, meeting residents; I attended dozens of house parties held for me to meet the voters; I rented out school auditoriums and went to various churches, religious centers, and PTA organizations so I could make presentations to hundreds of people at a time. I even held a debate with a former mayor who was against the project because it would bring too much traffic to Pacifica.

Almost everybody who watched the debate thought I won it hands down, presenting what the new town center would do for Pacifica in terms of revenue stream and employment opportunities. Even the leaders of the opposition thought I did a great job of presenting the facts and figures for our proposed project. But I also wanted to address the town's concern for its future infrastructure, in and beyond the new town center. So I began making a series of concessions.

I now understand why politicians frequently have a tough time keeping all the promises they make during a campaign: They make too many of them. They get caught up in the moment, trying to win by making promises they later can't keep. In my case the pledges were in writing, and I had no option but to live up to them.

In my determination to win the vote, I promised first to fix the traffic situation, pledging millions to not only pay for all the new public roadways associated with my project but also to improve the town's existing roads. I then pledged to donate land to enable the city to build a new city hall and a new public library in the heart of the city core I was creating, followed by agreeing to build a new aquatic center where swim meets could be held and residents could swim. I also promised to take two city-owned lots and finance two state-of-the-art athletic fields, with lights, scoreboards, and bleachers—and to maintain those fields for ten years.

All this I promised just for the right to make an application to a no-growth city council for a project that included no more than 355 residential units. A week or so before the election, I began to calculate the economic impact of the project limitations I had agreed to accept and the cost of the benefits I proffered the community. The figures were astounding: over $10 million in direct benefits and tens of millions in economic impact on the project due to various concessions. I had made the same mistake so many politicians make; in my zeal I had given away too much. But in my case I had no way to take any of it back. I began to envision a hollow victory.

In the end none of this mattered. When the votes were finally counted after that November 7 election, our measure lost by 509 votes out of about 15,000 cast.

At first I was disappointed; I could not understand why

a majority of the voters didn't see the tremendous value of the project and what it would bring to Pacifica. Part of it was, I'm sure, the negative messages from my opponents. They attacked me for everything from being an anti-environmentalist to being a litigious East Coaster. One of our opponents in particular would repeatedly disrupt our presentations to make it known that our site was a habitat for the red-legged frog, now on the endangered species list; she even paraded around the city's annual arts and crafts Fog Festival, dressed as a big frog. The *Pacifica Tribune* ran a front-page photo of the frog hugging me. I was wearing a "Vote Yes" T-shirt and thought it was great publicity. I had pledged that 45 percent of the entire project would be put aside as open space, accessible to the public and suitable for frogs as well as humans.

None of it was enough, however. When election day rolled around, I lost by the slimmest margin imaginable. I was truly shocked that the vast majority of Pacifica did not embrace our vision, a vision they had helped create during the charrette process back in May. Perhaps the fact that I was voluntarily giving them these benefits made them more suspect; the opposition fought me literally to win nothing, rather than new opportunities for their community. They were blinded by fear of change, misinformation, and a distrust of developers.

On my side of the equation, I began to rethink the situation and to reflect on my pre-election economic analysis. Ultimately I realized that, once again, I had been delivered an advantage by something that initially appeared to be a setback. I also realized that I had been too swept up in my zeal to create a coastal urban community.

In my effort to win voter approval not only had I

promised the city new civic buildings and roadways and playing fields and open space, I had promised to use local union labor for the construction, to limit the hotel forever to 350 rooms, and to make 15 percent of the mix affordable housing. I had also promised to follow whatever recommendations urban planner Andrés Duany recommended, including the creation of apartments above retail stores, live-work spaces and town houses. These were marginal for us in terms of profit and made it seem like we wanted way too many housing units: 355 in all. I would have settled for less than half that, all high-end single-family homes.

I nonetheless made these promises because at the time the residential housing market was still red hot. That's just what Trammel Crow saw when they had their option on the site. What they didn't see, in those post-9/11 days when the hospitality industry was crippled, was the hotel and resort potential. They had walked away, like horses with blinders, not seeing the incredible value of the commercial zoning of the property.

Today the hospitality sector is booming, and my development option on the quarry site includes creating a luxury resort hotel, with a wellness center like a Canyon Ranch or Phoenician Spa located in Tucson and Phoenix, Arizona. I have enough land for an equestrian center so that guests can horseback ride along the shore and participate in many other outdoor activities. We can attract regional and national corporate groups for conferences and retreats along with leisure travelers from San Francisco and around the globe. Without the cap on the number of rooms, we can develop time-share and condo-hotel units and, as business grows, expand the hotel by adding more rooms and suites. In fact, the very day after the election, Daniel and I met with top executives from one of the world's largest and most prestigious hotel operators. They were truly impressed with the site and expressed their interest in branding and operating a five-star spa resort and fractional ownership complex on the property. (A few days later the *Pacifica Tribune* reported that a one-acre oceanfront site with an outdated motel on it three blocks south of the quarry sold for $12 million, further reinforcement of the great value we have in the Pacifica quarry site.)

We can also use some of the land for a regional, high-end, premium brand outlet mall—right now 50,000 cars a day pass the edge of the property on California Highway 1, and that figure will reach 75,000 when the state completes construction of a nearby tunnel connecting the highway to the south and bypassing the often-closed Devil's Slide span of Highway 1.

And whereas Trammel Crow was turned down by a two-to-one margin, we won the active backing of half the voters. Not bad in the heart of no-growth country. The election process allowed me to build a great deal of goodwill with the residents and community leaders. Ultimately the "no" side will wake up and realize just what they lost, and will likely try to get me back to the table with incentives; it will be another case of opportunities arising from an apparent setback. We might even consider running another referendum, which always remains an option. Even without it, the quarry project will still revive the existing community, creating significant jobs and tax revenues, and it will be one of my company's signature projects. So stay tuned.

EPILOGUE TO CHAPTER 10

As the final deal for this book, Pacifica is worthy, not only because of its sheer size and its astounding return on investment, but because it illustrates most if not all of the Peebles Principles. I will leave you to figure those out.

This deal also revealed something of the corporate culture at my firm. As I mentioned, anyone who brings in a new deal gets to keep part of the action. It is a nice incentive program, but there is more to it than that. I don't give excessive salaries or guaranteed bonuses. My key executives are fairly paid and rank above the average levels for the industry when it comes to base salaries, but they work in an entrepreneurial environment where they can make much more. Basically, if our deals do well, they do well. So they end up being compensated well above the top end of the market. It's really all about creating parallel interests. Everyone becomes an integral part of the firm, doing anything they can to help out. It creates an atmosphere of tremendous energy and motivation where everybody can act as an entrepreneur within the company envelope. It's important to me that we keep the nimble, entrepreneurial spirit and not grow into a dinosaur. My goal is to make sure that all of our employees are exposed to great opportunities and that all of our key executives can become multimillionaires.

Which brings us to the final Peebles Principle, and what the Pacifica deal best illustrated: the importance of seeing value. The property was a true diamond in the rough, an abandoned rock quarry in a small, financially strapped community with limited resources and a very vocal opposition. You had to have a lot of vision to see what it could become. It was not even on the market at the time, so it took even more foresight to go after something before it got out to the general public and to buy something that had been beaten up. It's the same sort of vision, for example, that led to the gentrification of New York's Soho district: a bunch of old loft warehouses that weren't being marketed as residences, but which the pioneers, looking through fresh eyes, saw for their inherent value and went after well ahead of the general public.

In the case of Pacifica, I was not the first person to see the value of the land. Two different developers had come before me, tried to win a residential referendum, and failed. One of them, a national company, had gotten trounced. So people familiar with the property thought it couldn't be developed, that the idea was flawed. I tried to win the same referendum, came damn close, then realized there was nothing wrong with the first idea we had come west with, the concept of creating a remarkable resort destination. I had tried to hit another home run with the residential referendum—and you should never be afraid to push the envelope, especially when your downside is covered—and was nearly snared in the ultimate trap of the entrepreneur. What is that greatest danger? The very thing that makes being an entrepreneur possible: becoming so excited about an idea that you get caught up in the moment, knocked over by the energies that bring ideas to life, those very opportunities that others fail even to see.

PEEBLES GROUND RULES

- Look under the rocks: The best deals are rarely advertised; more often they are discovered.

- Don't be afraid to make a lowball offer.

- Incentives are more important than salaries for creating an entrepreneurial spirit.

- People don't always appreciate getting something for free. It seems more valuable if you have to fight for it.

- Beware getting caught up in the moment: Never win a deal just for the sake of winning it.

Peebles Principle #12: Seeing Value Is Everything

The hallmark of the entrepreneur is to see value that other people do not see or have overlooked. Even when lots of people are presented with the same deal you are, few can see its hidden value.

❧ *Appendix* ❧

The Importance of Politics

Understanding the political process is a science. Understanding how to use it is an art.

Politics played a part in all of the deals described in this book. In some, the political process was the very essence of the deal—the winning of the Royal Palm, for example. In others, politics was more of an enhancement, a way to maximize profits. The quarry property in Pacifica initially generated a huge return without any politics. The political process then amplified its potential.

You can look at politics from many vantage points. You can consider it an abstract principle, and see its process in virtually any industry. There is no business out there that does not require an understanding of who the gatekeepers are, where the points of power lie, and how to move and manage those forces. This is a great deal of what politics is about: Webster's dictionary defines "politic" as an adjective meaning shrewdness in the promotion of a policy. This is as good a generic definition as any.

The politics described in this book, however, are of the more literal type, referring to our publicly elected officials and to the people who administer local and national government. This is the nature of the political animal in real estate development. It is a regulated industry and, as such, requires you to play politics in the literal sense.

Politics plays a part in other industries as well, some of which are closely related to real estate development—construction, for example. Others are farther afield: you might be an energy consultant, or a manufacturer, or a telephony services provider.

In all these cases, what politics does—and by that I mean what doing business with the government does—is to give an aspiring entrepreneur the opportunity to start a business. Access to the government provides an entrée to business opportunities. Ironically enough, that includes entrée to the private sector, to corporate America. Politics allows first comers to start a business and develop a client base, and then it facilitates the growth of that business. You can have relationships with the government as a contractor or vendor in a whole array of industries, providing a whole array of goods and services. This is true whether you are an individual consultant doing information technology work or a big general contractor doing roadwork or building bridges.

In simplest terms, what I am talking about here is the winning of government contracts. In more complex situations, the "win" relates to more subtle changes, like a change in local zoning or a shift in regulations that can ripple through an entire industry. But whether I am talking about the award of a contract to build a parking lot or the creation of a new environmental law, the process takes place in a political environment. The very process itself is political, no matter where you are in this country, so understanding politics is very important and embracing the political process will put you on the road to success.

The most basic form of politics is the game of who you know. It's the person you know in the building permit department who can process your paperwork in a timely fashion or the phone call you can make to get your factory inspection done efficiently. These things don't create wealth in the sense of paying you money, but they make you money because they save you time. They are politics with a small *p*.

Other political relationships are on a grander scale. Because politicians talk to each other, I was able to use my contacts when going from one market into another—for example, when we asked the mayor of New Orleans to call the mayor of San Francisco and arrange an introduction. Or when I had Congressman Ron Dellums's office call HUD to help open a door for me there.

This idea of using relationships to make connections—like the concept of six degrees of separation—is key to using politics. Once you have a political relationship, you can use it to gain access to other politicians, government officials, even to private sector people. Political relationships can also get you access to information. You can get more information about what's happening now and what's going to happen in the future.

How, then, are political relationships born, and how are they managed? Political relationships are developed because of mutual need.

Unless they are independently wealthy, politicians have to rely on the public—and that generally means the business community—to finance their elections. Helping raise those funds is an essential ingredient for building political relationships. Politicians need to raise money, and businesspeople need access to those politicians. So businesspeople support them financially and introduce them to other people who will support them financially. Sometimes it's more a matter of giving politicians business advice in terms of running their campaigns, or ideas on how to improve their city. This is only natural, since the business community interacts with the government on a regular basis—with a building or planning department, for instance—and can provide the candidates with some real insight. Essentially, however, political relationships revolve around the power to raise money.

Of course, the primary thing that politicians need to win is votes. Financial or intellectual contributions are just different ways to help win those votes. If you can get a politician those votes directly, or can arrange access to people who can get them those votes, you can build a relationship that way. If you are a community leader, for example, you have the ability to introduce candidates to large numbers of potential voters. But whether it's through money or through access to the public, politicians want to build relationships with people who can help them get votes. That's the nature of the beast, and that's the beauty of it, too, and the ease of creating a relationship in politics. All you have to do is go through a couple of election cycles and you can become a player.

What you do with that political relationship, however, is what the average person doesn't understand.

A political relationship is a unique and sophisticated type of relationship. Just because you raise money for somebody's campaign doesn't mean you own them. It doesn't mean they're going to vote for you. I have seen so many situations where businesspeople think that because they've given money, the politician is supposed to do what they want. Wrong. You still have to treat politicians respectfully. Nobody wants to be perceived as being bribed, unless they are really dishonest people, and you don't want to bribe anybody. As a businessperson, what you want is a level playing field. What you want is access.

One of my favorite quotes is from Lyndon Johnson, who once said, "If you support me early, you get access. If you support me late, you get good government." What a political relationship gets you is access to a fair shake. My approach has always been that I don't need to have an inside advantage. I just want a fair shot at winning. Don't get me wrong—I want to win every time. But I want to win when I deserve to win, and that is easier said than done. What good political relationships do is to make all things equal and permit you to win where you should.

If you don't understand this, you will squander your political connections. A person who is going to be successful in building and maintaining long-term political relationships cannot ask his or her political friends to do something that's not in their best interests, and certainly not in the best interests of their constituencies. You can't ask them to do you a special favor that runs contrary to their interests or those of their constituents. All you really want them to do is insure that you are not treated unfairly.

This is more important than you might think, especially as your public profile grows. There are going to be times, at higher levels, when you become controversial. You can expect weak-kneed politicians to run from that. What you expect from your true political friends is that they have courage to stand up and continue to treat you fairly, even in an environment where the mood may be to treat you unfairly. That's what you want.

When you understand this, you can be very successful in the political arena. My view has always been that I want to protect my political friends, not abuse them, and to make it easy for them to support what I am doing. On the flip side, I expect my political friends to tell the truth and stand up for me if somebody is attacking me unfairly. In the Washington, D.C., lease deal that is the subject of Chapter 4, I presented the city with a lease that was $58 million less expensive than the competing proposal. It should have been an easy proposition to support. The reason I left Washington was that Mayor Barry lacked the courage to stand up and support me. He violated our relationship.

If my proposal had less merit, or had required a special favor to push it through, I would have understood Barry's behavior. I have always taken care not to use my political relationships for anything that is borderline, either in terms of its importance for me or its value to the community. You never want to be a pest and call on politicians for every single thing you need done. More importantly, you never want to ask politicians to do something unethical or something that goes against their political interests. Political favors are a precious currency and should be used wisely.

If you do manage your political relationships well, they'll endure for long periods of time, and they will evolve and lead to other relationships. Ultimately you will end up having connections with people in other political arenas, in ways that you cannot foresee. Congressman Ron Dellums, for whom I worked as a young man in Washington, D.C., is now the mayor of Oakland. One of his staff, who supervised me when I worked for him, now holds his old congressional seat. Prior to that, I supported her campaigns to be a California state representative and senator. You should always support those who have helped you; you must be there for your friends, otherwise you have no right to expect their loyalty when you need it. The point is that you should maintain your relationships with politicians with the long term in mind, since some of them will be successful and go on to other places. And that ends up helping you in the long term.

Overall, I believe the key to managing the political process is to manage your expectations and to be realistic. You don't ever want to be in a position where you do something that is ethically questionable. A financial contribution is not a bribe, and if someone *is* expecting a bribe, you don't want to be the one bribing them. That's not what it's all about. You never go to a politician and say, Hey, I supported you financially and you've got to do this for me. Your approach is that your proposal is a good thing for their constituency, and for their community, and that you need their support. What you are counting on is for them to treat you fairly. That is the sophisticated way of politics and how it works around the country; understanding this is one of the reasons I have been successful.

One other thing: When it comes to the power of politics, perception is king. Just the perception of a political relationship helps. In my early career in Washington, I rarely had to call on Mayor Barry. The perception was that everybody knew I could. That perception would get me business opportunities; it would even get me cooperation from his staff. The perception was such that government officials who worked under him would treat me fairly, because they didn't want me to have to call their boss. When it came to getting my bid for the Marriott in Washington honored, the perceived relationship I had with President Clinton was enough. This is another important lesson about politics—the use of perceptions—which is the ultimate extension of the power of who you know.

❧ *Index* ❧